GUINNESS
MOVIE
FACTS & FEATS

PATRICK ROBERTSON

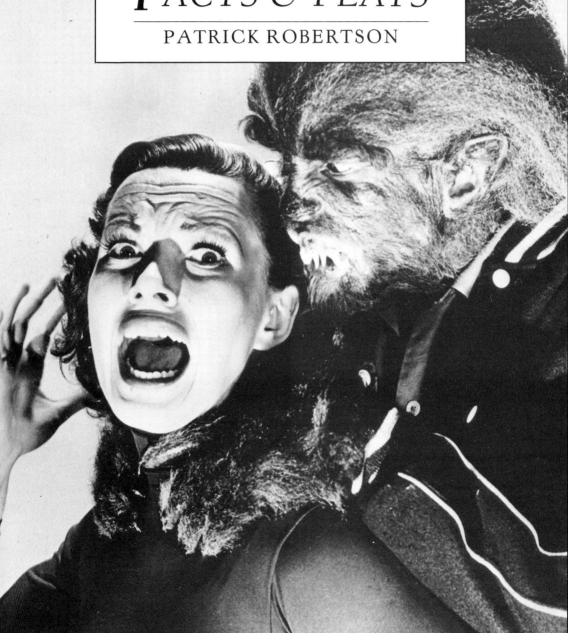

GUINNESS BOOKS

Project Editor: Honor Head
Editor: Anne Marshall
Design: Christie Archer
Picture Editor: Alex Goldberg

Published in Great Britain by Guinness Publishing
Limited
33 London Road, Enfield, Middlesex

Distributed by Sterling Publishing Co. Inc.
2 Park Avenue, New York, USA

Typeset in Great Britain by
Ace Filmsetting Ltd, Frome, Somerset
Printed and bound in Great Britain by
Hazell Watson & Viney Ltd, Aylesbury

**British Library Cataloguing in Publication
Data**
Robertson, Patrick
    The Guinness book of movie facts and feats.—
3rd ed.
    1. Cinema films
    I. Title   II. Robertson, Patrick.
    Guinness film facts and feats
    791.43'09

    ISBN 0-85112-899-8

PICTURE CREDITS FOR MOVIE FACTS & FEATS 1988

Barnes Museum	ILN (Illustrated London News)	Punch Magazine
British Film Archive	Library of Congress	Patrick Robertson
Bruce Coleman	Kobal Collection	Science Museum
Bruce Torrance Collection	Museum of London	SI (Syndication International—Picturegoer
Rob Burt	National Film Archive	Library)
Eon Productions Ltd	New Zealand Film Archive	Spectrum Colour Library
E.T. Archive	Nordisk	Stiftung Deutsche Kinemathek
Gamma	Peter Jackson Collection	20th Century Fox
Grant Lobban Collection	Popperfoto	Weidenfeld (Publishers)

Frontispiece: I Was a Teenage Werewolf. (Rob Burt)

CONTENTS

PREFACE

Most books on films are concerned about quality—the cinema as art. This book is unashamedly about *quantity*—together with 'firsts', records, oddities, remarkable achievements, historic landmarks and the wilder extravagances of the motion picture business during the 100 years of its colourful history. It is not the place to seek potted biographies of favourite stars or great directors, but it does offer a gamut of film facts, ranging from the significant to the absurd, many of which have never appeared in any film book before. For the historically minded there are old orthodoxies explored and often rejected—Who really 'invented' the close-up? What was the first western? Where did full-length feature films begin? Hollywood receives due attention, of course, as the centre of world film production, but many other countries—no less than 80 in all—have been approached for information. There is something about each of them, including a chart which records the number of features made each year by every film producing nation since the earliest days (pp. 14–15).

Devotees of Dracula will find a complete filmography; Shakespeare buffs a listing of all 40 versions of Hamlet, including the four in which the Prince was played by a woman; film fans may read about other film fans, including Queen Victoria, Stalin, Hitler and the last Emperor of China (who wore Harold Lloyd spectacles as a tribute to his favourite star). Records range from the largest and smallest cinema theatres, the longest career in movies, the biggest cast (300,000) and the most remakes to the heaviest actress, the last silent picture and the longest and shortest film titles.

This is the third edition of the *Guinness Movie Facts & Feats*. It contains not only updated and revised material, but many new features. There is a comprehensive analysis of movies about sport, with all those which have been the subject of Hollywood features fully quantified; a statistical run-down of the change-over from black-and-white to colour movies; and a survey of foreign locales used as the setting for Hollywood movies from 1920 to the present. On the lighter side there is a gallery of all the Bond Girls and a listing of the less complimentary things that stars have said about each other.

Corrections, updates and suggestions for new features will always be welcome. There are two things in particular we would like readers to help us with. The filmography of films in which US Presidents have been portrayed has been greatly expanded and we are confident that it is now within an ace of being complete. But because many of these portrayals were cameo parts, often they were uncredited. Any help in identifying the actors whose names have not been listed will be most gratefully received. There is also an important record we have been trying to establish ever since the first edition of this book and it still eludes us. So anyone who can tell us which is the oldest cinema in the world, please get in touch. It has to have started operating before February 1910 to precede the oldest cinema in Britain.

And while on the subject of longevity, we would like to draw attention to the fact that the third edition of the *Guinness Book of Movie Facts & Feats*, like the second, is dedicated to the actress with the longest cinema career in the history of motion pictures. For us she is 'The First Lady of the Silver Screen'—Miss Lillian Gish.

COUNTRY ABBREVIATIONS

Abbr	Country	Abbr	Country	Abbr	Country	Abbr	Country
Afg	Afghanistan	Fin	Finland	Jap	Japan	SA	South Africa
Alg	Algeria	Fr	France	Ken	Kenya	Sp	Spain
Arg	Argentina	Ger	Germany	Kor	Korea	Swe	Sweden
Aus	Australia	GDR	Germany, East	Lby	Libya	Swz	Switzerland
Aut	Austria	FRG	Germany, West	Mex	Mexico	Syr	Syria
Ban	Bangladesh	Gha	Ghana	Mor	Morocco	Sen	Senegal
Bel	Belgium	Gre	Greece	Moz	Mozambique	S. Kor	South Korea
Bra	Brazil	Gab	Gabon	Mau	Mauritania	Tai	Taiwan
Bul	Bulgaria	HK	Hong Kong	Neth	Netherlands	Tha	Thailand
Can	Canada	Hun	Hungary	NZ	New Zealand	Tun	Tunisia
Chn	China	Ind	India	Nor	Norway	Tur	Turkey
Col	Colombia	Ice	Iceland	Phi	Philippines	US	United States
Cz	Czechoslovakia	Ire	Ireland	Pol	Poland	Uru	Uruguay
CayI	Cayman Islands	Isr	Israel	Por	Portugal	Ven	Venezuela
Cur	Curacao	It	Italy	Rom	Romania	Yug	Yugoslavia
Den	Denmark	IvC	Ivory Coast	Rus	Russia		
Egy	Egypt	Jam	Jamaica	Sin	Singapore		

ONE

FADE IN

The first motion picture films were taken with a camera patented in Britain by French-born Louis Aimé Augustin Le Prince (1842–90?) in November 1888. Two fragments survive: one taken at a speed of 10–12 frames per second early in October 1888 in the garden of his father-in-law, Mr Joseph Whitley, at Roundhay, Leeds; the other taken at 20 frames per second later in the month and showing traffic crossing Leeds Bridge. According to Le Prince's mechanic, James Longley, the latter film was shown on a projector incorporating a Maltese cross for intermittent picture shift. He claimed that the image obtained was sufficiently clear for smoke to be visible rising from the pipe of a lounger on the bridge. Both films were made on sensitized paper rolls 2⅛ in wide and it was not until a year later that Le Prince was able to obtain Eastman celluloid roll film, which had just been introduced into Britain. This provided a far more suitable support material and it seems likely that the inventor was able to start the commercial development of his motion picture process by the beginning of 1890. A new

projector was built so that a demonstration could be given before M. Mobisson, the Secretary of the Paris Opera. On 16 September 1890 Le Prince boarded a train at Dijon bound for Paris with his apparatus and films. He never arrived. No trace of his body or his equipment was ever found and after exhaustive enquiries the police were unable to offer any rational explanation of his disappearance. The mystery has never been solved.

The first commercially developed motion picture process was instigated by Thomas Alva Edison (1847–1931), American electrical engineer. His initial attempt to produce an illusion of movement, by means of an apparatus called the 'optical phonograph', resulted in failure, and in January 1889 Edison assigned William Kennedy Laurie Dickson (1860–1935), an assistant at his laboratories in West Orange, NJ, to work on the development of what was to become the Kinetoscope, a film-viewing machine designed for use in amusement arcades. Dickson, the French-born son of English parents, had early training as a photographer and was better suited to this kind of research than his mentor who knew little of optics. Abandoning the use of rectangular sheets of celluloid for camera work, he substituted 50 ft lengths of celluloid film produced by the firm of Merwin Hulbert. These long rolls were first purchased on 18 March 1891, which is the earliest date at which it seems likely that Dickson could have made successful films for viewing in the peep-show Kinetoscope apparatus.

The first public demonstration of motion pictures took place at the Edison Laboratories at West Orange, NJ, on 22 May 1891, when 147 representatives of the National Federation of Women's Clubs, having lunched with Mrs Edison at Glenmont, were taken over her husband's workshops and allowed to view the new Kinetoscope. The New York *Sun* reported: 'The surprised and pleased clubwomen saw a small pine box standing on the floor. There were some wheels and belts near the box, and a workman who had them in charge. In the top of the box was a hole perhaps an inch in diameter. As they looked through the hole they saw the picture of a man. It was a most marvellous picture. It bowed and smiled and waved its hands and took off its hat with the most perfect naturalness and grace. Every motion was perfect....' The film used for this demonstration appears to have been taken with a horizontal-feed camera without sprockets. This

The LePrince camera of 1888.

Probably the earliest pictorial poster advertising a cinema show in Britain, believed to date from the latter half of 1897. The claim to have been the 'first' was advertising puffery. In fact the Egyptian Hall was the third place of entertainment to show films in London. (*Museum of London*)

would have been an imperfect apparatus at best, and not until October 1892 is there evidence that William Dickson had built an effective vertical-feed camera using perforated film. In that month the *Phonogram* published an illustration showing sequences from four films evidently taken with such a device. These included pictures of Dickson himself, together with his helper, William Heise, and for bringing the invention to fruition. Most historians were content to accept Edison's own version of events until the appearance in 1961 of a painstaking work of scholarship titled *The Edison Motion Picture Myth*. The author, Gordon Hendricks, demonstrates by reference to hitherto unpublished papers in the Edison archives that all the experimental work on the Kinetoscope was conducted by Dickson, or under his direction, and that Edison himself can be credited with little more than instigating the research programme and providing facilities for carrying it out.

The practical development of motion pictures in Britain can be dated from a camera built in 1895 by Birt Acres (1854–1918) and R. W. Paul (1869–1943) at the latter's optical instrument works in Saffron Hill. Paul's interest in films had been aroused the previous October when he was approached by a Greek showman, George Trajedis, with a request to manufacture some Edison Kinetoscopes. This Paul agreed to do on learning that Edison had omitted to patent the machine in Britain. Since Edison's agents understandably refused to sell films for the pirated machines, Paul approached Acres with the suggestion that they should construct a camera together (later each claimed to have been the only begetter of the apparatus) so that they could make their own Kinetoscope subjects, Acres to be the cameraman. Using film obtained from the American Celluloid Co. of Newark, NJ, Acres tried out the camera for the first time with a scene of a cricketer (his assistant Henry Short) coming out of Acres' home in Barnet, Clovelly Cottage. This was followed by what Paul described as 'our first saleable film', *The Oxford and Cambridge University Boat Race*, which was premièred in a Kinetoscope at the India Exhibition, Earls Court on 27 May 1896. This film, together with *The Derby* and *The Opening of the Kiel Canal* (see News Film, p. 220), formed the first programme presented on screen in Britain since Le Prince's experiments, when Acres gave a private show with his Kineopticon projector in a coach-house at Wrotham Cottage, Barnet in August 1895. Acres was also the first to give a public screening (see below), while Paul became the first manufacturer of projectors (q.v.) and Britain's pioneer film producer.

The first commercial presentation of motion pictures took place at Holland Bros' Kinetoscope Parlor, 1155 Broadway, New York, which opened for business on 14 April 1894. The Kinetoscopes were arranged in two rows of five, and for 25c viewers were allowed to watch five films—to see the whole programme they had to pay double entrance money. The first day's take of $120 suggests that this first 'cinema audience' totalled nearly 500. The films, made in the Edison 'Black Maria' (see Film Studio, p. 134) at West Orange, were titled:

also shots of wrestling and fencing. By this date, then, it can be positively asserted that Dickson had overcome all the obstacles that had stood in the way of making films suitable for commercial exhibition. He was to receive little thanks for his work. After Dickson left West Orange in 1895, following a dispute with his employer, Edison steadfastly refused to concede that anyone but himself was responsible

Few inventions have spread more rapidly than cinematography. By the end of 1896, a mere twelve months after the real start of commercial cinema in France, nearly all the major countries of the western world had witnessed their first demonstration of the new art. It is clear from the following chronology that the Lumière brothers of Lyon were the most positive force in introducing motion pictures to the world. (The designation 'Lumière' below signifies that the programme was made up of Lumière films.) The presentations listed were public shows before a paying audience unless otherwise indicated.

1895

March 22 FRANCE *La Sortie des Ouvriers des l'Usine Lumière* (Fr 94), presented by Louis and Auguste Lumière before the Société d'Encouragement pour l'Industrie Nationale at 44 rue de Rennes, Paris (see below).

May 20 UNITED STATES *Young Griffo v. Battling Charles Barnett* (US 95) presented before paying audience at 153 Broadway, New York (see below).

November 1 GERMANY Eight short films (for subjects, see Production: firsts by countries, p. 8) presented by Max and Emil Skladanowski at Berlin Wintergarten.

November 10 BELGIUM Lumière programme before invited audience of scientists etc., in Brussels. First before paying audience at 7 de la Galerie du Roi, Brussels, 1 Mar 1896.

1896

January 14 UNITED KINGDOM Programme (subjects see below) presented by Birt Acres before Royal Photographic Society, London. First before paying audience: Lumière programme by F. Trewey at Regent Street Polytechnic, London, 20 Feb 1896.

February ?? ITALY Lumière presented by Vittorio Calcina at the Ospedale di Carita, Turin.

March 19 AUSTRIA Lumière presented by E. J. Dupont at the Graphic Arts Teaching & Research Centre, Vienna.

April 6 NORWAY Skladanowski programme presented at Circus Variété, Oslo.

April 20 IRELAND Unidentified programme presented at Star of Erin Variety Theatre, Dublin.

May 4 RUSSIA Lumière presented by Francis Doublier at Aquarium Theatre, St Petersburg.

May 6 SOUTH AFRICA R. W. Paul's Theatrograph programme—*Highland Dancers* (GB 96), *Street Scenes in London* (GB 96), *Trilby Dance* (GB 96), *A Military Parade* (GB 96), *The Soldier's Courtship* (GB 96)—presented at Empire Theatre of Varieties, Johannesburg.

May 10 HUNGARY Lumière presented at Royal Hotel, Budapest. Included street scenes taken in front of Opera House and Chain Bridge, Budapest, and Hungarian Millenary Procession.

May 15 SPAIN Lumière presented by M. Promio at 34 Carrera de San Jeronimo, Madrid.

May 27 ROMANIA Lumière presented at Salon l'Independenta Romana, Bucharest.

June 7 YUGOSLAVIA (SERBIA) Lumière presented at Kod Zlatnog Krsta Café, Belgrade.

June 7 DENMARK Lumière presented by Vilhelm Pacht in Raadhuspladsen, Copenhagen.

June 9 NETHERLANDS Lumière presented at the Kurhaus, Scheveningen.

June 18 PORTUGAL Lumière (?) presented by Erwin Rousby at Real Coliseu, Rua da Palma, Lisbon.

June 28 SWEDEN Lumière presented by C. V. Roikjer at the Industrial Exhibition, Malmö.

June 28 FINLAND Lumière presented at the Societetshuset, Helsinki.

July 7 INDIA Lumière presented at Watson's Hotel, Bombay.

July 8 BRAZIL 'Omniographo' presented at 57 Rua do Ouvidor, Rio de Janiero.

July 15 CZECHOSLOVAKIA Lumière presented at the Lázenský dům, Karoly Vary.

July 21 CANADA Edison Vitascope programme presented at West End Park, Ottawa.

July 28 ARGENTINA Lumière presented by Francisco Pastos and Eustaquio Pellier at Colón Theatre, Buenos Aires.

August 11 CHINA French programme (negative evidence suggests *not* Lumière) presented as act of variety show at Hsu Gardens, Shanghai.

August 15 MEXICO Lumière presented by engineering student Salvador Toscano Barragan at 17 Calle de Jesus, Mexico City.

August 22 AUSTRALIA R. W. Paul programme presented by conjurer Carl Hertz at Melbourne Opera House.

September 26 GUATEMALA Lumière presented by Arnold Tobler at 11 Passage Aycinena, Guatemala City.

October 13 NEW ZEALAND R. W. Paul (?) programme of English films presented by Profs Hausmann and Gow at Auckland Opera House.

October ?? POLAND Edison programme presented at Lvov.

Date unknown EGYPT unidentified programme at Zavani Café, Alexandria.

1897

January 24 CUBA Lumière presented by Gabriel Veyre at Teatro Tacón, Havana.

January 28 VENEZUELA Edison presented by Manuel Trujillo at Teatro Baralt, Maracaibo.

February/March ?? BULGARIA Lumière presented in port town of Russe.

March 2 PERU Edison Vitascope presented on the Plaza de Armas, Lima.

June 10 THAILAND Lumière presented by S. G. Marchovsky in Bangkok.

June ?? JAPAN Lumière presented by Katsutaro Inahata at Osaka.

December 25 URUGUAY Lumière at Montevideo.

Date unknown TUNISIA Lumière at store show established by Albert Samama on rue Es-Sadika, Tunis.

1898

Spring GREECE Lumière at Place Kolokotronis, Athens.

1899

Date unknown TURKEY unidentified programme presented privately before Sultan by Spaniard Don Ramirez and then publicly at his Electric Circus, Constantinople.

1900

November 30 (?) INDONESIA Nederlandsche Bioscope Maatschappij presented at Batavia.

Date unknown KOREA free film show sponsored by Anglo-American Tobacco Co. of Shanghai. Admission in exchange for cigarette coupons.

Date unknown SENEGAL Lumière presented at Dakar.

Date unknown IRAN unidentified programme presented before Shah by Mirza Ebrahim Khan at Royal Palace, Teheran. First public show opened in Avenue Cheraq Gaz, Teheran, by Sahâf Bâshi in 1905.

Sandow, Bertholdi (mouth support), Horse Shoeing, Bertholdi (table contortion), Barber Shop, Blacksmiths, Cock Fight, Highland Dance, Wrestling, Trapeze.

The first commercial presentation of films in Britain took place at the Kinetoscope parlour opened by the Continental Commerce Co. of New York at 70 Oxford Street, London, on 18 October 1894. The twelve machines offered such titillating delights as *Carmencita* (a buxom vaudeville artiste) and *Annabelle Serpentine Dance*, as well as more prosaic fare like *Blacksmith Shop, Wrestling Match* and *The Bar Room*.

The first film presented publicly on screen was *La Sortie des Ouvriers de l'Usine Lumière* (Fr 94) which was shown before members of the Société d'Encouragement pour l'Industrie Nationale by Auguste and Louis Lumière at 44 rue de Rennes, Paris, on 22 March 1895. Believed to have been taken in August or September 1894, the film showed workers leaving the Lumière photographic factory at Lyons for their dinner-hour.

The first public screening in Britain was given by Birt Acres at the London headquarters of the Royal Photographic Society, 14 Hanover Square on 14 January 1896. The programme, comprised of films taken by Acres himself, consisted of *The Opening of the Kiel Canal, The Derby, Boxers, Three Skirt Dancers* and *Rough Seas at Dover*.

The first film to be screened before a paying audience was a four-minute boxing subject, *Young Griffo v. Battling Charles Barnett*, presented by Major Woodville Latham of the Lamda Co. at 153 Broadway, New York on 20 May 1895. The projec-

The earliest known motion-picture film—*Traffic Crossing Leeds Bridge* (GB 88).

tor was a primitive and imperfect machine called the Eidoloscope, designed for the Lamda Co. (the first film company established as such) by former Edison employee Eugene Lauste. Although some authorities have cast doubt on the Eidoloscope's ability to create an illusion of movement on a screen, it must have achieved a sufficient level of technical acceptability, however jerky and inadequate the picture, for Latham to have attracted paying customers. Another commercial show was given by C. Francis Jenkins and Thomas Armat, using a projector they had designed themselves, at a purpose-built temporary cinema at the Cotton States Exposition at Atlanta, Ga., in September 1895. After making various improvements to the machine, Armat came to an arrangement with Thomas Edison, who had failed to produce a workable projector himself, by which the celebrated inventor would be allowed to exploit it as his own. As the Edison Vitascope, the improved machine was debuted at Koster and Bial's Music Hall on Broadway on 23 April 1896, an occasion which has often and erroneously been heralded as the first time that motion pictures were presented on a screen to a paying audience.

The first screening before a paying audience in Europe was given by Max and Emil Skladanowski with a projector of their own invention at the Berlin Wintergarten on 1 November 1895. The films were made up of endless loops and the action lasted only a few seconds before it was repeated. Taken at the rate of eight pictures a second, the films were flickering and jerky, but the fact that there was movement on the screen at all was sufficient for the Nazis to claim, some 40 years later, that Germany was the cradle of the cinema industry. In fact neither the work of Lauste and Latham in America, nor that of the Skladanowskis in Germany was destined to have any lasting effect on the development of the cinema. It is generally agreed that the première of the Lumière brothers' show, before a paying audience at the Grand Café, 14 Boulevard des Capucines, Paris, on 28 December 1895, marks the debut of the motion picture as a regular entertainment medium. Their projector was the first to advance beyond the experimental stage and the first to be offered for sale.

The first screening before a paying audience in Britain took place at the Regent Street Polytechnic on 20 February 1896, when the French magician Felicien Trewey exhibited the Lumière Cinématographe with accompanying commentary by M. Francis Pochet. Admission was 1s and the engagement lasted three weeks, hours 2–4 p.m. The opening programme included the Lumière films *Arrival of a Train at a Station, The Baby and the Goldfish, The Family Tea Table* and *M. Trewey: Prestigidateur.* The first commercial show outside London was by Birt Acres at Cardiff Town Hall on 5 May 1896.

TWO

THE INDUSTRY

FEATURE FILMS

The world's first full-length feature film was *The Story of the Kelly Gang* (Aus 06), made in Australia in 1906. No other country established regular production of features until 1911. (*Backnumbers*)

The first feature film, according with the Cinématheque Française definition of a feature being a commercially made film over one hour duration, was Charles Tait's *The Story of the Kelly Gang* (Aus 06), which was 4000 ft (1219 m) long and had a running time of 60–70 min. A biopic of Victoria's notorious bushranger Ned Kelly (1855–80), the film was produced by the theatrical company J. & N. Tait of Melbourne, Victoria, and shot on location over a period of about six months at Whitehorse Road, Mitcham (Glenrowan Hotel scenes, including the last stand of the Kelly Gang); at Rosanna (railway scenes); and on Charles Tait's property at Heidelberg, Vic. (all other scenes). The actual armour which had belonged to Ned Kelly—a bullet-proof helmet and jerkin fashioned from ploughshares—was borrowed from the Victorian Museum and worn by the actor playing the role, an unidentified Canadian from the Bland Holt touring company who disappeared before the film was finished. It had to be completed with an extra standing in as Ned, all these scenes being taken in long shot. Elizabeth Veitch played Kate Kelly, and others in the cast included Ollie Wilson, Frank Mills, Bella Cole and Vera Linden.

Made on a budget of £450, *The Story of the Kelly Gang* was premièred at the Athenaeum Hall, Melbourne, on 24 December 1906 and recovered its cost within a week, eventually grossing some £25,000, including receipts from the English release. No complete print survives but stills from the film were issued as picture postcards and give the impression of a vigorous, all-action drama made with imaginative use of outdoor locations—a significant advance on the studio-bound one-reelers being turned out in Europe and America at this period. It was long believed that the film had been totally lost, but recently a 210 ft (64 m) long fragment was discovered in Melbourne. Other versions of the Ned Kelly story survive. There were remakes in 1910, 1917, 1920, 1923, 1934, 1951 and 1970, all of them Australian productions except the last, a British film with Mick Jagger in the title role.

Australia was the only country in the world to have established regular production of feature-length films prior to 1911. For figures on early output, see Production: World Output (pp. 14–15).

The first feature-length film made in Europe was Michel Carré's 90-minute long production *L'Enfant prodigue* (Fr 07), premièred at the Théâtre des Variétés in the Boulevard Montmartre, Paris, on 20 June 1907. This was a screen representation of a stage play, with little or no adaptation.

THE FIRST 12 FEATURE FILMS PRODUCED IN THE USA

June 1912 *Oliver Twist* (5 reels) H. A. Spanuth
Dec 1912 *The Beloved Vagabond* (6 reels) Gold
  Rooster
Jan 1913 *Cleopatra* (6 reels) United States Film
  Co.
Jan 1913 *From the Manger to the Cross* (6 reels)
  Kalem
Aug 1913 *Moths* (5 reels) Thanhouser

Aug 1913 *Arizona* (6 reels) All Star Feature
  Corp.
Oct 1913 *In the Bishop's Carriage* (5 reels)
  Famous Players
Nov 1913 *The Count of Monte Cristo* (5 reels)
  Famous Players
Nov 1913 *Traffic in Souls* (6 reels) Imp
Dec 1913 *The Sea-Wolf* (7 reels) Bosworth

Dec 1913 *Ten Nights in a Bar-room* (5 reels)
  Photo Drama
Dec 1913 *Hoodman Blind* (5 reels) Pilot
It is worthy of note that neither Cecil B.
DeMille's *The Squaw Man* (US 14) nor D. W.
Griffith's *Judith of Bethulia* (US 14), each of
which has been cited as the first feature
produced in the US, appears above.

THE FIRST 12 FEATURE FILMS PRODUCED IN THE UK

Aug 1912 *Oliver Twist* (4 reels) Hepworth
Dec 1912 *Lorna Doone* (5 reels) Clarendon
May 1913 *East Lynne* (6 reels) Barker
July 1913 *The Battle of Waterloo* (5 reels) British
  & Colonial
July 1913 *Ivanhoe* (6 reels) Zenith Films

July 1913 *A Message from Mars* (4 reels)
  United Kingdom Films
Aug 1913 *David Copperfield* (8 reels) Hepworth
Sept 1913 *King Charles* (4 reels) Clarendon
Sept 1913 *A Cigarette-Maker's Romance*
  (4 reels) Hepworth

Sept 1913 *The House of Temperley* (5 reels)
  London Films
Oct 1913 *The Grip* (4 reels) Britannic Films
Oct 1913 *Hamlet* (6 reels) Hepworth

COUNTRIES PRODUCING FEATURE FILMS BY 1914

By the outbreak of World War I, the following countries had commenced feature-film production:

1906 Australia
1909 France
1911 Denmark, Germany, Italy, Poland, Russia,
  Spain, Yugoslavia (Serbia)

1912 Austria, Greece, Hungary, Japan, Norway,
  Romania, United Kingdom, United States

1913 Brazil, Finland, India, Netherlands,
  Sweden, Venezuela, Canada

FILM PRODUCING NATIONS

The following list chronicles, wherever known, the first motion picture production, the first dramatized (i.e. acted) production, the first feature film (over one hour duration) and the first talkie feature of each of the film-producing countries of the world, signified by the abbreviations Film, Drama, Feature, Talkie. The first feature film in natural colour is included for major film-producing nations. The first motion picture production means a film made by a native or permanent resident of the country, as opposed to a visiting cameraman or non-resident producer. Where a category has been omitted no information is available. Drama/Feature and Feature/Talkie signify respectively that the first feature-length film was also the first dramatic production of any length and that the first talkie was also the first feature-length production. Other abbreviations: doc. = documentary; f. = filmed; d. = directed; pr. = première; prod. = produced.

ALGERIA
Film: *La Prière du muezzin* (1906), d. Felix
  Mesguich.
Drama: *Ali Bouf a l'huile* (1907), d. Felix
  Mesguich.
Feature/Talkie: *Peuple en marche* (1963), d.
  Ahmed Rachedi and René Vautier.

ANGOLA
Film: *Monangambé* (1968), d. Sarah Maldoror.
Feature/Talkie: *Des fusils pour Banta* (1970), d.
  Sarah Maldoror.

ARGENTINA
Film: *La Bandera Argentina* (1897), d. Eugenio
  Py.
Drama: *El Fusilamiento de Dorrego* (1908), d.
  Mario Gallo and Salvador Rosich.
Feature: *Nobleza Gaucha* (1915), d. Humberto
  Cairo.
Talkie: *Muñequitas porteñas* (1931), with Maria
  Turguenova—Vitaphone system.

AUSTRALIA
Film: *The Melbourne Cup* (3 Nov 1896), d.
  Marius Sestier.

Drama: untitled 75 ft drama by Joseph Perry of
  the Salvation Army about man sent to gaol for
  stealing bread and helped by Army's 'prison-
  gate brigade' on release, c. 1897.
Feature: *The Story of the Kelly Gang* (pr. 26 Dec
  1906), d. Charles Tait. (NB: **First feature
  film** (q.v.) **in world.**)
Talkie: *Fellers* (press shown 23 May 1930), d.
  Arthur Higgins and Austin Fay, prod. Artaus
  Films, starring Arthur Tauchert.

AUSTRIA
Drama: *Ein Walzertraum* (scene from opera)
  f. 2 Mar 1907.
Feature: *Zweierlei Blut* (1912), starring Luise
  Kohn and Jakob Fleck.
Talkie: *G'schichten aus der Steiermark* (pr. 23
  Aug 1929), d. Hans Otto Löwenstein, prod.
  Eagle Film and Ottoton film, starring Hilde
  Maria and Anny Burg.

BANGLADESH
Feature/Talkie: *Mukh O Mukhosh* (1956), d.
  Jabbar Khan.

BELGIUM
Film: *Le Marché aux poissons de Bruxelles* (1897)
  and other actualities, d. M. Alexandre.
Drama: *'chand d'habits* (1897), d. M. Alexandre.
Feature: *Belgique meurtrie* (1920), d. Paul Flon.
Talkie: *La Famille Klepkens* (1930), d. Gaston
  Schoukens and Paul Flon.

BOLIVIA
Film: actualities by Luis Castillo, 1913.
Feature: *La Profecia del Lago* (1923), d. José
  Maria Velasco Maidana (film banned).
Talkie: *La Guerra del Chaco* (1936), d. José Luis
  Bazoberry.

BRAZIL
Film: *View of Guanabara Bay* (f. 19 July 1898),
  d. Alfonso Segreto.
Drama: *Os Estranguladores* (1906) —crime film
  based on true story in police files, d. Isaac
  Sandenberg.
Feature: *O Crime dos Banhados* (1913), d.
  Francisco Santos, prod. Guarany Film.

Talkie: *Acabaram-se os Otarios* (1930), country
  comedy d. Luis de Barros, starring Genésio
  Arruda and Tom Bill.

BULGARIA
Film: actuality about Bulgarian army, 1910.
Drama: *Such is the War* (1914).
Feature: *The Bulgar is a Gentleman* (1915),
  satire about Sofia snobbery, d. Vassil
  Guendov, starring ditto and Mara Lipina.
Talkie: *A Song of the Balkan Mountains* (1934),
  d. Peter Stoychev.

BURMA
Film: *The Funeral of U Tun Shein* (1920)
  actuality made by U Ohn Maung.
Feature: *Dana Pratap* (1925), prod. London Art
  Photo Co. of Rangoon.
Talkie: *Shwe ein the* (1932), prod. British Burma
  Film Co.

CAMEROON
Film: *L'Aventure en France* (1962), d. Jean-Paul
  N'Gassa.
Feature/Talkie (doc.): *Une Nation est née*
  (1972).
Feature/Talkie (drama): *Pousse-pousse* (1975),
  d. Daniel Karawa.

CANADA
Film: actualities of life on the prairies made by
  James Freer of Brandon, Manitoba, 1897.
Drama: *The Great Unknown* (1913), d. Oscar
  Lund, starring Barbara Tennent and Fred
  Truesdell.
Feature: *Evangeline* (1913), d. E. P. Sullivan and
  W. H. Cavanaugh, prod. Canadian Bioscope
  Co., starring Laura Lyman and John F.
  Carleton.
Talkie (English): *North of '49* (1929), d. Neal
  Hart, prod. British Canadian Pictures.
Talkie (French): *A la croisée des chemins*
  (1943), d. and starring Paul Guévrement.
Colour: *Talbot of Canada* (1938), Kodachrome.

CAPE VERDE ISLANDS
Feature/Talkie: *Os Flagelados do Vento Leste*
  (1988), d. António Faria, starring Carlos
  Alhinho and Arciolinda Almeida.

FILM PRODUCING NATIONS (continued)

CHILE

Film: *Un Ejercicio General de Bomberos*, pr. 26 May 1902.

Feature: *La Baraja de la muerte* (1916), d. Salvador Giambastiane.

Talkie: *Norte y Sur* (1934), d. Jorge Délano.

CHINA

Film/Drama: *Tingchun Mountain* (1908), d. Lin Tenlun of the Feng Tai Photo Shop, Peking, starring Tan Hsin-pei.

Feature: *Yen Rei-sun* (1921), about embezzler who murders prostitute, d. Ren Pun-yen, prod. China Film Research Society, starring Chun Tso-Tze and Wang Tsai-yun.

Talkie: *Singsong Girl Red Peony* (1930), d. Chang Shih-chuan, prod. Star Film Co., starring Butterfly Wu.

COLOMBIA

Film/Drama: *The Life of General Rafael Uribe* (1914), d. brothers Di Domenico.

Feature: *La Maria* (1922), d. Alfredo Del Diestro.

Talkie: *Flowers of the Valley* (1939), d. Pedro Moreno Garzón.

CONGO

Film: *Kayako* (c. 1967), d. Sébastien Kamba.

Feature/Talkie: *La Rançon d'une alliänce* (1973), d. Sébastien Kamba.

COSTA RICA

Drama: *El Retorno* (1926), d. Romulo Bertoni.

Feature: *La Segua* (1984), d. Antonio Yglesias.

CUBA

Film: *El Brujo desapareciendo* (1898), d. José E. Casasús

Drama: *El Cabildo de ña Romualda* (1908), d. Enrique Diaz Quesada, prod. Metropolitan Films.

Feature: *El Rey de los campos de Cuba* (1913), d. Enrique Diaz Quesada, starring Gerardo Artecona and Evangelina Adams.

Talkie: *El Caballero de Max* (1930), d. Jaime San-Andrews, starring Nancy Norton and Wilfredo Genier—Vitaphone. (The Cuban government had made a sound-on-film documentary by the Phonofilm process in 1926.)

CYPRUS

Feature/Talkie: *Avrianos Polemistis/Tomorrow's Warrior* (1981), d. Michael Papas, prod. Cyprian (MP) Films, starring Christos Zannidea.

CZECHOSLOVAKIA

Film/Drama: *Výstavní Párkař a Lepič Plakátů* (1898), *Dostavencíčko Ve Mlýnici* (1898), *Pláč a Smích* (1898), etc., actualities and short comedies featuring Bohemian cabaret artiste Josef Šváb-Malostranský, d. Prague student Jan Křiženecký.

Feature: *Pražští Adamité* (1917), d. Antonín Fencl, prod. Lucernafilm, starring Josef Vošalik.

Talkie (Czech): *Tonka of the Gallows* (1930), d. Karel Anton. Talkie (Slovak): *The Singing Land* (1932), d. Karel Plicka.

Colour: *Jan Roháč of Duba* (1947), d. Vladamír Borský.

DAHOMEY (BENIN)

Film: *Ganvié, mon village* (1966), d. Pascal Abikanlou.

Feature/Talkie: *Sous le signe du Vaudoun* (1974), d. Pascal Abikanlou.

DENMARK

Film: *Kørsel med grønlandske Hunde* (1896), d. Peter Elfelt.

Drama: *Henrettelsen* (1903), d. Peter Elfelt, starring Francesca Nathansen and Victor Betzonich.

Feature: *Den sorte Drøm* (pr. 4 Sept 1911), circus drama, d. Urban Gad, starring Valdemar Psilander and Asta Nielsen.

Talkie: *Eskimo* (pr. 9 Oct 1930), d. G. Schneevogt, starring Mona Martenson and Paul Richter.

Colour: *Tricks* (pr. 7 May 1956), d. Erik Balling.

DOMINICAN REPUBLIC

Drama: *Las Emboscados de Cupido* (1924), d. Francisco Palau.

Feature/Talkie: *La Serpiente de la Luna de los Piratas* (1972), d. Jean-Louis Jorge.

ECUADOR

Feature/Talkie: *Se Conocieron en Guayaquil* (1949), d. Alberto Sanatana, prod. Ecuador Sono Films.

EGYPT

Film: *Dans les rues d'Alexandrie* (1912), d. M. de Lagarne.

Drama: *Sharaf el Badawi* (1918), prod. Italo-Egyptian Cinematographic Co.

Feature: *Koubla Fil Sahara'a* (1927), d. Ibrahim Lama, prod. Condor Film. (NB: Shooting on *Laila* (1927), generally credited as first Egyptian feature, started earlier, but the film was released later.)

Talkie: *Onchoudet el Fouad* (pr. 14 Apr 1932), d. Mario Volpi.

FINLAND

Film: *Pupils of Nikolai Street School during Break* (1904).

Drama: *Salaviinanpolttajat* (1907), d. Louis Sparre, starring Teuvo Puro and Jussi Snellman.

Feature: *Kun Onni Pettää* (pr. 23 Nov 1913), d. Konrad Tallroth, starring Axel Precht and Sigrid Precht.

Talkie: *The Log-Driver's Bride* (1931), d. Erkki Karu.

FRANCE

Film: *La Sortie des Usines* (1894), d. Louis Lumière.

Drama: *L'Arroseur arrosé* (1895), d. Louis Lumière, starring Lumière's gardener M. Clerc and apprentice boy Duval.

Feature: *L'Enfant prodigue* (pr. 20 June 1907), d. Michel Carré.

Talkie: *Les Trois masques* (1929), d. André Hugon, prod. Pathé-Natan, starring Renée Heribel and Marcel Vibert.

Colour: *L'Eternal amour* (1921), d. Gaston Colombani in Héraute Colour.

GABON

Film: *M'Bolo Gabon* (1967).

Feature/Talkie: *Où vas-tu Koumba* (1971), d. Alain Ferrari and Simon Auré.

GERMANY

Films: *Italian Dance, Kangaroo Boxer, Juggler, Acrobats, Russian Dance, Serpentine Dance, Lutte, Apothéose* (all pr. 1 Nov 1895), d. Max and Emil Skladanowski.

Feature: *In dem grossen Augenblick* (pr. 11 Aug 1911), d. Urban Gad, prod. Deutsche Bioscop GmbH, starring Asta Nielsen and Hugo Hink.

Talkie: *Melodie der Welt* (pr. 12 Mar 1929), d. Walter Ruttman, starring J. Kowal Samborsky and Renée Stobrawa.

GHANA

Drama: *Amenu's Child* (1949), d. Sean Graham.

Feature/Talkie: *Boy Kumasenu* (1951), d. Sean Graham.

GIBRALTAR

Feature/Talkie: *Instant Justice* (1985), d. Denis Amar, prod. Mulloway Ltd, starring Michael Paré and Tawny Kitaen.

GREECE

Film: Olympic Games actuality (1906).

Drama: *Quo Vadis Spiridion* (1911), comedy, d. Spiros Dimitracopoulos, prod. Athina Films.

Feature: *Golfo* (1912), d. Costas Bahatoris from Spiros Peressiadis' folk-story play.

Talkie: *Les Apaches d'Athenes* (1930), musical, d. D. Gaziadis, prod. Dag Films, starring Mary Sayannou and Petros Epitropakis.

GUATEMALA

Drama: *Agent No 13* (1912), d. Alberto de la Riva.

Feature/Talkie: *El Sombreron* (1950).

GUINEA

Film: *Mouramani Mamadou Touré* (1953).

Feature/Talkie: *Sergeant Bakary Woolén* (1966), d. Lamine Akin.

GUINEA-BISSAU

Feature/Talkie: *Ntturudu* (1986), d. Umban U'Kset, prod. Republic of Guinea-Bissau, starring Mario Acqlino.

GUYANA

Feature/Talkie: *Aggro Seizeman* (1975), d. James Mannas and Brian Stuart-Young, starring Gordon Case and Martha Gonsalves.

HONG KONG

Dramas: *The Widowed Empress, The Unfilial Son, Revealed by the Pot, Stealing the Cooked Ducks* (all 1909), d. Benjamin Polaski, prod. Asia Film Co.

HUNGARY

Film: *The Emperor Franz Josef opening the Millenial Exhibition* (1896), d. Arnold Sziklay.

Drama: *Siófoki kaland* (pr. 29 Apr 1898) — shown as sequence in stage production *Mozgáfényképek/Moving Pictures.*

Feature: *Ma és holnap* (1912), d. Mihály Kertész (Michael Curtiz).

Talkie: *A Kék Bálvány* (pr. 25 Sept 1931), d. Lajos Lázár, starring Pál Jávor.

Colour: *Ludas Matyi* (1949), d. K. Nádasdy.

ICELAND

Film: various short subjects shot 1904.

Drama: *Aevintýri Jóns og Gvendar/The Adventures of Jön and Gvendur* (1923), d. Loftur Gudmundsson.

Feature/Talkie: *Milli fjalls og fjöru/Between Mountain and Shore* (1948), d. Loftur Gudmundsson.

INDIA

Film: *Cocoanut Fair* (1897), maker unknown, probably English. First by Indian: *The Wrestlers* (f. Nov 1899), d. Harishchandra S. Bhatvadekar of Bombay.

Drama: *Pundalik* (pr. 18 May 1912), d. R. G. Torney.

Feature: *Raja Harischandra* (pr. 17 May 1913), d. D. G. Phalke of Bombay.

Talkie (Hindi): *Alam Ara* (pr. 14 Mar 1931), d. A. M. Irani, prod. Imperial Film Co., starring Master Vithal and Zubeida.

Talkie (Bengali): *Jamai Sasthi* (1931), prod. Madan Theatres.

Colour: *Kisan Kanya* (1937), d. Moti B. Gidwani, prod. Imperial Film Co.—Cinecolor.

India's first full-length feature film, D. G. Phalke's *Raja Harischandra* (Ind 12).

emigrant returning from USA, d. Jordano Pidutti.
Talkie: *In the Ruins of Ba'albak* (1936), d. George Costi, prod. Lumnar Film Co.

LIBYA
Feature/Talkie: *Lorsque le destin s'acharne* (1972), d. A. Zarrouk.

LUXEMBOURG
Feature/Talkie: *Wât huet e gesôt?* (1980), d. Paul Scheuer, prod. AFO-Film.

MADAGASCAR
Film: Centenary celebrations of martyrdom of Malagasy hero Rasalama, d. M. Raberono 1937.
Feature/Talkie: *Le Retour* (1973), d. Randrasana Ignace Solo.

MALAYSIA (MALAYA)
Talkie: *Chandu* (1939), prod. Malayan Films Inc.

MALI
Drama: *Bambo* (1968).
Feature/Talkie: *Les Wandyalankas* (1973), d. Alkaly Kaba.

MALTA
Feature/Talkie: *Katarin* (1977), d. Cecil Satariano, starring Anna Stafrace.

MAURITANIA
Feature/Talkie: *Soleil O* (1971), d. Med Hondo.

MEXICO
Drama: *Don Juan Tenorio* (1898), d. Salvador Toxano Barragan.
Feature: *Fatal Orgullo* (1916), prod. México Lux.
Talkie: *Más fuerte que el deber* (1930), d. Raphael J. Sevilla.
Colour: *Novillero* (1936), d. Boris Maicon—Cinecolor.

MOROCCO
Feature/Talkie: *Itto* (1934), d. Jean Benoit-Levy.

NEPAL
Feature/Talkie: *Harischandra* (1951).

NETHERLANDS
Drama: *Muis Hamel bij den Criffeur* (1904), d. Albert and Willy Mullens.
Feature: *De Levende Ladder* (1913), d. Maurits H. Binger, prod. Hollandia.
Talkie: *Vader des Vaderlands* (1933), d. G. J. Teunissen.

NEW ZEALAND
Film: *Opening of the Auckland Exhibition* (f. 1 Dec 1898), d. A. E. Whitehouse.
Drama: *A Message from Mars* (1903), d. W. F. Brown.
Feature: *The Test* (1916), d. and starring Rawdon Blandford.
Talkie: *Down on the Farm* (1935), d. Lee Hill and Stuart Pitt, prod. Sound Film Productions Ltd.

NICARAGUA
Feature/Talkie: *Alsino y el Condor* (1982), d. Miguel Littin.

NIGER
Film: *Aouré* (1962), d. Mustapha Allasane.
Feature/Talkie: *FVVA* (1971), d. Mustapha Allasane.

NIGERIA
Drama: *My Father's Burden* (1961), d. Segun Olusola.
Feature/Talkie: *Two Men and a Goat* (1966), d. Edward Jones Horatio.

INDONESIA
Feature: *Loetoeng Kasaroeng* (1927), d. G. Kruger at Bandung.
Talkie: *Njai Dasima* (1931), d. Lie Tek Soi and Bakhtiar Effendi, prod. Tan's Film.

IRAN
Film: scenes of religious procession and of Shah's private zoo, d. Mirza Ebrahim Khan (Court Photographer to Shah Mozaffareddin) 1900.
Drama/Feature: *Abi and Rabi* (1932), comedy, d. Ohanian.
Talkie: *Dokhta Lor* (1934), d. Abdol Hoseyn Sepenta.

IRAQ
Drama/Feature/Talkie: *Leila in Iraq* (1949).

IRELAND
Drama: *Fun at Finglas Fair* (1915), d. F. J. McCormick. Never released, as all prints destroyed in Easter Rising.
Feature: *Knocknagow* (1918), d. Fred O'Donovan, prod. Film Co. of Ireland, starring Fred O'Donovan and Kathleen Murphy, featuring Master Cyril Cusack in screen debut.
Talkie (English): *The Voice of Ireland* (1932), d. Col Victor Haddick. Talkie (Irish): see Languages: Irish Gaelic (p. 152).

ISRAEL
Film: documentary about Jewish settlement in Palestine (1912), d. Akiva Arie Weiss.
Drama: *Yerahmiel the Shlemiel* and other short comedies (1926), d. Nathan Axelrod.
Feature: *Oded Hanoded* (1933), d. Nathan Axelrod.
Talkie: *Me'al Hekhoravot* (1936), d. Nathan Axelrod.

ITALY
Film: *Arrivo del treno stazione di Milano* (1896), d. Italo Pacchioni.
Drama: *La Presa di Roma* (1905), d. Filoteo Albernini, starring Carlo Rosaspina.
Feature: *La Portatrice di pane* (1911), d. S. De Montépin, prod. Vesuvio Films, Naples.
Colour Feature: *Cyrano de Bergerac* (1925), d. Augusto Genina, prod. Unione

Cinematographica Italia, starring Pierre Magnier.
Talkie: *La Canzone dell' amore* (1930), d. Genarro Righelli.

IVORY COAST
Film: *Sur la dune de la solitude* (1964), d. Timité Bassori.
Feature/Talkie: *Korogo* (1964), d. Georges Keita.

JAMAICA
Feature/Talkie: *The Harder They Come* (1972), d. Perry Henzell, starring Jimmy Cliff and Janet Bartley.

JAPAN
Film: street scenes in Tokyo's Ginza and shots of geisha from Shimbasi and Gion districts, d. Tsunekichi Shibata of the Mitsukoshi Department Store's photo dept., 1897.
Drama: *Momiji-gari* (1897), Noh drama, d. Tsunekichi Shibata, starring Kikugoro V and Danjuro IX.
Feature: *The Life Story of Tasuke Shiobara* (1912).
Talkie: *Taii no Musume* (1929), prod. Nikkatsu Co.
Colour: *Karumen Kokyo ni Kaeru* (1951).

JORDAN
Feature/Talkie: *Watani Habibi* (1964).

KOREA
Drama: *The Righteous Revenge* (1919), d. Kim Do-san.
Feature: *A Pledge in the Moonlight* (1923), morality tale about importance of keeping money in banks, d. Yun Paek-nam.
Talkie: *Chun Hyang-jon* (1939), d. Yi Pil-u and Yi Myong-u.

KUWAIT
Feature/Talkie: *Bas Ya Bahar* (1972), d. Khaled el Seddik, starring Mohamad Monsour and Amal Baker.

LAOS
Feature/Talkie: *Gun Shots in the Valley of the Jugs* (1983).

LEBANON
Drama/Feature: *The Adventures of Elias Mabrouk* (1929), comedy about Lebanese

NORWAY
Film: reception of the newly-elected King Haakon VII in Oslo, 1905.
Drama: *Thje Dangerous Life of a Fisherman* (1907), prod. Norsk Kinematograf A/S, starring Alma Lund.
Feature: *Anny—Story of a Prostitute* (1912), d. Adam Eriksen, starring Julie Jansen.
Talkie: *The Great Christening* (pr. 26 Dec 1931), d. Einar Sissener and Tancred Ibsen, starring Einar Sissener.

OUTER MONGOLIA
Feature/Talkie: *At the Frontier* (1937).

PAKISTAN
Feature/Talkie: *Teri Yaad* (1948), prod. Dewan Pictures, d. Dawood Chand, starring Asha Posley and Nasir Khan. Urdu.

PARAGUAY
Feature/Talkie: *Cerro Cora* (1978), starring Rosa Ros and Roberto de Felice, d. Ladislao Gonzalez.

PERU
Film: *Peruvian Centaurs* (1908), actuality of cavalry manoeuvres.
Drama: *Negocio al Agua* (1913), d. Frederico Blume.
Feature: *Luis Pardo* (1927), biopic of brigand of that name, d. and starred Enrique Cornejo Villanueva.
Talkie: *Resaca* (1934), d. Alberto Santana.

PHILIPPINES
Film: *El Fusilamiento de Rizal.*
Feature: *Dalagang Bukid* (1919), d. José Nepomuceno.
Talkie: *Punyal na Ginto* (1932).

POLAND
Film: actualities made by Kazimierz Proszynski with a camera of his own invention—the 'pleograph'—1894.
Drama: *His First Visit to Warsaw* (1908), comedy starring Antoni Fertner.
Feature: *Dzieje Grzechu* (pr. 26 Aug 1911), d. Antoni Bednarczyk, starring Maria Mirska and Teodor Roland.
Talkie: *The Morals of Madame Dulska* (1930), d. B. Newolyn.

PORTUGAL
Film: *Leaving the Factory* (1896), d. Aurelio Da Paz Dos Reis.
Drama: *Rapto duma Actriz* (1907), d. Lino Ferreira, starring Carlos Leal and Luz Velozo.
Feature: *A Rosa do Adro* (1919).
Talkie: *A Severa* (pr. 17 June 1931), d. Jose Leitao de Barros, prod. Super-Filmes, starring Dina Teresa and Conde Marialava.

ROMANIA
Film: actualities of Bucharest race-course, a fair and the Capsa coffee house (1897), d. Paul Menu.
Drama: *Amor fatal* (pr. 26 Sept 1911), d. Grigore Brezeanu, starring Lucia Sturdza and Tony Bulandra.
Feature: *Razboiul Independentei* (pr. 1 Sept 1912), d. Grigore Brezeanu, starring C. Nottra and Ar. Demetriade.
Talkie: *Ciuleandra* (pr. 30 Oct 1930), d. Martin Berger, starring Jeana Popovici-Voinea.

SENEGAL
Film: *C'était il y a 4 ans* (1955), d. Paulin Vieyra.
Feature/Talkie: *La Noire de . . .* (1967), d. Ousmane Sembène.

SINGAPORE
Feature/Talkie: *White Golden Dragon* (1936).

SOMALIA
Film/Drama: *The Love that Knows no Barrier* (1961), d. Hossein Manrok.
Feature/Talkie: *Town and Village* (1968), d. El Hadji Mohamed Giumale.

SOUTH AFRICA
Film: scene taken from front of tram travelling down Commissioner Street, Johannesburg, d. Edgar Hyman, 1896.
Drama: *The Star of the South* (1911), about theft of diamond found on banks of Vaal by a Hottentot, prod. Springbok Film Co.
Feature: *De Voortrekkers* (pr. 16 Dec 1916), d. Harold Shaw, prod. African Film Productions Ltd, starring Dick Cruickshanks and Zulu actor Goba as Dingaan. Claimed (in S. Africa) that *The Covered Wagon* (US 23) was inspired by this film.
Talkie (Afrikaans): *Mocdertjie* (1931), d. Joseph Albrecht, starring Carl Ricjter and Joan du Toit.
Talkie (English): *They Built a Nation* (1938), d. Joseph Albrecht, prod. African Film Productions Ltd.

SPAIN
Film: *Salida de misa de doce en la Iglesia del Pilar en Zaragoza* (1896), d. Eduardo Jimeno.
Drama: *Riña en un Café* (1897), d. Fructuoso Gelabert.
Feature: *Lucha por la herencia* (1911), d. Otto Mulhauser, prod. Alhambra Films.
Talkie: *Yo quiero que me lleven a Hollywood* (pr. 20 June 1932), d. Edgar Neville.
Colour: *En un rincon de España* (1949), d. Jerónimo Mihura.

SRI LANKA
Feature/Talkie: *Banda Nagarayata Pemineema* (1953).

SUDAN
Feature/Talkie: *Hopes and Dreams* (1969), d. Al Rachid Mehdi.

SURINAM
Feature/Talkie: *Wan Pipel* (1976), d. Pim de la Parra, starring Borger Breeveld and Diana Gangaram.

SWEDEN
Film/Drama: *Slagsmål i Gamla Stockholm* (pr. 3 July 1897), two 17th-century cavaliers fighting over a girl, d. Ernest Florman, prod. Numa Handels & Fabriks AB.
Feature: *Blodets Röst* (pr. 20 Oct 1913), d. Victor Sjöström, prod. Svenska Biografteatern, starring Victor Sjöström and Ragna Wettergreen.
Talkie: *Konstgjorda Svensson* (pr. 14 Oct 1929), d. Gustaf Edgren, prod. Film AB Minerva, starring Fridolf Rhudin and Brita Apelgren.
Colour: *The Bells in Old Town* (1947), d. Ragnar Hylton-Cavallier, prod. Europa Film—Cinecolor, starring Edvard Person.

SWITZERLAND
Films: *Zurcher Sechseläuten-Umzag* (c. 1901) and *Montreux Fête des Narcisses* (c. 1901), d. Georges Hipleh-Walt.
Feature: *Der Bergführer* (1917), d. Eduard Bienz, prod. La Société Bâloise EOS.
Talkie: *Bünzli's Grosstadtabenteuer* (1930), d. Robert Wohlmut, starring Freddy Scheim.

SYRIA
Drama/Feature: *Al Moutaham al Bari* (1928), gangster movie, d. and starring Ayoub Badri,

prod. Hermon Film.
Talkie: *Leila Al-Amira* (1947), d. Niazi Mustafa.

TAIWAN
Drama: *The Orphan who Saved his Grandfather* (1922).

TANZANIA
Feature/Talkie: *Gumu* (1935).

THAILAND
Drama/Feature: *Miss Suwan* (1922), d. and prod. Henry McRay and the Wasuvati family. Performers were 'noble families and high-ranking government officials'.

TRINIDAD
Drama: *Callaloo* (1937), starring Ursula Johnson.
Feature/Talkie: *The Right and Wrong* (1970), d. Harbance Kumar, prod. De Luxe Films, starring Ralph Maharaj and Jesse Macdonald.

TUNISIA
Drama: *Ain el Ghezal* (1924), d. Haydée Samama-Chikly, starring Si Haj Hadi Djeheli.
Feature: *The Secret of Fatouma* (1928), d. Dedoncloit, starring Véra de Yourgaince.
Talkie: *Majnunal Kairouan* (1937), d. J. A. Creuzi, starring Fliza Chamia and Habib el Manaa.

TURKEY
Film: *Collapse of the Russian Monument in Ayestafanos* (1914), d. Fuat Uzkinay.
Drama: *The Wedding of Himmet Aga* (1916).
Feature: *Pençe* (1917), d. Sedat Simavi.
Talkie: *Istanbul Sokaklarinda* (1931), d. Muhsin Ertugrul, prod. Ipek Film.

UK
Film: *Traffic Crossing Leeds Bridge* (1888), d. Louis Aimé Augustin Le Prince.
Drama: *The Soldier's Courtship* (f. Apr 1896), d. Robert Paul, starring Fred Storey.
Feature: *Oliver Twist* (1912), d. Thomas Bentley, prod. Hepworth, starring Ivy Millais and Alma Taylor.
Colour Feature: *The World, the Flesh and the Devil* (1914), d. F. Martin Thornton, prod. Union Jack Photoplays and Natural Colour Kinematograph Co., starring Frank Esmond.
Talkie: *Blackmail* (pr. 21 June 1929), d. Alfred Hitchcock, prod. British International Pictures, starring Anny Ondra and John Longden.

UPPER VOLTA
Film: *A Minuit . . . l'Independence* (1960).
Feature/Talkie: *Le Sang des parias* (1973), d. Mamadou Djim Kolla.

URUGUAY
Film: *Una Carrera de Ciclismo en el Velodrome de Arroyo Seco* (1898), d. Felix Oliver.
Drama: *Oliver, Juncal 108* (1900), d. and starring Felix Oliver.
Feature: *Del Pingo al Volante* (1928), d. Roberto Kouri, prod. Bonne Garde.
Talkie: *Dos Destinos* (1936), d. Juan Etchebchere, prod. Estudios Ciclolux, starring Pepe Corbi.

USA
Film: actualities of fencers and wrestlers, etc., d. W. K. L. Dickson, prod. Edison Co., 1892.
Drama: *The Execution of Mary Queen of Scots* (f. 28 Aug 1895), d. Alfred Clark, prod. Raff & Gammon and Edison Co., starring Mr R. L. Thomas (as Mary!).
Feature: *Oliver Twist* (pr. 1 June 1912), prod. H. A. Spanuth, starring Nat C. Goodwin and Winnie Burns.

Colour Feature: *The Gulf Between* (pr. 21 Sept 1917), prod. Technicolor Motion Picture Corp., starring Grace Darmond and Niles Welch.

Talkie: *The Jazz Singer* (pr. 6 Oct 1927), d. Alan Crosland, prod. Warner Bros, starring Al Jolson.

USSR

Film: *Cossack Trick Riders* (f. 29 Sept 1896), d. amateur cinematographer A. P. Fedetsky at Kharkov.

Drama: *Boris Gudonov* (1907), d. A. O. Drankov, starring F. G. Martini and Z. Lopanskaya.

Feature: *Story of Sin* (pr. 15 Nov 1911), d. unknown, prod. S. Mintus of Riga, starring M. Mirskaya and S. Zheromsky.

Soviet Feature: *Signal* (1918), d. Alexander Arkatov, prod. Moscow Cinema Committee, starring Grabevetskaya.

Talkie: *The Earth Thirsts* (1930), d. Yuli Raizman.

Colour: *Nightingale, Little Nightingale* (1936), d. Nikolai Ekk.

VENEZUELA

Film: *Muchachas bañádose en el Lago* (1897) and *Un gran especialista sacando muelas en el Hotel Europa* (1897), d. Manuel Trujillo Durán at Maracaibo.

Drama: *Carnival in Caracas* (1909), d. Augusto Gonzalez Vidal and M. A. Gonham.

Feature: *The Lady of Cayenas* (1913), parody of *Camille*, d. E. Zimmerman.

Talkie: *El Rompimiento* (1938), d. Antonio Delgado Gomez, starring Rafael Guinard.

VIETNAM

Drama: *Vie du Detham* (1910), biopic of guerilla leader, d. Rene Batisson.

Talkie: *Canh dong ma* (1940).

YUGOSLAVIA

Film: *Odhod od mase v Ljutomeru* (1905), made in 17.5 mm by Ljutomer lawyer Karl Grossman.

Drama/Feature: *Zivot i Dela Besmrtnog Vožda Karadjordje* (pr. 17 Nov 1911), biopic of 'Immortal Leader Karadjordje', d. I. Stojadinović, starring M. Petrović.

Talkie: *Nevinost Bez Zastite* (1939), d. D. Aleksić.

ZAIRE

Feature/Talkie: *La Nièce captive* (1969), d. Luc Michez.

The first European feature film scripted for the screen was a four-reel version of *Les Misérables* (Fr 09), produced by Pathé from the novel by Victor Hugo.

The first feature film exhibited in the United Kingdom was Charles Tait's *The Story of the Kelly Gang* (Aus 06), which had its British première at the Assembly Rooms, Bath, in January 1908. The film was released by the Colonial Picture Combine.

The first feature film produced in the United Kingdom was Thomas Bentley's *Oliver Twist* (GB 12), a Hepworth production in four reels starring ex-beauty queen Ivy Millais as Oliver Twist, Alma Taylor as Nancy and John McMahon as Fagin. It was released in August 1912, two months after Vitagraph's version in America (see below).

The first feature film produced in the United States was Vitagraph's four-reel production of *Les Misérables* (US 09), released in separate one-reel parts between 18 September and 27 November 1909. Charles Kent's Vitagraph production of *The Life of Moses* (US 09), in five reels, was also released in separate parts (4 December 1909–19 February 1910) because the producers did not consider that the American public were prepared to sit through a film that lasted over an hour. The first feature film to be released in its entirety in the USA was *Dante's Inferno* (It 11) in August 1911. *Queen Elizabeth* (Fr 12), which is nearly always cited as the first feature film shown in America, was in fact the third, because in the meantime the first domestic feature-length production to be shown whole had been released. This was *Oliver Twist* (US 12), produced by H. A. Spanuth and starring Nat C. Goodwin and Winnie Burns, which was premièred on 1 June 1912, nearly six weeks before *Queen Elizabeth* (12 July 1912). However, the prejudice against long films was so insistent in America (at least amongst producers and distributors) that even in 1913 the major European success of that year, August Blom's feature *Atlantis* (Den 13), had to be compressed into a half-length version for US release. Domestic production was a modest two in 1912 and twelve in 1913, the real watershed being

in 1914, when no less than 212 features were produced. The delay in going over to feature-film making suggests that the impact of *Queen Elizabeth*'s successful exploitation by Adolph Zukor in 1912 may not have been so influential as historians of the cinema have generally believed. Competition from the major European film-producing nations, most of whom had a two-year lead on America in feature production (see p. 7), may in fact have been the deciding factor.

*P*RODUCTION OUTPUT

Total world output of feature films is nearly 4000 annually. Asian countries (including Australasia) account for approx. 50 per cent of output, European countries (including USSR) for approx. 33 per cent, the Middle East and Africa for approx. 5.5 per cent, North America for approx. 6 per cent, and Latin America for approx. 5.5 per cent.

The country with the largest production output in the world is India, with a total of 806 full-length feature releases in 1987 and an annual output that has exceeded 700 each year since 1979.

The twelve major film-producing countries of the past decade in terms of output are the following (average annual output in brackets): India (770); Japan (330); USA (229); France (175); Philippines (159); USSR (150); Turkey (c. 150); Thailand (131); Hong Kong (123); Italy (116); Taiwan (c. 110); China (c. 100).

FEATURE-FILM PRODUCTION

The following countries have held the production record since the inception of feature films:

1906–11 Australia	1922–32 Japan	1940 Japan
1912 Hungary	1933–35 USA	1941–53 USA
1913 Germany	1936–38 Japan	1954–70 Japan
1914–22 USA	1939 USA	1971– India

The smallest country with an established film industry is Iceland, whose population of 220,000 are among the most frequent filmgoers in the world with an average of 10 to 11 visits a year (about four times the Scandinavian average). Feature production began in 1948 with Loftur Gudmundsson's *Between Mountain and Shore* and continued sporadically through the next three decades with a dozen features made up to 1977. The breakthrough for the establishment of a permanent film industry came in 1978 with the setting up of the Icelandic Film Fund by Act of Parliament. The first grants from the fund were made the following year and three full-length features went into production immediately. The number of features released annually since then has fluctuated between two and five, and it is estimated that the more successful productions are seen by as many as a quarter of the population of the nation.

Iceland's first full-scale film studio able to accommodate the making of feature films was built in 1988 by Jon Thor Hannesson and Snorri Thorisson.

The best year for UK film production was 1936, with 192 features released. The most productive year of the silent era was 1920, with 155 features.

The worst years for UK film production (since 1914) were 1986 and 1987 when only 30 features were released. The worst years of silent pictures were 1925 and 1926 with 33 releases. On two occasions in the past 65 years, production in Britain has come to a total halt. No films were made during November 1924 and for a three-week period in 1975.

The best year for US film production was 1921 with 854 feature releases.

The worst year for US film production (since 1913) was 1963 with 121 feature releases.

The highest output of any Hollywood studio was 101 features from Paramount in 1921; highest of the sound era was 68 by Paramount in 1936 and the same number from Warner's in 1937. Currently, the studio with the highest output is Columbia, with 20 starts in 1987.

The largest number of foreign films released in the USA in any one year was 361 in 1964. The number of domestic releases was 141. The lowest number of foreign films was 30 in 1943, against 397 Hollywood productions.

Worldwide Production of Feature Films 1906–87

The figures given in the chart on pp. 14–15 refer to feature films of an hour or more in length, including co-productions and feature-length documentaries. Television movies (TVMs) are excluded unless they have had a theatrical release. Production is attributed to the country in which the production company is registered. The figure quoted for any year represents the number of features completed and released.

In addition to the countries listed in the chart, the following have a significant annual output but were excluded because of insufficient data: Burma (approx. 45 p.a.); Iran (post-revolution approx. 75 p.a.); Mongolia (approx. 10 p.a.); Taiwan (approx. 110 p.a.); Vietnam (approx. 35 p.a.); Albania (approx. 10 p.a.).

ACCIDENTS

The largest number of fatalities incurred in the production of a film was 27 when the ship *Viking* blew up off Newfoundland on 15 March 1931 during the shooting of *The Viking* (Can 31), a drama about the seal fishing industry. The producer, Varick Frissell, was amongst those killed.

Reports of prodigious death rolls on Hollywood movies tend to be exaggerated. Neither version of *Ben Hur* (US 25 and US 59) resulted in any deaths, except of horses. **Hollywood's worst accident** took place during production of *Such Men Are Dangerous* (US 30), when two planes collided on the way to shoot a scene. Ten members of the film crew were killed.

Deaths in the course of production have a macabre tendency to come in threes. A helicopter crash during the making of *Twilight Zone* (US 82) resulted in three dead, two of them child actors; three stuntmen were killed shooting the Cooper River rapids for *The Trail of '98* (US 28); three extras were drowned in the *Noah's Ark* (US 28) flood scenes; three aerial stuntmen were killed on *Hell's Angels* (US 30), though only one of them while actually filming; three horsemen died in the cavalry charge in *They Died with Their Boots On* (US 41). One of the latter was Bill Mead, whose horse tripped as he rode by the side of Errol Flynn. He had the presence of mind to fling his sword forward to avoid falling with it, but by incredible mischance the hilt stuck in the ground and Mead fell on the tip of the blade, impaling himself.

Greater safety precautions on Hollywood sets since the *Twilight Zone* disaster noted above have resulted in a sharp decline in accidents. In 1982 there were 214 accidents involving members of the Screen Actors Guild; in 1986 the figure was down to 65, though this included two deaths—stuntmen Dar Robinson and Vic Magnotta.

It is rare for scenes of actual deaths during filming to be retained in the completed picture, but one known example is the anti-British propaganda drama *Mein Leben für Irland* (Ger 41). In the final battle scene several extras were killed when one stepped on a live land-mine, and the footage was included in the release prints.

ARCHIVES

The first film archive was the Danish Statens Arkiv for historiske Film og Stemmer, which had its origins in the spring of 1910 when Anker Kirkeby of the Copenhagen newspaper *Politiken* approached Ole Olsen of Nordisk Films with the idea of preserving a selection of films likely to be of historic interest in the future. During the ensuing three years a collection of films was assembled, including a number, specially taken for the archive, which showed prominent Danish writers, scientists, politicians, etc., and shots of parts of old Copenhagen due for redevelopment. The archive was formally established at the Royal Library in Copenhagen on 9 April 1913.

By the outbreak of war in 1914, film collections had been formed at the Louvre in Paris, the National Records Office in Madrid, the New York Public Library, and in Brussels, Rome, Berlin, and the Indian state of Baroda. These pioneer efforts, and those that followed in the 1920s, were generally concerned with the preservation of films as a record of national or civic history.

The first National Film Archive formed as a record of the film industry, rather than as a retrospective of public events, was the Reichsfilmarchiv established in Germany at the instigation of Arnold Raether on 4 February 1935. The Svenska Filminstituter Archive claims an earlier date of foundation, but it originated with the Filmhistorika Samlingarna, a private collection formed in 1933 by Einar Lauritzen.

Two other major archives were founded in 1935. The British Film Institute (founded 1933) set up the National Film Archive under Ernest Lindgren in May, and in New York Iris Barry and John Abbott established the Museum of Modern Art Film Library. The following year, Henri Langlois formed the Cinémathèque Française from his own private film collection and this rapidly grew into a national institution, though the government support enjoyed since the end of World War II was withdrawn in 1969 when the French government established its own archive. The USSR's giant Gosfilmofond, which occupies a 150-acre site at Bielye Stolbi near Moscow and employs a staff of 600, was not founded until 1948.

The largest collection of films in the world is preserved by the Motion Picture, Broadcasting and Recorded Sound Division of the Library of Congress, Washington, DC, which has over 90,000 titles spanning a period of some 90 years. **The oldest film in the collection**, which is also **the oldest American film in existence** anywhere in the world, is catalogued as *Indian Club Swinger*. Made by W. K. L. Dickson at the Edison laboratory at West Orange, NJ, it shows a young man exercising with Indian clubs and was made either in 1892 or 1893.

The Library of Congress's Motion Picture Division is a copyright repository rather than a film archive in the conventional sense. **The world's largest service film archive** is Britain's National Film Archive, with 87,000 films. The Cinémathèque Française and the archive of the Centre Nationale de la Cinématographie, both based in Paris, each claim to hold 60,000 films, while the Soviet Union's Gosfilmofond has about 50,000.

The smallest national archive is the Icelandic Film Archive, which contains some 200 films about or made in Iceland.

Lost Films

Films believed irretrievably lost continue to resurface from time to time, often in unlikely places. A recent notable find was the first three reels of John Ford's *The Gunfighting Gentleman* (US 19), starring Harry Carey in a performance which the dean of silent film conservators, Kevin Brownlow, describes as 'strikingly prefiguring the look and style of John Wayne in his sound-era westerns'. They were retrieved from a cache of 900,000 ft of mainly silent pictures dating from 1907 to 1933 discovered in Holland. Brownlow has now begun a worldwide quest to locate the two missing reels of *The Gunfighting Gentleman*, made two years after Ford's debut as a director.

> It is estimated that half of all the feature films made before 1951 have been irretrievably lost; three out of every four feature films made before 1930; and four out of every five features made before 1920.

Hailed as the most important discovery of a 'lost' film in recent years, some 18 to 20 hours of black-and-white footage from Orson Welles's uncompleted documentary *It's All True*, shot in Brazil for RKO in 1942, were found in 300 cans in the Paramount stock footage vault in 1986. The footage included one of

This was the only known copy of an historic New Zealand film, *The Birth of New Zealand* (NZ 22). Archives all over the world are racing against time to transfer old nitrate prints to acetate film before they decompose like this one. (*New Zealand Film Archive*)

WORLDWIDE FEATURE FILM PRODUCTION 1906–1987

Year	Algeria	Argentina	Australia	Austria	Bangladesh	Belgium	Brazil	Bulgaria	Canada[1]	China[4]	Cuba	Czechoslovakia	Denmark	Egypt	Eire	Finland	France	Germany, Fed. Rep.	Germany, Dem. Rep.	Greece	Hong Kong[3]	Hungary	India	Indonesia[2]	Iraq
1906	0	0	1	0		0	0	0	0	0	0	0	0	0	0	0	0	0		0	—	0	0	0	0
1907	0	0	2	0		0	0	0	0	0	0	0	0	0	0	0	1	0		0	—	0	0	0	0
1908	0	0	0	0		0	0	0	0	0	0	0	0	0	0	0	0	0		0	—	0	0	0	0
1909	0	0	0	0		0	0	0	0	0	0	0	0	0	0	0	1	0		0	—	0	0	0	0
1910	0	0	0	0		0	0	0	0	0	0	0	0	0	0	0	0	0		0	—	0	0	0	0
1911	0	0	16	0		0	0	0	0	0	0	0	1	0	0	0	1	0		0	—	0	0	0	0
1912	0	0	8	1		0	0	0	0	0	0	0	2	0	0	0	3	0		1	—	14	0	0	0
1913	0	0	4	6		3	2	0	1	0	1	0	13	0	0	1	—	49		0	—	11	3	0	0
1914	0	0	3	9		0	—	0	0	0	1	0	16	0	0	1	—	29		0	—	19	1	0	0
1915	0	4	8	10		0	3	1	1	0	1	0	24	0	0	0	—	60		0	—	27	0	0	0
1916	0	12	15	7		0	6	0	2	0	1	0	34	0	0	1	—	107		1	—	52	0	0	0
1917	0	16	6	9		0	4	2	2	0	3	1	40	0	1	0	—	117		0	—	77	3	0	0
1918	0	2	13	40		0	2	0	1	0	1	13	21	0	0	0	—	211		1	—	107	7	0	0
1919	0	15	16	56		1	6	0	2	0	2	23	20	0	0	0	—	345		0	—	48	8	0	0
1920	0	5	10	48		1	6	0	2	0	5	17	8	0	3	1	—	485		0	—	54	27	0	0
1921	0	11	15	47		7	2	3	0	—	8	25	10	0	0	2	—	646		0	—	25	44	0	0
1922	0	10	7	64		8	4	3	8	—	5	30	8	0	3	3	—	474		3	—	6	64	0	0
1923	0	15	7	45		3	6	1	2	—	0	18	15	0	0	3	—	347		2	—	13	52	0	0
1924	0	13	10	30		4	4	0	0	—	0	8	9	0	0	4	68	271		1	—	9	54	0	0
1925	0	15	9	24		10	12	1	0	—	1	17	8	0	2	2	73	228		2	—	3	86	0	0
1926	0	7	16	17		2	12	0	0	80	3	31	7	0	0	2	55	195		2	—	3	94	1	0
1927	0	6	4	18		2	10	2	2	75	2	24	6	1	0	6	74	241		2	—	8	90	1	0
1928	0	6	13	19		1	10	2	3	50	1	16	4	4	0	3	94	226		2	—	2	109	2	0
1929	0	4	3	22		4	13	7	0	40	3	35	3	2	0	7	52	194		4	—	5	140	5	0
1930	0	5	3	17		3	14	3	1	—	2	23	5	4	0	2	98	180		13	—	3	194	7	0
1931	0	4	6	9		3	4	2	0	—	0	23	4	2	0	7	157	199		6	—	3	228	5	0
1932	0	2	4	11		5	8	0	0	60	0	24	6	6	1	3	156	150		6	—	8	148	5	0
1933	0	6	7	18		1	6	2	1	—	0	44	10	6	0	5	152	129		2	—	9	144	1	0
1934	0	6	9	17		6	2	2	2	69	0	34	8	7	0	4	119	142		1	—	12	171	3	0
1935	0	13	3	32		5	2	0	3	80	0	34	11	12	1	5	128	111		0	—	18	233	3	0
1936	0	15	6	25		3	3	1	5	—	0	31	6	13	1	9	145	128		0	—	28	217	2	0
1937	0	28	5	18		7	0	1	6	75	1	49	13	17	0	12	124	108		1	150	36	179	3	0
1938	0	41	7	11		5	3	1	0	86	2	41	10	10	2	20	122	113		3	55	35	172	4	0
1939	0	50	4	11		3	2	1	1	58	8	41	9	15	0	21	94	118		1	100	27	165	4	0
1940	0	49	3	10		2	7	2	0	—	2	31	12	12	0	22	40	89		0	—	39	170	13	0
1941	0	47	3	5		3	1	4	0	—	1	21	16	12	0	15	41	71		1	—	41	167	31	0
1942	0	56	1	6		5	1	1	0	—	1	11	18	22	0	18	74	64		0	—	48	173	1	0
1943	0	36	0	10		1	1	3	0	—	3	10	18	15	0	22	81	83		3	—	53	161	0	0
1944	0	24	1	8		1	7	1	1	—	1	9	18	23	0	16	27	75		2	—	22	127	6	0
1945	0	23	1	1		9	5	2	0	—	2	3	10	42	0	20	50	72		5	—	3	99	0	0
1946	0	32	3	4		8	11	4	3	—	1	11	13	52	0	16	81	1	3	4	—	2	200	0	0
1947	0	38	1	13	0	3	9	3	0	—	2	19	13	55	0	15	88	6	4	6	—	4	281	0	2
1948	0	41	1	25	0	3	14	0	2	—	2	17	10	49	0	16	84	21	7	6	—	5	263	3	0
1949	0	47	4	25	0	1	18	0	5	7	4	20	8	44	0	16	97	56	12	8	256	7	291	8	3
1950	0	56	1	17	0	2	30	1	3	26	10	20	14	48	0	14	104	61	10	6	202	4	241	23	0
1951	0	53	3	28	0	1	22	2	3	—	5	8	18	52	0	19	109	69	8	12	192	9	221	40	0
1952	0	35	1	19	0	2	31	2	1	—	5	16	12	59	0	28	100	73	6	17	259	5	233	42	0
1953	0	37	1	28	0	4	31	1	2	17	4	18	12	62	0	25	111	103	7	19	188	6	260	50	0
1954	0	45	2	22	0	5	25	4	2	—	11	14	13	65	0	28	98	109	9	19	167	8	278	59	0
1955	0	43	2	28	0	5	24	2	0	24	7	16	13	51	0	30	110	123	13	16	235	10	289	64	0
1956	0	36	2	37	1	8	21	9	2	42	5	21	13	39	0	18	129	122	19	26	311	10	295	36	1
1957	0	15	3	26	0	3	36	5	3	—	3	25	16	40	1	21	142	107	22	28	223	15	294	21	3
1958	0	32	1	23	0	12	41	9	3	52	6	29	16	55	3	17	126	115	17	38	237	13	294	19	5
1959	0	22	2	19	3	6	30	3	4	70	5	33	14	58	2	15	133	106	28	59	239	18	304	16	1
1960	0	31	2	20	2	9	29	10	2	82	2	30	19	59	0	18	158	94	24	68	293	14	318	38	2
1961	0	25	1	23	5	9	36	9	5	85	2	39	22	52	1	18	167	80	27	56	303	19	298	37	0
1962	0	32	1	20	5	11	28	8	4	80	2	35	23	49	0	21	125	61	24	78	261	17	315	12	7
1963	1	27	0	15	4	4	21	9	5	—	4	36	21	48	0	14	141	66	20	66	260	21	302	19	6
1964	0	37	0	19	17	2	23	10	14	—	6	38	19	45	0	6	148	77	16	94	235	18	310	19	3
1965	3	30	0	16	12	5	26	8	15	47	4	40	16	43	0	9	142	69	14	96	204	20	322	15	1
1966	1	34	3	18	24	3	30	12	10	4	2	31	18	39	0	7	130	60	16	106	171	20	311	13	1
1967	2	27	2	12	22	31	41	15	11	2	3	40	20	33	0	3	120	96	20	76	169	22	329	13	4
1968	4	32	1	7	34	10	47	6	13	4	4	36	19	40	1	12	117	107	16	95	156	21	349	8	1
1969	2	29	6	3	30	15	46	14	25	—	1	25	23	44	0	9	154	121	13	88	158	20	379	9	2
1970	8	28	14	7	41	12	70	25	46	1	0	28	28	48	0	13	138	113	—	86	138	20	398	21	2
1971	1	38	10	5	6	16	69	18	32	1	4	37	33	46	0	9	127	99	12	83	127	20	432	52	1
1972	9	32	7	9	28	20	81	22	32	5	2	35	17	41	1	6	169	85	17	63	133	21	411	50	1
1973	6	39	12	6	31	27	58	18	43	6	3	36	12	43	0	8	200	98	16	63	201	18	448	58	0
1974	10	38	11	8	30	16	82	19	41	5	2	38	14	44	0	3	234	80	15	38	147	19	432	84	0
1975	3	33	24	6	34	21	90	25	39	9	2	39	17	49	0	5	222	81	16	47	109	19	470	39	1
1976	4	21	16	5	44	11	78	20	30	13	5	46	20	47	0	9	214	61	17	38	112	17	507	58	0
1977	1	21	17	8	31	30	73	21	39	—	3	42	20	50	1	7	142	60	15	21	116	19	555	124	3
1978	5	22	10	3	42	20	101	21	39	—	3	46	16	51	2	10	227	64	17	18	135	23	612	81	2
1979	2	33	18	9	52	10	93	22	55	12	6	46	11	39	0	9	234	66	17	—	125	25	714	51	3
1980	0	34	14	8	44	21	102	21	54	82	4	45	12	34	—	11	189	49	15	26	132	21	742	68	—
1981	0	24	9	11	39	9	80	—	33	—	0	44	12	43	—	16	231	76	16	25	127	24	737	71	—
1982	5	17	21	13	42	5	86	17	27	105	3	44	7	41	1	19	164	70	16	46	126	27	763	52	—
1983	3	17	19	11	45	11	84	22	34	114	8	41	12	46	2	17	131	77	16	48	114	26	741	74	—
1984	3	31	15	14	50	8	90	20	27	—	6	34	13	63	3	20	161	77	—	37	125	23	800*	78	—
1985	5	24	16	18	63	7	83	17	58	—	7	44	8	75	2	15	151	77	19	23	105	27	912	62	—
1986	3	37	23	12	70	6	79	23	63	—	—	56	10	91	2	29	134	73	16	26	109	26	840	64	—
1987	4	33	23	14	65	12	60	21	61	—	—	39	11	70	2	15	133	74	—	22	113	34	806	52	—

— No data available   [1] Completions per year   [2] Starts per year   [3] Financial year April–March   [4] 1949–66: 614   * estimated

Japan	Korea, South	Malaysia	Mexico	Netherlands	New Zealand	Norway	Pakistan	Philippines	Poland	Portugal	Romania	Singapore	South Africa	Spain	Sri Lanka	Sweden[3]	Switzerland	Thailand	Tunisia	Turkey	UK	Uruguay	USA	USSR	Venezuela	Yugoslavia
0	0	0	0	0	0	0		0	0	0	0	0	0	0	0	0	0	0	0	0	0	0	0	0	0	0
0	0	0	0	0	0	0		0	0	0	0	0	0	0	0	0	0	0	0	0	0	0	0	0	0	0
0	0	0	0	0	0	0		0	0	0	0	0	0	0	0	0	0	0	0	0	0	0	0	0	0	0
0	0	0	0	0	0	0		0	0	0	0	0	0	0	0	0	0	0	0	0	0	0	0	0	0	0
0	0	0	0	0	0	0		0	3	0	0	0	0	—	0	0	0	0	0	0	0	0	0	1	0	1
2	0	0	0	0	0	1		0	2	0	1	0	0	—	0	0	0	0	0	0	2	0	2	9	0	—
0	0	0	0	1	0	0		0	5	0	10	0	0	—	0	4	0	0	0	0	18	0	12	31	1	—
5	0	0	0	5	0	0		0	5	0	0	0	0	—	0	5	0	0	0	0	15	0	212	17	0	—
3	0	0	0	7	0	0		0	3	0	0	0	0	—	0	2	0	0	0	0	73	0	419	44	1	—
—	0	0	1	9	1	2		0	5	0	0	0	14	—	0	4	0	0	0	0	107	0	677	74	0	—
—	0	0	11	5	0	3		—	7	0	0	0	0	7	0	7	—	0	0	2	66	0	687	57	0	—
—	0	0	6	10	0	3		—	6	0	0	0	0	5	0	6	—	0	0	1	76	0	841	27	0	6
—	0	0	13	5	0	2		—	7	4	0	0	6	17	0	11	—	0	0	3	122	0	646	12	0	—
—	0	0	7	10	0	2		—	8	2	2	0	4	12	0	20	—	0	0	0	155	1	797	8	0	—
—	0	0	8	10	0	3		—	17	3	1	0	2	8	0	7	—	0	1	3	137	0	854	5	0	—
—	0	0	4	11	2	3		—	15	2	0	0	3	4	0	11	—	1	2	2	110	0	748	9	0	—
—	—	0	3	6	0	1		—	11	7	1	0	1	8	0	23	—	1	0	3	68	1	576	12	0	—
875	—	0	0	6	1	1		—	8	3	1	0	1	10	0	16	—	1	1	1	49	0	579	41	1	—
—	—	0	7	2	1	2		—	5	0	6	0	1	38	0	18	—	2	0	0	33	0	579	76	0	—
—	—	0	4	4	0	5		3	8	1	4	0	0	39	0	18	—	3	0	0	33	0	740	77	1	—
648	—	0	2	1	2	5		4	12	1	3	0	0	25	0	11	—	3	2	0	48	1	678	106	0	—
798	—	0	2	1	1	3		—	12	1	4	0	0	12	0	6	—	8	2	1	80	1	641	125	3	0
850	—	0	2	1	0	2		—	16	1	5	0	0	21	0	6	—	1	1	1	81	1	562	103	1	—
—	—	0	1	1	0	2		—	12	5	3	0	0	8	0	13	—	—	1	0	75	0	509	123	0	—
—	—	0	1	0	0	1		16	10	2	0	0	2	2	0	24	—	—	0	1	93	1	501	88	1	—
498	—	0	6	1	0	5		20	14	0	1	0	0	9	0	22	—	—	0	1	110	0	489	67	1	4
450	—	0	21	0	0	3		—	11	0	0	0	0	17	0	22	—	—	0	7	115	0	507	35	3	2
413	—	0	23	8	0	2		—	14	3	2	0	0	23	0	19	6	—	0	3	145	0	480	59	0	0
470	—	0	22	9	1	1		—	14	1	0	0	0	44	0	20	—	—	2	0	165	0	525	34	0	0
558	—	0	25	11	3	1		15	24	1	0	1	1	19	0	28	—	—	0	0	192	1	522	49	0	0
583	5	0	38	5	0	2		32	28	3	1	—	0	10	0	22	3	—	1	1	176	0	538	45	1	0
554	—	0	57	3	0	5		55	21	4	0	—	1	4	0	27	1	10	1	1	134	3	455	41	0	0
437	—	0	37	4	0	4		—	18	1	3	—	1	20	0	30	1	12	0	4	84	0	483	52	2	1
497	—	6	29	2	1	4		—	0	3	0	0	3	40	0	36	9	—	0	4	50	0	477	50	1	0
232	—	0	37	—	1	4		—	0	2	0	0	0	33	0	34	11	—	0	1	46	0	492	50	1	0
87	—	1	47	—	0	5		—	0	4	1	0	0	49	0	34	13	—	0	2	39	0	488	26	2	0
61	—	0	70	—	0	4		—	0	4	2	0	0	53	0	43	5	—	0	2	47	0	397	27	0	0
46	—	0	73	—	0	3		—	0	3	0	0	1	34	0	43	—	—	0	2	35	0	401	21	0	0
38	—	0	82	2	0	4		—	0	4	1	0	0	33	0	44	—	—	0	3	39	0	350	20	4	0
57	—	0	72	1	0	6		10	1	6	4	—	4	41	0	36	0	—	0	6	41	1	378	19	1	0
97	—	2	58	0	0	1	0	24	2	7	0	—	2	48	0	43	2	—	0	12	58	1	369	22	0	2
123	—	3	81	2	0	4	0	—	2	4	0	—	1	44	0	40	2	—	1	16	74	1	366	22	3	4
156	—	3	108	2	0	3	4	—	3	7	1	—	4	37	0	34	1	10	0	18	101	2	356	13	4	3
215	—	8	124	0	0	2	15	—	4	2	0	—	2	49	0	25	1	—	0	21	81	2	383	14	4	3
212	—	11	101	1	0	7	10	—	2	2	2	15	5	41	0	31	1	—	1	32	75	1	391	10	1	6
258	—	18	99	1	1	7	7	—	4	8	1	14	1	41	0	25	4	—	0	52	101	2	324	20	3	5
302	—	16	83	2	0	6	10	—	3	4	2	21	5	43	6	31	0	—	0	50	102	0	344	42	1	9
370	—	11	105	0	0	9	7	—	3	3	3	13	5	69	5	30	1	—	1	53	110	0	253	35	1	7
423	26	9	84	2	0	9	19	—	8	0	4	20	4	56	7	30	3	—	0	64	95	0	254	84	2	14
514	40	9	87	0	0	8	31	—	6	4	3	12	2	75	7	34	3	—	0	52	91	0	272	98	3	10
443	44	16	106	3	0	9	27	16	1	8	13	2	3	72	8	32	3	—	0	60	115	1	300	144	2	15
516	80	23	92	4	0	9	33	97	16	4	4	19	5	75	9	29	3	—	1	80	111	2	241	130	1	15
500	109	28	84	1	0	8	34	92	16	5	4	17	6	68	9	24	5	50	1	71	99	1	187	145	1	14
555	85	13	64	6	0	8	38	112	21	2	9	12	8	73	9	23	7	43	0	68	110	1	154	139	1	14
537	91	19	49	1	0	6	34	108	23	2	10	19	19	91	8	18	9	35	0	116	109	0	131	137	0	32
378	115	18	—	5	0	5	34	152	23	5	8	27	13	89	6	17	4	96	0	127	126	0	147	97	3	22
363	146	15	—	2	0	6	46	142	26	8	10	21	7	113	11	18	4	48	0	125	107	0	121	96	4	18
346	148	13	—	3	1	6	67	161	25	8	11	19	8	123	15	24	4	44	0	178	75	0	141	108	9	17
487	189	12	52	1	0	8	54	161	20	6	14	11	6	133	15	19	10	44	1	214	80	0	153	127	3	20
442	124	9	—	6	1	7	72	201	26	5	15	12	10	152	20	25	5	54	2	238	69	0	156	131	3	21
410	155	10	48	7	0	6	66	180	21	7	14	14	9	138	21	27	4	51	7	206	89	0	178	136	2	31
494	219	11	90	4	0	6	99	175	18	4	7	5	12	117	20	34	7	52	3	177	73	0	180	121	5	36
494	229	11	93	6	0	5	91	169	22	4	12	5	12	123	20	24	—	64	5	229	85	0	177	141	1	29
423	209	9	—	3	0	11	85	194	25	4	8	4	17	105	17	20	7	73	4	225	103	0	231	130	4	23
421	202	2	—	4	1	6	79	253	25	7	13	3	17	107	14	19	—	74	2	266	97	0	223	133	4	23
400	122	2	81	6	0	8	99	181	20	8	16	3	24	104	20	14	—	70	4	298	90	0	224	127	1	21
405	125	3	48	11	1	12	93	146	25	6	16	4	22	112	18	18	18	81	2	208	80	0	201	150	5	16
333	141	6	44	9	0	12	107	120	31	11	18	1	34	115	41	24	15	83	2	188	81	0	179	140	3	11
333	94	4	40	14	1	14	111	143	36	10	23	4	30	102	31	20	15	90	3	124	80	0	161	148	5	19
356	134	4	43	8	0	12	109	174	28	18	22	2	25	90	30	16	10	130	1	164	64	0	188	149	13	18
337	102	3	59	8	4	10	74	141	32	19	20	2	24	97	75	22	—	98	2	225	43	0	157	143	29	15
326	117	4	63	9	2	6	87	135	27	5	23	0	19	79	35	17	10	148	3	123	49	0	162	141	12	16
335	96	5	85	14	3	13	80	170	32	6	28	0	22	73	29	18	—	150	2	195	38	1	167	151	9	24
320	91	9	108	7	2	10	58	173	37	13	32	0	20	110	75	26	—	142	4	—	41	1	200	151	5	26
332	87	14	87	11	5	10	84	179	41	8	31	0	20	92	56	25	16	138	3	—	32	1	181	145	4	24
322	97	13	74	13	5	10	66	149	33	7	30	0	15	146	65	18	13	117	3	—	37	—	187	158	7	32
363	91	15	80	15	4	7	85	143	32	4	32	0	35	99	33	23	17	109	3	—	33	—	231	148	9	28
379	81	13	77	12	8	7	82	138	32	8	26	0	80	75	34	23	17	141	3	—	42	—	262	150	15	34
329	80	8	73	16	12	10	92	158	41	2	—	0	85	77	26	20	21	134	—	—	47	—	264	—	—	30
311	80*	10	88	12	5	10	106	177	33	4	—	0	56	60	18	27	28	102	—	—	30	—	311	156	—	24
286	—	13	82	—	6	8	76	167	29	5	—	0	78	77*	18	25	36	130	—	—	30	—	329	—	15	26

the main segments of the film, the record of an epic 1650-mile river journey by raft by four poor fishermen bent on personally lobbying dictator Getulio Vergas to seek economic aid. Triumph and tragedy mingled when their leader died as the raft finally entered Rio harbour. Missing is most of the colour footage of Carnival shot by Welles in Rio and dumped in Santa Monica Bay on the order of studio executives some 20 years later. It is generally reckoned that the making of *It's All True* was the beginning of the downfall of Welles's brilliant early career, since RKO put it about that he was profligate, undisciplined and unable to complete a film on time or to specification. A major restoration job is now being undertaken on the nitrate film stock, most of which has shrunk, and a feature-length documentary film is planned about the shoot, including much of the best of what has been retrieved. According to those who have already seen some of the footage, its public exhibition after some 45 years is likely to give the lie to RKO's claims that Welles was out of control.

The biggest single loss of archive film occurred in March 1982 when 6506 films were destroyed by fire and explosions at the Cineteca Nacional in Mexico City. A commentator described the disaster as 'the most terrible cultural loss in modern Mexican history—the filmic memory of our country is erased'.

The largest collection of film stills in the world is the four million housed at the Department of Film of the Museum of Modern Art in New York.

The largest collection of film stills in Europe is the National Film Archive Stills Collection in London, which consists of three million black-and-white stills and 750,000 colour transparencies from over 50,000 films.

According to the organizers of Nitrate Project 2000, there is 189,786,700 ft of pre-1953 nitrate film in the UK, totalling some 35,000 hours of running time. This is equivalent in length to about 20,000 full-length feature films. Cost of transferring all of the footage to acetate is estimated at £14.5 million. Nitrate Project 2000's aim is to save the best of it by the end of the century.

CO-PRODUCTIONS

The first co-production was *Das Geheimnis der Lüfte* (Aut/Fr 13), a full-length feature thriller starring Julius Brandt. The Austrian production company was Wiener Autorenfilm; the French company is believed to have been Pathé.

The first Anglo-American co-production was *Charley's Aunt* (US/GB 25), starring Syd Chaplin,

a Christie comedy co-produced with Ideal Films Ltd of London, which opened at the Colony Theater, New York, on 8 February 1925.

The first Anglo-Soviet co-production was *Anna Pavlova* (USSR/GB 85), made by Mosfilm (Moscow) and Poseidon films (London) and starring Galina Belayeva as Pavlova, Martin Scorcese and James Fox.

The most cosmopolitan co-productions are the seven-nation films *Soldaty svobody* (USSR/Bul/Hun/GDR/Pol/Rom/Cz 77) and *West Indies Story* (Tun/Mali/IvC/Mau/Alg/Sen/Fr 79). *Soldaty svobody* involved the most production companies, namely Mosfilm (USSR), Za Ugrakbu Film (Bul), Mafilm (Hun), Defa (GDR), PRF EF (Pol), Bukuresti (Rom), Barrandov (Cz) and Koliba (Cz).

Films co-produced by five different countries have included *The Behest of the Inca* (Bul/FRG/It/Sp/Peru 66); *Love at 20* (Fr/It/Jap/Pol/FRG 63); *Marco the Magnificent* (Afg/Egy/Fr/It/Yug 66); *The Call of the Wild* (GB/FRG/Sp/It/Fr 72).

HOLLYWOOD

The first European inhabitant of the area now known as Hollywood, then called Nopalera, was Mexican-born Don Tomas Urquidez, who built an adobe dwelling in 1853 at what is now the northwest corner of Franklin and Sycamore Avenues.

The name 'Hollywood' was conferred on her Cahuenga Valley ranch by Mrs Harvey Henderson Wilcox, wife of one of the district's earliest real-estate developers, in 1886. The name had nothing to do with holly-bushes imported from England, as some accounts have it. Mrs Wilcox had been travelling by train to her old home in the east when she met a lady with a summer home near Chicago called 'Hollywood'. She was so charmed by the name that she decided to borrow it for her own property. In 1903 the village of Hollywood and its environs were incorporated as a municipality, but in 1910 the citizens voted to become a district of Los Angeles in order to secure water supplies. At that date the population was 5000; by 1919 it was 35,000 and by 1925 it had grown to 130,000.

Beverly Hills

The exodus of Hollywood's upper crust to Beverly Hills began when Douglas Fairbanks rented sports goods manufacturer Syl Spaulding's 36-room house on Summit Drive in 1919. At that time Beverly Hills was mainly agricultural land given over to the cultivation of beans and there was only one house between Fairbanks' rented property and the sea seven miles away. Early in 1920 he bought a hunting lodge adjacent to the Spaulding mansion and rebuilt it in a style befitting his new bride, Mary Pickford. Named *Pickfair* after the first syllables of their names, Doug's wedding gift to Mary was, and remained, Beverly Hills' most regal establishment, a magnet that drew the elite of the film colony to what was soon to become America's richest suburb. In 1980, following the death of Mary Pickford, the 45-room mansion was put up for sale, but it was not until 1988 that international financier Meshulam Riklis paid the equivalent of £12 million for it as a home for his diminutive actress wife Pia Zadora. Riklis announced that he would spend another £3.5 million to 'spruce it up'.

> *Plus ça change* . . . According to black magician Aleister Crowley, who visited Hollywood in 1916, what he described as 'the cinema crowd' consisted of 'cocaine-crazed sexual lunatics'.

The first dramatic film made in the Los Angeles area was Francis Boggs' *The Count of Monte Cristo* (US 08), a Selig production made partly in Colorado and partly in the Laguna and Venice districts of what is now Greater Los Angeles. The first made wholly in LA was Francis Boggs' *The Power of the Sultan* (US 09), starring Hobart Bosworth, a Broadway actor who had lost his voice through TB and was seeking recuperative sunshine. The movie was shot in three days, 8–10 May 1909, on a rented lot next to a Chinese laundry on Olive and Seventh Streets, Los Angeles. Boggs, who might have become prominent as California's pioneer director, was unfortunately cut down in his prime, murdered by a crazed Japanese studio gardener in 1911.

The first studio in the Los Angeles area was established by the Selig Co. at 1845 Allesandro Street, Edendale. Construction began in August 1909 and enlargements were made in 1910 and again in 1911, so that within two years of opening it was occupying a 230×220 ft (70×67 m) building.

The first film made in Hollywood was D. W. Griffith's *In Old California* (US 10), a Biograph melodrama about the liaison between a Spanish maiden (Marion Leonard) and a dashing hero, destined to become Governor of California (Frank Grandin), who have an illegitimate wastrel son (Arthur Johnson). It was shot in two days, 2–3 February 1910, and released on 10 March.

> At the 1984 American Film Institute Life Achievement Award presentation to 90-year-old Lillian Gish, John Houseman recalled that many years ago Miss Gish and her sister Dorothy were offered the chance of buying the Sunset Strip in Hollywood for $300. The Gish sisters talked the matter over, weighing the pros and cons. They then went down to fashionable Bullock's and bought a dress each instead.

The Nestor Studios on Sunset Boulevard 1911. Formerly a derelict roadhouse, it was Hollywood's first studio.

The first studio in Hollywood was established there as the result of a toss of a coin. Al Christie, chief director of the Centaur Co., wanted to make westerns in California, since he was tired of having to simulate sagebrush country in New Jersey. Centaur's owner, David Horsley, thought that Florida would be better, but agreed to abide by a heads-or-tails decision. Christie tossed and won. After viewing various possible sites in Southern California, he found a derelict roadhouse on Sunset Boulevard which looked suitable and cost only $40 a month to rent. This building was converted into a studio in October 1911. It was called the Nestor Studio, after the name of the western branch of the company. Today the site is occupied by the West Coast headquarters of CBS. By the end of the following year there were 15 film companies operating in Hollywood. Uninterrupted sunshine and a comforting distance from the agents of the Patents Co. were not the only attractions of Southern California as a film-making base. The astonishing range and variety of its scenery enabled locations to be found that could reasonably represent any terrain from Cornwall to the Urals; westerns could be located in the real west rather than New Jersey, South Sea island pictures could be shot on Catalina and neighbouring islands, an oil field in Los Angeles itself served for Texan oilman dramas, Spanish missions set the scene for old Mexico, and there were even sufficient baronial mansions to cater for the needs of pictures playing in Hollywood's England. Only a jungle was missing, but studios like Selig and Universal established their own zoos and built their African locales on the back-lot.

The first talking picture made in Hollywood was a Fox Movietone short *They're Coming to Get Me* (US 26), with comedian Chic Sale, released in May 1926.

The Celebrated Hollywood Sign

The sign was erected on Hollywood Hills in 1923 at a cost of $21,000. Originally it spelt out the word HOLLYWOODLAND, in letters 30 ft wide and 50 ft tall and built up from 3×9 ft sheet metal panels attached to a scaffolding frame. Each letter was studded with 20-watt light bulbs at eight-inch intervals. A man called Albert Kothe, who lived on the job—in a hut behind one of the 'L's'—was employed full time to change the bulbs when they burned out. The sign has often been featured in movies as a means of establishing locale, for example as shown in *The Day of the Locust* (US 75) and *1941* (US 79). It has been put to more macabre use for frequent suicide attempts. First to take a death dive from the top of the sign was failed starlet Peg Entwhistle in 1932.

Declared an historic landmark in 1973, the original and much dilapidated sign was replaced five years later after a fund for this purpose had been established by Gene Autry, Alice Cooper and Playboy chief Hugh Hefner. The new sign cost $27,000 for each letter. The remains of the old one were sold to a Mr Hank Berger, who cut the scrap metal into one-inch squares and retailed them to the more obsessive nostalgia buffs at $29.95 a time.

A group calling themselves 'The Environmental Pranksters' have made newspaper headlines several times recently by their depredations on the famous sign. Using black plastic sheeting to cover up whole letters, or parts of letters, they converted HOLLYWOOD to HOLYWOOD to celebrate the Pope's visit in 1987, to HOLLYWEED after laws on marijuana possession had been relaxed, and to OLLYWOOD in tribute to Col. 'Olly' North's performance at the Senate's Irangate hearings.

The first footprints outside Grauman's Chinese Theater in Hollywood were Norma Talmadge's on 18 May 1927. Legend has it that she stepped on the wet cement by accident, thereby giving Sid Grauman the idea for his celebrated and still continuing publicity stunt.

Selection for the Hollywood Walk of Fame is a high honour for those who have achieved distinction in the motion picture and entertainment business. It is also expensive for the recipient of the honour. The Hollywood Historic Trust, which adminsters the Walk of Fame, recently upped the price to $3500. Most celebrities are prepared to pay, though a few have refused to dip into their own pockets as the price of sidewalk immortality. By June 1988 there were 1871 stars embedded in the concrete, with 632 remaining slots.

Biting the Hand . . .

☆ 'A town that has to be seen to be disbelieved'—Walter Winchell

☆ 'It's a great place to live—if you're an orange'—Fred Allen

☆ 'Hollywood is a sewer—with service from the Ritz Carlton'—Wilson Mizner

☆ 'There is one word which aptly describes Hollywood—*nervous!*'—Frank Capra

☆ 'They've great respect for the dead in Hollywood, but none for the living'—Errol Flynn

☆ 'Hollywood is the only community in the world where the entire population is suffering from rumourtism'—Bert Lahr

☆ 'Hollywood is pretty painful even in small quantities'—Constance Bennett. (It grew a little less painful when her salary leaped from $8000 a week to $30,000 a week—the highest in Hollywood—shortly after saying this.)

☆ 'It's somehow symbolic of Hollywood that Tara was just a facade, with no rooms inside'—David O Selznick

☆ 'Hollywood stinks'—Frank Sinatra

☆ 'I saw Hollywood born and I've seen it die . . .'—Mary Pickford in old age

☆ 'Hollywood is a place where they'll pay you $50,000 for a kiss and 50c for your soul'—Marilyn Monroe

> About one quarter of Hollywood's film community consists of Canadians.

LONGEST FILMS

The longest film ever made was the 85-hr *The Cure for Insomnia* (US 87), directed by John Henry Timmis IV and premièred in its entirety at the School of Art Institute of Chicago on 31 January 1987. Much of the film consists of L. D. Groban reading his own 4080 page poem, also titled *The Cure for Insomnia*, interspersed with scenes of rock band J.T.4 and Cosmic Lightning and what the makers describe as some 'X-rated footage'. A short 'clean' version lasting a mere 80 hours is available without the erotic scenes.

The longest commercially-made film was *The Burning of the Red Lotus Temple* (Chn 28–31), adapted by the Star Film Co. from a newspaper serial *Strange Tales of the Adventurer in the Wild Country* by Shang K'ai-jan. It was released in 18 feature-length parts over a period of three years. Although never shown publicly in its 27-hr entirety, some cinemas would put on all-day performances of half-a-dozen parts in sequence.

The longest commercially-made American movie to be released uncut was Erich von Stroheim's *Foolish Wives* (US 22), which was distributed to Latin American countries in its original 6 hr 24 min version. In the United States, however, it was seen only in a severely cut form, a 12-reel version for the road show and a 10-reel version for general release.

The 42-reel version of von Stroheim's masterpiece *Greed* (US 24)—**Hollywood's longest-ever film in its original form**—was shown only once at a 9-hr screening at MGM on 12 January 1924. Idwal Jones, drama critic of the *San Francisco Daily News*, who was present, commented that it had 'every comma of the book put in'. It was subsequently cut to 24 reels by an aggrieved von Stroheim, who had already spent four unpaid months editing the original footage down to 48 reels; then to 18 reels by Rex Ingram, and finally 10 reels by Joe Farnham. The 32 reels of cut negative were melted down by MGM to retrieve the minute quantity of silver nitrate they contained.

The longest commercially-made American movie released in America was the ill-fated $43 million epic *Cleopatra* (US 63) at a seemingly endless 4 hr 3 min. The only other Hollywood productions longer than *Gone with the Wind* (US 39), which ran for 3 hr 40 min, were *The Greatest Story Ever Told* (US 65) at 3 hr 45 min and Bob Dylan's 3 hr 55 min *Renaldo and Clara* (US 77). Otto Preminger's *Exodus* (US 60) was exactly the same length as *Gone with the Wind*. Prior to *Gone with the Wind* the record for the longest Hollywood talkie was held by MGM's *The Great Ziegfeld* (US 36), which ran for 2 hr 59 min.

The longest commercially-made British film was Christine Edzard's monumental screen adaptation of Charles Dickens's *Little Dorrit* (GB 87), starring Sir Alec Guinness, Derek Jacobi and talented newcomer Sarah Pickering in the title role. With a total running time of 5 hr 57 min, the film was released in two parts, playing on alternate days, the first part of 2 hr 56 min duration, the second 3 hr 1 min.

> Contrary to general belief, Eisenstein's celebrated uncompleted masterpiece *Que Viva Mexico!* (US 32) did receive a public showing in its fullest form. A cinema on New York's 14th Street asked to show the original uncut version which Eisenstein had consigned to Sol Lesser. There were nearly 90 reels and Lesser agreed on the proviso that the entire 20-hour epic was shown non-stop. Before the first third of the film was over, the cinema was empty.

The longest film to be shown commercially in its entirety was Rainer Werner Fassbinder's 15 hr 21 min opus *Berlin Alexanderplatz* (FRG 83) at the Vista cinema in Hollywood on 6–7 August 1983. Tickets cost $20 and there was a two-hour break for dinner. The slightly longer *Heimat* (FRG 84), at 15 hr 40 min, was shown in several German cities and at the London Film Festival during 1984, but these were weekend shows with a night in between the first half and the second.

FILMS RUNNING FOUR HOURS

The following are films shown in public in a version lasting four hours or longer. The list includes films issued in parts, but not serials. The duration of the silent films listed is calculated on the assumption that they were projected at 16 f.p.s.

Hours	Film	Hours	Film	Hours	Film
4 hr	Chusingura (Jap 55)		Le Chagrin et la Pitié (Fr 70)	6 hr 30 min	Sleep (US 63)
	Gosta Berlings Saga (Swe 24)		La Hora de los Hornos (Arg 68)	6 hr 40 min	Hitler: a Film from Germany (FRG 77)
	Heaven's Gate (US 81) [1]	4 hr 34 min	Atvaltozas/Point of Departure (Hun 84)		
	Ludwig (It/Fr/FRG 73) [2]			7 hr	Der Hund von Baskerville (Ger 14–20)
	Manon des Sources (Fr 54)	4 hr 38 min	The Memory of Justice (FRG 76)	7 hr 45 min	Francais si vous savez (Fr 73)
4 hr 3 min	Cleopatra (US 63)	4 hr 40 min	Amerikanske Billeder (Den 81)	7 hr 58 min	Iskry Plamja (Rus 25)
4 hr 5 min	The Keys of Happiness (Rus 13)		The Prodigal Son (GB 23)	8 hr	Empire (US 64)
	Siberiade (USSR 79)	4 hr 45 min	Rameau's Nephew by Diderot (Can 74)	8 hr 27 min	War and Peace (USSR 63–67) [6]
4 hr 12 min	L'Amour Fou (Fr 68)			8 hr 32 min	La Roue (Fr 21) [7]
4 hr 15 min	Parsifal (FRG/Fr 82)	4 hr 58 min	Percal (Mex 50)	9 hr	Wagner (GB/Hun/Aut 83) [8]
	Paths of Life (GDR 81)	5 hr 2 min	Winifred Wagner und die Geschichte des Hauses Wahnfried (FRG 75)		Napoleon (Fr 27) [9]
	Molière (Fr 78)			9 hr 21 min	Shoah (Fr/Swz 85)
	Out 1: Spectre (Fr 72)	5 hr 5 min	Les Misérables (Fr 27)	9 hr 29 min	The Human Condition (Jap 58–60)
	Mera Naam Joker (Ind 70)	5 hr 6 min	Petersburgskije truscoby (Rus 15)	12 hr 40 min	Out 1: Noli me Tangerey (Fr 71) [10]
4 hr 16 min	The Age of Cosimo de Medici (It 72)	5 hr 14 min	Potop/The Deluge (Pol 74)	12 hr 43 min	Comment Yukong deplace les montagnes (Fr 76)
	Gustaf Wasa (Swe 28)	5 hr 16 min	1900 (It 78)	13 hr	The Old Testament (It 22)
4 hr 17 min	Les Plouffe (Can 81)	5 hr 20 min	Vindicta (Fr 23)	14 hr 33 min	The Journey (Can 87)
4 hr 20 min	Amor der Perdicao (Por 80)	5 hr 32 min	Les Misérables (Fr 33)	15 hr 21 min	Berlin Alexanderplatz (FRG/It 80) [11]
	Boris I (Bul 85)	5 hr 50 min	Fanny and Alexander (Swe 83) [4]	15 hr 40 min	Heimat (FRG 84)
	The Greatest Story Ever Told (US 62) [3]	5 hr 54 min	Soldati Svobodi (USSR/Bul/Hun/Cz/GDR/Rom/Pol 77)	24 hr	* * * * (US 67) [12]
	Rubens (Neth 78)	5 hr 57 min	Little Dorrit (GB 87)	27 hr	The Burning of the Red Lotus Temple (Chn 28–31)
4 hr 25 min	The Idiot (Jap 51)	6 hr	Charles XII (Swe 27)	48 hr	The Longest Most Meaningless Movie in the World (GB 70) [13]
	The Tokyo Trial (Jap 85)		Idade de Terra (Bra 79)	50 hr	Mondo Teeth (US 70)
4 hr 30 min	Measure for Measure (Bul 81)		Khan Asparouch (Bul 82)	85 hr	The Cure for Insomnia (US 87)
	Imagen de Caracas (Ven 68)	6 hr 10 min	Die Nibelungen (Ger 24)		
	The Great Citizen (USSR 38)	6 hr 24 min	Foolish Wives (US 22) [5]		

[1] Long version shown Venice Film Festival 1982 and elsewhere.
[2] General release print 3 hr; 4-hr version shown Rome 1980, Paris 1983.
[3] At première only. Release prints were 3 hr 58 min.
[4] Long version shown at Venice Film Festival 1983.
[5] Released at this length in South America only. US general release: 10 reels.
[6] Russian language version. English language version 6 hr 13 min.
[7] Released in 4-hr version, but VGIK in Moscow has print of 8½ hr original.
[8] Premièred in 9-hr entirety at Dominion, Tottenham Court Road, May 1983. Release version 5 hr.
[9] Abel Gance's 42-reel version définitive; trade and press shown at the Apollo, Paris in 1927 and believed to have been shown commercially in Nice and other provincial centres. The version shown at the Paris première was 3 hr 40 min. The 7½-hr version reconstructed by Kevin Brownlow was first shown at Don Bosch, Netherlands on 24 November 1984.
[10] Shown only once at this length, then re-edited as 4½-hr Out 1: Spectre.
[11] Long version: see **Longest film shown commercially** entry above.
[12] Shown only once, then re-edited as two features of conventional length.
[13] Premièred at this length, then cut to 1½ hr.

Rainer Werner Fassbinder's *Berlin Alexanderplatz* (FRG/It 80) was the longest film to be shown commercially in its entirety. Presented at Hollywood's Vista theatre, it ran for 15 hours 21 minutes.

*C*INEMA MUSEUMS

The first cinema museum was the Česco-slovenskyé Filmové Museum, founded by Jindřich Brichta at Prague in 1923.

The first cinema museum in America was the Crocker Museum which Charles Chaplin's assistant Harry Crocker, who had a mania for collecting movie memorabilia, established on Sunset Boulevard, Hollywood in 1928. The exhibits consisted of props and costumes from silent movies, including Chaplin's original tramp costume, Harold Lloyd's glasses, William S. Hart's first leather chaps, Keaton's pancake boater, Gloria Swanson's 'Sadie Thompson' costume, the cabin that tottered on the brink from *The Gold Rush* (US 24), and the winning chariot from *Ben Hur* (US 26).

---

*CI*NEMA MUSEUMS

The following museums are either wholly devoted to cinema or have substantial cinema collections. Film archives are only included if they also administer a museum.

ARGENTINA
Museo Municipal de Arte Moderno, Mendoza.

AUSTRALIA
Australian Film Institute Museum, Canberra.
Movie Museum, Buderim.

AUSTRIA
Osterreichisches Filmmuseum, Vienna.

BELGIUM
Musée du Cinéma, Brussels.
Musée de la Photographie et du Cinéma, Brussels.
Provinciaal Museum voor Kunstambachten het Sterckshof, Deurne.

BRAZIL
Embrafilme Cinema Museum, Rio de Janeiro.
The Cinema Museum, São Paulo.

CZECHOSLOVAKIA
Museum of Animated and Puppet Films, Kratochvile Castle, Bohemia.

DENMARK
Det Danske Filmmuseum, Copenhagen.

FRANCE
Henri Langlois Film Museum, Palais de Chaillot, Paris.
Musée du Cinéma, Rue de Courcelles, Paris.
Musée du Cinéma, Lyons (Lumière collection).
Pirates Galleon Museum, Cannes. The only museum devoted to a single film—housed in the galleon built at a cost of £7m for Roman Polanski's *Pirates* (US/Tun 86).

GERMANY, DEM. REP. OF
Kreismuseum, Bitterfeld.

GERMANY, FED. REP. OF
Munich City Museum (Film and Photography Department).
Deutsches Film Museum, Frankfurt-am-Main.

GREAT BRITAIN
Barnes Museum of Cinematography, St Ives, Cornwall.
The National Museum of Photography, Film and Television, Bradford.
Laurel & Hardy Museum, Ulverston, Cumbria (birthplace of Stan Laurel).
Buckingham Movie Museum (home movies).
The Museum of the Moving Image, South Bank, London (opened autumn 1988).
Movie Memorabilia, Warwick. Claimed by its proprietors as 'the first museum-type gallery in the world—specializing in original film art from the major studios; and all this displayed in a museum setting with costumes, props and artefacts used in the movies'.

HUNGARY
The Ciné-Museum, Kaposvár.

ITALY
Museo Nazionale del Cinema, Turin.

MEXICO
Cinematica Luis Bunuel, Puebla.
Cinematica Mexicana, Mexico City.
Anda Museum, Mexico City. Established 1987 by actors' union Anda to preserve momentos of Mexican stars.

NETHERLANDS
Stichting Nederlands Filmmuseum, Amsterdam.

NORWAY
Norsk Filminstitutt, Oslo.

SWEDEN
Asta Nielsen Filmmuseum, Lund.

SWITZERLAND
Museum des Films, Basel.

USA
Tom Mix Museum, Dewey, Oklahoma.
Will Rogers Memorial, Claremore, Oklahoma.
International Museum of Photography, George Eastman House, Rochester, NY.
Museum of Modern Art, New York.
Hollywood Stuntmen's Hall of Fame, Mojave, California.
The Hollywood Museum, 7051 Hollywood Boulevard (opened 1984).
Hollywood Studio Museum, opened 1987 in what was formerly known as the De Mille Barn, site of the original Lasky Studio where Cecil B. De Mille filmed *The Squaw Man* in 1913.
American Museum of the Moving Image, Kaufman Astoria Studios, Queens, New York. Opened May 1988. Billed as first museum in the US devoted to 'the art, history and technology of motion pictures and television'.

USSR
Ukrainian State Museum of Theatrical, Musical and Cinema Art, Kiev.
Cinema History Museum, Odessa (history of cinema in Georgia).
The Eisenstein Museum, Moscow (housed in Eisenstein's widow's small apartment).

YUGOSLAVIA
Muzej Jugoslavenske Kinoteke, Belgrade.

---

*P*UBLICITY

The largest publicity budget was the $24 million spent by the Samuel Goldwyn Co. on the launch of *The Care Bears Movie* (US 85). It is not unknown for the publicity budget to exceed the production cost of a film. A notable example was the Brooke Shields starrer *The Blue Lagoon* (US 80), which cost $4.5 million to make but $6.3 million to promote.

Slogans

Slogans extolling movies have tended towards hyperbole ever since impresario George Belmont announced his presentation of the 'Theatrograph' at Sadler's Wells in 1896 with the words: 'A mighty mirror of Promethean Photographs and a superb, brilliant, and electrifying entertainment specially adapted to cheer the toiling millions'.

A travelling bioscope showman encountered by a correspondent of *The Pelican* in a Kentish village in 1908 stretched credulity with a sign proclaiming: 'The most extraordinary invention of modern times, as presented before the Emperor Napoleon!'

Innocence of a different type during the early years of the movies is represented by a local billsheet for a Mary Pickford film showing in Haddington, Scotland. It proffered 'What Happened to Mary Twice Nightly'.

Impressive figures have often engaged the attention of publicists. India's first feature film *Raja Harischandra* (Ind 12) was advertised as 'a performance with 57,000 photographs . . . a picture two miles in length . . . all for only three annas!' *After Rain, Clear Sky* (Chn 31), one of China's earliest all-talkies, was promoted with the information that 'on the 977 occasions for dialogue, 6935 sentences are spoken'. The quantitative attractions of Twentieth Century-Fox's *The Egyptian* (US 54) stimulated a slogan writer to even greater flights of figurative fancy with the claim that it had '10,965 pyramids, 5337 dancing girls, one million swaying bulrushes, 802 sacred bulls'.

Promoting a film to the wrong audience may be deliberate, in the case of a weak attraction, or perpetrated through sheer ignorance. In 1918 a Chicago theatre urged: 'Tomorrow—Ibsen's *Doll's House*— Bring the Kiddies!' Equally inappropriate was a Toronto cinema's slogan for David Lean's gentle evocation of middle-aged suburban romance *Brief Encounter* (GB 45): 'Girls who live dangerously'. A cinema on New York's 42nd Street, an area noted for vice, booked a nature film titled *The Love Life of a Gorilla* (US 37) and brought the crowds flocking in with a poster asking the searing question 'Do native women live with apes?' Anyone paying good money to see the film was rewarded with the answer—they don't.

Carl Laemmle knew that what audiences really want is escapist nonsense and signalled the fact loud and clear by billing his *Fighting American* (US 24) as the picture 'guaranteed not to make you think'.

Attempts to summarize the story in a phrase could involve criminal assault on the English language. *Bridal Suite* (US 39) was encapsulated: 'Howl Bent for Laugh Heaven, Four Zanies Tangle with Cock-Eyed Love'. Real extravagance of prose style, though, was reserved for the epics. Cecil B. De Mille's *King of Kings* (US 27) was advertised in New York as abounding in 'Dramatic Magnificence, Spectacular Splendor, Riotous Joy, Tigerish Rage, Undying Love, Terrifying Tempests, Appalling Earthquakes'. (Audiences might be forgiven for not recognizing this as the story of the Gospels.)

In contrast, publicity could hardly be more downbeat than the announcement on the marquee of a drive-in in Cleveland County, NC in 1960: 'Two Features'. The manager explained that he never advertised the titles of the films because 'the people who patronize this drive-in don't care what's playing'.

Devastating honesty was seldom an attribute of movie publicists, but individual cinema managers would occasionally give a frank opinion of their offerings. In 1947 an exhibitor in Hastings, Neb. announced: 'Double Feature—One Good Show and One Stinker'.

Slogans could be used to take a side-swipe at another star. Fox's advertising to promote George O'Brien in *The Iron Horse* (US 24), which declared 'He's not a Sheik or a Caveman or a Lounge Lizard— He is a Man's Man and An Idol of Women', was clearly meant to draw a denigratory comparison with Latin lover Rudolph Valentino.

If the star was not the main attraction, someone else might be. When Oscar, the well-known Negro bootblack on the Paramount lot, played a bit part in *Gambling Ship* (US 33), a black cinema on Los Angeles' Central Avenue billed the film with the legend: 'Sensational star in *Gambling Ship*, Oscar supported by Cary Grant'. The pictures outside were entirely of Oscar.

There is nothing like a good scandal to hype an indifferent picture. Released at the time of the Profumo affair, *The Man who Couldn't Walk* (US/ Can 64) was billed as 'the story behind the scandal that shocked London . . . baring untold secrets of vice, intrigue and international party girls'. What was actually delivered on screen amounted to no more than a routine meller about safecrackers. There was no character remotely resembling the Defence Minister and none that bore any connection with Miss Keeler.

Another attempt at topicality was made by the British distributors of a florid Indian romance titled *Red Rose* (Ind 82). The original slogan ran 'Petals from a beautiful film flower named Red Rose', to which some enterprising publicist had added 'Adapted from "The Yorkshire Ripper"'.

Howard Hughes made immediate impact with the posters promoting his controversial picture *The Outlaw* (US 43) when it was briefly released in 1943 before being withdrawn again. The slogan—'Mean, Moody and Magnificent'—was spread below a picture of a rampant-breasted Jane Russell standing bare-legged bestride a haystack with a pistol in each fist. When released in 1946 a far more decorous though equally striking copy-line had taken its place, a quote from Judge Twain Michelsen, who had tried the film for indecency: 'We have seen Jane Russell. She is an attractive specimen of American womanhood. God made her what she is.'

Briefer, but equally apt, was the slogan promoting Tony Richardson's *The Loved One* (US 65): 'The Picture with Something to Offend Everyone'. Briefer still and perhaps even more effective was the slogan accompanying *Baby Doll* (US 56): 'Condemned by Cardinal Spellman'.

In the twenties and thirties every big picture was ballyhooed with publicity stunts organized by local exhibitors. This not very hostile looking tank was helping to boost *The Big Parade* (US 25) into the biggest grossing silent picture of them all.

Publicity Stunts

These began decorously enough in the early days of cinema and became progressively more outrageous during the days of Hollywood's greatest extravagances, the 1920s. Initially a little ingenuity was made to go a long way. One of the earliest stunts, reported by *Kinematograph Weekly* in 1907, was dreamed up by the proprietor of a Chicago nickelodeon who had letters printed in simulated handwriting purporting to be from a girl called Lizzie, on a visit to the city, writing to her friend Mary about an exciting excursion to the cinema. They were scattered in the streets and the advertiser relied on the baser human impulse to read other people's letters. Other gimmicks employed in the USA prior to World War I included making arrangements with grocers to give 13 eggs for every dozen ordered, the extra egg being paid for by the cinema and stamped with details of the next attraction; distributing oversized neckties of a garish hue and offering free

seats to any man willing to wear one throughout the performance; and giving free admission to anyone slender enough to pass through a narrow wicket set up in the lobby or alternatively short enough to pass under a low bar.

The Vaudette Theater of West Point, Ga. announced that they would be giving away a free 'one-piece coat and garment hanger' to every patron on an advertised date in 1914. Those who attended were handed a very small envelope which contained a two-inch nail. The distributors of *Neptune's Daughter* (US 14), in which Annette Kellerman was clad in rather less than that customary for the period, sent out 36-inch tape measures which bore, at appropriate intervals, Miss Kellerman's vital statistics.

When Kalem reissued *The Colleen Bawn* (US 11), they had several tons of earth shipped from Killarney to New York and made up into four foot square sods for distribution to cinemas exhibiting the film. For the price of a theatre ticket, Irish immigrants could savour the pleasure of once again standing on Irish soil.

One of the most sure-fire stunts, repeated in small towns all over the USA from about 1912, was known as 'Giving Away a Baby'. The exhibitor announced that a baby would be given away on the stage on a certain day. He then arranged for someone to write to the local newspaper deploring this act of inhumanity, to which the cinema manager would reply in a hurt tone saying that the baby had made no objection and the mother was indifferent to its fate. This would provoke a shoal of letters, a lively public debate in the community, and threats of police prosecution. On the appointed night a packed house, usually including a contingent of police, would see the manager give away a baby pig.

The first of the great press agent hoaxes was perpetrated by the publicist for Thanhouser's serial *The Million Dollar Mystery* (US 14), who gave an anonymous tip-off to the police and newspapers that an heiress had disappeared. For seven days the police hunt continued, while Thanhouser's press agent fed them with information that paralleled the action of the forthcoming film. When the deception was exposed, the 'missing heiress' turned out to be the heroine of *The Million Dollar Mystery.*

Ace publicist Harry Reichenbach stimulated public interest in *The Virgin of Stamboul* (US 20) by conning the New York police into dragging a lake in Central Park for the body of the virgin. Meanwhile a Turkish Government Commission (recruited from loafers in Turkish coffee houses on the East Side) was installed at the Hotel Navarre to provide a focus for press attention.

As a promotion for the serial *Bride 13* (US 20), the manager of the Lyric Theater at Easley, S. Carolina persuaded an engaged couple to be married in front of the screen immediately following the first episode. A capacity audience watched the event, which included an unscheduled moment of drama when the bride's mother, who was present but had no idea that her daughter was involved in the stunt, shouted 'Stop!' from the stalls. She was persuaded, in the interests of her daughter's happiness and the manager's profits, to let the show go on.

Hollywood's tsars were not above a little stunt work themselves. Carl Laemmle turned the expensive luxury of employing Erich von Stroheim as a director to good account by erecting a mammoth electric sign on Broadway flashing out the prodigious budget allocated for *Foolish Wives* (US 22), then in the course of its year-long shooting schedule. As von Stroheim's extravagances pushed the budget ever higher, Laemmle arranged for the New York Fire Brigade to tear down Broadway every Wednesday to change the light bulbs to the latest spiralling figure. The 'S' in

Stroheim was replaced on the billboard by a $ sign.

It was about this period that publicity stunts involving stars reached their apogee. During a dip in Valentino's popularity, Harry Reichenbach, arch-exponent of ballyhoo, persuaded the great lover to grow a beard, and then proceeded to orchestrate a chorus of protest from outraged legions of female fans and the proprietors of barber shops. A few months later he arranged a ceremonial debearding by experts nominated by the Master Barbers of America.

To promote Raoul Walsh's *The Honor System* (US 25), the producers arranged for a practical demonstration of the 'honor' system in action, with a prisoner being released for a single day on his honour to return. Alas, he was not seen again.

Another stunt that backfired was the misguided one perpetrated by Universal when *The Phantom of the Opera* (US 25) was brought to England. By some means the studio publicity department persuaded Lt. Col W. H. Barrell, Commanding Officer of the 153rd Heavy Brigade of the Royal Artillery, to give the English release prints a military escort from Southampton docks to the station and from Waterloo to Wardour Street. For the ceremonial march through London, the prints were preceded not only by troops but also an armoured car and a full regimental band. Press and public were equally scandalized by the vulgarity of the operation and the 'outrage on British troops', as one newspaper put it. There was a full-scale War Office enquiry and questions were asked in the House. To make matters worse, Universal's English representative, James Bryson, confessed that the military had been escorting empty boxes, since the prints of *The Phantom of the Opera* had been left safely in his trunks on the *Berengaria*, the liner which had brought them from New York. The uproar was so great that the film was never released in Britain and when, some years later, there was a second and more discreet attempt to bring it over, permission was flatly refused.

> What Hollywood publicists lack in finesse they make up for in originality. Patrons of *Blood Feast* (US 63) were supplied with paper bags to be sick into.

When *The Man I Killed* (US 32) went on release, an American exhibitor engaged a man to be buried alive for 24 hours. Unfortunately a storm during the night obliterated the grave marker and long after the 24 hours were up a team of 30 rescuers were desperately digging to release the entombed man. His first demand on being brought to the surface was for overtime pay.

Publicist Pete Smith was inspired with the idea of getting Sam Goldwyn to say that there were only 13 real actors in Hollywood and to name them. Goldwyn liked the stunt, but for the fact that he felt that as a result he would only be on speaking terms with 13 actors. He found the solution himself, naming twelve of the actors and leaving Hollywood to guess the name of the 13th.

Mom and Dad aka *A Family Story* (US 47), an exploitation movie with a live childbirth scene, was shown to sexually segregated audiences. According to publicity, this was 'so as not to offend the delicate'. To improve the effect, promotional manager Joe Solomon arranged to have a nauseous chemical put into the ventilation system and then called the local press to take pictures of the women reeling and retching out of the cinema. This ensured a full house of men in the evening.

When *Psycho* (US 60) was released, producer-director Alfred Hitchcock had it written into every booking contract that no one was to be admitted after the film began. The master showman created a publicity gimmick that was actually enforceable in law.

The distributors of *Snuff* (Arg/US 74), a tasteless exploitation movie based on the unfounded rumours then circulating that young girls were being killed for real on camera in Latin America sex pix, hired rentamob to picket cinemas showing the film in order to attract adverse but none the less beneficial publicity.

When *Too Scared to Scream* (US 85) premièred at Hollywood's Paramount Theater a contest was held on the sidewalk outside to find the girl who could scream loudest and scariest. One hundred contestants were judged for howl quality by the picture's producer and star Mike Connors.

Hollywood hype continues unabated. *Million Dollar Mystery* (US 87) is the story of $4 million of loot that gets dispersed into four stashes of $1 million each. Three of the stashes are located as the narrative unfolds, but at the end of the pic $1 million remains hidden—for anyone in the audience who has followed the clues to find for real. *Variety* remained unimpressed. 'Offer people enough money' sniffed filmdom's bible, 'and they'll do a lot of things, including watch a bad movie over and over again'.

REMAKES

The longest interval between remakes with the same actor playing the same role was 34 years in the case of Tito Lusiardo's performances in *El Dia que me Quitas/The Day You Leave Me* (US 35 and Arg 69).

The story which has been remade the most times is *Cinderella*, of which there have been 84

Possibly the only film to actually declare itself a remake in the credits is the Gene Hackman father-son drama *Misunderstood* (US 84). Although its primary source is Florence Montgomery's turn of the century novel, an end credit adds that it is a 'remake and adaptation' of Luigi Comencini's *Incompreso* (It 67). In the remake, Hackman is the stiff and unbending widower father, an American living in Tunisia; the Italian film had Anthony Quayle as an equally stiff and unbending father, but a British consul based in Rome.

productions, including cartoon, modern, ballet, operatic, pornographic and parody versions, from *Cinderella and the Fairy Godmother* (GB 98), starring Laura Bayley, to Beta Film's *Cinderella* (W. Ger i.p. 88).

In addition to *Cinderella*, the following works have been the subject of twelve or more movie remakes: Shakespeare's *Hamlet* – 45+13 parody versions; *Carmen* (Merimée's story and Bizet's opera – 54+2 parodies; *Faust* (Marlowe, Goethe and Gounod's opera) – 51; R. L. Stevenson's *Dr Jekyll and Mr Hyde* – 47 (including parodies and variants); Shakespeare's *Romeo and Juliet* – 32+6 modern+9 parodies; Defoe's *Robinson Crusoe* – 43 (inc. 2 porno); Dumas fils' *La Dame aux camelias* – 36; Cervantes's *Don Quixote* – 35; Shakespeare's *Macbeth* – 27+3 modern+1 parody; Hugo's *Les Miserables* – 31; Dumas père's *The Three Musketeers* – 30+10 variants featuring the character d'Artagnan; the Hindu epic *Harischandra* – 25 in 9 languages; Tolstoy's *Resurrection* – 23; Dumas père's *The Count of Monte Cristo* – 21+13 variants featuring the character Edmund Dantes; Dickens's *Oliver Twist* – 21; Shakespeare's *A Midsummer Night's Dream* – 20; Shakespeare's *Julius Caesar* – 18+1 modern; Dickens's *A Christmas Carol* – 19; Tolstoy's *Anna Karenina* – 18; *William Tell* (Schiller and legend) – 15; Dostoevsky's *Crime and Punishment* – 15; *Othello* (Shakespeare and Verdi's opera) – 15; Shakespeare's *King Lear* – 15 including Godard's 'free' version (the director admitted he had not read the play); Harriet Beecher Stowe's *Uncle Tom's Cabin* – 14; Lewis Carroll's *Alice in Wonderland* – 14; Tolstoy's *The Living Corpse* – 13; Dumas père's *The Corsican Brothers* – 13; Mrs Henry Wood's *East Lynne* – 13; Sir Arthur Conan Doyle's *The Hound of the Baskervilles* – 12.

'If I had my life to live over I would do everything the exact same way—with the possible exception of seeing the movie remake of *Lost Horizon*.'—Woody Allen

SEQUELS

It took a surprisingly long time for the idea of making sequels to popular movies to emerge—despite the enormous output of the major film-producing nations during the 1910s and 1920s, there was not a single sequel during the silent era. **The first sequel** was the Fox production *Cock-eyed World* (US 29), with Victor McLaglen and Edmund Lowe reprising their roles as the bawdy Marines of *What Price Glory* (US 26). The same director, Raoul Walsh, and the same writers, Laurence Stallings and Maxwell Anderson, worked on both movies. As has often happened since, the sequel failed to live up to the original at the box office.

The longest interval between a sequel and its original was 34 years in the case of *The Maltese Falcon* (US 41) and *The Black Bird* (US 75) and a similar period between *National Velvet* (US 44) and *International Velvet* (GB 78). In *The Black Bird*

Lee Patrick looks as if she had a higher regard for the cigarette-smoking Humphrey Bogart in *The Maltese Falcon* (US 41) (*below*) than she had for cigar-chomping George Segal in the sequel, *The Black Bird* (US 75).

George Segal played Sam Spade's son, who has inherited Effie (Lee Patrick), the elder Spade's secretary in *The Maltese Falcon*, along with his father's detective agency. Miss Patrick had also played Effie in the 1941 picture. The role of Velvet grown up in *International Velvet* was offered to Elizabeth Taylor, who had played the child Velvet when she was 12 years old, but she turned it down and the role was played with mature dignity and charm by Nanette Newman. The star of the picture was Tatum O'Neal as Velvet's niece from America who comes to live with her aunt in Britain, becomes a showjumper, and wins an Olympic Gold Medal.

The longest interval between a sequel and its original with the same stars was 20 years and one day in the case of Claude Lelouche's *A Man and a Woman* (Fr 66), which premièred at the Cannes Film Festival on 10 May 1966, and *A Man and a Woman: 20 Years Later* (Fr 86), which also bowed

Above: Bette Davis as the middle-aged Regina Hubbard in *The Little Foxes* (US 41) (*Popperfoto*). *Left*: Ann Blyth played the same character 20 years younger in the prequel *Another Part of the Forest* (US 48). (*Kobal*)

at Cannes, on 11 May 1986. The co-stars of both pictures were Jean-Louis Trintignant and Anouk Aimée. Lelouche has promised *A Man and a Woman: 40 Years Later* for May 2006.

The first 'roman numeral' sequel was *Quatermass II* (GB 57), the follow-up to *The Quatermass Experiment* (GB 54).

The longest interval between a 'I' and 'II' picture was 23 years in the case of Alfred Hitchcock's *Psycho* (US 60) and Richard Franklin's *Psycho II* (US 83). Anthony Perkins returned in his role as the psychotic murderer Norman Bates, released after spending 22 years in a mental institution.

The sequel that wasn't. *Surf II* (US 82) was a cod—there had never been a *Surf I*.

'Prequels'

These are sequels that relate the story that *preceded* the original film. *Another Part of the Forest* (US 47) recounted the earlier lives of the Hubbard family portrayed in *The Little Foxes* (US 41); Steve McQueen's title role in *Nevada Smith* (US 66) centred on the earlier life of the character played by Alan Ladd in *The Carpetbaggers* (US 64); Michael Winner's *The Night Comers* (GB 71) told the story of how the ghosts in *The Innocents* (GB 61)—the manservant Quint and the 'former governess'—lost their lives; *Rhapsody* (US 54), from Henry Handel Richardson's novel *Maurice Guest*, was followed 25 years later by the film of the preceding volume of the story, *The Getting of Wisdom* (Aus 79); Richard Lester's *Butch and Sundance—The Early Days* (US 79) recounts the story of how the outlaw pair (Tom Berenger and William Katt) met and teamed up together, while the earlier George Roy Hill picture *Butch Cassidy and the*

Sundance Kid (US 69) related the events leading up to the death of Butch and Sundance (Paul Newman and Robert Redford) in a shoot-out with the Bolivian army. Zoltán Fábri brought Jósef Baláz's novel *Hungarians* (Hun 79) to the screen before embarking on the preceding story of the hero's father in his youth, told in *Bálint Fábián's Encounter with God* (Hun 80). Both Bálint Fábián and his son András were played by the same actor, Gábor Koncz. *Indiana Jones and the Temple of Doom* (US 84) was set in 1935, preceding by three years the action of the earlier Indiana Jones caper *Raiders of the Lost Ark* (US 81). *Missing in Action 2—The Beginning* (US 85) related what happened to Col. Braddock (Chuck Norris) in Vietnam before his escape to the US and return to Vietnam to locate missing comrades, as depicted in *Missing in Action* (US 84).

The only prequel–sequel movie was Francis Ford Coppola's *The Godfather Part II*, which ranged back and forth in time to reveal events which had taken place before those in *The Godfather* (US 71) as well as events which followed on. A rare instance of a sequel–prequel–sequel arose with Claude Berri's *Jean de Florette* (Fr 86), from the Marcel Pagnol story of the destruction of a hunchback townsman (Gerard Depardieu) who seeks to settle on the land in Provence in the 1920s, which was the prequel to Pagnol's own film *Manon des Sources* (Fr 53), in which the hunchback's daughter (Jacqueline Pagnol) wreaks vengeance on the village. A remake of *Manon des Sources* (Fr 87), also by Claude Berri and with Emanuelle Béart in the title role, provided a new sequel to the prequel.

THREE

BOX OFFICE AND BUDGETS

BOX OFFICE

The film with the highest earnings worldwide is *E.T. The Extra-Terrestrial* (US 82), which has earned a gross $700 million in rentals. Distributor MCA estimates that some 240 million cinemagoers have seen the picture.

Previous box office champions were *Snow White and the Seven Dwarfs* (US 37), which was the first talkie to overtake the record for silent pictures set by *The Big Parade* (US 25) (see below); *Gone with the Wind* (US 39), which held the record from 1940 until overtaken by *The Sound of Music* (US 65) in August 1966 and again in 1971–2 as the result of a reissue; *The Godfather* (US 72), which set a new record the year of its release; and *Jaws* (US 75), also a record-breaker in its first year and box office champion until surpassed by *Star Wars* in 1977. The crown passed to *E.T. The Extra-Terrestrial* (US 82) in January 1983, 31 weeks after its release.

The top grossing silent film was King Vidor's *The Big Parade* (US 25), with worldwide rentals of $22 million. No exact figure is available for D. W. Griffith's *The Birth of a Nation* (US 15), which was long thought of as the top grossing silent, with estimates of up to $50 million receipts in the domestic

---

ANNUAL TOP MONEYMAKER USA

Prior to 1947 there are no consistent records. Since that date *Variety* has identified the following pictures as top moneymaker of the year in the domestic market (US and Canada). Where the top moneymaker is a non-American production, the top American grosser is listed second:

1947 *The Best Years of Our Lives*
1948 *The Road to Rio*
1949 *Jolson Sings Again*
1950 *Samson and Delilah*
1951 *David and Bathsheba*
1952 *The Greatest Show on Earth*
1953 *The Robe*
1954 *White Christmas*
1955 *Cinerama Holiday*
1956 *Guys and Dolls*
1957 *The Ten Commandments*
1958 *The Bridge on the River Kwai* (GB)
 Peyton Place (US)
1959 *Auntie Mame*
1960 *Ben Hur*

1961 *The Guns of Navarone* (GB)
 The Absent-Minded Professor (US)
1962 *Spartacus*
1963 *Cleopatra*
1964 *The Carpetbaggers*
1965 *Mary Poppins*
1966 *Thunderball* (GB)
 Doctor Zhivago (US)
1967 *The Dirty Dozen*
1968 *The Graduate*
1969 *The Love Bug*
1970 *Airport*
1971 *Love Story*
1972 *The Godfather*
1973 *The Poseidon Adventure*
1974 *The Sting*
1975 *Jaws*
1976 *One Flew Over the Cuckoo's Nest*
1977 *Star Wars*
1978 *Grease*
1979 *Superman* (GB)
 Every Which Way But Loose (US)

1980 *The Empire Strikes Back*
1981 *Raiders of the Lost Ark*
1982 *E. T. The Extra-Terrestrial*
1983 *Return of the Jedi*
1984 *Ghostbusters*
1985 *Back to the Future*
1986 *Top Gun*
1987 *Beverly Hills Cop II*

Of the 45 top grossers listed above, 9 were contemporary dramas, 8 were historical epics, 7 were comedies, 6 were musicals, 5 were science-fiction, 4 were war films, 2 were adventure films, one was a Bond movie and one a Cinerama travelogue. Only one was a straight crime drama (*The Godfather*).

Usually the top grosser in the US is also the top grosser worldwide. A notable exception occurred in 1986, when *Top Gun* wasn't; it was outgunned by Australia's all-time sleeper *Crocodile Dundee*.

ANNUAL TOP MONEYMAKER GB

The following have been the annual top moneymaking British films in the domestic market since 1936:

1936 *The Ghost Goes West*
1937 *Good Morning Boys*
1938 *A Yank at Oxford*
1939 *Pygmalion*
1940 *Convoy*
1941 *49th Parallel*
1942 *The First of the Few*
1943 *In Which We Serve*
1944 *This Happy Breed*
1945 *The Seventh Veil*
1946 *The Wicked Lady*
1947 *The Courtneys of Curzon Street*
1948 *Spring in Park Lane*
1949 *The Third Man*
1950 *The Blue Lamp*
1951 *Laughter in Paradise*
1952 *Where No Vultures Fly*
1953 *The Cruel Sea*

1954 *Doctor in the House*
1955 *The Dam Busters*
1956 *Reach for the Sky*
1957 *Doctor at Large*
1958 *The Bridge on the River Kwai*
1959 *Carry on Nurse*
1960 *Doctor in Love*
1961 *The Swiss Family Robinson*
1962 *The Young Ones*
1963 *From Russia with Love*
1964 *Goldfinger*
1965 *Help!*
1966 *Thunderball*
1967 *You Only Live Twice*
1968 *Up the Junction*
1969 *Oliver!*
1970 *Battle of Britain*
1971 *On the Buses*
1972 *Diamonds are Forever*
1973 *Live and Let Die*
1974 *Confessions of a Window Cleaner*

1975 *The Man with the Golden Gun*
1976 *The Return of the Pink Panther*
1977 *The Spy Who Loved Me*
1978 *The Revenge of the Pink Panther*
1979 *Moonraker*
1980 *Monty Python's Life of Brian*
1981 *Superman II*
1982 *Chariots of Fire*
1983 *Octopussy*
1984 *Never Say Never Again*
1985 *A View to a Kill*
1986 *Santa Claus—The Movie*
1987 *The Living Daylights*

Of the 52 films listed, 17 were comedies, 9 were war films, 13 were Bond movies, 7 were contemporary dramas, 3 were historical, 2 were musicals, and one was science-fiction. Significantly only one straight crime drama (*The Blue Lamp*) is included.

market alone. This is now considered to be a wildly exaggerated figure, and *Variety* quotes $5 million as a reasonable 'guestimate'. Griffith himself stated in 1929 that the film had earned $10 million world-wide.

The highest grossing film from outside the USA was the phenomenal Australian success *Crocodile Dundee* (Aus 86), starring Paul Hogan as the irrepressible crocodile hunter from the Northern Territory who takes on New York and wins hands down. It took $70 million in rentals in North America, some $80 million in the rest of the world, and earned a worldwide gross estimated at $375 million. It was also the highest grossing film of all time in Britain, taking over £20 million at the box office.

The highest grossing film from a Third World country was Jamie Uys's *The Gods Must Be Crazy* (Botswana 81), an engaging tale about a Kalahari Bushman's encounters with western civilization as he journeys to 'the edge of the world' to jettison a Coca Cola bottle whose descent from a passing aeroplane has caused dissention in his tribe. Made on the kind of budget major advertisers spend on a single TV commercial, it opened without fanfare and to generally negative reviews. Word of mouth from audiences charmed by much the same kind of unpretentious good humour that made *Crocodile Dundee* so popular had a snowballing effect and it became the No. 1 foreign film in Japan in 1982 and the box office champion in France in 1983. In all,

Britain's top moneymaker of 1958 was David Lean's *The Bridge on the River Kwai* (GB 57). It was also the top moneymaker of the year in the US, the first time a British film achieved this distinction.

THE TWENTY-FIVE TOP GROSSING FILMS

The list below was published by the American trade paper *Variety* in 1988 and represents the North American (US and Canada) rentals for the 25 top grossing films of all time. As a very approximate guide, films which are successful in the North American market can usually expect to earn about the same in overseas rentals as they do in domestic rentals.

1	*E.T. The Extra-Terrestrial* (US 82)	$228,379,346
2	*Star Wars* (US 77)	$193,500,000
3	*Return of the Jedi* (US 83)	$168,002,414
4	*The Empire Strikes Back* (US 80)	$141,600,000
5	*Jaws* (US 75)	$129,549,242
6	*Ghostbusters* (US 84)	$128,264,005
7	*Raiders of the Lost Ark* (US 81)	$115,598,000
8	*Indiana Jones and the Temple of Doom* (US 84)	$109,000,000
9	*Beverly Hills Cops* (US 84)	$108,000,000
10	*Back to the Future* (US 85)	$104,237,346
11	*Grease* (US 78)	$96,300,000
12	*Tootsie* (US 82)	$95,268,806
13	*The Exorcist* (US 73)	$89,000,000
14	*The Godfather* (US 72)	$86,275,000
15	*Superman* (GB 78)	$82,800,000
16	*Close Encounters of the Third Kind* (US 77/80)	$82,750,000
17	*Beverly Hills Cop II* (US 87)	$80,857,776
18	*The Sound of Music* (US 65)	$79,748,000
19	*Gremlins* (US 84)	$79,500,000
20	*Top Gun* (US 86)	$79,400,000
21	*Rambo: First Blood Part II* (US 85)	$78,919,250
22	*Gone With the Wind* (US 39)	$77,612,077
23	*Rocky IV* (US 85)	$75,974,593
24	*Saturday Night Fever* (US 77)	$74,100,000
25	*The Sting* (US 73)	$70,227,100

Gods grossed over $85 million from as far apart as Bulgaria, where it won the Grand Prize at the International Festival of Comic Films, to Australia, where it ran for 84 weeks and where a woman had to be carried out of a cinema in Sydney after becoming helpless with laughter. In America, where the film had performed poorly on its first outing, it took nearly $13 million on its triumphant return in 1985. Only in Britain was *Gods* a total failure—after a one-week run in the Haymarket, anti-South African activists ensured that it never got a repeat showing.

> 'There will never be any real money in these galloping tintypes . . .'—William De Mille (brother of Cecil) to David Belasco, 1911.

The country with the highest box office gross is the USA, whose record year was 1987 with 1089 million paid admissions worth $4253 million.

Indiana Jones and the Temple of Doom (US 84) took a record $9.3 million at the box office in a single day.

What Hollywood Earns

Worldwide theatrical rentals of feature films released by the major US distributors totalled $1960 million in 1986, of which $1170 million was earned in the domestic market and the balance overseas. Top foreign market for Hollywood pictures is Japan, which returned $102.6 million to the distributors in 1986. Britain is in sixth place in the export league, notching up $49 million in rentals.

The highest single day gross for any film was achieved by Paramount's *Indiana Jones and the Temple of Doom* (US 84), which took $9,324,760 at 1687 sites on Sunday 27 May 1984. The same picture also earned the **highest week's gross** at $45,709,328 in its opening week. **The highest opening day gross** was scored by *Return of the Jedi* (US 83) on Wednesday 25 May 1983 with a take of $6,219,629 at 1002 sites.

> With Japan as Hollywood's biggest export market, it behoves tiro producers to take note of Nipponese preferences. Per one Japanese buyer: 'The picture has to open with a bang. Every five minutes there should be another bang and the picture should end with a bang. The story doesn't matter.'

The lowest reported box office gross for any film in the last decade was $1500 for *Contaminacion* (Col 82).

The highest loss on any film was incurred by United Artists on the ill-fated *Heaven's Gate* (US 80), which earned $1,500,000 in North American rentals against an estimated negative cost of $44 million and a total cost, including distribution and studio overheads, of $57 million. It brought in a better return (or lesser loss) per dollar, however, than the $24 million *Honky Tonk Freeway* (US 81), which earned only $500,000 in North American rentals and in terms of budget/box office ratio is Hollywood's biggest box office flop of all time.

Box Office Disasters

Megabuck pix which have returned less than a tenth of their budget in North American rentals:

The Clan of the Cave Bear (US 86)
    Cost $18 million Earned $1.5 million
8 Million Ways To Die (US 86)
    Cost $18 million Earned $0.5 million
The Fall of the Roman Empire (US 64)
    Cost $20 million Earned $1.9 million
Five Days One Summer (US 82)
    Cost $15 million Earned under $1 million
Heaven's Gate (US 80)
    Cost $44 million Earned $1.5 million
Honky Tonk Freeway (US 81)
    Cost $24 million Earned $0.5 million
Inchon (Kor 82)
    Cost $46 million Earned $1.9 million
Jinxed (US 82)
    Cost $14 million Earned under $1 million
The King of Comedy (US 83)
    Cost $19 million Earned $1.2 million
King Kong Lives (US 86)
    Cost $18 million Earned $1.7 million
Lookin' to Get Out (US 82)
    Cost $17 million Earned under $1 million
My Science Project (US 85)
    Cost $14 million Earned $1.1 million

Omar Mukhtar—Lion of the Desert
(GB/Lby/US 81)
 Cost $30 million Earned $1.5 million
Once Upon a Time in America (US 84)
 Cost $30 million Earned $2.5 million
One from the Heart (US 82)
 Cost $26 million Earned under $1 million
Orphans (US 87)
 Cost $15 million Earned under $1 million
Pirates (US/Tun 86)
 Cost $31 million Earned under $1 million
Revolution (GB 85)
 Cost $28 million Earned under $1 million
Sky Bandits (GB 86)
 Cost $18 million Earned under $1 million
The Squeeze (US 87)
 Cost $19 million Earned $1 million
Tai-Pan (US 86)
 Cost $25 million Earned $2 million
Waterloo (It/USSR 70)
 Cost $25 million Earned $1.4 million

BUDGETS

The most expensive film ever made is believed to be the Carolco production *Rambo III* (US 88), of which the negative cost is estimated by *Variety* to have been $63 million. Higher estimates have been made for *Superman II* (GB 80), but the same source quotes $54 million. Producer Alexander Salkind told *Variety* in June 1983 that *Superman I* had cost as much as $80 million, attributing this to the trial and error on the special effects and because 'the distributor wasn't a partner in that one and wasn't too worried about expenses'. It is likely that this figure includes additional costs such as interest charges, prints, etc. Per *Variety* the negative cost was $55 million.

The most expensive silent film was Fred Niblo's *Ben Hur* (US 25) at $3.9 million.

The record for the most expensive production has been held successively by the films listed below. Figures quoted are those reported at the time the films were produced and in most cases are impossible to verify.

$30,000 *Napoleon* (US 08)	
$34,000 *For the Term of his Natural Life* (Aus 08)	$3,900,000 *Ben Hur* (US 25)
$47,500 *Queen Elizabeth* (Fr 12)	$3,950,000 *Hell's Angels* (US 30)
$50,000 *The Prisoner of Zenda* (US 13)	$4,250,000 *Gone with the Wind* (US 39)
$210,000 *Cabiria* (It 14)	$5,200,000 *Wilson* (US 44)
$575,000 *Intolerance* (US 16)	$6,000,000 *Duel in the Sun* (US 46)
$1,000,000 *A Daughter of the Gods* (US 16)	$8,250,000 *Quo Vadis* (US 51)
$1,100,000 *Foolish Wives* (US 22)	$13,500,000 *The Ten Commandments* (US 56)
$1,500,000 *When Knighthood was in Flower* (US 22)	$15,000,000 *Ben Hur* (US 59)
$1,800,000 *The Ten Commandments* (US 23)	$19,000,000 *Mutiny on the Bounty* (US 62)
$2,000,000 *The Thief of Baghdad* (US 24)	$44,000,000 *Cleopatra* (US 63)
	$55,000,000 *Superman* (GB 78)
	$63,000,000 *Rambo III* (US 88)

The following films have cost over $40 million (note: studios seldom reveal budgets and varying estimates have been made of the 'bottom line' cost of some of these megabuck movies. Figures quoted should therefore be regarded as 'probable') : *Dune* (US 84) $42 million; *Cleopatra* (US 63) $44 million; *Heaven's Gate* (US 80) $44 million; *Ishtar* (US 87) $45 million; *Inchon* (Kor 82) $46 million; *Star Trek* (US 79) $46 million; *Santa Claus* (GB 85) $50 million; *The Cotton Club* (US 84) $51 million; *Annie* (US 82) $51.5 million; *Reds* (US 81) $52 million; *Superman II* (GB 80) $54 million; *Superman* (GB 78) $55 million; *Rambo III* (US 88) $63 million.

The least expensive full-length feature film on record is Victorian Film Productions' part-colour *The Shattered Illusion* (Aus 27), which took twelve months to complete and included spectacular scenes of a ship being overwhelmed by a storm. Total cost of production was £300 ($1460).

The least expensive all-colour talkie was Pat Rocco's 80-minute psychological drama *Someone* (US 65), with Joe Adair and four other paid performers, which was made on an eight-day schedule for $1200 (£500).

Other low budget movies which have achieved box office and/or critical success include Marco Bellocchio's *I Pugni in Tasca* (It 66), which cost $78,000; Truffaut's *The Four Hundred Blows* (Fr 59), $65,000; *Never on Sunday* (Gre 59), $100,000; Nasser Gholam-Rezai's highly acclaimed *How Starry was My Night* (Iran 77), $28,000; Philippe Garrel's *La Concentration* (Fr 68), $14,000; Celestino Coronado's *Hamlet* (GB 77), $5000; Jon Jost's colour feature *Angel City* (US 76), $6000; Ingmar Bergman's *The Seventh Seal* (Swe 57), $40,000; Ermano Olmi's *Il Posto* (It 61), $15,000; Akira Kurosawa's *Rashomon* (Jap 50), $40,000; Claude Lelouch's *Smic, Smac, Smoc* (Fr 71), $30,000; Wim Verstappen's award-winning *Joszef Katus* (Neth 67), $2400; Jon Jost's *Last Chants for a Slow Dance* (US 77), $3000; Josef Rodel's *Albert—Why* (FRG 78), winner of the 1979 German Critics' Film Prize, $5000. *The Night of the Living Dead* (US 68) was made for $114,000 and brought in $12 million in worldwide rentals; John Waters' *Pink Flamingos* (US 72), billed as 'An Exercise in Poor Taste' and described in one review as 'the sickest movie ever made', cost $12,000 to produce and grossed $1,250,000 in two years; while the notorious *Deep Throat* (US 71), made for $25,000, grossed $4.6 million over the same length of time. Wayne Wang's thriller *Chan is Missing* (US 81), set in San Francisco's China Town, came in at $20,000.

In a rather higher bracket at $262,000, but still comparable with the cost of many 30-second TV commercials, was the Canadian sleeper *I've Heard the Mermaids Singing* (Can 87), which sold to 32 countries after winning the Prix de Jeunesse at the

1987 Cannes Film Festival. Writer, director, editor and co-producer Patricia Rozema recounted how her two main sources of funds, Telefilm Canada and the Ontario Film Development Company, had tried to persuade her to accept more money, but she had refused as she 'didn't want to be obligated to have a huge audience'. Among the highpoints in the picture is a scene in which the heroine Polly takes off into the air and flies effortlessly over Toronto. Per Ms Rozema: 'The special-effect flying was a $60 effect. A fan, some scaffolding, a little bit of smoke and there you go.'

The lowest budgeted British film to win an international release was Bill Forsyth's *That Sinking Feeling* (GB 79), made for £6000. Cost of dubbing new voices for the North American release in 1983—the original Glaswegian accents were impenetrable to US audiences—exceeded the budget of the picture.

The record budget/box office ratio was 1:285 in the case of the $350,000 Australian production *Mad Max* (Aus 80), which grossed $100 million in its first two years of international distribution.

Average Budgets

The earliest feature films made in Britain prior to World War I cost in the region of £4000–£5000, a figure which by the early twenties had risen to £6000–£7000. By the end of the twenties the average budget had virtually doubled, one estimate in 1927 being £17,000. There could be wide disparity though—supporting features were probably still within the £8000–£10,000 range, while Michael Balcon has quoted £30,000–£35,000 as a reasonable average for good-class pictures at the end of the silent era. The 1930s saw a vast outpouring of 'Quota Quickies' with budgets determined solely by length, the fixed rate being £1 per foot of screened film. The average length being 6000 ft, the average budget was £6000, allowing for a 12-day shooting schedule.

Average budgets of Hollywood features from the earliest days to the present are listed below. As in Britain, a lot of budgets were way below the general level. The 'B' pictures of the thirties and forties ground out at $15,000–$20,000, the budget set to realize an anticipated profit margin of $2000–$3000. Failure to reap the forecast return could put a small Poverty Row studio into serious financial difficulties. Quality was hardly a consideration. Sam Newfield, who could manufacture a 'B' western in three or four days with quite a bit of stock footage as padding, was once urged by a studio executive to hurry things up on a particular picture: 'You don't really mean', he drawled in reply, 'that there's someone out there waiting to see this junk'. Amongst the lowest budget features ever made in the USA were the so-called 'Ghetto movies'—all-black films for all-black audi-

ences. Budgets could be trimmed to as little as $5000 by the simple expedient of failing to pay the actors.

AVERAGE HOLLYWOOD BUDGETS FOR FEATURE FILMS ($)

1913 13,000 (5 reels)	1948 1,000,000	1978 5,300,000
1915 21,800 (5 reels)	1955 900,000	1979 6,700,000
1919 60,000 (5 reels)	1960 1,000,000	1980 7,500,000
1924 300,000	1965 1,500,000	1981 9,750,000
1932 153,000	1970 1,750,000	1982 10,900,000
1935 209,000	1972 1,890,000	1983 9,700,000
1940 314,000	1974 2,500,000	1984 11,300,000
1941 400,000	1976 4,000,000	1986 11,900,000
		1987 12,500,000

Figures prior to 1972 are quoted from *Motion Picture Almanac*. The decrease in the average budget between 1924 and the early 1930s may be accounted for by the increase in the number of cheap 'B' pictures, economies forced on studios by the Depression, and a decline in the general index of prices. Early talkies also tended to have smaller casts and less elaborate sets than the silent features of the 1920s. The apparent stability between 1948 and 1960 is harder to explain, particularly as this period saw a vogue for expensive historical epics, a substantial increase in the use of colour, and the demise of the 'B' picture. The figures quoted for this decade should therefore be regarded with caution.

Raising Coin

Finding finance for films is never easy in India, but director John Abraham literally drummed up the money for his award-winning *Amma Ariyan* (Ind 87). He spent six years touring round remote villages soliciting funds by banging a drum as he went. Master film-maker Shyam Benegal also believes in involving the common people. When he made a film called *Manthan* (Ind 76) which was set in a milk co-operative, the money came from the co-op's own members. His acclaimed *Susman* (Ind 87), about the handloom weavers of Andra Pradesh, was financed by the weavers themselves.

The budget for *The Diary of a Madman* (Fr 87), from Gogol's short story, was mustered by producers Fanny Cotençon and Roger Coggio, who also star in the film, by the simple device of selling tickets in advance. Six months before release they had managed to sell 300,000 tickets at 23 francs (about £2.35) apiece. Debut black helmer Robert Townsend raised the seed coin for his comedy *Hollywood Shuffle* (US 87), about Hollywood's perceptions of blacks, by using 10 different unsolicited credit cards to charge up $40,000 of expenses. The film stock came free when he succeeded in begging the short-ends from two films he was acting in, *Ratboy* and *Odd Jobs*. Using his salary from these performances, plus the money he earned as a stand-up comic, he was able to finance the film entirely from his own resources—a total of some $100,000—but the 17 days of shooting had to be spread over two years to enable him to take to the road again whenever funds ran low.

Not all newcomers have to exercise such ingenuity. According to Paul Hogan, when he decided it was 'time to have a go at this film-making business', Aussie investors were so eager to put up coin for *Crocodile Dundee* (Aus 86) that 'we had to send $3,500,000 back'.

FOUR

STORY AND SCRIPT

AUTHORS

Producers began turning to literature for their plots soon after the turn of the century. In 1902 Ferdinand Zecca of Pathé succeeded in compressing Zola's *L'Assommoir* into five minutes of screen time as *Les Victimes d l'Alcolisme* (Fr 02), while Edwin S. Porter of the Edison Co. presented *Uncle Tom's Cabin* (US 02) in 14 'tableaux' lasting some 17 minutes. Probably the first novel to be adapted at sufficient length for an adequate presentation of the story was *Robbery Under Arms*, by Rolf Boldrewood, which was brought to the screen by the Australian producer C. McMahon in a five-reel version premièred at the Athenaeum Theatre, Melbourne, on 2 November 1907. The first in Europe was Viggo Larsen's three-reel version of Guy Boothby's *Dr. Nicola* (Den 09), starring August Blom. In America the same year Vitagraph produced a four-reel version of Dickens' *Oliver Twist* (US 09) and soon found they had set a trend, eight versions of the story appearing in various countries during the following three years. Among them was Britain's first essay at a 'full-length' screen adaptation, Thomas Bentley's *Oliver Twist* (GB 12), with Ivy Millais in the title role.

The payment of film rights was first put on an organized basis in France, where the Société Cinématographique des Auteurs et Gens de Lettres was established in 1908 to act as a performing rights society interceding between companies like Film d'Art—who based all their films on works of literature—and the members of the two leading literary associations, the Société des Auteurs and the Société des Gens de Lettres.

It was only the previous year that the matter of film rights to an author's work had arisen for the first time, when the Kalem Co. produced a one-reel version of *Ben Hur* (US 07). The publishers of Lew Wallace's novel, Harper's, and the producers of the very successful play based on the book, promptly sued. Kalem defended themselves on the grounds that neither publisher nor author had suffered damage and that the film was a good advertisement for the book and the play. The case lasted four years, Kalem finally conceding defeat and settling for $25,000.

The first copyright fee paid in the US for film rights had been negotiated in the meantime between Biograph and Little, Brown & Co., publishers of Helen Hunt Jackson's *Ramona*, a bestselling romance about an Indian maiden, originally

Some books have been turned into movies for the unlikeliest of reasons. Orson Welles decided to make a movie of Sherwood King's novel *If I Die Before I Wake* without having read so much as a synopsis. In a desperate financial situation over a stage play he was producing in Boston, Welles called Harry Cohn of Columbia to ask him for a $50,000 loan. When Cohn sounded reluctant, Welles offered to direct a film for him and added that he had an excellent thriller in mind which could be produced very inexpensively. The director was momentarily nonplussed when Cohn asked the title, but glancing over his shoulder he noticed that the wardrobe mistress was reading a paperback and signalled to her to hold it up so that he could see the cover. He told Cohn the title was *If I Die Before I Wake* and was promised a loan in exchange for making the film. It was released as *The Lady from Shanghai* (US 48) with Welles himself playing opposite Rita Hayworth.

published in 1884. The film of *Ramona* (US 10) was directed by D. W. Griffith with Mary Pickford in the title role. The fee was $100 and the authoress received the rare distinction of a credit following the main title.

Film rights were not to remain on this modest level for long. In Italy Gabriele D'Annunzio (1863–1938) signed an historic contract with Ambrosio Films in May 1911 disposing of rights to six of his works at 40,000 lire each, equivalent to $7845 at the then rate of exchange. Ambrosio later bought eight more, but far from delighting in this good fortune D'Annunzio displayed only contempt for the medium which had so wholeheartedly embraced his work. He saw only one of the films, *La Leda senza cigno* (It 12), which he dismissed as 'childish and grotesque'. So far as the 40,000 lire fees were concerned, he declared that they were just a means of buying meat for his dogs.

The record fees noted below do not take account of *The Birth of a Nation* (US 15), for which the copyright fee was paid on a royalty basis. The film was based on a disagreeably racist novel called *The Clansman*, for which author Thomas Dixon had demanded an unprecedented (for the US) rights fee of $25,000. Producer–director D. W. Griffith was unable to raise such a sum and offered him a $2000 advance against a 25 per cent royalty instead. Dixon ultimately received some $750,000, **the highest sum made by the author of any silent film property.**

The highest sum made by any novelist in film history has almost certainly accrued to William Peter Blatty, author of *The Exorcist.* The amount of money involved is indeterminate, since Mr Blatty, as producer of the film, was on 40 per cent of the gross. *The Exorcist* (US 73) has grossed over $89 million in North American rentals alone.

The highest price ever paid for film rights is the $9,500,000 (£4,950,000) by Columbia in 1978 for Charles Strouse's Broadway musical *Annie.* When the $35 million picture was eventually released in 1982, *Variety* remarked in a thumbs-down review that the price of the rights was 'about what the whole film should have cost'.

The highest sum paid for rights during the silent era was $600,000 (£170,000) by the Classical Cinematograph Corporation in 1921 for *Ben Hur*, the Lew Wallace novel made into a 1925 movie.

The first million dollar property was Garson Kanin's Broadway show *Born Yesterday.* Kanin had instructed his agent to refuse any offers from Columbia owing to a long-standing feud with production chief Harry Cohn. The unprecedented size of the offer undermined Kanin's resolve and Columbia made the picture (US 50) with Judy Holliday and Broderick Crawford.

The highest ratio of rights to budget was 78 per cent in the case of Pathé's *Les Misérables* (Fr 11). The film had a budget of 230,000f, of which 180,000f was paid to the Victor Hugo estate for the rights.

Starring . . . The Author

Novelists and playwrights have occasionally appeared in the screen versions of their own works, the earliest known example being Jean Richepin's starring role as the Count de la Roque in *Gypsy Passion* (Fr 22), from his story *Miarka, the Child of the Bear.* Elinor Glyn, the one who preferred to sin on a tiger skin, played herself in her own *It* (US 27), overshadowed only by the 'It Girl' herself, Clara Bow. The same year, Ivor Novello starred in the film of his own play *The Vortex* (GB 27), reprising the role of the drug addicted youth Nicky Lancaster. With the coming of sound Peter Frauchen, author of bestseller *Der Eskimo*, featured as the villain in MGM's *Eskimo* (US 33), but no other examples are noted until after the war, when Sir Compton Mackenzie played Captain Buncher in *Whisky Galore!* (GB 49), from his popular novel of the same name—for US release the picture was retitled *Tight Little Island*—and author

Mickey Spillane as his own creation Mike Hammer in *The Girl Hunters* (US 63). Britain's Shirley Eaton is the girlfriend. *(SI)*

Birgit Tengroth took a leading role in Ingmar Bergman's sombre rendering of *Törst/Thirst* (Swe 49). The first American writer to literally get into the act was black novelist Richard Wright, who took the lead in an Argentinian film, *Native Son* (Arg 50), from his story about a black youth afflicted by racism in the Chicago ghetto. Eynon Evans was cast as Amos in *The Happiness of Three Women* (GB 54), based on his play *The Wishing Well* and a few years later Erich Maria Remarque, author of *All Quiet on the Western Front*, put in a distinguished performance as the schoolmaster Pohlmann in the film of his novel *A Time to Love and a Time to Die* (US 58). The role of private eye Mike Hammer was played by his creator Mickey Spillane in *The Girl Hunters* (US 63) and paperback queen Jacqueline Susann did a bit part as an interviewer in her own *Valley of the Dolls* (US 67). Another cameo role by the author was Peter Benchley as the reporter in his mighty *Jaws* (US 75). Gore Vidal appeared as a senator in the film of his play *The Best Man* (US 64). Anne-Cath Vestly starred in *Mormor og de Atte Ungene I Byen* (Nor 76), based on her own short stories, while another Norwegian film, *Anette* (Nor 80), not only featured the author of the novel, Astri Nustad, but was directed by her son. Amos Kolek, son of the Mayor of Jerusalem, had the satisfaction of playing a character based on himself in the film of his autobiographical novel *Don't Ask Me Why I Love* (Isr 79). Another autobiographical novel brought to the screen was Vergilio Ferreira's *Manha Submersa* (Por 80), in which the author played the rector of a seminary to which a boy is sent against his will to train for the priesthood. The boy's experiences were based on

Ferreira's own. Similarly, Gavino Ledda, the shepherd lad whose deprived childhood was so movingly portrayed in *Padre Padrone* (It 77), starred in as well as wrote and directed the autobiographical *Ybris/Habris* (It 84), which recounted the story of the scholar shepherd grown to manhood. Recent examples of authors performing in the films of their own works have come from Switzerland, where Ingrid Puganigg played the title role in *Martha Dubronski* (Swz 85), and Canada, where Gordon Pinsent directed and starred in the film of his novel *John and the Missus* (Can 87), a mining drama set in the economically depressed Newfoundland of the early sixties.

The most filmed author is William Shakespeare (1564–1616), whose plays have been presented in 279 straight or relatively straight film versions, 37 'modern versions' (where the story line has been loosely based on Shakespeare, e.g. *West Side Story*) and innumerable parodies. Not surprisingly *Hamlet* has appealed most to film-makers, with 58 movie versions (see filmography and also Remakes, p. 25), followed by *Romeo and Juliet*, which has been filmed 47 times, and *Macbeth*, filmed 31 times.

It will be noted from the checklist below that on four occasions Hamlet has been played by a woman: Sarah Bernhardt in a French synchronized sound short of 1900 (see also Sound Film, First, p. 144); the great Danish star Asta Nielsen in a German version of 1920 where Hamlet is revealed at the very end to have been a girl raised as a boy; Caroline Johnson, who interchanged with male thespian Rick McKenna in the 1971 film version of Toronto's Theatre of God production; and, recently, Fatma Girik in the explicitly titled *Female Hamlet* (Tur 77).

Among the more bizarre film versions of Shakespeare's greatest play is one in which the Prince of Denmark has undergone a metamorphosis into a gunslinger in the Wild West—*Quella sporca storia del West* (It 68). Hamlet has yet to meet Frankenstein's Monster, but one fears this is only a matter of time. Even the most well-intentioned treatment of Shakespeare's work can be subject to the grossest liberties. One of the most inexplicable is the translation of the sub-titles on the US/GB release prints of Grigori Kozintsev's *Hamlet* (USSR 64), intended as a word-for-word film version of the play. The title-writer has given a modern English rendering of Boris Pasternak's scrupulous Russian translation of Shakespeare's original text. Other debasements of the bard's work have been more deliberate. We may be thankful that there has been no follow-up to the soft-porn British film *The Secret Sex Life of Romeo and Juliet* (GB 70) and even more so that among the many projected Shakespeare films that have failed to go into production was Joseph Goebbels' viciously anti-semitic version of *The Merchant of Venice*.

No one has ever shot *Hamlet* without the Prince, but Orson Welles succeeded in shooting *The Merchant of Venice* (It 70) without Portia. The role was to have been assigned to Yugoslavian sculptress turned actress Oja Kodar, Welles's live-in companion for the last two decades of his life, but she turned it down on the grounds that her English was not good enough. Not wanting anyone else in the part, Welles simply rewrote Shakespeare to dispense with one of the bard's most celebrated heroines. Audiences never had an opportunity to see this novel interpretation, which had Welles himself playing Shylock. Two of the workprint reels were stolen from the production office in Rome and consequently the film has remained unreleased.

HAMLET FILMOGRAPHY

Fr 00 with Sarah Bernhardt
Fr 07 with Georges Méliès
It 08 (Cornerio)
It 08 (Milano)
It 08 (Cines)
Fr 09
It 10 with Dante Capelli
Fr 10 with Jacques Grétillat
Den 10 with Alwin Neuss
GB 12 with Charles Raymond
Fr 13 with Paul Mounet-Sully
GB 13 with Sir Johnston Forbes-Robertson
It 14 with Hamilton A. Revelle
US 14 with James Young
GB 14 with Eric Williams
US 14 with Alla Nazimova (there is some doubt whether this film was ever made, nor is it known whether Nazimova played Hamlet or Ophelia if it was)
It 17 with Ruggero Ruggeri
Ger 20 with Asta Nielsen

Ind 28
US 33 with John Barrymore (test reel of Act I Scene 5 and Act II Scene 2)
Ind 35 with Sohrab Modi
GB 48 with Sir Laurence Olivier
Ind 54 with Kishore Sahu
US 58 (Baylor Theater production)
US 59 (Encyclopaedia Britannica 16 mm production)
Ger 60 with Maximilian Schell
Pol 60 (short directed by Jerzy Skolimowski)
US 64 with Richard Burton
USSR 64 with Innokenti Smoktunowski
Hamile aka *The Tongo Hamlet* Gha 65 with Kofi Middleton-Mends
Hun 65 (animated)
GB 69 with Nicol Williamson
US 70 with Richard Chamberlain (TVM)
Heranca aka *Hamlet* Bra 70 with David Cardaso
US 71 with David Suchet (16 mm)

Can 71 (musical) with Rick McKenna and Caroline Johnson
Un Amleto di meno It 73 with Carmelo Bene
Dogg's Troupe Hamlet GB 77
Female Hamlet Tur 77 with Fatma Girik
GB 78 with Anthony and David Meyer
Dome to Elsinore USSR 78—made by workers of the Paris Commune Shoe Factory, Moscow.
MODERN VERSIONS
Der Rest ist Schweigen Ger 59 with Hardy Kruger
Ophelia Fr 61 with André Jocelyn
Ithele na yini vasilas/He Wanted to be King Gre 67 with Angelos Theodoropoulos
Quella sporca storia del West It 68 with Enio Girolami.
PARODIES

GB 15	GB 19	US 19	US 37
US 16	GB 19	Den 22	It 52
US 16	GB 19	Den 32	Fin 88
It 16			

Edgar Wallace, the most filmed 20th-century writer, whose works were made into 179 motion pictures. (*Popperfoto*)

The most filmed novelist is Edgar Wallace (1875–1932), whose books and short stories have been made into at least 179 British, American and German films. In addition there have been other films based on Edgar Wallace plays, scripts and unidentified sources, making him the most filmed 20th-century writer. The first movie derived from one of Wallace's works of fiction was *The Man who Bought London* (GB 16), from his novel of the same name. Despite the royalties from his prodigious literary output, his film rights (over 50 of the films were made in his lifetime), and fees for scriptwriting, directing, and chairing the board of British Lion, Edgar Wallace died owing $315,000.

The most filmed American writers are the western novelist Zane Grey (1875–1939) and the pioneer mystery writer Edgar Allan Poe (1809–49), each with 103 films of their works. Those of the former began with *Riders of the Purple Sage* (US 18) and ended with *The Maverick Queen* (US 56). All but one were American movies (including a Spanish language western), the exception being *Rangle River* (Aus 37). Grey wrote over a hundred novels, not all of which have been filmed, though a number have been made four times. Zane Grey movies nearly always featured on the bottom half of the bill and the finish of Hollywood 'B' movie production in the mid-fifties brought an end to the filming of his works.

Since both the Edgar Wallace and Zane Grey liter-

ary lodes seem to have been fully worked (the last Wallace was made in 1976), it seems probable that their records will be overtaken within a few years by one of the runners-up, all of them writers of enduring quality. Sandwiched between Wallace and Grey are Alexandre Dumas (père) (1802–70), author of *The Count of Monte Cristo* and *The Three Musketeers*, whose works have been brought to the screen in 118 films, and Charles Dickens (1812–70) with 113 films to his credit, while Count Leo Tolstoy (1828–1910) scores 106.

The most filmed living writer is the Swedish children's novelist Astrid Lindgren (1907–), whose works have been adapted for 31 movies.

CLASHES

The simultaneous release of Gregory Ratoff's *Oscar Wilde* (GB 60), with Robert Morley, and Ken Hughes's *The Trials of Oscar Wilde* (GB 60), with Peter Finch, drew attention to a phenomenon which has been commoner in the history of movies than is generally realized. As early as 1912 the first feature film made in Britain and the first feature film made in America were rival versions of *Oliver Twist* and that same year no less than three different productions of *The Last Days of Pompeii* were made in Italy. Here are some of the more notable examples of movie 'clashes':

☆ Two Russian adaptations of *War and Peace* were actually released on the same day, 13 February 1915, and the same thing happened the next year in America when both the Francis X. Bushman–Beverly Bayne and Harry Hilliard–Theda Bara versions of *Romeo and Juliet* were premièred on 22 October 1916.

☆ As many as eight biopics of the rascally monk Rasputin were made in 1917, four in Russia, three in the USA and one in Germany.

☆ In 1934 Marlene Dietrich's bravura performance in and as *The Scarlet Empress* (US 34) eclipsed Elizabeth Bergner's less vibrant interpretation of *Catherine the Great* (GB 34).

☆ The following year there was another clash of costume dramas with Josef von Sternberg's American version of *Crime and Punishment*, starring Peter Lorre, and Pierre Chanal's French production with Pierre Blanchar.

☆ America and France clashed again in 1936 when audiences could choose between the Hollywood biopic *Louis Pasteur* with Paul Muni or the more authentic portrayal of the great scientist by Sacha Guitry in the version titled simply *Pasteur*.

☆ Two feature-length cartoon versions of *Cinderella* appeared in 1950, one from Walt Disney in America, the other from Estela Film in Spain.

☆ Disney had competition again the following year

when his cartoon version of *Alice in Wonderland* was on release at the same time as Lou Bunin's puppet and live-action version with Carol Marsh as Alice.

☆ Twin films about the July plot to kill Hitler, one titled *The 20th July*, the other *It Happened on 20th July*, were released in Germany on successive days in 1955.

☆ Mario Lanza was not the only actor to play *The Great Caruso* in 1951. Ermanno Randi starred in a rival Italian biopic, titled *Enrico Caruso, Legend of a Voice*.

☆ When the Italian director Franco Zeffirelli made a British production of *Romeo and Juliet* in 1968 with Leonard Whiting and Olivia Hussey, an Italian production of the great love story was made by Ricardo Freda with Gerald Meynier and Rosemarie Dexter. This version was brought to London for dubbing, but hoping to penetrate the lucrative American market, Signor Freda chose to have it done in that most unromantic of accents, Brooklynese!

☆ Another clash of classics—this time with some real competition at the box office—came in 1975 with the simultaneous release of Patrick Garland's *A Doll's House*, with Claire Bloom as Nora, and Joseph Losey's *A Doll's House* with Jane Fonda. Both these were British productions, but there was also a German version the same year, directed by Rainer Werner Fassbinder and starring Margit Carstensen.

☆ Two biopics titled *Harlow* (US 65), one with Carroll Baker as the thirties star, the other with Carol Lynley, were joined by a third from the Andy Warhol stable titled *Harlot* (US 65). In this rather unconventional version, the Blonde Venus was portrayed by Mario Montez in drag.

☆ The well-loved children's classic *The Little Mermaid* appeared in three different versions in 1976—a Czech production, a Finnish production, and a USSR–Bulgarian co-production.

☆ *The Elephant Man* (GB 80), with John Hurt, was one of the box office successes of 1980, but not many people were aware of the Canadian version produced the same year.

☆ Released within twelve months of each other, if not the same year, were the three treatments of the Entebbe Raid story, *Victory at Entebbe* (US 76), *Raid on Entebbe* (US 76), and the most accurate version of the events, *Operation Thunderbolt* (Isr 77).

☆ Opera buffs were confronted with no less than seven versions of *Carmen* in 1984, albeit three of them from the same director. Peter Brook filmed his French stage production with three different casts, the title role being taken by Helene Delavault, Zehava Gal and Eva Saurova. Julia Migenes-Johnson took the part in Francesco Rossi's Italian-French co-production, Anne-Marie Mühle in Roland Sterner's Swedish production, Stefania Toczyska in Mate Rabinovski's French production and Laura del Sol in Carlos Saura's Spanish production. An eighth version of Carmen, based on Merimée's story rather than Bizet's opera, was *Carmen Nue* with Pamela Prati in the title role.

☆ *Wills and Burke* (Aus 85) was released a week before *Burke and Wills* (Aus 85). The latter is a straight presentation of the story of Australia's most celebrated explorers, the former a parody. Uniquely in a clash situation there were two actors, Peter Collingwood and Chris Haywood, who appeared in both versions. (Any listing of either actor's credits is going to read like a mistake.)

☆ Raymond Radiguet's novel *La Diable au corps*, about a love affair between a 17-year-old boy and a married woman, was filmed by Scott Murray with a World War II Australian setting as *Devil in the Flesh* (Aus 86) and by Marco Bellocchio with a 1985 Rome setting as *Il Diavolo in Corpo* (It 86). The Australian version did not contain the fellatio scene which caused Bellocchio censorship problems in the Italian version.

☆ In 1987 both mainland China and Taiwan produced rival biopics of the leader of the 1911 revolution and 'Father of modern China' Dr Sun Yat-Sen. As the two films had the same booking dates, audiences were understandably confused as to which version was which. There were also two biopics of China's last Emperor, Pu Yi, Bertolucci's *The Last Emperor* (It/GB/Chn 87) and the Chinese production *The Last Empress* (Chn 87). The latter concentrates mainly on Pu Yi's relationship with his official wife Wanrong and his two concubines Wenxlu and Tan Yuling.

☆ 1988 saw the release of two *Robinson Crusoe* movies, one directed by Calen Deschanel and starring Aidan Quinn; the other by Sherry Sneller with John Lynch.

*S*CRIPT

The first scriptwriter was New York journalist Roy McCardell, who was hired in 1900 by Henry Marvin of the American Mutoscope & Biograph Co. to write ten scenarios a week at $15 each. Since most of the films made by Biograph at that time were 50–100 ft in length (about 1½ minutes), McCardell found he was able to complete his first week's assignment in a single afternoon.

The first contract writer (i.e. full-time employee of a studio) was Louis Feuillade, who joined the Gaumont Studios in Paris in 1905.

Britain's first regular scriptwriter was Harold Brett, engaged by H. O. Martinek of the British & Colonial Kinematograph Co., whose earliest known scenario was for a spy picture called *A Soldier's Honour* (GB 11). Previously it had been the custom of British film producers to shoot without a script or write their own screenplays.

The first writer of literary distinction to be

engaged to produce a scenario was the French playwright Henri Lavedan, whose *L'Assassination du Duc de Guise* (Fr 08) was made by Film d'Art.

In the USA the first eminent writer under contract was Emmett Campbell Hall, who was engaged by D. W. Griffith to script the Biograph pictures *His Trust* (US 11) and *His Trust Fulfilled* (US 11), a two-part story of the American Civil War.

> Cecil B. DeMille, on returning a writer's script: 'What I have crossed out I didn't like. What I haven't crossed out I am dissatisfied with.'

The first scriptwriter to 'have his name in lights'—in other words, to be credited on a cinema marquee—was H. H. Van Loon, author and adaptor of *The Virgin of Stamboul* (US 20), who was afforded this tribute by the Strand Theater, San Francisco, in November 1920.

The first scriptwriters to write dialogue for a sound feature film were Joseph Jackson and Edward T. Lowe Jr., who composed the four talking sequences of Warner Bros' crime melodrama *Tenderloin* (US 28). The dialogue was so ludicrous that two of the sequences were cut after the first week of the film's run. (The dialogue sequences in *The Jazz Singer* (US 27) had been ad libbed by Al Jolson in the title role.)

The shortest dialogue script since the introduction of talkies was written for Mel Brooks' *Silent Movie* (US 76), which had only one spoken word throughout. The dialogue sequence in the otherwise silent movie occurs when mime artist Marcel Marceau, having been invited by telephone (silently) to appear in a silent movie, replies (audibly) 'Non!'. The person making the call is asked (according to the inter-title) 'What did he say?' Response, also by inter-title: 'I don't know. I don't understand French.'

The only other film with but a single word of dialogue, Paul Fejos's *Marie, A Hungarian Legend* (Hun 32), used a longer word—the name 'Marie'.

The most co-writers credited for any film was 21 in the case of *Forever and a Day* (US 43). They included C. S. Forester, John van Druten, Christopher Isherwood, R. C. Sherriff, James Hilton and Frederick Lonsdale.

A Yank at Oxford (GB 38) credited only eight scriptwriters, but at least 31 are known to have been employed by MGM on the screenplay. Among those uncredited were Herman J. Mankiewicz, John Paddy Carstairs, Hugh Walpole and F. Scott Fitzgerald.

The lowest fee paid for the script of a major Hollywood feature was the $10 earned by Preston Sturges for *The Great McGinty* (US 40).

Sturges was a scriptwriter who wanted to direct. The deal with Paramount was that he should be given the opportunity in return for doing the script for a nominal fee.

The longest delay between the completion of a movie script and the making of the movie was 39 years in the case of Freddie Francis's *The Doctor and the Devils* (GB 86), starring Timothy Dalton. The script, about the Edinburgh grave robbers Burke and Hare, was written by the Welsh poet Dylan Thomas in 1947. It was originally to have been filmed by the Rank Organization. When this came to naught, further attempts were made by Nicholas Roeg in the 1960s and by Mel Brooks in 1983 before it was finally brought to the screen by Brooksfilm in an adaptation by Ronald Harwood.

Profanities, Obscenities and Expletives

It is Hollywood myth that Clark Gable's celebrated closing line in *Gone with the Wind* (US 39)— 'Frankly, my dear, I don't give a damn'—was the first occasion on which the word 'damn' had been spoken on the screen. It was said by both Leslie Howard and Marie Lohr in *Pygmalion* (GB 38) and had featured in at least two earlier Hollywood pictures. Fred Stone said 'Damn you!' to the heroine's boss (who had wronged her) in *Alice Adams* (US 35) and three years before that Emma Dunn had exclaimed 'Well, I'll be damned' in *Blessed Event* (US 32). Nothing stronger was allowed until the sixties, the obscenities voiced by Mickey Shaughnessy in *Don't Go Near the Water* (US 56) being bleeped out.

British censors had less reserve about the use of realistic language where it was appropriate. 'Bloody' was heard for the first time in *Pygmalion* (GB 38), 'fanny' in *Convoy* (GB 40), 'arse' in *The Guinea Pig* (GB 49) and 'bastard' in *The Blue Lamp* (GB 49). The British also pioneered the on-screen use of 'bugger' in *Poor Cow* (GB 67) and the most over-used four-letter word in *I'll Never Forget Whatshisname* (GB 68), in which Marianne Faithful made a little piece of film history by breaking the ultimate 'word barrier'. (Critic Kenneth Tynan had, however, said it earlier on television.) The Americans were first, however, with 'shit', which was heard in *In Cold Blood* (US 67) a year earlier than its first appearance on a British soundtrack in *Boom!* (GB 68), while the permissive Danes led with the first on-screen use of a four-letter word in reference to female genitalia in *Quiet Days in Clichy* (Den 69). This was the era of the permissive society and the breakdown of old taboos, aptly summed up by Bob Hope in 1968: 'Last year Hollywood made the first pictures with dirty words. This year we made the pictures to go with them.'

The film with the doubtful distinction of over-using the most over-used four letter word the most times was *Scarface* (US 84), in which it is spoken 206 times—an average of once every 29 seconds.

Most of the above words had been used at one time or other by actors in silent films. When Edmund Lowe and Victor McLaglen indulged in a fine exchange of Billingsgate in *What Price Glory* (US 26), the studio received hundreds of letters of protest from outraged lip-readers. Likewise in *Sadie Thompson* (US 28), lip-readers would be the only ones to appreciate the full rich flavour of Gloria Swanson's language as Sadie—which made no concessions to the censors. The title cards only reproduced what she was *not* saying.

Dialogue in the hit Australian comedy *Crocodile Dundee* (Aus 86) had to be rejigged for the pic's American release. 'Stone the bloody crows' was elbowed along with 'I'm a bit crook', while 'stickybeak' was changed to the much less picturesque 'busybody'. One commentator noted that the result of sanitizing gutsy Antipodean quirks of speech is to give the impression that Australians have no colloquialisms of their own.

The most hackneyed line in movie scripts is 'Let's get outta here'. A survey of 150 American features of the period 1938–74 (revived on British television) showed that it was used at least once in 84 per cent of Hollywood productions and more than once in 17 per cent. Film critic David McGillivray disputes this finding with the assertion that no single phrase has been so overworked in movie scripts as 'Try to get some sleep now'.

The most improbable scenario ever to reach the screen must be a matter of opinion, but the editor would like to nominate George Dewhurst's plot for the Hepworth production *Mist in the Valley* (GB 23), in which Alma Taylor played an ex-nun who marries an amnesia victim and is framed for allegedly murdering a usurping uncle who was posing as her father.

The longest monologue in a dramatic film is a 20-minute speech by Edwige Feuillère in *L'Aigle à deux têtes/The Eagle has Two Heads* (Fr 48).

The longest monologue in a Hollywood movie is by Lionel Barrymore in *A Free Soul* (US 31). Six cameras were used to film the 14-minute speech in one take, since sound editing had yet to be perfected.

Statesmen as Scriptwriters

A number of statesmen have turned their hands to scriptwriting, including Sir Winston Churchill, who was under contract to London Films from 1934 until the war and worked on such films as *The Twenty Five Year Reign of King George V* (uncompleted) and *Conquest of the Air* (GB 38). He is also said to have contributed a speech to the script of *Lady Hamilton/ US That Hamilton Woman* (GB 42). On the other side of the Atlantic, President Roosevelt wrote the original scenario for *The President's Mystery* (US 36), about a lawyer (Henry Wilcoxson) who fakes his own death so that he can right the wrongs he did in the name of big business. Carmine Gallone's vast and sprawling epic *Scipio Africanus* (It 37), a story of Roman victories in Africa intended to parallel Mussolini's contemporary victories in Abyssinia, was alleged to have been written by Il Duce himself. Some years earlier Mussolini's melodrama *The Cardinal's Mistress* had been made into a successful silent movie. Another dictator with a screenplay to his credit was General Franco who wrote the scenario for *The Spirit of Race* (Sp 41), an adaptation of his own novel, under the pen-name Jaime de Andrade. He also scripted and shot his own animated cartoons. In more recent times former Thailand Prime Minister Kukrit Pramoj wrote *Fai Dang/The Red Bamboo* (Phi 79). Field Marshal Idi Amin Dada, before he was deposed as President-for-Life of Uganda, scripted an adulatory biopic of himself, but happily this was never made. India's former premier Moraji Desai is probably the only world leader to have scripted a film while in office. Having committed himself to producer J. G. Mohla before being gaoled under Mrs Gandhi's State of Emergency, and finding himself Prime Minister shortly after his release, he nevertheless felt under an obligation to fulfil his undertaking. Working in the early mornings he completed his English-language script of *Yogeshwar Krishna*, the story of Lord Krishna, a few months later. Originally written as a play, Pope John Paul II's *The Jeweller's Shop*, first performed in Poland in 1960, was filmed in Montreal in 1987 with Burt Lancaster, Ben Cross and Olivia Hussey in the leading roles.

'If my books had been any worse I should not have been invited to Hollywood, and if they had been any better I should not have come'— Raymond Chandler.

FIVE

CHARACTER AND THEMES

SCREEN CHARACTERS

The character most often portrayed on screen since the inception of the story film has been Sherlock Holmes, the master detective created by Sir Arthur Conan Doyle (1859–1930), who has been played by 69 actors, including one black (Sam Robinson), in 193 films produced between 1900 and 1988 (see filmography). The only actor to have played both Sherlock Holmes and Dr Watson was Reginald Owen, who was Watson in *Sherlock Holmes* (US 32) and Holmes in *A Study in Scarlet* (US 33).

When the Allies reached Berlin in 1945, the contents of Hitler's bunker revealed a number of interesting sidelights to his character and tastes. The two movies they found were both Sherlock Holmes adventures—*The Hound of the Baskervilles* (Ger 37) and *The Man Who Was Sherlock Holmes* (Ger 37).

Peter Cushing in *The Hound of the Baskervilles* (GB 59).

SHERLOCK HOLMES FILMOGRAPHY

The filmography below includes feature-length TVMs, but excludes filmed television series. Where known the actor playing Sherlock Holmes is included.

Sherlock Holmes Baffled (US 00)
Maurice Costello *The Adventures of Sherlock Holmes* (US 03)
Sherlock Holmes Returns (US? 06?)
Bauman Károly *Sherlock Holmes* (Hun 08)
Viggo Larsen *Sherlock Holmes I Livsfare* (Den 08); *Sherlock Holmes II* (Den 08); *Sherlock Holmes III* (Den 08)
Sherlock Holmes in the Great Murder Mystery (US 09)
Viggo Larsen *Sangerindens Diamanter* (Den 09)
August Blom *Droske No 519* (Den 09)
Viggo Larsen *Den Graa Dame* (Den 09)
The Latest Triumph of Sherlock Holmes (Fr 09)
Sherlock Holmes (It 09?)
Viggo Larsen *Der Alte Sekretar* (Ger 10); *Der Blaue Diamant* (Ger 10); *Die Falschen Rembrandts* (Ger 10); *Die Flucht* (Ger 10)
Otto Lagoni *Sherlock Holmes I Bondefangerklør* (Den 10)
Forrect Holger-Madsen (?) *Forklaedte Barnepige* (Den 11)
Holger Rasmussen *Medlem af den Sorte Hand* (Den 11)
Alwin Neuss *Millionobligation* (Den 11)
Hotel Mysterierne (Den 11)
Viggo Larsen *Arsène Lupins Ende* (Ger 11); *Sherlock Holmes contra Professor Moriarty* (Ger 11)
Henri Gouget *Les Aventures de Sherlock Holmes* (Fr 11)

Schlau, Schlauer, am Schlauesten (Fr 12) French title unknown
Georges Treville *The Speckled Band* (GB 12); *The Reigate Squires* (GB 12); *The Beryl Coronet* (GB 12); *The Adventure of the Copper Beeches* (GB 12); *A Mystery of Boscombe Vale* (GB 12); *The Stolen Papers* (GB 12); *Silver Blaze* (GB 12); *The Musgrave Ritual* (GB 13)
Verrater Zigarette (Ger 13)
Schwarze Kappe (Ger 13)
Gli artigli di griffard (It 13)
Forte di Sherlock Holmes (It 13)
Harry Benham *Sherlock Holmes Solves the Sign of Four* (US 13)
Ferdinand Bonn *Sherlock Holmes contra Dr Mors* (Ger 14)
En Raedsom Nat (Den 14)
Em Gregers (?) *Hvem er Hun?* (Den 14)
James Bragington *A Study in Scarlet* (GB 14)
Francis Ford *A Study in Scarlet* (US 14)
Alwin Neuss *Der Hund von Baskerville* (Ger 14); *Der Hund von Baskerville II* (Ger 14); *Der Hund von Baskerville III* (Ger 15); *Der Hund von Baskerville IV* (Ger 15)
Eugen Burg *Der Hund von Baskerville V* (Ger 15)
Alwin Neuss *Ein Schrei in der Nacht* (Ger 15)
Bloomer *Tricks Sherlock Holmes* (It 15)
Alwin Neuss *William Voss* (Ger 15)
William Gillette *Sherlock Holmes* (US 16)
H. A. Saintsbury *The Valley of Fear* (GB 16)
Alwin Neuss *Sherlock Holmes auf Urlaub* (Ger 16); *Sherlock Holmes Nächtliche Begegnung* (Ger 16)

Hugo Flink *Der Erstrommotor* (Ger 17); *Die Kasette* (Ger 17); *Der Schlangenring* (Ger 17); *Die Indische Spinne* (Ger 18)
Viggo Larsen *Rotterdam-Amsterdam* (Ger 18)
Ferdinand Bonn *Was er im Spiegel sar* (Ger 18); *Die Giftplombe* (Ger 18); *Das Schicksal der Renate Yongk* (Ger 18); *Die Dose des Kardinals* (Ger 18)
Sam Robinson *Black Sherlock Holmes* (US 18) only time Holmes has been played by a black
Viggo Larsen *Drei Tage Tot* (Ger 19)
Kurt Brenkendorff *Der Mord im Splendid Hotel* (Ger 19)
Erich Kaiser-Titz (?) *Dr Macdonald's Sanitorium* (Ger 20)
Adolf D'Arnaz (?) *Harry Hill contra Sherlock Holmes* (Ger 20)
Lu Jurgens (?) *Das Haus ohne Fenster* (Ger 20)
Eille Norwood *The Dying Detective* (GB 21); *The Devil's Foot* (GB 21); *A Case of Identity* (GB 21); *The Yellow Face* (GB 21); *The Red-Headed League* (GB 21); *The Resident Patient* (GB 21); *A Scandal in Bohemia* (GB 21); *The Man with the Twisted Lip* (GB 21); *The Beryl Coronet* (GB 21); *The Noble Bachelor* (GB 21); *The Copper Beeches* (GB 21); *The Empty House* (GB 21); *The Tiger of San Pedro* (GB 21); *The Priory School* (GB 21); *The Solitary Cyclist* (GB 21); *The Hound of the Baskervilles* (GB 21); *Charles Augustus Milverton* (GB 22); *The Abbey Grange* (GB 22); *The Norwood Builder* (GB 22); *The Reigate Squires* (GB 22); *The Naval Treaty* (GB 22); *The Second Stain* (GB 22); *The Red Circle* (GB 22); *The Six Napoleons* (GB 22); *Black Peter*

(GB 22); *The Bruce-Partington Plans* (GB 22); *The Stockbroker's Clerk* (GB 22); *The Boscombe Valley Mystery* (GB 22); *The Musgrave Ritual* (GB 22); *The Golden Pinz-Nez* (GB 22); *The Greek Interpreter* (GB 22)
John Barrymore *Sherlock Holmes* (US 22)
Eman Fiala *The Abduction of Banker Fusee* (Cz 23)
Eille Norwood *Silver Blaze* (GB 23); *The Speckled Band* (GB 23); *The Gloria Scott* (GB 23); *The Blue Carbuncle* (GB 23); *The Engineer's Thumb* (GB 23); *His Last Bow* (GB 23); *The Cardboard Box* (GB 23); *Lady Frances Carfax* (GB 23); *The Three Students* (GB 23); *The Missing Three-Quarter* (GB 23); *Thor Bridge* (GB 23); *The Stone of Mazarin* (GB 23); *The Dancing Men* (GB 23); *The Crooked Man* (GB 23); *The Final Problem* (GB 23); *The Sign of Four* (GB 23)
Philip Beck *Kobenhavns Sherlock Holmes* (Den 25)
Carlyle Blackwell *Der Hund von Baskerville* (Ger 29)
Clive Brook *The Return of Sherlock Holmes* (US 29); *Paramount on Parade* (US 30)
Arthur Wontner *The Sleeping Cardinal* (GB 31)
Raymond Massey *The Speckled Band* (GB 31)
Robert Rendel *The Hound of the Baskervilles* (GB 32)
Clive Brook *Sherlock Holmes* (US 32)
Arthur Wontner *The Sign of Four* (GB 32); *The Missing Rembrandt* (GB 32)
Martin Fric *Lelicek ve Sluzbach Sherlocka Holmese* (Cz 32)
Richard Gordon *The Radio Murder Mystery* (US 33)
Reginald Owen *A Study in Scarlet* (US 33)
Arthur Wontner *The Triumph of Sherlock Holmes* (GB 35); *Silver Blaze* (GB 37)
Bruno Güttner *Der Hund von Baskerville* (Ger 37)
Hermann Speelmans *Die Graue Dame* (Ger 37)

Hans Albers *Der Mann, der Sherlock Holmes War* (Ger 37)
Basil Rathbone *The Hound of the Baskervilles* (US 39); *The Adventures of Sherlock Holmes* (US 39); *Sherlock Holmes and the Voice of Terror* (US 42); *Sherlock Holmes and the Secret Weapon* (US 42); (cameo role) *Crazy House* (US 43); *Sherlock Holmes in Washington* (US 43); *Sherlock Holmes Faces Death* (US 43); *Sherlock Holmes and the Spider Woman* (US 44); *The Scarlet Claw* (US 44); *The Pearl of Death* (US 44); *The House of Fear* (US 45); *The Woman in Green* (US 45); *Pursuit to Algiers* (US 45); *Terror by Night* (US 45); *Dressed to Kill* (US 45)
John Longden *The Man with the Twisted Lip* (GB 51)
Peter Cushing *The Hound of the Baskervilles* (GB 59)
Christopher Lee *Sherlock Holmes und das Halsband des Todes* (FRG 62)
Jerome Raphel *The Double-Barrelled Detective Story* (US 65)
John Neville *A Study in Terror* (GB 65)
Nando Gazzolo *La Valle della paura* (It 68, TVM); *L'Ultimo dei Baskerville* (It 68)
Uncredited *The Best House in London* (GB 69)
Robert Stephens *The Private Life of Sherlock Holmes* (GB 70)
Radovan Lukavsky *Touha Sherlocka Holmese* (Cz 71)
George C. Scott *They Might Be Giants* (US 72)
The Case of the Metal-Sheathed Elements (GB 72) cartoon
Stewart Granger *The Hound of the Baskervilles* (US 72, TVM)
Keith McConnell *Murder in Northumberland* (GB 74)
Rolf Becker *Monsieur Sherlok Holmes* (Fr 74, TVM)
Harry Reems *Sherlock Holmes* (US 75) porno

Douglas Wilmer *The Adventure of Sherlock Holmes' Smarter Brother* (GB 75)
Roger Moore *Sherlock Holmes in New York* (US 76, TVM) released theatrically in Europe
Keith McConnell *Murder by Death* (US 76) SH role cut in some release prints
Sherlock Holmes (Swz 76)
A Case of Royal Murder (GB 77)
The Case of the Exhumed Client (GB 77)
Nicol Williamson *The Seven-Per-Cent Solution* (GB 77)
Trevor Ainsley *The Case of the Mounting Fortune* (GB 78)
Peter Cook *The Hound of the Baskervilles* (GB 78)
Christopher Plummer *Murder by Decree* (GB/Can 79)
Jeremy Young *The Case of the Fantastical Passbook* (GB 79)
Aljgis Masjulis *The Blue Carbuncle* (USSR 80, TVM)
Peter O'Toole (voice) *Sherlock Holmes and the Baskerville Curse* (Aus 82) —animated
Ian Richardson *The Hound of the Baskervilles* (GB 83); *The Sign of Four* (GB 83)
Vassily Livanov *The Sign of Four* (USSR 83); *Trouble in Bohemia* (USSR 83)
Guy Rolfe *The Case of Marcel Duchamp* (Fr 83)
Peter Cushing *The Masks of Death* (GB 84, TVM)
Nicholas Rowe *Young Sherlock Holmes* (GB 86)
Vassily Livanov (voice) *Sherlock Holmes and I* (USSR 86) —animated
Basil Rathbone (voice—posthumously) *The Great Mouse Detective* (US 86) —animated
Jeremy Brett *The Sign of Four* (GB 87)
Michael Caine *Sherlock and Me* (US 88) (NB Caine character is imposter)
Peter Cushing *The Abbot's Egg* (GB i.p., TVM)
Jeremy Brett *The Hound of the Baskervilles* (GB i.p., TVM)

The other fictitious or legendary characters most frequently represented on screen have been Count Dracula—155 films (see p. 50); Frankenstein's monster—109; Tarzan—94; Zorro—69; Hopalong Cassidy—66 (see p. 103); Robin Hood—55; Charlie Chan—49.

COMIC STRIP CHARACTERS

A host of comic strip characters have been portrayed on screen in live action feature-length movies. This list is confined to English language films. The name following the abbreviation 'Orig' is that of the originator of the comic strip.

☆ Ginger Meggs, cartoon larrikin in Australian newspapers, was played by Ray Griffin in *Those Terrible Twins* (Aus 25). Orig: James Bancks.
☆ *Ella Cinders* (US 26) with Colleen Moore. Orig: William Counselman and Charles Plumb.
☆ Fatty Finn, an urchin of the backstreets of Sydney, was played by 'Pop' Ordell in *The Kid Stakes* (Aus 26). Orig: Syd Nicholls.
☆ *Tillie the Toiler* (US 27) with Marion Davies as the office girl heroine. Orig: Russ Westover in the *New York American*.
☆ *Harold Teen* (US 28) with Arthur Lake. Orig: Carl Ed.
☆ J. Farrell MacDonald played Jiggs and Polly Moran played Maggie in *Bringing Up Father* (US 28). Orig: George McManus.
☆ *Skippy* (US 30) with Jackie Cooper. Orig: Percy Crosby.
☆ *Sooky* (US 31) with Robert Coogan in the name part and Jackie Cooper as Skippy. Orig: Percy Crosby.

☆ *Little Orphan Annie* (US 32) with Mitzi Green. Orig: Harold Gray and Al Lowenthal.
☆ *Harold Teen* (US 34) with Hal LeRoy. Orig: Carl Ed.
☆ *Tailspin Tommy* (US 34) with Maurice Murphy as the young flying ace. First serial based on comic strip. Orig: Hal Forrest.
☆ *Palooka* (US 34) with Stuart Erwin. Orig: Ham Fisher.
☆ *Tailspin Tommy and the Great Air Mystery* (US 35) with Maurice Murphy. Orig: Hal Forrest.
☆ *Flash Gordon* (US 36) with Buster Crabbe. Serial. Orig: Alex Raymond.
☆ *Jungle Jim* (US 37) with Grant Withers. Serial. Orig: Alex Raymond.
☆ *Tim Tyler's Luck* (US 37) with Frankie Thomas. Serial. Orig: Lyman Young.
☆ *Dick Tracy* (US 37) with Ralph Byrd. Serial. Orig: Chester Gould.
☆ *Radio Patrol* (US 37) with Grant Withers. Serial. Orig: Eddie Sullivan and Charles Schmidt.
☆ *Blondie* (US 38) with Penny Singleton in the title role and Arthur Lake as Dagwood. First of a series of 28 supporting features made by Columbia 1938-50. Orig: Chic Young.

☆ *Little Orphan Annie* (US 38) with Ann Gillis. Orig: Harold Gray and Al Lowenthal.
☆ *Flash Gordon's Trip to Mars* (US 38) with Buster Crabbe. Serial. Orig: Alex Raymond.
☆ *Dick Tracy Returns* (US 38) with Ralph Byrd. Serial. *Tracy's G-Men* (US 39). Orig: Chester Gould.
☆ John Trent as Tailspin Tommy in *Sky Patrol* (US 39). Serial. Orig: Hal Forrest.
☆ *Planet Outlaws* (US 39) with Buster Crabbe as Buck Rogers. Orig: Dick Calkins and Phil Nolan.
☆ *Buck Rogers* (US 39) with Buster Crabbe. Serial. Orig: Dick Calkins and Phil Nolan.
☆ *Li'l Abner* (US 40) with Granville Owen. Orig: Al Capp.
☆ *Flash Gordon Conquers the Universe* (US 40) with Buster Crabbe. Serial. Orig: Alex Raymond.
☆ *Adventures of Captain Marvel* (US 41) with Tom Tyler. Orig: C. C. Beck.
☆ *Tillie the Toiler* (US 41) with Kay Harris. Orig: Russ Westover.
☆ *Private Snuffy Smith* (US 42) with Bud Duncan. Orig: Billy de Beck.
☆ Bud Duncan as Snuffy Smith in *Hillbilly Blitzkrieg* (US 42). Orig: Billy de Beck.

COMIC STRIP CHARACTERS (continued)

Buster Crabbe doubled as comic book heroes Buck Rogers and Flash Gordon in the Saturday morning serials of the thirties and forties. (*Kobal*)

☆ *Winslow of the Navy* (US 42) with Don Terry. Serial. Orig: Lt Com Frank Martinek.
☆ *Don Winslow of the Coastguard* (US 43) with Don Terry. Serial. Orig: Lt Com Frank Martinek.
☆ *The Phantom* (US 43) with Tom Tyler. Serial. Orig: Lee Falk.
☆ *Dixie Dugan* (US 43) with Lois Andrews. Orig: Joseph McEvoy. In this case McEvoy's strip had itself been based on a film—*Show Girl* (US 28).
☆ *Captain America* (US 44) with Dick Purcell. Orig: Jack Kirby and Joe Simon.
☆ *Dick Tracy* (US 45) with Morgan Conway. Orig: Chester Gould.
☆ *Joe Palooka, Champ* (US 46) with Joe Kirkwood, who also starred in eight other Palooka movies 1947–51. Orig: Ham Fisher.
☆ Joe Yule as Jiggs and Renie Riano as Maggie in *Bringing Up Father* (US 46); also in *Jiggs and Maggie in Society* (US 48) and *Jiggs and Maggie Out West* (US 50). Orig: George McManus.
☆ *Dick Tracy vs Cueball* (US 46) with Morgan Conway. Orig: Chester Gould.
☆ *Dick Tracy's Dilemma* (US 47) and *Dick Tracy Meets Gruesome* (US 47) with Ralph Byrd. Orig: Chester Gould.
☆ *Superman* (US 48) with Kirk Alyn. Serial. Orig: Jerry Siegel and Joe Schuster.
☆ *Jungle Jim* (US 48) with Johnny Weissmuller in this and seven other Columbia low budgeters. Orig: Alex Raymond.
☆ *Bomba the Jungle Boy* (US 49) with Johnny Sheffield; first of series of 12 which continued to 1955. Orig: Roy Rockwell.
☆ *The Adventures of Jane* (GB 49) with Christabel Leighton-Porter. Orig: Norman Pett.
☆ *Atom Man vs Superman* (US 50) with Kirk Alyn as Superman. Serial. Orig: Jerry Siegel and Joe Schuster.
☆ Scotty Beckett as Corky and Jimmy Lydon as Skeezix in *Gasoline Alley* and *Corky of Gasoline Alley* (both US 51). Orig: Frank O. King.
☆ *Superman and the Mole Men* (US 51) with George Reeves. Orig: Jerry Siegel and Joe Schuster.
☆ *Blackhawk* (US 52) with Kirk Alyn. Orig: Reed Crandall and Charles Guidera.
☆ *Prince Valiant* (US 54) with Robert Wagner. Produced in colour and Cinemascope, this was the first major motion picture of the talkie era to be based on a comic strip. Orig: Harold Foster.
☆ *The Sad Sack* (US 57) with Jerry Lewis. Orig: George Baker.
☆ *Li'l Abner* (US 59) with Peter Palmer. Orig: Al Capp.
☆ *Dondi* (US 61) with David Kory. Orig: Gus Edson and Irwin Hasen.
☆ *Modesty Blaise* (GB 66) with Monica Vitti in title role and Terence Stamp as Willie Garvin. Orig: Peter O'Donnell and Jim Holdaway.
☆ *Batman* (US 66) with Adam West in title role and Burt Ward as Robin. Orig: Bob Kane.
☆ *Barbarella* (Fr/It 67) with Jane Fonda. Orig: Jean-Claude Forest.
☆ *The Adventures of Barry McKenzie* (Aus 72) with Barry Crocker; sequel *Barry McKenzie Holds His Own* (Aus 74). Orig: Barry Humphries—the only comic strip artist to have appeared in the films based on his strip.
☆ *Tiffany Jones* (GB 73) with Anouska Hempel. Orig: Pat Tourret and Jenny Butterworth.
☆ *Wonder Woman* (US 74, TVM) with tennis star Cathy Lee Crosby and *The New, Original Wonder Woman* (US 75, TVM) with Lynda Carter. Orig: Charles Moulton.
☆ *Friday Foster* (US 75) with Pam Grier, based on first comic strip with black heroine. Orig: Jorge Langaron.
☆ *Brenda Starr* (US 75, TVM) with Jill St John. Orig: Dale Messick.
☆ *The Incredible Hulk* (US 77, TVM) with Lou Ferrigno. Orig: Stan Lee.
☆ *Spider-Man* (US 77, TVM), *Spider-Man Strikes Back* (US 78) and *The Dragon's Challenge* (US 80) with Nicholas Hammond. Orig: Stan Lee.
☆ *Superman* (GB 78) with Christopher Reeve; followed by *Superman II* (GB 81), *Superman III* (GB 84) and *Superman IV* (GB 87). The first in the series was claimed to have been the most expensive film ever made. Orig: Jerry Siegel and Joe Schuster.
☆ *Captain America* (US 79, TVM) with Reb Brown. Orig: Jack Kirby and Joe Simon.
☆ *Mandrake* (US 79, TVM) with Anthony Herrerra. Orig: Lee Falf.
☆ *Buck Rogers* (US 79) with Gil Gerard. Orig: Dick Calkins.
☆ *Fatty Finn* (Aus 80) with Ben Oxenbould. Orig: Syd Nicholls.
☆ *Flash Gordon* (GB 80) with Sam J. Jones. Orig: Alex Raymond.
☆ *Swamp Thing* (US 82) with Dick Durock as the Thing. Orig: DC Comics.
☆ *Conan the Barbarian* (82) with Arnold Schwarzenegger. Orig: Robert E. Howard.
☆ *Annie* (US 82) with Aileen Quinn as Little Orphan Annie. Orig: Harold Gray and Al Lowenthal.
☆ *Ginger Meggs* (Aus 82) with Paul Daniel. Orig: James Bancks.
☆ *Supergirl* (GB 84) with Helen Slater. Orig: Otto Binder.
☆ *Conan the Destroyer* (US 84) with Arnold Schwarzenegger. Orig: Robert E. Howard.
☆ *Sheena Queen of the Jungle* (US 84) with Tanya Roberts. Orig: Sam Iger and Will Eisner.
☆ *Howard the Duck* (US 86) with Ed Gale, Chip Zien, Tim Rose, Steve Sleap, Peter Baird, Mary Wells, Lisa Sturz and Jordan Prentice taking it in turns to play the eponymous hero. Orig: Steve Gerber.
☆ *Jane and the Lost City* (GB 87) with Kirsten Hughes. Orig: Norman Pett.
☆ *Brenda Starr* (US 88) with Brooke Shields. Orig: Dale Messick.

Kirk Alyn had the misfortune to be probably the only lead player in history to get no billing at all. Although the star of the early *Superman* movies of the forties and fifties, the producers decreed that he would have to remain anonymous as they thought the kids would be disappointed to learn that the Man of Steel was a mere mortal actor.

BIOPICS

The historical character who has been represented most often on screen is Napoléon Bonaparte (1769–1821), Emperor of the French. The role has been played in at least 179 films to date.

Other historical characters most often represented on screen include Jesus Christ, of whom there are 147 recorded film portrayals; Vladymir Ilich Lenin (1870–1924)—76; Adolf Hitler (1889–1945)—65; Cleopatra (69–30 BC)—40; Queen Victoria (1819–1901)—37; Henry VIII (1491–1547)—34; Queen Elizabeth I (1553–1603)—32; Grigori Rasputin (1871?–1916)—29; Josef Stalin (1879–1953)—31; Pancho Villa (1877–1923)—27; St Joan of Arc (*c*. 1412–31)—25; Sir Winston Churchill (1874–1965)—19. The US President most often portrayed on screen has been Abraham Lincoln in 130 films. See p. 44. Chairman Mao Tse-Tung (1893–1976) was portrayed for the first time in *The Great Flowering River* (Chn 79) and Queen Elizabeth II (1926–) by Jeanette Charles in *Marcia* (GB 77). The first screen portrayal of Mrs Thatcher (1925–) was by Janet Brown in the James Bond movie *For Your Eyes Only* (GB 81). See also Western heroes (p. 64).

The first portrayal of a reigning British monarch was by Thomas R. Mills, who played King George V (1865–1936) in a fictionalized version of Sir Roger Casement's life *Whom the Gods Destroy* (US 16).

Adolf Hitler has been portrayed on screen 65 times. *Top*: Ward Bond in *Hitler—Dead or Alive* (US 42). *Right*: Robert Watson in *The Hitler Gang* (US 43), flanked by Maryin Kosleck as Goebbels, Alexander Pope as Goering, Victor Varconi as Hess and Luis van Rooten as Himmler. (*SI*)

US PRESIDENTS

The President of the United States **most often portrayed on film**, as well as **America's most oft portrayed historical character**, is Abraham Lincoln (1809–65). The role has been played in the 130 films listed, as well as a quantity of educational subjects. This filmography of representations of US Presidents cites the actor playing the presidential role where known, though in some films the actor has been uncredited. The date preceding the presidents' names is the year of inauguration.

1789 GEORGE WASHINGTON (1732–99)
Washington at Valley Forge (US 08)
Barbara Freitchie (US 08)
Benedict Arnold and Major Andre (US 09)
Phillips Smalley *A Heroine of '76* (US 11)
Washington at Valley Forge (US 14)
William Worthington *The Spy* (US 14)
Charles Ogle *Molly, the Drummer Boy* (US 14)
Joseph Kilgour *The Battle Cry of Peace* (US 15)
George MacQuarrie *Betsy Ross* (US 17)
Noah Beery *The Spirit of '76* (US 17)
A Daughter of War (US 17)
George MacQuarrie *The Beautiful Mrs Reynolds* (US 18)

Harold Judson *Deliverence* (US 19)
Schoolmaster Matsumoto (Jap 19)
Arthur Dewey *America* (US 24)
Joseph Kilgour *Janice Meredith* (US 24)
Francis X. Bushman *The Flag* (US 27)
Edward Hern *The Winners of the Wilderness* (US 27)
Alan Mowbray *Alexander Hamilton* (US 31); *The Phantom President* (US 32)
Aaron Edwards *Are We Civilized?* (US 34)
George Houston *The Howards of Virginia* (US 40)
Montague Love *Remarkable Andrew* (US 42)
Alan Mowbray *Where Do We Go From Here?* (US 45)
Douglass Dumbrille *Monsieur Beaucaire* (US 46)
Robert Barrat *The Time of their Lives* (US 46)
Richard Gaines *Unconquered* (US 47)
James Seay *When the Redskins Rode* (US 51)
John Crawford *John Paul Jones* (US 59)
Howard St John *Lafayette* (Fr 62)
Washington at Valley Forge (US 71)
Lorne Green *Washington—The Man* (US *c*. 75)
Patrick O'Neal *Independence* (US 76)

Frank Windsor *Revolution* (GB 86)

1797 JOHN ADAMS (1735–1826)
Jack Drumier *The Beautiful Mrs Reynolds* (US 18)
John Paul Jones (US 59)
William Daniels *1776* (US 72)
Pat Hingle *Independence* (US 76)

1801 THOMAS JEFFERSON (1743–1826)
Albert Hart *The Beautiful Mrs Reynolds* (US 18)
P. R. Scammon *My Own United States* (US 18)
Lionel Adams *Janice Meredith* (US 24)
Frank Walsh *America* (US 24)
Albert Hart *The Man Without a Country* (US 25)
Old Ironsides (US 26)
Montague Love *Alexander Hamilton* (US 31)
The Phantom President (US 32)
George Irving *Hearts Divided* (US 36)
Guy Bates Post *Maytime* (US 37)
The Howards of Virginia (US 40)
Gilbert Emery *The Remarkable Andrew* (US 42); *The Loves of Edgar Allan Poe* (US 42)
Grandon Rhodes *The Magnificent Doll* (US 46)

US PRESIDENTS (continued)

Holmes Herbert *Barbary Pirate* (US 49)
Herbert Heyes *The Far Horizons* (US 55)
John Paul Jones (US 59)
Ken Howard *1776* (US 72); *Independence* (US 76)

1809 JAMES MADISON (1751–1836)
Burgess Meredith *The Magnificent Doll* (US 46)

1817 JAMES MONROE (1758–1831)
Charles Brandt *The Beautiful Mrs Reynolds* (US 18)
Emmett King *The Man Without a Country* (US 25)
Morgan Wallace *Alexander Hamilton* (US 31)

1825 JOHN QUINCY ADAMS (1767–1848)
No portrayals on screen

1829 ANDREW JACKSON (1767–1845)
F. C. Earle *My Own United States* (US 18)
George Irving *The Eagle of the Sea* (US 26)
Russell Simpson *The Frontiersman* (US 27)
Lionel Barrymore *The Gorgeous Hussy* (US 36)
Hugh Sothern *The Buccaneer* (US 38)
Edward Ellis *Man of Conquest* (US 39)
Brian Donlevy *The Remarkable Andrew* (US 42)
Der unendliche Weg (Ger 43)
Lionel Barrymore *Lone Star* (US 52)
Charlton Heston *The President's Lady* (US 53)
Basil Ruysdael *Davy Crockett, King of the Wild Frontier* (US 55)
Carl Brenton Reid *The First Texan* (US 56)
Charlton Heston *The Buccaneer* (US 58)
John Anderson *Bridger* (US 76, TVM)

1837 MARTIN VAN BUREN (1782–1862)
Charles Trowbridge *The Gorgeous Hussy* (US 36)

1841 WILLIAM HENRY HARRISON (1773–1841)
Douglass Dumbrille *Ten Gentlemen from West Point* (US 42)
George Eldredge *Brave Warrior* (US 52)

1841 JOHN TYLER (1790–1862)
No portrayals on screen

1845 JAMES KNOX POLK (1795–1849)
Addison Richards *The Oregon Trail* (US 59)

1849 ZACHARY TAYLOR (1784–1850)
The Fall of Black Hawk (US 12)
Harry Holden *The Yankee Clipper* (US 27)
Robert Barrat *Distant Drums* (US 51)
Fay Roope *Seminole* (US 53)

1850 MILLARD FILLMORE (1800–74)
No portrayals on screen

1853 FRANKLIN PIERCE (1804–69)
Porter Hall *The Great Moment* (US 44)

1857 JAMES BUCHANAN (1791–1868)
No portrayals on screen

1861 ABRAHAM LINCOLN (1809–65)
Uncle Tom's Cabin (US 03)
The Blue and the Grey (US 08)
The Reprieve (US 08)
The Life of Abraham Lincoln (US 08)
The Assassination of Abraham Lincoln (US 09)
Stirring Days in Old Virginia (US 09)
George Stelle *The Sleeping Sentinel* (US 10)
Abraham Lincoln's Clemency (US 11)
The Old Man and Jim (US 11)
The Fortunes of War (US 11)
James Dayton *Lieutenant Grey* (US 11)
Ralph Ince *Under One Flag* (US 11)
A Romance of the '60's (US 11)
Ralph Ince *The Battle Hymn of the Republic* (US 11)
Grant and Lincoln (US 11)
Ralph Ince *The Seventh Son* (US 12)

H. G. Lonsdale *The Fall of Black Hawk* (US 12)
Ralph Ince *Lincoln's Gettysburg Address* (US 12)
Francis Ford *On Secret Service* (US 12); *When Lincoln Paid* (US 12)
When Lincoln was President (US 13)
Hugh Ford *With Lee in Virginia* (US 13)
From Rail Splitter to President (US 13)
William Clifford *The Toll of War* (US 13)
Lincoln for the Defense (US 13)
Ralph Ince *Songbird of the North* (US 13)
Willard Mack *The Battle of Gettysburg* (US 13)
Ralph Ince *Lincoln the Lover* (US 14); *The Man Who Knew Lincoln* (US 14)
Benjamin Chapin *Lincoln's Thanksgiving Story* (US 14) not released
The Sleeping Sentinel (US 14)
Benjamin Chapin *Old Abe* (US 15)
The Magistrate's Story (US 15)
Joseph Henabery *The Birth of a Nation* (US 15)
Francis Ford *The Heart of Lincoln* (US 15)
William Ferguson *The Battle Cry of Peace* (US 15)
Frank McGlynn *The Life of Abraham Lincoln* (US 15)
The Heart of Maryland (US 15)
Samuel Drane *The Crisis* (US 16)
Benjamin Chapin 10 one-reelers collectively known as *The Lincoln Cycle* (US 17)
Ralph Ince *Battle Hymn of the Republic* (US 17)
Gerald Day *My Own United States* (US 18)
Benjamin Chapin *Down the River* (US 18)
Rolf Leslie *Victory and Peace* (GB 18)
Benjain Chapin *Lincoln's Thanksgiving Story* (US 18); *Children of Democracy* (US 18); *Son of Democracy* (US 18)
Meyer F. Stroell *The Copperhead* (US 19)
The Land of Opportunity (US 20)
Ralph Ince *The Highest Law* (US 21)
Ellery Paine *Lincoln's Gettysburg Address* (US 22) talkie
Wild Bill Hickock (US 23)
The Heart of Abraham Lincoln (US 24)
Ellery Paine (?) *An Episode in the Life of Abraham Lincoln* (US 24) talkie
George A. Billings *Barbara Freitchie* (US 24); *The Dramatic Life of Abraham Lincoln* (US 24)
Charles E. Bull *The Iron Horse* (US 24)
Abraham Lincoln (US 25)
George A. Billings *The Man Without a Country* (US 25); *Hands Up* (US 26)
Charles E. Bull *The Heart of Maryland* (US 27)
Rev. Lincoln Caswell *Lincoln's Gettysburg Address* (US 27) talkie
Uncle Tom's Cabin (US 27)
The Heart of Lincoln (US 27)
Frank Austin *Court Martial* (US 28)
Walter Huston *Two Americans* (US 29)
George A. Billings *Lincoln's Gettysburg Address* (US 30)
Only the Brave (US 30)
Walter Huston *Abraham Lincoln* (US 30)
The Phantom President (US 32)
Frank McGlynn *Abraham Lincoln, the Pioneer* (US 33); *Abraham Lincoln, the Statesman* (US 33); *Are We Civilized?* (US 34); *The Littlest Rebel* (US 35); *Roaring West* (US 35)
Chic Sale *The Perfect Tribute* (US 35)
Frank McGlynn *The Prisoner of Shark Island* (US 36); *Hearts in Bondage* (US 36)
Segraren vid Hampton Roads (Swe c. 36)
Bud Buster *Cavalry* (US 36)
Frank McGlynn *Western Gold* (US 37); *Wells Fargo* (US 37); *The Man without a Country* (US 37); *The Plainsman* (US 37)
Albert Russell *Courage of the West* (US 37)
Triumph (GB? 37)
Percy Parsons *Victoria the Great* (GB 37)

Frank McGlynn *The Lone Ranger* (US 37); *The Mad Empress* (Mex 39)
A Failure at Fifty (US 39)
Frank McGlynn *Lincoln in the White House* (US 39)
Frank McGlynn and Walter Houston *Land of Liberty* (US 39) compilation film
John Carradine *Of Human Hearts* (US 39)
Henry Fonda *Young Mr Lincoln* (US 39)
Raymond Massey *Abe Lincoln in Illinois* (US 39)
Gene Reynolds *The Blue Bird* (US 40)
Victor Killain *Virginia City* (US 40)
Charles Middleton *Sante Fe Trail* (US 40)
A Dispatch from Reuters (US 40)
Dreams (US 40)
Not Long Remember (US 41)
Charles Middleton *They Died With Their Boots On* (US 41)
Ed O'Neill *Tennessee Johnson* (US 42)
Joel Day *The Days of Buffalo Bill* (US 46)
Charles Middleton *The Decision of Christopher Blake* (US 48)
Jeff Corey *Rock Island Trail* (US 50); *Transcontinent Express* (US 50)
G. William Horsley *Lincoln in Illinois* (US 50)
Hans Conreid *New Mexico* (US 51)
Leslie Kimmell *The Tall Target* (US 51)
Thomas Mitchell (?) *The Lincoln-Holmes Incident, a Folktale* (US 52)
Richard Hale *San Antone* (US 53)
Suddenly (US 54)
James Griffith *Apache Ambush* (US 55)
Stanley Hall *The Prince of Players* (US 55)
The Palmetto Conspiracy (US 55)
Tom Tryon *Springfield Incident* (US 55)
The Abductors (US 57) corpse only
Austin Green *The Story of Mankind* (US 57)
Royal Dano *Lincoln: The Young Years* (US c. 59, TVM)
Lincoln at Gettysburg (US 60)
The Boyhood of Abraham Lincoln (US 62)
Raymond Massey *How the West was Won* (US 63)
Uncle Tom's Cabin (FRG 65)
Dennis Weaver *The Great Man's Whiskers* (US 71)
Charlton Heston *Lincoln's Gettysburg Address* (US 73)
Arthur Hill *The Rivalry* (US 75)
William Deprato *The Faking of the President* (US 76)
John Anderson *The Lincoln Conspiracy* (US 77)
Ford Rainey *Guardian of the Wilderness* (US 77)
Sam Waterston *Lincoln* (US 88, TVM)

1865 ANDREW JOHNSON (1808–75)
Van Heflin *Tennessee Johnson* (US 42)

1869 ULYSSES SIMPSON GRANT (1822–85)
Barbara Freitchie (US 08)
Stirring Days in Old Virginia (US 08)
The Blue and the Gray (US 08)
The Old Soldier's Story (US 09)
The Bugle Call (US 09)
From Wallace to Grant (US 11)
Alvin Wyckoff *Lieutenant Grey of the Confederacy* (US 11)
Grant and Lincoln (US 11)
With Lee in Virginia (US 13)
The Littlest Rebel (US 14)
Paul Scardon *The Battle Cry of Peace* (US 15)
Donald Crisp *The Birth of a Nation* (US 15)
Frank Murray *My Own United States* (US 18)
Wilbur J. Fox *The Warrens of Virginia* (US 24)
Walter Rogers *Abraham Lincoln* (US 24)
Dixie (US 24)
Walter Rogers *Flaming Frontier* (US 26); *The Heart of Maryland* (US 27); *The Little*

Shepherd of Kingdom Come (US 28)
Court-Martial (US 28)
Fred Warren *Abraham Lincoln* (US 30)
Guy Oliver *Only the Brave* (US 30)
Fred Warren *Secret Service* (US 31)
Walter Rogers *Silver Dollar* (US 32)
Fred Warren *Operator 13* (US 34)
Gold is Where You Find It (US 38)
Joseph Crehan *Union Pacific* (US 39);
    Geronimo (US 39)
Harrison Greene *The Son of Davy Crockett* (US
    41); *Tennessee Johnson* (US 42)
Joseph Crehan *They Died With Their Boots On*
    (US 42); *The Adventures of Mark Twain* (US
    44)
Reginald Sheffield *Centennial Summer* (US 46)
John Hamilton *The Fabulous Texan* (US 47)
Joseph Crehan *Silver River* (US 48)
Sunset at Appotomax (US 53)
John Hamilton *Sitting Bull* (US 54)
Hayden Rorke *Drum Beat* (US 54)
Morris Ankrum *From the Earth to the Moon* (US
    58)
Stan Jones *The Horse Soldiers* (US 59)
Henry Morgan *How the West was Won* (US 63)
Buffalo Bill, l'eroe del Far West (It/Fr/FRG 65)
Antonio Albaisin (?) *Ringo e Gringo contro tutti*
    (It 66)
Jason Robards *The Legend of the Lone Ranger*
    (US 81)

1877 RUTHERFORD BIRCHARD HAYES (1822–93)
John Dilson *Buffalo Bill* (US 44)

1881 JAMES ABRAM GARFIELD (1831–81)
Night Raiders (US 39)
Lawrence Wolf *No More Excuses* (US 68)
Van Johnson *Il prezzo del potere* (It/Sp 69)

1881 CHESTER ALAN ARTHUR (1831–86)
Emmett Corrigan *Silver Dollar* (US 32)
Larry Gates *Cattle King* (US 63)

1885 and **1893** STEPHEN GROVER CLEVELAND
    (1837–1908)
Topack *Lively Political Debate* (US 94)
William B. Davison *Lillian Russell* (US 40)

Pat McCormick *Buffalo Bill and the Indians* (US
    76)
Wilford A. Brimley *The Wild Wild West
    Revisited* (US 79, TVM)
Haji Washington (Iran 83)

1889 BENJAMIN HARRISON (1833–1901)
Steele *Lively Political Debate* (US 94)
Roy Gordon *Stars and Stripes Forever* (US 52)

1897 WILLIAM MCKINLEY (1843–1901)
Del Henderson *A Message to Garcia* (US 36)
Frank Conroy *This is My Affair* (US 37)

1901 THEODORE ROOSEVELT (1858–1919)
Terrible Teddy, The Grizzly King (US 01)
The 'Teddy' Bears (US 07)
Big Game Hunting in Africa (US 09) recon-
    struction newsfilm with actor portraying T.R.
Up San Juan Hill (US 09)
T.R. as himself in unidentified one-reel comedy
    starring Matty Roubert (US 14)
T.R. himself in *Womanhood, the Glory of a
    Nation* (US 17)
W. E. Whittle *General Pershing* (US 19)
The Fighting Roosevelts (US 19)
Jack Ridgway *The Copperhead* (US 19)
E. J. Radcliffe *Sundown* (US 24)
Buck Black *Lights of Old Broadway* (US 25)
Frank Hopper *The Rough Riders* (US 27)
The Man Who Dared (US 33)
Erle C. Kent *The End of the Trail* (US 36)
Sidney Blackmer *This Is My Affair* (US 37)
Wallis Clark *Jack London* (US 43)
Sidney Blackmer *In Old Oklahoma* (US 43);
    Buffalo Bill (US 44)
John Morton *I Wonder Who's Kissing Her Now?*
    (US 47)
Sidney Blackmer *My Girl Tisa* (US 48)
John Alexander *Fancy Pants* (US 50)
Edward Cassidy *The First Travelling Saleslady*
    (US 56)
Karl Swenson *Brighty of the Grand Canyon* (US
    66)
Brian Keith *The Wind and the Lion* (US 75)
William Phipps *Eleanor and Franklin* (US 76,
    TVM)

David Healy *Eleanor and Franklin: The White
    House Years* (US 77, TVM)
James Whitmore *Bully* (US 78)
Bob Boyd *The Indominatable Teddy Roosevelt*
    (US 85)

1909 WILLIAM HOWARD TAFT (1857–1930)
The Sculptor's Nightmare (US 08)
Ross Durfee *The Winds of Kitty Hawk* (US 78,
    TVM)

1913 THOMAS WOODROW WILSON (1856–1924)
himself in introduction to *The Battle Cry of Peace*
    (US 15)
himself in *Womanhood, the Glory of a Nation*
    (US 17)
The Great Victory (US 18)
Orlo Eastman *The Kaiser: The Beast of Berlin*
    (US 18)
R. A. Faulkner *General Pershing* (US 19)
Turn Back the Clock (US 33)
Alexander Knox *Wilson* (US 44)
Earl Lee *The Story of Will Rogers* (US 52)
L. Kovsakov *The Unforgettable Year 1919* (USSR
    52)
Frank Forsyth *Oh! What a Lovely War* (GB 69)
Jerzy Kaliszewski *Polonia Restituta* (Pol/USSR/
    Hun/Cz/GDR 81)

1921 WARREN GAMALIEL HARDING (1865–1923)
No portrayals on screen

1923 JOHN CALVIN COOLIDGE (1872–1933)
Ian Wolfe *The Court Martial of Billy Mitchell*
    (US 55)

1929 HERBERT CLARK HOOVER (1874–1964)
Tom Jensen *Fires of Youth* (US 31)
The Day the Bubble Burst (US 82, TVM)

1933 FRANKLIN DELANO ROOSEVELT (1882–1945)
Capt. Jack Young *Yankee Doodle Dandy* (US
    42); *This Is the Army* (US 43)

Left: John Fitzgerald Kennedy as
a young PT boat commander
during World War II. **Right**: Cliff
Robertson as the future President
in *PT 109* (US 63).

Herr Roosevelt Plaudert (Ger 43)
Jack Young Mission to Moscow (US 43)
Godfrey Tearle The Beginning or the End (US 47)
Nikolai Cherkasov The First Front (USSR 49)
Secret Mission (USSR 50)
Beau James (US 57)
Ralph Bellamy Sunrise at Campobello (US 60)
Richard Nelson The Pigeon that Took Rome (US 62)
McHale's Navy Joins the Air Force (US 68)
Stephen Roberts First to Fight (US 67)
Stanislav Jaskevik Liberation (USSR 70–71)
Edward Herrmann Eleanor and Franklin (US 76, TVM)
Dan O'Herlihy MacArthur—The Rebel General (US 77)
Stephen Roberts Ring of Passion (US 77, TVM)
Edward Herrmann Eleanor and Franklin: The White House Years (US 77, TVM)
Howard Da Silva The Private Files of J. Edgar Hoover (US 78)
Stephen Roberts Ring of Passion (US 78, TVM)
Teheran '43 (USSR/Fr/Swz 81)
Jason Robards F.D.R.: The Last Year (US 81, TVM)
Edward Herrmann Annie (US 82)

1945 HARRY S. TRUMAN (1884–1972)
Art Baker The Beginning or the End (US 47)
Secret Mission (USSR 50)
Call Me Madam (US 53)
uncredited child Alias Jesse James (US 59)
James Whitmore Give 'Em Hell, Harry! (US 75)
E. G. Marshall Collision Course (US 76)

Ed Flanders MacArthur—The Rebel General (US 77)
Robert Symonds Tail Gunner Joe (US 77, TVM)
Enola Gay (US 80, TVM)
Algimantas Masiulis Victory (USSR 86)

1953 DWIGHT DAVID EISENHOWER (1890–1969)
Willis Bouchey Red Planet Mars (US 52)
The Outsider (US 61)
Harry Carey Jr The Long Grey Line (US 55)
Henry Grace The Longest Day (US 72)
James Flavin Francis Gary Powers (US 76, TVM)
Andrew Duggan Tail Gunner Joe (US 77, TVM)
Robert Beer The Right Stuff (US 83)

1961 JOHN FITZGERALD KENNEDY (1917–63)
Kennedy in his True Colours (Chn 62)
Cliff Robertson PT 109 (US 63)
William Jordan The Private Files of J. Edgar Hoover (US 77)
Sam Chew Young Joe, the Forgotten Kennedy (US 77, TVM)
Paul Rudd Johnny We Hardly Knew Ye (US 77, TVM)
James Franciscus Jacqueline Bouvier Kennedy (US 82, TVM)
Robert Hogan Prince Jack (US 84, TVM)

1963 LYNDON BAINES JOHNSON (1908–73)
Ivan Treisault How to Succeed in Business without Really Trying (US 67)
Colpo di Stato (It 68)
The Wrecking Crew (US 69)

Andrew Duggan The Private Files of J. Edgar Hoover (US 77)
Donald Moffat The Right Stuff (US 83)
Kenneth Mars Prince Jack (US 84, TVM)

1969 RICHARD MILHOUS NIXON (1913–)
Jean-Pierre Biesse Made in USA (Fr 67)
The Statue (US 70)
Cold Turkey (US 70)
Million Dollar Duck (US 70)
Jim Dixon Is There Sex After Death? (US 71)
Dan Resin as young Nixon and Richard Dixon as older Nixon in Richard (US 72)
Richard Dixon The Faking of the President 1974 (US 76) ; The Private Files of J. Edgar Hoover (US 77)
Anderson Humphreys The Cayman Triangle (CayI 77)
Harry Spillman Born Again (US 78)
Richard M. Dixon Hopscotch (US 80) ; Where the Buffalo Roam (US 80)
Philip Baker Hall Secret Honor: The Last Testament of Richard M. Nixon (US 84, TVM)

1974 GERALD RUDOLPH FORD (1913–)
Dick Crockett The Pink Panther Strikes Again (GB 76)

1977 JAMES EARL CARTER (1924–)
Ed Beheler The Cayman Triangle (CayI 77)
Black Sunday (US 77)
himself Special Counsel (US 88)

1981 RONALD REAGAN (1911–)
himself in It's a Great Feeling (US 49)

BLACK FILMS

The first black film was The Railroad Porter (US 12), a chase comedy with an all-black cast directed by pioneer black film-maker Bill Foster.

The first black production company was the Lincoln Motion Picture Co., founded in Los Angeles in 1915 by black actors Clarence Brooks and Noble Johnson, a prosperous black druggist called James T. Smith and white cameraman Harry Grant. The company's first release was The Realisation of a

> The only archive in the world devoted exclusively to films with black casts and films made by blacks is the Black Film Collection at Tyler, Texas.

Negro's Ambition (US 16), with Noble Johnson starring as an oil engineer who makes good.

The first black feature film was the Frederick Douglass Film Co.'s six-reel The Coloured American Winning his Suit (US 16), which was premièred at Jersey City on 14 July 1916. The all-black cast was largely amateur, made up of 'young men and women of the race from . . . the best families in New Jersey'.

The first black talkie was Christie Comedies' two-reel Melancholy Dame (US 28), featuring Roberta Hyson and Spencer Williams. The picture was about black 'high society' in Birmingham, Ala.

The first feature-length black talkie was MGM's Hallelujah! (US 29), directed by King Vidor and starring Daniel Haynes. **The first made by a black production company** was the Oscar Micheaux Corporation's The Exile (US 31), directed by Oscar Micheaux and starring Stanley Murrell.

The first feature-length film produced by blacks in Britain was Horace Ove's Reggae (GB 70), a 60-min documentary about the distinctive Jamaican music form. **The first dramatic feature** was Horace Ove's Pressure, made on location in the Ladbroke Grove area of London in 1974, but not released until February 1978. Originally commissioned by the BBC, but rejected as 'too heavy', the film told the story of a British-born younger son (Herbert Norville) of an immigrant family from Trinidad who finds himself adrift between two cultures. **The first dramatic feature released** in Britain was Black Joy (GB 77), a delightful comedy about an innocent and unsophisticated Guyanan immigrant (Trevor Thomas) exposed to the 'hustlin'' way of life of the Brixton ghetto.

Black Films Made by the Major Studios

During the silent period the 'majors' showed little or no interest in black movies and even when black characters were required they were generally played by white actors in black-face. D. W. Griffith's The Birth of a Nation (US 15) had a large cast of black

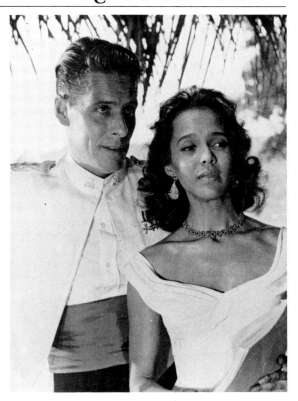

Romance between white and black was treated for the first time in an English-language film in *Pool of London* (GB 50), with Susan Shaw and Earl Cameron (*top left*). In America the subject remained too hot to handle until *Island in the Sun* (US 59) offered twin romances between John Justin and Dorothy Dandridge (*above*) and Harry Belafonte and Joan Fontaine (*left*).

roles, since the controversial plot revolved round the black 'takeover' of the South following the Civil War, yet only one genuine black—the curiously named Madame Sul-Te-Wan—was employed on the film.

The coming of sound altered the picture, since the trend towards greater realism demanded that blacks be played by blacks, though their roles were generally confined to the menial or the comic (usually both combined). At the same time the major studios began to turn out the occasional all-black picture, most of them dependent upon the vocal talents of the black American and aimed principally at white audiences. Those made prior to the sudden explosion of 'superspade' black exploitation pictures in the late sixties were as follows: *Hallelujah!* (MGM 29) with Daniel Haynes; *Hearts in Dixie*

(Fox 29) with Clarence Muse; *Green Pastures* (Warner 36) with Rex Ingram; *Stormy Weather* (TCF 43) with Bill Robinson, Lena Horne; *Cabin in the Sky* (MGM 43) with Eddie Anderson, Lena Horne; *Bright Road* (MGM 51) with Dorothy Dandridge; *Carmen Jones* (TCF 54) with Harry Belafonte, Dorothy Dandridge; *Anna Lucasta* (United Artists 58) with Sammy Davis Jr., *Porgy and Bess* (Goldwyn 59) with Sidney Poitier, Dorothy Dandridge.

No Hollywood films took the subject of contemporary race relations as a main theme until 1949 when three such films came to the screen almost simultaneously, led by *Home of the Brave*, the story of a black veteran undergoing psychiatric treatment following traumatic war experiences. The other two films, *Pinky* and *Lost Boundaries*, dealt with light-skinned blacks passing for white.

The Hays Code ban on miscegenation as a theme was breached by *Island in the Sun* (US 59), which offered twin romances between John Justin and Dorothy Dandridge (who marry in the end) and Harry Belafonte and Joan Fontaine (who part). In

Britain the subject had been tackled much earlier in *Pool of London* (GB 50), which depicted the relationship between a Jamaican ship's steward (Earl Cameron) and a white cinema cashier (Susan Shaw).

Production output: A total of 49 all-black silent features are recorded in the US for the period 1917–30; exactly 150 all-black talkies were made in the US 1931–50.

Blacks in Leading Roles

The fortunes of black leading actors rose in the late 1960s, following the success of the civil rights movement and the cult of 'black consciousness'. A peak was reached in about 1973, when 45 American-made features, 21 of them from major distributors, starred black leading players. By 1982 only eight films had blacks in starring roles, three of which top-lined Richard Pryor. According to the National Association for the Advancement of Colored People, Hollywood films featuring blacks in 'significant' roles totalled no more than 12 in 1981, 22 in 1982 and 14 in 1983.

The first black film with an all-African cast was the Stoll Co.'s *Nionga* (GB 25), about a young betrothed couple in Central Africa and the tragic ending to their romance, the man being accidentally killed and the bride burned alive in her hut according to local custom. Such films were rare, the only other pre-war examples on record being *Zeliv* (It 28), a story of tribal life enacted entirely by Zulus, *Samba* (Ger 28) and *Stampede* (GB 30). All these films were aimed at white audiences, a fact made abundantly clear in the sub-titles to *Nionga*, which referred to its protagonists as 'the savages'.
The first African film drama made by a black African was Ousmane Sembene's *La Noire de . . .* (Sen 67), premièred at the Théâtre Sorano in Dakar on 4 February 1967.

JEWISH FILMS

The first Jewish film with an all-Jewish cast was Stanisław Sebel's screen version of Gordin's *Satan* (Pol 12), produced by Madame Yelizariantz's Sila Co. with a cast drawn from Warsaw's Fishon Theatre. Within a year there were four Polish companies specializing in Jewish films, Sila having been joined by Variag (also run by a woman, Madame Stern), Mintus and Kosmofilm.
The first British example was *The Jewish King Lear* (GB 12), filmed at the Pavilion Theatre and premièred at New King's Hall in the Commercial Road.
America's first Jewish picture was *A Passover Miracle* (US 14), released by Kalem in two versions, one with English sub-titles, the other with Yiddish.
The first talkie in Yiddish was Sidney M. Goldin's *Style and Class* (US 29), a Judea Films production with Goldie Eisenman and Marty Baratz.

Production Output

According to Rob Edelman's filmography of feature films in Yiddish (*Films in Review* June/July 1978), there were 53 produced in America 1924–61, 17 in Poland pre-1940, 4 in Russia 1925–33 and solitary examples from West Germany in 1948 and Italy in 1949. Mr Edelman believes there may also have been Romanian and Hungarian Yiddish features.

After *Three Daughters* (US 61), production ceased entirely for nearly 20 years. Then in 1980 came Samy

---

Molly Picon, seen here in Joseph Green's *Mamele/ Little Mother* (Pol c. 37), was the Yiddish cinema's foremost star.

Szlingerbaum's *Brussels-Transit* (Bel 80), a story of Polish-born survivors of the holocaust settling in Brussels after World War II. The film, which had a Yiddish commentary and part-Yiddish dialogue, was followed by *The Dybbuk* (Pol 82), a Jewish State Theatre of Poland production from the play by Syymon Szurmiez, and an Israeli offering called *If They Give, Take* (Isr 82). A short directed by David Greenwald, *The Well* (US 84), may herald renewed production of Yiddish films in America.

The revival of interest in Yiddish films was stimulated by the founding of the National Centre for Jewish Film at Brandeis University, Waltham, Mass., established in 1976 with 30 mainly incomplete films from the estate of producer Joseph Seiden. It now houses over 2000 films on Jewish subjects as well as an extensive photo and rare book collection. Despite the lack of any recent product, a Yiddish Film Festival was held in New York in 1978 and the following year a season of Yiddish films ran at Cineplex in Toronto. In Europe, retrospectives of Yiddish cinema were held in Frankfurt by Walter Schobert in 1980, 1982 and 1984. Two feature-length documentaries, *Das Jiddische Kino* (FRG 83) and *Almonds and Raisins* (GB 84), have also been made on the history of Yiddish films. The former introduced a season of Yiddish features on West Germany's ZDF television station in April 1983. As part of London's 1987 Jewish East End celebration, the National Film Theatre presented a retrospective of Yiddish films dating back to the Molly Picon comedy *East and West* (Aut 23).

Anti-Semitic Films

These have been rare. In 1935, when Joseph Goebbels ordered a search to be made for foreign anti-Semitic films that could be released in Germany, the only example that could be obtained was a primitive Swedish talkie called *Pettersson and Bendel* (Swe 33). Curiously the Nazi-controlled film industry of the Third Reich made no overtly anti-Semitic pictures until just before the war, when Hans Heinz Zerlett directed *Robert und Bertram* (Ger 39), a comedy about two German tramps who get the better of a rascally Jew and save the innkeeper's lovely Aryan daughter from the fate of marrying him. The following year cinematic Jew-baiting began in earnest with *Jud Süss* (Ger 40), *Die Rothschilds* (Ger 40) and *Der ewige Jude* (Ger 40), three films whose virulent hatred was a presage of the vengeance to be wreaked on the race they vilified. Of these *Jud Süss* is undoubtedly the most notorious; it is also the only one to have been released since the war. Dubbed in Arabic, it was distributed in the Arab states in 1955 by the USSR agency Sovexport.

After the collapse of the Third Reich, anti-Semitic films were mercifully sparse, but in 1952 the semi-official Cifesca company of Spain produced Luis Marquina's *Amaya* (Sp 52). This film blamed the Muslim conquest of Spain on treacherous Jews who were portrayed as funding the invasion in order to make more profit as part of the Islamic empire. One of the characters states that to the Jews, a Christian is no different from a Muslim, simply someone to be exploited for profit. The Jews in the film are depicted as rascally, cunning and devious; the Spanish characters are not unlike the Nordic heroes and heroines in similar types of Nazi film.

HORROR

The character most frequently portrayed in horror films is Count Dracula, the creation of the Irish writer Bram Stoker (1847–1912), whose novel *Dracula* was published in 1897. Representations of the Count or his immediate descendants on screen outnumber those of his closest rival, Frankenstein's monster, by 155 to 109 (see filmography).

The peak year for production of horror films was 1972, with a total of 189. Of these, 83 emanated from the USA. The horror boom rapidly abated, with only 58 screamers going into production worldwide in 1975.

> In *Friday the 13th Part VI: Jason Lives* (US 86), Jason may but hardly anybody else does. *Variety* reviewer 'Cart' totted up 18 corpses, which worked out at an average of one stiff to every 4.83 minutes of running time.

Bela Lugosi in the role that made him a screen legend. When he died he was buried in his Dracula cloak. (*Popperfoto*)

DRACULA FILMOGRAPHY

The filmography excludes the frequent appearances that Dracula has made in cartoon films. The name of the artiste portraying the vampire is given before the title where this is known. (* amateur productions)

Drakula (Hun 21)
Max Schreck *Nosferatu, eine Symphonie des Grauens* (Ger 22)
Bela Lugosi *Dracula* (US 31)
Carlos Villarias *Dracula* (US 31) Spanish language
Gloria Holden *Dracula's Daughter* (US 36) Dracula himself seen as corpse only
Lon Chaney Jnr *Son of Dracula* (US 43) despite title, Chaney plays Dracula himself, there is no son in the picture
John Carradine *House of Frankenstein* (US 44); *House of Dracula* (US 45)
Bela Lugosi *Abbott and Costello Meet Frankenstein* (US 48)
Atif Kaptan *Drakula Istanbula* (Tur 53)
El Fantasma de la operatta (Arg 55)
German Robles *El Castillo de los monstruos* (Mex 57)
Victor Fabian *Frankenstein Meets Dracula* (US 57); *Return of the Wolfman* (US 57); *Revenge of Dracula* (US 57)
Francis Lederer *The Return of Dracula* (US 58)
*Black Inferno** (US 58)
Christopher Lee *Dracula* (GB 58)
*Castle of Dracula** (GB 58)
*Dracula** (US 59)
Gene Gronemeyer *The Teenage Frankenstein** (US 59); *Slave of the Vampire** (US 59)
Donald Glut (as Dracula's son) *I Was a Teenage Vampire** (US 59)
Richard Christy *Pawns of Satan** (US 59)
Chimi Kim *The Bad Flower* (S. Kor 61)
Frankenstein, el vampiro y cia (Mex 61)
Donald Glut (as Dracula's son) *Monster Rumble** (US 61)
Yechoon Lee *Ahkea Khots* (S. Kor 61)
Jeffrey Smithers *House on Bare Mountain* (US 62)
Donald Glut (as Dracula's son) *Dragstrip Dracula** (US 62)
Escala en Hi-Fi (Sp 63)
Kiss Me Quick! (US 64)
Sexy Proibitissimo (It 64)
Jack Smith *Batman Dracula* (US 64)
John Carradine *Billy the Kid versus Dracula* (US 65)
Mga Manugang ni Drakula (Phi 65)
Christopher Lee *Dracula—Prince of Darkness* (GB 65)
Pluto Felix *The Worst Crime of All!* (US 66)
Glenn Sherrard *Horror of Dracula** (US 66)
Mitch Evans *Dr Terror's Gallery of Horrors* (US 66)
Cesar Del Campo (?) *El Imperio de Dracula* (Mex 66)
Chappaqua (US 66)
Cesar Silva *La Sombra del murcielago* (Mèx 66)
Dracula's Wedding Day (US 67)
Harrison Marks *Vampire* (GB 67)
Dante Rivero *Batman Fights Dracula* (Phi 67)
Harrison Marks *The Naked World of Harrison Marks* (GB 67)
Bill Rogers (as descendant of Dracula) *A Taste of Blood* (US 67)
John Carradine *Las Vampiras* (Mex 67)
Christopher Lee *Dracula Has Risen from the Grave* (GB 68)

Santo en el tesoro de Dracula (Mex 68)
Dracula Meets the Outer Space Chicks (US 68)
Mondo Keyhole (US (?) 68)
Isabell, A Dream (It 68)
Aldo Monti *El Vampiro y el Sexo* (Mex 68)
Vince Kelly (as descendant of Dracula) *Dracula, the Dirty Old Man* (US 69)
Men of Action Meet Women of Dracula (Phi 69)
Christopher Lee *One More Time* (GB 69)
Alex d'Arcy *The Blood of Dracula's Castle* (US 69)
Tales of Blood and Terror (US/GB 69)
Does Dracula Really Suck (US 69) homosexual Dracula
Gabby Paul (?) *Il Risveglio di Dracula* (It 69)
Christopher Lee *El Conde Dracula* (FRG/Sp/It 69)
Marty Feldman *Every Home Should Have One* (GB 70)
Des Roberts *Guess What Happened to Count Dracula?* (US 70)
Dennis Price *Vampyros Lesbos/Die Erbin des Dracula* (Sp/FRG 70)
Tunnel Under the World (It 70)
Christopher Lee *Taste the Blood of Dracula* (GB 70); *The Scars of Dracula* (GB 70)
Eva Renzi (as descendant of Dracula) *Beiss mich Liebling* (FRG 70)
Des Roberts *Dracula's lusterne vampire/ Dracula's Vampire Lust* (Swz 70)
Paul Albert Krumm *Jonathan, Vampire sterben nicht* (FRG 70)
Denholm Elliott *Dracula* (GB 71, TVM)
Britt Nichols (as Dracula's Daughter) *La Fille de Dracula* (Fr/FRG 71)
Mori Kishida *Chi o Su Me/Lake of Dracula* (Jap 71)
Paul Naschy *Hombre que vino de ummo* (Sp/ FRG 71)
Zandor Vorkov *Dracula versus Frankenstein* aka *Blood of Frankenstein* (US 71)
Howard Vernon *Dracula contra el Dr Frankenstein* (Sp/Fr 71)
Jim Parker *The Mad Lust of a Hot Vampire* (US 71)
The Lust of Dracula (US 71)
Once Upon a Prime Time (Can 71)
Ferdy Mayne *Happening der Vampire* (FRG 71)
Charles McCauley *Blacula* (US 72)
Dennis Price *Go For a Take* (GB 72)
Dracula, A Family Romance (US 72)
Paul Naschy *La Messe nere della Contessa Dracula* (It 72)
Narciso Ibañez Menta *La Saga de los Draculas* (Sp 72)
Des Roberts *Dracula Vampire Sexuel* (Swz 72)
Howard Vernon *La Hija de Dracula* (Sp 72)
Christopher Lee *Dracula AD 1972* (GB 72)
David Azivu (?) *Santo y Blue Demon contra Dracula y el Hombre Lobo* (Mex 72)
Cesar Silva *La Invasion de los Muertos* (Mex 72)
Chabelo y Pepito contra los monstruos (Mex 73)
Paul Naschy *El Gran amor del Conde Dracula* (Sp 73)
Udo Kier *Blood for Dracula* (It/Fr 73)
Christopher Lee *The Satanic Rites of Dracula* (GB 73)
Harry Nillson (as Dracula's son) *Son of Dracula* (GB 73)
The House of Dracula's Daughter (US 73)
Christopher Lee *Tendre Dracula* (Fr 73)
Shadow of Dracula (Can 73)
Jack Palance *Dracula* (GB 74, TVM)

John Forbes-Robertson *Legend of the 7 Golden Vampires* (GB/HK 74)
David Niven *Vampira* (GB 74)
Dracula's Blood (US 74)
Hope Stansbury (as Dracula's daughter) *Blood* (US 74)
Dracula Goes to RP (Phi 74)
Tiempos duros para Drácula (Arg/Sp 75)
Peter Wechsburg (as illegitimate son of Dracula) *Deafula* (US 74)
Dracula is not Dead (GB 75)
Evil of Dracula (Jap 75)
Jay Robinson *Train Ride to Hollywood* (US 75)
El Jovencito Dracula (Sp 76)
Joe Rigoli (?) *El Pobrecito Dracula* (Mex 76)
Rossano Brazzi (?) *Il cav. constante nicosia demoniaco ovvero Dracula in Brianza* (It 76)
Christopher Lee *Dracula Père et Fils* (Fr 77)
Evelyne Kraft *Lady Dracula* (FRG 77)
Louis Jourdan *Count Dracula* (GB 77, TVM)
Geoffrey Land *Doctor Dracula* (US 77)
Suzanne Krazna as Countess Dracula in *Halloween with the Addams Family* (US 77, TVM)
Michael Pataki (as Dracula's grandson) *Dracula's Dog* (US 78)
John Carradine *Nocturna* (US 78) 'the first soft-porn-vampire-disco-rock movie'
Christopher Lee *Count Dracula and His Vampire Bride* (GB 78)
Fabian Forte *La Dinastia Dracula* (Mex 78)
Enrique Alvarez Felix *Dracula* (Mex 78)
Stefan Sileanu (as the historical Dracula, Vlad the Impaler) *Vlad Tepes/US: The True Life of Dracula* (Rom 79)
George Hamilton *Love at First Bite* (US 79)
Klaus Kinski *Nosferatu: Phantom der Nacht* (FRG 79)
Judd Hirsch *Halloween That Almost Wasn't* (US 79, TVM)
Frank Langella *Dracula* (US 79)
Gianni Garko *Dracula in Oberbayern* (FRG 79)
The Diabolic Loves of Nosferatu (Sp 79)
Peter Lowey *Dracula Bites the Big Apple* (US 79)
Johnny Harden *Star Virgin* (US 79)
Masumi Okada *Kyuketsuki Dorakyura Kobe Ni Arawaru: Akuma wa Onna wo Utsukushiku Suru* (Jap 79)
Jamie Gillis *Dracula Sucks* (US 80)
Gerald Fielding *Dracula's Last Rites* (US 80)
Andreas Voutsinas *Les Charlots Chez Dracula Junior* (Fr 80)
Louise Fletcher *Mama Dracula* (Fr/Bel 80)
Andres Garcia *El Macho Bionico* (Mex 81)
Jamie Gillis *Dracula Exotica* (US 81)
Les Jeux de la Comtesse Dolingen de Gratz (Fr 81)
Charlie Callas *Hysterical* (US 82)
Buenas Noches, Senor Monstruo (Sp 82)
Kung Fu from Beyond the Grave (HK 82?)
Dracula, Sovereign of the Damned (US? 83)
Kostas Soumas *Dracula Tan Exarchia* (Gre 83)
Gayracula (US 83)
Edmund Purdom (?) *Fracchia contro Dracula* (It 86)
Duncan Regehr *Monster Squad* (US 87)
Ferdy Mayne *Freckles and Ghosts* (Cz 88)
Brenden Hughes *To Die For* (US 88)
Klaus Kinski *Nosferatu in Venice* (FRG i.p.)

MUSICALS

The first musical with an original score was MGM's *The Broadway Melody* (US 29), with Bessie Love, Anita Page and Charles King, which was premièred at Grauman's Chinese Theatre in Hollywood on 1 February 1929. The songs were: *Give My Regards to Broadway* (George M. Cohan); *The Wedding Day of the Painted Doll, Love Boat, Broadway Melody, Boy Friend, You Were Meant For Me* (Arthur Freed and Herb Brown); and *Truthful Deacon Brown* (Willard Robison).

The first British musical was BIP's *Raise the Roof* (GB 30), directed by Walter Summers with Betty Balfour as an actress bribed by a rich man to ruin his son's touring review.

The first musical in colour was Warner Bros' *On With the Show*, directed by Alan Crosland in two-colour Technicolor with Betty Compson and Joe E. Brown and premièred in New York on 28 May 1929. **The first British** was BIP's *Harmony Heaven* (GB 30) with Polly Ward and Stuart Hall.

The musical with the most song numbers was Madan Theatres' *Indra Sabha* (Ind 32), a Hindi movie with 71 songs.

The Hollywood musical with the most songs was RKO's *The Story of Vernon and Irene Castle* (US 39). In the course of its 93 minutes running time the film proffered, in the words of *Variety*, 'one original song and 40 old pop songs by divers tunesmiths'.

Birth of the musical—*Broadway Melody* (US 29) was all-singin', all-dancin' and starred Bessie Love, a veteran of Hollywood's earliest days who went on performing in movies for over 60 years.

Not many movies attract an audience of blind patrons, but there was a recent exception. In February 1983 the Linda Ronstadt musical *The Pirates of Penzance* (GB 83) opened in Miami and Fort Lauderdale with a braille libretto available on request. Prepared by blind Pittsburgh writer–composer Linda Marcus, the braille text included stage directions and keywords to indicate action and scene changes.

SERIES

The longest series of films was the 85 Hong Kong-made features about the 19th-century martial arts hero Huang Fei-Hong, starting with *The True Story of Huang Fei-Hong* (HK 49) and continuing to *Magnificent Butcher* (HK 80). Of the total, 77 starred Kwan Tak-Hing and no less than 25 of the films premièred in a single year, 1956. All but five were in Cantonese, the others, all made in the 1970s, being in Mandarin.

The longest series still continuing is Shochiku Studios' *Tora-San* comedy series, of which the first was premièred in August 1969 and the fortieth in August 1988. The hero of the series, played by

Kiyoshi Atsumi, is a Chaplinesque 'little man' who owns nothing, does little or no work and gets into scrapes. All the films have almost identical plots— ne'er do well pedlar Tora-San returns from his wanderings to home and family, who try to persuade him to marry and settle down. He falls in love with his 'madonna'—a different girl each time—whom he always loses before setting off again on his travels. Tora-San was originally devised as an antidote to Japan's national characteristics of ruthless efficiency and success-at-any-price. The formula was spectacularly successful; whilst the first Tora-San movie was seen by 282,000 people, the audience nowadays for each new film averages 3 million with a box office take of some $20 million.

The longest series of English language films still continuing is United Artists' James Bond movies, which began in 1962 with *Dr No* (GB 62). The series marked its silver anniversary with the 15th in the UA sequence of movies, *The Living Daylights* (GB 87). In addition there has been a spoof Bond film, Columbia's *Casino Royale* (GB 67) with David Niven as an ageing and sexually timid 007 brought out of retirement, and Warner Bros' *Never Say Never Again* (GB 83), in which Sean Connery, who had said 'never again' very firmly after *Diamonds Are Forever* (GB 71), reprised the role after an offer of $5 million for his services proved difficult to refuse. No member of the cast has appeared in all

> Ian Fleming, creator of James Bond, named agent 007 after an American ornithologist known for the standard text on West Indian birds. 'It struck me,' recalled the writer, 'that his name, brief, unromantic and yet very masculine, was just what I needed'.

THE BOND MOVIES

Title	Distributor	Bond	Villain	'M'	Bond girl
Dr No (GB 62) d. Terence Young	United Artists	Sean Connery	Joseph Wiseman as Dr Julius	Bernard Lee	Ursula Andress as Honeychile Rider
From Russia with Love (GB 63) d. Terence Young	United Artists	Sean Connery	Lotte Lenya as Rosa Klebb	Bernard Lee	Daniella Bianchi as Tatiana Romanova
Goldfinger (GB 64) d. Guy Hamilton	United Artists	Sean Connery	Gert Frobe as Auric Goldfinger	Bernard Lee	Honor Blackman as Pussy Galore
Thunderball (GB 65) d. Terence Young	United Artists	Sean Connery	Adolfo Cali as Emilio Largo	Bernard Lee	Claudine Auger as Domino
Casino Royale (GB 67) d. John Huston, Ken Hughes, Val Guest, Robert Parrish, Joe McGrath, Richard Talmadge, Anthony Squire	Columbia	David Niven	Woody Allen as nephew Jimmy Bond	John Huston	Ursula Andress as Vespa Lynd
You Only Live Twice (GB 67) d. Lewis Gilbert	United Artists	Sean Connery	Donald Pleasance as Ernst Stavro Blofeld	Bernard Lee	Mie Hama as Kissy Suzuki
On Her Majesty's Secret Service (GB 69) d. Peter Hunt	United Artists	George Lazenby	Telly Savalas as Ernst Stavro Blofeld	Bernard Lee	Diana Rigg as Tracy Vicenzo
Diamonds Are Forever (GB 71) d. Guy Hamilton	United Artists	Sean Connery	Charles Gray as Ernst Stavro Blofeld	Bernard Lee	Jill St John as Tiffany Case
Live and Let Die (GB 73) d. Guy Hamilton	United Artists	Roger Moore	Yaphet Kotto as Dr Kananga	Bernard Lee	Jane Seymour as Solitaire
The Man with the Golden Gun (GB 74) d. Guy Hamilton	United Artists	Roger Moore	Christopher Lee as Scaramanga	Bernard Lee	Britt Ekland as Mary Goodnight
The Spy Who Loved Me (GB 77) d. Lewis Gilbert	United Artists	Roger Moore	Curt Jurgens as Stromberg	Bernard Lee	Barbara Bach as Major Anya Amasova
Moonraker (GB 79) d. Lewis Gilbert	United Artists	Roger Moore	Michael Lonsdale as Hugo Drax	Bernard Lee	Lois Chiles as Holly Goodhead
For Your Eyes Only (GB 81) d. John Glen	United Artists	Roger Moore	Julian Glover as Kristatos	—	Carole Bouquet as Melina
Octopussy (GB 83) d. John Glen	MGM/ United Artists	Roger Moore	Louis Jourdan as Prince Kamel Khan	Robert Brown	Maud Adams as Octopussy
Never Say Never Again (GB 83) d. John Glen	Warner Bros	Sean Connery	Klaus Maria Brandauer as Largo	Edward Fox	Kim Basinger as Domino
A View to a Kill (GB 85) d. John Glen	MGM/ United Artists	Roger Moore	Christopher Walken as Max Zorin	Robert Brown	Tanya Roberts as Stacey Sutton
The Living Daylights (GB 87) d. John Glen	MGM/ United Artists	Timothy Dalton	Jeroen Krabbe as Gen. Georgi Koskov	Robert Brown	Maryam d'Abo as Kara Milovy

the UA Bond movies, but Canadian actress Lois Maxwell has scored the most appearances, playing M's lovelorn secretary Miss Moneypenny in the first 14 films. At least a dozen of the crew working on *The Living Daylights* (GB 87) were second generation members of the 'Bond family' whose fathers or mothers had worked on the earlier 007 pictures.

The most successful series at the box office has been United Artists' and Eon Productions' British-made James Bond movies, which topped $2000 million in worldwide aggregate rentals with the release of their 15th 007 adventure *The Living Daylights* (GB 87).

United Artists' Bond Girls

© Danjaq S.A. 1962–87, Eon Productions Ltd

Ursula Andress as Honeychile Rider in *Dr No* (GB 62).

Daniella Bianchi as Tatiana Romanova in *From Russia with Love* (GB 63).

Honor Blackman as Pussy Galore in *Goldfinger* (GB 64).

Claudine Auger as Domino in *Thunderball* (GB 65).

Mie Hama as Kissy Suzuki in *You Only Live Twice* (GB 67).

Diana Rigg as Tracy Vicenzo in *On Her Majesty's Secret Service* (GB 69).

Jill St John as Tiffany Case in *Diamonds Are Forever* (GB 71).

Jane Seymour as Solitaire in *Live and Let Die* (GB 73).

Britt Ekland as Mary Goodnight in *The Man with the Golden Gun* (GB 74).

Barbara Bach as Major Anya Amasova in *The Spy Who Loved Me* (GB 77).

Lois Chiles as Holly Goodhead in *Moonraker* (GB 79).

Carole Bouquet as Melina in *For Your Eyes Only* (GB 81).

Maud Adams as Octopussy in *Octopussy* (GB 83).

Tanya Roberts as Stacey Sutton in *A View to a Kill* (GB 85).

Maryam d'Abo as Kara Milovy in *The Living Daylights* (GB 87).

Ursula Andress moonlighted as a Bond Girl Mark II when she played Vespa Lynd in Columbia's spoof 007 pic *Casino Royale* (GB 67). In this one the gratuitous violence was unaccompanied by sex— Bond was frightened of women. (*Kobal*)
Inset: Kim Basinger as Domino in Warner Bros' *Never Say Never Again* (GB 83).

SEX

Sex on screen followed rapidly on the emergence of cinema as a public entertainment. The pioneer producer of sex films was Eugène Pirou, beginning with a three-minute long production titled *Le Coucher de la mariée* (Fr 96), starring blonde and chubby Mlle Willy. Based on an act performed by Mlle Willy at the Olympia music-hall in Paris the previous year, the film showed a newly-wed couple preparing for bed. The girl's husband removes her satin slipper and presses it ecstatically to his lips, then she disrobes and puts on her night attire while her husband watches with evident desire. Finally Mlle Willy does a provocative little dance before the couple retire to bed. The film caused a sensation when it was premièred in the basement of the Café de Paris in November 1896 and was soon showing at two other *salles* as well, one in the boulevard Bonne-Nouvelle and the other at 86 rue de Clichy. Pirou followed this success with other sex subjects, such as *Bain de la Parisienne* (Fr 97), *Lever de la Parisienne* (Fr 97) and *La Puce* (Fr 97), most of them based on strip-tease acts playing in the Paris music halls. *La Puce*, for example, showed a maiden afflicted with a flea who removes her garments one by one to locate the offending insect.

Pirou's chief rival in the blue-movie field was Georges Méliès, whose *Les Indiscrets/The Peeping Toms* (Fr 96) came out at the end of 1896. Méliès was the man who brought nudity to the screen in *Après le bal* (Fr 97) and won a wide following with such sensational subjects as *En Cabinet particulier/A Private Dinner* (Fr 97), *L'Indiscret aux Bains de mer/ Peeping Tom at the Seaside* (Fr 97) and *La Modèle irascible/An Irritable Model* (Fr 97). In England these films were distributed by the Warwick Trading Co., who described them as 'welcome at any smoking concert or stag party'.

The earliest known American film on a sexual theme is American Mutoscope & Biograph's *The Downward Path* (US 02), a five-scene melodrama about a share-cropper's daughter who follows a downward path to prostitution—in one of the scenes she is encountered soliciting in the streets.

While most of the above films were very much of the 'What the Butler Saw' genre, the longer sex drama designed for general release emerged with Fotorama's *The White Slave Traffic* (Den 10), a two-reel shocker of such drawing power at the box office that within a few months Nordisk had produced a rival version with the same name. It was no less sensational. A publicity still shows a scene of a kidnapped girl being savagely beaten. Ole Olsen of Nordisk recalled that at the trade show in Berlin, the German cinema managers all clambered on to their seats for a better view. It was the success of these Danish sexploitation films—other titles included *The Last Victim of the White Slave Traffic* (Den 11) and *Dealer in Girls* (Den 12)—that inspired George Loane Tucker to make the first American feature-length sex picture, *Traffic in Souls* (US 13), starring Jane Gail and Matt Moore. Made clandestinely—not because

Probably the earliest surviving still from a pornographic film. Title and date unknown but probably French, *c.* 1900. (*Kobal*)

of the subject, but because Universal did not believe that the American public were ready for feature films—Tucker's $5700 movie garnered record earnings of $450,000.

> Former British Board of Film Censors Secretary John Trevelyan recalled an occasion when Customs officers seized an imported film titled *Games in Bed.* On screening the film they found it was about ways of entertaining a sick child.

Nudity on Screen

Female leads appeared in the nude for the first time in two feature films released in the same week in October 1916. In the Fox production *Daughter of the Gods* (US 16), filmed on location in the lush settings of St Augusta, Jamaica, the nymph-like figure of Australian-born star Annette Kellerman was seen as nature had intended. Miss Kellerman, the Esther Williams of silent movies, was a former professional swimmer who had been the centre of controversy five years earlier when she wore the first one-piece bathing suit. In fact Esther Williams played her in the biopic *Million Dollar Mermaid* (US 52), but by that date the austere provisions of the Hays Code precluded any presentation of the naked human form. The other film with a nude leading lady released the same week was also a Fox feature, *The Ragged Princess* (US 16), a melodrama top-lining winsome 16-year-old blue-eyed blonde newcomer June Caprice. Escaping from an orphanage, where she has been cruelly treated, the ragged waif comes across a woodland lake, strips off her clothes, and runs naked through the trees to plunge into the cooling waters.

The sensation caused in the 1930s by Hedy Lamarr's nude bathing scenes in *Extase* (Cz 33) has given wide currency to the mistaken idea that Miss Lamarr was the first nude actress on screen. She was not even the first nude in Czech movies, a distinction earned by Ira Rina in Gustav Muchaty's *Eroticon* (Cz 29).

Other nude scenes of the pre-*Extase* period were legion. Celio Film's *Idolo Infranto* (It 13) contained a scene set in an artist's studio with a nude model. 'The Naked Truth' was represented by a nude girl in woman director Lois Weber's *The Hypocrites* (US 15). This Paramount release was banned in Ohio and the Mayor of Boston demanded that clothes be painted on to the image of 'Naked Truth', frame by frame. The nude was uncredited, but has been variously claimed as a Miss Margaret Edwards and Lois Weber herself.

D. W. Griffith hired a number of prostitutes to appear naked in the Belshazar's Feast sequence of *Intolerance* (US 16). Joseph Hanabery, Griffith's assistant, had been ordered to shoot nude scenes, but decided it was more than he could get away with and had his actresses lightly draped for the orgy. Meanwhile Griffith, who was back in New York, did some close shots of nude prostitutes and these were intercut with Hanabery's more discreet scenes. When the film was reissued, in 1942, the New York Censor Board insisted that Griffith's nude inserts be cut.

Australia's Annette Kellerman became the first star to appear on screen in the nude in *Daughter of the Gods* (US16).

A nude girl on a crucifix was portrayed in *The Penitentes* (US 16) and a 'Miss Ray' appeared nude

> Romain Gary shot two versions of *Kill* (US 71), one clothed and the other unclothed. The undraped version, he explained, was for Protestant countries and the other for Catholic countries.

in *Le Film du Diable* (Bra 17). In *The Tree of Knowledge* (US 20), Yvonne Gardelle appeared naked as Lillith, the temptress who seeks to seduce Adam in the Garden of Eden before the creation of Eve. There were nude bathing scenes in *The Branding Iron* (US 20), *Isle of Love* (US 22) —in the night club scene naked girls threw themselves into a swimming pool as midnight struck—and in Henry Hathaway's *To the Last Man* (US 33), with Esther Ralston as one of the participants. Clara Bow took to nude bathing in *Hula* (US 27).

Lili Damita was seen in the buff in *Red Heels* (US 26) and Hope Hampton in *Lovers' Island* (US 26), while in *In Line of Duty* (US 32), a picture set in Arctic regions, Sue Carol bravely stripped off twice. Sally Rand performed an alfresco dance wearing nothing but a pair of shoes in *Paris at Midnight* (US 26) and a rather more circumspect Elissa Landi played a naked Christian girl bound to the stake in a Roman arena in *The Sign of the Cross* (US 32). Jean Vigo's *A Propos de Nice* (Fr 30) contains a scene of a nude sitting at a cafe table. The 35 mm prints of the film imported into Britain had the scene cut, but the sub-standard gauge prints retained it, since 16 mm film is not subject to censorship in Britain. A full-length nude is observed in the prison scene in *The Yellow Ticket* (US 31), about prostitution in Czarist Russia. The first nude scene in a Russian film, of a widow hysterically mourning in *Earth* (USSR 30), was cut by order of the authorities.

Nude scenes also appeared in *A Man's World* (US 18), *The Tree of Knowledge* (US 20), *Man, Woman and Marriage* (US 21), *Heedless Moths* (US 21) —the earliest known instance of a nude stand-in being used for the star, Jane Thomas—*Quo Vadis* (Ger/It 24), *Dante's Inferno* (US 24), *Wege zur Kraft und Schonheit* (Ger 25), *Metropolis* (Ger 26), *Beatrice Cenci* (It 26), *Casanova* (Fr/It 26), *Faust* (Ger 26), *Mandrin* (Fr 28?) and *Secrets of the Orient* (Ger/Fr 28). In most of these films the nakedness was tastefully discrete. Stefan and Franciszka Themerson's *Europa* (Pol 30) had what has been claimed as 'the first full-frontal nude'. The censor demanded that the scene should be cut, but Stefan neglected to do so and the film was released intact.

Following the introduction of the 1934 Hays Code, nudity disappeared from the Hollywood screen for 30 years. The first picture to bypass the ban was Sidney Lumet's *The Pawnbroker* (US 64), in which a woman was shown naked to the waist. The film was passed uncut by the Production Code Administration on the grounds that the scene was an essential element in the narrative. This decision opened the way for artistically valid scenes of nudity and sexual explicitness; it also hastened the end of the Administration itself, since a more liberal attitude towards sex on screen was difficult to accommodate within a code of prohibitions, and a ratings system was adopted instead.

The first film containing nude scenes to be passed by the British Board of Film Censors was *One Summer of Happiness* (Swe 51), in which a young couple were seen embracing in a pool of bulrushes. The decision was based on the fact that, in the words of former

> The first real 'nudie pic' was a UFA documentary on naturism titled *The Way to Strength and Beauty* (Ger 27). *Variety* referred to the 'dumb-looking German women' as 'very sturdy heifers'.

BBFC Secretary John Trevelyan, 'it was generally accepted in this country that in Scandinavia people bathed in the nude'. The prohibition of nudity, which had remained absolute since the founding of the Board in 1913 until this breach in 1952, was abandoned for good the following year after a naturist movie called *The Garden of Eden* (US 53) was banned by the BBFC but certified for exhibition by over 180 local authorities including the LCC. Some even gave it a U Certificate. The Board wisely decided that its original decision had been out of keeping with changing social attitudes and modified its policy on nudity. Another 14 years were to pass, however, before the Board felt the public was ready to accept a full frontal nude, and again it was a Swedish film which stimulated the change. *Hugs and Kisses* (Swe 66) was passed by the BBFC in 1967 complete with a scene in which a girl undressed in front of a full-length mirror. This was also the first time that pubic hair was displayed so forthrightly, though there had been some revealing 'flashes' during the scene in *Blow Up* (GB 67) in which David Hemmings wrestles on the floor with Jane Birkin and Gillian Hills.

The cinema of the Eastern world took longer to come to terms with nudity. The same year that *The Pawnbroker* (US 64) was restoring bare bosoms to the American screen, the first Indian films were released in which girls were permitted to be seen in bathing costumes—*April Fool* (Ind 64) and *Sangam* (Ind 64). India still bans nudity and has only recently allowed kissing (q.v.). In Japan, however, nudity had arrived on screen in the fifties, with a scene in *The Princess Yang* (Jap 55) where the heroine enters the bath. Since the heroine was the distinguished dramatic actress Machiko Kyo, it was unthinkable that she should be seen *in person* in the nude, so a stripper was hired from the Ginza to double for her. Foreign films continued to be subject to strict censorship, though not always simply by cutting. In the Japanese release prints of *A Clockwork Orange* (GB 71) the nude scenes went out of focus, while *Woodstock* (US 69) had the emulsion scraped off the footage containing nudes. Nevertheless, Japan has come a long way since a scene of Cary Grant embracing Sylvia Sidney in *Madame Butterfly* (US 32) was cut by the Japanese censor because Miss Sidney's elbow was exposed. Among the last of the Far Eastern countries to succumb was Red China, where nudity reached the screen in 1985 with a picture called *The Rickshaw Boy* (Chn 85). In this a girl was seen totally naked— but from the rear only.

The first full-frontal male nudity to be seen on screen appeared fleetingly in *Dante's Inferno* (It 12). The first explicit scene revealing male genitalia in a commercial feature was the nude wrestling match between Alan Bates and Oliver Reed in Ken Russell's *Women in Love* (GB 69).

The naked form in serious films is usually justified on 'artistic' grounds. Derek Jarman, director of the all-male *Sebastiane* (GB 75), vouchsafed a refreshingly practical explanation for the abundant nudity in this study of religious sexuality in Romano-Britain: 'the budget wouldn't run to authentic costumes'.

According to director Derek Jarman, the reason for all the nudity in *Sebastiane* (GB 75) was because 'the budget wouldn't run to authentic costumes'. At least it was cultural—the dialogue was in Latin.

The first film made for theatrical release in which the sex act was depicted was *Extase* (Cz 33). The young heroine (Hedwig Kiesler, later known as Hedy Lamarr), who has flown from an impotent husband, runs naked through the woods, bathes, and then has sex with a young engineer in a hut. Curiously *Extase* is celebrated as the first motion picture containing a nude scene, which it was not, rather than the first to show sexual intercourse, which it was.

The first theatrical release to contain a scene of unsimulated sexual intercourse was Jan Lindqvist and Stefan Jarl's *Dom Kallar Oss Mods/ They Call Us Misfits* (Swe 67), starring Kenta Gustafsson and Stoffe Svensson.

The earliest known pornographic film which can definitely be dated is *A l'Ecu d'Or ou la bonne auberge* (Fr 08).

There is no doubt that pornographic film-making was well established even by this early date, though for obvious reasons records are sparse. It was in the same year as *A l'Ecu d'Or* was released, 1908, that Russia enacted a law against obscene movies, known there as 'the Paris Genre'. In Moscow the Mephistopholes Kino decided to test its enforcement by presenting a full programme of such films and was promptly closed down.

The earliest known American pornographic film is *A Free Ride* aka *A Grass Sandwich* (US 15).

Pornography received 'professional recognition' in the USA in 1974, when the Screen Actors Guild relaxed the rule against its members appearing in hardcore movies. Formerly any SAG members performing in porno pics did so anonymously.

The first full-length erotic cartoon film was Osamu Tezuka's *A Thousand and One Nights* (Jap 69) —claimed (inaccurately) as 'the first animated film for adults'. David Grant's *Sinderella* (GB 72) was declared obscene by both Bow Street Magistrates' Court and the High Court of Appeal, but later passed by the British Board of Film Censors with cuts amounting to only 26 seconds.

'Soft porn' for theatrical release first started in Japan in 1950 with a wave of teenage sexploitation

---

Porno films are usually shot on tacky sets, reflecting small ambitions and smaller budgets. Not so the sadomasochistic hard porn pic *The Story of Joanna* (US 75), which takes place in the stately mansion owned by the brother of the then New York Governor Hugh Carey. When the owner and his family returned from vacation unexpectedly early and saw what was taking place on their dining-room table under the harsh glare of brute lights, the film-makers had to beat a very hasty retreat.

films with titles like *Teenager's Sex-Manual, Virgin's Clinic, A Virgin's Sex Manual, Bitch* and *Bad Girl*. The title role in the latter was played by the aristocratic Yoshiko Kuga, daughter of a Japanese peer, which gave it an added piquancy for some. The films reflected—and exploited—the revolution in social values of post-war Japan, where a confused generation of teenagers was apt to identify freedom with license. Remarkably the production of these movies began only three years after the first Japanese screen kiss.

The genesis of the American 'skinflick' is generally attributed to ex-Signal Corps cameraman Russ Meyer, who made his soft-porn debut with *The Immoral Mr Teas* (US 59), a comedy about a man with the unusual ability to undress girls mentally. This modest pioneer effort, shot on a budget of $24,000 in four days, inspired no less than 150 imitations within a year of its release.

Although sexploitation movies are generally profitable in relation to their modest budgets, the first to achieve an outstanding box office success, even by comparison with major studio productions, was *Emmanuelle* (Fr 74). Of the 607 new films released in Paris in 1974 *Emmanuelle* scored the highest number of admissions (1,342,921), ahead of such notable box-office draws as *The Sting* (US 73) — 1,154,952 admissions and *The Exorcist* (US 73) — 655,092 admissions.

The most prolific producer of pornographic films is the Nikkatsu Company of Tokyo, Japan, which released 57 'roman porno' movies (the Japanese name for soft porn) in 1986 and just over 50 in 1987. No hardcore films are produced, as they are illegal in Japan. Average budget per picture is $152,000.

The first film about homosexuality was Richard Oswald's *Anders als die Andern* (Ger 19), starring Conrad Veidt, which dared to confront the cinemagoing public with a subject still proscribed in literature. Following the resumption of censorship, male homosexuality received no further attention until Gustaf Gründgens' *Zwei Welten* (Ger 40). The story by Felix Lutzkendorff was an innocuous romance about two boys and two girls working together on a farm in the summer holidays. Under the direction of Gründgens it became transformed into an idyll between the two boys.

Elsewhere the theme attracted less sympathetic treatment. During the Japanese occupation of Shanghai, the Japanese made a film in China for native consumption called *Chu Hai-tang* (Jap/Chn 43), which attempted to propagate the idea of the Chinese as a decadent race with the story of a Chinese General embroiled with a female impersonator from the Peking Opera.

In Britain the subject remained unbroached on screen until Terence Young's *Serious Charge* (GB 59), about a priest (Anthony Quayle) falsely accused by a youth (Andrew Ray) of making homosexual advances. This made relatively little

> The earliest gay gag in a movie features in Mutual's Charlie Chaplin comedy *Behind the Screen* (US 16). Eric Campbell as the heavy, thinking the heroine Edna Purviance, dressed in male clothing, is a boy, goes all coy and twee, protruding his bottom provocatively.

impact, and it was left to Basil Deardon to make a film sufficiently explicit to actually use the word 'homosexual' in the dialogue. The picture was *Victim* (GB 61), in which Dirk Bogarde portrayed a respected barrister who becomes the victim of blackmail as a result of his relationship with a young vagrant (Peter McEnery). In the meantime American director Joseph Mankiewicz had directed Gore Vidal's screen adaptation of *Suddenly, Last Summer* (GB 59), the story of a homosexual poet whose beautiful cousin (Elizabeth Taylor) lures Italian beach boys for his delectation. Other British films on homosexual themes followed *Victim* in fairly quick succession, including *A Taste of Honey* (GB 61), *The Leather Boys* (GB 63) and *The Servant* (GB 63), but there was little further development of the theme by American film-makers between *Suddenly, Last Summer* and John Huston's *Reflections in a Golden Eye* (US 67), again with Elizabeth Taylor, this time as the wife of an army officer (Marlon Brando) infatuated with a young recruit.

The first film to deal explicitly with homosexuality was *Anders als die Andern* (Ger 19). The two lovers at a gay ball were played by Conrad Veidt and Reinhold Schünzel. (*Stiftung Deutsche Kinemathek*)

Lesbian love was treated with delicacy and discretion in Leontine Sagan's *Mädchen in Uniform* (Ger 31), a tender study of a girl's infatuation for a teacher in a repressive Prussian boarding school.

> At one time Samuel Goldwyn was contemplating buying the screen rights to Radcliffe Hall's controversial novel *The Well of Loneliness*. 'You can't do that,' warned an aide, 'It's about lesbians—you'll never get it past the Hays Office'. 'That's all right,' Goldwyn assured him, 'We'll make them Americans'.

The first explicitly lesbian film from the USA was *The Children's Hour* (US 62), the second film version of Lillian Hellman's play of the same name. Both pictures were directed by William Wyler, but in the earlier version, titled *These Three* (US 36), the original story of two schoolmistresses having an affair was changed to a heterosexual triangle involving two female teachers and a man. Wyler's remake had Shirley Maclaine and Audrey Hepburn in a sensitively-handled adaptation true to the spirit and the purpose of the play.

Kissing

The first screen kiss was performed in close up by May Irwin and John Rice in a filmed scene from the stage play *The Widow Jones* (US 96) and was described by a contemporary journal, *The Chap Book*, as 'absolutely disgusting'.

The first far eastern country to permit kissing in films was China, the first oriental screen kiss being bestowed on Miss Mamie Lee in *Two Women in the House* (Chn 26). In Japan, where kissing was considered 'unclean, immodest, indecorous, ungraceful and likely to spread disease'—at least by Tokyo's Prefect of Police—some 800,000 ft of kissing scenes were cut from American movies that same year. Indians reacted much the same way, though with less rigour about cuts. According to *The Report of the Indian Cinematograph Committee* (1928), during western films 'when a kissing scene is shown, the ladies turn their heads away'.

Japan's first screen kiss was seen in *Hatachi no Seishun/Twenty-Year-Old Youth* (Jap 46), directed by Yasushi Sasaki. The honour of directing the inaugural kiss should have gone to Yasuki Chiba, who was planning to introduce the daring innovation in his aptly titled *Aru Yo no Seppun/A Certain Night's Kiss* (Jap 46), but he lost his nerve at the last moment and the big clinch between the two lovers was discreetly obscured by an open umbrella. Only four years later the sex act itself was brought to the Japanese screen in *Yuki Fujin Ezu/Picture of Madame Yuki* (Jap 50).

Kissing in Indian Films

Kissing was voluntarily renounced by the film producers themselves in the mid-thirties on the grounds that Indians did not kiss in public, and to see them doing so on the screen was pandering to an alien custom. After Independence, when the producers decided that there were sound commercial reasons for a little occidental decadence, they found themselves up against the stern morality of the censors. Some latitude was permitted, however, if at least one of the partners in the act was a foreigner, or in the case of 'international' versions of films for overseas release only. In one instance two Indians were allowed to be seen kissing each other because the girl was playing the part of a Portuguese. The breakthrough came only in 1977, when for the first time in over 40 years two Indians playing Indians were able to kiss in a major film shown in their own country. The historic embrace took place between Zeenat Aman, a former Miss Asia, and the sub-continent's most romantic leading man, Shashi Kapoor, in Raj Kapoor's *Satyam Shivam Sundaram* (Ind 77), a musical melodrama about a man who falls in love with the compelling voice of an adivasi girl and only learns on their wedding night that half of her face is hideously disfigured by a burn.

The last major film-producing country still banning kissing on screen is Turkey.

The longest screen kiss in a commercial feature movie occupied 3 min 5 sec of Regis Toomey's and Jane Wyman's time in *You're in the Army Now* (US 40). Naomi Levine spent the full duration of Andy Warhol's non-commercial 50 min *Kiss* (US 63) kissing Rufus Collins, Gerald Malanga and Ed Saunders.

> Singapore has special rules about 'suggestive prolonged kissing': it is not allowed in Malay language films, but is acceptable in others. In Pennsylvania in the 1930s, horizontal screen kisses were banned, vertical allowed.

The most kisses in a single film were the 127 bestowed by John Barrymore on Mary Astor and Estelle Taylor in *Don Juan* (US 26).

The only Hollywood leading lady who never kissed her leading man on screen was the Chinese-American star Anna May Wong (1907–61). She nearly achieved it in *The Road to Dishonour* (GB 29); indeed her kissing scene with John Longden was shot, but cut by the censor on the grounds that inter-racial love would be offensive to some patrons. One other heroine of the American screen also faced a kissing ban: Marguerite Clark (1881–1940), at one time Mary Pickford's chief rival as 'America's Sweetheart'. In this case the ban was imposed by her husband, Harry Palmerson-Williams, whom she married in 1918. Although she made another dozen films, her career was severely damaged by the marital edict and she retired in 1921.

Cinema and the Call of Nature

It was sometimes remarked, in the days before stark realism invaded the screen, that nobody in films ever seemed to feel the call of nature. As early as 1912, though, a Hungarian company called Hunnia had made a film titled *Bitter Love or Hunyadi János* (Hun 12) which was entirely about going to the lavatory—the plot centring round an aperient water called Hunyadi János which had an extraordinarily stimulating effect on the bowels. Not surprisingly, Hollywood was a good deal more reticent on the subject and it was not until 1928 that King Vidor's *The Crowd* (US 28), better remembered as the first feature film to make extensive use of outdoor New York locations, pioneered in another direction with a bathroom set which actually showed a lavatory bowl. The first film in which people are depicted performing the natural functions on screen was the Soviet production *Earth* (USSR 30). Like most Russian films of the period it is about tractors, and during the scene in question one of them runs out of water and peasants urinate in the radiator. Many years were to pass before the bowel action was depicted on screen and it was the uninhibited Australians who led the way with *The Office Picnic* (Aus 72), in which a character is seen seated on the lavatory with the door open. In a French film of the same year, *La Grande Bouffe* (Fr 72), Michel Piccoli perishes in his own excrement as a result of overeating. This was also the first film in which a character audibly breaks wind.

SPORT

Olympic Movies

Considering the drama as well as the popular appeal of the Olympics, it is perhaps surprising that they are not more often used as the setting for movies. These are the ones that have been made to date:

☆ *The Olympic Hero* (US 28) Comedy starring Charley Paddock, the American sprinter portrayed by Dennis Christopher in *Chariots of Fire* (GB 81).

☆ *Olympic Honeymoon* (GB 36) A light-hearted romp in which Claude Hulbert, as an estranged honeymooner, is mistaken for an ice hockey champion and helps Britain win the gold at the Winter Olympics. (The British team did in fact win in 1936.)

☆ *Charlie Chan at the Olympics* (US 37) Hokum about spies being pursued by the inscrutable Chinese detective to Berlin, where 'No. 1 Son' is a member of the US swimming team competing at the Olympics.

☆ *Jim Thorpe—All-American* (US 51) Biopic with Burt Lancaster as the Oklahoma Indian who won the decathlon and pentathlon events at Stockholm in 1912, but was forced to return his medals when it was found he had played a few games of semi-pro baseball for coffee-and-cake money.

☆ *The Bob Mathias Story* (US 54) Autobiopic with Bob Mathias, who won the decathlon twice, at London in 1948 and Helsinki in 1952, playing himself and his wife Melba playing herself.

☆ *Geordie* (GB 55) Bill Travers as a weakly Scots lad who takes a body-building course and wins the hammer throwing event at the Melbourne Olympics.

☆ *It Happened in Athens* (US 62) Trax Cotton as untrained Greek shepherd lad winning the marathon at the first modern Olympics at Athens in 1896.

☆ *Walk, Don't Run* (US 66) Cary Grant, in his last film appearance, as one of an ill-assorted group who wind up living in Samantha Eggar's flat during the Tokyo Olympics due to shortage of accommodation.

☆ *The Games* (GB 70) Story of four marathon runners from different countries competing at Rome Olympics. Starring Ryan O'Neal and Michael Crawford.

☆ *Wilma* (US 77) TVM story of Wilma Rudolph (Shirley Jo Finney), Tennessee girl who overcame physical handicaps to become champion sprinter and winner of three golds at the 1960 Rome Olympics.

☆ *International Velvet* (GB 78) Tatum O'Neal as niece of the Velvet played by Elizabeth Taylor as a child in *National Velvet* (US 44). Orphan comes to Britain from US, has difficulty settling down, takes to show-jumping at prompting of Velvet (Nanette Newman), and eventually triumphs in Olympics.

☆ *Running* (Can 79) Michael Douglas as American marathon runner overcoming injury at the Montreal Olympics. (It is typical of Canadian films that the hero is American rather than Canadian.)

☆ *Dawn* (Aus 79) Bronwyn Mackay-Payne plays the big Aussie swimmer Dawn Fraser who won three golds at Melbourne 1956, Rome 1960 and Tokyo 1964 and was then banned for ten years for stealing a flag at the Tokyo Games.

☆ *Goldengirl* (US 79) Susan Anton as lissom blonde runner brainwashed and physically coerced by unscrupulous coach and adoptive father into winning three golds at the 1980 Moscow Olympics. (As the US did not compete, all the agony would have been for nothing.)

☆ *Chariots of Fire* (GB 81) David Puttnam's quadruple Oscar winner about Jewish athlete, Harold Abrahams (Ben Cross), who provoked controversy by hiring a professional coach to train him for the 1924 Paris Olympics, and Eric Liddel (Ian Charleson), the Scottish sprinter who refused to race on the Sabbath.

Robby Benson strikes gold as Sioux Indian athlete Billy Mills in *Running Brave* (Can 83). (*Kobal*)

☆ *Running Brave* (Can 83) Biopic of Sioux Indian Billy Mills, winner of the 10,000 metres at the 1964 Tokyo Games.
☆ *Nadia* (US 84) Leslie Weiner and Johann Carlo as the younger and older Nadia Comaneci, elf-like Romanian who took the triple gold for gymnastics at the 1976 Montreal Olympics.
☆ *Spiker* (US 85) Fictional story of how the US Olympic volleyball team is selected and trained. Unusually the good ol' USA loses in this one.
☆ *Going for Gold* (US/Can 88) Comedy about an overweight athlete who resurrects the forgotten sport of Bosnonian coneball in order to compete in the Olympics.

HOLLYWOOD AND SPORT—THE LEAGUE TABLE

Hollywood had made a total of 727 feature films with a sports background up to the end of 1987. The most popular sport as a subject for screen drama is boxing, with just under 25 per cent of the total, followed by horse racing with 16.2 per cent and American Football with 14.2 per cent. The number of films devoted to each sport in each decade is listed below, with the various sports in rank order according to their individual totals. Only films about competitive sport have been included, so few of the films of Esther Williams, for example, have been counted under swimming.

	1910–19	1920–29	1930–39	1940–49	1950–59	1960–69	1970–79	1980–87	Total
Boxing	–	61	39	29	28	4	11	7	179
Horse Racing	1	32	44	21	11	5	3	1	118
American Football	2	23	38	14	10	5	8	3	103
Motor Racing	2	23	20	3	10	16	8	–	82
Baseball	5	9	7	7	13	1	7	4	53
Athletics	–	8	2	–	3	3	8	5	29
Basketball	–	2	2	–	3	2	12	4	25
Wrestling	–	–	2	1	–	–	7	6	16
Golf	–	1	4	–	3	4	1	2	15
Motor Cycle Racing	–	2	1	–	1	3	6	1	14
Polo	–	6	4	–	–	–	–	–	10
Speedboat Racing	–	1	6	–	–	–	2	–	9
Rowing	–	5	4	–	–	–	–	–	9
Skiing	–	–	1	1	–	2	2	3	9
Ice Hockey	–	–	3	1	1	–	1	1	7
Tennis	–	1	1	–	1	–	3	1	7
Swimming	–	2	–	–	1	–	1	2	6
Cycle Racing	–	–	1	–	–	–	1	4	6
Roller Skating	–	–	–	–	1	–	4	–	5
Pool	–	–	–	–	–	1	1	2	4
Soccer	–	–	–	–	–	–	–	3	3
Gymnastics	–	–	–	–	–	–	–	2	2
Ice Skating	–	–	1	–	–	–	1	–	2
Showjumping	–	–	–	–	–	1	–	1	2
Skateboarding	–	–	–	–	–	–	2	–	2
Yacht Racing	–	–	1	–	–	1	–	–	2
Angling	–	–	–	–	–	1	–	–	1
Bowling	–	–	–	–	–	–	1	–	1
Cockfighting	–	–	–	–	–	–	1	–	1
Dog Racing	–	–	1	–	–	–	–	–	1
Fencing	–	1	–	–	–	–	–	–	1
Ice Yachting	–	1	–	–	–	–	–	–	1
Volleyball	–	–	–	–	–	–	–	1	1
Weightlifting	–	–	–	–	–	–	1	–	1

SOCCER FILMOGRAPHY

Soccer is not only the most popular spectator sport in the world, it is also the most international of all sports in film terms. Although far fewer feature films have been made about soccer than about boxing or horse racing, they emanate from a much wider range of countries. No other sport has produced fiction features from as many countries as these: Argentina, Austria, Belgium, Brazil, Britain, Bulgaria, Czechoslovakia, Denmark, Egypt, France, Germany, Hong Kong, Hungary, India, Israel, Italy, Japan, Korea, Poland, Portugal, Romania, Spain, Sweden, Tunisia, Uruguay, USA, USSR, Yugoslavia. The filmography below contains the titles of all known soccer films to the end of 1987.

The Winning Goal (GB 20)
The Ball of Fortune (GB 26)
Monsieur mon chauffeur (Bel 28)
Der König der Mittelstürmer (Ger 28)
Die Elf Teufel (Ger 28)
The Great Game (GB 30)
Soccerfans (Cz 31)
Up for the Cup (GB 31)
Our Football Eleven (Cz 36)
Goal! (Arg 36)
The Goalkeeper (USSR 36)
The Klapzuba Football Eleven (Cz 38)
Alma e Corpo de Uma Raça (Bra 38)
The Arsenal Stadium Mystery (GB 39)
Bola ao Centro (Por 47)
Plavi 9 (Yug 50)
The Football Parson (Den 51)
The Merry Duel (Cz 51)
In the Penalty Area (Cz 51)
Women Who Have Run Off-Side (Cz 51)
The Great Game (GB 53)

Small Town Story (GB 53)
11:1 (GDR 55)
A Football Star (Hun 56)
Saeta Rubia (Sp 56)
The Goalkeeper Lives in our Street (Cz 57)
Favourite No 13 (Bul 58)
Gambe d'oro (It 58)
Il Nemico di mia moglie/My Wife's Enemy (It 59)
Our Lads (Rom 59)
Los Economicamente debiles (Sp 60)
Football Fans (Cz 60)
The Last Goal (Hun 61)
Comrade President the Centre-Forward (Yug 62)
Ivana in the Forward Line (Cz 63)
Pelota de cuero (Arg 63)
Third Time (USSR 63)
Allez France (Fr 64)
Fadni odpoledne (Cz 65)
Let's Go Wakadaisho (Jap 67)
Somos los mejores! (Arg 67)
Fish, Football and Girls (Isr 68)
Volver a vivi (Sp 68)
Fight for the Glory (Jap 69)
Aconteceu no Maracanã (Bra 69)
Il Presidente del Borgorosso Football Club (It 70)
Shoot Paragon! (Pol 70)
Sekundomer/Stop Watch (USSR 70)
Women Offside (Cz 71)
The Goalkeeper's Fear of the Penalty (FRG/Aut 71)
Bloomfield (Isr 71)
I Due maghi de pallone (It 71)
Mother Love (S.Kor 72)
Willi wird das Kind schon schaukeln (FRG 72)
Tochka, Tochka, Zapiataia/Dot, Dot, a Comma (USSR 72)
Football of the Good Old Days (Hun 73)

A Goal, Another Goal (USSR 73)
Stubby (Swe 74)
Pandhattam/Play Ball (Ind 74)
Pirveli Mertskhali/The First Swallow (USSR 75)
Eleven Hopefuls (USSR 76)
Furia Española (Sp 76)
The Memorable Day (Bul 76)
Takaya Ona, Igra (USSR 77)
The Boys in Company C (HK 77)
Trener/The Coach (Yug 78)
Striker (Ind 78)
Yesterday's Hero (GB 79)
Everything for Football (Rom 79)
Coup de Tête (Fr 80)
Mundita lito (Uru 81)
The Match (Hun 81)
Gregory's Girl (GB 81)
Escape to Victory (US 81)
At Start of Play (USSR 82)
Pra Frente Brazil (Bra 82)
Eccezzziunale . . . Veramente (It 82)
White Wing (Bra 82)
Referees, Fans and Soccer Players (It 82)
Copa de Ora (Uru 82)
Soccer Attack Centre (It 83)
El Harrif/Street Player (Egy 83)
Was Kostet der Sieg/What Price Victory (Aut 83)
The Champions (HK 83)
Those Glory, Glory Days (GB 83)
Young Giants (US 83)
Excuse Me—Are You Watching Football? (GDR 83)
The Football Master (It 84)
A Mort L'Arbitre (Fr 84)
The Cup (Tun 86)
Ultimo Momento (It 87)
Hotshot (US 87)

Above: Bill Forsyth's all-Scottish *Gregory's Girl* (GB 81) charmed audiences with its story of first love on the football field. Dee Hepburn played the girl soccer ace, object of inept goalie John Gordon Sinclair's attentions.
Right: Love is not the only emotion inspired by women on the football field. This lady referee has aroused the hostility of both teams at once in *Women Offside* (Cz 71).

*W*ESTERNS

The earliest subjects of western interest were *Sioux Indian Ghost Dance, Indian War Council* and *Buffalo Dance*, made by the Edison Co. at West Orange, NJ on 24 September 1894. *Bucking Broncho* followed on 16 October and is notable for the first appearance of a cowboy in a film—Lee Martin of Colorado, who is seen riding *Sunfish* in a corral, while his 'pardner' Frank Hammit stands on the rails and discharges the first of many tens of thousands of pistol shots that were to be seen (and later heard) in almost every western that followed. Annie Oakley, immortalized in *Annie Get Your Gun* (US 50), made her film debut a fortnight later on 1 November 1894.

The first westerns were copyrighted by the American Mutoscope & Biograph Co. on 21 September 1903. One was titled *Kit Carson* (US 03) and related the story of its hero's capture by Indians and subsequent escape through the agency of a beautiful Indian maiden. There were 11 scenes and the film had a running time of 21 minutes, making it the longest dramatic picture (other than Passion Plays) produced in America at that time. The other film, titled *The Pioneers* (US 03), showed the burning of a settler's homestead by Indians, who kill the homesteader and his wife and carry off his daughter. The picture ends with the dramatic rescue of the child by frontiersmen who have found the bodies of her parents. Running time was approximately 15 minutes. Both pictures were directed by Wallace McCutcheon and filmed on location in the Adirondack Mountains of New York State. *Kit Carson* was made on 8 September 1903 and *The Pioneers* two days later.

The more celebrated *The Great Train Robbery* (US 03), generally and erroneously described as the first western and often as the first film to tell a story, was copyrighted by the Edison Co. some six weeks later, on 1 December 1903.

Until 1906 all westerns were shot in the Eastern states, generally in New Jersey. **The first western made in the West** was Biograph's *A California Hold Up* (US 06), shot by O. M. Grove.

The first feature-length western was Lawrence B. McGill's *Arizona* (US 13), an All Star Feature Corporation production with Cyril Scott and Gertrude Shipman. It was released in August 1913, six months before Cecil B. DeMille's *The Squaw Man* (US 14), usually credited as the first feature.

The first western in colour was a British production by a Dutch director, Theo Bouwmeester's *Fate* (GB 11), made in Kinemacolor by the Natural Colour Kinematograph Co. Set in Texas, it was about an Englishman who becomes leader of a tribe of renegade Indians.

The first feature-length colour western was the Famous Players–Lasky production *Wanderer of the Wasteland* (US 24), a Zane Grey horse opera from the novel of the same name. Photographed in two-colour Technicolor by Arthur Ball, it was directed by Irvin Willar, starred Jack Holt, Noah Beery and Billie Dove, and was premièred in Los Angeles on 21 June 1924.

The first western talkie was Fox-Movietone's *In Old Arizona* (US 28), directed by Raoul Walsh and Irving Cummings and starring Edmund Lowe,

> There has been at least one western in which not a single gunshot is heard. *They Passed This Way* aka *Four Faces West* (US 48) starred Joel McCrea as a bank robber on the run from Charles Bickford's Pat Garrett. Strong characterization and suspense proved no substitute for the traditional showdown in Main Street as far as the fans were concerned and the film bombed at the box office.

Warner Baxter and Dorothy Burgess. It was premièred at the Criterion Theater, Los Angeles, on 25 December 1928.

The first feature-length film with an all-Indian cast was Edward S. Curtis's *The Land of the Head Hunters* (US 14), a story of the son of a tribal chief and his quest for manhood. It was filmed on location on the North-West coast of America.

The first western with Indian dialogue was Universal's talkie serial *The Indians Are Coming* (US 31), in which Chief Thunderbird spoke in his native Sioux. In 1970 Dame Judith Anderson, an Australian, successfully coped with all-Sioux dialogue in her role as Buffalo Cow Head in *A Man Called Horse* (US 70).

The highest earning western was *Butch Cassidy and the Sundance Kid* (US 69), with North American rentals during its initial release of $29.2 million. According to David Pirie's *Anatomy of the Movies* (London, 1981), however, it is beaten into second place if inflation is taken into account. Applying the US cost of living index to the rentals earned during initial release, the real value of the $10 million returned by *Duel in the Sun* (US 47), a David O Selznick production starring Joseph Cotten and Gregory Peck, exceeds the inflation adjusted value of *Butch Cassidy*'s rentals.

The first western star was G. M. 'Broncho Billy' Anderson (1881–1971), who was to have been cast as one of the villains for his western debut in *The Great Train Robbery* (US 03), but proved so inept on a horse that he had to be relegated to extra work. Notwithstanding this inauspicious start to a career dedicated to the relationship of man and horse, Anderson starred in *Life of an American Cowboy* (US 06) and then went west with a Selig location crew to make one of the earliest westerns shot in the real west—*The Girl from Montana* (US 07). The following year he established a West Coast studio for Essany at Niles, California, and decided to embark on a series of one-reelers based on a central character, reasoning that the weakness of the Edison, Selig and Essany westerns he had played in was that they lacked clearly-defined heroes. His original intention had been to find an actor expert in horsemanship whom he could direct, but actors of any kind being in short supply in California, he eventually decided to cast himself in the role. *Broncho Billy and the Baby* (US 10), a sentimental story of a man-gone-wrong who is reformed by the love of a good woman, was the first in a series of nearly 400 Broncho Billy pictures which established Anderson as a major star. A curious feature of the films was their total lack of continuity. If Broncho Billy married in one picture, he would be a bachelor again in the next; he would be reformed inexhaustibly by a succession of good women; and death would only interrupt his career in the saddle until the opening scenes of the next one-reeler. He turned to features in 1918, but competition from his successors, Tom Mix and W. S.

Hart, was too strong. After a period of producing Stan Laurel comedies for Metro, he retired in 1923. Nearly half a century after his last silent western role in *The Son of a Gun* (US 18), he made a single excursion into talkies with a guest appearance in *The Bounty Killer* (US 67).

The most popular western star was determined annually with a poll of exhibitors conducted by *Motion Picture Herald* between 1936 and 1954 (when the 'B' western ended). Buck Jones won in 1936, Gene Autry each year from 1937–42, and Roy Rogers from 1943–54 inclusive.

The western hero most often portrayed on screen has been William Frederick Cody (1846–1917), otherwise known as 'Buffalo Bill', a character who has appeared in 49 dramatic films to date. William Bonney (1860–81), alias Billy the Kid, has been portrayed in 46 films; Jesse James (1847–82) in 37 films; Wild Bill Hickock (1837–76) in 36 films; General George Armstrong Custer (1839–76) in 31 films; and Wyatt Earp (1848–1929) in 22 films.

The most prolific western directors were Lesley Selander (1900–79), with at least 107 known feature-length westerns made between 1935 and 1967, and Lambert Hillyer (1893–), with 106 recorded titles between 1917 and 1949.

The only western directed by a woman was Ruth Ann Baldwin's curiously titled Universal production *'49-'17* (US 17).

Gene Autry was voted most popular Western star for the third time in 1939, the year he made this goodwill visit to Britain with his horse 'Champion'.

> The days of the 'real West' overlapped with the movies' version to the extent that there were still authentic western heroes alive—such as 'Buffalo Bill' Cody (d. 1917) and Marshal Wyatt Earp (d. 1929)—when Hollywood was busy creating mythology. One early western, the Selig Co.'s *Custer's Last Stand* (US 08), included among its cast three aged Sioux Indians who had actually participated in the Battle of the Little Big Horn (1876) as young warriors. The producer's hope that he could depend on them as historical advisers came, however, to naught. 'The most we could get out of them,' he declared, 'was that the fight was over so quickly that they could' remember little about it.'

Western Output

It is estimated that there have been over 3500 multi-reel westerns made since the first two-reeler, the Oklahoma Natural Mutoscene Co.'s *The Bank Robbery* (US 08).

SIX

PERFORMERS

The first motion picture film to employ the use of actors was a brief costume drama, *The Execution of Mary Queen of Scots* (US 95), which was shot by Alfred Clark of Raff & Gammon, Kinetoscope proprietors, at West Orange, NJ on 28 August 1895. The part of Mary was played by Mr R. L. Thomas, Secretary and Treasurer of the Kinetoscope Co. After approaching the block and laying his head on it, Thomas removed himself, the camera was stopped, and a dummy substituted. The camera was then started again for the decapitation scene. This was **the first use of trick photography or special effect work** in a film.

The first person employed to play a comedy role in a film was M. Clerc, a gardener employed by Mme Lumière at Lyons, France. He was aptly cast in the part of the gardener in the Lumière production *L'Arroseur arrosé* (Fr 95), a film premièred at the Grand Café in Paris on 28 December 1895. Clerc is seen watering flowerbeds with a hose. A mischievous boy, played by a 14-year-old Lumière apprentice called Duval, creeps up behind the gardener and places his foot on the hose to stop the flow of water. As the perplexed gardener holds the nozzle up to his eye to see if there is a blockage, young Duval removes his foot and capers with joy as a burst of water gushes into M. Clerc's face. Clerc and Duval were the first performers to be seen on the screen, as *The Execution of Mary Queen of Scots* had been made for viewing in Edison's 'peep-show' Kinetoscope.

The first professional actors to perform in movies made their screen debuts almost simultaneously on either side of the Atlantic. In America John Rice and May Irwin performed the first screen kiss in *The Widow Jones* aka *May Irwin Kiss* (US 96), which was a scene from the Broadway comedy *The Widow Jones* filmed by Raff and Gammon in April 1896. At about the same time in Britain, Fred Storey played the title role in R. W. Paul's *The Soldier's Courtship* (GB 96), a short comedy made on the roof of the Alhambra Theatre, Leicester Square, and premièred underneath. Storey also got to kiss the heroine, Julie Seale of the Alhambra Ballet. Performers of established reputation rarely appeared in films prior to about 1908 in France and Britain and later elsewhere. There were, however, a few notable exceptions during the primitive period, including Auguste van Biene's role as the cellist in Esme Collings' *The Broken Melody* (GB 96), from the play of the same name; Joseph Jefferson's performance in American Mutoscope & Biograph's *Rip Van Winkle* (US 96); Beerbohm Tree and Julia Neilson in *King John* (GB 99); Sarah Bernhardt in *Hamlet* (Fr 00); Coquelin in *Cyrano de Bergerac* (Fr 00); Marie Tempest and Hayden Coffin in *San Toy* (GB 00); and Marie Tempest, Ben Webster and H. B. Warner in *English Nell* (GB 00). The only one of these to make a career as a screen actor was H. B. Warner (1876–1958), whose most notable performances were in *King of Kings* (US 27) as Jesus Christ, *Mr Deeds Goes to Town* (US 36), *Lost Horizon* (US 37) and *Victoria the Great* (GB 37).

The Star System

This emerged in the United States and Europe simultaneously. Previous to 1910 it was the deliberate policy of film-makers not to give their lead players any star billing, lest they should overvalue their services. First to break with this was the American production company Kalem, which in January 1910 began issuing star portraits and posters with the artistes names credited. A few weeks later Carl Laemmle, who had succeeded in luring the still anonymous Florence Lawrence away from Biograph to work for IMP, pulled the kind of outrageous publicity stunt that has enlivened and bedevilled the industry ever since, and in the process created the first real movie star. He began by arranging for a story to break in the St Louis papers that the actress had been killed in a street-car accident. Public interest in the supposed tragedy having been fully aroused, Laemmle placed the following advertisement in the same papers on 10 March 1910: 'The blackest and at the same time the silliest lie yet circulated by the enemies of IMP was the story foisted on the public of St Louis last week to the effect that Miss Lawrence, "The Imp Girl", formerly known as "The Biograph Girl", had been killed by a street car. It was a black lie so cowardly. We now announce our next film *The Broken Path*.' This was followed up with personal appearances by Miss Lawrence and a long interview in the *St Louis Post-Dispatch*; within a year her name was appearing on film posters in larger type than the title.

In Europe the practice of publicizing star names began the same year with the outstanding success of two films, one from Denmark, the other from Germany. Asta Nielsen's bravura performance in *The Abyss* (Den 10), one of the first long films to demonstrate a true sense of dramatic construction, brought a hitherto little-known actress almost immediate international recognition and the first of the really prodigious star salaries (c.f. Artistes' earnings, pp.

67–70). Germany's box office success of the year was *Das Liebesglück der Blinden/The Love of the Blind Girl* (Ger 10), starring 'The Messter Girl', a designation that cloaked the identity of Oskar Messter's leading player Henny Porten, who had also scripted the picture. It was received with such acclaim by filmgoers that Messter was persuaded to reveal her name. Once her name was on the credits, Henny proceeded to justify the producers' worst fears by demanding an increase in salary—from the equivalent of $50 a month to $56. Messter refused and she walked straight out of the studio. Having failed to call what he thought was a bluff, the producer sent his assistant, Kurt Stark, to fetch the girl back with a promise that she could have the raise. Henny returned to the studio, married Stark, and went on to become Germany's idol of the silent screen.

Right: Katsuo Mikoshiba, the Nipponese Chaplin.

Below: The lunatics take over the asylum. Doug 'n' Mary and Charlie Chaplin have something to look happy about. Already the three highest paid stars in Hollywood, they had just combined forces as United Artists to ensure they got the lion's share of the profits from their movies. (*SI*)

Not Charlie Chaplin

No actor has been portrayed on screen by *other* actors as often as Charlie Chaplin. It started with Leslie Henson playing Chaplin in a satire by James Barrie called *The Real Thing At Last* (GB 16), which was about an American film producer modernizing *Macbeth*. In the same year Fred Evans did a Chaplin role in *Pimple—Himself and Others* (GB 16) and meanwhile Australia's Ern Vockler was doing Chaplin impersonations on stage and appeared as the little tramp in a film titled *Charlie at the Sydney Show* (Aus 16). Essany followed with *Chase Me Charlie* (US

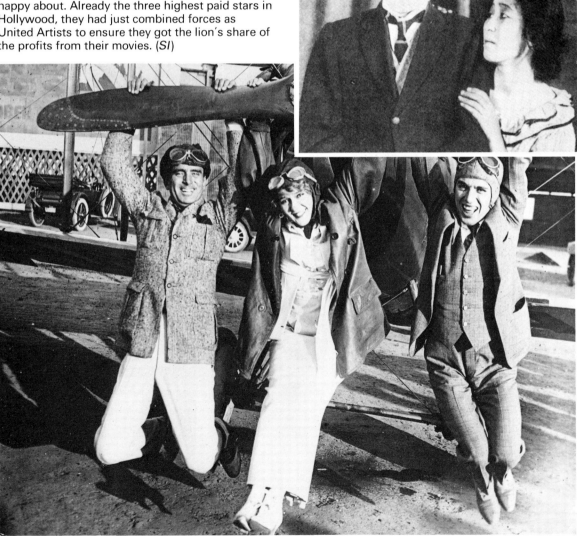

17), in which Graham Douglas impersonated Chaplin (who had left Essany for Mutual) in a compilation of genuine Chaplin extracts made into a story with linking footage. The Ming Hsing Film Co. of Shanghai made two 'Chaplin films' in the early twenties—*The King of Comedy Visits China* (Chn 22) and *Disturbance at a Peculiar Theatre* (Chn 22)—with British amateur actor Richard Bell taking the part of Charlie. Japan also had a home-grown Chaplin in the person of Katsuo Mikoshiba, who looked almost indistinguishable from the real thing in his baggy pants, bowler and toothbrush moustache, and Germany had her own Charlie Kaplin. The Chaplin impersonation industry seems to have come to a halt with a full-scale biopic, an unauthorized *Life Story of Charles Chaplin* (GB 26) starring Chick Wango in the title role, which was suppressed and never shown. Recently, however, there has been a Chaplin 'comeback'. Chinese comedian Dean Saki played the title role in *Chinese Chaplin and the Kung Fu Kid in Laughing Times* (HK 81), in which the little tramp befriends a poor but beautiful orphan girl obviously inspired by Paulette Goddard's barefoot waif in *Modern Times* (US 36).

Artistes' Earnings

Earnings which have now reached as much as $20 million for a single film began at a level commensurate with the penny gaff milieu of early film-making. The earliest known wage rate was the gold Louis ($4.30 or 17s) per day paid in the late 1890s by Star Films of Paris, but not all production companies were so generous. Gene Gauntier was offered $3 to play the lead in Biograph's *The Paymaster* (US 06), the story of a mill-girl in love with the manly young paymaster of the mill. Miss Gauntier was required to be thrown into the millstream by the villain, which she allowed him to do, not liking to mention that she was unable to swim. The producer was so pleased with her pluck that the $3 fee was raised to $5. Alma Lund, who played the female lead in the first film drama made in Norway—*Dangerous Life of a Fisherman* (Nor 07)—was paid the equivalent of $1.50 for her part; the boy who played her son got 75c. R. W. Paul paid Britain's first professional film actor, Johnny Butt, a daily wage of 5s ($1.25) in 1899, which was rather better than the 4s ($1) a day accorded to Chrissie White when she joined the Hepworth Co. at Walton-on-Thames in 1908. 'When I really got on,' she recalled, 'I received 8s a day, and when I was a star they paid me 50—shillings, not pounds.' Dave Aylott, who joined Cricks & Martin of Mitcham in 1909, remembered that their terms were 7s 6d a day for principal parts, 5s for minor parts, plus 1s 6d travelling expenses to Mitcham and a bread and cheese lunch with beer. In America at this time the $5 a day received by Mary Pickford when she joined Biograph in 1909 seems to

have become standard throughout the industry, nothing extra being paid for 'star' roles.

The escalation in salaries, when it came, was rapid and had to do with two factors: the use of major names from the stage, who had to be paid highly to demean themselves in this way; and the introduction of the 'star' system (c.f. Star system, p. 65) from 1910 onwards. The change began with Film d'Art in Paris, a company established in 1908 to produce prestige films with prestige players. Their leading artistes were paid the equivalent of $40 for each rehearsal and $200 for the actual shoot. Featured players, however, received as little as $2 to $3 a day for services in a major film like *Germinal* (Fr 13), for which the star, Henry Krauss, was paid $700. In England Will Barker paid Sir Herbert Beerbohm Tree a record £1000 to play Wolsey in *Henry VIII* (GB 11), a two-reeler which was shot in a single day. How far this was from the norm is indicated by the fact that the following year Barker was able to secure the lead player of his *Hamlet* (GB 12), Charles Raymond, for just 10s— which included his services as director of the film!

The first superstar salary was earned not by any of the rising American players, but by Denmark's Asta Nielsen. For her debut in *The Abyss* (Den 10) she was paid a modest 200kr ($53.60), but the film rocketed her to stardom and by the end of 1912 she was under contract to Berlin producer Paul Davidson with guaranteed annual earnings of $80,000. Compared to Asta Nielsen's salary of over $1500 a week, the highest paid stars in America were Gene Gauntier at $200 a week and Florence Lawrence at $250 a week. At this time Mary Pickford, who was soon to eclipse them all, was trailing at $175 a week at Biograph. The following year, however, Adolph Zukor lured her to Famous Players at $500 a week and this was doubled in 1914 and doubled again in 1915. Already the highest paid woman in the world, on 24 June 1916 she signed a new contract that put her on a par with the highest paid man in the world— Charles Chaplin, who had contracted with Mutual earlier in the year at a salary of $670,000. Miss Pickford's earnings were now half the profits of all her pictures, with a $10,000 p.w. minimum, plus a $300,000 single payment bonus, plus $150,000 p.a. to her mother for 'goodwill', plus $40,000 for examining scenarios prior to signing.

> Samuel Goldwyn on doing business with Mary Pickford: 'It took longer to make one of Mary's contracts than it did to make one of Mary's pictures.'

In the meantime Francesca Bertini, Italian 'diva', had become Europe's highest paid star in 1915 at $175,000 p.a., only slightly behind the $200,000 p.a. that Mary Pickford was then earning. European earnings, however, were never to rise above this before World War II, apart from the $450,000 that Alexander Korda paid Marlene Dietrich to star in *Knight Without Armour* (GB 37). American earnings continued to spiral upward, but with the three highest paid stars—Mary Pickford, Charlie Chaplin and Douglas Fairbanks—combined together as producers under the distribution banner of United Artists from 1919 onwards, it is hard to assess their new earning power. In that same year Roscoe 'Fatty' Arbuckle had become the first star with a guaranteed minimum of $1 million a year, but his contract with Paramount only lasted until scandal destroyed his career in 1922 and he became the first star to be formally banned.

No other star of the silent era matched Arbuckle's salary, but Nazimova was reported to be the highest salaried woman star in 1920 at $13,000 p.w., Tom Mix, the most popular cowboy star of the silents, was earning $17,500 p.w. in 1925 and Harold Lloyd's weekly wage was reported to be $40,000 p.w. in 1926. Salaries in Britain were a sad contrast. Alma Taylor, the most popular female star of the early twenties, was paid £60 p.w. by the Hepworth Co., but they were less generous with their leading male actor, Stewart Rome, who earned only £10 p.w. Ivor Novello, a matinee idol with a strong stage reputation, could command £3000–£4000 per film at his height in the late twenties, while the highest sum for a silent film was the £10,000 paid to music hall artiste Sir Harry Lauder for his role as a retired grocer in George Pearson's *Huntingtower* (GB 27).

The coming of sound and the Depression, almost simultaneously, forced most star salaries downward. In 1927 over 40 stars were reputedly earning $5000 or more a week. By 1931 only 23 stars had salaries of $3500 or more. Top earners in that year were Constance Bennett and John Barrymore at $30,000 p.w., a sum soon to be matched by Greta Garbo, who earned $250,000 for *The Painted Veil* (US 34) and the same for *Anna Karenina* (US 35). Highest earnings of 1935 were the $480,833 reported by Mae West to the tax authorities, well in excess of the highest earnings of 1938—Shirley Temple's $307,014, or 1939—James Cagney's $368,333, or even 1946 when Bing Crosby topped both at the box office (rated No. 1 in the Quigley Poll) and at the bank with $325,000. During the forties and fifties top star salaries per film were generally in the $250,000–$400,000 region, with a new peak of $500,000 for a British film—Elizabeth Taylor in *Suddenly Last Summer* (GB 59)—and $750,000 for an American production, earned by both John Wayne and William Holden (plus 20 per cent of the net) on *The Horse Soldiers* (US 59). The 1960s saw the era of the $1 million star salary for single pictures and in the 1970s the multi-million dollar contract. In the mid 1970s Charles Bronson was reported to be earning $20,000–$30,000, plus

$2500 living allowance, per day. However, this was far exceeded by Marlon Brando's reputed $3.5 million for 12 days shooting on *Superman* (GB 78), which works out at $290,000 per day. According to a special *Newsweek* report on Hollywood in 1978, the world's highest paid stars were Paul Newman, Robert Redford and Steve McQueen, commanding some $3 million per picture. Each of the three had turned down a $4 million offer to take the starring role in *Superman* (GB 78). Dustin Hoffman accepted precisely that amount for his transvestite role in *Tootsie* (US 82), but an even higher figure of $5 million plus percentage had already been paid to Burt Reynolds for *The Cannonball Run* (US 81). Sean Connery became the highest paid British star when he was lured back into Bond movies with a $5 million bait for *Never Say Never Again* (GB 83).

The highest paid actresses are Meryl Streep, who earned $4 million for *Out of Africa* (US 85) and the same for *Heartburn* (US 86), and Barbra Streisand, who became the first woman to reach the $5 million plateau with the less than sensational *Nuts* (US 88). Meanwhile the men were continuing to outstrip their female colleagues. Hoffman and Redford each took home $5.5 million for the much abused *Ishtar* (US 87), though Redford had already earned $6 mil-

Meryl Streep's paycheck for *Out of Africa* (US 85) was $4 million. (*Kobal*)

lion for *Out of Africa* (US 85) and $6.5 million for *Legal Eagles* (US 86). Clint Eastwood collected $6 million on *Heartbreak Ridge* (US 87) and Eddie Murphy consolidated his position as the highest-paid black film star when he banked $7 million for fast talking his way through *Beverly Hills Cop II* (US 87). The contract he signed with Paramount after his runaway success in the original *Beverly Hills Cop* (US 84), which was to give him $25 million for six films, has now been renegotiated at an undisclosed figure. The only hint Murphy would give was that he certainly hadn't negotiated down.

None of these multi-million dollar stars approach the earning capacity of the man who has now replaced Clint Eastwood as the world's most bankable star. Sylvester Stallone has not only broken the $10 million barrier but seems well on his way to doubling that, taking a comparatively modest $12 million for *Cobra* (US 86) and the same for *Over the Top* (US 87) before breaking his own record very handsomely with a reported $16 million (covering director's and writer's chores as well) for *Rocky IV* (US 87) and nearly $20 million for *Rambo III* (US 88). With the latter film Stallone topped the record formerly held by Marlon Brando for the highest sum earned by an actor for a single movie. On *Superman* (GB 78), Brando was originally paid nearly $3.5 million for 12 days shooting in his role as Superman's father—a not ungenerous $290,000 a day. In 1982 an out-of-court settlement awarded him a further $15 million, representing 11.3 per cent of the box-office gross, making a total of $18.5 million for his ten minutes of screen time.

With gross earnings, including royalties, of $74 million during the two years 1985 and 1986, Stallone's total wealth has been estimated by *Forbes Magazine* at $650 million, making him by far the richest star in the history of motion pictures.

The lowest salaries of recent years have seldom fallen below the £1500 that Olivia Hussey claimed she was paid for 11 months work while she was playing the female lead in Zeffirelli's *Romeo and Juliet* (GB 68)—at least in the west. In eastern countries and even Eastern Europe, different standards prevail. Teresa Izewska, star of the award-winning *Kanal* (Pol 57), revealed at the Cannes Film Festival that she earned the equivalent of $12 a month and that the Polish authorities had bought her one dress and one pair of shoes in order to represent them at the Festival. In 1973 *Variety* reported that China's biggest box office star, Shih Chung-chin, drew a salary of $20 a month. She slept in a communal dormitory with other actresses. Things are looking up, however, on the other side of the bamboo curtain. By 1980 a top Chinese star could earn a maximum of 250 yuan ($168) a month, though not all were so generously recompensed.

Sylvester Stallone, now the highest paid star in the world, claims that his total payment for playing this role in *The Lords of Flatbush* (US 74) was 25 free T-shirts. (*Kobal*)

Joan Chen, star of the first Anglo-Chinese co-production *The Last Emperor* (It/GB/Chn 88), was earning less than $8 a month in 1980 when she won the 100 Blossoms award as most popular actress. Her salary then went up to $24 a month. Top salary per film for Soviet stars is 6000 roubles (approx. £3750) for a 50-day schedule, and this modest emolument is subject to a 10 per cent withholding tax.

The lowest paid players in American pictures were found in black movies. White director Edgar G. Ulmer recalls paying the 50 chorus girls in *Moon Over Harlem* (US 39) 25c a day each. The shooting schedule was four days and the girls had to pay their car fares from Harlem to the studio in Jersey out of the $1 they earned for a week's work. A record zero budget for an entire cast was achieved by Action Pictures Co. for their all-black feature *Sugar Hill Baby* (US 38). The casting director announced with disarming frankness that there was no money available for salaries, the only inducement offered being the somewhat doubtful 'chance to continue to work in future in productions at good salaries'.

Leading players in Hollywood films expect rather more immediate rewards, but even for major motion pictures salaries may, on occasions, be modest. For what many fans reckon to be the most memorable role in movie history, that of Scarlett O'Hara in *Gone With the Wind* (US 39), Vivien Leigh (by no means a newcomer to the screen) was paid a not very princely $15,000. This was less than ice-skating champion turned film star Sonja Henie was then being paid for a week's work. Frank Sinatra earned only $8000 for his Oscar-winning performance in *From Here to Eternity* (US 53). Nodules on his throat had brought his singing career to a temporary halt and he was desperate to get back into movies at any price. A few years later his co-star in *The Man with the Golden Arm* (US 56), Kim Novak, was hired at her regular salary from Columbia of $100 a week, though producer Otto Preminger had to pay the studio $100,000 for her services. In the mid-1950s Paul Newman was getting a relatively meagre $17,500 for each of his Warner Bros' pictures; by the mid-1960s he was on $750,000 a film plus percentage. In the same kind of price bracket was James Dean, paid $18,000 for his standout performance in *East of Eden* (US 55). It was his fifth film but his first starring role and it rocketed him to instant stardom.

The most highly-paid stars have sometimes been victims of ingenious attempts by the unscrupulous to benefit from their box office drawing power without the formality of payment. In 1917 a film processor in Chicago created his own Chaplin feature film—at a time when Chaplin was the highest paid star in the world—by matching together shots from his old comedies and then interpolating material from Fox's sensational *The Daughter of the Gods* (US 16), in which Australian star Annette Kellerman appeared in the nude. By clever optical work, he succeeded in creating scenes in which Chaplin and the naked Antipodean beauty appeared to be performing together. The film was released to the underground trade as *Charlie, Son of the Gods*.

Even more audacious was Soviet director Sergei Komarov's deception that secured him the gratuitous services of not one but two superstars, Mary Pickford and Douglas Fairbanks. During the visit of the couple to Moscow in July 1926, Komarov posed as a newsreel cameraman and followed them round with a camera, shooting enough footage to piece together a full-length comedy feature after their departure. Titled *The Kiss of Mary Pickford* (USSR 26), it was an engaging tale of a film extra who is determined to kiss the 'world's sweetheart'—and succeeds! Most remarkable of all was the climactic sequence of the close embrace between Soviet hero and Hollywood heroine. Although the film has now been shown publicly in the west, no one has been able to offer a convincing explanation of how Komarov managed to contrive this scene.

Perhaps the last of the great western stars, Clint Eastwood had already been in movies for ten not very productive years when he was offered $15,000 to appear in a spaghetti western called *A Fistful of Dollars* (It 64). By 1972 he was the No. 1 star at the box office and between the mid-seventies and mid-eighties his pictures grossed a record $1400 million. Another star who found fame and fortune in the sixties was Dustin Hoffman. His worth was rated at $17,000 for the smash hit *The Graduate* (US 67) and $425,000 a couple of years later for the floppo *John and Mary* (US 69).

All of these stars were generously remunerated in comparison with Steve McQueen, whose total reward for playing the lead in tacky horror movie *The Blob* (US 58) was $3000. He was not invited to appear in the sequel, *Son of Blob* (US 71). By that time his fee would have been several times the whole budget of the movie. According to Sylvester Stallone, the world's highest paid film star, the only recompense he received for playing a leading role in *The Lords of Flatbush* (US 74) was 25 free T-shirts. Today as ever a performer may be bargain basement one moment and in the megabuck league the next. One Stephen J. Lewicki cast an unknown rock singer for the lead in *A Certain Feeling* (US 84) and has since been able to congratulate himself all the way to the bank that he secured the services of Madonna for $100 all in.

The first screen artiste to work on percentage was Nellie Stewart, who was paid £1000 plus a per cent of the gross for her role in *Sweet Nell of Old Drury* (Aus 11).

The first American artiste to receive a percentage deal was James O'Neill (father of Eugene), who played the wronged Edmond Dantes in Famous Players' maiden production *The Count of Monte Cristo* (US 13). O'Neill had played the part on stage no less than 4000 times over a period of 30 years and was both too old (65) and too ham for the screen version, but Daniel Frohman knew that his was the name which would draw theatregoers to the cinema and he offered the star 20 per cent of the net profits as an inducement. Returns were undermined by a rival Selig version of *The Count of Monte Cristo*, but the Famous Players version eventually grossed $45,539.32, of which O'Neill received $3813.32. As far as Hollywood was concerned, the major studios resisted allowing their players any cut of the profits until James Stewart succeeded in wresting a percentage from Universal-International for his memorable performance in *Winchester '73* (US 50). His share of the profits was $600,000, rather more than the 'King of Hollywood', Clark Gable, was paid by MGM for a year's work.

BIOPICS OF SCREEN STARS

These are relatively rare and have often concentrated on an aspect of the performer's life other than their screen career. The biopics of Diana Barrymore and Lillian Roth were concerned with their subjects' alcoholism, those of Eddie Cantor and Al Jolson dwelt mainly on their singing careers, and Annette Kellerman's on her swimming exploits, while *The George Raft Story* recounted the star's pre-Hollywood days in the gangster milieu of 20s New York. The following performers have had their life stories, in whole or in part, portrayed in feature movies:

BUD ABBOTT (1895–1974) and LOU COSTELLO (1906–59) *Bud and Lou* (US 78, TVM). Harvey Korman and Buddy Hackett in a behind-the-scenes story of the comedy duo's stormy personal relationship.

DIANA BARRYMORE (1921–60) *Too Much Too Soon* (US 58) with Dorothy Malone in the story, based on Miss Barrymore's memoirs, of how she went to Hollywood to look after her alcoholic father John Barrymore (Errol Flynn) and herself succumbed to drink.

HUMPHREY BOGART (1899–1957) *Bogie* (US 80, TVM) with Kevin O'Connor, based on Joe Hyams' biography of the same title.

EDDIE CANTOR (1892–1964) *The Eddie Cantor Story* (US 53) with Keefe Brasselle in the name role. Cantor himself played a bit part and also sang the songs off-screen.

LON CHANEY (1883–1930) *The Man of a Thousand Faces* (US 57) with James Cagney as the character actor and contortionist extraordinary of the silent screen.

CHARLES CHAPLIN (1889–1977) *The Life Story of Charles Chaplin* (GB 26) with Chick Wango in a British attempt to cash in on the popularity of the cockney lad who had made it in Hollywood. The first biopic of a screen star, but never released due to a threat of legal action from its subject.

JOAN CRAWFORD (1906–77) *Mommie Dearest* (US 81) was based on Christina Crawford's controversial expose of her adoptive mother, here portrayed by Faye Dunaway as an insecure but savagely egotistical woman given to beating her children with coathangers.

JAMES DEAN (1931–55) *James Dean* (US 76, TVM) was scripted by the moody rebel's friend Bill Bast and recounted the story of their lives together as aspiring young actors when they were room-mates in the early fifties. Dean was portrayed by Stephen McHattie, Bast by Michael Brandon.

LEILA DINIZ (194?–6?) *Leila Diniz* (Bra 87) with Louise Cardoso as the unconventional and rebellious Brazilian star of the sixties who became a symbol of the period before perishing in a plane crash at the age of 27.

FRANCES FARMER (1914–70) *Committed* (US 84) was an earnest black-and-white docu-drama with Sheila McLaughlin in an intense performance as the overwrought, alcoholic, leftist and eventually lobotomized Hollywood beauty whose neuroses led to commitment to an asylum. The title is a play on words signifying Farmer's other commitment, to various 'progressive' causes.

Jessica Lange underwent the straitjacketing and lobotomy in a stand-out performance in Graeme Clifford's *Frances* (US 82), a version with less emphasis on politics and more on the relationship with monstrous mother Lillian Farmer, played for hisses by Kim Stanley.

W. C. FIELDS (1879–1946) *W. C. Fields and Me* (US 76) with Rod Steiger in another study of a star disintegrating from drink. The 'Me' of the title was Fields' mistress Carlotta Monti (Valerie Perrine), who nursed the tyrant comic through his alcoholism to the detriment of her own career.

ERROL FLYNN (1909–59) *My Wicked, Wicked Ways—The Legend of Errol Flynn* (US 85, TVM) with Canadian Duncan Regehr as the swashbuckling Australian. Barbara Hershey played his fiery Spanish actress wife Lili Damita, Barrie Ingham his fellow drunk John Barrymore and Lee Purcell the too perfect Olivia de Havilland.

CLARK GABLE (1901–60) *Gable and Lombard* (US 76) with James Brolin struggling bravely in a generally misconceived attempt to portray 'the man rather than the star'.

JUDY GARLAND (1922–69) *Rainbow* (US 78, TVM) Judy's early life from her days starting out in vaudeville aged 10 to her triumph in *The Wizard of Oz* (US 39) when she was 17. Andrea McArdle played Judy, Moosie Drier the teenage Mickey Rooney and Johnny Doran played Jackie Cooper, who directed *Rainbow*. Probably the only occasion the director of a movie has been portrayed in it.

CORINNE GRIFFITH (1898–1979) *Papa's Delicate Condition* (US 63), based on silent screen heroine Corinne Griffith's own book, is the only other biopic about the childhood of a star. Linda Bruhl played the six-year-old Corrie, Jackie Gleason her inebriate father.

Left: Joan Crawford with adopted daughter Christina (*SI*). *Right*: Faye Dunaway as Joan Crawford, Mara Hobel as Christina, in *Mommie Dearest* (US 81), biopic based on Christina's biography which revealed her mother's true and deeply unloving nature. (*Kobal*)

BIOPICS OF SCREEN STARS (continued)

JEAN HARLOW (1911-37) *Harlow* (US 65) with Carroll Baker in a travesty of the star's life of which the producer, director and screen-writer should be thoroughly ashamed. *Harlow* (US 65) with Carol Lynley in a rather better attempt at the subject, released in an Electronovision version.

AL JOLSON (1886-1950) *The Jolson Story* (US 46) and *Jolson Sings Again* (US 49) with Larry Parks in both highly successful films. Jolson himself did the voice-over for the songs and is also seen in long shot during the 'Swanee' sequence of the first picture.

BUSTER KEATON (1895-1966) *The Buster Keaton Story* (US 57) with Donald O'Connor in what Leslie Halliwell has described as 'a dismal tribute'. Once again the theme is one of drink being the curse of the starring classes.

ANNETTE KELLERMAN (1888-1978) *Million Dollar Mermaid* (US 53) with Esther Williams playing the Australian girl who invented the one-piece bathing suit and became the first star actress to appear on the screen in the nude (not depicted in the biopic).

BRUCE LEE (1940-73) *A Dragon Story*/GB: *The Bruce Lee Story* (US 74) with Hsiao Lung as the Chinese-American actor who achieved international stardom in Hong Kong martial arts movies.

A succession of wholly or semi-fictitious martial arts films followed which purported to portray Bruce Lee: *The Story of the Dragon* (HK 76) with Ho Tsung-tao (Bruce Li); *Bruce Lee—True Story* (HK 76) with Bruce Li; *Bruce Lee and I* (HK 76) with Li Msiu Hsien; *The Dragon Lives* (HK 78) with Bruce Li; *Bruce Lee: the Man, the Myth* (HK 78) with Bruce Li; *Bruce Lee, The Tiger of Manchuria* (HK 78) with Hang Yong Chul; *Young Bruce Lee* (HK 79) with Chuck Norris; *Sexy Isla Meets Bruce Lee in the Devil's Triangle* (Can 7?); *Bruce Lee versus the Gay Power* (Bra 7?). *The Death of Bruce Lee* (HK 76) merely invoked the name, not the character.

CAROLE LOMBARD (1908-42) *Gable and Lombard* (US 76) with Jill Clayburgh as the love of Gable's life, killed tragically in an aeroplane accident at the age of 34. The film failed to illuminate either the romantic myth of the legendary affair or the earthy reality (Lombard commented to a friend 'He's not what you'd call a helluva great lay'). Though even Hollywood could not bring itself to nominate the film for an Oscar, it did succeed in picking up Harvard Lampoon's 1976 Victor Mature Memorial Award for the most embarrassing line of dialogue. The citation read: 'Gable and Lombard, for the screen's greatest insouciant comment following the incendiary demise of his beloved in a plane crash, as he gazes fondly over the twisted wreckage: "She should have taken the train".'

MARILYN MONROE (1926-62) *Goodbye, Norma Jean* (US/Aus 75) with Misty Rowe, a reasonable look-alike but nothing more, in an exploitation movie that concentrates on Norma Jean Baker's seedy and often degrading existence before her metamorphosis into Marilyn Monroe superstar.

Catherine Hicks essayed the difficult role of legendary sex goddess in *Marilyn the Untold Story* (US 80), a TVM theatrically released in Europe. Based on Norman Mailer's biography, it in fact told little that had not been told before, but then neither did the book. One unusual feature was the portrayal of living and active stars by other actors—Tony Curtis by Bruce Neckels, Jack Lemmon by Brad Blaisdell and Laurence Olivier by Anthony Gordon.

GEORGE RAFT (1895-1986) *The George Raft Story* (US 61) with Ray Danton as the professional athlete, gambler, nightclub dancer and intimate of gangsters who turned it all to good account in Hollywood.

BILL 'BOJANGLES' ROBINSON (1878-1949) *Stormy Weather* (US 43) with 'Bojangles' himself in an all-black fictionalized version of his own life story. Also subject of 1979 Broadway musical *Bojangles.*

WILL ROGERS (1879-1935) *The Story of Will Rogers* (US 50) with Will Rogers Jnr playing his father in a bland homage to the celebrated crackerbarrel philosopher and latecomer movie star.

LILLIAN ROTH (1910-) *I'll Cry Tomorrow* (US 55) with Susan Hayward as the Broadway/Hollywood star of the early thirties whose career became another write-off to alcoholism.

KINUYO TANAKA (1910-77) *Actress* (Jap 87). Sayuri Yoshinaga as one of the greatest Japanese screen actresses, star of the first successful talkie made in Japan *A Madame and a Wife* (Jap 31). Almost a potted history of the Japanese film industry, the picture includes recreated scenes of Kenji Mizoguchi (played by Bunta Sugawara) directing Tanaka in his masterpiece *The Life of Oharu* (Jap 52).

RUDOLPH VALENTINO (1895-1926) *Valentino* (US 51) with Anthony Dexter in a flat biopic made at a time when Hollywood's attempts to portray the twenties invariably mixed period cliché with blundering anachronisms.

The Legend of Valentino (US 75) with Franco Nero in a version billed as 'romantic fiction'—a precaution against litigation from any of the surviving personalities in Valentino's tempestuous life.

Valentino (GB 77) with Rudolf Nureyev charismatic in Ken Russell's lush and stimulating evocation of man, myth, place and period.

HANSA WADKAR (1920-71) *Bhumika* (Ind 78) with Smita Patil as the popular Hindi star of the thirties and forties. One of the few foreign-language star biopics.

PEARL WHITE (1889-1938) *The Perils of Pauline* (US 47) with Betty Hutton recreating the career of the silent serial queen in uncompromisingly forties style.

Extras

The first film with a 'cast of thousands' in a literal sense was Luigi Maggi's Napoleonic epic *Il Granatiere Rolland* (It 10), for which 2000 extras were employed. A similar number participated in Britain's first extravaganza, Charles Weston's feature-length *The Battle of Waterloo* (GB 13).

The largest number of extras employed on a film appeared in the funeral scene of Sir Richard Attenborough's *Gandhi* (GB 82) and comprised a crowd believed to have been in excess of 300,000. Announcements by loudspeaker van, in newspapers and on television and radio summoned over 200,000 volunteer extras to Delhi's ceremonial mall, the Raj-path, where they were supplemented by another 94,560 contracted performers, the majority of whom were paid a fee equivalent to 40p each. The sequence had to be shot in a single morning, that of Saturday 31 January 1981, the 33rd anniversary of Gandhi's funeral. Eleven camera crews shot 20,000 ft of film, more than the total footage of the 188-minute release print of the movie. The edited funeral sequence with its 300,000 performers ran for only 125 seconds of screen time.

The largest number of soldiers used as extras was 187,000 in the last Nazi-made motion picture epic *Kolberg* (Ger 45). For this story about Napoleon's siege of Kolberg, whole army divisions were diverted from the front to play Napoleonic soldiers

In Samuel Fuller's war picture *Big Red One* (US 80), all the Nazi concentration camp guards were played by Jews. The location was a military base in Israel and the jackbooted jailers were Israeli soldiers lent for the production.

at a time when Germany was facing the prospect of her defeat. The film was started in 1943 and completed at the end of the following year, with drafts of fresh extras continuously replacing those who had to return to more earnest military duties. Released in January 1945, at a time when few Berlin cinemas were still functioning, *Kolberg* was seen by a considerably smaller total audience than the number which had appeared in it.

Other considerable casts include: 157,000 for monster movie *Wang Ma Gwi/Monster Wangmagwi* (S.Kor 67); 120,000 for *War and Peace* (USSR 67); 106,000 for *Ilya Muromets* (USSR 56); 80,000 for *The War of Independence* (Rom 12); 68,894 for *Around the World in 80 Days* (US 56); 60,000 for *Intolerance* (US 16) —publicity for the picture claimed 125,000; 60,000 for *Dny Zrady* (Cz 72); 50,000 for *Ben Hur* (US 59), *Exodus* (US 60), *Inchon* (Kor/US 81) and *Khan Asparouch* (Bul 82); 36,000 in *Metropolis* (Ger 26), including 1100 bald men in the Tower of Babel sequence; and 30,000 in *Michael the Brave* (Rom 70).

When Mario Mattoli was filming his comedy *Imputato, alzateri!/Defendant Stand Up!* (It 39) at Cinecitta Studios in Rome, he was dismayed to hear that on the last day of shooting he had to play host to 200 Japanese tourists. Knowing that it would be all but impossible to control such a herd of non-Italian speaking oriental shutterbugs, he made the best of a bad job. Hastily rewriting the script, Mattoli devised an end scene involving a mob of Japanese tourists and filmed his 200 unpaid extras to hilarious effect.

The cast of *Metropolis* (Ger 26) included 1100 bald extras in the Tower of Babel sequence. *(Kobal)*

The year that the largest number of extras were employed in Hollywood was 1927, when a total of 330,397 days were worked (227,415 by men, 102,892 by women), an average daily call of 1056. Since there were 14,000 extras registered with Central Casting that year, average employment rate was approximately one day in 14.

Extras who Became Stars

Comparatively few major stars began their film careers as extras, the majority having had stage or, latterly, television experience before entering movies. Those who did do extra work include Theda Bara, Gary Cooper, Marlene Dietrich, Clark Gable, Janet Gaynor, John Gilbert, Paulette Goddard, Stewart Granger, Jean Harlow, Harold Lloyd, Sophia Loren, Marilyn Monroe, David Niven, Ramon Novarro, Merle Oberon, Norma Shearer, Erich von Stroheim, Constance Talmadge, Rudolph Valentino, Michael Wilding and Loretta Young.

Despite the fact that he was registered at Central Casting as 'Anglo-Saxon type 2008', David Niven's first role was as a Mexican in a blanket in a Hopalong Cassidy oater. He was subsequently an extra in 26 other westerns.

Sadly the reverse process could also apply. Leading players who ended their careers as extras were King Baggot, Mae Busch, Ethel Clayton, Grace Cunard, western star Franklyn Farnum, Flora Finch, Francis Ford (brother of John Ford and a leading man in the late teens), John Ince (brother of early mogul Thomas Ince), Douglas Fairbanks' leading lady Julanne Johnston, Alice Lake, original 'Biograph Girl' Florence Lawrence, western star Kermit Maynard, Marshall Neilan, who had once commanded $125,000 per picture, Florence Turner, who was the first star to be put under contract, and 'country boy' hero Charles Ray. May McAvoy, romantic lead of the twenties who played opposite Al Jolson in *The Jazz Singer* (US 27), retired when talkies took over but later tried to make a comeback as a character actress. She never succeeded in securing a speaking part and ended her career as an extra with MGM in the 1940s.

The dream of stardom via Central Casting occasionally comes true even today. Sixteen-year-old French schoolgirl Sandrine Bonnaire applied for a role as an extra in Maurice Pialat's *A Nos Amours* (Fr 83). She was given the lead instead, winning plaudits from the critics for her performance and sharing in the accolade of a César award, the French Oscar, for 'Best Film' of the year.

Black Extras

Demand for black extras in the USA began with the flood of Civil War movies that followed the 50th anniversary in 1911. Tarzan and other jungle movies, together with epics of the ancient world, maintained a steady flow of work and the number of blacks registered with Central Casting peaked at 6816 in 1926. The following year was the best for employment, with some 10,000 black roles cast—the total for the previous three years had been 17,000. There was a decline with the coming of talkies and generally the films of the thirties were more confined in their settings than those of the silent era, requiring smaller crowd scenes. World War II brought an almost complete stop to black casting; despite the million black Americans under arms, Hollywood's doughboy was resolutely white. After the war there was little improvement—in 1948 only 130 black roles were cast in pictures.

> Crowd scenes are no problem to Bulgarian producers. Extras, mainly housewives, pensioners, schoolchildren and the star-struck, are easily recruited at 10 to 20 lev a day— equivalent to 8p to 16p.

Contracts, Legal and Binding . . .

In the days when studios 'owned' stars, the price of security and gigantic salaries was often freedom of behaviour. All big stars had morality clauses in their contracts (first to sign had been Maryon Aye in 1922), but Joan Crawford's with MGM in 1930 even specified the hour by which she had to be in bed. Mary Miles Minter's contract with the Realart Co. in 1919 was dependent upon her remaining unmarried for 3½ years. Others enjoined to remain single were Clara Bow, at Paramount's insistence, and Alice White, whose contract with First National further obliged her to learn two languages during the course of 1930, preferably French and Spanish. Walter Pidgeon, much in demand for musicals before he became a father figure, was forbidden to sing tenor lest he impair his rich baritone voice. Buster Keaton's famous unsmiling face was a contractual obligation. His contract with MGM in the twenties precluded him from smiling on screen, while Charles Butterworth's with Warner Bros prevented him from smiling in public. Similarly, Roscoe Ates' stutter was legally binding in his contract with RKO. First National demanded of Douglas Fairbanks Jnr that he never travel in 'planes. Joe E. Brown was forbidden to grow a moustache. A clause in teetotaller Frank McHugh's contract with First National required that he play drunkards whenever required, while Maurice Chevalier's with Paramount, signed as talkies were coming in, insisted that he remain in character—it was rendered invalid if he ever lost his French accent. In 1931 boxing fan Vivienne Segal was directed by her contract with Warner's not to yell at prize fights in case she strained her voice.

Possibly the most difficult contractual obligation to enforce was the one enjoined on Lois Moran not to grow sophisticated for a year after the release of *Stella Dallas* (US 26). Clara Bow was offered a $500,000 bonus by Paramount in 1926 provided she kept herself free of scandal during its tenure. She failed to collect. All the cast of Cecil B. DeMille's reverential life of Christ, *King of Kings* (US 27), were bound by contract not to accept any roles without DeMille's consent for ten years after the film's release. Dorothy Cummings, who played the Madonna, was further denied the right to divorce, which she promptly did 3 months after the première.

Occasionally the stars were able to impose unusual conditions on their masters, the studios. At the Warner studios in the early thirties, George Arliss's contract provided that he did not have to remain on set after 4.30 p.m., while John Barrymore's gave him the privilege of not being on set before 10.30 a.m. Moran and Mack, the Two Black Crows, were the only Paramount stars allowed to drive their car within the studio gates. Garbo's desire to be alone was protected by a clause preventing MGM from demands that she make any public appearances. When stage player Margaret Sullavan was persuaded by director John Stahl to accept the lead in *Only Yesterday* (US 33), she was so reluctant to enter films that she had a clause inserted in her contract to the effect that she could quit after ten days if she disliked Hollywood as much as she anticipated. Although she loathed Tinsel Town, she completed the picture and many others. Joe E. Brown's contract with Warner's demanded that the studio co-operate with him in running a baseball team. Virginal Evelyn Venable's contract with Paramount in 1933 had a clause inserted by her father preventing her from being kissed on screen. The rather less virginal Clara Bow wrote into her contract with Paramount that none of

the workmen or technicians were to use profane language to her or in her presence.

Even today, producers are known to make grudging concessions if the name of the star is big enough. Roger Moore will not sign any contract unless he is guaranteed an unlimited supply of hand-rolled Monte Cristo cigars from Cuba. On one of the Bond movies, the bill of 007's cigars came to £3176.50. Audrey Hepburn also knows how to wipe the thin-lipped smile from producers' faces. Before agreeing to star in *Sidney Sheldon's Bloodline* (US/FRG 83), she imposed a condition that all her costumes were to be designed by Paris couturier Givenchy; and furthermore that, when filming was completed, she would be given the $100,000 wardrobe.

FILM STARS WHO HAVE PLAYED THEMSELVES IN MOVIES

June Allyson *Words and Music* (US 48)
Fred Astaire *Dancing Lady* (US 33)
Mary Astor *Hollywood* (US 23)
Lew Ayres *The Cohens and the Kellys in Hollywood* (US 32)
Lauren Bacall *Two Guys from Milwaukee* (US 46)
Anne Bancroft *Silent Movie* (US 76)
Tallulah Bankhead *Stage Door Canteen* (US 43); *Main Street to Broadway* (US 53)
Brigitte Bardot *Dear Brigitte* (US 65)
Wendy Barrie *It Should Happen to You* (US 54)
Ethel Barrymore *Main Street to Broadway* (US 53)
Lionel Barrymore *Free and Easy* (US 30); *Main Street to Broadway* (US 53)
Freddie Bartholomew *Sepia Cinderella* (US 47)
Noah Beery *Hollywood* (US 23)
Dorothy Bellew *The Kinema Girl* (GB 14)
William Bendix *Duffy's Tavern* (US 45); *Variety Girl* (US 47)
Constance Bennett *It Should Happen to You* (US 54)
Edgar Bergen *Stage Door Canteen* (US 43); *Song of the Open Road* (US 44)
Milton Berle *Let's Make Love* (US 60); *Broadway Danny Rose* (US 84)
Humphrey Bogart *Thank Your Lucky Stars* (US 43); *Two Guys from Milwaukee* (US 46); *Always Together* (US 47); *The Love Lottery* (US 54)
John Boles *Stand Up and Cheer* (US 34)
Ray Bolger *The Great Ziegfeld* (US 36)
Clara Bow *Fascinating Youth* (US 26)
Joe E. Brown *Hollywood Canteen* (US 44)
Johnny Mack Brown *The Marshal's Daughter* (US 53)
Coral Browne (as herself in 1958) *An Englishman Abroad* (GB 84)
James Caan *Silent Movie* (US 76)
Eddie Cantor *Thank Your Lucky Stars* (US 43); *Hollywood Canteen* (US 44); *The Story of Will Rogers* (US 52)
Jack Carson *It's a Great Feeling* (US 49)
Charles Chaplin *Show People* (US 29)
Cyd Charisse *Words and Music* (US 48)
Maurice Chevalier (also plays hero) *L'Homme du Jour* (Fr 37); *Pepe* (US 60)
Julie Christie *Nashville* (US 75)
Betty Compson *Hollywood* (US 23); *Hollywood Boulevard* (US 36)
Chester Conklin *Fascinating Youth* (US 26); *The Perils of Pauline* (US 47)
Eddie Constantine *Les Sept péchés capitaux* (Fr/It 62); *Warnung vor einer Heiligen Nutte* (FRG/It 71); *Flight to Berlin* (GB 84)

It is hard to imagine Maurice Chevalier without his inimitable French accent, but Paramount were taking no chances. His contract lapsed if he lost it. *(Popperfoto)*

Jackie Coogan *Free and Easy* (US 30)
Gary Cooper *Variety Girl* (US 47); *It's a Great Feeling* (US 49); *Starlift* (US 51)
Ricardo Cortez *Hollywood* (US 23)
Broderick Crawford *A Little Romance* (US 79)
Joan Crawford *Hollywood Canteen* (US 44); *It's a Great Feeling* (US 49)
Bing Crosby *Star Spangled Rhythm* (US 42); *Duffy's Tavern* (US 45); *Variety Girl* (US 47); *Angels in the Outfield* (US 52); *The Greatest Show on Earth* (US 52); *Let's Make Love* (US 60); *Pepe* (US 60)
Finlay Currie *6.5. Special* (GB 58)
Karl Dane *Free and Easy* (US 30)
Bette Davis *Thank Your Lucky Stars* (US 43); *Hollywood Canteen* (US 44)
Sammy Davis Jnr *Pepe* (US 60)
Doris Day *Starlift* (US 51)

Olivia de Havilland *Thank Your Luck Stars* (US 43)
Dolores Del Rio *Torero!* (Mex 56)
Catherine Deneuve *L'Enfante de l'Art* (Fr 88)
Marlene Dietrich *Follow the Boys* (US 44); *Jigsaw* (US 49)
Richard Dix *Fascinating Youth* (US 26)
Diana Dors *Allez France* (Fr 64)
Jimmy Durante *Pepe* (US 60)
Douglas Fairbanks *Hollywood* (US 23); *The Kiss of Mary Pickford* (USSR 26); *Show People* (US 29)
Marianne Faithful *Made in USA* (Fr 67)
Peter Falk *Der Himmel uber Berlin* (FRG/Fr 87)
William Farnum *The Perils of Pauline* (US 47)
Alice Faye *Four Jills in a Jeep* (US 44)
Stepin Fetchit *Stand Up and Cheer* (US 34)
Gracie Fields *Stage Door Canteen* (US 43)
W. C. Fields *Sensations of 1945* (US 44); *Song of the Open Road* (US 44); *Follow the Boys* (US 44)
Barry Fitzgerald *Variety Girl* (US 47)
Rhonda Fleming *The Patsy* (US 64)
Cyril Fletcher *Yellow Canary* (GB 43)
Errol Flynn *Always Together* (US 47); *It's a Great Feeling* (US 49)
Henry Fonda *Jigsaw* (US 49); *Main Street to Broadway* (US 53); *Fedora* (FRG 78)
Jane Fonda *Leonard Part 6* (US 87)
Kay Francis *Four Jills in a Jeep* (US 44)
Zsa Zsa Gabor *Pepe* (US 60); *Smart Alex* (US 86)
Greta Garbo *A Man's Man* (US 29)
Ava Gardner *The Band Wagon* (US 53)
John Garfield *Thank Your Lucky Stars* (US 43); *Hollywood Canteen* (US 44); *Jigsaw* (US 49)
Judy Garland *Words and Music* (US 48)
Greer Garson *The Youngest Profession* (US 43); *Pepe* (US 60)
John Gilbert *Married Flirts* (US 24); *A Man's Man* (US 29)
Paulette Goddard *Star Spangled Rhythm* (US 42); *Variety Girl* (US 47)
Elliott Gould *Nashville* (US 75); *The Muppets Take Manhattan* (US 84)
Betty Grable *Four Jills in a Jeep* (US 44)
Cary Grant *Without Reservations* (US 46)
Greta Gynt *I'm a Stranger* (GB 52)
Larry Hagman *I am Blushing* (Swe 81)
Creighton Hale *Mary of the Movies* (US 23)
Rex Harrison *Main Street to Broadway* (US 53)
W. S. Hart *Hollywood* (US 23); *Show People* (US 29)
Laurence Harvey *The Magic Christian* (GB 70) as self playing Hamlet

FILM STARS WHO HAVE PLAYED THEMSELVES IN MOVIES (continued)

Sessue Hayakawa *Night Life in Hollywood* (US 22)

Sterling Hayden *Variety Girl* (US 47)

Susan Hayward *Star Spangled Rhythm* (US 42)

Sonja Henie *Hello London* (GB 58)

Katharine Hepburn *Stage Door Canteen* (US 43)

William Holden *Variety Girl* (US 47)

Jack Holt *Hollywood Speaks* (US 32)

Bob Hope *Duffy's Tavern* (US 45) ; *Variety Girl* (US 47) ; *The Greatest Show on Earth* (US 52) ; *The Oscar* (US 66)

John Hurt *Spaceballs* (US 87)

Betty Hutton *Star Spangled Rhythm* (US 42) ; *Duffy's Tavern* (US 45)

Sidney James *The Beauty Contest* (GB 64)

Al Jolson *Hollywood Cavalcade* (US 39) ; *Rhapsody in Blue* (US 44) ; *Jolson Sings Again* (US 49) —scene of Jolson meeting Larry Parks and congratulating him on his portrayal of Jolson in *The Jolson Story*

Boris Karloff *The Cohens and the Kellys in Hollywood* (US 32) ; *Bikini Beach* (US 64)

Danny Kaye *It's a Great Feeling* (US 49)

Buster Keaton *Hollywood Cavalcade* (US 39) ; *Sunset Boulevard* (US 50)

Gene Kelly *Words and Music* (US 48) ; *Love is Better than Ever* (US 52) ; *Let's Make Love* (US 60)

George Kennedy *The Legend of Lylah Clare* (US 68) ; *Modern Romance* (US 81)

Alan Ladd *Star Spangled Rhythm* (US 42) ; *Duffy's Tavern* (US 45) ; *Variety Girl* (US 47)

Veronica Lake *Star Spangled Rhythm* (US 42) ; *Variety Girl* (US 47)

Dorothy Lamour *Star Spangled Rhythm* (US 42) ; *Duffy's Tavern* (US 45) ; *Variety Girl* (US 47) ; *Here Comes the Groom* (US 51)

Carole Landis *Four Jills in a Jeep* (US 44)

Laurel and Hardy *Pick a Star* (US 37)

Peter Lawford *Pepe* (US 60)

Janet Leigh *Pepe* (US 60)

Jack Lemmon *Pepe* (US 60)

Ronald Reagan played himself in *It's a Great Feeling* (US 49).

Peter Lorre *Hollywood Canteen* (US 44)

Bessie Love *Night Life in Hollywood* (US 22) ; *Mary of the Movies* (US 23)

Linda Lovelace *Linda Lovelace for President* (US 75)

Ida Lupino *Thank Your Lucky Stars* (US 43)

Jeanette MacDonald *Follow the Boys* (US 44)

Virginia McKenna *An Elephant called Slowly* (GB 69) ; *The Lion at World's End* (GB 71)

Fred MacMurray *Star Spangled Rhythm* (US 42)

Gordon MacRae *Starlift* (US 51)

George Marshall *Variety Girl* (US 47)

Marcello Mastroianni *L'Ingorgo/Bottleneck* (It/Fr/Sp/FRG 79)

Victure Mature *Head* (US 68)

Harpo Marx *Stage Door Canteen* (US 43)

Virginia Mayo *Starlift* (US 51)

Adolphe Menjou *Fascinating Youth* (US 26)

Burgess Meredith *Jigsaw* (US 49)

Ray Milland *Star Spangled Rhythm* (US 42) ; *Variety Girl* (US 47)

Liza Minnelli *Silent Movie* (US 76) ; *The Muppets Take Manhattan* (US 84)

Tom Mix *The Cohens and the Kellys in Hollywood* (US 32)

Bull Montana *Hollywood* (US 23)

Owen Moore *Hollywood* (US 23)

Dennis Morgan *It's a Great Feeling* (US 49)

Paul Muni *Stage Door Canteen* (US 43)

Mae Murray *Married Flirts* (US 24) ; *Show People* (US 29)

Ornella Muti *Grandi Magazzini* (It 86)

Nita Naldi *Hollywood* (US 23)

Patricia Neal *It's a Great Feeling* (US 49)

Pola Negri *Hollywood* (US 23)

Paul Newman *Silent Movie* (US 76)

Anna Q. Nillson *Sunset Boulevard* (US 50)

Kim Novak *Pepe* (US 60)

Merle Oberon *Stage Door Canteen* (US 43) ; *The Oscar* (US 66)

Donald O'Connor *Follow the Boys* (US 44)

Lili Palmer *Main Street to Broadway* (US 53) ; *Le Rendezvous de Minuit* (Fr 66) (also played two fictitious characters) ; *Jack of Diamonds* (FRG/GB 66)

Larry Parks *Jolson Sings Again* (US 49) —also played Jolson

Mary Pickford *Hollywood* (US 23) ; *The Kiss of Mary Pickford* (USSR 26) made by Sergei Komorov without Miss Pickford being aware of her own participation

Walter Pidgeon *The Youngest Profession* (US 43)

Zasu Pitts *Mary of the Movies* (US 23) ; *Make Me a Star* (US 32)

Eddie Polo *Dangerous Hour* (US 23)

Dick Powell *Star Spangled Rhythm* (US 42)

Jane Powell *Song of the Open Road* (US 44)

William Powell *The Youngest Profession* (US 43)

Robert Preston *Variety Girl* (US 47)

Dennis Price *Go for a Take* (GB 72)

George Raft *Broadway* (US 42) ; *Stage Door Canteen* (US 43) ; *The Patsy* (US 64) ; *Casino Royale* (GB 67) ; *Sextette* (US 78)

Tony Randall *The King of Comedy* (US 83)

Ronald Reagan *It's a Great Feeling* (US 49)

Wallace Reid *Night Life in Hollywood* (US 22)

Michael Rennie *The Body Said No!* (GB 50)

Burt Reynolds *Silent Movie* (US 76)

Debbie Reynolds *Pepe* (US 60)

Ralph Richardson *The Volunteer* (GB 43)

Tex Ritter *Nashville Rebel* (US 66) ; *What Am I Bid?* (US 67)

Joan Rivers as President of the USA *Joan Rivers in Les Patterson Saves the World* (Aus 87)

Edward G. Robinson *It's a Great Feeling* (US 49)

May Robson *How Molly Made Good* (US 15)

Patricia Roc *Holiday Camp* (GB 47)

Eddie Rochester *Star Spangled Rhythm* (US 42)

Roy Rogers *Hollywood Canteen* (US 44)

Will Rogers *Hollywood* (US 23)

Sabrina *Just My Luck* (GB 57)

Randolph Scott *Starlift* (US 51)

Larry Semon *Go Straight* (US 25)

Norma Shearer *Married Flirts* (US 24)

Martin Sheen *In the King of Prussia* (US 82)

Brooke Shields *The Muppets Take Manhattan* (US 84)

Sylvia Sidney *Make Me a Star* (US 32)

Phil Silvers *Take It or Leave It* (US 44)

Frank Sinatra *Pepe* (US 60) ; *The Oscar* (US

Gloria Swanson as herself in *Airport 75* (US 74). More than half a century earlier she had also played herself in *Hollywood* (US 23).

66); *Cannonball Run II* (US 83)
Barbara Stanwyck *Hollywood Canteen* (US 44); *Variety Girl* (US 47)
Tommy Steele *Kill Me Tomorrow* (GB 55); *The Tommy Steele Story* (GB 57)
Anita Stewart *Mary of the Movies* (US 23); *Hollywood* (US 23); *Go Straight* (US 25)
Gloria Swanson *Hollywood* (US 23); *Airport 75* (US 74)
Blanche Sweet *Souls for Sale* (US 23)
Constance Talmadge *In Hollywood with Potash and Perlmutter* (US 24)
Norma Talmadge *In Hollywood with Potash and Perlmutter* (US 24); *Show People* (US 29)
Estelle Taylor *Mary of the Movies* (US 23); *Hollywood* (US 23)
Robert Taylor *The Youngest Profession* (US 43)
Bill Travers *An Elephant called Slowly* (GB 69); *The Lion at World's End* (GB 71)
Lana Turner *The Youngest Profession* (US 43)
Ben Turpin *Hollywood* (US 23); *Make Me a Star* (US 32)
Liv Ullman *Players* (US 79)
Peter Ustinov *Players* (US 79)
Conrad Veidt *Die Grosse Sehnsacht* (Ger 30)
Vera-Ellen *Words and Music* (US 48)
H. B. Warner *Sunset Boulevard* (US 50)
Paul Wegener *The Golem and the Dancer* (Ger 14)
Johnny Weissmuller *Stage Door Canteen* (US 43)
Orson Welles *Follow the Boys* (US 44); *Someone to Love* (US 87)
Cornel Wilde *Main Street to Broadway* (US 53)
Michael Wilding *Hello London* (GB 58)
Natalie Wood *The Candidate* (US 72); *Willie and Phil* (US 81)
Monty Woolley *Night and Day* (US 46)
Jane Wyman *Hollywood Canteen* (US 44); *It's a Great Feeling* (US 49); *Starlift* (US 51)
Ed Wynn *The Patsy* (US 64)
Michael York *Fedora* (FRG 78)
Susannah York *Scruggs* (GB 66) —also played heroine; *Long Shot* (GB 78)

NON-ACTORS WHO HAVE PLAYED THEMSELVES IN FILMS

The list excludes the many bandleaders and vocalists appearing in sound movies.
(* Autobiopics)

Princess Aicha Abidir *Pierrot-le-Feu* (Fr/It 65)
Frankie Albert, All-American quarterback *The Spirit of Stanford** (US 42)
Buzz Aldrin, astronaut *The Boy in the Plastic Bubble* (US 76, TVM)
Dragljub Aleksić, acrobat *Nevinost bez Zastite** (Yug 68)
Queen Alexandra *The Great Love* (US 18); *Women Who Win* (GB 19)
Muhammed Ali, heavyweight boxing champion *The Greatest** (US 77); *Body and Soul* (US 81)
Alfredo Alvarado, exhibition dancer *El Rey del Jorapo** (Ven 80)
Vijay Amritraj, Indian tennis champion *Octopussy* (GB 83)
Mario Andretti, motor-racing driver *Speed Fever* (It 78)
Lady Astor, first woman MP to sit in House of Commons *Royal Cavalcade* (GB 35)
Lt-Commander Auten VC, RNR re-enacted exploit which won him VC in *Q Ships* (GB 28)
Lord Baden-Powell, defender of Mafeking and founder of the Scout movement *Boys of the Otter Patrol* (GB 18); *The Man Who Changed His Mind* (GB 28); *The Woodpigeon Patrol* (GB 30)

Admiral Badger *Victory* (US 13)
Max Baer, boxer *The Prizefighter and the Lady* (US 33)
Bruce Bairnsfather, creator of cartoon character 'Old Bill' *Old Bill Through the Ages* (GB 24)
Joan Bakewell, TV personality *The Touchables* (GB 67)
Adolf Beck, convicted of false murder charge *The Martydom of Adolf Beck** (GB 09)
The Duchess of Bedford *The Beauty Contest* (GB 64)
The Duke of Bedford *The Iron Maiden* (GB 62)
Alec Bedser, cricketer *The Final Test* (GB 53)
Saul Bellow, novelist *Zelig* (US 83)
Sonny Berger, Hell's Angels leader *Hell's Angels* (US 69)
Yogi Berra, baseball star *That Touch of Mink* (US 62)
Daniel and Phillip Berrigan, radical Jesuits *In the King of Prussia* (US 82)
Roy Best, Warden of Canon City Penitentiary *Canon City* (US 48)
Ronald Biggs, train robber *The Great Rock 'n' Roll Swindle* (GB 80); *Honeymoon* (FRG 80)
Danny Blanchflower, soccer star *Those Glory Glory Days* (GB 83)
Jasmine Bligh, TV announcer *Band Wagon* (GB 40)
Ada Bodart, assisted Nurse Edith Cavell in establishing her World War I escape organization *Dawn* (GB 28)

Evangeline Booth, Commandant of US Salvation Army *Fires of Faith* (US 19)
Lord Boothby, politician *Rockets Galore* (GB 58)
Bjorn Borg, tennis champion *Racquet* (US 79)
Horatio Bottomley, politician and financier, three times charged with fraud (convicted 1922) *Was It He?* (GB 14)
The Bowen Family, of Guyra, NSW, victims of psychic phenomena *The Guyra Ghost Mystery* (Aus 21)
Jack Brabham, motor-racing driver *The Green Helmet* (GB 61)
Sir David Brand, premier of Western Australia *Nickel Queen* (Aus 71)
RSM Ronald Brittain, Regimental Sergeant Major of ferocious demeanour *You Lucky People* (GB 55)
Dr Joyce Brothers, sexologist *Stand Up and Be Counted* (US 71); *Embryo* (US 76); *The Lonely Guy* (US 84)
Joe Brown, New York speakeasy proprietor *Dressed to Kill* (US 28)
Judge Willis Brown of Salt Lake Juvenile Court *A Boy and the Law* (US 14)
Maurice Buckmaster, spy-master *Odette* (GB 50)
Sir Matt Busby, football manager *Cup Fever* (GB 65)
José Capablanca, chess Grand Master *Chess Fever* (USSR 25)

NON-ACTORS WHO HAVE PLAYED THEMSELVES IN FILMS (continued)

Andrew Carnegie, multi-millionaire industrialist *Our Mutual Girl* (US 14)

James Earl Carter, US President *Special Counsel* (US/Is 88)

George Washington Carver, distinguished black scientist *George Washington Carver** (US 40)

Dick Cavett, TV chat show presenter *Health* (US 80)

César, sculptor who created the César (French Oscar) *T'es folle ou quoi?* (Fr 82)

Arthur Christiansen, ex-editor of the *Daily Express The Day the Earth Caught Fire* (GB 61)

M. E. Clifton-James, ex-actor who impersonated Montgomery to deceive Nazi Intelligence *I Was Monty's Double** (GB 58)

Ty Cobb, baseball player *Somewhere in Georgia* (US 17); *Angels in the Outfield* (US 51)

Sir Alan Cobham, aviator *The Flight Commander* (GB 27)

William Cody, Buffalo Bill *The Life of Buffalo Bill** (US 09); *Buffalo Bill's Far West and Pawnee Bill's Far East* (US 10); *The Indian Wars* (US 13); *Sitting Bull—The Hostile Indian Chief* (US 14); *Patsy of the Circus* (US 15)

Dennis Compton, cricketer *The Final Test* (GB 53)

Douglas 'Wrong Way' Corrigan, aviator *The Flying Irishman** (US 39)

Michael Curtiz, film director *It's a Great Feeling* (US 49)

Emmett Dalton, youngest of the Dalton brothers, notorious desperadoes *Beyond the Law* (US 18)

Josephus Daniels, US Secretary of the Navy *Victory* (US 13)

Jimmie Davis, Governor of Louisiana *Louisiana** (US 47)

Moshe Dayan, Israeli Minister of Defence *Operation Thunderbolt* (Isr 77)

Count de Bauford in unidentified Carl Laemmle film (US 10) about his romance with an American heiress

Cecil B. DeMille, film producer and director *Hollywood* (US 23); *Free and Easy* (US 30); *Star Spangled Rhythm* (US 42); *Variety Girl* (US 47); *Sunset Boulevard* (US 50)

Jack Dempsey, heavyweight boxing champion *Sweet Surrender* (US 53); *Big City* (US 37); *Off Limits* (US 53); *Requiem for a Heavyweight* (US 62)

Joe Di Maggio, baseball player *Angels in the Outfield* (US 51)

Richard Dimbleby, BBC commentator *The Twenty Questions Murder* (GB 50); *John and Julie* (GB 55); *Rockets Galore* (GB 58); *Libel* (GB 59)

Georgi Dimitrov, communist revolutionary tried and acquitted in the 1933 Reichstag Fire trial, Prime Minister of Bulgaria 1946–49 *Kämpfer* (USSR 36)

Walt Disney, creator of Mickey Mouse, etc *Once Upon a Time* (US 44)

Sir Arthur Conan Doyle, novelist and creator of Sherlock Holmes *The $5,000,000 Counterfeiting Plot* (US 14)

Joni Eareckson, paraplegic *Joni** (US 80)

Sgt Arthur Guy Empsey, war hero *Over the Top** (US 18)

Godfrey Evans, cricketer *The Final Test* (GB 53)

Robert Fabian, police detective *Passport to Shame* (GB 59)

Emerson Fittipaldi, motor-racing driver *Speed Fever* (It 78)

Margot Fonteyn, prima ballerina *The Little Ballerina* (GB 51)

Michael Foot, socialist politician *Rockets Galore* (GB 58)

John Ford, director *Big Time* (US 29)

Joe Frazier, boxer *Rocky* (US 77)

Tito Fuentes, baseball player *Solomon King* (US 74)

Samuel Fuller, director *Pierrot-le-Feu* (Fr 65); *Scotch Myths—The Movie* (GB 83)

Paul Gallico, novelist *Madison Square Garden* (US 32)

Dorothy Gibson, Titanic survivor *Saved from the Titanic* (GB 12)

André Gide, writer *La Vie commence demain* (Fr 52)

Frank Gifford, American footballer *Paper Lion* (US 68); *Viva Knievel!* (US 77)

Alan Ginsberg, poet *Ciao! Manhattan* (US 72)

Raymond Glendenning, sports commentator *The Galloping Major* (GB 51); *Make Mine a Million* (GB 59); *The Iron Maiden* (GB 62)

Elinor Glyn, pioneer of the sex novel and creator of 'It' *It* (US 27); *Show People* (US 29)

Barbara Goalen, model *Wonderful Things!* (GB 58)

Pancho Gonzales, tennis coach *Players* (US 79)

John Gorton, Prime Minister of Australia *Don's Party* (Aus 76)

Billy Graham, American evangelist *Souls in Conflict* (GB 55); *Two a Penny* (GB 67)

Sheila Graham, journalist and mistress of F. Scott Fitzgerald (played by Deborah Kerr in biopic *Beloved Infidel* (US 59)) *College Confidential* (US 60)

Angèle Grammont, who escaped from old people's home near Lausanne *Angèle** (Swz 68)

Zane Grey, Western novelist *White Death* (Aus 36)

Merv Griffin, TV anchorman *The Lonely Guy* (US 84)

Grock, clown *Grock** (Ger 31)

Earl Haig, World War I Commander-in-Chief *Remembrance* (GB 27)

Ernest Haigh, ex-Chief Inspector of Police *Leaves from My Life** (GB 21)

Giscele Halimi, defence counsel in notable 1972 abortion trial *L'Une chante l'autre pas* (Fr/Bel/Cur 76)

David Hamilton, photographer *Tiffany Jones* (GB 73)

General Sir Ian Hamilton, leader of the Gallipoli Expedition *Tell England* (GB 31)

Oscar Hammerstein, composer *Main Street to Broadway* (US 53)

Judge James Hannon, judge who tried Arlo Guthrie for casting litter *Alice's Restaurant* (US 69)

Gilbert Harding, crusty TV personality, famous for rudeness *Simon and Laura* (GB 55); *As Long as They're Happy* (GB 55); *An Alligator Named Daisy* (GB 55); *My Wife'f Family* (GB 56); *Left, Right and Centre* (GB 59); *Expresso Bongo* (GB 59)

Mickey Hargitay, ex-Mr Universe, ex-husband of Jayne Mansfield *Mr Universe* (Hun 88)

Tom Harmon, All-American quarterback *Harmon of Michigan** (US 41)

Norman Hartnell, couturier *The Beauty Contest* (GB 64)

Len Harvey, boxer *The Bermondsey Kid* (GB 33)

Edith Head, Hollywood costume designer *The Oscar* (US 66)

Hugh Hefner, founder of Playboy empire *How Did a Nice Girl Like You Ever Get Into This Business* (FRG 70); Hefner played by Cliff Robertson in *Star 80* (US 83)

Graham Hill, motor-racing driver *The Fast Lady* (GB 62)

> A disclaimer before the end credits of *Players* (US 79) insisted that all the characters in the film were wholly fictitious; it was immediately followed by a cast list that included no less than 14 famous tennis personalities, including John McEnroe, playing themselves.

Dennis Hills, captive of Idi Amin *The Rise and Fall of Idi Amin* (Ken 81)

David Hockney, artist *A Bigger Splash** (GB 74)

John Hodge MP, Minister of Pensions *Broken in the Wars* (GB 19)

Ben Hogan, golfer *The Caddy* (US 53)

Hedda Hopper, movie gossip columnist *Sunset Boulevard* (US 50); *Pepe* (US 60); *The Patsy* (US 64)

William Morris Hughes, Prime Minister of Australia *Smithy* (Aus 46)

Hubert Humphrey, US Senator *The Candidate* (US 72)

James Hunt, motor-racing driver *Speed Fever* (It 78)

Len Hutton, cricketer *The Final Test* (GB 53)

Father Iliodor, rascally monk, first protégé then opponent of Rasputin *The Fall of the Romanoffs* (US 18)

David Jacobs, broadcaster *Otley* (GB 68)

James J. Jeffries, boxing champion *Pennington's Choice* (US 15)

Admiral Lord Jellicoe *Q Ships* (GB 28)

Al Jennings, convicted bank and train robber *The Bank Robbery* (US 08); *Beating Back** (US 15)

Amy Johnson, aviatrix *Dual Control* (GB 32)

Jack Johnson, boxer *Jack Johnson's Adventures in Paris* (Fr 13); *As the World Rolls on* (US 21)

José José, alcohol and drug addicted popular singer *Gavilán o Paloma** (Mex 85)

Helen Keller, deaf-blind scholar *Deliverance** (US 19)

Murray King, Long Island insurance salesman *Murray, King** (US 69)

Evel Knievel, motorcycle stuntman *Viva Knievel!* (US 77)

Somchai Koonperm, village chief *Kamnan Poh** (Tha 80)

Jim Laker, cricketer *The Final Test* (GB 53)

Fritz Lang, film director (played by Marcel Hillaire in *Take the Money and Run* (US 69)); *Contempt* (Fr 64)

Nikki Lauda, motor-racing driver *Speed Fever* (It 78)

Ed Koch, Mayor of New York *The Muppets Take Manhattan* (US 84)

Henry Lawson, Australian poet *While the Billy Boils* (Aus 21)

Dr Timothy Leary, guru of LSD *Cheech and Chong's Nice Dreams* (US 81)

Mitchell Leisen, film director *Hold Back the Dawn* (US 41)

Suzanne Lenglen, Wimbledon tennis champion *Things Are Looking Up* (GB 35)

Oscar Levant, composer *Rhapsody in Blue* (US 45); *Humoresque* (US 47)

Bernard Levin, journalist *Nothing But the Best* (GB 63)

Prinz Eduard von und zu Liechtenstein, of the Royal House of Liechtenstein *Johann Strauss an der Schönen blauen Donau* (Aut 13)

Sir Thomas Lipton, millionaire grocer and yachtsman *The Lipton Cup* (US 13)

Vincent Lombardi, American footballer *Paper Lion* (US 68)

Chief Lomoiro, Masai tribal leader *Visit to a Chief's Son* (US 74)

Captain James Lovell, astronaut *The Man Who Fell to Earth* (GB 76)

Joan Lowell, yachtswoman *Adventure Girl** (US 34)

Paul and Linda McCartney, ex-Beatle and photographer wife *Give My Regards to Broad Street* (GB 84) ; Paul only in *Eat the Rich* (GB 87)

Windsor McCay, cartoonist (*Little Nemo*, etc) and pioneer film animator *The Great White Way* (US 24)

Jem Mace, boxer *There's Life in the Old Dog Yet* (GB 08)

John McEnroe, tennis champion *Players* (US 79)

George McGovern, US Senator *The Candidate* (US 72)

Marshall McLuhan, Canadian academic, expert on media and communications *Annie Hall* (US 77)

George McManus, cartoonist (*Bringing Up Father*, etc) *The Great White Way* (US 24)

Alice Marble, tennis champion *Pat and Mike* (US 52)

Queen Mary *Women Who Win* (GB 19)

Dan Maskell, tennis player *Players* (US 79)

Bob Mathias, twice winner of Olympic decathlon *The Bob Mathias Story** (US 54)

Yehudi Menuhin, violinist *Stage Door Canteen* (US 43)

Cliff Michelmore, TV personality *A Jolly Bad Fellow* (GB 63)

Lewis Milestone, film director *Fascinating Youth* (US 26)

Freddie Mills, boxer *6.5 Special* (GB 58)

Leslie Mitchell, Britain's first TV announcer (1936) and Movietone commentator *Geneviève* (GB 53)

Jim Mollison, aviator who made first east–west crossing of N. Atlantic *Dual Control* (GB 32)

Gussie Moran, tennis champion *Pat and Mike* (US 52)

Stirling Moss, motor-racing driver *The Beauty Contest* (GB 64)

James Mossman, broadcaster *Masquerade* (GB 64)

Malcolm Muggeridge, journalist and pundit *I'm All Right Jack* (GB 59) ; *Heavens Above* (GB 63) ; *Herostratus* (GB 67) ; *The Naked Bunyip* (Aus 70)

Audie Murphy, most decorated US Soldier of World War II and subsequently professional actor *To Hell and Back** (US 55)

Pete Murray, disc jockey *6.5 Special* (GB 58)

Albert Namatjira, Aboriginal artist *The Phantom Stockman* (Aus 53)

Ilie Nastase, Romanian tennis champion *Players* (US 79)

Bess Nielsen, Parisian girl given to amorous adventures *On n'est pas serieux quand on a 17 ans** (Fr 74)

Officer Obie, policeman who arrested Arlo Guthrie for casting litter *Alice's Restaurant* (US 69)

Dan O'Brien, San Francisco Chief of Police *Poison* (US 24)

Barney Oldfield, motor-racing driver *Barney Oldfield's Race for Life* (US 16)

Ignace Paderewski, pianist, Prime Minister and later President of Poland *Moonlight Sonata* (GB 37)

The most decorated GI of World War II, Audie Murphy, played himself in *To Hell and Back* (US 55). *(Kobal)*

Arnold Palmer, golfer *Call Me Bwana* (GB 63)

Huang Pao-Mei, girl spinner in China's Cotton Mill No 17 *Huang Pao-mei** (Chn 58)

Michael Parkinson, TV personality *Madhouse* (GB 74)

Louella Parsons, movie gossip columnist *Hollywood Hotel* (US 37) ; *Stagedoor Canteen* (US 43)

Nicholas Parsons, TV personality *Mr Jolly Lives Next Door* (GB 87)

Princess Patricia *Women Who Win* (GB 19)

Lieutenant Harold R. Peat *Private Peat** (US 18)

Betty Ting Pei, Bruce Lee's lover *Bruce Lee and I** (HK 76)

Pele, Brazilian soccer player *Young Giants* (US 83)

Shimon Peres, Prime Minister of Israel *Special Counsel* (US/Isr 88)

Marshal Pétain, French Commander-in-Chief World War I, Head of Vichy Government World War II *Verdun, Visions d'Histoire* (Fr 28)

Pablo Picasso, artist *La Vie commence demain* (Fr 52) ; *Le Testament d'Orphée* (Fr 60)

Wiley Post, first aviator to circumnavigate world solo *Air Hawks* (US 35)

Andre Previn, conductor *Pepe* (US 60)

Luis Procuna, matador *Torero!** (Mex 56)

Yizhak Rabin, Prime Minister of Israel *Operation Thunderbolt* (Isr 77) ; *Special Counsel* (US/Isr 88)

Dame Marie Rambert, founder of the Ballet Rambert *The Red Shoes* (GB 48)

Paul Raymond, eroticist *Erotica* (GB 81)

Jean Renoir, film director *The Christian Licorice Store* (US 71)

Carlos Reutemann, motor-racing driver *Speed Fever* (It 78)

Robert Ripley, originator of *Believe It or Not* *The Great White Way* (US 24)

Charlie Rivel, circus clown *Scö-ö-ön** (Ger 43)

Jackie Robinson, first black to play major league baseball *The Jackie Robinson Story** (US 50)

Robert Robinson, broadcaster *French Dressing* (GB 64)

Sugar Ray Robinson, boxer *Paper Lion* (US 68)

Richard Rodgers, composer *Main Street to Broadway* (US 53)

Theodore Roosevelt, ex-President of the USA *Womanhood, The Glory of a Nation* (US 17)

Lady 'Bubbles' Rothermere, society hostess *The Stud* (GB 78)

Damon Runyon, writer *The Great White Way* (US 24) ; *O, Baby* (US 26) ; *Madison Square Garden* (US 32)

Gunther Sachs, millionaire industrialist and playboy *Cadillac* (FRG 69)

Margaret Sanger, birth control pioneer *Birth Control* (US 17)

Jean-Paul Satre, philosopher *La Vie commence demain* (Fr 52)

Ichijo Sayuri, stripper *Ichijo Sayuri: Wet Desire** (Jap 74)

Joe Schmidt, American footballer *Paper Lion* (US 68)

Charles E. Sebastian, ex-Mayor of Los Angeles *The Downfall of a Mayor** (US 17)

Mlle Segree, lover of Landru, murderer of 11 women *Landru* (Ger 23)

Caporal Sellier, bugler who sounded the World War I armistice, re-enacted scene in *The Soul of France* (Fr 28)

Mack Sennet, founder of the Keystone Kops *Hollywood Cavalcade* (US 39)

NON-ACTORS WHO HAVE PLAYED THEMSELVES IN FILMS (continued)

Ma Sha, reformed pimp and killer *The First Error Step** (Sin 79)

Barry Sheene, world motorcycling champion, and his girlfriend Stephanie McLean *Space Riders* (GB 83)

William Shirer, historian *The Magic Face* (US 51)

Harry Siegenberg, bookmaker *The Stolen Favourite* (SA 19)

O. J. Simpson, football player *The Klansman* (US 74)

George R. Sims, crusading journalist gaoled in celebrated 1885 Maiden Tribute of Modern Babylon case *The Martyrdom of Adolf Beck* (GB 09)

Sir Charles Kingsford Smith, Australian aviator *Splendid Fellows* (Aus 34)

Kate Smith, singer *Hello Everybody* (US 33) (fictionalized biopic)

Susan Sontag, writer *Zelig* (US 83)

Mickey Spillane, thriller writer *Ring of Fear* (US 54)

Ringo Starr, ex-Beatle *Give My Regards to Broad Street* (GB 84)

Isobel Lillian Steele, American victim of Gestapo *Captive of Nazi Germany** (US 36)

Charles Stragusa, narcotics agent who led 10-year quest to nail mobster Lucky Luciano *Re: Lucky Luciano* (It/Fr 73)

Preston Sturges, film director *Star Spangled Rhythm* (US 42)

Anne Sullivan, who taught blind deaf-mute Helen Keller to speak and read *Deliverance* (US 19)

Ed Sullivan, TV personality *The Patsy* (US 64)

Hannen Swaffer, journalist *Spellbound* (GB 41)

Crown Princess of Sweden *Women Who Win* (GB 19)

Fuji Takeshi, world junior welterweight boxing champion *Fuji Takeshi Monogatari** (Jap 68)

Yukio Tani, martial arts exponent *Ju-Jitsu to the Rescue* (GB 13)

Alderman C. E. Tatham, Mayor of Blackpool *Sing As We Go* (GB 34)

A. J. P. Taylor, historian *Rockets Galore* (GB 58)

Evelyn Nesbitt Thaw, beauty whose husband murdered her lover, architect Stanford White (played by Joan Collins in *The Girl in the Red Velvet Swing* (US 55) and by Elizabeth McGovern in *Ragtime* (US 81)) *The Great Thaw Trial* (US 07) ; *Redemption* (US 17)

Wynford Vaughan Thomas, broadcaster *John and Julie* (GB 55)

William 'Big Bill' Thompson, Mayor of Chicago *Is Your Daughter Safe?* (US 27)

W. M. Tilgham, Marshal of Cache, Oklahoma *The Bank Robbery* (US 08)

Mark Twain, humorous writer *A Curious Dream* (US 07)

Senator Jo Valentine of Western Australia *The Pursuit of Happiness* (Aus 88)

John van Druten, playwright *Main Street to Broadway* (US 53)

Princess Victoria *Women Who Win* (GB 19)

King Vidor, film director *It's a Great Feeling* (US 49)

Guillermo Vilas, tennis player *Players* (US 79)

The Prince of Wales, later King Edward VIII *The Warrior Strain* (GB 19) ; *The Power of Right* (GB 19) ; *Remembrance* (GB 27)

Lech Walesa, founder of Solidarity *Man of Iron* (Pol 81)

Jimmy Walker, Mayor of New York *Glorifying the American Girl* (US 29)

Raoul Walsh, film director *It's a Great Feeling* (US 49)

Cyril Washbrook, cricketer *The Final Test* (GB 53)

Alan Whicker, TV commentator *The Angry Silence* (GB 60)

Gough Whitlam, Prime Minister of Australia *Barry McKenzie Holds His Own* (Aus 74)

District Attorney Whitman *Our Mutual Girl* (US 14) ; *Smashing the Vice Trust* (US 14)

Frank Wills, Watergate security guard who discovered break-in *All the President's Men* (US 76)

Peter Wilson, Chairman of Sotheby's *Laughter in the Dark* (GB 69)

Woodrow Wilson, President of the USA *Womanhood, The Glory of a Nation* (US 17)

Walter Winchell, influential American columnist (played by Lew Ayres in *Okay America!* (US 32)) ; *Wake Up and Live* (US 37) ; *Love and Hisses* (US 37) ; *The Helen Morgan Story* (US 57) ; *College Confidential* (US 60) ; *Wild in the Streets* (US 68)

Godfrey Winn, journalist *Very Important Person* (GB 61) ; *Billy Liar!* (GB 63)

Maharishi Narish Yogi, guru *Candy Baby* (US 69)

Sam Yorty, Mayor of Los Angeles *The Candidate* (US 72)

Jimmy Young, broadcaster *Otley* (GB 68)

Krzysztof Zanussi, film director *Amator/Camera Buff* (Pol 79)

Florenz Ziegfeld, impresario *Glorifying the American Girl* (US 29)

Adolf Zukor, film producer *Glorifying the American Girl* (US 29)

The only British monarch to have acted in films was King Edward VIII when he was Prince of Wales. In March 1919 he performed in two patriotic war dramas—like Indian stars of today he economized on time by playing his scenes for both films at the same time. This was made easier by the fact that he was portraying himself in each and that they had remarkably similar plots. *The Power of Right* (GB 19), directed by F. Martin Thornton for Harma Photoplays, was about a colonel's son who joins the cadets and succeeds in killing an escaped German internee, while *The Warrior Strain* (GB 19) was also about a cadet, this time an Earl's son, who foils a dastardly plot by a German baron to signal the enemy from Brighton. In the latter film the Prince played a scene with Sydney Wood (as the boy's father), and another in which he presents each of the members of the cadet section with a gold watch as a reward for thwarting the wicked baron. Some years later he again played himself in BIP's *Remembrance* (GB 27), a story about disabled war veterans.

NON-ACTORS IN FILMS

Personalities who have played roles other than themselves (see also Personalities playing themselves. pp. 77–80) include:

Horacio Accavallo, world flyweight boxing champion, lead in *Destino para dos* (Arg 67)

Muhammed Ali, world heavyweight boxing champion, as young fighter in *Requiem for a Heavyweight* (US 62) ; as Gideon Jackson, first black US Senator, in *Freedom Road* (US 79, TVM)

Viscount Althorp, brother of Princess of Wales, as public schoolboy in *Another Country* (GB 84)

Max Baer, boxer, in *The Prizefighter and the Lady* (US 33)

Mrs Morgan Belmont, society leader and member of New York's '400', played the upper crust Diana Tremont in *Way Down East* (US 20)

Peter Benchley, author of *Jaws*, played a reporter in *Jaws* (US 75)

Godfrey Binaisa, President of Uganda, bit parts in *King Solomon's Mines* (US 50) and *The African Queen* (GB 51)

Ex-Detective Sergeant Bishop as Detective Sergeant in *Blackmail* (GB 29)

Bricktop, black nightclub proprietor famous in cafe society, as mother figure in *Honeybaby, Honeybaby* (US 74)

RSM Ronald Brittain, Regimental Sergeant Major at Sandhurst Military Academy during 1950s, appeared (usually as a Sergeant Major) in *Carrington VC* (GB 54), *The Missing Note* (GB 61), *The Amorous Prawn* (GB 62), *Joey Boy* (GB 65) and *The Spy with a Cold Nose* (GB 66)

Dr Joyce Brothers, sexologist, in *Burnin' Love* (US 87)

William Burroughs, sex writer, as a mafia don in *It Don't Pay to be an Honest Citizen* (US 85)

Truman Capote, author, leading role in detective fiction parody *Murder by Death* (US 76)

Primo Carnera, boxer, as boxer in *The Prizefighter and the Lady* (US 33) ; as Pyrhon Macklin in *A Kid for Two Farthings* (GB 55) ; as Corfa in *Casanova's Big Night* (US 54)

Georges Carpentier, boxer, as hero in *Toboggan* (Fr 34)

Viscount Castlerosse, bon viveur, as the man in the bath chair in *Kipps* (GB 41)

Fidel Castro, dictator, bit player in *Holiday in Mexico* (US 46)

Juan Chacon, trade union leader, as Mexican strike leader in *Salt of the Earth* (US 54)

G. K. Chesterton, author, in *Rosy Rapture—The Pride of the Beauty Chorus* (GB 14)

Michael Chow, restaurateur, as underworld boss Fong Wei Tan in *Hammett* (US 82)

Daniel Cohn-Bendit, revolutionary, in Godard's *Vent d'est* (FRG/It 70); as friend of heroine who bemoans his resemblance to Daniel Cohn-Bendit in *Un Amour à Paris* (Fr 87)

Henry Cooper, boxer, as prizefighter John Gully in *Royal Flash* (GB 75)

Carmine Coppola, composer, as man in the lift in Francis Coppola's *One from the Heart* (US 82)

James John Corbett, world heavyweight boxing champion, in *The Midnight Man* (US 19)

Quentin Crisp, homosexual liberationist, played Polonius in *Hamlet* (GB 76); as Dr Zahlus in *The Bride* (GB 85)

Jack Dempsey, boxer, as boxer in *The Prizefighter and the Lady* (US 33)

Dionne Quins, world's first surviving quintuplets, in *The Country Doctor* (US 36), *Reunion* (US 36) and *Five of a Kind* (US 38)

Steve Donaghue, champion jockey, as Steve Baxter, hero of *Riding for a King* (GB 26), *Beating the Book* (GB 26), *The Golden Spurs* (GB 26) and *The Stolen Favourite* (GB 26)

Terry Downes, boxer, as Chunky in Sherlock Holmes movie *A Study in Terror* (GB 65)

Gertrude Ederle, first woman to swim the English Channel, in *Swim, Girl, Swim* (US 28)

Princess Elizabeth of Toro, as the Sharma in *Sheena—Queen of the Jungle* (US 84)

David Frost, television commentator, as reporter in *The VIPs* (GB 63)

Paul Getty III, grandson of oil tycoon, as film scriptwriter Dennis in *The State of Things* (US/Por 82)

Althea Gibson, black tennis star, as maid in John Ford's *The Horse Soldiers* (US 59)

Allen Ginsberg, poet, as a lawyer in *It Don't Pay to be an Honest Citizen* (US 85)

Robert Graves, poet and novelist, as partygoer in *Deadfall* (GB 68)

Graham Greene, author, as the insurance representative in *Day for Night* (Fr 73)

Germaine Greer, women's liberationist, as Clara Bowden in *Universal Soldier* (GB 71)

Jerry Hall, statuesque model and Mrs Mick Jagger, in *Running Out of Luck* (US 85) and *Topo Galileo* (It 88)

Lorenz Hart, of Rodgers and Hart, played the bank teller in *Hallelujah, I'm a Bum* (US 33)

Len Harvey, British boxing champion, played a glass collector turned boxer in *Excuse My Glove* (GB 36)

Hugh Hefner, founder of Playboy empire, as pipe smoking ancient Roman in *History of the World—Part I* (US 81)

Ernest Hemingway, author, uncredited bit part in *The Old Man and the Sea* (US 58)

Xaviera Hollander, prostitute and writer, lead in *My Pleasure is My Business* (Can 74)

Bianca Jagger, jet-setter, leads in *Flesh Colour* (US 79) and *The Great American Success Company* (US 79)

Clive James, Australian pundit, as most drunken of Bazza's mates in *Barry McKenzie Holds His Own* (Aus 77)

James Jones, novelist, as a poker player in *The Marseilles Contract* (GB/Fr 74)

Thomas Keneally, Australian novelist, as Father Marshall in *The Devil's Playground* (Aus 76)

Jomo Kenyatta, President of Kenya 1963–78, played an African chief in *Sanders of the River* (GB 35)

Jerzy Kosinksy, controversial Polish-American novelist, as Bolshevik revolutionary Zinoviev in *Reds* (US 81)

Dr Emmanuel Lasker, world chess champion, played Napoleon's chess partner in Lupu Pick's *Napoléon a Sainte-Hélène* (Fr 29)

Tad Lincoln, son of Abraham Lincoln, in *The Highest Law* (US 21); he himself played by Dickie Moore in *Lincoln in the White House* (US 39)

John Lindsay, Mayor of New York, played Senator Donnovan in *Rosebud* (US 75)

Joe Louis, boxer, played lead as young fighter in all-black *Spirit of Youth* (US 38)

Victor Lowndes, chairman of Playboy UK, as Reeve Passmore in *Fledglings* (GB 65)

Compton MacKenzie, author, as Capt Buncher in film of his own novel *Whisky Galore!* (GB 49); as Sir Robert Dysart in *Chance of a Lifetime* (GB 50)

Norman Mailer, writer, as 'The Prince' in *Wild 90* (US 68); as Lt Francis Xavier Pope of NY Police in *Beyond the Law* (US 68); as film director and presidential candidate 'Kingsley' in *Maidstone* (US 70); as New York architect Stanford White (murdered in celebrated turn-of-century crime of passion) in *Ragtime* (US 81); as Lear (in opening scenes—Burgess Meredith then takes over) in *King Lear* (US/Swz 87)

Yehudi Menuhin, violinist, in *The Magic Bow* (GB 46)

Freddie Mills, British champion boxer, in *Emergency Call* (GB 52), *Kill Me Tomorrow* (GB 55), *Fun at St Fanny's* (GB 56), *Breakaway* (GB 56), *Chain of Events* (GB 58), *Carry on Constable* (GB 60), *Carry on Regardless* (GB 61), *The Comedy Man* (GB 63), *Saturday Night Out* (GB 64)

Jóan Miró, Spanish painter, played the museum curator in *El Umbracle* (Sp 73)

Stirling Moss, motor-racing driver, in *Casino Royale* (GB 67)

Benito Mussolini, Italian dictator, extra in *The Eternal City* (US 14)

Beverly Nichols, author, as the Hon. Richard Wells in *Glamour* (GB 31)

Mrs Richard Nixon, wife of ex-President Nixon, walk-on parts in *Becky Sharp* (US 36) and *Small Town Girl* (US 37)

HRH Nana Agyefi Kwame II de Nsein, as the mad King Bossa Ahadee in *Cobra Verde* (FRG 88)

John O'Hara, novelist, as a reporter on a train in *The General Died at Dawn* (US 36)

Charley Paddock, US Olympic athlete (played by Dennis Christopher in *Chariots of Fire* (GB 81)) as hero in *The Olympic Hero* (US 28)

Princess Pearl, daughter of White Rajah of Sarawak, as Princess Paula in Ruritanian romance *Everything is Rhythm* (GB 36)

Pelé, Brazilian football star, as soccer hero in *Hotshot* (US 87)

Harold Pinter, playwright, as 'society man' in *The Servant* (GB 63); as lawyer Saul Abrahams in *Rogue Male* (GB 76); as bookshop customer in *Turtle Diary* (GB 85)

Nosher Powell, minder, in lead role as Home Secretary in *Eat the Rich* (GB 87)

Kukrit Pramoj, Prime Minister of Thailand (1974), as Prime Minister of the fictitious state of 'Sarkhan' in *The Ugly American* (US 62)

Erich Maria Remarque, author of *All Quiet on the Western Front*, as the schoolmaster Pohlmann in the film of his novel *A Time to Love and a Time to Die* (US 58)

David Robinson, film critic of *The Times*, in *If* (GB 60), *Fragments of Life* (Hun 70),

---

Kukrit Pramoj (*left*) played a fictitious prime minister in *The Ugly American* (US 62). Twelve years later he played the role for real when he became prime minister of Thailand. (*Kobal*)

NON-ACTORS IN FILMS (continued)

Britannia Hospital (GB 81), and as 1930s drama critic of *The Times* in *Mephisto* (Hun 81)

Sugar Ray Robinson, boxer, as Zero in *Candy* (It/Fr 68)

Babe Ruth, baseball player, subject of *The Babe Ruth Story.* (US 48), acted in *Headin' Home* (US 19)

Pierre Salinger, John F. Kennedy's Press Secretary, as poker player in *The Marseilles Connection* (GB/Fr 73)

Max Schmeling, boxer, as hero Max Breuer, playing opposite wife Anny Ondra, in *Knockout* (Ger 36)

Martin Scorsese, film director, as the Director of the Metropolitan Open House in *Pavlova—A Woman for All Time* (GB/USSR 83)

George Bernard Shaw, playright, in *Rosy Rapture—The Pride of the Beauty Chorus* (GB 14)

Jean Shrimpton, model, leading lady in *Privilege* (GB 67)

Ex-Empress Soraya in triple role as herself, Linda and Mrs Melville in *I Tre Volti* (It 65)

Steven Spielberg, producer/director, as Cook County Clerk in *The Blue Brothers* (US 80)

Mickey Spillane, author, played his own creation Mike Hammer in *The Girl Hunters* (US 63)

Jacqueline Susann, novelist, in *Valley of the Dolls* (US 67)

Leslie 'Squizzy' Taylor, Melbourne gangster gunned down in 1927, in race-track drama *Bound to Win* (Aus 19)

Bill Tilden, tennis champion, as Joles in *The Music Master* (US 27)

Franz von Trauberg, first post-war Mayor of Berlin, as kidnapped ambassador in *Guernica* (It 72)

Leon Trotsky, revolutionary and founder of the Red Army, played a bit part as a nihilist in Vitagraph's spy drama *My Official Wife* (US 14) and also appeared in *The Battle Cry of Peace* (US 15)

Margaret Trudeau, estranged wife of Premier of Canada, Pierre Trudeau, starred in *The Guardian Angel* (Can 78) and *Kings and Desperate Men* (Can 79)

Gene Tunney, heavyweight boxing champion, in Pathé serial *The Fighting Marine* (US 26)

Hugh Walpole, author, as the vicar in *David Copperfield* (US 35)

Senator John Warner, ex 'Mr Elizabeth Taylor', as a fisherman in *The Mirror Crack'd* (GB 81)

Judge Joseph N. Welch, presiding judge at the McCarthy hearings, played a judge in *Anatomy of a Murder* (US 59)

Bombardier Billy Wells, British boxing champion, starred as the pilot in *The Silver Lining* (GB 19) and played the hangman in *The Beggar's Opera* (GB 53)

White Man-Runs Him, last survivor of the Battle of the Little Big Horn (at which Gen. Custer's force was massacred in 1876), played in a Ken Maynard western *The Red Raiders* (US 27)

Gough Whitlam, Prime Minister of Australia, as 'man in night club' in *The Broken Melody* (Aus 38); see also under Non-actors who have played themselves

Godfrey Winn, journalist, played an announcer in *The Bargee* (GB 64) and Truelove in *The Great St Trinian's Train Robbery* (GB 65)

Jersey Joe Walcott, boxer, as 'George' in *The Harder They Fall* (US 56)

Alexander Woolcott, writer and critic, as literary sophisticate Vanderveer Veyden in *The Scoundrel* (US 35)

Brig. Gen. Chuck Yeager, first pilot to break sound barrier and US astronaut, as Fred the barman in *The Right Stuff* (US 83). Yeager portrayed in same film by Sam Shepard—one of the rare instances of a name appearing on both sides of the cast list

Yevgeny Yevtushenko, poet, played leading role as Russian space pioneer Konstantin Tsiolkovsky in *Take-Off* (USSR 79)

In 1938 *Motion Picture Magazine* conducted a survey which showed that divorce was almost twice as prevalent among Hollywood stars as among other Americans. At a time when just over 16 per cent of American marriages ended in divorce, 29 per cent of married stars from Hollywood's 'Top 400' had divorced at least once. Of the 313 who had been married:

212 claimed to have been married only once (71 per cent)

 63 claimed to have been married twice (20 per cent)

 24 claimed to have been married three times (8 per cent)

  5 claimed to have been married four times or more (1.5 per cent)

Only 194 children were claimed by these 'Top 400' stars, and of these 19 had been adopted.

Things appear to have got worse rather than better following World War II. Dr Robert L. Sumner, a Southern Baptist minister, focused attention on the sorry state of matrimony in the movie capital with a computation that in 1949 there were 42 marriages involving a prominent screen star and 180 divorces.

The highest incidence of divorce occurs where both partners are prominent stars. According to a recent estimate, no less than 74 per cent of such marriages contracted since 1916 have ended in divorce.

The most married stars in the Hollywood galaxy have been Lana Turner, Mickey Rooney, Zsa Zsa Gabor, Stan Laurel and Georgia Holt, each with eight marriages. The latter two hold the record for most repeat marriages to the same person, with Georgia Holt marrying John Sarkisian, the father of Cher, three times, and Stan Laurel marrying Virginia Rogers three times.

Black Actors

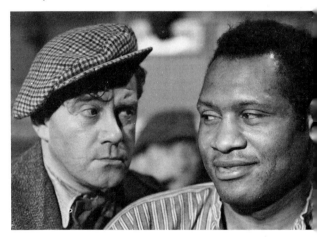

The idea of blacks as members of the community was novel to English audiences when Paul Robeson took the lead as a London docker in *Song of Freedom* (GB 37). (SI)

The first black actor to play a leading role in a feature film was Sam Lucas, cast in the title role of *Uncle Tom's Cabin* (US 14).

The first black actor to make a career in films was Noble Johnson, who made his debut in a Lubin western in 1914 playing an Indian chief. After arriving in Hollywood in 1915, he graduated from stunt work and bit parts with the formation of the Lincoln Motion Picture Co., an all-black production company specializing in ghetto films, of which he was president as well as leading player. Johnson starred in three Lincoln productions—*The Realisation of a Negro's Ambition* (US 16), *The Trooper of Company K* (US 17) and *The Law of Nature* (US 18)—before leaving the company to concentrate on the Universal serials he had been making between Lincoln pictures.

Britain's first black screen actor was Bermuda-born Ernest Trimmingham, who made his debut in the British & Colonial production *Her Bachelor Guardian* (GB 12). **The first black actor to play a leading role in a British film** was Paul Robeson as Bosambo in Alexander Korda's *Sanders of the River* (GB 35). He also starred in *Song of Freedom* (GB 37), *Big Fella* (GB 37), *King Solomon's Mines* (GB 37) and *Jericho* (GB 37).

Not Starring

Often a role that appears to have been tailor made for a particular star was intended for someone else altogether.

☆ George Jessel, initial choice for the lead in *The Jazz Singer* (US 27), lost the opportunity to be the first star of a talking picture because he demanded an extra $10,000 for singing on top of the $30,000 Warner Bros offered him for the role. Next choice was Eddie Cantor, who turned down the role because he thought it could and should only be played by Jessel. Al Jolson upped the ante with a demand of $75,000 and a by then desperate Jack Warner capitulated.

☆ Noel Coward was Stanley Kubrick's first choice for the hapless child-lover in *Lolita* (GB 62), a role tackled with relish by James Mason, who considered it his best film.

☆ Stars practically queued up not to have to play the washed-up has-been opposite Judy Garland in *A Star Is Born* (US 54). Among those rejecting the role before James Mason took it on were Humphrey Bogart, Cary Grant (who first accepted, then backed out), Gary Cooper, Marlon Brando and Montgomery Clift.

☆ Henry Fonda turned down the part which won Peter Finch his posthumous Oscar in *Network* (US 76) as 'too hysterical'.

☆ Robert Montgomery was scheduled to play Clark Gable's Oscar winning role in *It Happened One Night* (US 34), but Columbia backed away at the last moment when MGM released another Montgomery picture, *Fugitive Lovers* (US 34), with a similar story-line. Instead MGM offered them Gable as a punishment for refusing a role opposite Joan Crawford.

☆ Robert Redford rejected the George Segal role in *Who's Afraid of Virginia Woolf* (US 66), the Dustin Hoffman role in *The Graduate* (US 67) and the John Cassavetes role in *Rosemary's Baby* (US 68)—all before he became a major star.

☆ Judy Garland secured the lead in *The Wizard of Oz* (US 39) only because Fox refused to loan Shirley Temple to MGM for the role. Shirley was the right age for the part of Dorothy—Judy was 17 playing a 9-year-old.

☆ Cary Grant was originally top-lined for *The Third Man* (GB 49) in the Joseph Cotten role; for *Sabrina* (US 54) in the Bogart role; and for *A Star Is Born* (US 54) in the James Mason role. He was also first choice for Professor Higgins in *My Fair Lady* (US 64).

☆ Olivia de Havilland was first choice for the role of Blanche, which won Vivien Leigh an Oscar, in *A Streetcar Named Desire* (US 51). John Garfield was offered the Brando role as Stanley Kowalski, but rejected it because he felt the male lead was much inferior to the female lead.

☆ Vivien Leigh was replaced by Elizabeth Taylor after having a breakdown on *Elephant Walk* (US 53), but did not disappear from the film altogether. Lynx-eyed Leigh fans have spotted her in a number of long shots which were not retaken.

☆ Eli Wallach was chosen for the Sinatra role in *From Here to Eternity* (US 53), but withdrew mysteriously without stating a reason, thereby fuelling the rumours that Sinatra had got the part through Mafia pressure.

☆ Betty Hutton got the chance to play what was undoubtedly her best role in *Annie Get Your Gun* (US 49) after Judy Garland had walked off the set halfway through shooting.

☆ Vanessa Redgrave backed out of *Georgy Girl* (GB 66) at the last moment, leaving the role open to sister Lynn.

☆ Jean-Louis Trintignant turned down James Fox's role as the decadent aristo in *The Servant* (GB 67).

☆ If Kevin McClory, holder of the rights to the James Bond story *Thunderball* (GB 65), had succeeded in getting financial backing, Richard Burton would have become the second actor to play 007. As it was, McClory had to do a deal with Cubby Broccoli, producer of the previous two Bond movies, and Sean Connery toplined again.

☆ The search for a new James Bond to replace 007 Roger Moore appeared to be over with the selection of *Remington Steele* star Pierce Brosnan. When Brosnan was unexpectedly called back for a fifth year of *Remington Steele*, Bond producer Cubby Broccoli told United Artists he wanted a star who would be wholly identified with the 007 role, not one associated with another screen personality. Brosnan was nixed in favour of Timothy Dalton, who made his 'licensed to kill' debut in United Artists' 15th Bond excursion *The Living Daylights* (GB 87).

☆ Despite the fact that he had triumphed in the Broadway production of *The Music Man*, Robert Preston was by no means first choice for the role of lovable rogue Harold Hill in the 1961 movie version. Among the many actors offered the part was Cary Grant, who responded 'Not only won't I play it, but unless Robert Preston plays it, I won't even go to see the picture'.

☆ Robert Redford accepted the lead in Richard Zanuck's production of *The Verdict* (US 82). Having flown to Boston, where the story was set, for a script conference, he found to his dismay that he was expected to play a drunken, balding slob. He made an excuse to leave the meeting, saying he wanted to freshen up before dinner, checked out of the hotel and flew back to LA. Zanuck replaced him with Paul Newman, who scored an Oscar nomination for the role.

☆ Exceptional example of a film shot twice over with substantially different casts was Woody Allen's *September* (US 88), a Checkhovian-style tale of angst amongst a group of people yearning for the unattainable in the remote Vermont country home of Mia Farrow. In the version which never made it to the screen, the role of Mia Farrow's mother, a great star of yester-year, was played by Mia Farrow's own real mother and star of yester-year Maureen O'Sullivan, but in the reshoot it was taken by Elaine Stritch. Denholm Elliott started out as Maureen O'Sullivan's husband but was recast as the neighbour in love with Mia Farrow, with Jack Warden replacing Elliott when Elliott replaced Charles Durning, the original lover. Sam Shepherd and Christopher Walken both essayed the role of the man Farrow is in love with, but Sam Waterston took over in the version that made it to the screen.

☆ Lee Marvin and Rod Steiger both opted out of playing the role that conferred superstar status on George C. Scott in *Patton: Lust for Glory* (US 70). Steiger considered it glorified militarism; he was later to be offered roles George C. Scott had rejected.

☆ The role which won Claudette Colbert her Best Actress Oscar in *It Happened One Night* was turned down successively by Myrna Loy, Margaret Sullavan, Miriam Hopkins and Constance Bennett. Colbert only accepted it on condition that shooting was completed in four weeks and that her usual salary of $25,000 per picture was doubled to $50,000.

☆ Greer Garson was talked into playing *Mrs Miniver* (US 42) because Norma Shearer refused to play a mother role. Garson was equally reluctant but had less pull on the studio lot. Ironically her Oscar winning performance catapulted her to the top of the studio tree.

☆ When Robert Donat failed to turn up in Hollywood for *Captain Blood* (US 35), Warner Bros asked Brian Aherne to step into the lead, but he turned it down. Finally the studio took a chance and cast an unknown young Australian in the part—Errol Flynn.

☆ Jeanne Moreau was first choice for Mrs Robinson (Anne Bancroft) in *The Graduate* (US 67).

☆ Audrey Hepburn turned down the title role in *The Diary of Anne Frank* (US 59) in favour of the flop *Green Mansions* (US 59). As the only Dutch actress of international repute, she may have regretted passing up the opportunity to play the Dutch girl who has come to symbolize the tragedy of the holocaust.

☆ Deborah Kerr won her celebrated role in *From Here to Eternity* (US 53) because Joan Crawford, announced for the part, hated the costumes.

☆ Princess Grace of Monaco was originally scheduled to play Tippi Hedren's title role in Hitchcock's *Marnie* (US 64). Prince Rainier had agreed to her returning to the screen, but the Monagesques were shocked at the idea and it was dropped.

☆ Ginger Rogers replaced Eleanor Parker who replaced Rita Hayworth who replaced Judy Garland as Jean Harlow's mother in *Harlow* (US 65).

☆ George Raft gave the thumbs down to leading roles in *Dead End* (US 37), *High Sierra* (US 41) and *The Maltese Falcon* (US 41). They all went to Bogey.

☆ Michael Caine established his inimitable cockney persona in *Alfie* (GB 66) after the part had been turned down by Anthony Newley, James Booth, Terence Stamp and Laurence Harvey.

☆ Bogart was second choice for *The African Queen* (GB 51), as was Katharine Hepburn. The intention was to cast John Mills and Bette Davis.

☆ Perhaps a unique example of a starring role intended for an actor going instead to an actress was the lead in *The Spanish Dancer* (US 20). Written for Rudolph Valentino, it was rewritten for Pola Negri.

☆ Rip Torn was originally signed for the cameo role of the Texan lawyer in *Easy Rider* (US 69) that brought overnight celebrity to veteran supporting player Jack Nicholson.

☆ The *Road to . . .* films were not designed for Bob Hope and Bing Crosby; they were meant for Fred MacMurray and George Burns.

☆ Charles Laughton began the part of Micawber in *David Copperfield* (US 35), but after three days of shooting became convinced that W. C. Fields was the only actor suitable for it. Paramount agreed to replace him, but with a condition written into Fields's contract that he had to speak in an English accent—an obligation he signally failed to fulfil!

☆ George Segal actually began filming *10* (US 79), but quit due to 'creative difficulties'—to be replaced by Dudley Moore in the role that shot the diminutive Englishman to Hollywood stardom.

☆ Bob Hoskins was signed for the role of Al Capone in *The Untouchables* (US 87), but given a $200,000 pay-off when Robert de Niro became available to play the part.

The performer who played in the most movies was Tom London (1883–1963), who was born in Louisville, Ky., and made the first of his over 2000 appearances on screen in *The Great Train Robbery* (US 03). He was given the role of the locomotive driver, which was also his job in real life. By 1919 he was playing starring roles at Universal under his real name, Leonard Clapham, which he changed to Tom London in 1924. When he became too old for lead roles he receded comfortably into character parts, specializing in sheriffs in 'B' westerns. His last picture was Willard Parker's *The Lone Texan* (US 59).

The performer who has played the most leading roles in feature films is the Indian comedienne Manorama, who made her screen debut in 1958 and completed her 1000th film in 1985. Of the total, 999 were in Tamil and one in Hindi (a language she does not speak). Manorama works on as many as 30 films at the same time.

The Hollywood star who played the most leading roles in feature films was John Wayne (1907–79), who appeared in 153 movies from *The Drop Kick* (US 27) to *The Shootist* (US 76). In all except 11 of these films he played leading roles. The Duke summed up his simple yet enduring qualities thus: 'I've never had a goddam artistic problem in my life, never, and I've worked with the best of them. John Ford isn't exactly a bum, is he? Yet he never gave me any manure about art.' And: 'I play John Wayne in every part regardless of the character, and I've been doing okay, haven't I?'

Of Hollywood stars still performing, the record for the most screen credits is held by John Carradine (1906–), who has featured or starred in 244 films from *Tol'able David* (US 30) to *Evil Spawn* (US 87). In addition he has performed in over 180 plays. Repeated claims that each of the veteran actor's new films is his 500th may be discounted.

The British star with the most screen credits who is still performing in movies is Christopher Lee (1922–), star of English, French, Spanish, German, Italian, Swedish, Norwegian, Russian, American and Australian films. The 157 feature films and two shorts he has played in from *Corridor of Mirrors* (GB 47) to *The Avalon Awakening* (GB 88) include 14 in which he recreated his most celebrated role, that of Count Dracula, and one in which he played HRH Prince Philip.

John Wayne playing his first starring role in *The Big Trail* (US 29). He was to achieve the record for the most leading roles in Hollywood pictures. (*SI*)

The Most Popular Actors and Actresses

The earliest recorded popularity poll was conducted by a Russian fan magazine in 1911 and was headed by dapper French comedian Max Linder, followed by Denmark's tragic actress Asta Nielsen, with another Danish star, Valdemar Psilander, in third place. America's first poll was staged by *Motion Picture Story Magazine* in March 1912 and resulted in Maurice Costello being voted most popular male star and the now forgotten Dolores Cassinelli most popular actress. By 1914 Mary Pickford, 12th in the 1912 poll, had displaced her and for the next ten years 'the girl with the golden curls', otherwise known as 'America's sweetheart', topped virtually every popularity poll held throughout the world, including those conducted in Soviet Russia (where her husband Douglas Fairbanks was voted most popular male star in 1925). The most durable star of talkies would appear to be John Wayne, who featured in the annual 'Ten Top Box Office Stars' Quigley Poll 25 times 1949–74 and headed it in 1950, 1951, 1954 and 1971. For the most popular Hollywood stars of the 1970s, see Quigley Poll results.

The first popularity poll confined to British-born stars was conducted by *Pictures and the Picturegoer* in 1915 with the following results: 1 Alma Taylor; 2 Elizabeth Risdon; 3 Charles Chaplin; 4 Stewart Rome; 5 Chrissie White; 6 Fred Evans.

Ten years later the *Daily News* poll showed Alma Taylor and Chrissie White, both of whom had joined the Hepworth Co. as child actresses in 1908, still firmly in the public favour: 1 Betty Balfour; 2 Alma Taylor; 3 Gladys Cooper; 4 Violet Hopson; 5 Matheson Lang; 6 Fay Compton; 7 Chrissie White; 8 Stewart Rome; 9 Owen Nares; 10 Ivor Novello.

During the 1930s America's box office was dominated by children, elderly ladies and gentlemen, and a mouse. Marie Dressler topped the Quigley Poll at age 63 in 1932 and again in 1933; Will Rogers came first aged 55 in 1934; then Shirley Temple rose to the top, aged 7, and remained there for the following three years, until 1939, when Mickey Rooney, 18 years old and playing a high school kid in the *Andy Hardy* series, took the lead and held first place for three years. Mickey Mouse was not eligible for the Quigley Poll, but he beat Emil Jannings by 400,000 votes as No. 1 star in a popularity contest held in Australia in 1931, and knocked Wallace Beery into second place in Japan in 1936.

Bridging this period and the John Wayne era were the Bing Crosby–Betty Grable years of the 1940s.

Cumulative Quigley Poll results for the 1960s give the following hierarchy of the biggest box-office draws of the decade: 1 John Wayne; 2 Doris Day; 3 Cary Grant, Rock Hudson and Elizabeth Taylor; 4 Jack Lemmon; 5 Julie Andrews; 6 Paul Newman; 7 Sean Connery; 8 Elvis Presley; 9 Sidney Poitier; 10 Lee Marvin. (Of course no such list is definitive. Sophia Loren, who never appeared in the annual Top Ten, was nevertheless voted the most popular star in the world by the US Foreign Press Corps in 1969.) The order for the 1970s: 1 Clint Eastwood; 2 Burt Reynolds; 3 Barbra Streisand; 4 Paul Newman; 5 Robert Redford; 6 Steve McQueen; 7 John Wayne; 8 Woody Allen; 9 Dustin Hoffman; 10 Sylvester Stallone. The mid-1980s saw the end of Clint Eastwood's and Burt Reynolds's dominance of the poll, but a Rambo–Rocky inspired return to the top for Sylvester Stallone. There is little consistency in the public's choice of favourite actresses, which tends to depend on the drawing power of a single film with a strong female leading role.

QUIGLEY PUBLICATIONS POLL

The annual Quigley Poll is a poll of exhibitors to determine the top box-office draws. Listed below are the top male and the top female star for each year—the rating of whichever was not No. 1 is given in brackets after the name.

1915 William S. Hart / Mary Pickford (2)
1916 William S. Hart / Mary Pickford (2)
1917 Douglas Fairbanks / Anita Stewart (3)
1918 Douglas Fairbanks / Mary Pickford (2)
1919 Wallace Reid / Mary Pickford (3)
1920 Wallace Reid / Marguerite Clark (2)
1921 Mary Pickford / Douglas Fairbanks (2)
1922 Mary Pickford / Douglas Fairbanks (2)
1923 Thomas Meighan / Norma Talmadge (2)
1924 Norma Talmadge / Rudolph Valentino (3)
1925 Rudolph Valentino / Norma Talmadge (2)
1926 Colleen Moore / Tom Mix (2)
1927 Tom Mix / Colleen Moore (2)
1928 Clara Bow / Lon Chaney (2)
1929 Clara Bow / Lon Chaney (2)
1930 Joan Crawford / William Haines (2)
1931 Janet Gaynor / Charles Farrell (2)
1932 Marie Dressler / Charles Farrell (4)
1933 Marie Dressler / Will Rogers (2)
1934 Will Rogers / Janet Gaynor (3)
1935 Shirley Temple / Will Rogers (2)
1936 Shirley Temple / Clark Gable (2)
1937 Shirley Temple / Clark Gable (2)
1938 Shirley Temple / Clark Gable (2)
1939 Mickey Rooney / Shirley Temple (5)
1940 Mickey Rooney / Bette Davis (9)
1941 Mickey Rooney / Bette Davis (8)
1942 Abbott & Costello / Betty Grable (8)
1943 Betty Grable / Bob Hope (2)
1944 Bing Crosby / Betty Grable (4)
1945 Bing Crosby / Greer Garson (3)
1946 Bing Crosby / Ingrid Bergman (2)
1947 Bing Crosby / Betty Grable (2)
1948 Bing Crosby / Betty Grable (2)
1949 Bob Hope / Betty Grable (7)
1950 John Wayne / Betty Grable (4)
1951 John Wayne / Betty Grable (3)
1952 Dean Martin and Jerry Lewis / Doris Day (7)
1953 Gary Cooper / Marilyn Monroe (6)
1954 John Wayne / Marilyn Monroe (5)
1955 James Stewart / Grace Kelly (2)
1956 William Holden / Marilyn Monroe (8)
1957 Rock Hudson / Kim Novak (11)
1958 Glenn Ford / Elizabeth Taylor (2)
1959 Rock Hudson / Doris Day (4)

In the 1950s this was the way Middle America liked its screen heroes. John Wayne topped the Quigley Poll in 1950, 1951 and 1954—and bounced back to the top again in 1971. (*SI*)

1960	Doris Day
	Rock Hudson (2)
1961	Elizabeth Taylor
	Rock Hudson (2)
1962	Doris Day
	Rock Hudson (2)
1963	Doris Day
	John Wayne (2)
1964	Doris Day
	Jack Lemmon (2)
1965	Sean Connery
	Doris Day (3)
1966	Julie Andrews
	Sean Connery (2)
1967	Julie Andrews
	Lee Marvin (2)
1968	Sidney Poitier
	Julie Andrews (3)
1969	Paul Newman
	Katharine Hepburn (9)
1970	Paul Newman
	Barbra Streisand (9)
1971	John Wayne
	Ali MacGraw (8)
1972	Clint Eastwood
	Barbra Streisand (5)
1973	Clint Eastwood
	Barbra Streisand (6)
1974	Robert Redford
	Barbra Streisand (4)
1975	Robert Redford
	Barbra Streisand (2)
1976	Robert Redford
	Tatum O'Neal (8)
1977	Sylvester Stallone
	Barbra Streisand (2)
1978	Burt Reynolds
	Diane Keaton (7)
1979	Burt Reynolds
	Jane Fonda (3)
1980	Burt Reynolds
	Jane Fonda (4)
1981	Burt Reynolds
	Dolly Parton (4)

1982	Burt Reynolds
	Dolly Parton (6)
1983	Clint Eastwood
	Meryl Streep (12)
1984	Clint Eastwood
	Sally Field (5)
1985	Sylvester Stallone
	Meryl Streep (10)
1986	Tom Cruise
	Bette Midler (5)
1987	Eddie Murphy
	Glenn Close (7)

Hollywood still offers the allure of instant stardom. How many ordinary cinemagoers had heard of Glenn Close in 1986? Yet the following year she demonstrated her *Fatal Attraction* (US 87) by topping the Quigley Poll as most popular actress.

Left: Paul Newman is still the most popular actor in Italy, even if the boyish good looks have faded a little since this picture was taken. By 1987 he was no longer among the top 25 stars in the USA. (*Rob Burt*)

Paul Newman is the favourite actor of both Italian men and women, according to a poll conducted in 1986. Favourite actress for men was home-grown star Ornella Mutie, favourite for women Catherine Deneuve.

The overseas star with the highest-ever popularity rating in the USA was Brigitte Bardot, who came 7th in the Quigley Poll of 1958.

The largest number of members of one family to have appeared in films is 31 in the case of the Luevas of Los Angeles. Matriarch Augustina Lueva (b. La Refugio, Mexico 1852), 18 of her 21 children and 12 of her grandchildren were reported to be actively employed as film actors in 1928. Six of the children and four of the grandchildren appeared together in an unidentified film of that year.

Other films in which families have appeared together are: *Hearts of the World* (US 18), in which Bobby Harron played the lead, his mother played a French woman, her two daughters Jessie and Mary played her screen daughters, and Bobby's brother Johnny played 'a boy with a barrel'; *Mr Smith Goes to Washington* (US 39) with brothers and sisters Coy, Vivian, Gloria, Louise, Harry, Billy, Delmar, Garry and Bobs Watson playing the Governor of Montana's children; and *Ein Tag ist Schoener als der Andere* (FRG 70), featuring the seven von Eichborn children, Clarissa, Justina, Evelyn, Jacqueline, Wolfram, Holger and Isabella. More recently Blake Edwards's *That's Life* (US 86) starred his wife Julie Andrews opposite Jack Lemmon, and featured his own daughter Jennifer Edwards and Jack's son Chris Lemmon, as well as Julie's daughter Emma Walton and Jack's wife Felicia Farr. When Mia Farrow starred as Hannah in *Hannah and Her Sisters* (US 86), there were no sisters around, but her mother Maureen O'Sullivan, her three children by André Prévin and four of her adopted children were all in the picture. Three generations were also represented in *Kung Fu Master* (Fr 88), with Jane Birkin's parents (mother is actress Judy Campbell) playing her parents in the film, and her children Charlotte Gainsbourg and Lou Doillon playing her on-screen daughters.

Some film families deliberately avoided working with each other. All six McLaglen brothers were film actors, Victor in America, the others mainly in Britain. When the youngest, Leopold, tried to break into Hollywood pictures in the mid-1930s, eldest brother Victor took out an injunction restraining him. 'There's only room for one McLaglen in Hollywood,' asserted Victor.

The most generations of screen actors in a family is four in the case of the Redgraves. Roy Redgrave (1872–1922), father of Sir Michael, made his screen debut in *The Christian* (Aus 11) and continued to appear in Australian movies until 1920. Sir Michael Redgrave (1908–85) married actress Rachel Kempson (1910–), and their two daughters Vanessa (1937–) and Lynn (1943–) and son Corin (1939–) all went into movies. Vanessa's daughters Natasha and Joely made their debut in *The Charge of the Light Brigade* (GB 68) and subsequently appeared in *Dead Cert* (GB 74) and *Joseph Andrews* (GB 77), while Corin's daughter Jemima appeared for the first time in *Joseph Andrews*. All three actress members of the fourth generation have successfully transferred to adult leading roles, Joely in *Wetherby* (GB 85), Natasha in *Gothic* (GB 86) and *A Month in the Country* (GB 87) and Jemma (her adult name) in *The Dream Demon* (GB 88).

Mums and Dads

A number of artistes have portrayed their own parents in films. Marie Lloyd Jnr played 'Queen of the Halls' Marie Lloyd Snr in *Variety Jubilee* (GB 43), while on the other side of the Channel playwright Sacha Guitry took the role of his father, actor Lucien Guitry, in *The Private Life of an Actor* (Fr 48) —he also played himself. Will Rogers Jnr portrayed Will Rogers Snr in three films—*Look for the Silver Lining* (US 49), *The Story of Will Rogers* (US 52) and *The Eddie Cantor Story* (US 53). Dick Powell Jnr was seen in a cameo role as lookalike father Dick Powell Snr in *The Day of the Locust* (US 74) and Marcel Cerdan Jnr had a leading role as his father in *Edith and Marcel* (Fr 84), the story of Edith Piaf's love affair with middleweight boxing champion Marcel Cerdan Snr. In *Adolf Hitler—My Part in His Downfall* (GB 72), Jim Dale plays Spike Milligan, while Milligan appears as his own father. Most recent example has been beauty Chynna Phillips playing her own mother Michelle Phillips, formerly of the sixties pop group The Mamas and the Papas and ex live-in lover of both Jack Nicholson and Warren Beatty, in *California Dreamin'* (US 88). The only recorded example of a character being played by his own brother is in Raj Kapoor's two autobiographical movies *Awara* (Ind 51) and *Shree 420* (Ind 55), with Shashi Kapoor in the roles based on Raj Kapoor.

Put Downs

Hollywood luminaries have a tendency to venerate each other, at least in public. It is reassuring to know that they do not always express such cloying sentiments in private.

JULIE ANDREWS
'Working with her is like being hit over the head with a Valentine card'—Christopher Plummer

TALLULAH BANKHEAD
'A day away from Tallulah is like a month in the country'—Howard Dietz

DIANA BARRYMORE
'Diana is a horse's arse, quite a pretty one, but still a horse's arse'—her father, John Barrymore

JOHN BARRYMORE
'It takes an earthquake to get Jack out of bed, a flood to make him wash, and the United States Army to put him to work'—his brother, Lionel Barrymore

HUMPHREY BOGART
'Bogey's a helluva nice guy until 11.30 p.m. After that he thinks he's Bogart'—Dave Chasen

Dynasty. Not many stars can say their great grandfather was a movie star—and their grandfather and grandmother—and their mother. *Left to right*: Natasha Richardson in *A Month in the Country* (GB 87); her mother Vanessa Redgrave in *Wetherby* (GB 85)—her sister Joely co-starred; her grandfather Michael Redgrave in *Kipps* (GB 41) (*SI*); her great grandfather Roy Redgrave in *In My Mind's Eye* (Aus 11) (*Weidenfeld (Publishers)*).

'He sounds like he has a mouth full of wet toilet paper'—Rex Reed on Marlon Brando. Looks like it too. (*SI*)

MARLON BRANDO
'Most of the time he sounds like he has a mouth full of wet toilet paper'—Rex Reed

CAPUCINE
Laurence Harvey to Capucine during filming of *Walk on the Wild Side* (US 62): 'If you were more of a woman, I would be more of a man. Kissing you is like kissing the side of a beer bottle'

MAURICE CHEVALIER
'A great artiste, but a small human being'—Josephine Baker

CLAUDETTE COLBERT
Noel Coward to CC: 'I'd wring your neck, if you had one'

GARY COOPER
'When he puts his arms around me, I feel like a horse'—Clara Bow
'He's got a reputation as a great actor just by thinking hard about the next line'—King Vidor

JOAN CRAWFORD
'The best time I ever had with Joan Crawford was when I pushed her down the stairs in *Whatever Happened to Baby Jane*'—Bette Davis
'There is not enough money in Hollywood to lure me into making another film with Joan Crawford'—Sterling Hayden after co-starring with her in *Johnny Guitar* (US 54)

BETTE DAVIS
'As much sex appeal as Slim Somerville'—Carl Laemmle on BD in her youth

'I can't imagine any guy giving her a tumble'—Carl Laemmle again
'Surely no one but a mother could have loved Bette Davis at the height of her career'—Brian Ahearne

DORIS DAY
'I knew Doris Day before she was a virgin'—Oscar Levant
'Doris Day is as wholesome as a bowl of cornflakes and at least as sexy'—Dwight MacDonald

JAMES DEAN
'He was a hero to the people who saw him only as a little waif, when actually he was a pudding of hatred'—Elia Kazan

KIRK DOUGLAS
'Boastful, egotistical, resentful of criticism—if anyone dare give it'—Sheilah Graham

NELSON EDDY
'The ham of hams'—Allan Dwan

FRANCES FARMER
'The nicest thing I can say about Frances Farmer is that she is unbearable'—William Wyler

Bette Davis said the best time she ever had with Joan Crawford was when she pushed her down the stairs in *Whatever Happened to Baby Jane* (US 62). Kicking her in the face must have been a bundle of fun too. (*SI*)

ERROL FLYNN
'A fifty-year trespass against good taste'—Leslie Mallory

CLARK GABLE
'Clark Gable took the humour and sex from the characters he played'—Joan Crawford
'To tell the honest truth, he isn't such of a helluva good lay'—his lover, subsequently his wife, Carole Lombard

GRETA GARBO
'Boiled down to essentials, she is a plain mortal girl with large feet'—Herbert Kretzmer
'The most inhibited person I've ever worked with'—Ernst Lubitsch
'Making a film with Greta Garbo does not constitute an introduction'—Robert Montgomery

CARY GRANT
'An incredible boor'—Joan Fontaine

PAUL HENREID
'He looks as if his idea of fun would be to find a nice cold damp grave and sit in it'—Richard Winnington

KATHARINE HEPBURN
'She ran the gamut of emotions from A to B'— Dorothy Parker on Hepburn's performance in the Broadway play *The Lake*
'Katherine of Arrogance'—sobriquet she acquired at RKO in the thirties

MIRIAM HOPKINS
'Puerile and silly and snobbish'—Edward G. Robinson
'I don't think there was ever a more difficult female in the world'— Bette Davis (whom some reckoned the second most difficult)
'The least desirable companion on a desert island'—Harvard Lampoon's citation to MH 1940

ALAN LADD
'Alan Ladd is hard, bitter and occasionally charming, but he is, after all, a small boy's idea of a tough guy'—Raymond Chandler

BURT LANCASTER
'Burt Lancaster! Before he can pick up an ashtray, he discusses his motivation for an hour or two. You want to say "Just pick up the ashtray, and shut up!"'—Jeanne Moreau

VIVIEN LEIGH
'She made life hell for everybody near her, unless they did everything she wished, as she wished and when she wished'—Wolfe Kaufman

'She is good as a peasant but incapable of playing a lady'—Sophia Loren on Gina Lollobrigida, seen here not playing a lady in *The Hunchback of Notre Dame* (Fr 57).

JERRY LEWIS
'One of the most hostile, unpleasant guys I've ever seen . . . arrogant, sour, ceremonial, piously chauvinistic egomaniac'—Elliott Gould on his childhood idol

GINA LOLLOBRIGIDA
'Her personality is limited. She is good as a peasant but incapable of playing a lady'—Sophia Loren

SOPHIA LOREN
'Sophia is a very pretty girl but she cannot threaten me because she is incapable of playing my roles'— Gina Lollobrigida

They may look lovey-dovey, but after completing *Desperately Seeking Susan* (US 85) Rosanna Arquette expressed the view that Madonna should have learned to act before jumping into the movie game. (*Kobal*)

MADONNA
'She's jumped right into the movie game . . . but I think people should learn to act first, you know what I mean?'—Rosanna Arquette, her co-star in *Desperately Seeking Susan* (US 85)

VICTOR MATURE
'Hollywood's self-avowed disciple of conceit and vulgarity'—W. H. Mooring

MARILYN MONROE
'She's just an arrogant little tail-twitcher who's learned to throw sex in your face'—Nunnally Johnson
'There's a broad with a future behind her'—Constance Bennett
'A fat cow'—Harry Cohn (given what he said about other people, this could be taken as moderately complimentary)
'A professional amateur'—Laurence Olivier

DAVID NIVEN
'An extremely mean and deeply heartless figure'—fellow actor Peter Willes

MAUREEN O'HARA
'She looked as if butter wouldn't melt in her mouth—or anywhere else'—Elsa Lanchester

MARY PICKFORD
'That prissy bitch'—Mabel Normand
'She was the girl every young man wanted to have—as his sister'—Alistair Cooke

RONALD REAGAN
'I can't stand the sight of Ronnie Reagan. I'd like to stick my Oscar up his arse'—Gloria Grahame

ROBERT REDFORD
'Well, at least he has finally found his true love—what a pity he can't marry himself'—Frank Sinatra

GEORGE C. SCOTT
'A jerk'—Joseph Levine

NORMA SHEARER
'A face unclouded by thought'—Lillian Hellman
'I love to play bitches, and she certainly helped me in this part'—Joan Crawford after co-starring with her in *The Women* (US 39)

FRANK SINATRA
'When Frank Sinatra was down he was sweet, but when he got back up he was hell'—Ava Gardner
'He's the kind of guy that, when he dies, he's going up to heaven and give God a bad time for making him bald'—Marlon Brando
'Terribly nice one minute and . . . well, not so nice the next'—HRH Prince Charles
'I think he's an ill-bred swine who operates on the level of an animal'—David Susskind

SYLVESTER STALLONE
'Repugant and ill-mannered'—anonymous producer

BARBRA STREISAND
Walter Matthau to BS during filming of *Hello Dolly* (US 69): 'I have more talent in my smallest fart than you have in your entire body'
   And on considering the matter further, Matthau again: 'She is the most extraordinarily uninteresting person I have ever met. I just find her a terrible bore'
'The most pretentious woman the cinema has ever known'—producer Jon Peters

ELIZABETH TAYLOR
On herself: 'I have the face and body of a woman and the mind of a child'

LANA TURNER
'She is not even an actress . . . only a trollop'—Gloria Swanson

RAQUEL WELCH
'Silicone from the knees up'—George Masters, make-up artist

ORSON WELLES
'There but for the grace of God, goes God'—Herman Mankiewicz

ESTHER WILLIAMS
'Wet she's a star, dry she ain't'—Joe Pasternak
'I can't honestly say that Esther Williams ever acted in an Andy Hardy picture, but she swam in one'—Mickey Rooney

LORETTA YOUNG
'Whatever it is this actress never had, she still hasn't got it'—*New York Times* critic Bosley Crowther

The largest cast of credited performers in a film was 260 in *Dny Zrady/Days of Treason* (Cz 72), the story of the betrayal of Czechoslovakia in 1938, including Gunnar Möllar as Hitler, Jaroslav Radimecky as Chamberlain, Alexander Fred as Goebbels, Rudolf Jurda as Goering and Vladamir Stach as Mussolini.

Sacha Guitry's *Napoleon* (Fr 54) had 101 credited roles, but was claimed to have 300 speaking parts. MGM claimed 365 speaking parts (73 credited) for *Ben Hur* (US 59), but this seems impossible for a 217-minute film unless it includes groups of people all speaking at once. As many as 430 speaking parts were claimed for the 188 minute *Gandhi* (GB 83), with 138 credited. The British film with the largest cast of credited performers is *Little Dorrit* (GB 87) with 211.

Other films with large casts (credited) include: *Mission to Moscow* (US 43) with 195; *Rottenknechte* (GDR 70) with 194; *Baron Muenchhausen* (Ger 45) with 150; *Sweden for the Swedes* (Swe 80) with 142; *Around the World in 80 Days* (US 56) with 138; *A Bridge Too Far* (GB 77) with 137; *Oh! What a Lovely War* (GB 69) with 125; and Karl Ritter's *Pour la Merité* (Ger 38) with 102.

For **the largest cast including extras**, see p. 72.

The largest all-female cast consisted of the 135 speaking roles in MGM's *The Women* (US 39), starring Joan Crawford, Norma Shearer, Rosalind Russell, Paulette Goddard and Joan Fontaine.

The smallest cast in a live-action dramatic feature, excluding movies with an all-animal cast, is none. Kostas Sfikas' *Model* (Gre 74) had no performers, only robots seen in a single set representing a factory yard. The 1 hr 45 min film was intended as a critique of the 'implacable process that transforms mankind into negotiable goods and mere accessories of an industrial machine'.

There have been a number of movies with a cast of one. Olaf Fønns, leading Danish romantic hero of the World War I period, played alone in Fritz Magnussen's *Remorse* (Den 19), made for Dansk Astra Film. The story is of a wealthy man who is ruined and loses his mistress (represented only by a pair of arms), then returns to her in a starving condition, is rejected and kills her. He restores his fortune but, relentlessly pursued by his own accusing shadow, eventually gives himself up. In addition to its solo performance, the film was distinguished by having no inter-titles.

Sunil Dutt's *Yaadein/Recollections* (Ind 64), in which he starred as well as directed and produced, was a single set, solo movie about a husband deserted by his wife. At the end of the film the woman's shadow seen against a wall indicates that she has returned to him. Robert Carlisle's *Sofi* (US 68), an adaptation of Gogol's *Diary of a Madman*, had Tom Troupe as its only performer. Thierry

Zeno's *Vase de noces* (Bel 73) starred Dominique Garny, who does not speak throughout the film. It tells the story of a simple man living alone amongst his poultry and pigs who eventually hangs himself. Danilo-Bata Stojković played alone as a man fleeing from imaginary pursuers in Milos Radivojević's *Testament* (Yug 75), which was also without speech. Jean-Pierre Lefebvre's *L'Amour blessé* (*Confidences de la nuit*) (Can 75) starred Louise Cuerrier as a lonely woman spending a dull evening in her room listening to a talk show, while Britain's only single artiste film had Monica Buferd in the rather more compelling role of *St Joan* (GB 77). James Whitmore gave a standout performance as Harry S. Truman in his solo biopic of the President's life and times *Give 'Em Hell, Harry!* (US 75).

Other examples of solo performances are by Anne Flannery in *A State of Siege* (NZ 78), Willeke van Ammelrooy in Frans Zwartje's *It's Me* (Neth 79), and by Alain Cavalier in *Ce repondent ne prend pas de message* (Fr 79).

More recently Julie Harris has played Charlotte Brontë in Delbert Mann's evocation of the author's life and times *Brontë* (US/Ire 83). Interaction with the other members of the Brontë family was conveyed by having Charlotte handle both sides of the conversation. Another powerful portrayal of a real-life character was by Philip Baker Hall as Richard Nixon in Robert Altman's *Secret Honor* (US 84), delivering an 80-min monologue described as 'a fictional meditation'.

Unusual Casts

☆ The only feature-length film with a cast composed entirely of American Indians was *The Silent Enemy* (US 30).

☆ The only feature film with a cast composed entirely of Lapps was *The Pathfinder* (Nor 87).

☆ There have been two fiction films with all-Eskimo casts, *Kivalina of the Ice Lands* (US 25) and *Igloo* (US 32), and three Hollywood movies with all-Balinese casts—*Virgins of Bali* (US 32); *Goona-Goona* (US 32) and *Legond, Dance of the Virgins* (US 32). One American film has been made with an all-Siamese cast, *Chang* (US 27); and one with an all-Sudanese cast, *Stampede* (US 30).

☆ In *Sitting Bull* (US 54), the Indians and the US Cavalry were all played by Mexicans. In Samuel Fuller's war picture *Big Red One* (US 80), all the Nazi concentration camp guards were played by Jews.

☆ *The Writing on the Wall* (Fr/Bel 82) was a story of the Northern Ireland troubles in which all the Protestants were played by Catholics and the Catholics by Protestants.

☆ There have been many films about nuns, but only one in which they were actually played by nuns.

Francesca (FRG 87) is about a fictitious star of yester-year who was raised by nuns in Bavaria. The Mother Superior is played by real-life Mother Superior Roswitha Schneider and the nuns by the Sisters of St Mary's Convent in Niederviebach, Bavaria.

☆ Nearly all the performers in *Amy* (US 81) were deaf—they were recruited from the California School for the Deaf at Riverside. Mentally-handicapped actor Richard Mulligan was cast as the most brilliant and intellectual teacher on campus in the off-beat high-school social comedy, *Teachers* (US 84). The title role in *Annie's Coming Out* (Aus 84), based on a true story about a brain damaged teenager, was played by real-life spastic Tina Arhondis.

☆ Members of the International Brigade played in André Malraux's *Man's Hope* (Sp 45), filmed from his own novel during the bombardment of Barcelona in 1938. For three allied fliers who were shot down over Switzerland in World War II, not only was it the end of their war but the opportunity to star in a film. John Hoy and E. G. Morrison of the RAF and Ray Reagan, USAAF sergeant, were given the leading roles in the Swiss film *Last Chance* (Swz 45), playing escaped prisoners leading a party of refugees over the Alps to neutral Switzerland. The refugees, all of different nationalities, were played by real refugees.

☆ All the leading players in *Dionysus* (Fr 84), about a US university professor who comes to Paris to defend a thesis on Dionysus and ends up running an assembly line at Citroen, were played by real life university professors.

☆ Beauty queens have often been given a chance to break into movies, but never so many all at once as in *Yankee Pasha* (US 54). A costumer about a New England girl sold into a Moroccan harem, the cast included the Misses USA, Japan, Panama, Norway, Uruguay, South Africa, Australia and Miss Universe, Christiane Martel.

☆ RKO tried an unusual experiment in 1944 with a film called *Days of Glory* (US 44), in which all 19 featured players were making their screen debut. One of the 19 went on to stardom—Gregory Peck.

☆ Von Stroheim used real hookers to play the prostitutes in *The Wedding March* (US 27) and similarly the inmates of the bordello in John Huston's *Under the Volcano* (US 85) were real-life members of their calling. Not so in *Maya* (Fr 49). A set representing a red light district was built in false perspective to give an illusion of depth. The prostitutes seen at the far end of the street were played by little girls of 6 to 8 years old outfitted in the gaudy raiment of harlotry.

☆ When lesbian producer/star Nazimova starred in her own production of *Salome* (US 23), she employed only gay actors as a 'homage' to Oscar Wilde.

☆ The masochists receiving the punishing attentions of Bulle Ogier in *Maitresse* (Fr 79) were not actors. They were deviants who were invited to bring along their own chains and whips.

☆ The extras engaged to play convicts in *Hell's Highway* (US 32) were all ex-cons themselves.

☆ A lot of films have been set in gaols, and a few have been shot in real prisons, but only one has had a cast made up entirely of prisoners and 'screws'. *A Time to Learn* (US 87) was made by the inmates of the Virginia State Penitentiary at Richmond, Va for the State Department of Correctional Education. It told of a black basketball-playing high school dropout and a white farm boy who meet up in prison and find that not being able to read prevents them from winning a place in normal society—Virginia has a 'no read, no bail' policy. The performers included a number of killers and rapists.

☆ There have been many prison dramas and war films with all male casts, but very few films with all-female casts. Best known is probably *The Women* (US 39), whose 135 speaking roles included those played by Joan Crawford, Norma Shearer, Rosalind Russell, Paulette Goddard and Joan Fontaine. Others have been: *Maedchen in Uniform* (Ger 31) with Dorothea Wieck; *The Mad Parade* (US 31) with Evelyn Brent; *The Blossoms Have Fallen* (Jap 38), about the constraints of life in a geisha house; *The Bitter Tears of Petra von Kant* (FRG 72) with Margit Carstensen; *Cries and Whispers* (Swe 72) with Harriet Andersson, Ingrid Thulin and Liv Ulmann; and *Friendships, Secrets and Lies* (US 79) with Sondra Locke, Tina Louise and Paula Prentiss. All-women films of the 1980s include *Black Mirror* (Can 81), a French-Canadian movie set in a women's prison, *Les Chicks* (Fr 85) and *Les Nanas* (Fr 85) with Marie-France Pisier.

☆ Equally rare are films with all-child casts. There have been four in which the children are playing children. Peter Brook's *The Lord of the Flies* (GB 63) was from William Golding's novel about schoolboy castaways on an uninhabited island who revert to barbarism, while *Leave Us Alone* (Den 75) had a similar theme of children adapting to life on a desert island. Mexico's *Poison for Fairies* (Mex 86), winner of five Ariels (Mexico's equivalent to the Oscar), is set in a girls' school and confronts the dangerous world of childhood fantasies. The only adult characters are represented by an arm or a leg seen at the side of the screen. *Maramao* (Fr/It 87) had a cast composed entirely of 5 to 13 year olds, headed by Italian moppet Vanessa Grevina. In addition there have been three films in which children play adults. *General Spanky* (US 37), starring Spanky McFarland of Our Gang fame, was a burlesque melodrama of the Civil War, while *Bugsy Malone* (GB 76) parodied the gangster movies of the thirties with a then unknown Jodie Foster as a 13-year-old femme fatale. The cast of *The Annunciation* (Hun 84), in which Adam, the first man, is guided through the darker passages of man's tormented history, were all between 8 and 12, with the part of Satan played by a 9-year-old girl.

☆ There have been isolated examples of children playing adults in straight dramas. Blanche Sweet played a married woman at the age of 13 in *A Man with Three Lives* (US 09) and 12-year-old Gladys Leslie took the role of a debutante in *The Beloved Imposter* (US 19). Mickey Rooney played an adult midget in *Orchids and Ermine* (US 27) at the age of 7 and this led to a persistent rumour that the child star was in reality a midget posing as a child. The reverse principle, of adults playing children, was not uncommon in silent days, when actresses like Mary Pickford and Lillian Gish specialized in such roles. More unusual examples are the 33-year-old Richard Barthelmess playing a 6-year-old boy in the opening scenes of *The Little Shepherd of Kingdom Come* (US 28) and Bette Davis's portrayal of a 13-year-old in *Payment on Demand* (US 51) when she was 43.

☆ There have been two films with all-midget casts: a western called *The Terror of Tiny Town* (US 38) and Werner Herzog's *Even Dwarfs Started Small* (FRG 70).

☆ Veteran producer Mario Cecchi Gori assembled a mammoth cast for his 125th picture *The Department Store* (It 86) which included every available performer who had appeared in his previous 124 films.

The longest screen career is that of Berlin comedian and character actor Curt Bois (b. 1900), who made his film debut in 1909 at the age of nine in *Mutterliebe* (Ger 09). Bois left Germany in 1933 on the accession of the Nazis and made his way to the US via Prague, Vienna, London and Paris. He went to New York to star in a stage play which closed after only one night and thence to Hollywood in 1938. He appeared in such notable films as *Casablanca* (US 42) and Max Ophuls' *Caught* (US 49) before returning to Berlin in the early fifties. Recent films include *Der Himmel uber Berlin* (FRG/Fr 87).

The actress with the longest screen career is Helen Hayes (b. 1900), who made her debut in *Jean and the Calico Doll* (US 10) at the age of 10. Since her screen work in the last ten years has been confined to television movies, the record for the most enduring actress of the large screen goes to Lillian Gish (b. 1893), first seen as a 19 year old in *An Unseen Enemy* (US 12) and more recently playing leading roles in *Hambone and Hillie* (US 84), *Sweet Liberty* (US 85) and *The Whales of August* (US 87).

Half Century Up

The following performers have had screen careers spanning 50 years or more.

☆ 50 Years

Melvyn Douglas (1901–81) *Tonight or Never* (US 31) *Ghost Story* (US 81)

Hermione Gingold (1897–1987) *Someone at the Door* (GB 36) *Garbo Talks* (US 86)

Rex Ingram (1895–1969) *Tarzan of the Apes* (US 18) *Journey to Shiloh* (US 68)

Gaston Modot (1887–1970) *Onésime* (Fr 09) *Les Testaments du Docteur Cordelier* (Fr 59)

Pola Negri (1897) *Love and Passion* (Pol 14) *The Moonspinners* (US 64)

Vincent Prince (1911–) *Service de Luxe* (US 38). Still active 1988

Sir Ralph Richardson (1902–83) *The Ghoul* (GB 33) *Give My Regards to Broad Street* (GB 84)

Michel Simon (1897–1975) *La Vocation d'André Carrel* (Swz 25) *The Red Ibis* (Fr 75)

☆ 51 Years

Tullio Carminati (1895–1971) *Il Bacio di Margherita de Cortona* (It 12) *Swordsman of Siena* (It/Fr 63)

Dorothy Gish (1898?–1968) *An Unseen Enemy* (US 12) *The Cardinal* (US 63)

Sir Cedric Hardwicke (1893–1964) *Riches and Rogues* (GB 13) *The Pumpkin Eater* (GB 64)

Paul Lukas (1895–1971) *Sphynx* (Hun 17) *Sol Madrid* (US 68)

Pedro Regas (1892–1974) debut 1921 *High Plains Drifter* (US 72)

Nora Swinburne (1902–) *Branded* (GB 20) *Up the Chastity Belt* (GB 71)

☆ 52 Years

Reginald Denny (1891–1967) debut 1914 *Batman* (GB 66)

Isabel Jeans (1891–1985/6?) *The Profligate* (GB 17) *The Magic Christian* (GB 69)

Walter Pidgeon (1897–1984) *Mannequin* (US 25) *Sextette* (US 77)

☆ 53 Years

Chester Conklin (1888–1971) one-reel comedies 1913 *A Big Hand for a Little Lady* (US 66)

Bob Steele (1907–) *The Adventures of Bill and Bob* (US 19). Reported to be playing bit parts 1972

Olga Tschechowa (1896–1980) *Todesreigen* (Ger 21) *Freihling auf Immenhof* (FRG 74)

☆ 54 Years

James Cagney (1899–1986) *Sinner's Holiday* (US 30) *Terrible Joe Moran* (US 84, TVM)

Bill Kerr (1922–) *Harmony Row* (US 34). Still active 1988

☆ 55 Years

Richard Arlen (1899–1976) *Ladies Must Live* (US 21) *A Whale of a Tale* (US 76)

Francis X. Bushman (1883–1966) *Fate's Funny Frolic* (US 11) *The Ghost in the Invisible Bikini* (US 66)

Sir Alec Guinness (1914–) *Evensong* (GB 33). Still active 1988

Stanley Holloway (1890–1982) *The Rotters* (GB 21) *Journey Through Fear* (GB 76)

Spanky McFarland (1928–) (fat boy of *Our Gang* comedies) *Day of Reckoning* (US 33). Still active 1988

Sylvia Sidney (1910–) *Broadway Nights* (US 27) *Hammett* (US 82)

☆ **56 Years**

Elizabeth Bergner (1898–1986) *Der Evangelimann* (Ger 23) *Whitsun Holiday* (FRG 79)

Charles Boyer (1899–1978) *L'Homme du Large* (Fr 20) *A Matter of Time* (It/US 76)

Fay Compton (1894–1978) *She Stoops to Conquer* (GB 14) *The Virgin and the Gypsy* (GB 70)

Gladys Cooper (1888–1971) *The Eleventh Commandment* (GB 13) *A Nice Girl Like Me* (US 69)

Marlene Dietrich (1901–) *So Sind die Männer* (Ger 22) *Just a Gigolo* (FRG 78)

Raymond Hatton (1887–1971) debut 1911 *In Cold Blood* (US 67)

Esmond Knight (1906–1987) *The Blue Peter* (GB 28) *Forbrydelsens Element* (Den 84)

Mae Marsh (1895–1968) *Man's Genesis* (US 12) *Arabella* (US 68)

Ray Milland (1905–85) *The Plaything* (GB 29) *The Sea Serpent* (It 85)

Sir John Mills (1908–) *The Midshipmaid* (GB 32). Still active 1988

☆ **57 Years**

Donald Crisp (1880–1974) *The French Maid* (US 06) *Spencer's Mountain* (US 63)

Constance Cummings (1910–) *The Criminal Code* (US 31). Still active 1988

Finlay Currie (1878–1968) *The War in the Air* (GB 08) *Bunny Lake is Missing* (GB 65)

Bette Davis (1908–) *The Bad Sister* (US 31). Still active 1988

Sylvie (1885–1970) *Britannicus* (Fr 12) *Le Ciel des fons* (Fr 69)

☆ **58 Years**

John Carradine (1906–) *Tol'able David* (US 30). Still active 1988

Minta Durfee (1890–1975) *His Wife's Mistake* (US 13) *Willard* (US 71)

Myrna Loy (1905–) *The Ten Commandments* (US 23) *Summer Solstice* (US 81, TVM)

Sir Laurence Olivier (1907–) *Hocus Pocus* (Ger 30). Still active 1988

Maureen O'Sullivan (1911–) *Song of My Heart* (GB 30). Still active 1988

John Stuart (1898–1979) *Her Son* (GB 20) *Superman* (GB 78)

H. B. Warner (1876–1958) *English Nell* (GB 00) *Darby's Rangers* (US 58)

☆ **59 Years**

Maurice Chevalier (1888–1972) *Trop credules* (Fr 08) *Monkeys Go Home* (US 67)

George Burns (1896–) *Lamb Chops* (US 29). Still active 1988

Madge Kennedy (1891–1987) *Baby Mine* (US 17) *Marathon Man* (US 76)

Cathleen Nesbitt (1889–1982) *The Faithful Heart* (GB 22) *The Second Star to the Right* (GB 81)

Françoise Rosay (1891–1974) *Falstaff* (Fr 13) *Pas folie la guêpe* (Fr 72)

☆ **60 Years**

Jackie Cooper (1921–) *Our Gang* shorts (US 27). Still active 1988

Lil Dagover (1897–1980) *Harakiri* (Ger 19) *Tales from the Vienna Woods* (FRG/Aus 79)

Fritz Rasp (1891–1976) *Der Phantom* (Ger 15) *Lina Braake* (FRG 75)

Gilbert Roland (1905–1985) *Blood and Sand* (US 22) *Barbarossa* (US 82)

Gloria Swanson (1897–1983) *At the End of a Perfect Day* (US 14) *Airport 75* (US 74)

☆ **61 Years**

Dame Edith Evans (1888–1976) *A Welsh Singer* (GB 15) *Nasty Habits* (GB 76)

Douglas Fairbanks Jr (1909–) *Party Girl* (US 20) *Ghost Story* (US 81)

Ann Sothern (1909–) *Broadway Nights* (US 27). Still active 1988

☆ **62 Years**

Mickey Rooney (1920–) *Not to be Trusted* (US 26). Still active 1988

☆ **64 Years**

Sir John Gielgud (1904–) *Who Is the Man?* (GB 24). Still active 1988

☆ **65 Years**

Margit Makay (1892–19??) *Bitter Love* (Hun 12) *A Very Moral Night* (Hun 77)

☆ **68 Years**

Bessie Love (1898–1986) *The Flying Torpedo* (US 15) *The Hunter* (US 83)

☆ **69 Years**

Iron Eyes Cody (1907–) *Back to God's Country* (US 19). Still active 1988

☆ **70 Years**

Cyril Cusack (1910–) *Knocknagow* (Ire 18). Still active 1988

Ruth Gordon (1896–1985) *Camille* (US 15) *Maxie* (US 85)

☆ **72 Years**

Francesca Bertini (1888–) *La Dea del Mare* (It 04) *1900* (It 76)

Seventy-five years separate Lillian Gish's performances in *An Unseen Enemy* (US 12)—kneeling on the right—and *The Whales of August* (US 87). (*Kobal*)

☆ **76 Years**

Lillian Gish (1893–) *An Unseen Enemy* (US 12). Still active 1988

Charles Vanel (1892–) *Jim Crow* (Fr 12). Still active 1988

☆ **78 Years**

Helen Hayes (1900–) *Jean and the Calico Doll* (US 10). Still active 1988

☆ **79 Years**

Curt Bois (1900–) *Mutterliebe* (Ger 09). Still active 1988

The largest number of roles played by one actor in a single film is not, as generally believed, the eight members of the d'Ascoyne family portrayed by Alec Guinness in *Kind Hearts and Coronets* (GB 49), but the 27 parts taken by Rolf Leslie in Will Barker's life story of Queen Victoria *Sixty Years a Queen* (GB 13). Others who have equalled or exceeded Sir Alec's eight roles are Lupino Lane, who played all 24 parts in *Only Me* (US 29), Joseph Henabery, cast as Abraham Lincoln and 13 other characters in *The Birth of a Nation* (US 15), Robert Hirsch, seen in 12 roles in *No Questions on Saturday* (US 64), Michael Ripper, with nine in *What a Crazy World* (GB 63), Flavio Migliaccio, who had eight parts in *Como Vai, Vai Bem* (Bra 69) and Rolv Wesenlund, portraying eight characters in the comedy *Norske Byggeklosser* (Nor 71). Perhaps the most economically casted film of recent years was *The Great McGonagall* (GB 74) which had five actors playing 34 parts between them.

Actresses Who Have Played Men

There have been many examples of films in which female characters disguised themselves in male attire and in silent days it was not infrequent for young women to play boys, but few actresses have played adult males. Those who have:

☆ Francesca Bertini in the title role of *Histoire d'un Pierrot* (It 13).

☆ Mathilde Comont as the Persian prince in *The Thief of Bagdad* (US 24).

☆ Elspeth Dudgeon (billed as 'John Dudgeon') as the aged man in the upstairs bedroom in *The Old Dark House* (US 32).

☆ Signe Hasso as 'Mr Christopher', Nazi agent masquerading as a woman, in *The House on 92nd Street* (US 45).

☆ Virginia Engels as old man who falls down the stairs during saloon brawl in *San Antonio* (US 45).

☆ Sena Jurinac as Octavian in *Der Rosenkavalier* (GB 62).

☆ Ivy Ling Po as the hero Chang in *The Mermaid* (HK 66).

☆ Caroline Johnson as the Prince of Denmark in *Hamlet* (Can 71).

☆ Anne Heywood as Roy, a transsexual man, in *I Want What I Want* (GB 72).

☆ Victoria Abril as an effeminate young man who undergoes a sex change in *I Want To Be a Woman* (Sp 77).

☆ Ethel Merman as a shell-shocked soldier suffering from the delusion he is Ethel Merman in *Airplane* (US 80).

☆ Linda Hunt, 4 ft 9 in American actress, as the male Eurasian cameraman Billy Kwan in *The Year of Living Dangerously* (Aus 82).

☆ Eva Mattes as a male film director based on Rainer Werner Fassbinder in *A Man Like Eva* (FRG 83).

☆ Gillian Jones as Sebastian (also Viola) in *Twelfth Night* (Aus 86).

☆ Debra Winger as redheaded male archangel Emmett, who is in charge of Heaven, in *Made in Heaven* (US 87). (Ms Winger played the role on condition she was neither credited nor identified.)

☆ Theresa Russell as King Zog of Albania in husband Ken Russell's segment of portmanteau film *Aria* (GB 87).

☆ Lanah Pellay as black waiter-turned-revolutionary Alex in *Eat the Rich* (GB 87).

Names

The most usual reasons for actors and actresses changing their names are that those they were born with are too long, too difficult to pronounce, or simply unglamorous. It is not hard to understand why Herbert Charles Angelo Kuchacewich ze Schluderpacheru decided to drop it in favour Herbert Lom, or why Derek Julius Gaspard Ulrich Niven van den Bogaerde thought he would go further with a name like Dirk Bogarde. Equally Larushka Mischa Skikne had good reason to change his to Laurence Harvey and nobody complained when Walter Matasschanskayasky chose to call himself Matthau instead (though he was billed as Walter Matasschanskayasky when he played a recurring cameo role as a drunk in *Earthquake* (US 74)).

Briefer names may be just as unacceptable. Sarah Jane Fulks was distasteful to Jane Wyman, as was Alexandra Zuck to Sandra Dee and Diana Fluck to Diana Dors. Olga Kronk preferred Claire Windsor, and not surprisingly Doris Day was as relieved to be free of Doris Kappelhoff as was Cyd Charisse not to have to answer to Tula Finklea. Burl Ivanhoe substituted Ives, while Fabian Forte Bonaparte was satisfied to get along with just his first name. Robert Taylor had rather more appeal for a romantic hero than Spangler Arlington Brugh and Septimus Ryott was undoubtedly correct in thinking that his female fans would prefer him as Stewart Rome. Austrian actor Jake Kratz doubted he would be able to play hot-blooded Latin lovers with a name like that and changed it to Ricardo Cortez. Many performers born with Latin names preferred something Anglo-Saxon: Dino Crocetti opted for Dean Martin, Margarita Carmen Cansino for Rita Hayworth, Luis Antonio Damaso de Alonso for Gilbert Roland and Anna Maria Luisa Italiano for Anne Bancroft. A few

> Juvenile actor River Phoenix, who became an overnight star with his performance in *The Mosquito Coast* (US 86), is one of a number of siblings with unusual names. His brother Leaf and sister Summer appear with him in *Russkies* (US 88), while yet to make their screen debut are Rainbow and Liberty. All are real, not screen names.

reversed the process, and changed Anglo-Saxon names into something more exotic: Bonar Sullivan became Bonar Colleano, Peggy Middleton assumed the more romantic Yvonne de Carlo and Muriel Harding decided that Olga Petrova held a greater air of mystery for a *femme fatale*.

Some actors chose names that others had discarded. Bernard Schwarz chose Tony Curtis, while the real Tony Curtis had become Italy's best loved comedian Toto. American actor Bud Flanagan changed his name to Dennis O'Keefe, while British actor Robert Winthrop altered his to Bud Flanagan. It was fortunate for James Stewart that his British namesake had already decided to change James Stewart into Stewart Granger before the other James Stewart went into movies.

Alternatively an artiste could sometimes get away with adopting a name which already had cachet. Cambodia's leading female star before the communist takeover, Kim Nova, selected her screen name in unabashed imitation of Kim Novak. In 1974 a Cambodian starlet called herself Kim Novy in imitation of the imitation. Charles Chaplin sued a Mexican comedian called Charles Amador who had changed his name to Charles Aplin, but was unable to do anything about a German comedian who appeared on screen as Charlie Kaplin. Hong Kong's Bruce Li found fame and fortune treading in the footsteps of the late Bruce Lee.

It was also perfectly possible to have several actors with a legitimate claim to the same name. There were three Robert Lee's working in Hollywood during the 1920s and four Charles Mack's, two of them styled themselves Charles E. Mack, and additionally a Mrs Charles Mack, who performed under that name.

Some were satisfied simply to change their Christian name: Leslie/Bob Hope; James/David Niven; William/Pat O'Brien; Clarence/Robert Cummings; Hubert/Rudy Vallee; John/Arthur Kennedy; Julius/Groucho Marx; Virginia/Bebe Daniels; Sari/Zsa Zsa Gabor; Marilyn/Kim Novak; Adolf/Anton Walbrook; Julia/Lana Turner; Ruth/Bette Davis.

Joseph Keaton assumed the first name of 'Buster' at the age of six months when he fell downstairs and Harry Houdini, a family friend, remarked to his father: 'That's some buster your baby took!' Harry Crosby acquired 'Bing' from avid reading of a comic strip called *The Bingville Bugle* when he was at school.

Even simpler was to change a single letter of the name: Conrad Veidt (Weidt); Beulah Bondi (Bondy); George Raft (Ranft); May Robson (Robison); Ronald Squire (Squirl); Gerard Philipe (Philippe); Dorothy Malone (Maloney); Warren Beatty (Beaty); Yul Brynner (Bryner). James Baumgarner was content to drop the 'Baum', Anna Maria Pierangeli split her surname down the middle and eschewed her first names, while Banky Vilma just switched to Vilma Banky.

Choice of a new name is dictated by varied circumstances. Judy Garland (Frances Gumm) took her stage surname from the theatre pages of a Chicago newspaper, whose reviews were written by Robert Garland. It was chosen by George Jessel, to whom the 11-year-old Miss Gumm had appealed for help after being billed as Glumm at the theatre where they were both appearing. Her first name came from a Hoagy Carmichael song *Judy*, of which she was fond. French comedian Fernandel was born Fernand Constandin. His wife called him *Fernand d'elle* (*her Fernand*). Luis Alonso selected his new name of Gilbert Roland as a tribute to the two stars he most admired, John Gilbert and Ruth Roland. Stepin Fetchit, the startled black manservant of twenties and thirties Hollywood movies, named himself after a racehorse which had obliged him by winning. Marilyn Monroe's Christian name was selected for her by Fox talent scout Ben Lyon because of his admiration for Marilyn Miller—the Monroe was her mother's maiden name. Bette (Ruth) Davis took her screen Christian name from Balzac's *Cousin Bette*. Gary (Frank J.) Cooper was named after his agent's hometown, Gary, Indiana. The actor's own hometown would hardly have been appropriate—he came from Helena, Montana. MGM ran a fan contest in 1925 to find a new name for the extravagantly named

Lucille Le Sueur. The winner came up with Joan Arden, but as there was already an actress of that name in Hollywood, Miss Le Sueur adopted the name suggested by the runner-up instead—Joan Crawford. Gretchen Young had her first name changed to Loretta by Colleen Moore, who discovered her as a 14-year-old extra in *Her Wild Oat* (US 26). Loretta, said Miss Moore, was the name of 'the most beautiful doll I ever had'. Bela Lugosi, real name Bela Blasko, took his screen surname from his

America and Britain both produced circus movies in 1938 and each had basically the same plot. *The Show Goes On* (GB 38) starred Anna Neagle; *Under the Big Top* (US 38) starred Anna Nagle.

hometown of Lugos in Hungary. Richard Burton, formerly Richard Jenkins, assumed the name of his old teacher in Port Talbot. Gig Young (Byron Barr) took the name of the character he played in *The Gay Sisters* (US 42) and former child star Dawn O'Day switched to Anne Shirley to play the heroine of that name in *Anne of Green Gables* (US 34). The story put about by her studio (and still believed in some quarters) that Theda Bara's name was an anagram of 'Arab Death' was so much hokum: the name was selected by director Frank Powell on learning that she had a relative called Barranger. Equally unromantic was Carole Lombard's (Jane Peters) decision to call herself after the Carroll, Lombardi Pharmacy on Lexington and 65th in New York. Greta Garbo might easily have become Greta Gabor. Long before meeting young Greta Gustafsson, her mentor Mauritz Stiller had cherished the dream of discovering and moulding a great star. He asked his manuscript assistant, Arthur Norden, to select a name. Norden, an historian, chose Gábor, after the Hungarian king, Gábor Bethlen. Stiller wanted something less East European, however, and amended it to Garbo. Another monarch was rather more personally involved in naming Lili Damita (Lilliane Carré). Holidaying at Biarritz in 1921 when she was 17, she attracted the attention of the King of Spain, who enquired after the *damita del maillo rojo* (*young lady in a red bathing dress*).

Those who retain their own names may also have cogent reasons for doing so. 'Bradford Dillman', said that actor, 'sounded like a distinguished, phoney, theatrical name—so I kept it.'

The most enduring screen team was that of Indian superstars Prem Nazir and Sheela, who had played opposite each other in 130 movies by 1975.

The Hollywood record pales by comparison. Excluding performers billed together solely in 'series' films, the most enduring screen partners are husband-and-wife team Charles Bronson and Jill

Could You

Use $500?

If So

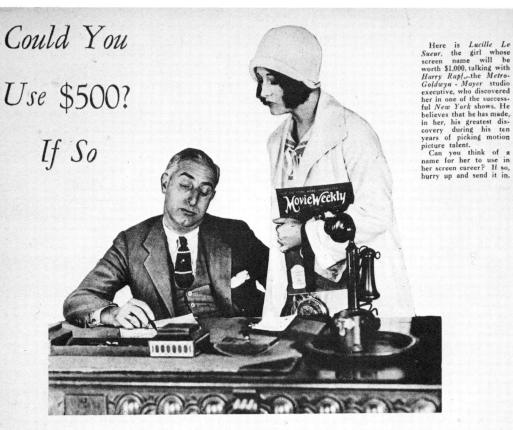

Here is *Lucille Le Sueur*, the girl whose screen name will be worth $1,000, talking with *Harry Rapf*, the *Metro-Goldwyn - Mayer* studio executive, who discovered her in one of the successful *New York* shows. He believes that he has made, in her, his greatest discovery during his ten years of picking motion picture talent.

Can you think of a name for her to use in her screen career? If so, hurry up and send it in.

Hurry Up and Enter

The $1,000 for a Name Contest

NAMES, names, names and more names! The Movie Weekly Contest Editor has been deluged with names. Every mail the postman staggers in under a load of hundreds more. It has seemed like a bombardment of telephone and city directories. Short names, long names, simple names and tongue twisters. First names from Fifi to Prudence and Mary to Hydrodendron. Last names from Smith to de la Montparnasse. Enough of them to name every parlor car that ever will be made.

But among the thousands that have been submitted, we have not selected THE name as yet. You still have a chance to win that $500 prize!

Readers of this magazine are helping us select a suitable screen name for Lucille Le Sueur, newest and one of the prettiest players signed by Metro-Goldwyn-Mayer. She will appear exclusively in films made by that big producing organization.

They have helped us to the extent of very nearly swamping us with suggestions. The response to our appeals, which were accompanied by the incentive of offering

a large cash prize for the name finally selected, has been tremendous. However, the judges will not choose one for the beautiful young actress until the contest has closed. The $500 still is all dressed up and no place to go.

Yes, it's all dressed up except the name after "Pay to the order of ...." Why don't you try to get yours there—by suggesting the winning *nom de screen* for Miss Le Sueur. You still have time. The contest hasn't closed yet. But you'll have to hurry. And we'll hurry with the $500 if you send in THE name.

Contestants may submit as many names as they can originate. Each one must be written on a separate sheet of paper with the senders' name and address on the same side. Read the rules carefully.

The cry for help in giving Miss Le Sueur a screen name that has not finally been answered yet came about this way:

Harry Rapf, Metro-Goldwyn-Mayer studio executive, who "discovered" Miss Le Sueur in one of the successful New York shows, believes he has made his greatest (Continued on page 31)

NAME COUPON

(Suggestions must be made on this coupon, a tracing of it or a similar one of your own making)

Name Suggested...

Your Name...

Your Address..

Left: Could you think of a better name for Lucille le Sueur. 18-year-old hopeful dreaming of stardom back in 1925? What about something plain and simple like Joan Crawford?

Ireland, who have co-starred in 15 films up to and including *Assassination* (US 87). Myrna Loy and William Powell played opposite each other in 13 pictures; Janet Gaynor starred with Charles Farrell and Sophia Loren with Marcello Mastroianni in 12 films; Lila Lee with Thomas Maighan and Ginger Rogers with Fred Astaire in 11 films; Judy Garland with Mickey Rooney and Katharine Hepburn with Spencer Tracy in 10 films; while three screen teams bring up the rear with 8 films together—Jeanette MacDonald and Nelson Eddy; Greer Garson and Walter Pidgeon; Olivia de Havilland and Errol Flynn.

The most extensive screen tests in the history of motion pictures were held for the role of Scarlett O'Hara in *Gone With the Wind* (US 39). MGM shot 149,000 ft of black-and-white test film and another 13,000 ft of colour with 60 actresses, none of whom got the part. Having discarded 27 hours of test film, producer David O Selznick narrowed the choice to three major stars and one unknown—Joan Bennett, Jean Arthur, Paulette Goddard and newcomer Vivien Leigh. The final tests required the four contenders to play the scenes of Scarlett getting into her corset, talking to Ashley in the paddock and drunkenly proposing to Rhett Butler. Miss Leigh's successful test was actually made after shooting of the movie had commenced—perhaps the only instance of a major motion picture going into production before the star role had been cast. Total cost of the 165,000 ft of tests was $105,000—approximately the budget then of an average second feature.

Hollywood's first nude screen tests were held for *Four for Texas* (US 63), which starred Ursula Andress and Anita Ekberg in the *femme* leads. Those actresses who had been unwilling to be tested need not have worried; all nude senes were cut by the censor.

Stars who Failed Screen Tests

Failing a screen test may not be a passport to stardom, but in some cases it has been no barrier. Bette Davis's first screen test was so appalling that she ran from the Goldwyn projection room screaming. Her next, with Universal, was successful enough for her to be given a job—as a stand-in girl for screen tests of male actors. Clark Gable failed a Warner screen test in 1930 because Jack Warner declared (in Gable's hearing) that he was only 'a big ape'. His next was at MGM, where his prominent ears told against him. Although he failed the test, MGM signed him any-

way and he stayed with the studio—contributing significantly to its ascendancy—for 23 years. Another star who failed the rigours of a MGM test was Maurice Chevalier, but he was signed by Paramount in 1928 on the strength of the *same* test.

Shirley Temple, probably the greatest box-office attraction of all time, failed a test for the *Our Gang* series. The screen's most prestigious luminary, Laurence Olivier, was turned down for *Queen Christina* (US 33) after testing opposite Greta Garbo, though it is widely held that Garbo deliberately sabotaged the test in order that the role should go to ex-lover John Gilbert, then in decline.

Paramount gave the thumbs down to young British thespian Archibald Leach on account of his thick neck and bandy legs. A couple of years later Paramount head B. P. Schulberg noticed Leach in the test of an aspiring actress in which he was merely the feed. Notwithstanding his neck and his legs, he was signed at $450 a week and given a brand new name to boot—Cary Grant.

Brigitte Bardot's puppy fat and spots caused her to fail a screen test with Marc Allégret when she was 16. Jane Russell also failed to pass muster! The report on her 1940 test for Fox read 'unphotogenic'. Warner's comments when she tested for them were 'no energy' and 'no spark'. Another star considered physically unsuitable was Robert Taylor. He failed his test for United Artists in 1933 because Sam Goldwyn thought he was too skinny.

Nothing was found wanting in Ava Gardner's physique. After seeing her test for MGM, Louis B. Mayer expostulated: 'She can't talk. She can't act. She's terrific.'

Less enthusiasm was expressed for Fred Astaire in a studio report on his first screen test, even if the words were much the same: 'Can't act. Can't sing. Can dance a little.'

Not even an established star could afford to be overconfident. According to Hollywood legend, at the height of her screen career Gloria Swanson took a test incognito wearing a blonde wig. She was turned down.

The shortest adult performer in movies is 2 ft 7 in tall Tamara de Treaux, an actress and singer from San Francisco. Tamara's most celebrated role to date was E.T., Steven Spielberg's lovable alien from outer space. Although in parts of the film E.T. was an electronic puppet, in others he was played by actors and actresses in costume—beside Tamara, there were 2 ft 10 in Pat Bilson and legless schoolboy Matthew de Merritt, who played the drunk scene walking on his hands inside the E.T. suit. Tamara's main scene was of E.T. shuffling into the spacecraft for his return home. Her weight—she considers she is too heavy at 2 st 12 lb—helped her to perfect what she described as 'a cute Daffy

'Can't act. Can't sing. Can dance a little.'—Studio report on Fred Astaire's first screen test.

Duck waddle'. Tamara was dwarfed by seven-year-old Drew Barrymore, who towered over her by 17 in.

The shortest actor to play the leading role in a film is Filipino paratrooper and black belt martial arts exponent Weng Weng, who has starred in *Agent 00* (Phi 81) and *For Your Height Only* (Phi 84). Weng Weng measures 2 ft 9 in.

The shortest actor to achieve celebrity in Hollywood and the only dwarf honoured in the Hollywood Walk of Fame is Billy Barty, a 3 ft 9 in veteran of 150 films and founder of The Little People of America Inc.

All-dwarf casts have been used in two films—a western *The Terror of Tiny Town* (US 38) and Werner Herzog's *Even Dwarfs Started Small* (FRG 70). *The Little Cigars* (US 73) had a cast of five midgets and one full-sized actress, described as 'a busty blonde'. The **largest cast of dwarves and midgets** was 116 in *The Wizard of Oz* (US 39), and an equal number in *Under the Rainbow* (US 81), which was the story of what the original Munchkins got up to on and off the set of *The Wizard of Oz* while they were staying at the Culver Hotel in 1938. (What they got up to was miniature mayhem.)

The most enduring dwarf actor is Angelo Rossitte, who debuted in Tod Browning's *Freaks* (US 32) and was recently featured in *From a Whisper to a Scream* (US 87).

The shortest artiste to play major roles, apart from dwarves and midgets, is 4 ft 9 in Linda Hunt, who made her debut in *Popeye* (US 80) as mother of the giant, Oxblood Oxheart, and won the Academy Award for Best Supporting Actress in 1984 for her role as Billy Kwan, a male Eurasian cameraman in Indonesia, in *The Year of Living Dangerously* (Aus 82). She has since been in the Merchant-Ivory version of Henry James's *The Bostonians* (GB 84), *Dune* (US 84) and as Gertrude Stein's lifetime companion Alice B. Toklas in *Waiting for the Moon* (US 87).

The only leading ladies under 5 ft were silent-screen heroines Florence Turner and Marguerite Clark, each 4 ft 10 in tall, 4 ft 11 in May McAvoy, who starred opposite Al Jolson in *The Jazz Singer* (US 27), and 4 ft 11½ in Gloria Swanson. Janet Gaynor and Mary Pickford were both 5 ft exactly, as was the lesser known Edith Roberts, whose height qualified her to play the title role in *Her Five-Foot Highness* (US 20).

The shortest leading man was French silent-star Max Linder, the impeccable dandy of the Paris boulevards, who was a mere 5 ft 2 in. Hollywood's shortest male stars are Mickey Rooney and Dudley Moore at 5 ft 3 in. Reports that Alan Ladd was only 5 ft tall were quite untrue; he was 5 ft 6 in, which made him an inch taller than Dustin Hoffman and the same height as Al Pacino. Nevertheless, Ladd's lack of inches was proverbial in Hollywood. Sophia Loren has confirmed that he had to stand on a box for his love scenes with her in *Boy on a Dolphin* (US 57) and James Mason, when he was invited to co-star with Ladd in *Botany Bay* (US 54), told the producer that he had no intention of standing in a trench for their scenes together.

The tallest screen artiste was Clifford Thompson, claimed to be 8 ft 6 in and then the tallest man in the world, who played opposite (and above) ZaSu Pitts in Hal Roach's *Seal Skins* (US 32). No other eight-footers are recorded. Artistes of 7 ft or over include Tex Erikson, 7 ft exactly, who was featured in *Jungle Jim in the Forbidden Land* (US 52); Johan Aasen, a 7 ft 2 in character actor who entered Hollywood pictures in 1923; Peter Mayhew, 7 ft 2 in ex-hospital porter, who played a mythical monster in *Sinbad and the Eye of the Tiger* (US 77) and the furry wookie Chewbacca in *Star Wars* (US 77); Richard Kiel, 7 ft 2 in without his size 16 shoes, who played the steel-teethed giant villain in Bond movies *The Spy Who Loved Me* (GB 77) and *Moonraker* (GB/Fr 79) and starred in the title role of *The Humanoid* (It 78); John Bloom, 7 ft 4 in, who was Frankenstein's monster in *Dracula v Frankenstein* (US 71); and Jack Tarver, 7 ft 10 in, the giant in Fox's feature-length children's picture *Jack and the Beanstalk* (US 17).

The tallest leading men were 6 ft 7 in James

James Mason declared that he had no intention of standing in a trench to play opposite diminutive Alan Ladd in *Botany Bay* (US 54). *(SI)*

Arness, who starred in *Them* (US 54) and *The First Travelling Saleslady* (US 56), and Bruce Spence, 6 ft 7 in, in *Stork* (Aus 71), which was scripted by 6 ft 7 in David Williamson, and *Wo die Grunen Ameisen Trauma* (FRG 84). Christopher Lee is the tallest major star at 6 ft 5 in, an inch taller than Clint Eastwood.

The heaviest screen artiste was Ethel Greer, who weighed 637 lb when she appeared with Clara Bow in *Hoopla* (US 33). Miss Greer's 140 lb husband, visiting the set, remarked of the slender 118 lb Miss Bow: 'I never could see why some fellows go for these skinny girls'.

The most generously proportioned leading lady of all time was Chesty Morgan, the possessor of a 73-in bust, who starred in *Deadly Weapons* (US 75).

> The most popular Hollywood actress in China is Deborah Raffin. This is on the strength of a TVM titled *Nightmare in Badham County* (US 77), one of the few American films released in China, which has been seen by over 200 million Chinese.

The actor who has played the same role the most times in feature films is the Hong Kong actor Kwan Tak-Hing, who portrayed the great South China martial arts hero Huang Fei-Hong (1847–1924) in 77 films out of a series of 85. His first appearance was in *The True Story of Huang Fei-Hong* (HK 49) and his last in *Magnificent Butcher* (HK 80). During the 1970s, when he played in only one Huang Fei-Hong movie, Kwan Tak-Hing continued the role in a television series.

The Hollywood actor to repeat the same role the most times in feature films was William Boyd (1898–1972), a major star of the twenties whose flagging career was revived in the thirties when Paramount chose him as the gentleman cowboy Hopalong Cassidy. Dressed always in black (usually reserved for villains in 'B' westerns), Boyd rode the range as 'Hoppy' in 66 full-length films, starting with *Hop-a-long Cassidy* aka *Hopalong Cassidy Enters* (US 35) and ending with *Strange Gamble* (US 48). The films were among the first American productions aired on television in the forties and Boyd then embarked on a long-running Hopalong Cassidy TV series, having already played the character in a network radio series.

A number of actors established a reputation for playing particular historical characters: Charles Vanel as Napoleon, Frank McGlynn as Abraham Lincoln and Robert Watson as Hitler. Silent player Roy Travers was cast as the Prince Consort eleven times and as Charles Dickens seven times. The most appearances in one historical role was probably by Mikhail Gelovani, who portrayed Stalin in more than 20 Soviet films. The dictator was so gratified by Gelovani's rather wooden projection of him as the wise, all-seeing, noble proletarian that he was never allowed to give the parts any other dimension.

Other actors have found their niche in occupational roles. Arthur Treacher and Charles Coleman seldom played anything but butlers throughout their screen careers, Irish-American actor Tom Dugan played a slow-witted new York cop in over 100 films following his debut in 1926, while Pat O'Brien was cast as a Roman Catholic priest in at least a dozen of his movies. In 1928 Guy Oliver claimed to have been cast as a sheriff in 150 of the 230 westerns he had made and in 1931 Frank Hagney, invariably seen as a boxer, declared ruefully that he had lost the world's heavyweight title no less than 29 times during his career. A number of performers specialized in courtroom dramas, but none with such dedication as Hollywood character actor Richard Tucker, who is known to have played the prosecuting attorney at least 54 times.

Among performers still active in films, the **record for playing the same occupational** role is claimed by veteran Bombay actor Jagdish Raaj. He has been cast as a uniformed police officer in 144 films (as of end 1987) over a period of 33 years.

Some were cast against type. German-born Peter

Bombay actor Jagdish Raaj has played a uniformed police officer in 144 films.

van Eyck, who became Hollywood's stock Nazi beast, only came to California because as an active anti-Nazi he was forced to flee Hitler's Germany. The ability to play a drunk well is a rare one, which enabled Jack Norton and Arthur Housman to specialize in amiable inebriates, seldom playing anything else. Some special talent must also have inspired producers to cast Carmen Nigro as a gorilla in 32 movies, or 33 if his claim to have played the title role in *King Kong* (US 33) can be sustained (it is generally accepted that all the gorilla scenes were

> In *Nous étions tous des noms d'arbres/The Writing on the Wall* (Fr/Bel 82), Armand Gatti's story of strife and sectarianism in present-day Northern Ireland, the Protestants are played by Roman Catholics and the Roman Catholics by Protestants.

acted with models). He last donned his ape suit for *Gorilla at Large* (US 54). 'Cowardly Lion' Bert Lahr was not so lucky. 'After *The Wizard of Oz*', he declared ruefully, 'I was typecast as a lion—and there aren't all that many parts for lions.'

Versatility is harder to quantify. However, it is doubtful whether any performer ever played with a greater variety of accents than Russian-born Hollywood actor Vladimir Sokoloff, who was cast as 35 nationalities during his career ranging from an Italian physicist in *Cloak and Dagger* (US 46) to a blind Chinese beggar in *Macao* (US 52). The only accent Sokoloff never succeeded in mastering was American.

The most delayed come-back: Of the many stars who have retired from films and made a comeback, the one with the longest absence from the screen was George Burns, with a 37-year interval between *Honolulu* (US 39) and *The Sunshine Boys* (US 76). The most delayed comeback by an actress was by Mae West, who retired from the screen after *The Heat's On* (US 43) and returned 35 years later in *Myra Breckinridge* (US 78).

The oldest performer to have played a major role in a movie is French veteran Charles Vanel (1892–), who was 95 on the completion of *Les Saisons du Plaisir* (Fr 88) in August 1987. The picture also marked his 75th anniversary as a screen actor. Set during a perfume manufacturers' convention in the south of France, it relates how a centenarian perfumier (Vanel) marries a 90-year-old bride (Denise Grey, who was playing her real age) and plans to name a successor to his dynasty. Vanel's co-star in his previous film, Claude Goretta's *Si le Soleil ne revenait pas* (Fr 87), was Catherine Mouchet, who was somewhat younger than Mme Grey—by 70 years. She had made her debut the previous year in *Thérèse* (Fr 86), 74 years after Vanel had made his debut in *Jim Crow* (Fr 12).

The oldest actress to have played a major role in a movie is Lillian Gish (1893–), who was 93 when she completed principal photography on *The Whales of August* (US 87), in which she co-starred with the comparatively juvenile 78-year-old Bette Davis, in December 1986. Other recent starring roles were in *Hambone and Hillie* (US 84) at the age of 90 and in *Sweet Liberty* (US 86) at the age of 92. Like Charles Vanel (see above), Miss Gish had made her screen debut in 1912. Neither, though, holds the record for the longest screen career (see p. 95), M. Vanel coming second to Curt Bois as the most enduring actor and Miss Gish coming second to Helen Hayes as the most enduring actress. (Note: most reference books cite Miss Gish's year of birth as either 1896 or 1898. In 1984 the American Film Institute was ungallant enough to make public its discovery of her birth certificate, which conclusively proves a birth date of 1893—and secures her place in the record books.)

The greatest age at which anyone has embarked on a regular movie career was 84 in the case of miniscule 4 ft 9 in character actress Lydia Yeamans Titus. She made her screen debut in the Rudolph Valentino film *All Night* (US 18) and played in over 50 features before her death in 1929 aged 95.

Mae West fans had to wait 35 years following her performance in *The Heat's On* (US 43) before she made a comeback in *Myra Breckinridge* (US 78). The picture may not have been worth the wait, but Mae still looked a cracker. (*Kobal*)

Nonagenerian Screen Artistes

Besides Charles Vanel (1892–), Lillian Gish (1893–) and Lydia Yeamans Titus (1834–1929) see above, other nonagenerian artistes have been A. E. Matthews (1869–1960) in *Inn for Trouble* (GB 60); Estelle Winwood (1883–1984) in *Murder by Death* (US 76); John Cromwell (1887–1979) in *The Wedding* (US 78); Catherine Nesbitt (1889–1982) in *Never Never Land* (US 80) and *The Second Star to the Right* (GB 81); Sam Jaffe (1891–1984) —who played the 200-year-old High Lama in *Lost Horizon* (US 37) —in *Nothing Lasts Forever* (US 82) and *On the Line* aka *Downstream* (US 84); and George Burns (1896–) in *18 Again* (US 88). Matty, as A. E. Matthews was known, once observed: 'I always wait for *The Times* each morning. I look at the obituary column, and if I'm not in it I go to work.' Estelle Winwood, born Lee, Kent, 24 January 1883, completed her role as Nurse Withers in *Murder by Death* (US 76) on her 93rd birthday. Miss Winwood was the oldest member of the Screen Actors Guild at the time of her death in California aged 101. She made

her professional debut at the Theatre Royal, Manchester, in 1898 and claimed to have been the first woman in America to wear lipstick in public.

At least two centenarians were professional extras. William H. 'Dad' Taylor, born Brownsville, Texas, 9 July 1828, appeared in Edwin Carewe's *Evangeline* (US 29) at the age of 101—a unique instance of a person born during the Georgian era playing in a talkie. The other was Walter 'Cap' Field (1874–1976), who joined the Mexican production company Ammex in 1913 and played his last role in *She's Too Hot to Handle* (US 76) when he was 101. He fondly remembered being 'killed or wounded four or five times' in various small roles in *Gone with the Wind* (US 39). The 'sage' in *The Man Who Would Be King* (US 75) was played by a 102-year-old Moroccan.

The youngest performer in a feature film was Balázs Monori, whose actual birth was shown in

Baby Leroy—a star at six months when he played opposite Maurice Chevalier in *Bedtime Story* (US 33).

Kilenc Hónap/Nine Months (Hun 76), the story of a pregnant woman (Lili Monori) torn between two men and striving to improve herself. The director, Márta Meszaros, was reported to be delighted that Balázs's screen debut was so accomplished that no second take was needed.

The youngest performer to receive star billing was Leroy Overacker, known on the screen as Baby Leroy, who was chosen at the age of six months to play the central juvenile role opposite Maurice Chevalier in *Bedtime Story* (US 33). Master Overacker's contract had to be signed by his grandfather, because not only the star but also his 16-year-old mother was under age. The film was about a gay bachelor who becomes encumbered with an abandoned baby whose protruding lower lip matches his own, a circumstance which leads everyone to believe that Chevalier is the father of the motherless child. All is unscrambled when it is found that the distinctive facial feature of the baby is accounted for by nothing more reprehensible than a button lodged under his lip.

Insurance

Insurance of stars' more notable physical accoutrements began when silent screen comedian John Bunny (1863-1915) insured his unlovely face for $100,000. Faces were most stars' fortunes and it was an enterprising Los Angeles underwriter, Arthur W. Stebbins, who originated the 'scarred face' policy taken out in the early 1920s by Rudolph Valentino, Douglas Fairbanks and Mary Pickford, the latter for $1 million. Some stars, though, owed their success to individual features, not always facial—Chaplin insured his feet for $150,000. Clara Kimball Young (1891-1960), often described as 'the most beautiful woman in films' at the peak of her career, c. 1918, insured her large and luminous eyes for the same amount. Cross-eyed Ben Turpin (1874-1940) insured to the tune of $100,000 against the possibility of his eyes ever becoming normal again—it would undoubtedly have cost him his career. Suave leading man Edmund Lowe (1890-1971) took out a $35,000 policy on his distinguished nose in the mid-1920s and at about the same time Kathleen Key had her lovely neck underwritten at $25,000. A decade later the most famous nose in the business carried a $100,000 risk for Jimmy Durante (1893-1980).

Alberta Vaughn took out a $25,000 policy in 1925 against the possibility of putting on 20 lb weight by 1 June 1927, while Walter Hiers—literally a Hollywood 'heavy'—insured for an equal sum against losing 45 lb. RKO insured Roscoe Ates' (1892-1962) inimitable nervous stutter in the early thirties. A year or two earlier, when sound arrived, First National had insured Corinne Griffith (1898-1979) against loss of voice. Ironically it was her unsuitability for talkies that finished her career. When Anthony Quinn (1915-) had his head shaved for the role of a Greek magician in *The Magus* (GB 68), he insured against the risk of his hair failing to grow.

Anthony Quinn insured against his hair failing to grow again after having his pate shaved for the role of Conchis in *The Magus* (GB 68). (*SI*)

The first actress to insure her legs was Hollywood extra Cecille Evans, whose appendages were underwritten for $100,000 in 1921. Miss Evans' speciality was 'doubling' her sensational legs for those of stars less well endowed. The 'Girl with the Million Dollar Legs', Betty Grable (1916–73), actually had them insured for more than that—the sum was $1,250,000. The legs may have been incomparable, but the policy did not stand comparison with the record risk of $5 million accepted on Cyd Charisse's (1921–) long and lovely limbs. No actor has ever been described as 'The Man with the Million Dollar Legs', but Fred Astaire (1899–1987) could have claimed the title—his were insured for just that sum.

It is not only performers who have had parts of their bodies insured. In 1939 the Fleischer Studio took out a $185,000 policy with Lloyd's of London to cover the hands of the 116 animators working on their first full-length cartoon feature *Mr Bug Goes to Town* (US 41).

The first artiste whose life was insured for the duration of a picture was Lillian Gish (1893–), covered for the sum of $1 million during the filming of *Way Down East* (US 20). The insurance company turned down director D. W. Griffith's application for insurance on the other principal players on health grounds. Had they known that Miss Gish was to be exposed on an ice floe in sub-zero temperature wearing only a thin frock every day for three weeks, and that she was to be rescued by the hero just before the floe went over the falls without any trick or stunt work, nor any safety precautions in case the rescue failed, doubtless the application on her behalf would have been refused with even greater promptitude.

When seven-year-old Shirley Temple's life (1928–) was insured with Lloyd's, the contract stipulated that no benefit would be paid if the child met death or injury while drunk.

Siobhan McKenna's insurance policy for *Of Human Bondage* (GB 64) forbade her to drive a car while the picture was in production. The first time the Irish actress had taken the wheel she had ended in a ditch, the second time against a wall, the third time up a tree.

SEVEN

FILM MAKING AND FILM MAKERS

ANIMALS

The first animal star to appear regularly in films was 'Hepworth Picture Player Rover', an English collie belonging to pioneer producer Cecil Hepworth who made his debut in his master's outstandingly successful low-budget (£7 13s 9d) box-office hit *Rescued by Rover* (GB 05). A simple melodrama about a dog rescuing a baby who has been kidnapped by gypsies, it was in such demand by exhibitors that the negative wore out and the film had to be made twice. Rover, whose real name was Blair, starred in at least seven other films before his death in February 1914. American historian Kenneth Macgowan dryly observed that Rover was the first screen performer who did not overact.

One of the first animals to achieve something akin to 'superstar' status was Strongheart, an ex-Red Cross dog who had served in the trenches in World War I. Strongheart was a consummate screen actor, but had an aversion to being made to howl. According to Lawrence Trimble, who directed Strongheart in most of his films, he would get so depressed that his work would be below par for several days afterwards. Once he had graduated to canine stardom, however, there was little choice but to indulge these displays of temperament. A double would be brought in to do the howling for him.

Serving on the other side of the line in World War I was the German Army dog Rin Tin Tin (1916–32), who came to Hollywood in the early twenties and became an animal 'megastar'. He was the only dog in America with a valet, a personal chef, his own limousine and a chauffeur for his exclusive use. He also had a five-room dressing room complex of his own on the studio lot.

The largest cast of living creatures in a film were the 22 million bees employed by Irwin Allen in *The Swarm* (US 78).

The largest number of horses ever assembled for a film was 11,000 in the case of Alexander Ptushko's

> The hit moppet picture *Benji* (US 74), about a dog who rescues two children from kidnappers, was shot mainly at a height of 18 in (46 cm) from the ground—the camera was showing the action from Benji's viewpoint. In Samuel Fuller's *White Dog* (US 84), the story of a dog trained to attack black people, all shots through the eyes of the dog were in black and white—dogs are colour blind.

Ilya Muromets/Sword and the Dragon aka *The Epic Hero and the Beast* (USSR 56). The Hollywood record was established the same year when King Vidor used 8000 horses in *War and Peace* (US 56).

The largest assemblage of assorted animals in a movie totalled 8552 in *Around the World in Eighty Days* (US 56), to wit: 3800 sheep, 2448 buffalo, 950 donkeys, 800 horses, 512 monkeys, 17 bulls, 15 elephants, 6 skunks, 4 ostriches.

Feline Films

Dogs have been hogging the screen ever since star dog Rover, superstar Strongheart and megastar Rin Tin Tin (see above). Moggies have seldom enjoyed the same drawing power, except in cartoons. Thanks, though, to a Japanese puss called Chatran (see below) the balance may be redressed. These are the cat movies which have paved the way:

☆ *The Black Cat* (US 41) Based on the Edgar Allan Poe story, the movie recounts how a flock of relatives of an eccentric old lady who is nuts about cats—she even maintains a cat crematorium—are eagerly awaiting her death so they can inherit. When she is murdered by one of them, they learn that no bequests will be paid until the last of her vast tribe of cats passes on.

☆ *Rhubarb* (US 51) About an alley cat called Rhubarb who inherits $30 million and a major league baseball club.

☆ *The Shadow of the Cat* (GB 61) Cat belonging to murdered woman seems to cause deaths of relatives seeking lost will.

☆ *Puss-in-Boots* (Mex 61) Mexican rendering of the well-loved fairy tale.

☆ *Gay Purr-ee* (US 62) Feature cartoon about a country cat called Mewsette (voice by Judy Garland) who comes to Paris and is kidnapped.

☆ *One Day, a Cat* (Cz 63) Engaging fantasy about a cat who wears glasses and the strange effect on the villagers when he takes them off.

☆ *Three Lives of Thomasina* (GB 63) Thomasina, heroine of a novel by Paul Gallico, is a cat in a small Scottish town who recovers from three crises to the joy of her little mistress, Karen Dotrice.

☆ *Under the Yum Yum Tree* (US 63) Acrobatic feline follows lecherous landlord Jack Lemmon around as he attempts to seduce tenant, Carol Lynley.

☆ *The Incredible Journey* (US 63) Disney movie

about a Siamese cat and two dogs, separated from their owner, who cross hundreds of miles of rugged terrain in Canada to return home.

☆ *That Darn Cat* (US 63) Another Disney, in which cat hero helps the FBI solve a case.

☆ *Torture Garden* (GB 68) Michael Bryant tangles with a man-eating house cat after greed induces him to permit the death of a supposedly rich relative.

☆ *Eye of the Cat* (US 69) Michael Saarazin as young man with aelurophobia (fear of cats) plotting to do in his wealthy aunt but done in himself by hordes of malign moggies.

☆ *The Aristocats* (US 70) Disney cartoon feature in which two cats are deliberately lost by butler who fears they will inherit his mistress's wealth. Various animal friends restore them to their rightful place.

☆ *The Night of the Thousand Cats* (Mex 72) Demented aristo (Hugo Stiglitz) keeps a thousand man-eating pussies in his castle and feeds them on the flesh of attractive young ladies ill-advised enough to pay a visit.

☆ *Harry and Tonto* (US 74) Art Carney as Harry, old New York widower evicted from apartment, on odyssey across America with cat Tonto.

☆ *I Am a Cat* (Jap 75) A cat observes (via subjective camera) life of teacher in early 20th-century Japan and romantic entanglements of family.

☆ *The Cat from Outer Space* (US 78) Disney fantasy about spaceship commanded by cat forced to make emergency landing on Earth.

☆ *Our Johnny* (Aus 80) Cat called Johnny upsets even tenor of life in humdrum household.

☆ *Cat's Eye* (US 85) Three stories from Stephen King, each involving same cat in bizarre situations.

☆ *The Black Cat* (It 85) Patrick Magee as an experimenter in the paranormal. His cat is suspected by visiting American photographer, Mimsy Farmer, of being the perpetrator of mysterious deaths in an English village.

☆ *The Adventures of Chatran* (Jap 87) About a farm cat and his adventures with the other farm animals on the Japanese island of Hokkaido. The third highest grossing film ever released in Japan and the second most successful Japanese production, it became a national cult. In 1988 *Chatran* became one of the few Japanese 'entertainment movies' (as opposed to art films) to secure a coast-to-coast release in America.

Animal Casts

There have been four full-length fiction films with all-animal casts. *Bill and Coo* (US 48), produced by comedian Ken Murray, was a comedy feature with a cast of Love Birds in miniature sets. Most of Walt Disney's True Life Fantasies were documentaries about wildlife, but *Perri* (US 57) was based on a novel by Felix Salten about the life of a squirrel. There were no credited human performers in *Jona-*

than Livingstone Seagull (US 73), though some fishermen in a boat are seen in the opening sequence. Apart from this, the cast was composed entirely of seagulls. The story, adapted from the novel by Richard Bach (who also wrote the screenplay), is a mystical one of a seagull who acquires grace, is killed doing a noble act, rises from the dead and becomes a bird messiah. Kon Ichikawa's *The Adventures of Chatran* (Jap 87) (see above under Feline Films) had a cast of cats, dogs and farm animals with not a human in sight and became Japan's box office hit of the year.

CAMERA AND CAMERAWORK

The largest number of cameras used for a single scene was 48 for the sea battle in *Ben Hur* (US 25). Another 42 cameras were employed on the chariot-race scene. Concealed in statues, in pits in the ground, and behind soldiers' shields, the 42 operators took 53,000 ft of film—equivalent to seven full-length features—in a single day.

The practice of using more than one camera on a scene was introduced by D. W. Griffith, who used three for the big fight between Dorothy West and Mabel Normand in *The Squaw's Love* (US 14). The three cameramen on this occasion were Billy Bitzer, P. Higginson and Bobby Harron. The use of multiple cameras was not confined to special scenes in Hollywood's silent days. Nearly all feature films were shot with twin cameras, one supplying the master negative from which all release prints for the domestic market were struck, the other the negative for all overseas prints.

The largest number of cameras used on one film was 160 in the case of *One Day of War* (USSR 42). A feature-length documentary, the film was shot in a single day by 160 newsreel cameramen at the Russian Front and behind the lines.

The widest aperture lens ever used in production of a feature film was f0.7 by cameraman John Alcott on *Barry Lyndon* (GB 75). Developed for the US space programme, the lens was fitted to a specially modified camera and employed in filming an interior scene lit only by candlelight.

The first motorized camera (professional) in series production was the all-metal Bell & Howell of 1912, manufactured in the USA with the motor as an optional fitment.

The first British motorized camera was the Aeroscope, invented by Polish cinematographer Kazimierz Prosznski and manufactured in 1913 by Newman & Sinclair. It was used extensively for newsreel work and also by Cherry Kearton for wildlife cinematography.

The first feature film made with a motorized camera was *A Sainted Devil* (US 24) with Rudolph Valentino, which was photographed at

Famous Players' Long Island studio by Harry Fishbeck with an electrically-driven camera of unidentified make. Generally cameramen continued to crank by hand throughout the silent era, due to the fact that it enabled action to be speeded up or slowed down at will. The coming of sound rendered hand-cranking impractical, since variations in film speed would have caused a corresponding and unnatural variation in the delivery of synchronized speech.

The first film shot with a three-perforation pull-down camera was Allan Edwall's *Pirates of the Lakes* (Swe 87), which opened at the Grand, Stockholm on 20 February 1987 with a print made on a polyester base. The camera was a Golden Panaflex converted by Benji Othall of Filmteknik to the specification of cameraman Rune Ericsson. The innovation enables very significant economies in the use of film stock and is expected to be adopted worlwide.

The earliest known multi-shot scene (different camera positions being used within a single scene) occurs in G. A. Smith's *The Little Doctors* (GB 01), in which there is a cut from a shot of two children administering medicine to a sick kitten to a close-up of the kitten with the spoon in its mouth.

Prior to the recent rediscovery of this film (see *Sight & Sound*, Summer 1978), the innovation had generally been attributed to D. W. Griffith. In *For the Love of Gold* (US 08), Griffith used a medium shot and a three-quarter shot in a card-game scene where he wanted to register the expressions on the gamblers' faces, and this has been credited as the first use of camera movement within a scene. Another recent discovery of the use of close-up (q.v.) shots within a scene in *The Yale Laundry* (US 07), must cast doubt on whether Griffith was the pioneer of the multi-shot scene even as far as the US industry is concerned.

The first panning shots were used by Max Skladanowski in *Komische Begegnung im Tiergarten zu Stockholm* (Ger 96), a short comedy shot on location in Sweden, and by Lumière representative Eugène Promio in *View of St Mark's Square, Venice* (Fr 96), a panorama of the Square taken from a boat on the Grand Canal.

The earliest known British example of a panning shot appears in a news film of Queen Victoria's Diamond Jubilee Procession shot by R. W. Paul with his 'Kinematograph' camera on 20 June 1897. The camera was mounted on a specially designed tripod with a swivel head. The first in an acted film, a panning shot of Epsom Downs, opens Alfred Collins' *Welshed, a Derby Day Incident* (GB 03).

The first 360° panning shot was made by Edwin S. Porter in *Circular Panorama of the Electric Tower* (US 01), in which the whole of the exhibition grounds of the Pan-American Exposition at Buffalo, NY are seen as the camera slowly revolves. Porter used a geared mounting of his own design for this effect.

The first use of a 360° pan in a full-length dramatic film was by James Whale in *Frankenstein* (US 31), and the following year Rouben Mamoulian employed the technique in *Dr Jekyll and Mr Hyde* (US 32) to give an effect of vertigo during the transformation scene.

Other films with 360° pans are *Rain* (US 32), Herbert Wilcox's *Bitter Sweet* (GB 33)—notable for its double 360° pan (the second much faster than the first)—*La Signora di Tutti* (It 34), *La Strada* (It 54), *Lola Montes* (Fr/FRG 55), *Vertigo* (US 58), *On the Beach* (US 59), *Judgement at Nuremberg* (US 61), *The Manchurian Candidate* (US 62), *Providence* (Fr/Swz 77), *The Swarm* (US 78), *Eagle's Wing* (GB 79), and Mai Zetterling's *Scrubbers* (GB 82). *Laughter in the Dark* (GB 69) was another British film with a double 360° pan, while Brian de Palma's *Obsession* (US 76) is notable for both a 360° and a 540° pan. The latter shot shows all four walls of a room entered by Genevieve Bujold, then pans on past the door to pick her up on the side opposite.

The first slow-motion film was made in 1898 by Berlin cinematographer Oskar Messter, using a specially constructed high-speed 60 mm camera of his own design. Among the earliest sequences filmed with this camera was one that showed a cat falling off a wall, with a Hipp millisecond watch inset in one corner to indicate the rate of descent. This was shot at 66 frames a second—over four times normal speed—though the camera was capable of filming at speeds of up to 100 frames a second.

The technique has had its widest application in sports and scientific films. The earliest practical application of slow-motion cinematography was for the purpose of gauging the breaking strain of girders, according to Hopwood's *Living Pictures*, published in 1899.

The first time slow motion footage was presented with synchronized sound was in *Easter Parade* (US 48). Part of the sequence in which Fred Astaire dances to Irving Berlin's 'Stepping Out With My Baby' was shot at 96 frames a second, but the action remains synchronized with the music.

The fastest speed at which a camera has been operated on any feature film (or the slowest slow motion sequence) was 2500 frames per second for the giant explosion scene in *Star Trek: The Wrath of Khan* (US 82). The scene, shot by Industrial Light and Magic at the Cow Palace in San Francisco, took a single second to film but occupied 104 seconds on screen. The normal speed at which a 35mm motion picture camera operates is 24 fps.

The time lapse technique was pioneered by Oskar Messter of Berlin, who filmed the blooming and wilting of a flower in 1897. The lapse factor was 1500 frames per 24 hours.

The earliest known American example is a 1902 American Mutoscope and Biograph subject of the demolition of New York's Star Theater.

The earliest known wipe appears in G. A. Smith's *Mary Jane's Mishap: or, Don't Fool with the Paraffin* (GB 03), in which Mary Jane does and is blown out of the chimney. A line moving across the screen 'wiped' away the scene of her unfortunate demise and replaced it with one of her forlorn grave. Hitherto the introduction of the wipe has generally been attributed to Georges Méliès in *La Royaume des fées* (Fr 03), but Dr Barry Salt of the Slade School has established that this is a misconception. What looks like a wipe between scenes is in fact no more than the lifting of a backdrop.

The only full-length feature film to have been made without a camera was Barcelona artist José Antonio Sistiaga's remarkable 75-minute animated one-man production in Cinemascope *Ere Ereve Baleibu Icik Subua Arvaren/Scope, Colour, Muda* (Sp 70). Completed in 17 months between October 1968 and February 1970, Sistiaga painted each frame of the film separately and single-handed direct on to the film-stock.

The first close-up was a study of a man called Fred Ott sneezing, copyrighted on 7 January 1894 as *Edison Kinetoscopic Record of a Sneeze* (US 94).

The first close-up in a British film was a 50 ft study of a man enjoying a glass of beer, made by G. A. Smith of Brighton and released under the alternative titles of *Comic Face* and *Man Drinking* in September 1897. The man was played by Tom Green. Both the Edison film and Smith's film consisted of a single shot.

The first known film in which close-ups are interpolated with other shots is *Grandma's Reading Glass* (GB 00). A small boy is seen focusing a magnifying glass on various objects, including a watch, a newspaper, canary, kitten and Grandma's eye. These appear in close-up as seen by the boy, probably the earliest use of the subjective camera technique. The identity of the film-maker who pioneered the interpolated close-up is disputed. The film has generally been attributed to G. A. Smith of Brighton (see above), but Mrs Audrey Wadowska claims that it was made by her father, Arthur Melbourne Cooper of St Albans, and that the roles of Grandma and the small boy were played by Miss Bertha Melbourne Cooper and Master Bert Massey.

The earliest known interpolated close-ups in an American film are contained in American Mutoscope and Biograph's *Grandpa's Reading Glass* (US 02), a film so similar to the Smith/Melbourne Cooper subject above that it was almost certainly a plagiarism—common practice in the early days of film-making. The objects viewed by the grandchildren in this film are a bird, a printed page, the eye of a child, the head of an adult woman, the head of an infant, the head of a girl child holding a kitten, and a monkey.

Close-ups of inanimate objects or of hands or feet were not unusual in American films of the early years of the century, particularly in the productions of the American Mutoscope and Biograph Co. (AM & B). Examples include the fire alarm box in Edison's *The Life of an American Fireman* (US 03), a girl's pretty foot in Edison's *The Gay Shoe Clerk* (US 03), the contents of a jewel case in AM & B's *The Great Jewel Mystery* (US 05), gifts in AM & B's *The Silver Wedding* (US 06) and a newspaper article in AM & B's *Trial Marriages* (US 07). Facial close-ups were rarer, though the opening scenes of AM & B's *The Widow and the Only Man* (US 04) introduce the two principal characters with separate close-ups. The persistent claim of D. W. Griffith to have been the only begetter of the close-up—he even went so far as to suggest he could have patented the technique—has now been rejected by most film historians, though many still credit him with having been the first to employ the interpolated facial close-up as a dramatic device to register emotion. Even this had been accomplished a year before Griffith entered the film industry. In the AM & B production *The Yale Laundry* (US 07), a comedy about students at Yale playing a jape on their professors, close-ups are used to show surprise on the faces of the victims. It is precisely this technique of advancing the narrative by means of a close-up shot that Griffith was later to claim as his innovation and his alone. There is a certain irony in the fact that it had been used earlier by an uncredited director of the very company with which Griffith was to establish his reputation. The great director also seems to have overlooked the fact that he himself was the subject of a close-up when he played the part of a clown in *At the French Ball* (US 08), a film made shortly before his directorial debut at Biograph.

Despite the pioneering efforts of the Edison Co., AM & B and 'the Brighton school' (in England), elsewhere the notion that a film should give its audience the same view as a theatre audience received of the stage persisted for many years. As late as 1911 the leading production company in Scandinavia, Nordisk Film, was using a 16 ft long pole attached to the camera as an indication to the actors that they must come no closer. Albert E. Smith recalled that about this period at Vitagraph the actors were always positioned nine yards in front of the camera. Mary Pickford, who claimed that she had been the subject of 'the first close-up'

Helen Hayes in *A Farewell to Arms* (US 32), the film which contains the closest close-up. In one scene the camera was only two inches from her eyes. (*SI*)

in D. W. Griffith's *Friends* (US 12), said that the 'front office' at Biograph had vigorously protested at the idea on the grounds that audiences were paying to see the whole of the performer, not only the top half.

The closest close-up occurs in *A Farewell to Arms* (US 32). In one shot the camera was 2 in (5 cm) from Helen Hayes's eyes.

The longest close-up is to be seen in *Daaera* (Ind 53) and lasts 6½ minutes.

The first zoom lens was patented in 1929 by Joseph Walker (1892–1985), who was cameraman on over 160 films including *It Happened One Night* (US 34) and *Mr Deeds Goes to Town* (US 38).

The earliest recorded use of the telephoto lens (invented in 1891) with a cinematograph camera was by W. K. L. Dickson, the Biograph cameraman covering the Boer War in 1900. Dickson recorded in *The Biograph in Battle* (London 1901) how he had sought to film the Boer positions with a telephoto, an attempt frustrated by poor visibility caused by haze.

The first dissolve from one scene to another was used by Georges Méliès in *Cendrillon* (Fr 99).

The earliest known American example is to be seen in the Edison Co.'s *Life Rescue at Long Beach* (US 01), a 2½-minute drama in five scenes about the rescue of a young lady from drowning. The dissolve effects a transition from the fourth scene, in which the lifeguards are reviving the prostrate maiden, to the climax, in which, fully recovered, she embraces her rescuers. The film is believed to have been directed by Edwin S. Porter, better remembered for *The Life of an American Fireman* (US 03) and *The Great Train Robbery* (US 03).

The first feature film to end with a freeze frame was Abel Gance's epic melodrama *La Roue* (Fr 23), in which the device was used to intensify the moment of the old railwayman Sisif's death. The earliest Hollywood feature to culminate in a freeze frame was *Poor Little Rich Girl* (US 36), with the three principals, Shirley Temple, Jack Haley and Alice Faye, arrested in motion.

The first camera dolly was used by British pioneer cinematographer R. W. Paul at the studio he built at New Southgate in 1899. In a lecture he gave before the British Kinematographers' Society in 1936, Paul recalled: 'A trolley mounted on rails carried the camera, which could thus be set at any required distance from the stage, to suit the subject. Sometimes the trolley was run to and from the stage while the picture was being taken, thus giving a gradual enlargement or reduction of the image of the film.' It is not known whether Paul's dolly dates from the opening of the New Southgate studios, but a photograph taken in 1902 shows it in use.

The first use of a camera dolly in a feature film was by Spanish cameraman Segundo de Chomon for Giovanni Pastrone's *Cabiria* (It 14). De Chomon had developed his dolly while working for Pathé in Paris (1906–10) and Pastrone patented it in Italy in 1912.

The dolly arrived in America comparatively late, no examples of its use being known before 1915. Tracking shots were used in two feature films that year, by Allan Dwan on *David Harum* (US 15) to follow the hero as he walks down the street of his small hometown, and by William Bowman in *The Second-in-Command* (US 15). On this film, cameraman William F. Alder employed two dollies, one for forward and backward tracking and the other for sideways movement. This was a notable innovation which did not come to its full fruition until Chinese-born James Wong Howe introduced the 'crab dolly'—a dolly that moves in any direction, including sideways and diagonally—on *The Rough Riders* (US 27).

Britain, having pioneered the dolly, then completely forgot about it until the end of the silent era. The first use of 'mobile camera' in a feature film was by Graham Cutts on Gainsborough-Piccadilly's *The Triumph of the Rat* (GB 26), with Ivor Novello. Camera mobility could be achieved without the use of a dolly. F. W. Murnau overcame the problem of how to depict Emil Jannings' drunken view of the wedding feast in *The Last Laugh* (Ger 25) by mounting his camerman on roller skates. When Sidney Franklin decided to use a hand-held Bell & Howell Eyemo camera on *Quality Street* (US 27), he emulated Murnau's example, but here the scene was not a drunken one and the camera had to be kept steady. The solution was to have an assistant pushing the roller-skated camerman from behind. James Wong Howe also found roller-skates the answer for the prize fight scene in *Body and Soul* (US 47), but on *He Ran All the Way* (US 51) he needed higher camera angles. A squatting camera operator could not roller-skate, so Howe found another expedient—the cameraman was pushed in a wheelchair.

The hidden camera was pioneered simultaneously in the USSR and USA in 1924. Concealed cameras were used by Russia's master of the newsreel, Dziga Vertov, in making his feature-length documentary about everyday life in the early Soviet state, *Kino-Eye* (USSR 24). Cameraman Mikhail Kaufman filmed open air scenes at Pioneer camps, in markets, at stations, etc., as well as interiors of low life in bars, cafes and thieves kitchens, without his subjects ever being aware of the camera. In America a hidden camera was used by Erich von Stroheim for the scene in *Greed* (US 24) in which Trina rushes out of the junk shop after finding a murdered body. The film was made entirely on location and it was a real street into which ZaSu Pitts dashes distractedly, grabbing the arms of real passers-by as she shrieks her awful news. The reaction of those unwittingly involved was, as von Stroheim hoped, totally believable, as they registered horror and alarm before rushing for help.

These pioneer efforts were followed by a number of other noted uses of hidden camerawork during the twenties. George Webber filmed exterior scenes for *Night Life of New York* (US 25) from a van parked in the streets of the city. Most of *Berlin, Symphony of a Great City* (Ger 27) was filmed in this way by Karl Freund, but where a van was impracticable he concealed the camera in a suitcase, using a special film-stock that he had hypersensitized himself in order to shoot in poor lighting conditions. King Vidor shot most of the New York exteriors for *The Crowd* (US 28) with a hidden camera.

The first British film made with hidden cameras was *Knave of Hearts*/US: *Lovers, Happy Lovers* (GB 54). Director René Clément took the camera out into the streets of London wrapped as a paper bundle, filming at Charing Cross Station in the rush hour and amongst the crowds at Piccadilly Circus.

The first double exposure was accomplished by Georges Méliès in *La Caverne maudite*/*The Cave of*

the Demons (Fr 98), employing the technique of 'spirit photography'. The evil inhabitants of the cave were first filmed against a black backdrop, so that the background was not exposed, then the film was wound back and the cave setting filmed. The effect was of 'ghost' characters superimposed against a solid background.

The more normal use of double exposure was to achieve the effect of two characters played by the same performer appearing on screen simultaneously. This was done by 'duplex cinematography', also pioneered by Georges Méliès and at about the same time as the film above. Méliès adapted a technque already well known to still photographers, by which a small frame enclosing two swing doors was mounted in front of the camera lens. When one door was opened, half the scene was exposed on film. The film was then wound back, one door shut and the other opened, and the rest of the scene shot. If the same performer was filmed each time, he or she would appear to be two characters interacting. Méliès' first attempt at this technique was in *Un Homme de tête*/*The Four Troublesome Heads* (Fr 98), which shows a magician removing his head three times over and in which he used a combination of both spirit photography and duplex photography.

The first physical contact between two characters played by the same person was accomplished in *Little Lord Fauntleroy* (US 21) when Mary Pick-

Mary Pickford greets Mary Pickford in *Little Lord Fauntleroy* (US 21). Note the physical contact.

ford played both the boy and his mother 'Dearest'. Cameraman Charles Rosher used a 2000 lb camera to achieve absolute steadiness between one take and the next, but the exact details of his extraordinarily advanced technique are still not known. The preparations for each double exposure were amongst the most meticulous and precise in the history of camerawork. It took 15 hours to shoot the scene in which the boy kisses 'Dearest' on the cheek, a take which lasts three seconds on the screen. In another scene they embrace and, in the most spectacular of all, the Little Lord runs and jumps into his mother's arms. The complexity of the operation was enhanced by the fact that Mary Pickford the mother had to be nine inches taller than Mary Pickford the boy. For her adult role in the double exposure scenes she was given platform heels and stood on a concealed ramp, a hazardous operation since she fell off on a number of occasions.

The attempted suicide of Alex (Malcolm McDowell) in *A Clockwork Orange* (GB 71) was achieved by throwing a Newman Sinclair camera off the top of a building. On the sixth take the camera landed downward as intended. The lens was smashed, but the camera was found to be still in perfect working order.

Double exposure was temporarily abandoned when sound came in, because of the difficulty of post-synching. **The first double exposure with dialogue** was a scene in Fox Movietone's *Masquerade* (US 29) in which Alan Burmingham carried on a conversation with another character also played by Alan Burmingham.

The first triple exposure was achieved by cameraman Al Siegler in Universal's *The Twins' Double* (US 14), in which Grace Cunard played the twin heroines and the villainess, their double— all three characters appearing on the screen at the same time.

The first quadruple exposure was of Dorothy Dalton as four different characters all seen at once in the promo short *Trip to Paramountown* (US 22).

Nowadays multiple exposures tend to be used for naturalistic special effects rather than the trick of showing the same person simultaneously performing more than one role. A **septuple exposure** was used in *Star Trek* (US 79) for the elaborate sequence in which the starship *Enterprise* first approaches the alien invaders. The different exposures, which included shots of the spacecraft, fog, yellow lights, a star-field and cloud effects, were combined in a scene which occupied only 30 seconds of screen time but 48 hours of filming.

Back projection was first employed successfully by special effects maestro Willis O'Brien for a single scene in *The Lost World* (US 25). It is a technique by which outdoor scenes can be shot in the studio by placing the actors against a rear projected filmed background. The following year back projection was used in the making of *Metropolis* (Ger 26), but it was slow to catch on because of the technical difficulties involved. The breakthrough came with the development of the Teague Back Projector, which was employed for the first time on the Fox production *Just Imagine* (US 30), a science-fiction film set in 1980. Back projection was used to depict a city of the future, with stars Maureen O'Sullivan and John Garrick coasting along in their private aircraft in the foreground.

Back projection in colour was first used by William Wellman on *Nothing Sacred* (US 37).

The first camera crane was used by cameraman William F. Alder for obtaining elevated shots in Metro's *The Second in Command* (US 15), with Francis X. Bushman. At about the same time Allan Dwan devised a more sophisticated elevator on tracks for use in the Babylonian sequence of D. W. Griffith's *Intolerance* (US 16). The 115 ft (35 m) high structure enabled Griffith to secure a parabolic shot, commencing at the ramparts of the Palace and descending forwards over a sea of extras to ground level and a close shot of the leading players. These early uses of the crane were exceptional. It was not until F. W. Murnau introduced his 20-ton, 200-hp 'Go-Devil' on *The Four Devils* (US 29), and the appearance of an even larger 28-ton apparatus with a 60 ft (18.3 m) elevation on the set of *Broadway* (US 29), that the crane came to be regarded as standard studio equipment.

The first woman cameraman was Rosina Cianelli, who made her camera debut with Paolo Benedetti's *Uma transformista original* (Bra 09), a Méliès-style trick film made at Barbacena, Brazil, with the Lazzari brothers as stars.

The first American camerawoman was Grace Davison, who joined the Astor Film Corp. at its Long Island studios as an actress in 1915 but was taught to handle a camera by veteran Harry Fishbeck. Miss Davison photographed *The Honeymooners* (US 15), *Spring Onions* (US 15) and other one-reel comedies.

The first camerawoman to shoot a feature film was Tamara Lobova, who worked on *Suvorov* (USSR 41) together with her husband Anatolij Golovnja. First with a solo camera credit was Galina Pyshkova for *Songs of Abay* (USSR 46).

*C*HASE SEQUENCES

The most destructive chase sequence in a motion picture occurred in H. B. Halicki's *The Junkman* (US 82), in which the mayhem involved the wrecking of over 150 vehicles including two Cadillac Eldorados, two Chrysler Magnums, numerous boats, trucks and motorcycles and two Pitts high-performance aeroplanes.

*C*OSTUME

The largest number of costumes in any one film was 32,000 for *Quo Vadis* (US 51). *Waterloo* (It/USSR 70) used 29,000 costumes and *Cleopatra* (US 63) 26,000 costumes.

The largest number of costume changes by one performer was by Elizabeth Taylor in *Cleopatra* (US 63). The 65 costumes designed by Irene Sharaff for Miss Taylor cost $130,000. Another 40 costumes and head-dresses designed by Oliver Messel at a cost of $64,800 did not appear in the movie as released.

The largest number of costume changes in a silent movie was 50 by Theda Bara in the course of the eleven reels of *Cleopatra* (US 17).

The most expensive costume ever worn in a movie was the barzucine sable coat that enfolded Constance Bennett in *Madame X* (US 65). It was valued at $50,000.

The most expensive costume designed and made specially for a film was Edith Head's mink and sequins dance costume for Ginger Rogers in *Lady in the Dark* (US 44), which cost Paramount $35,000. By comparison, Elizabeth Taylor's dress of cloth-of-24-carat-gold in which she made her entry into Rome in *Cleopatra* (US 63) cost a modest $6500. However, the total cost of Miss Taylor's wardrobe, which amounted to $194,800, was **the highest sum ever expended on costumes for a single performer in any one film.**

The most expensive single costume of the silent era was made for Mary Pickford to wear in the title role of *Dorothy Vernon of Haddon Hall* (US 24). A sumptuous Elizabethan gown embroidered with real seed pearls, it was designed by Mitchell Leisen at a cost of $32,000.

   At the other end of the scale, costumes could cost next to nothing even in Hollywood's most extravagant days; except for the studios' insistence that nothing was worthwhile unless it was expensive. When a rough, workaday costume was needed for Ingrid Bergman in *For Whom the Bell Tolls* (US 43), designer Edith Head selected an old pair of men's trousers and a shirt from the extra's wardrobe. Producer David O Selznick was incensed and demanded that Miss Head should design a new costume. She did so, copying the old garments

Ingrid Bergman's costume in *For Whom the Bell Tolls* (US 43) may not look as if it has been specially designed for her, but the producer insisted. (*SI*)

exactly, then bleaching them and dying them to look as worn as the originals.

The record spent on costumes in relation to budget was the $1 million plus for wardrobe in the $7 million production *Chanel Solitaire* (US 81), a biopic of the legendary French fashion designer Coco Chanel.

The largest costume collection in the world is owned by Western Costume Co. and housed in a six-storey building at 5335 Melrose Avenue, Hollywood, California. The collection consists of approximately one million costumes valued at over $50 million.

   Western Costume was established in Los Angeles in 1912. In a curious way its fortune could be said to have been founded on dietary deficiency. Business was slow until a major break came with D. W. Griffith's order for all the Civil War costumes for *The Birth of a Nation* (US 15). Griffith, preoccupied with authenticity, had hoped to use genuine uniforms of the period, but found that progress in nutrition over the intervening 50 years had made the average actor of 1914 too large to fit the average soldier's uniform of the 1860s.

The largest costume collection in Europe is held by Berman and Nathan's of London, who have a stock of over 700,000 costumes.

Chaplin's Tramp Costume

The costume was devised in response to Mack Sennett's request that he 'get into a comedy make-up' for *Kid Auto Races at Venice* (US 14). Chaplin created the costume in a dressing room where Fatty Arbuckle and Chester Conklin were playing pinochle. The moustache was a scrap of crêpe hair borrowed from Mack Swain; the trousers were Fatty Arbuckle's—hence the bagginess—and the Derby came from Minta Durfee's father, Fatty's father-in-law; the cut-away coat belonged to Chester Conklin (or Charlie Avery, according to one account); the size 14 shoes were Ford Sterling's and Chaplin had to wear them on the wrong feet to keep them on. Only the whangee cane belonged to Charlie himself.

Chaplin gave the original costume to his assistant Harry Crocker in 1928 as a central exhibit in the newly-opened Crocker Museum of props and costumes on Sunset Boulevard. Nearly 60 years later, in 1987, Chaplin's bowler and cane came up for sale at Christie's in London, where they were bought by Danish shopping mall entrepreneur Jörgen Strecker for $150,000.

The truth is now out about the most celebrated bra in history, the cantilevered job designed by Howard Hughes to give Jane Russell support where he felt she needed it most. According to Jane's recent autobiography, the fabled garment did really exist, but she only wore it once and that was in the privacy of her own dressing room. Hughes had used engineering principles to design the ideal brassière for the well-endowed woman. It simply did not work. Jane found it 'uncomfortable and ridiculous' and changed back into her own custom-made bra. She went on set and everyone assumed she was wearing her mentor's creation. She never let on until years after Howard Hughes's death, but there is little doubt that the legend of the cantilevered bra will long outlive Jane Russell herself.

Fashion and the Movies

Movie costumes began to influence fashion as early as 1912, when it was reported that the natives of Tahiti had become so addicted to westerns that they had taken to wearing stetsons. A rather more far-reaching fashion was initiated by D. W. Griffith

when he invented the first pair of false eyelashes in order to give Seena Owen's eyes an abnormally large and lustrous appearance for her role as Princess Beloved in *Intolerance* (US 16). They were made by a wigmaker who wove human hair through the warp of a 24-inch strip of thin gauze. Each day two small pieces were cut from the end of the strip and gummed to Miss Owen's eyelids. The use of mascara and other eye make-up was directly inspired by the example of screen vamps Theda Bara and Pola Negri, who darkened their eyelids to give themselves an air of brooding mystery. Plucked eyebrows became the rage about 1930 after Jean Harlow had hers trimmed into a slender arch. Beauty editors advised her imitators to dab ether on their brows to ease the pain of plucking out the hairs.

Bessie Barriscale caused a sensation with the backless evening gown she wore in *Josselyn's Wife* (US 19) and soon the middle classes were aping a fashion formerly displayed only by their betters. All classes followed the trend to bobbed hair, which became the style of the twenties after Colleen Moore had created the archetypal flapper role in *Flaming Youth* (US 23). Pola Negri was not only the first to go barelegged and sandalled in summer, but was also the first to paint her toenails. She recalled that when she first did this in about 1923, using a bright red polish, a woman glanced down at her feet and shrieked 'She's bleeding'. Nevertheless, within a few weeks, Miss Negri claimed, women everywhere were lacquering their toenails. Joan Crawford was the first to go barelegged with evening clothes in 1926. She stated that she never wore stockings between then and 1930, when long dresses returned to fashion. Bare legs for ordinary 'streetwear' were pioneered by blonde starlet Rita Carewe in 1927. To preserve the proprieties, however, Miss Carewe had her legs *polished* to give the impression that she was wearing silk stockings.

Bejeaned teenagers might have made an earlier appearance but for the obduracy of D. W. Griffith. About 1914, 16-year-old Dorothy Gish became the first screen star and one of the first women in America to adopt jeans. She never wore them in films, however, and only once to the studio; a stern message to her mother from Griffith prevented such a solecism from ever being repeated. Another ten years were to pass before a woman wearing trousers as an article of feminine apparel (as opposed to male impersonation costume) appeared on screen in the person of Myrna Loy in *What Price Beauty* (US 24). This seems to have had little impact upon fashion at the time and it was not until Louise Brooks took to wearing silk trousers (indoors only) in 1927 that the practice became accepted amongst the more sophisticated followers of filmdom's fashion decrees. The real breakthrough for emancipated womanhood, though, had to await the release of von Sternberg's *Morocco*

(US 30), in which Marlene Dietrich concealed her celebrated legs in slacks. Von Sternberg's purpose was to emphasize the lesbian characterization of the role, but the innovation was imitated by the women of America to an extent that suggests its implication was wholly lost on them.

Probably the single most influential trendsetter, and the star who made least effort to be one, was Garbo. The enormous fur collars of the twenties owed their genesis to the broad collar designed by Max Ree to conceal her long neck in *The Torrent* (US 26). Garbo's berets, which she wore off-screen, became a universal fashion of the thirties and made a come-back in the sixties after Faye Dunaway had worn one as the thirties woman gangster in *Bonnie and Clyde* (US 67). The diagonally placed Eugénie hat, dipping over one eye, worn by Garbo in *Romance* (US 30), hastened the end of the cloche and introduced the basic configuration that was to dominate hat styles throughout the thirties. Although most fashion design of the period reflected a conscious rejection of the past, Adrian's Eugénie hat was created for a film that was set in the 1850s.

The other major trendsetter of the period was Joan Crawford, whom women fans watched spellbound as she suffered in mink. While her taste in furs was beyond the reach of the majority, the padded-shoulder costume Adrian designed for her to wear in *Today We Live* (US 33) started the vogue for tailored suits that sloped upwards from the neck. Crawford herself was so enamoured with the style that she went on wearing padded shoulders long after they had gone out of general fashion.

By this time the big studios were co-operating with the garment trade—most of the moguls had come from that industry themselves—so that the costumes designed for the new genre of 'women's pictures' could be in the shops by the time the film was released. It was another Adrian creation for Joan Crawford that began this mass marketing of star costumes, the celebrated *Letty Lynton* dress which she wore in the film of the same name (US 32). Over half a million copies were sold by Macy's of New York alone. The success of the venture encouraged its development. In 1933 a leading department store in Columbus, Ohio called Morehouse Martens 'completed an arrangement by which copies of movie stars' clothes are on sale at the store prior to or coincident with the opening of their pictures'. The initial offerings were a Joan Blondell double-duty dress, a Jean Arthur frock and Claire Dodd pyjamas. The same year Bamberger's of Newark, NJ opened a 'Cinema Shop' devoted exclusively to copies of the clothes worn by stars, and their lead was followed by other major stores from coast to coast, including such noted names as the Hecht Co. of Washington, Goldsmith's of Chicago, Joseph Horne of Pittsburgh ('The Hollywood Shop') and the May Co. of Los

The film was *On Golden Pond* (US 81). The stars were Henry Fonda and Katharine Hepburn. The hat was Spencer Tracy's.

The battered hat worn by Henry Fonda in *On Golden Pond* (US 81) was Spencer Tracy's. Katharine Hepburn, who surprisingly had never met Fonda in the 50 years they had each spent in Hollywood, presented it to him the first day on set.

Angeles. The desire to look like the stars was no less fervent in Britain, where a magazine devoted to the subject with the title *Film Fashionland* was started in 1934.

Generally, the adoption of a movie fashion brought fortunes either to the designer or to the entrepreneur who succeeded in adapting it to a mass market. The star who launched the style seldom derived any direct benefit, with the notable exception of Shirley Temple. The astute business sense of Mrs Temple ensured that when Fox sold the manufacturing rights to Shirley's party dresses from *Baby Takes a Bow* (US 35), it was Shirley who garnered the lion's share of the profits.

What stars did not wear could sometimes have as much impact on fashion trends as what they did wear. When Clark Gable opened his shirt to reveal a bare and matted torso in *It Happened One Night* (US 34), men's undershirt sales took a 40 per cent dive. Mae West also enjoyed a quite unlooked for effect on fashion, if the Kansas Restaurant Association is to be believed. In 1934 the Association publicly thanked Miss West for stemming the dieting craze stimulated by the sylph-like figures of Dietrich, Crawford and Harlow and for restoring well-rounded curves to healthy US women.

Marlon Brando's butch get-up in *The Wild One* (US 54) inspired the leather look amongst gays. (*Rob Burt*)

Hollywood also played its part in bringing an exotic touch to American fashion. When Dorothy Lamour wore the first of her celebrated series of sarongs in *Jungle Princess* (US 36), it generated a demand for tropical fabrics that lasted for the next ten years. The Latin-American look that swept the USA in the early forties was instigated by Edith Head's costumes for Barbara Stanwyck in *The Lady Eve* (US 41), and Charles LeMaire's designs for Jennifer Jones in *Love is a Many Splendoured Thing* (US 55) began a trend towards oriental fashion.

After World War II, Hollywood's main fashion influence was in the direction of casual wear, though even as early as 1922 American males had been persuaded to abandon their stiff collars after heart-throb Wallace Reid had played a romantic lead wearing a soft collar. By the 1950s it was mainly teenagers who took their fashion lead from movie idols. What we now regard as standard leather-biker costume only became so after Marlon Brando had appeared looking butch and menacing in zip-up jacket in *The Wild One* (US 54). It also inspired the leather look among gays. James Dean's windcheater in *Rebel Without a Cause* (US 55) and Elvis Presley's tight trousers in *Jailhouse Rock* (US 57) set the teenage-style of the later 1950s and early 1960s.

Footwear is less often influenced by the movies, but girls with slim ankles took to wearing slip-ons without socks or stockings after Bardot had sloughed off the conventions of the formal fifties in *And God Created Woman* (Fr 57). The sex kitten also made going barefoot acceptable—she seldom wore shoes off-screen—provided you were young and pretty. Ten years later Jane Fonda's knee-length white vinyl boots in *Barbarella* (Fr/It 67) became part of the uniform of the mini-skirt generation.

Hairstyles are often prone to the dictates of Hollywood, with Jean Seberg and Mia Farrow demonstrating that cropped hair went well with an elfin face. Blonde streaks in brunette hair was a fashion inspired by Audrey Hepburn in *Breakfast at Tiffany's* (US 61). Whatever it may or may not have done for the butter industry, *Last Tango in Paris* (Fr/It/US 72) gave the world frizzy hair, as exemplified by sultry Maria Schneider, and revived the neglected art of permanent waving.

Another kind of casual look, for highbrows rather than hoydens, involved wearing the kind of baggy, rumpled clothes sported by Diane Keaton with neurotic chic in *Annie Hall* (US 77). Youth and good looks were not really sufficient if you wanted to get away with this; a certain fey and anxious charm was also imperative.

The decline of the cinema as a cultural force has reduced its fashion impact in the west, but in the Orient, where cinema-going continues to increase, it appears to be breaking down traditional prejudices against western dress. Significant of the trend are reports that jeans are now being worn by Indian women since superstar Zeenat Aman began wearing them in public.

CREWS

The largest production crew on a movie consisted of the 556 craftsmen and technicians employed by producer Sukertaru Taguchi on Kon Ichikawa's *Tokyo Olympiad* (US 65). The largest number on a dramatic feature was 532 for the British World War I flying story *Sky Bandits* (GB 86).

DIRECTORS

The first director—The functions of director and producer were first separated for America's earliest 'spectacle' film *The Passion Play* (US 98). Rich G. Hollaman, the producer, engaged a distinguished stage director, L. J. Vincent of Niblo's Garden Theatre in New York, to direct the picture. Unfortunately, America's first movie director had never seen a movie and nothing could persuade him that the camera was capable of reproducing live action. Convinced that he had been engaged to direct a succession of lantern-slide tableaux, he would rush out on to the set whenever the performance of a scene was progressing favourably and scream 'Hold it!' The film was eventually made by subterfuge. Each afternoon cameraman William Paley would declare that the light was no longer strong enough to continue and as soon as Vincent had departed the actors would reassemble and shoot as much as possible before dark. The two-reel drama was a sensation when it was premièred at the Eden Musée on 30 January 1898, but it is difficult to know whether it would be more accurately described as the first film made by a professional director or the first dramatic film made with no director at all.

The first woman director was Alice Guy (1873–1968), originally secretary to Léon Gaumont, who was given an opportunity to direct after she had complained at the lack of variety in Gaumont productions. She made her debut with *La Fée aux choux*, about a young couple walking in the countryside who encounter a fairy in a cabbage patch and are presented with a child. The film is usually said to date from 1896, but since it is listed No. 370 in the Gaumont catalogue it seems more likely that it was made *c.* 1900. Mlle Guy was Gaumont's sole director of dramatic films until Zecca joined the studios at La Villette in 1905. In 1907 she emigrated to the USA, and founded the Solax Co. on Long Island three years later. Between 1919 and 1922 she directed for Pathé and Metro, then

The world's first woman director, Alice Guy, on the set of her first movie *La Fée aux choux* (Fr *c.* 00)

returned to France. Despite her long experience, she was unable to find work as a director in her own country and made a living writing stories based on film scenarios for pulp magazines.

The first feature film directed by a woman was the Rex production of *The Merchant of Venice* (US 14), which had Lois Weber as director. Miss Weber was also **the first American woman director**, starting with Gaumont Talking Pictures in New York in 1907, then working for Reliance in 1908, for Rex 1909–13, for the Bosworth Co. 1914–15 and for Universal 1915–19, after which she went independent. Her best known picture was Universal's highly successful *Where Are My Children?* (US 16), a treatise on birth control. As her films became increasingly controversial, she had difficulty in obtaining distribution, and her last picture, *White Heat* (US 34), about miscegenation, was not released.

Sharon Smith, in *Women Who Make Movies* (New York 75), has listed 36 women directors who were active in the United States during the silent era and believes there were others who directed anonymously. The only one to make the transition to sound was Dorothy Arzner, whose *Manhattan Cocktail* (US 28) was **the first talkie directed by a woman**. At the height of her career in the thirties she was listed as one of Hollywood's top ten directors.

The first woman to direct a British production was Jakidawdra Melford, who made her directorial debut with a highwayman picture called *The Inn on the Heath* (GB 14). The first feature by a woman was Dinah Shurey's *Carry On!* (GB 27), a naval war drama, and the first talkie was Elinor Glyn's *Knowing Men* (GB 30).

> Of the 7332 feature films distributed by the major Hollywood studios during the thirty years 1949 to 1979, only 14 were directed by women—less than one-fifth of one per cent.

The first director to direct himself in a full-length feature film was Harold Heath, who played the lead in Anchor Films' detective thriller *£1000 Reward* (GB 13).

The first black American director to direct a film aimed at multi-racial audiences was Melvin van Peebles, former San Francisco cable-car gripman, who made his directorial debut with *La Permission/The Story of a Three Day Pass* (Fr 67). Based on van Peebles' own novel, *The Pass*, it

Below left: If you ever wondered how a director made himself heard on a location set before the days of the electronic loudhailer, here's how. The picture was *Robin Hood* (US 22), the director Allan Dwan. Douglas Fairbanks starred as Robin, but not in those knickerbockers (*Popperfoto*). *Below right*: By the 1930s electronics had come to the aid of the director. (*Popperfoto*)

KEEP OFF C.B. de MILLE

related the story of a black GI on a three-day furlough who has a brief affair with a Parisian shop girl. His first American movie was *The Watermelon Man* (US 70), in which Godfrey Cambridge portrays the white insurance salesman who wakes up one morning to find he has turned black.

The first black American to direct an American film at a major studio was former *Life* photographer Gordon Parks, who directed *The Learning Tree* (US 69) for Warner Bros.

For **the first black director of black films** see p. 46.

The first black African director was Paulin Soumanou Vieyra, born in Dahomey in 1925, who made his directorial debut with *Afrique sur Seine* (Sen 55).

The first Maori to direct a feature film was Barry Barclay, whose *Ngati* (NZ 87) was selected for Critics' Week at the 1987 Cannes Film Festival and won the award for Best Film at the 1987 Taormina Film Festival.

The first director to make a film on percentage was D. W. Griffith, who made *The Birth of a Nation* (US 15) while earning his regular $300 a week with Majestic and was offered 37½ per cent of net profits after the film had been completed.

The first director to earn a million dollars for a single picture was Mike Nichols for *The Graduate* (US 67).

In South India, directors are paid a standard fee according to what language the film is being made in. Directors of Hindi films receive top whack at $7000, directors of Tamil and Telegu films get $5000 and directors of Kannada and Malalayam movies have to be content with $3330.

The longest directorial career lasted for 66 years in the case of King Vidor (1894–1982), beginning with a two-reel comedy about auto-racing called *The Tow* (US 14), filmed at Galveston, Texas, where he grew up, and culminating in another short, a documentary about painting called *The Metaphor* (US 80). Vidor's feature-film career had begun with a Christian Science melodrama titled *The Turn of the Road* (US 18); which oddly enough had been financed to the tune of $9000 by a consortium of ten doctors. Between this and his last feature, *Solomon and Sheba* (US 59), came such notable milestones in movie history as *The Big Parade* (US 25)—the most profitable silent film ever made (see p. 28)—his greatest artistic success *The Crowd* (US 28), the first major all-black movie *Hallelujah* (US 29)—see p. 46—a classic tear-jerker *The Champ* (US 31), and a beautifully crafted adaptation of A. J. Cronin's novel *The Citadel* (GB 38) with Robert Donat. Vidor was a romantic, both

on and off screen. Looking for a female lead for his first rather primitive comedy *The Tow*, he saw a beautiful girl passing in the back of a car. When he tracked her down, her father refused to let her debase herself in motion pictures. Vidor was determined to secure her services as an actress, but he had also fallen in love with her. They married and she became a major star of the silent screen as Florence Vidor.

Directors with a career spanning half a century:

KING VIDOR (1894–1982) 66 years from *The Tow* (US 14) to *The Metaphor* (US 80).

ABEL GANCE (1889–1982) 60 years from *La Digue* (Fr 11) to *Bonaparte et la Revolution* (Fr 71).

JORIS IVENS (1898–) 60 years from *De Brug* (Neth 28) to *La Vent* (Fr 88). Still active.

GRIGORI ALEXANDRANOV (1903–83) 59 years from *The Battleship Potemkin* (USSR 25), co-directed with Sergei Eisenstein, to *Lubov Orlova* (USSR 84).

MANOEL DE OLIVEIRA (1908–) 57 years from *Douru, Faina Fluvial* (Por 31). Still active.

YULI RAIZMAN (1908?–) 57 years from *A Circle* (USSR 27) to *A Time for Wishes* (USSR 84).

JOHN FORD (1895–1973) 54 years from *Lucille Love—The Girl of Mystery* (US 14) to *Vietnam, Vietnam* (US 68).

ALFRED HITCHCOCK (1899–1980) 53 years from *Always Tell Your Wife* (GB 23) to *Family Plot* (US 76).

GEORGE MARSHALL (1896–1975) 52 years from Harry Carey westerns and Ruth Roland serials in 1917 to *Hook, Line and Sinker* (US 69).

RAOUL WALSH (1887–1980) 52 years from *The Life of Villa* (US 12) to *A Distant Trumpet* (US 64).

RUDALL HAYWARD (189?–1974) 51 years from *The Bloke from Freeman's Bay* (NZ 20) to *To Love a Maori* (NZ 71).

GEORGE CUKOR (1899–1983) 51 years from *Grumpy* (US 30) to *Rich and Famous* (US 81).

MARK DONSKOI (1901–1981) 51 years from *Life* (USSR 27) to *The Orlovs* (USSR 78).

MICHAEL CURTIZ (1888–1962) 50 years from *Ma Es Holnap* (Hun 12) to *The Comancheros* (US 62).

Apart from Alfred Hitchcock, most of whose work was in America, **the most durable British director** was Maurice Elvey (1887–1967), whose directorial career spanned 44 years from *The Fallen Idol* (GB 13) to *Second Fiddle* (GB 57).

Hollywood's most prolific director was William Beaudine (1892–1970), who directed 182 full-length features from *Watch Your Step* (US 22) to *Jesse James Meets Frankenstein's Daughter* (US 60), of which 32 were silents and 144 were talkies. In addition he directed over 120 shorts from 1916. Runners up are as follows:

RICHARD THORPE (1896–) 179 features from *Burn 'em Up Barnes* (US 21) to *The Scorpio Letters* (US 67), of which 63 were silents and 116 were talkies.

MICHAEL CURTIZ (1888–1962) 164 features from *Ma Es Holnap* (Hun 12) to *The Comancheros* (US 62), of which 61 were made in Europe before 1926 and the remainder in Hollywood.

SAM NEWFIELD (1900–64) 140 talkies.

ALLAN DWAN (1885–1981) 132 features from *Richelieu* (US 14) to *The Most Dangerous Man Alive* (US 61), plus over 200 shorts from *Brandishing a Bad Man* (US 11). Dwan claimed to have been involved in the making of 1400 films since 1910 as writer, producer or director.

JOHN FORD (1895–1973) 132 features from *The Tornado* (US 17) to *Vietnam, Vietnam* (US 68).

Note: It has been claimed that George Marshall (1896–1975) directed 425 features during his career, but only 88 full-length pictures crediting him as director can be traced for the period 1917–69. Ford Beebe (1888–) is said to have directed over 200 westerns, 'B' pictures and serials from 1916, but only 72 known films give him director credit.

The most prolific British director was Darlington-born Maurice Elvey (1887–1967), who directed 149 full-length features from *Her Luck in London* (GB 14) to *Second Fiddle* (GB 57). In addition he directed 41 shorts (mainly two-reelers) from *The Fallen Idol* (GB 13).

The director to make the most films in a single year was Sam Newfield (1900–64), who directed 17 'B' westerns for eight different 'Poverty Row' studios during 1938.

The most co-directors on a single film was 16 in the case of *I misteri di Roma* (It 63), an anti-establishment view of 'one day in the life of the city' directed by Gianni Bisiach, Libero Bozzari, Mario Carbone, Angelo D'Alessandro, Nino del Fra, Luigi di Gianni, Giuseppe Ferrara, Ansano Giannarelli, Guilo Macchi, Lori Mazzetti, Massimo Mida, Enzo Mutti, Piero Nelli, Paolo Nuzzi, Dino Partesano and Giovanni Vento.

Deutschland in Herbst (FRG 78), *Love for Everyone* (Chn 42) and *Paramount on Parade* (US 30) each had eleven directors; *Dreams of Thirteen* (FRG/Neth 74 and *Aria* (US/GB 87) had ten; *If I Had a Million* (US 32) and *Forever and a Day* (US 43) had seven. All the foregoing were either non-fiction or episodic fiction films. The most directors on a straight fiction film was seven for *Casino Royale* (GB 67), a Bond movie directed by John Huston, Ken Hughes, Val Guest, Robert Parrish, Joe McGrath, Richard Talmadge and Anthony Squire; and the same number for *Dungeonmaster* aka *Ragewar* (US 85), which was the collective work of Rose-Marie Turko, John Buechler, Charles Band, David Allen, Steve Ford, Peter Manoogian and Ted Nicolaou.

The youngest director of a professionally-made 35mm film was 14-year-old Londoner Howard Selfe, whose 18-minute travelogue *Flower Island* (GB 84) was shot in Jersey in August 1981 during the island's flower festival. A Norwood Entertainments Ltd production, it was premièred in June 1984 at the Odeon, Leicester Square as a supporting film to Bryan Forbes's *The Naked Face* (GB 84) and subsequently went on general release. It was one of the last unsponsored supporting programme shorts made in Britain; the abolition of the 'Quota' and the Eady Levy making production of such films uneconomic. At the time that Howard Selfe made *Flower Island* he was a student at the Italia Conti Academy of Dramatic art. After a career as a child actor he left films to establish a retail business.

The youngest director of a professionally-made feature film was Lev Kuleshov (1899–1970), who was 17½ when he embarked on his four-reel *Proyekt inzhenera Praita/Engineer Prite's Project* (USSR 18) at the Khanzhonkov Studios in Moscow. Other teenage directors have been Japan's Masahiro Makino, who made his directorial debut in 1927 at the age of 18; George Palmer, 17½, of Melbourne, Vic., who directed the railroad drama *Northbound Ltd* (Aus 26); Yuli Raizman, director of *A Circle* (USSR 27) at the age of 19; Philippe Garrel, whose feature debut *Anemone* (Fr 66), made when he was 19, starred his father Maurice Garrel; Sam Raimi, a 19-year-old who hustled the money for *The Evil Dead* (US 82) on the strength of a 30-min pilot shot on 8 mm; and 18-year-old Laurent Boutonnat, *enfant terrible* responsible for *La Ballade de la Feconductrice* (Fr 80). Boutannat was just old enough to be allowed to see his own film—it won an adults-only rating for its depiction of castration, child slaughter and bestiality. The only teenage female director was 19-year-old French helmer Christine Ehm, who made her debut with *Simone* (Fr 87).

The oldest director is Joris Ivens, born in the Netherlands in 1898, who made the Franco–Italian co-production *Le Vent* (Fr/It 88) at the age of 89. This was 60 years after he had made his directorial debut with *De Brug* (Neth 28).

Hollywood's oldest director was George Cukor (1899–1983), 81 years old when he was signed by MGM in October 1980 to direct Jacqueline Bisset and Candice Bergen in *Rich and Famous* (US 81).

George Cukor (1899–1983) with Candice Bergen and Jacqueline Bisset during the making of *Rich and Famous* (US 81). At 81 he was the oldest director ever signed for a major Hollywood picture.

The most versatile film-maker in terms of the most credits for a single film is Polish director Andrzej Kondratiuk, whose *The Four Seasons* (Pol 85) credited him as producer, director, scriptwriter, cameraman, art director, composer, soundman, props buyer, lighting-man and star. The only technical credit to someone else went to editor Maryla Orlowska. Exceptionally for a professionally made film produced in an Eastern bloc country, *Four Seasons* was privately financed—by Andrzej Kondratiuk.

Most credits for a major motion picture went to Charles Chaplin for producing, directing, scripting, composing, editing, choreographing, costume-designing and starring in *Limelight* (US 52). Most versatile femme film-maker is Sweden's Ann Zacharias, director, producer, scriptwriter, production designer and star of *The Test* (Swe 87).

The first woman to take writer–director–star credit on a major feature was Elaine May for *A New Leaf* (US 70). First with producer–director–star credits was Barbra Streisand for the Jewish musical *Yentl* (GB 83).

*E*DITING

The most edited film in terms of total negative discarded was Howard Hughes' *Hell's Angels* (US 30), which consumed 2,254,750 ft of film during the four years it took to make. If all this footage had been shown unedited, it would have run for 560 hr or 23 days non-stop. The cost of the film stock was $225,475. The final release print was 9045 ft (2 hr 15 min running time), a reduction in the ratio of 249:1. A single scene without actors—a brief close-up of the valves of an aeroplane engine—occupied 20,000 ft of film (the length of four full-length features) before Hughes was satisfied.

In more recent times Michael Cimino shot 220 hours of film for his $57 million epic *Heaven's Gate* (US 81) to produce a release print which one critic described as 5 hours 25 minutes of 'staggering self-indulgence'. When the long version flopped, it was cut to 2½ hours.

Other films with extravagant shooting ratios: Fritz Lang's *Metropolis* (Ger 26) was reduced from 1,960,000 to 13,165 ft, a ratio of 149:1; Charles Chaplin's *City Lights* (US 31) was reduced from 975,000 to 7784 ft, a ratio of 125:1; *Uncle Tom's Cabin* (US 27) was reduced from 900,000 to 13,000 ft, a ratio of 69:1; Charles Chaplin's *The Kid* (US 20) was reduced from 400,000 to 6000 ft, a ratio of 67:1; Leni Riefenstahl's *Olympische Spiele* (Ger 38) was reduced from 1,300,000 to 20,000 ft, a ratio of 65:1; William Wyler's *Ben Hur* (US 59) was reduced from 1,125,000 to 23,838 ft, a ratio of 47:1; Howard Hughes' *The Outlaw* (US 46) was reduced from 470,000 to 10,451 ft, a ratio of 45:1;

Erich von Stroheim's *Foolish Wives* (US 21) was reduced from 360,000 to 10,000 ft, a ratio of 36:1; William Wyler's *The Best Years of Our Lives* (US 46) was reduced from 400,000 to 16,000 ft, a ratio of 25:1; Chuck Wein's *Rainbow Bridge* (US 71) was reduced from 252,000 to 10,300 ft, a ratio of 24:1; three with a ratio of 23:1 were D. W. Griffith's *Intolerance* (US 16), reduced from 300,000 to 13,000 ft, Sergei Eisenstein's *October* (USSR 27), also reduced from 300,000 to 13,000 ft, and *Gone With the Wind* (US 39), reduced from 474,538 to 20,300 ft; and *The Longest Day* (US 72), reduced from 360,000 to 17,000 ft, had a ratio of 21:1, or about twice the average.

The most edited single sequence of a movie was the chariot race scene in *Ben Hur* (US 25), for which editor Lloyd Nosler had to compress 200,000 ft of film into a sparse 750 ft, a ratio of 267:1. Histo-

> **RIGHT–LEFT**
> In 1928 a Marxist group in Germany called the Popular Association for Film Art presented a compilation film made up entirely of clips from old UFA newsreels, but cut in such a way as to present a revolutionary viewpoint. It brought outraged protests from audiences who had watched the original newsreels without demur and the film was promptly banned. The Marxists claimed that this effectively demonstrated the power of political prejudice; in fact what it most clearly showed was the extraordinary power of a skilled editor to transform a motion picture.

rian Kevin Brownlow commented: 'These 750 ft are among the most valuable in motion picture history.'

The least edited films include D. W. Griffith's *Broken Blossoms* (US 19), which was made with no retakes of any scene and had only 200 ft trimmed from its original length of 5500 ft; and William Wellman's *The Public Enemy* (US 31), which was reduced by only 360 ft from its original 8760 ft.

Narrative features which were released unedited include *My Hustler* (US 65); Andy Warhol's *Chelsea Girls* (US 66); and Laura Mulvey and Peter Wollen's *Penthesilea: Queen of the Amazons* (GB 74). The ultimate was achieved by *The Lacy Rituals* (GB 73), which was unedited to the extent of including shots of the clapperboard being clapped and even retained the director's cries of 'cut!' on the soundtrack.

The first woman editor was Viola Lawrence, who graduated from assistant editor to editor at New York's Vitagraph Studios in 1915.

> **R2 D2,** lovable robot hero of *Star Wars* (US 77), was named after a piece of film editors' jargon— it means 'Reel 2, Dialog 2'.

New Films for Old

Skilful editing can create an entirely new film from rearrangement of shots in an earlier one. This was achieved by Fred J. Balshofer, who had made a spy spoof called *An Adventuress* (US 20) in which the then unknown Rudolph Valentino played a bit part, and wanted to cash in on the Latin lover's meteoric rise to stardom. The locale of the new picture, *The Isle of Love* (US 22), was switched from World War I Germany to a desert island by the simple expedient of inserting stock shots of bathing beauties on a palm-fringed beach throughout the film. The problem of expanding Valentino's minor role in the original into the lead for the new picture was overcome in a number of ways. Various shots were repeated several times; long shots were blown up into close-up and intercut with other footage; some scenes were projected on a loop, so that Valentino repeated the same motions several times over; one scene was used as a flashback; and out-takes from the original were inserted into the new film, notably discarded footage of a car ride, which so expanded the scene as to make it seem interminable. Valentino, it is hardly necessary to add, received no recompense for this unauthorized 'star performance'.

Woody Allen successfully cannibalized and transmogrified a Japanese crime melodrama into a madcap comedy. Retitled *What's Up Tiger Lily?* (US 66), the comedic effect was achieved by re-editing, deliberately mismatching the dubbed dialogue, and by Allen's zany narration.

Blake Edwards did what was in effect a reconstruction job with *The Trail of the Pink Panther* (GB 82), the only film ever to have been embarked upon after the death of its star. Peter Sellers (1925–80) was seen once again as the accident-prone Inspector Clouseau in a story knit together from clips and left-over out-takes from five previous Pink Panther films. Linking shots were made with an uncredited look-alike filmed at a distance or heavily disguised, as in one scene where the Inspector sets off for England swathed in bandages from head to foot. When all the usable Sellers footage had been exhausted, the film resorted to flashbacks of a teenage Clouseau played by Daniel Peacock and an 8-year-old Clouseau in the person of Lucca Mezzofanti. All this ingenuity failed to pay off. The picture flopped and Sellers's widow Lynne Frederick won an award of $1,687,000 from United Artists for violation of her late husband's contractual rights; United Artists were also ordered to pay $214,000 in costs.

FILM STOCK

Transparent roll film of a kind suitable for motion picture use (though designed for still photography) **was first manufactured** by the Eastman Dry Plate and Film Co. of Rochester, NY in August 1889. Although Thomas Edison ordered some about this date for experiments in cinematography, it was found unsatisfactory and the first stock used for taking films for the Edison Kinetoscope was supplied by the Merwin Hulbert firm in 50 ft rolls on 18 March 1891. In the meantime, however, Louis Aimé Augustin Le Prince of Leeds, Yorkshire, had succeeded in making experimental cinematograph films on Eastman Kodak stock that he had ordered in the autumn of 1889.

The first commercially-produced films in Britain were made in 1895 by Robert Paul and Birt Acres using stock supplied by the European Blair Camera Co. Ltd of St Mary Cray, Kent. By the end of 1896, film stock specially cut and prepared for motion picture use was being advertised by the Celluloid Co. of New York, Dr J. H. Smith & Co. of Zurich, Switzerland, the Blair Co. of Cambridge, Mass. and London, England, the Eastman Kodak Co. of Rochester, NY and Fitch & Co. of London.

The first perforated film was used by Louis Aimé Augustin Le Prince (1842–90?) in his motion picture experiments conducted at Leeds, Yorkshire, in 1889. The inventor's assistant Longley recalled that 'we had brass eyelets fixed in the band [ie film] similar to the eyelets of boots'. The projector built by Le Prince in 1889 had a wheel with pins 'for gearing into the band of pictures'. Perforated film was not used by Thomas Edison until at least three years later.

Commercially-produced film stock was originally sold unperforated and it was not until 1904 that Eastman Kodak began offering perforation as an optional extra. Even as late as 1922 Richardson's *Handbook of Projection* states 'perforation is usually done by the producer'. Unperforated nitrate stock continued to be available from Eastman Kodak until September 1949.

The first safety film on an acetate base was introduced by Eastman Kodak of Rochester, NY, in the autumn of 1908, but its application was limited due to the fact that it tended to shrink and cockle. The negative safety stock was withdrawn in 1912, though positive safety film continued to be available for use with portable projectors in schools. Little record of production on safety film in the USA survives from this period and the earliest commercially-made movie known to have been released on safety stock, a 345 ft drama titled *La Vendetta del Groom* (It 09), was produced by Cines of Rome.

Sub-standard safety film was produced in 28 mm gauge by Pathé for use with the KOK home movie projector in France in 1912 and in 22 mm gauge by Kodak for use with the Edison Home Kinetoscope the same year.

Safety film continued to be confined to the sub-standard gauges until 1950, when Eastman Kodak

Top left: Captain America was one of many comic book heroes to make it to the big screen. For the others see p. 41.

Bottom left: How is your geography? There's something very wrong with this title. If you can't spot it, see p. 164.

Top right: India produces more feature movies than any other country in the world, peaking at a record 912 in 1985. That's about three times Hollywood's annual output. This not very typical Parisian scene was on display in Trivandrum, Kerala. (See p. 11.)

Bottom right: Abraham Lincoln has been portrayed on screen more times than any other US President—in 130 movies to date. Walter Huston played the role in Griffith's 1930 biopic. (See p. 43.)

Top: Steven Spielberg's *E.T. The Extra-Terrestrial* (US 82) remains the biggest box office hit of all time, with a worldwide gross of $700 million. (See p. 28.)

Bottom: The UFO landing site in Steven Spielberg's *Close Encounters of the Third Kind* (US 77) was the largest indoor set ever built. It was constructed inside a 10 million cubic feet dirigible hangar at Mobile, Alabama.

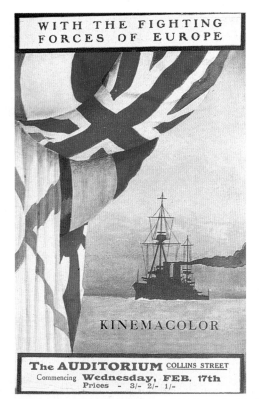

Left: How many people know that World War I was filmed in natural colour? This performance of newsreel films made in Charles Urban's pioneering Kinemacolor process was held at Melbourne, Australia in February 1915.

Below: The 'Croc' became the most successful non-American film of all time and shot Australia's Paul Hogan to international stardom. (See p. 29.) Incidentally the inverted commas round the first name were added by distributors 20th Century Fox because they feared the US public would think the picture was a nature subject about crocodiles.

A WARNER BROS. PICTURE

CASABLANCA

Above: The largest cast ever assembled for a motion picture. There were 300,000 extras in the funeral scene shot in Delhi's Rajpath for Richard Attenborough's *Gandhi* (GB 82). (See p. 72.)

Left: In 1983 the British Film Institute polled its members to determine their choice of the 30 best movies of all time. Out of a total of 2000 films nominated, *Casablanca* (US 42) was overwhelmingly the first choice And if you've ever wondered what the ultimate black and white movie would look like in colour—heaven forbid!—this lobby card shows what a travesty it would be.

Top: Walt Disney, record Oscar winner, with some of his 26 regular trophies and his six 'specials'. The seven miniatures to the left of the Oscar he is holding were in honour of *Snow White and the Seven Dwarfs* (US 37).

Bottom: James Dean was the teenage archetype of the fifties. Windcheaters became part of every young rebel's uniform after the moody star had stonekicked his way through *Rebel Without A Cause* (US 55). (See Fashion and the Movies, p. 116.)

Top: David Naughton before and after the 10-hour make-up job performed by Rick Bahe to transform him into *An American Werewolf in London* (GB 82). (See p. 130.)

Bottom: Linda Hunt (*aloft*) is one of the few actresses to have played a male role, as the Eurasian cameraman Billy Kwan in *The Year of Living Dangerously* (Aus 82). (See p. 98.) She is also Hollywood's shortest leading player at only 4 ft 9 in. (See p. 102.)

Above: Sherlock Holmes, portrayed in 193 films to date, has appeared on screen more often than any other character, real or imaginary. Eille Norwood (1861–1948) starred in 47 of them during the silent era. (See p. 40.)

Right: Elizabeth Taylor's wardrobe in *Cleopatra* (US 62) was the most expensive ever at $194,000. This little cloth-of-24-carat-gold number cost $6500. (See p. 115.)

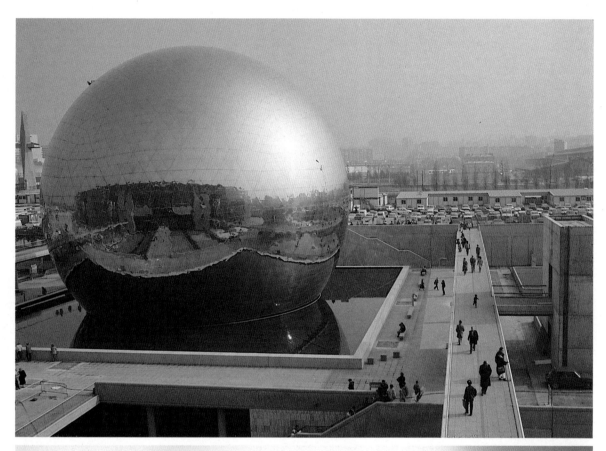

Canada's IMAX System uses the largest frame size of any film stock, ten times greater than standard 35 mm film. (See p. 125.) It renders a screen image of up to 115×85 ft, the height of an eight-storey building. (See p. 200.) Latest installation is the Geode in Paris, pictured above and below.

reintroduced 35 mm uninflammable stock, using a triacetate base immune from shrinkage. The revolution in film stock was total and immediate, so that since 1951 virtually no film has been made on the highly inflammable nitrate stock previously in use.

The largest frame format of any film stock was the 2.04 × 2.805 in dimension used in the 70 mm horizontal feed Imax system, developed by Multiscreen Corp. of Canada. The first film produced in this 5.242 sq in format, which is nine times the size of the standard 35 mm frame, was *Tiger Child* (Can/ Jap 70), presented at the Fuji Group's pavilion at Japan's Expo 70.

Film-makers worldwide will be able to save as much as $400 million a year in stock costs if a revolutionary new Panavision camera perfected by Sweden's Sandrews Film becomes standard in the industry. The innovation with such megabuck potential is a relatively simple device; instead of the frame being advanced by four perforations (one of them empty) each pull- down, as customary, the Sandrews camera moves the frame down only three perforations. This means that 25 per cent less stock is used, saving a quarter of the cost. The first feature film shot this way was Allan Edway's *The Pirates of the Lakes* (Swe 87) and the camera has also been adopted for shooting TV's *Dallas*.

The first film shot in High Definition Video System (HDVS) for theatrical release was *Julia and Julia* (It 87), starring Kathleen Turner, an English-language film made by RAI of Rome. HDVS was developed by Sony and NHK to enable feature films to be shot on tape and transferred to film without loss of quality. The video image has 1125 lines, about twice the definition of a television picture. The technique is claimed to cut below-the-line production costs by 20 to 30 per cent. The first HDTV feature produced in America was *Do It Up* (US 88), starring Robby Benson, which was made by the Rebo High Definition Studio, New York.

*G*AUGES

The standard gauge of 35 mm was adopted by Thomas Alva Edison (1847–1931) of West Orange, NJ, in the spring of 1891 for use with the Kineto- scope peep-show viewing apparatus developed by his assistant W. K. L. Dickson. Edison's choice of four perforations, giving a 4 × 3 format to the image, was probably dictated by the fact that the film was designed for showing in a viewing machine, not on screen. Had he anticipated that projection would become the normal method of presenting movies, he would doubtless have opted for a wider format, to give an aspect ratio approximating more closely to

58 mm film stock (*left*) used by Georges Méliès of Paris in 1896. The narrower gauge was Lumière film stock of approximately the same date. (*ILN*)

---

that of a theatre stage. The Lumière brothers of Lyon, France, who built the first commercially successful projectors, decided to conform to the gauge pioneered by Edison and it was undoubtedly their dominance of the nascent film industry in Europe that established 35 mm as the standard gauge. It was officially recognized as such by international agreement in 1907.

The first use of 70 mm film was by Birt Acres (1854–1918) of Barnet, Herts, for shooting scenes of Henley Regatta on 7–9 July 1896. He soon abandoned use of wide gauge film because of the high cost.

A 70 mm projector was produced by Herman Caster of Canatosta, NY, and introduced into Britain as *The American Biograph* on 17 March 1897 at the Palace Theatre.

The first 70 mm feature film was a special widescreen version of *Fox Movietone Follies of 1929*, premièred in the Grandeur process at the Gaiety Theater, New York, on 17 September 1929.

The first 16 mm feature film to be shot profes- sionally was Lambert Hillyer's *Sundown Riders* (US 44), a western made in Kodachrome and starring Russell Wade, Jay Kirby and Andy Clyde. The picture was shot in eight days at a negative cost of $30,000, less than the cost of a monochrome 'B' western of the time. Release was through voluntary bodies and other institutions. The first feature shot

GAUGES

3 mm	NASA, USA c. 1968	25 mm	Current Chinese broad gauge	60 mm	Demeny Chronophotographe, France 1895; Prestwich, GB 1898
4 mm	US Air Force 1950s	25.4 mm	Kinora, GB 1908		
4.75 mm	Pathé-Duplex, GB 1955	26 mm	Société Cinelux, France 1920	62 mm	American Mutoscope & Biograph Co., USA 1895
8 mm	Eastman Kodak, USA 1932	28 mm	Pathé KOK, France 1912		
8.75 mm	China 1950s (for use in mobile cinemas)	30 mm	France 1910 (three 10 mm frames laterally)	63 mm	Veriscope Co., USA 1897
9.5 mm	Pathé, France 1922	32 mm	Vincennes, France 1920 (two 16 mm frames laterally)	63.5 mm	Spoor-Berggren Natural Vision, USA 1929
11 mm	Duplex, USA c. 1903			65 mm	Warner Bros., USA 1930; Joseph Schenck, USA 1930; Todd-AO, USA 1955
13 mm	Prestwich, GB 1899; France c. 1925	35 mm	Edison, USA 1891; Lumière, France 1894; standard from 1907		
15 mm	Gaumont Pocket-Chrono 1900				
16 mm	Eastman Kodak, USA 1923	38 mm	Lee and Turner, GB 1901	68 mm	American Mutoscope & Biograph Co., USA c. 1898
17 mm	Pathé, Spain c. 1920	42 mm	Tri-Ergon sound system, Germany 1929		
17.5 mm	Birtac, GB 1898; Kino d'Ernemann, Germany 1903, etc.	45 mm	Claude-Autant Lara, France 1929 (three 15 mm frames laterally)	70 mm	Birt Acres, GB 1896; Herman Caster, USA 1897; Fox Grandeur, USA 1929, etc.
18 mm	USSR c. 1925				
20 mm	Mirographe, France c. 1920	48 mm	Blair Viventoscope, GB 1897	73 mm	American Mutosope & Biograph Co., GB c. 1897
21 mm	Mirographe, France 1900; Edison, USA c. 1905	50 mm	Le Prince, GB 1888; Graphophonoscope, France 1899	75 mm	Lumière, France 1900
22 mm	Edison Home Kinetoscope, USA 1912; Cinébloc, France 1921	51 mm	Latham, USA 1895		
		55 mm	Prestwich, GB c. 1902; Cinemascope 55, USA 1956		
24 mm	Société d'Exploutations Cinématographiques, France 1925	56 mm	Magnafilm, USA 1929		

on 16 mm and blown up to 35 mm for showing in cinemas—a common practice nowadays for low-budget movies—was Harry Fraser's Kodachrome *The People's Choice* (US 46), with Drew Kennedy as the slowly-turning worm and Louise Arthur as the ever-believing girl. Well-known films shot on 16 mm and blown up for theatrical release include *Doctor Zhivago* (US 65), *Medium Cool* (US 69), *Easy Rider* (US 69) and *Downhill Racer* (US 69).

The smallest gauge ever employed for filming was 3 mm, developed c. 1960 by Eric Berndt and used by NASA in manned space flights in the late 1960s. It had a centre frameline perforation.

The largest gauge ever employed in filming was 75 mm, used by the Lumière Co. of Lyons, France for special large screen presentations at the Paris Exposition of 1900.

*F*ILM STUDIES

The first course on cinematography was delivered by H. Vodnik at the Slovenija Technical College, Belgrade, Serbia (now Yugoslavia) during the winter semester of 1896–97.

The first in Britain was a course of evening classes commenced under the direction of Robert Mitchell at the Regent Street Polytechnic, London, on 1 October 1913.

The first film school was the State School of Cinematography, Moscow (later the Moscow State Film Institute or VGIK), founded on 1 September 1919 with the support of the Moscow Cinema Committee to train directors, actors, cameramen, lighting experts and art directors. Directors did a three-year course, actors a two-year course, and by government decree all studios were required to reserve a certain number of vacancies for the school's graduates each year. The first Principal was pioneer director Vladamir Gardin (1877–1965),

who made the earliest version of *War and Peace* (Rus 15), and notable teachers during the school's formative years were Eisenstein, Pudovkin, Kozintsev, Dovzhenko, Yutkevich and Tisse. During the first year of the school's existence, raw film stock was in such short supply that the students 'shot' imaginary films with no film in the camera.

The first in Britain was the AAT Film School, established at 14 Soho Square under the auspices of Associated Artist Technicians in 1938. The Director of the school was Edward Carrick (1905–) son of the distinguished stage designer Edward Gordon Craig and grandson of Ellen Terry. Classes were offered in scriptwriting, editing, sound, special effects, camerawork and art direction at a fee of 180 guineas for the full two-year course. The school closed down at the outbreak of war.

*F*LASHBACK

The first flashback was used in the Lubin production *A Yiddisher Boy* (US 08) and showed the hero involved in a boyhood street-fight 25 years earlier.

The first sound flashback, in which dialogue and sounds from the past are synchronized with an image of the present in order to conjure up a distant memory, was used by Rouben Mamoulian in *City Streets* (US 31). Dialogue heard earlier in the film was repeated over a huge close-up of Sylvia Sidney's tear-stained face as she recalls the past.

The first flashback within a flashback appeared in Jacques Feyder's *L'Atlantide* (Fr 21); thereafter it was bypassed by film-makers as too confusing until Michael Curtiz challenged the audience's comprehension with a flashback within a flashback within a flashback in *Passage to Marseilles* (US 44). The experiment was repeated in John Brahm's *The Locket* (US 46) and then happily relegated to the limbo of great ideas that do not work.

Unconventional Flashbacks

These include the multiple flashbacks out of sequence employed by William K. Howard in *The Power and the Glory* (US 33) and Orson Welles in *Citizen Kane* (US 41).

Andre Antoine's *La Coupable* (Fr 16) was told entirely in flashbacks, as was *Saragossa Manuscript* (Pol 74), a Decameron-type fantasy of erotic happenings in the 18th century, which went continuously backwards in time. The original version of Sergio Leone's *Once Upon a Time in America* (US 84) jumped backwards and forwards with such confusing irregularity that *Variety*'s correspondent at Cannes actually logged the sequences: 1933—22 min; 1968—14 min; childhood sequence of indeterminate date—54 min; 1920s—25 min; 1968—7 min; 1920s–30s—61 min; 1968—30 min; 1933—7 min.

Bertolucci's first feature *La Commare secca* (It 62), about the murder of a prostitute in Rome and the subsequent investigation, used the 'against the rules' technique of false flashbacks—deliberately intended to mislead—interspersed with true flashbacks. A charming device was adopted by Keisuke Kinoshita in *Nogiku no gotoku Kimi Nariki/She was like a Wild Chrysanthemum* (Jap 55) —about an old man revisiting his home-town after 60 years and recalling boyhood scenes—when he placed all the flashbacks in an oval-shaped vignette.

*L*IGHTING

The earliest use of lighting effects for their aesthetic value is generally attributed to D. W. Griffith, who employed artificial lighting to obtain a 'fireside glow' in *The Drunkard's Reformation* (US 09), for the 'sunlight effect' in *Pippa Passes* (US 09) and the 'dim, religious light' in *Threads of Destiny* (US 10). Griffith had to overcome the resistance of his cameramen Harry Marvin and Billy Bitzer, who regarded shadows as 'amateurish'.

The first backlighting by reflectors was introduced by D. W. Griffith's cameraman Billy Bitzer on *Enoch Arden* (US 11), which opens with a superbly backlighted shot of the villagers bidding the sailors goodbye. The technique had been discovered by accident. Normally the camera was never faced directly into the sun, but one day Bitzer turned it playfully on to Mary Pickford and Owen Moore as they sat at a shiny-topped table with the sun behind them. Instead of the couple appearing in silhouette, as he expected, Bitzer found that he had obtained a beautifully lit shot with the two artistes' faces bathed in radiance—suitably, since they were in love—the effect of the sun's light reflected in the table top. Bitzer devised a system whereby one mirror would reflect the sun into another, which could then be beamed to the back of a performer's head.

The most powerful lighting used on any film was the 58,000 amps that illuminated the set of *The King and I* (US 56). This is equivalent to the illumination of 258 'brute' arc lights.

The most powerful standard lighting unit currently on sale is the 350-amp Titan Molarc, manufactured by the Mole-Richardson Co. of Hollywood.

The most powerful single arc ever used was a giant 13,940 amp, 325 million candlepower lamp used by Colonel Tim McCoy on the western *California* (US 27). The lamp was 40 times the strength of the most powerful arc available today (see above), 54 times as powerful as the most brilliant lighthouse beam, and said to have a beam that would radiate for 90 miles (145 km).

On the set of *California* (US 27) with the most powerful lighting unit in the history of motion pictures.

*L*OCATIONS

Hollywood home and away: Out of a total of 114 US productions filmed partly or wholly overseas in 1986, the highest number were made in the UK with 24 or 22 per cent, followed by Canada with 21, Italy with 10, Mexico with 9 and France with 7. Hollywood films were lensed in 26 different countries outside the USA. On the domestic front, 121 out of 309 releases were made in California, representing 39 per cent. Next most popular state was New York with

45, followed by Illinois with 14, Texas with 13 and North Carolina with 11. There were 13 states in which no filming took place.

> Director Elaine May insisted on undulating sand dunes for her megabuck desert comedy *Ishtar* (US 87), starring Warren Beatty and Dustin Hoffman. Her location hunters scoured the desert for exactly the right vista. On Miss May's arrival, she took one look and decided that what she really wanted was a completely flat desert. Two weeks and hundreds of man hours later the set was ready for inspection—a whole square mile of perfectly level sand.

The first Hollywood movie in an urban setting to be filmed entirely on location was Universal's *The Naked City* (US 48), a murder story set in the teeming streets of New York. Directed by Jules Dassin, the film contained no studio sets, even the interior scenes, such as those in a police station, being shot in real locations.

The first feature film shot by a western film-maker in Communist China was *Pekin-Central* (Fr 86), a comedy-drama about a young French woman (Christine Citti) and her relationship with two married men (Yves Renier and Marco Bisson) during a group tour of China. Director Camille de Casablanca, making her helming debut, submitted a fake scenario to the Chinese authorities in order to get permission to film there.

> Robert Redford's *The Milagro Beanfield War* (US 87), about a conflict between locals who want to reclaim a beanfield farm and rapacious land developers who want to exploit the land, was originally set to be filmed in Chimayo, New Mexico. The picture had to be relocated to Truchas, NM when reality began to mirror art—a land developer succeeded in blocking the Chimayo shoot on the grounds that it would be disruptive.

Hollywood the World Over

Hollywood has made 3013 feature films set in 117 identifiable foreign countries during the period 1920-87. Comparatively few of these films were shot in the locales they represented, as overseas location shooting was exceptional before the 1950s. The table below, therefore, lists the 25 countries most often depicted in American movies, not necessarily the countries in which the films were actually shot. The most popular overseas locale over the whole period surveyed has been the UK with 548 films (27 of them set in Scotland) or 18.2 per cent of the total, followed closely by France, with 516 films or 17.1 per cent. Hollywood's love affair with Britain, though, has undergone a sharp decline from the 25 per cent of all overseas settings in the 1930s and 1940s to a mere 7.4 per cent (equal with Mexico) in the 1980s. The allure of France has also waned, as America looks beyond Europe, once the epitome of sophistication

THE 25 COUNTRIES MOST OFTEN DEPICTED IN AMERICAN MOVIES

	1920-29	%	1930-39	%	1940-49	%	1950-59	%	1960-69	%	1970-79	%	1980-87	%	Totals	%
Great Britain	151	20.7	160	25.4	134	25.3	53	10.7	24	7.7	11	9.7	15	7.4	548	18.2
France	162	22.2	119	18.9	63	11.9	83	16.8	54	17.3	16	14.2	19	9.4	516	17.1
Canada	91	12.5	45	7.1	25	4.7	20	4.0	4	1.3	4	3.5	6	3.0	195	6.5
Mexico	23	3.1	46	7.3	32	6.0	35	7.0	21	6.7	12	10.6	15	7.4	184	6.1
Italy	18	2.5	18	2.9	13	2.5	30	6.0	38	12.1	7	6.2	10	5.0	134	4.4
Germany	11	1.5	20	3.2	36	6.7	18	3.6	22	7.0	8	7.1	9	4.5	124	4.1
China	26	3.6	31	4.9	21	3.4	9	1.8	8	2.6	1	0.9	6	3.0	102	3.4
Spain	30	4.1	9	1.4	9	1.7	11	2.2	16	5.1	2	1.8	7	3.5	84	2.8
USSR	30	4.1	21	3.3	9	1.7	4	0.8	6	1.9	6	5.3	7	3.5	83	2.8
Austria	15	2.1	27	4.3	12	2.3	5	1.0	7	2.2	4	3.5	3	1.5	73	2.4
India	19	2.6	11	1.7	6	1.1	15	3.0	3	1.0	0	—	2	1.0	56	1.9
Philippines	2	0.3	2	0.3	11	2.1	7	1.4	12	3.8	3	2.7	4	2.0	41	1.4
Egypt	13	1.8	8	1.3	9	1.7	6	1.2	1	0.3	0	—	2	1.0	39	1.3
Korea	0	—	0	—	0	—	29	5.9	6	1.9	1	0.9	0	—	36	1.2
Japan	4	0.5	0	—	7	1.3	3	0.6	12	3.8	2	1.8	7	3.5	35	1.2
Cuba	9	1.2	5	0.8	5	1.0	12	2.4	1	0.3	2	1.8	0	—	34	1.1
Ireland	11	1.5	9	1.4	5	1.0	2	0.4	3	1.0	3	2.7	1	0.5	34	1.1
Vietnam	2	0.3	2	0.3	2	0.4	6	1.2	2	0.6	4	3.5	15	7.4	33	1.1
Hungary	10	1.4	8	1.3	5	1.0	5	1.0	1	0.3	0	—	3	1.5	32	1.1
Morocco	4	0.5	2	0.3	9	1.7	13	2.6	3	1.0	1	0.9	0	—	32	1.1
Switzerland	6	0.8	9	1.4	6	1.1	5	1.0	3	1.0	1	0.9	2	1.0	32	1.1
Brazil	3	0.4	3	0.5	9	1.7	6	1.2	3	1.0	1	0.9	3	1.5	28	0.9
South Africa	12	1.6	3	0.5	3	0.6	3	0.6	3	1.0	1	0.9	2	1.0	27	0.9
Argentina	11	1.5	5	0.8	6	1.1	1	0.2	1	0.3	0	—	1	0.5	25	0.8
Algeria	8	1.1	10	1.6	1	0.2	3	0.6	2	0.6	0	—	0	—	24	0.8
Others	59	8.1	58	9.2	92	17.4	110	22.3	57	18.2	23	20.0	63	31.2	462	15.3
Total	730		631		530		494		313		113		202		3013	

and romance, to farther flung and more exotic locales, many of them in the Far East. It remains to be seen whether the success of the first non-American picture to top the box office worldwide in any year, *Crocodile Dundee* (Aus 86), has Hollywood film-makers heading down under to a country which has never made the top 25 list and has been the setting for only three American pictures in a quarter of a century.

The largest number of different locations used on a motion picture was 168 in the case of Sergei Bondarchuk's four-part *War and Peace* (USSR 1963–67), of which the most prominent were the Battle of Borodino sequence, filmed at Borodino; the 'Moscow on Fire' sequence, filmed at Volokolamsk; and the 'Hunting in Otradnoye' sequence, filmed in the village of Boguslavskiy, near Kashira.

The provincial city most often used for film settings in Britain is Liverpool, which has been featured in 27 films to date: *Her Benny* (GB 20); *Grass Widowers* (GB 21); *Old English* (US 30); *The House of the Spaniard* (GB 36); *Souls at Sea* (GB 37); *Penny Paradise* (GB 38); *Spare a Copper* (GB 40); *Atlantic Ferry* (GB 41); *It Happened One Sunday* (GB 44); *Waterfront* (GB 50); *The Magnet* (GB 50); *These Dangerous Years* (GB 57); *The Key* (GB 58); *Violent Playground* (GB 58); *Sapphire* (GB 59); *In the Wake of a Stranger* (GB 59); *Ferry Across the Mersey* (GB 64); *The Little Ones* (GB 64); *Charlie Bubbles* (GB 67); *The Reckoning* (GB 69); *Letter to Brezhnev* (GB 85); *No Surrender* (GB 86); *Coast to Coast* (GB 86); *Business as Usual* (GB 87); *The Fruit Machine* (GB 88); *The Dressmaker* (GB 88); *Distant Voices, Still Lives* (GB 88). Fourteen films have been set in Glasgow, 11 in Blackpool, 10 in Brighton, 9 in Edinburgh and Oxford.

*M*AKE-UP

Little attention was paid to make-up in films before the advent of the close-up (q.v.). **The earliest motion picture in which it is apparent that the actors are wearing make-up** (other than blackface or whiskers) is Edwin S. Porter's *The Whole Dam Family and the Dam Dog* (US 05), in which the cast are made-up to create the illusion of a family resemblance. The pioneer of special make-up techniques for film as opposed to stage performances was D. W. Griffith, who began experiments to achieve a more naturalistic appearance for his performers at Biograph in about 1910. Stage actress Olga Petrova recalled of her film debut in *The Tiger* (US 14): 'I noticed immediately that my co-workers wore a make-up much darker, almost a beige, whereas I wore the usual light Leichner's 1.' There was a good reason for her co-workers' departure from stage practice. The orthochromatic film stock used at this date was insensitive to the red end of the spectrum (scarlet

It is all too easy for sophisticated audiences to take the wonders of film-making for granted. How many New Yorkers watching *84 Charing Cross Road* (US 86) paused to consider the simple fact that they were watching traffic flowing in both directions along Madison Avenue—one-way for the last 20 years? Easy if done on a set. But it wasn't done on a set—that was the real Madison Avenue 1986 and the cars and buses were defying the traffic regulations, courtesy of the Mayor's Office of Film, Theatre and Broadcasting. And how many Londoners were aware that the scene of Anne Bancroft visiting the bookshop at 84 Charing Cross Road, with the familiar thoroughfare visible through the window, was shot in New York?

registered as black) and consequently a heavy application of yellow make-up was necessary to create an impression of natural skin tone on screen.

The first make-up specifically for on-screen use was Supreme Greasepaint, introduced by Polish immigrant Max Factor in 1914. The need for special make-up was dictated by the increasing use of artificial lighting for filming from 1912 onwards. Freckles and skin blemishes photographed black, pink cheeks a murky grey, and skin tones a deathly white.

The first studio make-up department was established at First National in 1924 under British-born Perc Westmore (1904–70). Perc later became head of make-up at Warner's, his brother Bud became head of make-up at Universal, and his other brother Wally spent 38 years in make-up at Paramount.

The largest make-up budget was $1 million for *Planet of the Apes* (US 68), which represented nearly 17 per cent of the total production cost. A team of 78 make-up artists worked under the direction of Fox's make-up specialist John Chambers, who won a special Oscar for his remarkable achievement of creating wholly credible ape faces sufficiently mobile to register the full range of human emotions.

The longest make-up job ever performed on a single artiste was the tattooing applied to Rod Steiger in Warner Bros' *The Illustrated Man* (US 69). It took make-up artist Gordon Bau and his team of eight assistants ten hours to complete the torso and another full day was spent on the lower body, hands and legs. Bau's longest job previously had been Charles Laughton's make-up for the title role of *The Hunchback of Notre Dame* (US 39), which he finished in a mere 5½ hours.

Other marathon make-up jobs have included the 4 hours daily spent by Wally Westmore on Fredric March's Hyde in *Dr Jekyll and Mr Hyde* (US 32); 4 hours for Boris Karloff's monster in *Frankenstein* (US 31), and a similar time for Jean Marais' make-up in *La Belle et la Bête* (Fr 45); 4½ hours on Bull Montana's ape-man in *The Lost World* (US 25) and the same for Lon Chaney in *The Hunchback of Notre Dame* (US 23); 5 hours for the principal apes in *Planet of the Apes* (US 68) and also for the 121-year-old character played by Dustin Hoffman in *Little Big Man* (US 70); Klaus Kinski's Dracula make-up for *Nosferatu* (FRG 79) also took 5 hours daily to apply. Boris Karloff's make-up for *The Bride of Frankenstein* (US 35), an elaboration of Jack Pierce's original monster make-up for the 1931 *Frankenstein*, took 7 hours to complete each day. Shooting of scenes involving Karloff—he was in most—had to be delayed until 1 p.m. In the same film Elsa Lanchester's make-up as the female monster was so rigid she had to be fed lunch through a tube. John Hurt was unable to eat at all after the 7-hour ordeal of having his head monstrously deformed for the title role in *The Elephant Man* (GB 80). It was so exhausting that the full make-up could only be applied every second day.

The record for the longest make-up job in a British movie is the 10 hours it took Rick Baker to transform David Naughton into a hairy beast for *An American Werewolf in London* (GB 81).

> One actor who refuses ever to wear make-up is the veteran French star Charles Vanel. Active in movies since 1912, he has worn make-up for only one of his 200 roles to date. That was well over 60 years ago, and even then Vanel, now France's longest serving screen actor, appeared too old for his role as the romantic lead in Baroncelli's *Le Reveil* (Fr 25). A skilled make-up man made the prematurely middle-aged 32-year-old star look as if he was indeed in his early thirties.

PRODUCERS

The youngest producer to produce a feature-length film for commercial exhibition was 16-year-old George Palmer of Melbourne, Vic., whose thriller *The Mail Robbery* (Aus 25) was released in Victoria and New South Wales. The following year he produced, directed and starred in *Northbound Ltd* (Aus 26), a railroad drama he had written himself. On reaching man's estate Palmer retired from the film business to establish a successful travel agency, but retained an interest in experimental film-making.

Hollywood's youngest ever producer was Steven Paul, who produced and directed the Elliott Gould, Susannah York romance *Falling in Love Again* (US 80) at the age of 20.

Britain's youngest producer was 22-year-old Norman Hope-Bell, who made his professional debut at Cricklewood Studios with an Ernie Lotinga comedy called *Love Up the Pole* (GB 36).

The first woman producer was Alice Guy (see p. 119), who founded the Solax Co. at Flushing, New York, on 7 September 1910. The first of nearly 300 short films produced by her in the next three years was *A Child's Sacrifice* (US 10), starring 'The Solax Kid' (Magda Foy), which was released on 21 October 1910.

The first feature film produced by a woman was Eros Films' *The Definite Object* (GB 20), a gangster movie set in New York produced by Countess Bubna.

The first talkie produced by a woman was Elinor Glyn's Talkicolor production *Knowing Men* (GB 30), with Carl Brisson and Elissa Landi. She also directed. **The first Hollywood talkie by a woman** was Elsie Janis's *Paramount on Parade* (US 30), which was released in April 1930, two months after Miss Glyn's picture.

The first and only feature film produced by a Roman Catholic priest is *Romero* (US 88), made by Fr Ellwood Kieser for Paulist Pictures, a non-profit making production house operating under the auspices of the Los Angeles Archdiocese. *Romero* tells the true story of the Archbishop of that name who was assassinated after urging soldiers of the Salvadorean army to refuse to obey orders to attack dissident peasants. Fr Kieser intended to make the story as a TV drama, but decided to go for a full-scale cinema feature after being turned down by the three major TV networks on grounds that the subject was too controversial.

> Hollywood producers have often been accused of illiteracy, though generally they can read well enough to cope with the small print of a contract. In India there is a genuinely illiterate producer. Jayashree More, a 30-year-old tribal woman from Gujarat, has never learned to read or write but has recently produced the Hindi film *Zindagi ke Mele* (Ind 87), starring Satyen Kapro and Anita Raaj. An inability to read small or any other print did not prevent her from persuading a bank in Allahabadad from putting up the coin to make the picture.

The two most successful producer/directors in terms of box office revenue are George Lucas and Steven Spielberg, who between them are responsible for seven out of the nine films which have garnered more than $100 million in North American rentals. Spielberg has to his credit, as both producer and director, the top earner of all time, *E.T. The Extra-Terrestrial* (US 82), as well as directing *Jaws* (US 75), which was the first picture to break the $100 million barrier, and the two Indiana Jones blockbusters *Raiders of the Lost Ark* (US 81) and

The world's only blind film producer is Bhupat Giri (*right*), seen here with one of the stars of Bombay cinema Kadarkhan.

look impoverished by comparison, the likes of George Lucas, Steven Spielberg and Sylvester Stallone counting their millions in mere hundreds.

> Cannon's Yoram Globus on the way he and his cousin Menashem Golan got to where they are today: 'We found that if we could sell a black-and-white Hebrew language film to Japan, we could sell anything . . .'

PROPS

The most valuable assemblage of props ever to be brought together on a single set was the $10 million worth of paintings and sculptures used for the art gallery scenes in Universal's *Legal Eagles* (US 86), starring Robert Redford. They included works by Willem de Korning, Roy Lichtenstein, Alexander Calder and Pablo Picasso.

The most expensive single prop ever used on a movie was the full-scale replica of a Spanish galleon built for Roman Polanski's *Pirates* (US/Tun 86) at a cost of £7 million. Designed by Pierre Guffrey, its construction kept 2000 Maltese shipyard workers in jobs for a whole year.

The most expensive model was Darth Vader's *Star Destroyer* used in *Star Wars* (US 77) and its sequels. Built by Industrial Light and Magic at a cost of $100,000, it had more than 250,000 portholes lit from inside. There are probably numerous tacky 'B' movies which could lay claim to the cheapest model, but points for ingenuity should certainly go to the art director of an engaging Australian sci-fi movie called *As Time Goes By* (Aus 87), about an alien from outer space and his time machine-cum-space ship. Miniscule budget allowed for nothing more elaborate than a cocktail shaker to represent the latter.

The largest land-based prop ever constructed for a movie was the 60 ft long, 40 ft high Wooden Horse of Troy used in Robert Wise's *Helen of Troy* (US 54). It weighed 80 tons, and 30 full-grown trees and

Indiana Jones and the Temple of Doom (US 84). Both the latter were produced by George Lucas, who also directed *Star Wars* (US 77) and produced *The Empire Strikes Back* (US 80) and *Return of the Jedi* (US 83). (For rental figures, see Top 25 Earners chart p. 29.) Lucas also holds the record for the highest earnings from a single film. As producer of *Star Wars* he was entitled to 40 per cent of net profits, worth a sum of nearly $50 million. In addition, Lucas held all the merchandising rights, which Fox had allowed him under the contract because they could see little value in them. His cut of the $2.6 billion revenue from retail sales of *Star Wars* related products is undisclosed.

The highest paid executive in Hollywood is Barry Diller, Chairman of 20th Century Fox and its parent company TCF Holdings, whose annual salary on appointment in October 1984 was set at $3 million. In addition, his five-year contract allows him 25 per cent of any increase in the value of the equity of the company, plus 17.5 per cent of any increase during the three years following the termination of the contract.

The richest man in the motion picture business is Tamesaburo Furakawa of Tokyo, Japan, Chairman of Nippon Herald Films, who was reported to be worth $1298 million in mid-1986. This makes him the second wealthiest man in Japan, next to the $1818 million head of Matsushita Electronic, Konosuke Matsushita. Rich Hollywood movieites

> The green vomit that gushed out of Linda Blair in *The Exorcist* (US 73) was realistic enough to make some spectators throw up themselves. It was in fact only a simple concoction of split pea soup and oatmeal.
> The dank green slime that covered Natasha Richardson as she writhed on the muddy floor of a crypt in *Gothic* (GB 86) was actually spinach. Ken Russell's nightmare fantasy of the conception of Mary Shelley's *Frankenstein* is notable also for another prop worthy of that distinctive director—a 7 ft penis adorned with skulls and leeches.

over 1000 lb of nails were needed to build it. A modern air-conditioning system was fitted to save the 25 occupants from heat prostration.

SCHEDULES

The longest production schedule for a feature movie was the 18 years it took to complete Alvaro Henriques Goncalves' *Presente de Natal* (Bra 71). Goncalves, a lawyer by profession, worked on his full-length animated feature single-handed.

The longest production schedule for a dramatic film in terms of start date and completion date was 13 years for Leni Riefenstahl's *Tiefland* (FRG 53) and the same length of time for *Dr Bethune* (Chn 77), Chinese tribute to the Canadian chest surgeon who gave his life while serving as a volunteer with the Red Army in 1939. In the case of *Tiefland*, production of what promised to be the most expensive talkie then made was suspended in 1942 after expenditure of 5 million RMs and the complete breakdown of the director's health. At the end of the war Frl. Riefenstahl was banned from working in the film industry, but following her de-Nazification in 1952 she succeeded in reassembling the original cast and completed the film. It recouped its cost but Frl. Riefenstahl, dissatisfied with her work, then withdrew the picture from distribution and it has not been shown since.

Production of *Dr Bethune* started in 1964 but was halted at the outset of the Cultural Revolution on the personal orders of Mao's wife, Jiang Qing, who asserted that the documentary footage of *Dr Bethune* was sufficient to honour his memory. The cameraman who had taken the documentary footage, Wu Yinxian, was also the cameraman on the biopic. Production was resumed with the collapse of the Cultural Revolution.

The longest production schedule for a British film was the 8 years 20 days (6 May 1956–26 May 1964) it took Kevin Brownlow and Andrew Mollo to complete their fantasy of a Nazi-occupied Britain, *It Happened Here* (GB 66). The picture, which occupied a cumulative shooting schedule of ten weeks, started as an amateur production by a group of enthusiastic teenagers and ended as a professional film with a West End release. (Mr Brownlow has asked the editor to point out that in these circumstances he should not be accorded the title of the world's slowest director.)

Other protracted production schedules have included 11 years (1925–36) for Ladislas Starewitch's animated puppet film *Le Roman de Rénard* (Fr 40); 11 or possibly 12 years for *Pakeezah* (Ind 71), which was so long in the making that the original hero aged too much and had to be recast as the heroine's father; 10 years for Michael and Andy Jones's Newfoundland comedy *The Adventures of*

Faustus Bidgood (Can 86), which called on the services of almost every actor and actress in the province; 7 years for Harry Hoyt's *The Lost World* (US 25), Fred Zinnermann and Walter Mirisch's *Hawaii* (US 66), Michael Kohler's *The Experiencer* and *Flame Top* aka *Down to Earth* (Fin 81), a biopic of the enigmatic Finnish folklorist Maiju Lassila; 5½ years for Edgar Reitz's *Heimat* (FRG 84), which perhaps is not surprising for a film nearly 16 hours long; 5 years for George Stevens's *The Greatest Story Ever Told* (US 65) and David Lynch's *Eraserhead* (US 77), declared to contain 'one of the most repugnant scenes in film history'; and 4 years for Mel Ferrer's *Vendetta* (US 50), Rudall Hayward's *On the Friendly Road* (NZ 36), which would have been New Zealand's first talkie if he had managed to finish it a year earlier, Francis Ford Coppola's *Apocalypse Now* (US 79), Joseph L. Mankiewicz's *Cleopatra* (US 63) and Terence Young's Korean War epic *Inchon* (Kor/US 81), starring Laurence Olivier as General MacArthur. Sir Richard Attenborough's monumental biopic of *Gandhi* (GB 82) had a schedule of 20 months from the start of pre-production to delivery of prints, with 26 weeks spent on shooting. The gestation of the movie, however, lasted 17 years from the start of the first of twelve draft screenplays to the pre-production date. Attenborough estimated that during this time he gave up some 40 acting parts and a dozen directorial assignments in order to realize what he described as 'my love affair with this project'.

Even this may not represent the ultimate in patience and fortitude. Screenwriter Ted Allan, whose *Bethune: The Making of a Hero* (Can/Chn 88) is based on his own recollections of the Canadian doctor venerated in China for his services on the Long March, first took the project to Darryl F. Zanuck at Fox in 1942. The film went into pre-production with Canadian star Walter Pidgeon signed to play Bethune. When the deal fell through, Allan continued his fight to get the story of his hero on to the screen. Both Columbia and Warner picked up the option and Robert Redford and Paul Newman were amongst those canvassed for the title role. After various independent companies had toyed with the project, Allan finally brought the efforts of a lifetime to fruition when *Bethune* went before the cameras in China in 1986 as a Canadian/French/Chinese co-production starring Donald Sutherland, some 44 years after he had initiated it.

The shortest shooting schedule of all time was the one day for Paul Vecchialli's 80-minute feature film *Trou de Mémoire* (Fr 85). Starring Francoise Lebrun and Vecchialli himself, the picture was shot with film stock left over from a documentary he had been commissioned to make.

Other directors who haven't stood around on the

job are Rob Nilsson, whose *Heat and Sunlight* (US 87), about a fortyish photographer obsessed with a beautiful dancer, was shot in 60 hours, and Roger Corman, who completed his cult movie *The Little Shop of Horrors* (US 60) in just two days and three nights. Frank Oz's 1986 remake, by contrast, took seven months to shoot.

Also shot in two days (and a couple of hours) was Emile de Antonio's *In the King of Prussia* (US 82), a reconstruction of the attack on the General Electric warhead plant in the mid-west township of King of Prussia by anti-nuclear demonstrators and their subsequent trial. Starring Martin Sheen as himself, and with the defendants, known as the 'Plowshares Eight', as themselves, the film had to be shot in 50 hours to meet the deadline before the defendants had to report for sentencing.

The shortest production schedule for a full-length feature film was for *Twist Around the Clock* (US 61), released 28 days after Chubby Checker reached No. 1 in the charts and gave Sam Katsman the idea of making a movie to cash in on the new dance craze. Chubby Checker starred.

The shortest time between completion of shooting and the première of a feature film was five hours in the case of Alfred Rolfe's racing drama *The Cup Winner* (Aus 11). The final scenes, consisting of footage of the Melbourne Cup shot by six cameramen, were filmed on 7 November 1911 and the completed drama edited and processed in time for a simultaneous opening at five Melbourne cinemas the same night. It opened in Sydney, 450 miles away, the following day.

*S*ET

The largest film set ever built was the 1312 by 754 ft (400×230 m) Roman Forum designed by Veniero Colosanti and John Moore and built on a 55-acre site at Las Matas, outside Madrid, for the last great Hollywod epic of the ancient world, Samuel Bronston's production of *The Fall of the Roman Empire* (US 64). Commencing 10 October 1962, 1100 workmen spent seven months laying the surface of the Forum with 170,000 cement blocks, erecting 22,000 ft (6705 m) of concrete stairways, 601 columns and 350 statues, and constructing 27 full size buildings. The highest point on the set was the Temple of Jupiter, whose bronze equestrian statues surmounting the roof soared 260 ft (79 m) above the paving of the Forum.

The largest indoor set was the UFO landing site built for the climax of Steven Spielberg's *Close Encounters of the Third Kind* (US 77). With a height of 90 ft (27 m), length of 450 ft (137 m) and

Samuel Bronston's massive set for *The Fall of the Roman Empire* (US 64). It was the largest set ever built.

250 ft (76 m) breadth, the set was constructed inside a 10 million cubic ft dirigible hangar at Mobile, Alabama, which had six times the capacity of the largest sound stage in Hollywood. The structure included four miles (6.4 km) of scaffolding, 16,900 sq ft (1570 sq m) of fibreglass, 29,500 sq ft (2740 sq m) of nylon canopy and 'enough concrete to make a full-scale replica of the Washington monument'.

The largest single structure ever built as a movie set was the vast 450 ft (137 m) long, 90 ft (27 m) high medieval castle designed by Wilfred Buckland and erected at Pasadena, California, for Douglas Fairbanks' version of *Robin Hood* (US 22). No record survives of its other dimensions, but to be in proportion it must have been at least as big as the *Close Encounters* set (see above), which was exactly the same height and length.

The smallest set used for the entire action of a movie—in terms of confined acting space—was the lifeboat containing the nine protagonists of Alfred Hitchcock's *Lifeboat* (US 44).

One way of creating the illusion of vast settings on a stage of limited size is to create the set in false perspective. This makes the background look a lot more distant than it really is. One problem, though, in using this technique is the size of the performers at the back of the set. In *Maya* (Fr 49), a set representing a street in a red-light district was built in false perspective. The prostitutes seen at the far end of the street were played by little girls of six to eight years old outfitted in the gaudy raiment of harlotry.

Films which have been made on a single set include the submarine drama *Umini sul fondo* (It 41), the underground railway dramas *Subway Express* (US 31) and *Dutchman* (GB 66) and the Spanish pictures *Historia de una escalera* (Sp 50), set on a staircase, and *Noventa minutos* (Sp 50), which took place in a cellar. Alfred Hitchcock's *Rope* (US 48), the story of an unmotivated murder by two homosexual college men, takes place entirely in the apartment in which the crime was perpetrated and his *Lifeboat* (US 44) was confined to the craft of the title. Rex Harrison and Lilli Palmer were the only two characters in *The Four Poster* (GB 52), which takes them from marriage to old age and finally their deaths in a drama enacted out in the room which contains the eponymous bed. *La Morte al lavoro* (It 78), *Inserts* (GB 75), *La Droleuse* (Fr 78) and *Yaadein* (Ind 64) were also one-room dramas, while Kostas Sfikas' *Model* (Gre 74) took place entirely in a factory yard unpeopled by human beings (there were some robots). Louis Malle's *My Dinner with André* (US 81) was a two-hander consisting of a conversation overheard (by the audience) between a playwright (Wallace Shawn) and an actor (André Gregory) in a smart Manhattan restaurant; while Johnny Legends' spoof of Malle's film, titled *My Breakfast with Blassie* (US 83) cast Andy Kaufman and Freddie Blassie in the roles of two enormously egotistical individuals breakfasting at a Los Angeles fast-food emporium. Ettore Scola's *Le Bal* (Fr/It/Alg 84) recounted five decades of social change in France through the medium of dance. Besides having no dialogue, the entire action, covering such diverse episodes of French history as the Popular Front of the thirties, the German Occupation of the forties, the Algerian War of the fifties, and the Paris riots of the sixties, is enacted on a single set representing a typical French ballroom.

STUDIOS

The first film studio in the world was Thomas Edison's *Black Maria*, a frame building covered in black roofing-paper, built at the Edison Laboratories in West Orange, NJ, and completed at a cost of $637.67 on 1 February 1893. Here Edison made short vaudeville-act films for use in his Kinetoscope, a peep-show machine designed for amusement arcades. The building was so constructed that it could be revolved to face the direction of the sun.

The first studio in Europe and **the first in the world in which films were made by artificial light** was opened by Oskar Messter at 94a Friedrich Strasse, Berlin in November 1896. For illumination Messter used four Körting & Matthiessen 50-amp arc-lamps on portable stands. His earliest productions by artificial light included *From Tears to Laughter* (Ger 96) and *Lightning Artist Zigg* (Ger 96). The first artificially lit studio in the USA, the Biograph Studio at 11 East 14th Street, New York, was not opened until 1903.

The first film studio in Britain was built at the back of the Tivoli Theatre in the Strand in 1897 by the Mutosope & Biograph Co. Like Edison's *Black Maria*, the studio was mounted on a cup-and-ball fixture that enabled it to be turned in the direction of the sun. It could also be rocked to and fro for 'storm at sea' sequences and similar effects. The glass panels that made up the sides of the studio could be dismantled for 'outdoor' scenes.

The first purpose-built sound stage was Stage Three at Warner Bros Studios, Sunset Boulevard, Hollywood, erected in April 1927. Shooting of *The Jazz Singer* (US 27) commenced on Stage Three the following month.

The largest film studio in the world is Universal City, California, whose 34 sound stages and other buildings cover an area of 420 acres. As many as 6000 staff are employed at times of peak production.

Built by Carl Laemmle, the studio was originally opened on a 230-acre lot on 15 March 1915 and had the unique distinction of being a municipality in its own right. Besides the outdoor stages, indoor studio, prop stores, processing labs, zoo and stables, Universal City had its own Town Hall, fire station and police department.

Universal City will be overtaken in size when Universal Studios at Orlando, Florida is opened in 1989. The new studios will occupy 450.3 acres of land and the project is budgeted at $300 million.

The largest studio stage in the world is the 007 stage at Pinewood Studios, Buckinghamshire, England, which was built in 1976 at a cost of £350,000. It is 336 ft (102 m) long by 139 ft (42 m) wide and 41 ft (12 m) high. Designed by Ken Adam and Michael Brown, the stage was originally built for the James Bond film *The Spy Who Loved Me* (GB 77) and accommodated 1.2 million gallons of water, a full-scale 600,000-ton oil-tanker and three nuclear submarines. The 007 stage is owned by United Artists and Eon Productions and is rented out to other film production companies.

*S*TUNTS

The first stuntman was ex-US cavalryman Frank Hanaway, who won himself a part in Edwin S. Porter's *The Great Train Robbery* (US 03) for his ability to fall off a horse without injuring himself.

The first professional stuntwoman was Helen Gibson, who doubled for Helen Holmes in the first 26 episodes of Kalem's serial *The Hazards of Helen* (US 14). Trained as a trick rider and married to cowboy star Hoot Gibson, she was chosen for her ability to do stunts on horseback but proved herself adept at other hair-raising exploits, including jumping a speeding motorcycle on to a fast moving locomotive. Unlike most stunt people, she achieved stardom in her own right, replacing Helen Holmes' successor Elsie McCleod as the lead in the long-running *Hazards of Helen.* Generally at this period, actresses were doubled in dangerous scenes by men in drag. Since the introduction of the Sex Equality Act in the USA, it is illegal for stuntmen to double for actresses unless no stuntwoman is willing to take on the assignment.

The Stuntman as Star

The claim made by many stars that they performed all their own stunts seldom amounted to anything more than press agents' ballyhoo. Apart from Helen Gibson (see above), the only star who really did all his own stunting was Richard Talmadge (1896–). The reason was twofold—he was an accomplished stuntman himself; and he never became so valuable a star that the studio feared the consequences if he was put

Cricklewood Studios 1921. 'Outdoor' sets inside the studio were rare at this early date. The film was *The Adventures of Sherlock Holmes* (GB 21) and the Stoll Co. had attempted to shoot on location in Baker Street without success. So 221b had to be built in the studio. (*ILN*)

out of action. Perhaps the star most often trumpeted as his own stuntman was Douglas Fairbanks; ironically, it was Talmadge who did most of his stunts, including the celebrated slide down the sail in *The Black Pirate* (US 26). Present-day stars also like to cultivate a macho image by pretending to do stunts performed by professionals. No doubts need to be entertained though about Mel Gibson's claim to have done his own stunts in *Mad Max Beyond Thunderdrome* (Aus 85), since the credits list his name twice: as leading man and as one of the stuntmen.

The only stuntman who stands in for children is Bobby Porter, who at 4 ft 9 in (1.45 m) often substitutes for little girls as well as little boys. Among his more spectacular appearances was in the title role of *Annie* (US 82), in which he hung suspended from a 20-storey high drawbridge as stand-in for 9-year-old Aileen Quinn.

The greatest height from which a stuntman has leaped in a free fall was 1170 ft (356.6 m), a stunt performed for *Highpoint* (Can 79) by Los Angeles parachutist Dar Robinson from a ledge at the sum-

Stunting at MGM *c.* 1928, from an unlabelled publicity shot. Does anyone know the title of the film or the identity of the flying artiste? And why is he taking a dive over the car? (*Popperfoto*)

mit of the CN Tower in Toronto. Robinson opened his 'chute out of shot at a height estimated at 300–350 ft from the ground after six seconds of freefalling, one of reaction time and two for releasing the canopy. The fee, an unconfirmed $150,000, is believed to be a **record payment for a single stunt**.

The highest jump without a parachute by a movie stuntman was 232 ft by A. J. Bakunas, who was doubling for Burt Reynolds in *Hooper* (US 78). He fell on to an air mattress.

The longest leap in a car propelled by its own engine was performed by stunt driver Gary Davis in *Smokey and the Bandit II* (US 81). Davis raced a stripped-down Plymouth up a ramp butted up against the back of a double-tiered car-carrier at 80 mph (129 km/h) and described a trajectory of 163 ft (49.7 m) before landing safely on the desert floor.

*S*WORDFIGHTS, SHOOT-OUTS AND KUNG FU

The earliest known kung-fu movie was *Thief in the Car* (Chn 20), directed by Ren Pengnian for the Shang Wu company of Shanghai and starring Ding Yuanyi and Bao Guiying. **The first kung-fu talkie** was Yang Xiaozhong's *Story of the 'Red Sheep' Hero* (Chn 35) with Wang Huchen and Tong Yuejuan.

The longest swordfight sequence was the 22-minute climax to *Beach of the War Gods* (HK 73), in which Wang Yu as the Chinese superpatriot and swordsman Hsiao Feng destroys large numbers of hated Japanese before dropping dead himself.

Surprisingly the longest clash-of-steel sequence in a Hollywood movie does not exceed 6½ minutes. Stewart Granger was crossing swords with an ignoble marquis (Mel Ferrer) in *Scaramouche* (US 53).

The record for carnage in a shoot-out movie has yet to be positively established, but one critic took the trouble to count the number of deceased persons littering the screen at different times during the course of the spaghetti western *The Bounty Hunters* (It 70) and came up with a total of 116.

*T*AKES AND RETAKES

The longest take in a movie comprises the whole of the second reel of Andy Warhol's *Blue Movie* (US 68) and consists of a 35-minute uninterrupted scene of Viva and Louis Waldon making love.

The longest take in a commercially-made feature movie is a 14-minute uninterrupted monologue by Lionel Barrymore in *A Free Soul* (US 31). Since a reel of camera film only lasts ten minutes, the take was achieved by using more than one camera. Alfred Hitchcock's *Rope* (US 48), the story of two homosexual college men who kill a third for the

It took 342 takes to get this scene in *City Lights* (US 31). Chaplin spent 534 days making the movie, including 368 days when he shot nothing at all as he sought for a way of showing that the girl, who couldn't see, thought the tramp, who never spoke, was a wealthy tycoon.

intellectual thrill of it, was shot in eight ten-minute takes (apart from one cut to the housekeeper in the first reel). The effect was of one continuous shot, since the action of the story occupied the same period of time—80 minutes—as the length of the film.

The greatest number of retakes of a single scene was 342 for the episode in Chaplin's *City Lights* (US 31) in which a blind flower girl (Virginia Cherrill) sells the little tramp a flower under the misapprehension he is a rich man. Chaplin kept reshooting the scene because he was unable to find a satisfactory way of making the blind girl think that the tramp was wealthy. Finally he found a simple yet perfect solution. Chaplin is trying to cross a street jammed with traffic. Unable to reach the sidewalk, he sees a limousine parked by the kerb, gets in at one door and out at the other. The girl hears the door close and assumes it is the owner getting out. She hands him the flower, takes his last quarter, and keeps the change.

Difficult dialogue is the most common reason for prodigious numbers of retakes. One scene in *Dr Strangelove* (GB 63) was shot 48 times because Sterling Hayden, playing the mad base commander, fluffed his line 47 times. Marilyn Monroe did 59 takes of a scene in *Some Like It Hot* (US 59) in which her only line of dialogue was 'Where's the Bourbon?'. Hollywood rebel Dennis Hopper had an early run-in with veteran director Henry Hathaway when he was made to repeat a scene in *From Hell to*

Texas (US 57) no less than 85 times. 'Kid', Hathaway growled at the moody method actor after the 85th take, 'you'll never work in this town again'. It was in fact some ten years before Hopper was offered another worthwhile role. **The record number of takes of a dialogue sequence** is claimed to be the 127 demanded by Stanley Kubrick of a scene with Shelley Duval in *The Shining* (US 80).

One-Shot Directors

At the other end of the scale, there have been those who earned themselves reputations as 'one-shot' directors, notably G. W. Pabst, Cecil B. DeMille, W. S. 'One-Shot Woody' van Dyke, and D. W. Griffith. According to Lillian Gish, Griffith's masterwork *The Birth of a Nation* (US 15) was made with only one retake of one scene. The single repeat shot was necessitated, much to Mr Griffith's displeasure, by the fact that Mae Marsh forgot to drape herself in the Confederate flag for her suicide scene.

*T*ANK

The largest tank ever built for moviemaking was erected in a disused Zeppelin hangar at Berlin under the direction of art director Max Heilbronner for UFA's *Volga, Volga* (Ger 29), an historical epic about Cossack pirate Stenka Rasin. The tank, which was constructed to represent the Volga river, was 2000 ft long.

*W*OMEN

The first film made with an all-female crew was a comedy titled *Sally Sallies Forth* (GB 28), produced with a women-only cast by the lady members of the Amateur Cinema Association. The 'directress' (as she was called) was Frances Lascott, the camerawoman Mrs A. E. Low and the title role—an inexperienced maidservant who disrupts a pompous tea party—played by Sadie Andrews. It was premièred at the Camera Club on 12 December 1928 and *Film Weekly*'s male critic declared it 'a rattling good effort'.

The first professionally-made feature by women was Savithri Ganesh's *Chinnari Pappalu* (Ind 67), produced and scripted in Telegu by Mrs Sarojini Madhusudana Rao, with music by Mrs P. Leela and art direction by Mrs Mohana. **America's first *femme* production** was *The Waiting Room* (US 73), a psychological drama produced and directed by Karen Sperling (grand-daughter of Harry Warner) and Doro Bachrach. The 32-woman crew was selected from 300 applicants attracted from California, Canada, Europe and New York (where the film was made).

BLUNDERS

The most frequent mistakes made in movies are microphone booms visible within the frame, and camera crews reflected in plate-glass windows. Other blunders are legion. Some of the choicest include:

☆ Adventure caper *Jungle Raiders* (It 86) opens with a title reading 'Malaysia, 1938'. There was no such country at that date. The name 'Malaysia' was only adopted by the Federated Malay States in 1963.

☆ A character in Basil Dearden's *The Mind Benders* (GB 63) commits suicide by leaping from the right-hand side of a train. The body is then seen lying on the left-hand side of the track.

☆ The forest of Cannon's *Rumpelstiltskin* (US 87), set in the Mittel-Europa of traditional fairy tales, is curiously composed of eucalyptus trees. Location shooting in Israel accounts for the solecism.

☆ In *Ratboy* (US 86), the eponymous alien is seen being driven through Hollywood by black hipster Manny. Shots taken from Ratboy's side of the car show Hollywood Boulevard in the background, while those taken from Manny's side reveal Sunset Boulevard.

☆ Set in Depression-hit America in 1931, *Pocketful of Miracles* (US 61) has a scene in which someone removes a newspaper from a pile and pays for it with a nickel. The coin is a Jefferson head nickel, first minted in 1938.

☆ The credits for *Three Kinds of Heat* (US 87) include 'Page Three' girl Samantha Fox; not so the picture—she isn't in it.

☆ GI Dean Jagger walks girlfriend Anna Neagle through the London streets at night in Herbert Wilcox's *I Live in Grosvenor Square* (GB 45). Although the scene is done in a single shot, they pass the same backgrounds twice—evidently the set was circular.

☆ The Mexican picture *From Neither Here Nor There* (Mex 87) is about an Indian woman trying to survive in Los Angeles as an illegal immigrant. Either the English language dialogue was written by a Mexican with an imperfect grasp of the language or the gringo bit players were allowed to improvise. In a scene set in a Kentucky Fried Chicken, the young man behind the counter recommends the chicken 'because it is really greasy'.

☆ Editing mistakes are rare, but *The Drum* (GB 38), Zoltan Korda's flagwaving story of the Raj, in-

Not surprisingly it is very hard to find publicity stills which reveal a blunder. This shot from Warner Bros' *The Sea Hawk* (US 40), starring Errol Flynn, was actually released without anyone spotting it. Can you see what is wrong? (*Peter Jackson Collection*)

explicably—and possibly uniquely—contains successive takes of the same line being said twice over.

☆ The basic premise of *Deadly Impact* (It 86), about a computer expert aiming to break the bank at Las Vegas, is that slot machines are programmed to deliver a jackpot at predetermined times. They aren't. Slots operate on the principle that a proportion of the take is returned according to the laws of statistical probability.

☆ In Michael Powell's *The Edge of the World* (GB 37), Belle Crystal plays a barefoot Scottish lassie on the island of Foula. Well, sometimes barefoot. She is seen running down a hillside to the shore with nothing on her pretty feet. She runs up it again in shoes, without having paused to put them on, and she is definitely still shod when she reaches the top. Without removing her shoes, she sets off for the shore again and arrives on naked feet.

☆ Washington's Lincoln Memorial is located in New York in the German version of *Uncle Tom's Cabin* (FRG 65).

☆ The camera is reflected in a mirror in the Robert De Niro-Meryl Streep movie *Falling in Love* (US 85).

☆ Near the beginning of *Elmer Gantry* (US 60), which takes place in 1927, just after Burt Lancaster jumps from a moving train and is seen walking down the track, a mid-1950s Ford is plainly visible in the distance.

☆ Moviegoers confronted with any filmic version of Genesis should spare a glance at Adam's midriff. If, as in *The Bible* (US 66), he has a navel—well, he shouldn't, should he?

☆ The eponymous Britisher of Nana Dzhordzhadze's *My English Grandfather* (USSR 86) speaks with a Texas accent strong enough to pass muster in *Dallas*. Apparently the only English-speaker available for post-synching, a young American tourist in Tbilisi, swore to the non-English-speaking Dzhordzhadze that his accent was pukka British. (The UK distributor made it a condition of the contract that the grandfather's role should be redubbed in the Queen's English.)

☆ Not impossible, but implausible: the tape recorders seen in the Japanese police chief's office in the Bond movie *You Only Live Twice* (GB 67) are of British manufacture.

☆ The gung-ho flagwagger *The Marines Are Here* (US 38) showed a gallant marine scaling a very high wall by climbing on the shoulders of his buddy. The next scene shows him dropping to the ground on the other side—closely followed by his buddy, who has apparently scaled the wall unassisted.

☆ In *Jaws* (US 75), when the citizens of Amity celebrate 4 July, there are no leaves on the trees. (The scene was shot in May).

☆ The title cards of silent western *Hands Across the Border* (US 26) refer several times to wonder horse Silver King as 'she'. As the name suggests, Silver King was a stallion.

☆ In *The Barbarian and the Geisha* (US 58) John Wayne absentmindedly addresses Sam Jaffe, playing a character called Henry Heuken, as Sam instead of Henry.

☆ Kathleen Turner is wearing canvas slip-ons as she leaps from a roof-top on to a train in *The Jewel of the Nile* (US 86). As she stumbles and falls, clinging to the side of the train, she is wearing leather open-work sandals; but on being rescued, she struggles to her feet and the sandals have been replaced once more by the canvas slip-ons.

☆ The heroine of *Adelen 31* (Swe 69), set in 1931, removes her clothes in one scene and reveals bikini marks.

☆ Dynamite is exploded in *Tap Roots* (US 48), set in 1860. Dynamite was invented in 1867.

☆ The action of *The Sound of Music* (US 65) is set in the 1930s, yet in one scene an orange box can be discerned stamped 'Produce of Israel'.

☆ Anachronisms are usually visual or in the dialogue. In *The Draughtsman's Contract* (GB 83) it is a background noise that dispels, at least for ornithologists, the illusion of the film's 17th-century setting. The gentle cooing of a collared dove is not a sound that would have fallen on Jacobean ears. The species was unknown in Britain until 1955.

☆ All the cars seen in the London street scenes in the Danny Kaye movie *Knock on Wood* (US 54) are left-hand drive. In another Danny Kaye film, *Merry Andrew* (US 58), a London bus is progressing along the right-hand side of the road.

☆ As the students rush up the back stairs of Covent Garden Opera House to the gods in *The Red Shoes* (US 48), the wall distinctly wobbles as only canvas stretched on a wooden frame can wobble.

☆ A character in *Man About the House* (GB 74) hails a taxi outside what is clearly Thames Television Studios and asks the driver to take him to Thames TV. On arrival he is seen getting out at exactly the spot at which he got in.

☆ The hero's flat in Portman Square in *Twenty-Three Paces to Baker Street* (US 56) has a balcony overlooking the Thames. Portman Square is over two miles away from London's river.

☆ MGM/UA had to send a letter of apology to Alaskan State Senator Jan Falks after they had publicized *Red Dawn* (US 84) with the declaration: 'In our time, no foreign army has ever occupied American soil. Until now.' Someone in MGM/UA marketing was too young to remember the Japanese occupation of the Aleutians in World War II. The slogan continued to run, however, the distributors defending it with the somewhat specious argument that 'in our time' did not necessarily include the war.

☆ Mike Hammer (Ralph Meeker) in *Kiss Me Deadly* (US 55) goes up to a street kiosk, buys some popcorn, and walks away eating it, a sequence lasting a few seconds. The clock in the background shows 2.10 p.m. when he approaches the kiosk, 2.15 p.m. as he buys the popcorn, and 2.20 p.m. as he departs.

☆ Set in Vienna, *Wonder Child* (GB/Aut 51) was made with Austrian actors speaking English. For Austrian and German release the producers made the curious decision to have the film dubbed not by the original actors, but by Germans speaking in Berlin accents. The picture's reception in Vienna was less than favourable.

☆ A corpse in a battle scene in *Son of Ali Baba* (US 52) moves its arm just as someone is about to step on it.

☆ A scene in a bar in *The In-Laws* (US 79) with Peter Falk sitting at the counter next to a cabbie has the pair switching places in the cutaway shots.

☆ *Crash Landing* (US 58) begins at Lisbon Airport. The planes seen in the background are clearly marked 'Western Air Lines', a US domestic carrier.

☆ In Tony Richardson's film of Nabokov's *Laughter in the Dark* (GB 69), Nicol Williamson enters the Curzon Cinema but finds himself in the auditorium of the National Film Theatre.

☆ The credits of the Indian film *Shiraz* (Ind 28) headed the list of players with the word 'Caste'.

☆ In *The Private Life of Sherlock Holmes* (GB 70), Holmes refers to a newspaper he has spied at the bottom of a birdcage as the *Inverness Courier*. The infallible detective is wrong. It is the *Inverness Times*.

☆ The leading man in *Caught* (US 87), played by Jack Shepherd, gets mugged in Amsterdam and suffers severe facial laceration. In the next scene the wound has miraculously healed overnight without leaving a mark.

☆ In an old English country house scene in *Great Impersonation* (US 35), Edmund Lowe is seen going to bed by candlelight. When he is awoken during the night, there is an electric light switch handy.

☆ The much acclaimed *Julia* (US 77), with Jane Fonda as left-wing playwright Lillian Hellman on a dangerous mission to Nazi Germany to rendezvous with her resistance heroine friend Julia (Vanessa Redgrave), was based on a wholly false premise. Lillian Hellman claimed in her memoirs to have smuggled $50,000 into Germany sewn up in a Persian lamb hat, the money being for the anti-Fascist underground to buy back lives from the Nazis. This forms the central theme of the film. In reality there was no restriction on Americans bringing dollars into Nazi

The Sound of Music (US 65) was set in Austria 1938. The orange box beneath the stall is labelled 'Produce of Israel'—a nation which came into being in 1948.

Germany before World War II and therefore the whole heroic episode is rendered pointless. In fairness to the film-makers, they accepted Miss Hellman's memoirs at their face value. It has since been revealed that the playwright never ever met 'Julia' (real name Muriel Gardiner) and that the incident was a figment of her vivid imagination.

EIGHT

COLOUR, SOUND AND SCOPE

COLOUR

The first commercially successful natural colour process was two-colour Kinemacolor, developed by George Albert Smith of Brighton for the Urban Trading Co., London. Smith made his first colour film by this process outside his house at Southwick, Brighton, in July 1906. It showed his two children playing on the lawn, the boy dressed in blue and waving a Union Jack, the girl in white with a pink sash.

The first commercially produced film in natural colour was G. A. Smith's *A Visit to the Seaside* (GB 08), an eight-minute short featuring the White Coons pierrot troupe and the Band of the Cameron Highlanders which was trade shown in September 1908. Taken at Brighton, it showed children paddling and eating ice cream, a pretty girl falling out of a boat, and men peeping at the Bathing Belles changing in their bathing machines. The first public presentation of Kinemacolor before a paying audience took place at the Palace Theatre, Shaftesbury Avenue, on 26 February 1909 and consisted of 21 short films, including scenes taken at Aldershot, sailing at Southwick, the Water Carnival at Villefranche and the Children's Battle of Flowers at Nice.

The first dramatic film in natural colour was the Kinemacolor production *Checkmated* (GB 10), directed by Theo Bouwmeester, who has also played the lead role of Napoleon. **The first American dramatic film in natural colour** was Eclair's Kinemacolor production *La Tosca* (US 12), with Lillian Russell. A total of 54 dramatic films were produced in Kinemacolor in Britain from 1910–12. In the USA there were only three dramatic productions in Kinemacolor besides *La Tosca*. These were *Mission Bells* (US 13), *The Rivals* (US 13) and *The Scarlet Letter* (US 13), the latter starring D. W. Griffith's wife Linda Arvidson.

The first full-length feature film in colour was a five-reel melodrama, *The World, the Flesh and the Devil* (GB 14), produced by the Union Jack Co. in Kinemacolor from the play by Laurence Cowen. Starring Frank Esmond and Stella St Audrie, it opened at the Holborn Empire on 9 April 1914 billed as 'A £10,000 Picture Play in Actual Colours' in 'four parts and 120 scenes'. Like most of the Kinemacolor dramas, the acting and direction (F. Martin Thornton) were execrable, the colour impressive.

Kinemacolor was an additive process in which both filming and projection were done through red and green filters. The drawbacks were the cost of the special projector used and the wear on the film, which passed through the projector at twice normal speed. Nevertheless, it was installed at some 300 cinemas in Britain and achieved success overseas as well, notably in the United States and Japan. On the production side Kinemacolor was limited in its application because it could not be used for indoor work. There was also a virtue to this, since it encouraged location shooting at a time when black-and-white productions were becoming progressively more studio-bound. One enterprising Kinemacolor venture was **the first colour western**, Theo Bouwmeester's *Fate* (GB 11), set in Texas but filmed in Sussex! Kinemacolor was particularly well suited for films of pageantry, two of the most successful releases being a newsreel of King Edward VII's funeral in May 1910—at which no less than nine kings were present—and a spectacular two-hour presentation of the 1912 Delhi Durbar. Others included the Coronation of King George V, the Naval Review of June 1911 and the Investiture of the Prince of Wales at Caernarvon.

The first all-colour feature film, 1914.

THE WORLD THE FLESH AND THE DEVIL
By LAURENCE COWEN.

Reproduced with Stereoscopic Relief

in Four Parts

120 Scenes

Matinees only
Daily, 2.30 to 5 p.m. **THE HOLBORN EMPIRE**

The escape from the Mill.

A 100 Minute Thrill

The Greatest Photo-Play in London

Prices: 6d. to 5s.

Presented by **KINEMACOLOR**
A £10,000 Picture Play in Actual Colors.

A MELO-DRAMA seething with Sensations.
—
Don't miss it!

Also amazing Programme of the World's Wonders in Nature's Colors.
—
Matinees only

Box Office
Tel.: 5367 Holborn. **THE HOLBORN EMPIRE** Daily, 2.30 to 5 p.m.

Production came to a halt when Charles Urban, the guiding spirit behind Kinemacolor, left for the US in 1914 to propagate the British war effort through films.

The first colour talkie was Frans Lundberg Films' *Vals ur Solstrålen* (Swe 11), directed by Ernst Dittmer and starring Rosa Grünberg, which was premièred at the Stora Biografteatern in Malmö, Sweden, on 1 May 1911. The 215 ft short was made by the Biophon synchronized disc sound process. The colour process is not recorded, but it was probably stencilled.

The first feature-length sound film in colour was MGM's two-colour Technicolor production *The Viking* (US 28), directed by R. William Neill with Donald Crisp as Leif Ericsson, the legendary discoverer of America, and Pauline Starke as the lovely Helga. It was premièred on 2 November 1928 with synchronized score and sound effects.

The first all-colour talkie feature was Warner Bros' two-colour Technicolor musical *On With the Show* (US 29), directed by Alan Crosland with Betty Compson and Joe E. Brown, which was premièred at the Winter Garden, New York, on 28 May 1929.

The first British talking feature in colour was Talkicolor's *Knowing Men* (GB 30), produced, directed and scripted by Elinor Glyn from her own novel in French and English versions with Danish star Carl Brisson playing opposite Austrian actress Elissa Landi. Although made in colour, the film was released in black-and-white. The first to be released in colour was BIP's *A Romance of Seville* (GB 29), which was originally shown as a silent in 1929 but had sound added in July 1930. Colour process unknown. The first film made as a talkie to be released in colour was BIP's *Harmony Heaven* (GB 30), a musical about a composer (Stuart Hall) who wins fame and the hand of his girl (Polly Ward) despite the attentions of a flirtatious socialite (Trilby Clark).

The first Technicolor film was *The Gulf Between* (US 17), a five-reeler starring Grace Darmond and Niles Welch, produced by the Technicolor Motion Picture Corporation in a two-colour additive process and premièred at the Aeolian Hall, New York, on 21 September 1917. It was **the first full-length colour feature produced in the USA** and the third in the world.

> Kodak's Eastman Color SP print film, the stock used for most colour features from the mid-fifties onwards, had a life of seven to ten years before the colour faded. A new film stock, Eastman Color Print film 5384, introduced as standard for professional colour work in 1982, has a life of 90 to 100 years.

> The colour values of Van Gogh's celebrated painting of a cornfield are not true to nature, according to director Vincente Minnelli. When he made *Lust for Life* (US 56), there was a scene in which Van Gogh is seen painting the picture (the original was used in the film), followed by a dissolve to an actual cornfield. In order to make the real corn match the colours rendered in the painting, Minnelli was obliged to spray the entire field with golden dye.

The first feature in subtractive Technicolor was Chester Franklin's *The Toll of the Sea* (US 22), starring Anna May Wong, which was premièred at the Rialto Theater, New York, on 26 November 1922. **The first Technicolor interior shots** were taken for a colour sequence in *Cytherea* (US 24).

The Technicolor Motion Picture Corporation had been founded by Dr Herbert Kalmus of the Massachusetts Institute of Technology in 1915. The earliest Technicolor process was not unlike Kinemacolor and depended on the use of filters on both camera and projector. Following his development of a reasonably successful two-colour subtractive process, Dr Kalmus took Technicolor to Hollywood in 1923. The main problem was that the double-coated film was given to cupping and scratched more easily than monochrome. To most producers the cost at 27¢ a foot was prohibitive, compared with 8¢ a foot for monochrome stock, but with the coming of talkies the feverish search for novelty by the major studios encouraged its use and 45 Technicolor features were made in the three years 1929–31.

The first film in three-colour Technicolor was Walt Disney's Silly Symphony cartoon *Flowers and Trees* (US 32), premièred 17 July 1932 at Grauman's Chinese Theater, Hollywood. The first dramatic subject was *La Cucaracha* (US 34), released at the RKO-Hill Street Theater, Los Angeles, on 15 November 1934 and the first three-colour Technicolor sequence in a feature was in MGM's *The Cat and the Fiddle* (US 34).

The first feature made entirely in three-colour Technicolor was Rouben Mamoulian's *Becky Sharp* (US 35) with Cedric Hardwicke and Miriam Hopkins. Not everyone appreciated the innovation. A critic for *Liberty* magazine wrote that the performers looked like 'boiled salmon dipped in mayonnaise'. **The first in Britain** was *Wings of the Morning* (GB 37), a race-track drama starring Henry Fonda and French actress Annabella, which opened at the Capitol, Haymarket, in May 1937.

The first three-colour film stock which could be used in any standard 35 mm camera was

Technicolor Monopack, which was used for the first time on the exterior shots of *Lassie Come Home* (US 42). Formerly special cameras had to be rented for colour work.

The most widely used colour process: Technicolor held almost a monopoly of the three-colour field from 1932 until 1952, when *Royal Journey* (Can 52) was released in Kodak's new Eastman Color process. Within three years Technicolor had fallen into second place, with 112 films being produced in Eastman Color in 1955 against 90 in Technicolor. Eastman Color is now used for virtually all colour films produced in the West. Metrocolor, Warnercolor and De Luxe are all processes using Eastman Color stock and films credited 'Color by

Technicolor' are generally made with Eastman Color negative but printed by Technicolor laboratories.

The shortest colour sequence consisted of two frames of Alfred Hitchcock's *Spellbound* (US 45). Towards the end of the film, a split-second scene of a gun blast was presented in vivid red Technicolor.

Decline of Black-and-White Films

Not surprisingly the USA was the first country to produce more films in colour than black and white, with 157 out of a total of 237 full-length features being shot in colour in 1954. Rather more surprisingly, monochrome made something of a comeback in

COLOUR AND BLACK-AND-WHITE PRODUCTION IN THE US AND UK, 1920-70

	Full Colour		Part Colour		Black and White			
	US	UK	US	UK	US	%	UK	%
1920	0	0	0	0	797	100	155	100
1921	0	0	2	0	852	99.8	137	100
1922	2	1	0	1	746	99.7	108	98.2
1923	2	1	1	1	573	99.5	66	97.1
1924	1	1	1	0	577	99.7	48	98.0
1925	0	0	1	0	578	99.8	33	100
1926	1	0	8	0	731	98.8	33	100
1927	0	0	1	0	677	99.9	48	100
1928	1	0	2	0	638	99.5	80	100
1929	5	1	5	0	552	98.2	80	98.8
1930	14	1	14	1	481	94.2	73	97.3
1931	5	0	0	0	496	99.0	93	100
1932	1	0	0	0	488	99.8	110	100
1933	1	0	2	0	504	99.4	115	100
1934	0	0	3	0	477	99.4	145	100
1935	2	0	1	0	522	99.4	165	100
1936	4	0	0	0	518	99.2	192	100
1937	8	0	2	0	530	98.1	174	98.9
1938	10	3	0	0	445	97.8	131	97.8
1939	10	3	1	0	472	97.7	81	97.6
1940	16	1	1	0	460	96.4	49	98.0
1941	17	0	1	0	474	96.3	46	100
1942	15	1	0	0	473	96.9	38	97.4
1943	19	1	0	0	378	95.0	46	97.9
1944	26	1	1	0	374	92.3	34	97.1
1945	22	2	0	0	328	93.7	37	94.9
1946	30	6	0	0	348	92.1	35	85.4
1947	40	3	1	0	328	88.9	55	94.8
1948	58	7	0	0	308	84.2	67	90.5
1949	52	6	1	0	303	85.1	95	94.1
1950	61	5	0	0	322	84.1	76	93.8
1951	78	7	1	0	312	79.8	68	90.7
1952	108	14	0	0	216	66.7	87	86.1
1953	144	14	0	0	200	58.1	88	86.3
1954	157	32	0	0	80	33.8	78	70.9
1955	138	33	0	0	98	41.5	62	65.9
1956	134	35	0	0	139	50.9	56	61.5
1957	99	31	1	0	203	67.0	84	73.0
1958	91	23	2	0	164	63.8	88	79.3
1959	80	24	1	0	96	79.3	75	75.8
1960	77	20	0	0	74	49.0	90	81.8
1961	72	32	1	0	78	51.7	77	70.0
1962	67	25	1	0	60	46.9	101	80.2
1963	76	31	0	0	54	41.5	76	63.5
1964	80	34	0	0	58	42.0	41	54.7
1965	88	46	0	0	50	36.2	34	42.5
1966	115	58	0	0	24	17.3	11	15.9
1967	136	84	2	0	7	4.8	6	6.7
1968	170	72	1	0	9	5.0	1	1.4
1969	171	86	2	0	4	2.3	0	0
1970	227	103	3	0	1	0.4	3	2.8

Since 1970 nearly all production in the US and UK has been in colour.

the later 1950s, with nearly 80 per cent of 1959's releases being in black and white, but from 1962 onwards colour remained in the ascendant. The number of monochrome releases fell dramatically from year to year until in 1970 there was but a single black-and-white production. Elsewhere, the changeover took a little longer, delayed perhaps by a feeling that colour was inappropriate to naturalistic, 'social realism' films or to subjects of serious concern. In Britain colour became predominant in 1965, when 46 colour films were produced against only 34 monochrome. Only three years later monochrome production was down to a single picture, with 72 colour releases. 1969 was the first year in which British production was 100 per cent colour. France, long the bastion of grainy monochrome effects, had succumbed by 1967, when only four out of 120 films were shot in black and white. Japan had reached a 50–50 stage by 1965, but within three years the proportion of monochrome features had dropped to 25 per cent. Italy maintained some black-and-white feature productions up to 1968, when seven out of 153 films were shot in monochrome, but very few after that.

In the Far East the changeover was generally slower. Out of the total of 763 films produced in India in 1982, 43 were black and white. All Burmese films were black and white before 1983, the year a colour laboratory was established in Rangoon processing Fuji Colour.

Black and white output 1987. The year's output of monochrome 35 mm feature films from the established film producing nations was as follows: *Chronicle of a Lonely Child* (Arg); *Dragon Food* (FRG/Swz); *The Fatal Telephone* (Yug); *Une Flamme dans mon coeur* (Swz); *Heat and Sunlight* (US); *A Hungarian Fairy Tale* (Hun); *Love Is a Fat Woman* (Arg); *Regina* (It); *The Sea and Poison* (It); *While There Is Light* (Sp); *Zisehk* (FRG).

The first feature film shot in black and white to be converted to full colour was *Yankee Doodle Dandy* (US 42), biopic of George M. Cohan starring James Cagney. The special prints with their computer-applied colour were released by MGM on 4 July 1985. 'Colorization', as it is known, has become a controversial issue in the industry, with many directors and stars vehemently opposed to the practice on the grounds that it diminishes the visual quality of films never intended to be in colour. Nevertheless, it appears to be popular with a large section of the public—the colorized version of *Miracle on 34th Street* (US 47) achieved the highest ratings of any film on US television in 1985. Color Systems Technology, the company which developed the system, claims that it goes to great trouble to preserve the integrity of the films given their treatment, even maintaining a research department whose sole function is to ascertain the true

colour of props, buildings, vegetation, costumes and such physical attributes as hair and eyes.

> One of the less celebrated, but eminently repeatable Goldwynisms, was the master word scrambler's observation that he 'wouldn't believe Technicolor until I see it in black and white'.

SOUND

The first presentation of sound films before a paying audience was made by Oskar Messter at 21 Unter den Linden, Berlin, in September 1896. The sound system employed synchronized Berliner discs, but there is no record of the titles of the films or the performers in them. **The first artistes known to have performed in a sound film** were Giampetro and Fritzi Massary, who appeared in a scene from an operetta filmed by Max Skladanowski, probably before the end of 1896.

The earliest known talking films were presented by Clément Maurice of the Gaumont Co. at the Phono-Cinéma-Théâtre of the Paris Exposition on 8 June 1900. They included: Sarah Bernhardt and Pierre Magnier in the duel scene from *Hamlet*, playing Hamlet and Laertes respectively; Coquelin in Rostrand's *Cyrano de Bergerac*; Coquelin and Mesdames Esquilar and Kervich in Molière's *Les Précieuses Ridicules*; Felicia Mallet, Mme Reichenberg and Gabrielle Réjane of the Comédie Française in scenes from *Madame Sans-Gêne* and *Ma Cousine*. In addition there were synchronized opera films and ballet films.

The earliest known talking film with original dialogue was *Lolotte* (Fr 00), a comedy written and directed by Henri Joly and premièred at the Théâtre de la Grande Roue at the Paris Exposition. The scene takes place in a hotel bedroom and is played by three characters, a newly-married couple and the patron of the hotel, the latter performed by Joly himself. The dialogue script survives.

The first sound films produced in Britain were a series of song subjects made by Walter Gibbons in the autumn of 1900 under the name of Phono-Bio-Tableaux Films. They included Vesta Tilley singing *The Midnight Son*, *Algy the Piccadilly Johnny* and *Louisiana Lou* and G. H. Chirgwin giving a soulful rendering of *The Blind Boy*. There was also an actuality with sound effects titled *Turn Out the Fire Brigade*. **The earliest British talking film** was Hepworth's Vivaphone version of *Cinderella* (GB 13) with Gertie Potter.

The first sound-on-film process was patented by French-born Eugene Lauste of Stockwell, London, on 11 August 1906. It was not until 1910, however, that Lauste succeeded in recording and reproducing speech on film, employing an electromagnetic

Left: The first sound-track, recorded by Eugene Lauste in 1910. *Top*: Making an experimental talkie in Eugene Lauste's back garden in Stockwell *c*. 1914. (*ILN*). *Above*: World's first talking projector by Eugene Lauste 1913.

recorder and string galvanometer. He used a French gramophone record, selected at random, for the initial trial, and by coincidence the first words to be heard in the playback were 'J'entends très bien maintenant' ('I hear very well now'). A colleague in the film business, L. G. Egrot, recalled visiting Lauste at his home in Benedict Road about this time: 'He had already started building his camera to take pictures and sound together, the front part of the camera allowing to test the different systems he was experimenting with for sound recording . . . Very often on a Sunday, a bandmaster friend of his, Mr Norris, would come along with his band and play in the garden of the house where, in 1911, Mr Lauste had had a wooden building erected as an experimenting studio. The machine was taken out, with all leads, some pictures would be made and some sound recorded.'

Lauste completed his sound-on-film projector and reproducing apparatus in 1913, and was about to embark on the commercial exploitation of the process when war broke out. In 1916 he went to the USA with the idea of obtaining financial backing, but the entry of America into the war the following year put an end to his hopes.

The first sound-on-film productions to be presented in public were shown at the Alhambra Kino in Berlin on 17 September 1922 before an invited audience of 1000 people. The films were made by the Tri-Ergon process developed by Joseph Engl, Joseph Massolle and Hans Vogt and included **the first sound-on-film dramatic talkie**. Titled *Der Brandstifter/The Arsonist* (Ger 22), and adapted from Von Heyermann's play of the same name, it had a cast of three with Erwin Baron playing seven of the nine parts. The other films were mainly orchestral with vocal accompaniment. Press reaction was mixed, criticism being levelled not so much against the level of technical achievement, but at the notion of talking films, which it was said

Above: Filming from a sound-proof booth in 1928. The camera is separated from the action by a sheet of plate glass. (*ILN*)

Left: By 1930 the camera had been released from its sound-proof prison and was back on wheels. The picture was *City of Song* (GB 30), the studio Wembley, the girl Australia's Betty Stokfeld (1905–66) making her screen debut. (*Popperfoto*)

would destroy the essential art of the motion picture—mime—and detract from the cinema's international appeal.

The first American sound-on-film motion picture was *Lincoln's Gettysburg Address* (US 22), a monologue delivered by Ellery Paine, made by Polish-born Prof. Joseph Tykocinski-Tykociner, research professor of electrical engineering at the University of Illinois, and presented in the Physics Building on 9 June 1922. The film was not released commercially.

The first presentation of sound-on-film productions before a paying audience took place at the Rialto Theater, New York, on 15 April 1923, when Lee De Forest showed a number of singing and musical shorts made by the Phonofilm process. The sound films formed a supporting programme to the main (silent) feature, *Bella Donna* (US 23) with Pola Negri. During the following 12 months, 34 cinemas in the eastern United States were wired for Phonofilm sound. The films made at the De Forest Studios between 1923 and 1927 included monologue numbers by Eddie Cantor, George Jessel and Chic Sale; dialogues between Gloria Swanson and Thomas Meighan and between Weber and Fields; Folkina's *Swan Dance*; playlets with Raymond

Hitchcock; and orchestral subjects featuring Ben Bernie, Paul Sprecht and Otto Wolf Kahn.

The year 1924 saw three notable sound-on-film 'firsts' from Phonofilm. President Coolidge was filmed delivering a campaign speech on the White House lawn, **the first time that a President of the USA had spoken from the screen; the first Technicolor film with a sound-track** was made, the subject being Balieff's *Chauve Souris* danced in the open air; and **the first dramatic talkie film to be released commercially**, *Love's Old Sweet Song*, a two-reeler directed by J. Searle Dawley with Mary Mayo and Una Merkel in the leading roles. Although the first to exploit sound-on-film commercially, De Forest failed to establish talking pictures as a major entertainment medium and the Phonofilm patents were eventually taken over by

When primitive sound-on-disc 'talkies' were introduced during the Edwardian era, volume was sometimes considered rather more important than quality. William Haggar, proprietor of a cinema in Aberdare, Wales, advertised that his films 'can be heard two miles away'.

One of the effects of the introduction of talkies in the USA was to kill off the theatrical stock companies. In 1929 there were still 200 companies playing stock; by 1939 there were five.

William Fox together with those of the Tri-Ergon system.

The first public demonstration of sound-on-film in Britain took place at the Finsbury Park Cinema on 14 June 1923, when a programme of Phonofilm shorts was trade shown. The *Bioscope* reported: 'Several pictures were projected, including a vocalist rendering a song from *Carmen*, a dancer imitative of Pavlova with dying swan musical effects, and others. The synchronization was as near perfect as possible, but the articulation sounded to me somewhat throaty.'

The first sound-on-film production shown before a paying audience in Britain was the Technicolor dance subject *Chauve Souris* (US 24), which was shown with musical sound-track at the Tivoli in London in the summer of 1925. **The first talking film seen by a paying audience** introduced a programme of Phonofilm singing and orchestral shorts premièred at the Empire, Plumstead on 4 October 1926 and consisted of Sidney L. (now Lord) Bernstein explaining how Phonofilm worked.

The first sound-on-film talkie produced in Britain was De Forest Phonofilms' *The Gentleman* (GB 25), a comedy short directed and scripted by William J. Elliott. The following year four short dramas were produced at the Clapham Studios by the De Forest Phonofilm Co. of Great Britain and in 1927 there were films of Edith Sitwell reading her own poems and Sybil Thorndike in a scene from Shaw's *Saint Joan*.

The first full-length feature film with sound (in part) was D. W. Griffith's *Dream Street* (US 21), a United Artists release. Described by one cinema historian as 'a dreadful hodgepodge of allegory and symbolism', it was a total failure when originally presented as an all-silent picture at the Central Theater, New York, in April 1921. After it had closed, Griffith was persuaded by Wendell McMahill of Kellum Talking Pictures to add a sound sequence. On 27 April the star, Ralph Graves, was brought to the Kellum Studios on West 40th Street to record a love song on synchronized disc, and this was included when the film reopened at the Town Hall Civic Centre on 1 May. A fortnight later a second sound sequence was added, consisting of the shouts and whoops of Porter Strong shooting craps together with other background noises, and this version opened in Brooklyn on 29 May 1921.

The only other feature movie with vocal sound prior to *The Jazz Singer* (see below) was José A. Ferreya's *La Muchacha del Arrabal* (Arg 22), starring Lidia Lis.

When the talkies came to the island of Malta in 1930 with the Valetta première of *Broadway Melody* (US 29), the manager of the Royal Opera House asked all his patrons to wear tennis shoes to lessen the noise of late arrivals. Such precautions were not sufficient to make the innovation the success it had been in other parts of the world. The sound-on-disc system got out of sync, so that the men talked in women's voices and vice versa. Come the half-way interval, the show had to be abandoned because a man was found dead in the stalls.

The first talking feature film (in part) was Warner Bros' Vitaphone (sound-on-disc) production *The Jazz Singer* (US 27), directed by Alan Crosland and starring Al Jolson, which opened at the Warner Theatre on Broadway on 6 October 1927. The initial, historic talking sequence takes place in Coffee Dan's, where Jack Robin (Al Jolson) has been singing *Dirty Hands, Dirty Face*. Amidst the applause, Jolson holds up his hands and urges: 'Wait a minute. Wait a minute. You ain't heard nothin' yet! Wait a minute, I tell you. You ain't heard nothin'. You wanna hear *Toot-toot-tootsie*? All right. Hold on.' Turning to the band, Jolson says: 'Now listen: you play *Toot-toot-tootsie*. Three choruses, you understand, and in the third chorus I whistle. Now give it to 'em hard and heavy. Go right ahead . . .'

The second and only other talking sequence was longer and involved a conversation between Jack Robin and his mother (Eugenie Besserer). In view of the many conflicting claims concerning the amount of dialogue in *The Jazz Singer*, it is worth recording that exactly 354 words are spoken in the two talking sequences, 60 in the first and 294 in the second. Jolson speaks 340, Eugenie Besserer 13 and Warner Oland (as the father) one—'Stop!' The dialogue sequences were unscripted, because Warner Bros had only intended to make a film with synchronized music and singing, not a talkie. Jolson, however, ad libbed—the famous line 'You ain't heard nothin' yet' was in fact a catchphrase he used in his stage performances—and studio head Sam Warner liked the snatches of talk enough to keep them in.

The first all-talking feature was Warner Bros' *Lights of New York* (US 28), which was premièred at the Strand Theater, New York, on 6 July 1928. Starring Helene Costello, the picture was so determinedly all-talking that the dialogue continued non-stop from opening credits to end title. Warner's billed it as '100% Talking!'; *Variety* commented '100% Crude'.

The first sound-on-film feature was Fox's *The Air Circus* (US 28), with Louise Dresser and David Rollins, which opened at New York's Gaiety on 1 September 1928. The dialogue sequence lasted 15 minutes. **The first all-talking sound-on-film feature** was Raoul Walsh and Irving Cummins' Fox western *In Old Arizona* (US 28), with Edmund Lowe and Warner Baxter, which was also **the first talkie shot outdoors**. It opened 26 December 1928 at the Criterion, Los Angeles.

The first British talking feature was Marshall Neilan's *Black Waters* (GB 29), a melodrama about a mad captain posing as a clergyman to murder people aboard a fog-bound ship. Starring John Loder and Mary Brian, the picture was produced in the USA by Herbert Wilcox for British & Dominions Sono Art World Wide.

The first feature-length talkie made in Britain was Alfred Hitchcock's *Blackmail* (GB 29), produced by British Int. Pictures at Elstree with Anny Ondra and John Longden and premièred at the Regal, Marble Arch, on 21 June 1929. The first reel had incidental sound and music only, but the characters began to speak in the second as the plot unfolded. It was billed as '99 per cent talking', a pardonable exaggeration. The posters also carried the slogan 'See and Hear It—Our Mother Tongue As It Should Be Spoken'—a sideswipe at the American-English that had dominated the screen hitherto.

Britain's first all-talking feature was *The Clue of the New Pin* (GB 29) adapted from the Edgar Wallace novel of the same name and produced by British Lion in association with British Photophone. The film was directed by Arthur Maude, starred Donald Calthrop and Benita Hume, and was released on 16 December 1929. An undistinguished production, the film is chiefly memorable for the fact that a rising young stage performer called John Gielgud played a bit part in it.

The first dubbed film was Lee De Forest's Phonofilm production *Love's Old Sweet Song* (US 24). The film contains one exterior scene, in which Una Merkel is strolling down a street when she hears the title song being sung by Mary Mayo from indoors. Since the exterior footage had to be shot silent, the song was dubbed in afterwards.

The coming of sound presented the studios with unforeseen problems. Not least for MGM was getting Leo to roar on cue for its famous trademark. (*Popperfoto*)

The first occasion on which another actor's voice was substituted for that of a member of the cast was in *The Patriot* (US 28). The performer concerned, Emil Jannings, threatened legal proceedings if the new sound-track was not erased, and the dubbed voice was removed. The first film released with a substitute voice was *The Wolf of Wall Street* (US 29), in which the heavily accented Hungarian actor Paul Lukas played a partner in a firm of stockbrokers. His dialogue was dubbed by Lawford Davidson. Happily Lukas's accent did not hinder the development of his career—he continued to play major roles in Hollywood pictures for another 40 years.

The first British film to be dubbed was Alfred Hitchcock's *Blackmail* (GB 29). The female lead, Czech actress Anny Ondra, spoke almost no English and her voice was dubbed by Joan Barry (later the mother of heiress Henrietta Tiarks). This was done by the novel method of having Miss Barry read Miss Ondra's lines into a microphone while the latter was performing.

The first use of post-synchronization with the same actors in a feature film was by Ernst Lubitsch for *The Love Parade* (US 29), as a means of freeing the camera from the constraints of the immobile sound-proof booth used in early talkies. By using a silent camera, he was able to counter the static camera positions that marred most of the pioneer sound productions and dub in the dialogue afterwards.

The first film with stereophonic sound was the re-edited version of Abel Gance's *Napoleon Bonaparte* (Fr 27), which was presented with added dialogue and sound effects at the Paramount Cinema, Paris, in 1935. The stereophonic process used had been patented by Gance and André Debrie three years earlier.

The first American productions with stereophonic sound were the Warner Bros' productions *Santa Fe Trail* (US 40) and *Four Wives* (US 40), presented in Vitasound. The first successful system of stereophonic musical accompaniment was Fantasound, developed by Walt Disney Studios in association with RCA and first employed for the sound-track of Disney's feature-length cartoon *Fantasia* (US 41), with music by the Philadelphia Orchestra under the direction of Leopold Stokowski.

The first use of overlapping dialogue—The talking picture borrowed the stage convention, far removed from reality, whereby no more than one character speaks at once. Credit for introducing overlapping dialogue in the interests of naturalism is usually given to Orson Welles for *Citizen Kane* (US 41), but in fact the technique had been used a year earlier in Howard Hawks' wild and witty *His Girl Friday* (US 40), with Cary Grant and Rosalind Russell.

Pistol shots could not be recorded by the Vitaphone sound-on-disc system used for making *The Jazz Singer* (US 27) and other early Warner Bros talkies, since the intensity of the sound would have caused the stylus to jump the groove. A drummer simulated the noise instead.

A sound effects specialist of the pre-war talkies was Miss Colin Bell of Gaumont-British Studios, whose particular talent was for imitating screaming babies. She caterwauled in *The Passing of the Third Floor Back* (GB 35) and *The Thirty-Nine Steps* (GB 35) among others.

Dolby Sound

A noise reduction system designed to eliminate hiss from recorded sound—as its originator has expressed it, 'real high fidelity means reproducing the silence as accurately as the sound'. It was developed by American-born Ray Dolby in an old dressmaking factory in Fulham, where Dolby laboratories were established in May 1965 with four employees and a refusal of credit from the bank. The first practical application was by Decca for disc recording, the units being known as the S/N Stretcher because they were for stretching the signal-to-noise ratio. After Ray Dolby had heard some engineers at Pye referring to his equipment as 'a Dolby', he decided to change the name to his own. **The first film with Dolby sound** was Stanley Kubrick's *A Clockwork Orange* (GB 71). This used Dolby noise reduction on all pre-mixes and masters, though the release prints had a conventional optical sound-track. The first film with a Dolby encoded mono sound-track was *Callan* (GB 74) and the first with a Dolby encoded stereo optical sound-track was Ken Russell's *Lisztomania* (GB 75). At this point Dolby began to take off; less than 10 years later there were 6000 cinemas worldwide equipped to take the new system. The 1000th film with a Dolby stereo soundtrack, *Heartbreak Ridge* (US 86), was released in 1986.

The first commercial play-off of a movie with digital sound took place at the Plitt Century Plaza Theater in Century City, California over a four-week period during February and March 1985. A specially-recorded version of Disney's 1941 cartoon feature *Fantasia* (US 41) was used for the presentation, with the sound emanating from a digital audio playback unit synchronized with the projector. The process allows for the exact reproduction of sound.

The last wholly silent film (ie without a sound-track) **produced in America** for general distribution was George Melford's *The Poor Millionaire* (US 30), with Richard Talmadge (who played both the hero and the villain) and Constance Howard. It was released by Biltmore Pictures on 7 April 1930, just 30 months and a day after the presentation of the first talkie feature. Only four other silents had been issued in 1930, all of them low budget westerns. The following year there were no silents but four films with synchronized music and sound effects only, including Chaplin's *City Lights* and F. W. Murnau's *Tabu*. Silent production in America, however, was not finished for good. In 1950 Georges Sadoul reported that silent features in colour were being produced in San Francisco for the Chinese population of the United States.

The last British silent feature was Argyle Art Pictures' *Paradise Alley* (GB 31), starring John Argyle and Margaret Delane, the story of a miner who takes the blame when his brother shoots a man during a robbery. It was released in March 1931.

European production had made virtually a complete change-over to sound by the end of 1931. Elsewhere, the last silent feature from Soviet Russia—Alexander Medvekin's *Schastye/Happiness*—was released in 1935 and the last seven Indian silents were issued the same year. Japan took longer to make the change. In 1937, 209 out of 524 movies were without dialogue—50 with sound effects and music, 159 silent. The following year saw the virtual demise of the silent, with 16 'sound effects only' films and 15 wholly silent. As late as 1952 in Burma, where only two of the 22 production companies were equipped to make sound films, production totalled 40 silents and 6 talkies.

The last silent feature films for commercial distribution were produced in Thailand at the end of the 1960s. Although talkies had been produced in the 1930s, World War II totally disrupted both the Thai economy and its film industry and subsequently all films were shot silent on 16 mm stock until 1965. Dialogue was supplied by actors and actresses 'live dubbing' in cinemas from a cubicle next to the projection booth. After 1965 the popularity of Indian-style musicals stimulated producers to shoot sound song-and-dance sequences on 35 mm stock for interpolation with otherwise silent 16 mm footage. According to the Thai Motion Picture Producers' Association 'by 1970 all Thai films were shot on 35 mm with sound'.

Post-Sound Silents

A small number of non-dialogue dramatic films (usually with synchronized music and sound effects) have been produced since the last war. The following list excludes ballet films and similar mime productions and also the Burmese, Thai and Chinese-American silents referred to above.

Russel Rouse's atomic spy thriller *The Thief* (US 52) with Ray Milland; *Los Noces de Sable* (Fr 52)—

Jean Cocteau's update of Tristan and Isolde set in the Sahara; *Dementia* (US 55), described by *Variety* as 'the strangest film ever offered for theatrical release', about the dreams of a demented woman; Kaneto Shindo's *The Island* (Jap 60), about a family living on a tiny island, which won the One World Prize at Melbourne in 1962 for 'the feature film which can be most universally understood'; the Bengali production *Ingeet* (Ind 61); Luiz Rosemberg Filho's 2¼-hour *Imagens* (Bra 72), which had no music or sound effects; Yoichi Takabayashi's *Gaki Zoshi* (Jap 72); Andrej Brzozowski's *Obszar Zamkniety/The Closed Area* (Pol 72); *Bez/A Film without Words* (Yug 73); Terry Bourke's spinechilling horror meller *Night of Fear* (Aus 73), about a woman who is terrorized by a crazed hermit after her car crashes on a lonely road; the cast-of-one *Vase de noces* (Bel 73); the cast-of-none *Model* (Gre 74), directed by Kostas Sfikas; Morton Hellig's *Once* (US 74) with Christopher Mitchum; Milos Radivojević's *Testament* (Yug 75); *Robinson Columbus* (Den 75); Jérôme Savetry's *La Fille du garde barrière/The Gatekeeper's Daughter* (Fr 75); James Scott's *Coilin and Platonida* (GB 76); V. Miroshnichenko's *Lone Wolf* (USSR 77), from the Turgenev story about a giant woodsman endeavouring to bring up two motherless children as well as care for the estate; Gérard Myriam Benhamou's *Adom ou le sang d'Abel* (Fr 77), about Cain and Abel; *Pentimento* (Neth 78); Pim de la Parra's *Dirty Picture* (Neth 80); *Le Dernier Combat* (Fr 83), about an apocalypse in which the world has been left with only a handful of men and a single woman survivor; Jos Stelling's *De Illusionist* (Neth 83); *Rebelote* (Fr 84), made by youthful French director Jacques Richard as a tribute to the silent days and with a score by Pierre Jansen for performance by a live orchestra—the picture was billed, less than accurately, as 'The first truly silent film since the advent of sound in 1927' (a claim that ignored the large output of silents between 1927 and 1931, as well as the films listed here); and the only full-length cartoon feature without dialogue, Donyo Donev's *We Called Them Montagues and Capulets* (Bul 84), a social comedy loosely based on *Romeo and Juliet*; *Bolivar* (Ven 82) and *Orinoko-Nuevo* (Ven 84), both by Diego Risquez, the only director to have made two modern silents; *To Sleep so as to Dream* (Jap 86), a detective picture set in the 1920s with all the dialogue presented as inter-titles. Mel Brooks's *Silent Movie* (US 76) nearly qualifies for this list, but there was one word of dialogue.

*L*ANGUAGES

Hollywood's foreign language output was confined principally to the early talkie period, the largest proportion being in Spanish for the Latin American market. Beginning with a dubbed version of RKO's *Rio*

Rita (US 29), a total of 96 Spanish language movies were produced in the USA during the ensuing six years, the majority by Fox, and another 17 were made by Paramount at their Joinville studios in France 1930–33. **The first foreign language feature made in America with live dialogue** was *Sombras de Gloria/Blaze of Glory* (US 30). It was a Sono Art-World production.

During the period 1930–35 a total of 63 French language pictures were produced by MGM, First National, Paramount, Warner Bros, RKO, Universal, Fox, Columbia and Twentieth Century. The Paramount productions were made at Joinville, outside Paris, where they also produced in Spanish, German, Italian, Swedish, Portuguese, Romanian, Polish, Czech and Dutch.

The first foreign language talkie to be subtitled in English was *Two Hearts in Waltz Time* (Ger 29). The titles were written by Herman G. Weinberg (an American), who sub-titled a record

In order to simulate the language of the mutants in *Island of Lost Souls* (US 32), Paramount's director of recording Loren L. Ryder recorded a track consisting of a combination of animal sounds and foreign languages played backwards. He then alternately speeded up the loop and slowed it down, producing cadences that were strange and horrifying. Audience reaction was even more dramatic than had been anticipated; the vibratory effect on the eardrums induced instant nausea.

number of over 400 films during the ensuing 40 years.

The first talkie produced in different language versions was British International Pictures' trilingual *Atlantic* (GB 29), which was released with separate English, French and German sound-tracks. Besides its overseas release, the German version was shown at the Alhambra, Leicester Square, to cater for the large German population living in London prior to World War II.

Multilingual films in which foreign characters speak in their own language were comparatively rare before *The Longest Day* (US 62) broke with former Hollywood practice by having the Germans speaking German and the French speaking French. There had been occasional examples, however, from the earliest days of sound, starting with G. W. Pabst's *Westfront 1918* (Ger 30), with dialogue in French and German. Others included Pabst's *Kameradschaft* (Ger 31), about a mining disaster

involving French and German miners; Luis Trenker's *Der verlorene Sohn/The Prodigal Son* (Ger 34), in German and English; Jean Renoir's *La Grande Illusion* (Fr 37), in French, English and German; Nyrki Tapiovaara's *Stolen Death* (Fin 38), a thriller in Finnish, Swedish and Russian; *Carl Peters* (Ger 41), in German and English; *Die Letze Chance* (Swz 34), in German and French; Guy Hamilton's *The Colditz Story* (GB 54), in English and German; *La Chatte* (Fr 58), in French and German; and Jean-Luc Godard's quadrilingual *Le Mépris/Contempt* (Fr/It 63), in which Michel Piccoli spoke Italian, Brigitte Bardot spoke French, Jack Palance spoke American and Fritz Lang spoke German, the need for sub-titles being effectively reduced by Giogia Moll's role as the interpreter.

Even silent films could be multilingual. Rex Ingram stated in *Motion Picture Directing* (New York 1922) that when making films with foreign settings, he made his principals speak the language of the country. Explaining that 'it helps them materially in keeping to the required atmosphere', he admitted ruefully 'few of them like to go to this trouble . . .'

The most multilingual film producing country is India, which has produced films in the following 45 languages since 1931: Angami Naga, Arabic, Assamese, Avadhi, Badaga, Bengali, Brijbhasha, Burmese, Chhattisgadhi, Coorgi, Dogri, English, French, Garhwali, German, Gorkhali, Gujarati, Haryanavi, Hindi, Kannada, Kashmiri, Khasi, Konkani, Magadhi, Maithili, Malay, Malayalam, Manipuri, Marathi, Marwari, Nepalese, Oriya, Persian, Punjabi, Pushtu, Rajasthani, Sanskrit, Sindi, Sinhalese, Swahili, Tamil, Telegu, Thai, Tulu, Urdu.

The only film made in Latin was Derek Jarman's *Sebastiane* (GB 76), a homophile interpretation of the legend of St Sebastian. The translator, Jack Welch, used ingenious shifts to put Roman barrack-room language of the third century AD into comprehensible Latin, but in one instance had to resort to a Greek word, rendering the epithet *Motherfucker* as *Oedipus. Sebastiane* enjoys the unique distinction of being the only English film ever to have been released in Britain with English sub-titles.

The first talking film made in dialect was *Mieke* (Bel 30), a comedy made in Antwerp by Felix Bell (Gaston Schoukens) in the Anversois patois.

The only feature film made in Esperanto was *Incubus* (US 65), whose star William Shatner is familiar to TV viewers as Capt Kirk of *Star Trek*. The avowed purpose of using Esperanto dialogue was to give the movie an air of the supernatural. It is one of the few American films to have been released with English sub-titles.

The first Hindi film produced in Britain was the Cabana Film Co.'s comedy-thriller *Bhaag Re Bhaag*

(GB 78), which had its world première at Leytonstone State Cinema on 4 February 1978. Produced and directed by M. A. Qayyum, it was a cops and robbers caper set in London and Epping Forest, starring Saghir Rahi and an overweight young English lady credited only as Patsy.

The first Cantonese film produced in Britain was *Ping Pong* (GB 86), a comedy thriller starring David Yip and set in London's Chinatown.

The first feature film in Irish was Bob Quinn's *Poitín/Poteen* (Eire 78), with Cyril Cusack as a poteen maker attempting to evade the attentions of the Garda in Connemara.

The first feature film in Welsh was Tom Haydon's documentary reconstruction *The Last Tasmanian* (Aus/GB/Fr 79). The curious circumstance of a film set in Tasmania being filmed in Welsh (there were also English and French language versions) is explained by the fact that Haydon's partner in the enterprise was the Welsh anthropologist Rhys Jones.

The first Welsh language feature to go on general release was *Coming Up Roses* (GB 86), which opened at the Cannon, Cardiff on 6 March 1987 and then crossed the borders of the principality to charm the English (in a subtitled version) with its engaging story of a fleapit cinema in the valleys which staves off demolition when the projectionist (Dafydd Hywell) and usherette (Iola Gregory) turn it into a mushroom farm.

The first feature film in Gaelic was Barney Platts-Mills' *Hero* (GB 82), a medieval fable about sorcery and magic in a remote corner of the Scottish highlands.

The first feature film in Breton was Gerard Guerin's *Lo Pais* (Fr 73), starring Olivier Bousquet and Nada Stangcar, about a young man trying to make his way to Paris and finally deciding to go home to help his own people. It was premièred at the Cannes Film Festival in 1973.

The only full-length feature film made in pidgin English was *Wokabout Bilong Tonten* (Aus 73), filmed in New Guinea with Anton Sil and Taruk Wabei in the lead roles.

The first feature film in Red Indian was *Windwalker* (US 80), starring Trevor Howard, which was made entirely in the Cheyenne and Crow languages.

The first feature film in Sanskrit (the Indian classical language, no longer spoken) was *Sankaracharya* (Ind 82).

The first feature film in Frysian, a language spoken in part of North Holland, was *De Droom* (Neth 85).

The first feature film in Okinawan, the language of Okinawa in the Ryuku Is, was *Paradise View* (Jap 85).

The first feature film in Iban, the language of Sarawak, was *Bejalai* (Malaysia 87).

The first feature film in Lapp was Nils Gaup's *Ofelas* (Nor 87), starring Mikkel Gaup, Ailu Gaup and Sara Marit Gaup. A tale of Lapps resisting Tchude marauders in the Arctic North 800 years ago, it was filmed in temperatures of up to 40 below zero.

WIDE SCREEN

The first wide screen process used for a feature film was Panoramico Alberini, devised by Filoteo Alberini in 1914, which was employed by Enrico Guazzoni for a sequence of *Il Sacco di Roma* (It 23).

The first wide screen system to employ the use of an anamorphic lens—a lens that squeezes a wide image on to standard gauge film as in Cinemascope (see below)—was Henri Chrétien's Hypergonar, used by Claude Autant-Lara in making *Construire un feu* (Fr 27).

The first feature film in wide screen throughout was *Happy Days* (US 30), made in the 70 mm Fox Grandeur process.

The first wide screen system to incorporate both wide gauge film and the anamorphic lens was Camera 65, later renamed Ultra-Panavision, which was originally employed on *Raintree Country* (US 57).

Cinemascope

This was developed by the French inventor Henri Chrétien from his original anamorphic Hypergonar

Wide screen is almost as old as the movies. This wrestling match was filmed by the Lamda Co. in 1895 for showing on the Eidoloscope projector.

system of 1927. Fox bought the patent rights in 1952 and **the first Cinemascope feature film**, *The Robe* (US 53), was premièred at Grauman's Chinese Theater in Hollywood on 24 September 1953. **Britain's first Cinemascope production** was also her first wide screen feature: MGM's *Knights of the Round Table* (GB 54), with Robert Taylor and Ava Gardner.

> 'A wide screen just makes a bad film twice as bad'.—Sam Goldwyn

Cinerama

This was developed by self-taught inventor Frederick Waller of Huntington, New York, who had originated the idea as early as 1939 for an oil exhibit at the New York's Fair. His intention had been to project moving pictures all over the interior surface of the oil exhibit building, but technical difficulties persuaded him to compromise with a half-dome, using eleven 16 mm projectors to cover the vast area of screen. After the war he resumed work on the process, reducing the number of projectors to three and adopting a wide screen ratio of almost 3:1. The first production in the perfected process was *This is Cinerama* (US 52), which opened in New York on 30 September 1952 and ran for 122 weeks. **The first full-length Cinerama feature** was MGM's *The Wonderful World of the Brothers Grimm* (US 62).

The widest wide screen system ever was Raoul Grimoin-Sanson's Cinéorama, presented at the Paris Exposition of 1900. Ten synchronized projectors threw a 360° image on to a screen 330 ft (100 metres) in circumference. The audience sat on the roof of the projection booth, which was designed to simulate the basket of a giant balloon. The hand-coloured film took the audience on an aerial voyage of discovery, looking down on the great capitals of Europe. Unfortunately, the show had to be terminated after three performances, since the heat of the ten projectors constituted a fire risk. The concept of 'cinema-in-the-round' was not revived until Walt Disney introduced Circarama at the Brussels World Fair in 1958, though on a screen of more modest circumference.

SMELLIES

The first attempt at combining an appropriate odour with a film was made by S. L. Rothapfel—the celebrated showman 'Roxy'—at the Family Theater, Forest City, Pa., in 1906. Roxy dipped cotton wool in a rose essence and strung it in front of a powerful electric fan during the showing of a news film of the Pasadena Rose Bowl Game. Similar experiments were made in 1929, when Albert E. Fowler, manager of the Fenway Theater, Boston, used a pint of lilac scent tipped into the ventilating system to accompany the credits of *Lilac Time* (US 29). Synthetic orange blossom perfume was sprayed from the ceiling when *Broadway Melody* (US 29) opened on Broadway.

The first film made as a 'smellie' was a wide-screen travelogue about China, *Behind the Great Wall* (US 59), filmed in Totalscope, DeLuxe Color, stereophonic sound and the new wonder of Aromarama. Premièred at the DeMille Theater, New York, on 2 December 1959, the film was accompanied by a range of 72 smells that included incense, smoke, burning pitch, oranges, spices and a barnyard of geese. The process, devised by Charles Weiss, involved circulating the scents through the ventilating system. Unlike most novelty films, *Behind the Great Wall* had the smell of success even without the gimmicks. It won two awards when it was shown at the Brussels Film Exposition unaccompanied by Aromarama.

The first feature 'smellie' was Michael Todd Jnr's *Scent of Mystery* (US 60), a 70 mm Technicolor thriller made in Smell-O-Vision and premièred at the Cinestage, Chicago, on 12 January 1960. The scents used—ocean ozone, pipe tobacco, garlic, oil paint, wine, wood shavings, boot polish, etc.—were piped to each individual cinema seat on cue from the 'smell-track' of the film.

A less sophisticated technique was used to waft the scents of Odorama to spectators of the 'sickie smellie' *Polyester* (US 82), which starred the outsize transvestite Divine playing an all-American housewife whose life stinks. Each member of the audience was given a card numbered from one to ten. When a number was flashed on screen, the spectator scratched the card with a coin, releasing a revolting odour appropriate to whatever disgusting activity was taking place before his eyes.

THREE DIMENSIONAL FILMS

The first presentation of 3-D films before a paying audience took place at the Astor Theater, New York, on 10 June 1915. The programme consisted of three one-reelers, the first of rural scenes in the USA, the second a selection of scenes from Famous Players' *Jim, the Penman* (US 15), with John Mason and Maria Doro, and the third a travelogue of Niagara Falls. The anaglyphic process used, developed by Edwin S. Porter and W. E. Waddell, involved the use of red and green spectacles to create a single image from twin motion picture images photographed 2½ in apart. The experiment was not a success, for much the same

Gig Young throws a punch at the audience in MGM's first 3-D spectacle *Arena* (US 53). Once the novelty of being socked in the face by your favourite star had worn off, the craze for 3-D disappeared overnight. (*Kobal*)

> Alfred Hitchcock on the shortlived fad for 3-D in the early fifties: 'A nine-days' wonder—and I came in on the ninth day'.

reason that 3-D failed 40 years later. Lynde Denig wrote in *Moving Picture World*: 'Images shimmered like reflections on a lake and in its present form the method couldn't be commercial because it detracts from the plot'.

The first 3-D film in colour was *Rêve d'Opium* (Fr 21), produced by the Société Azur in the System César Parolini.

The first 3-D feature film was Nat Deverich's 5-reel melodrama *Power of Love* (US 22), starring Terry O'Neil and Barbara Bedford, premièred at the Ambassador Hotel Theater, Los Angeles, on 27 September 1922. Produced by Perfect Pictures in an anaglyphic process developed by Harry K. Fairall, it related the adventures of a young sea captain in California in the 1840s. The only other American feature in 3-D prior to *Bwana Devil* (US 52) was R. William Neill's *Mars* aka *Radio Mania* (US 22), with Grant Mitchell as an inventor who makes contact with Mars via television. It was produced in Laurens Hammond's Teleview process.

The first 3-D talkie was a De Forest Phonofilm comedy short titled *Lunacy* (US 24), which opened at the Rivoli and Rialto Theaters in New York as part of the supporting programme on 22 September 1924. The 3-D process was called Plastigram.

The first feature-length talkie in 3-D was Sante Bonaldo's *Nozze vagabonde* (It 36), starring Leda Gloria and Ermes Zacconi, which was produced by the Società Italiana Stéréocinématografica at the Cines-Caesar studios. The 3-D cameraman was Anchise Brizzi.

The first 3-D talkie in colour was an UFA short titled *Zum Greifen Nah/You Can Nearly Touch It* (Ger 37), premièred at the UFA Palast in Berlin on 27 May 1937.

The first feature-length talkie in colour and 3-D was Alexander Andreyevsky's Soyuzdetfilm production *Robinson Crusoe* (USSR 47), starring Pavel Kadochnikov as Crusoe and Y. Lyubimov as Friday. The process used, Stereokino, was the first to successfully dispense with anaglyphic spectacles. Developed by S. P. Ivanov, it employed what were known as 'radial raster stereoscreens'—a corrugated metal screen with 'raster' grooves designed to reflect the twin images separately to the left and right eye. The most difficult technical problem encountered during the production of *Robinson Crusoe* was persuading a wild cat to walk along a thin branch towards the camera. After five nights occupied with this one scene, the cameraman succeeded in getting a satisfactory shot. The effect, according to accounts, was riveting, the animal seeming to walk over the heads of the audience and disappear at the far end of the cinema.

3-D Output

During the 3-D boom that began with the low budget *Bwana Devil* (US 52), over 5000 cinemas in the USA were equipped to show 3-D movies, but the fad was shortlived. 3-D production figures were: 1952—1; 1953—27; 1954—16; 1955—1. In addition there were 3-D movies produced in Japan, Britain, Mexico, Germany and Hong Kong, but many of these (as well as some of the US productions) were released flat.

Sporadic production resumed in 1960 and since the release of the much-hyped *Comin' at Ya!* (US 81) there has been a hesitant revival. The roster to date:

September Storm (US 60) —the first Cinemascope movie in 3-D
The Mask (Can 61)
Wondrous Adventures of a Magician (Chn 62)
The Bubble aka *Fantastic Invasion of Planet Earth* (US 66)
La Marca del Hombre Lobo (Sp 69)
The Stewardesses (US 70)
The Four Dimensions of Greta (GB 72) —first British 3-D feature released as such
The Flesh and Blood Show (GB 72)
Domo Arrigato (Jap 72)
Flesh for Frankenstein (Fr/It 73)
Prison Girls (US 73)
Willie Nelson's Second Annual Fourth of July Picnic (US 74)
SOS over the Tayga (USSR 75)
Tiger Man (HK 76)
The Lollipop Girls in Hard Candy (US 76)
Ape (S.Kor 76)
Dynasty (Tai 77)
Thirteen Nuns (Tai 77)
The Porno Hostess in 3-D (It 79)
Remi (Jap 79)
The Surfer Girls (US 80)
The Capitol Hill Girls (US 80)
Love in 3-D (FRG 80)
What the Swedish Butler Saw (Swe 80)
The Magnificent Bodyguards (HK 81)
Rottweiler aka *Dogs of Hell* (US 81)

Comin' at Ya! (US 81)
Menage à Trois (Fr 82)
Parasite (US 82)
The Spooky Movie Show (US 82)
Friday the 13th Part 3 (US 82)
Treasure of the Four Crowns (Sp 82)
Abracadabra (Aus 82) – cartoon feature
Spacehunter: Adventures in the Forbidden Zone (US 83)
Laughing Laughing (Chn 83)
The Man Who Wasn't There (US 83)
Jaws 3-D (US 83)
Metalstorm (US 83)
Amityville 3-D (US 83)
Supergirls in 3-D (FRG 83)
Venus (Fr? 83)
Scoring! (US 84)
Blonde Emanuelle (Fr? 84)
Emmanuelle 4 (Fr 84)
Hyperspace (US 84)
Chain Gang (US 84)
Tales of the Third Dimension (US 84)
Hit the Road Running (US 84)
Kuftichathan (Ind 84) — Malalayam
Silent Madness aka *Omega Factor* aka *Night Killer* (US 84)
Starchaser: The Legend of Orin (US 85) – cartoon
Shira Ka Insaaf (Ind 85) —Hindi
Shaktiman (Ind 85) —Hindi

The first British 3-D films were four Stereo-Techniques' shorts directed by Raymond Spottiswoode and presented in the Tele-Cinema at the Festival of Britain in 1951: *A Solid Explanation*; *Royal River*; *The Black Swan* (ballet with Alicia Markova); *Now is the Time.*

The first British feature in 3-D was Montgomery Tully's *The Diamond*/US: *The Diamond Wizard* (GB 54), a thriller with Dennis O'Keefe and Margaret Sheridan. It was released 'flat'.

The first 3-D feature with stereophonic sound was Warner Bros' *House of Wax* (US 53). When it was premièred at the Paramount Theater, New York, with 25 speakers, the *Christian Science Monitor* was moved to deplore the 'cacophony of sound hurtling relentlessly at one from all directions'. André de Toth, director of the movie, may have been able to hear the cacophony, but was unable to see the 3-D effect, as he only had one eye.

> The old adage that the inventor is the last man to make money from his invention may often be true, but Milton L. Gunzburg stole a march on the entrepreneurs ready to reap the richest pickings from his enterprise. Inventor of the Natural Vision 3-D process used for *Bwana Devil* (US 52) etc., he secured the sole distribution rights for the Polaroid glasses necessary for viewing three-dimensional movies. Purchasing the glasses from the Polaroid Land Co. at 6c each, he sold them to theatres at 10c each. For a halcyon six months Gunzburg was distributing six million pairs a week till his contract ran out in July 1953. His $6,240,000 profit represented a better return than the box-office gross on any of the shortlived 3-D movies.

HOLOGRAPHY

The first successful demonstration of holographic film was given before the Twelfth Congress of the International Union of Technical Association Cinematographers in Moscow in 1977. The system was developed by Prof. Victor Komar of the Cinema and Photo Research Institute and gives an illusion of three-dimensional substance without the use of anaglyphic spectacles. Komar's method involved the deployment of laser beams to create a representation of objects in depth based on wave interference. If a spectator moved from one vantage position to another, he would see the object represented from a different angle, as in natural vision. The first film made in holography was a 30-second experimental subject showing a beautiful girl putting jewellery into a glass case. It could be viewed by a maximum of four spectators at a time.

NINE

MUSIC

Cinema music is almost as old as cinema. Felicien Trewey's presentation of films at the Regent Street Polytechnic in February 1896, the first before a paying audience in Britain, had a piano accompaniment described in a contemporary newspaper report as 'a trifle meagre'. It was not long before presenters began to recognize the virtue of appropriate music, though whether the quartet of saxophones engaged by the Cinématographe Lumière when it opened in the Boulevard Saint-Denis, Paris, in March 1897 was able to produce something apposite for every item on the programme is not recorded. In America, Albert E. Smith of Vitagraph recalled that the first of their productions to be shown with musical accompaniment was a news film of the burial of the victims of the sinking of the USN *Maine*, premièred at a disused opera house on Lexington Avenue, New York, in March 1898 with an orchestra playing a funeral dirge. Similarly, Henry Hopwood recorded in his book *Living Pictures* (1899) that a news film of the Albion launch disaster, screened only 30 hours after the event, was accompanied by an orchestra playing *Rocked in the Cradle of the Deep*.

The resident cinema orchestra is recorded as early as 1901, when Britain's first picture house, Mohawk's Hall, in Islington, appointed the 16-piece Fonobian Orchestra under the direction of Mr W. Neale. This remained rare, though, until the advent of the super-cinemas after 1914, which generally employed large orchestras under competent if not distinguished conductors. At the smaller houses, a single pianist would do the job, sometimes far from competent, but occasionally brilliant—Shostakovich supported himself while writing his first symphony in 1924 by playing the piano in an 'old, draughty and smelly' backstreet cinema in Leningrad. (He lost the job a year later because he stopped playing during an American comedy to roar with laughter.) Less brilliant at the keyboard, but later to achieve celebrity in another walk of life, was the pianist at the Market Street Cinema in Manchester, about the same time. She was Violet Carson, the hairnetted Ena Sharples of television's *Coronation Street*.

Picture houses that could not afford even the meagre wages of a pianist might fall back on the humble phonograph, which was adequate only if there was no intention that the music should relate to the mood of the film being shown. The manager of the first cinema in Leicester, opened in 1906, recalled that he installed a gramophone (later replaced by a mechanical organ) operated by the girl in the pay-box, but that the choice of records bore no relation to the action on the screen, their only purpose being to drown the noise of the projector.

Inappropriate music could easily destroy the enjoyment of an otherwise meritorious picture, and in the USA the usual practice was for production companies to issue 'cue sheets' of suitable mood music with screen cues, an idea inaugurated by the Edison Co. in 1910 and copied by Vitagraph the following year. The consequence of leaving the choice of music to individual accompanists could be disastrous. Paul McCartney's father Jim McCartney recalls leading a small orchestra providing the music for *The Queen of Sheba* (US 21) when it was presented in Liverpool. For the chariot race sequence they played *Thanks for the Buggy Ride* and for the tragic culmination of the picture, the death of the Queen, they chose *Horsey Keep Your Tail Up*.

The first purpose-built cinema organ (i.e. a unit organ) was designed by Robert Hope-Jones, a Liverpudlian who joined the Wurtlitzer Co. of North Tonawanda, New York, in 1910 and killed himself four years later after his employers, exasperated at the expense incurred by his constant improvements in design, had locked him out of the factory on full salary. The first Wurlitzer cinema organs were installed in theatres in 1911.

The first cinema organ in Britain was built by Jardine & Co. to the specification of organist George Tootell in 1913 and installed at the Palace Cinema in Accrington, Lancashire.

The majority of cinema organs which have survived are now in the hands of collectors or preservation societies. Some, though, have been put to practical use. One of the less probable last resting places of a cinema organ is the Chapel of St Francis in Wormwood Scrubs Prison, where the prisoners are uplifted by the strains of the Ealing ABC's Compton.

Britain's first Mighty Wurlitzer was a Model D Unit Orchestra Organ, with six units on two manuals, installed at the Picture House, Walsall, Staffs, in January 1925. Although removed in 1955, the Organ is still in use at the Congregational Church at Beer, South Devon.

The largest cinema organ in the world was the Wurlitzer installed at Radio City Music Hall, New York, in 1932. Still in use, it has 58 ranks of pipes

The mammoth 2500 pipe Christie organ at the Regal Theatre, Marble Arch, could create all the effects illustrated. It would also simulate most orchestral instruments as well as a 32-note carillon and a 25-note cathedral chime. But it was too late: the year was 1929 and already movies were being made with all the sound effects recorded on film. (*ILN*)

controlled from either or both of the twin four-manual consoles.

The largest organ ever installed in a cinema in Britain was a Christie 4/30 (30 units on four manuals), installed at the Regal (now Odeon), Marble Arch and first played by Quentin Maclean in 1928. It incorporated a piano and a carillon, the latter feature being unique.

The first film music to be specially composed for the screen was by Romolo Bacchini for the Cines productions *Malia dell'Oro* (It 06) and *Pierrot Innamorato* (It 06).

Italy was the first country whose major films were regularly supplied with an original score, a practice that did not become widespread elsewhere until the 1920s. Notable early examples were *Lo Schiavo di Cartagine* (It 10), with music by Osvaldo Brunetti, *La Legenda della Passiflora* (It 11), for which Mazzuchi composed the music, and rival scores by Walter Graziani and Colombio Aron for the two simultaneous productions of *The Last Days of Pompeii* (It 13). Pizetti's *Fire Symphony* was written to accompany the sequence in *Cabiria* (It 13) in which the young maidens are sacrificed to the fire god Moloch. Mario Costa wrote a distinctive score

for *Storia del Pierrot* (It 13) and Tosti lent prestige to *A marechiare ce sta 'na fenesta* (It 15).

The first composition for a French film was Wormser's score for Michel Carré's six-reel production of *L'Enfant prodigue* (Fr 07), the longest film made anywhere in the world at that date. It preceded by a year the score which is usually said to have been the world's first specially composed film music, written by Camille Saint-Saëns for Film d'Art's inaugural production *L'Assassinat du Duc de Guise* (Fr 08). This was an arrangement for piano, two violins, viola, cello, bass violin and harmonium. Other pioneer film composers were: Mikhail Ippolitov-Ivanov, who composed scores for *Stenka Razin* (Rus 08), Russia's first dramatic film, and for Vasili Goncharov's *Song About the Merchant Kalashnikov* (Rus 08); R. N. McAnally, whose composition, originally thought to be for the Salvation Army's *Soldiers of the Cross* (Aus 00), is now believed to have been for their similarly titled religious feature *Heroes of the Cross* (Aus 09); the Brazilian Costa Junior, composer of a score for *Paz e Amor* (Bra 10), a two-reel 'talkie' with dialogue spoken by actors behind the screen; and V. Strizhevsky, who wrote the music for *Zaporozhskaya Syetch* (Rus 11).

America and Britain trailed behind the countries mentioned above. **The first original score to accompany an American production** was composed by Walter Cleveland Simon for Sidney Olcott's *Arrah-Na-Pough* (US 11), while **the first for a full-length American feature production** was by Victor Schertzinger for *Civilization* (US 15). The same year Joseph Carl Breil became **the first American composer to receive screen credit**, for his score to accompany D. W. Griffith's *The Birth of a Nation* (US 15), but this was not a wholly original work. The 151-page score comprised excerpts from the works of a dozen famous composers, including Beethoven, Schubert, Schumann, Weber and Wagner, together with some original themes by Breil himself, notably the *Love Strain* reflecting the final love scene of the Little Colonel (Henry B. Walthall) and Elsie Stoneman (Lillian Gish).

The first composer to write music for a British film was Sir Edward German, who was paid 50 gns by W. G. Barker for 16 bars of music to accompany the Coronation scene in *Henry VIII* (GB 11). It was reported at the time that Barker 'personally supervised rehearsals of special music which he thinks important in adding to the effectiveness of the subject', which suggests that there may have been a rather more complete score than the single theme by German.

The first film music composed for a sound film was commissioned by Erich Pommer, Gaumont manager for Central and Eastern Europe, for *Les*

Heures (Fr 13) aka *Die Stunden*, a 55-minute non-acted 'visual impression' of a day—morning, noon and night. The score was recorded on disc and synchronized with the film. The name of the composer is not known.

The first sound-on-film score was Hugo Riesenfeld's music for Fritz Lang's *Siegfried* (Gerr 22), recorded on Phonofilm for its presentation at the Century Theater, New York, in 1925. This was a year earlier than the sound-on-disc Vitaphone accompaniment to Warner Bros' *Don Juan* (US 26), usually claimed as the first synchronized sound feature film.

The first film in which the music was dubbed (ie post-recorded) was *Innocents of Paris* (US 29), a Maurice Chevalier confection whose success was mainly due to the theme song *Louise*.

The first song specially composed for a motion picture was *Mother I Still Have You*, written by Louis Silvers and sung by Al Jolson in *The Jazz Singer* (US 27).

The first hit-song from a movie was 'Sonny Boy', also an Al Jolson number, from *The Singing Fool* (US 28), composed by Buddy De Sylva, Lew Brown and Ray Henderson. Within nine months of the film's release, the sales of 'Sonny Boy' records had reached 2 million and sheet music 1¼ million.

The first record of a song from a movie was *Mother o' Mine* from *The Jazz Singer* (US 27), sung by Al Jolson and released on the Brunswick label on 6 October 1927 concurrently with the film's première.

The first golden disc awarded for a record selling one million copies was presented to bandleader Glenn Miller on 10 February 1942 for *Chattanooga Choo Choo*, the hit song he and his orchestra had performed in the Fox musical *Sun Valley Serenade* (US 41).

The biggest selling record of a song from a movie is Irving Berlin's *White Christmas*, performed by Bing Crosby in *Holiday Inn* (US 42), which has sold over 30 million copies to date.

The biggest selling soundtrack album is of John Williams's symphony for *Star Wars* (US 77), which has sold over three million copies.

The first sound film with a full symphonic score was RKO's *The Bird of Paradise* (US 32), with music by Viennese composer Max Steiner. It was also the **first complete film score to be issued on disc**, released by RCA Victor as an album of 78s. Formerly producers had been unwilling to have music coming from an unidentified source, on the premise that audiences would be confused by hearing music where there was no visible orchestra. Hence, early sound films tended to confine the musical accompaniment to the front and end credits or to passages of the action where it could be clearly seen to emanate from a radio or gramophone. There is no evidence that audiences were confused, for once Steiner had established the symphonic score as integral to certain types of movie the source was never questioned. Steiner scored no less than 290 films during his seven years with RKO and 30 years with Warner Bros, including *King Kong* (US 33), *Gone with the Wind* (US 39), and his two Oscar-winning movies *New Voyager* (US 42) and *Since You Went Away* (US 44). The symphonic score fell into disfavour in the 1960s with the rise of pop and jazz accompaniments, but after a slow climb back in the 1970s reached its apogee with John Williams's Oscar-winning music for *Star Wars* (US 77).

The only time an orchestra composed entirely of strings has been used to record the musical accompaniment to a movie was for *Psycho* (US 60). Hitchcock wanted music that would help to terrify the audience and composer Bernard Herrman responded with what he described as a black-and-white sound to complement a black-and-white film of a black-and-white story. The shrieking violin strings played a significant part in making *Psycho* the film that many people remember as the most frightening they have ever seen.

The first feature-length rock concert film was Lee Robinson's *Rock 'n Roll* (Aus 59), an all-star performance from Sydney Stadium.

The first woman film composer was Jadan Bai, founder of the Sangeet Film Co. and mother of India's superstar Nargis, who made her musical debut with the score of *Talash-e-Huq* (Ind 35).

The first woman composer to write a complete score for a Hollywood feature was Elizabeth Firestone, daughter of tyre magnate Harvey S. F. Firestone, who scored the Robert Montgomery comedy *Once More, My Darling* (US 47).

The first woman to compose for a British feature was Elizabeth Lutyens, whose score accompanied the Christopher Lee–Diana Dors low-budget thriller *Penny and the Pownall Case* (GB 48).

The most successful film composer of all time—in terms of scoring the music for box-office hits—is Boston Pops resident conductor John T. Williams (1932–) who has composed the scores of seven of the eight highest earning films in history: *E.T.* (US 82), *Star Wars* (US 77), *The Empire Strikes Back* (US 80), *Jaws* (US 75), *Raiders of the Lost Ark* (US 81), *Return of the Jedi* (US 83) and *Indiana Jones and the Temple of Doom* (US 84). He has won four Oscars for Best Original Score.

Music on Set

Providing music on set to create 'mood' for the performers, a common practice during the production of silent dramas, is usually said to have originated with

The Philharmonia Orchestra recording Sir William Walton's score for *Hamlet* (GB 48) at Denham.

actors in emoting during the production of *La Vie du Christ* (Fr 06).

On occasions the practice got out of hand. Garbo was not satisfied with unadorned orchestral music and insisted on being sung to on set, it was reported in 1927. A soloist would join the studio orchestra and serenade her through a megaphone. Another demanding star caused an even greater onslaught of melody, though not entirely of her own volition. During an epic feud between Pola Negri and Gloria Swanson, whose respective egos were too great to be accommodated together in one studio, Swanson's director Allan Dwan hired a 70-strong brass band to drown the noise being made on Negri's adjacent set and persuade his opposite number to control the temperamental Polish star. In another instance the practice was itself instrumental in inflating a performer's ego to the point of affecting his career. Erich von Stroheim had commanded that whenever Anton Wawerka, who played the Emperor Franz Josef in *The Merry-Go-Round* (US 22) and in *The Wedding March* (US 28) appeared on set, the orchestra should strike up the Austrian national anthem. The custom even prevailed off set, all the Hollywood restaurants honouring Wawerka with the anthem whenever he entered their doors. The actor became so accustomed to this regal treatment that he suffered a breakdown when *The Wedding March* was completed and his imperial privileges withdrawn.

The Star as Composer

Charles Chaplin composed the score for all his films from *City Lights* (US 31) onwards. Noel Coward produced, directed, scripted and starred in *In Which We Serve* (GB 42) as well as composing the music. Less well known instances are: Robert Mitchum's composition of the music for the songs *The Ballad of Thunder Road* and *Whipporwill* in *Thunder Road* (US 58); the use of a portion of Lionel Barrymore's symphony *Tableau Russe* in *Dr Kildare's Wedding Day* (US 41); David McCallum's theme song for *Three Bites of the Apple* (US 67); teenager John Rubinstein's score for *All Together Now* (US 75, TVM) — son of legendary pianist Artur Rubinstein, he also starred; and Brazilian soccer star Pele's score for his auto-biopic *Pele* (Mex 78).

D. W. Griffith's *Judith of Bethulia* (US 14), though the star of the film, Blanche Sweet, says she has no recollection of it. In fact the idea had originated in Europe at an earlier date, pioneer woman director Alice Guy playing a gramophone on set to assist the

TEN

TITLES AND CREDITS

TITLES

The Twelve Longest Film Titles

☆ Lina Wertmüller's *Un Fatto di sangue nel commune di Siculiana fra due uomini per causa di una vedova si sospettano moventi politici. Amore · Morte · Shimmy. Lugano belle. Tarantelle. Tarallucci é vino.* (It 79). The English language title was *Revenge.*

☆ *The Persecution and Assassination of Jean-Paul Marat as Performed by the Inmates of the Asylum of Charenton under the Direction of the Marquis de Sade* (GB 66).

☆ *Les yeux ne veulent pas en tout temps se fermer ou peut-être qu'un jour Rome se permettre de choisir à son tour* (Fr/FRG 70).

☆ *Why Do I Believe You When You Tell Me That You Love Me, When I Known You've Been a Liar All Your Life* (GB 83).

☆ *La' il cielo é la terra si univano, la' le quattro stagioni si ricongiungevano la' il vento é la pioggia si incontravano* (It 72).

☆ *Mais que'es-ce que J'ai fait au Bon Dieu pour avoir une femme qui boir dans les cafés avec les hommes?* (Fr 80).

☆ *Those Magnificent Men in Their Flying Machines: or, How I Flew from London to Paris in 25 Hours and 11 Minutes* (GB 65).

☆ *Film d'amore é d'anarchia, ovvero stamattina alle 10, in via dei Fiori, nella nota casa di tolleranza* (It 72).

☆ *Izrada i otkrivanje spomenika velikom srpskom satiricaru Radoju Domanoviću kao i druge manifestacije povodom 100-godisnjice njegovog rodenja* (Yug 75).

☆ *Cafeteria or How Are You Going to Keep Her Down on the Farm after She's Seen Paris Twice* (US 73). Described as 'the short and sweet story of a girl and her 26 cows', this, the longest titled American fiction film, runs precisely one minute.

☆ *F.F.S.S. Cioé: 'Che mi hai portato a fare sopra a posillipo se non mi vuoi pui' bene?'* (It 83).

☆ *The Saga of the Viking Women and their Voyage to the Waters of the Great Sea Serpent* (US 57).

The Shortest Film Titles

These have all had one letter or digit: (an asterisk signifies a feature movie): *A* (Fr 64); *A* (It 69); *B* (It 69); *C* (It 70); *D* (It 70); *E* (Can 82)*; *F* (US 80); *G* (US 72); *G* (GB/FRG 74)*; *G* (Swe 83)*; *H* (US 60); *I* (Rom 66); *I* (Swe 66)*; *M* (Ger 31)*; *M* (US 51)*; *M* (Cz 64); *O* (GB 32); *O* (Jap 75); *P* (Neth 64); *Q* (Fr/It/Bel 74)*; *Q* (US 83)*; *V* (It 68); *V* (US 83)* TVM; *W* (US 73)*; *W* (Phi 85)*; *X* (Ger 28)*; *X* (Swe 57); *X* (US 62); *X* (Nor 87)*; *Y* (Swe 87)*; *Z* (Fr/It 68)*; *$* (US 72)*; *3* (US 56); *3* (US c. 80).

Odd Titles

Writing in *Films and Filming*, David McGillivray nominated *Betta, Betta in the Wall, Who's the Fattest Fish of All* (US 69) and *She Ee Clit Soak* (US 71) as 'the most preposterous movie titles ever conceived'. Other unusual titles include *Ojojoj* (Swe 66); *RoGoPaG* (It 63); *I-Ro-Ha-Ni-Ho-He-Yo* (Jap 60); *Ha, Ha, Hee, Hee, Hoo Hoo* (Ind 55); *Sssssss* (US 73); *Phffft* (US 54). Rather more comprehensible curiosities are *Telephone Girl, Typist Girl or Why I Became a Christian* (Ind 25); *After the Balled-Up Ball* (US 17); *In My Time Boys Didn't Use Hair Cream* (Arg 37); *The Film That Rises to the Surface of Clarified Butter* (US 68) and *How to Make Love to a Negro without getting Tired* (Can/Fr i.p. 88), but some explanation might be needed for *Egg! Egg?* (Swe 75) and *Cash? Cash!* (Bel 69). *Yes* (Hun 64) was followed by *No* (Hun 65) and the situation remained equally unclear with *Yes No Maybe Maybe Not* (GB 75), though things get less indecisive with *Certain, Very Certain, As a Matter of Fact . . . Probable* (It 70). *I Go Oh No* (Tai 84) invites the injunction *Hurry, Hurry* (Sp 81), but then the answer will probably be *I Can't . . . I Can't* (Eire 69). The response to *I Know that You Know I Know* (It 82) might be *Okay Okay* (It 83) or perhaps *Augh! Augh!* (It 80), while *I'm Married. Ha Ha* (Mex 62) might elicit something more sympathetic like *Come to My Place, I'm Living at My Girl Friend's* (Fr 81) if the problem is *Feudin', Fussin' and A-Fightin'* (US 48). If *The End of the World is our Usual Bed in a Night Full of Rain* (It 78) anyone might say *It Seemed Like a Good Idea at the Time* (Can 75), *And So It Is* (Bolivia 68). No answers were vouchsafed to the important questions *Who Created the Yoyo? Who Created the Moon Buggy?* (Phi c. 80), though another, unspoken question, met with the response *No Thanks, Coffee Makes Me Nervous* (It c. 81).

Some odd titles make more sense than first appears. *P'Tang Yang Kipperbang* (GB 83) is a recurring phrase in the film's dialogue, representing part of the codes and rituals of teenagers at school in the 1940s. A sci-fi comedy called *Recharge Grandmothers*

The longest single word in a movie title, and undoubtedly the most unpronounceable, occurs in *Schwarzhuhnbraunhuhnschwarzhuhnweiss-huhnrothuhnweiss oder Put-Putt* (FRG 67).

Exactly! (Cz 84) was about robot grandmothers who take over the running of households. *Down by Law* (US 86) was released in Italy as *Daunbailò*. No, that isn't an Italian dialect word—that's *Down by Law* spelt phonetically. Similarly, *Nocaut* (Mex 84) is not an unfamiliar word in Spanish, but simply the phonetic spelling of 'Knockout'—the picture is about boxing. Wordless titles include Warhol's well-known **** (US 67); ... (Arg 71) —the English language title was *Dot Dot Dot*; and Michael Snow's ↔ (Can 69). Rather less inventive, but eminently explicit, is *A 100% Brazilian Film* (Bra 87), which is a 100% Brazilian film. Casting about for an apt title for an animated film, Aleksander Skrocynski made an inspired choice with *An Animated Film* (Pol 84), while Netherlands producer Jos Stelling figured that if you are trying to sell a Dutch movie, you might as well call it that, so *Dutch Movie* (Neth 84) it was. *Film Without Title* (FRG 47) was the title of a Rudolph Jugert movie, but it was not apparent whether Vincenzo Ferrari's *Untitled* (It 73) had one or not. The makers of *Don't Worry, We'll Think of a Title* (US 65) evidently had trouble in doing so.

Home Town

Most of the world's big cities and many of the smaller ones have been used in movie titles. This list is confined to titles which consist only of the names of towns.

Abilene Town (US 46); *Albuquerque* (US 48); *Atlantic City* (US 44) (Can/Fr 81); *Bagdad* (US 49); *Bar-cel-ona* (Sp 87); *Baton-Rouge* (Fr 85); *Bengazi* (US 55); *Benghazi* (It 42); *Berlin* (Ger 27); *Bilbao* (Sp 78); *Birdsville* (Aus 86); *Cairo* (GB 42) (GB 63); *Calcutta* (US 47); *Canon City* (US 48); *Carson City* (US 52); *Casablanca* (US 42); *Casablanca, Casablanca* (It 85); *Cheyenne* (US 47); *Chicago* (US 27); *Coronado* (US 35); *Dallas* (US 50); *Dimboola* (Aus 79); *Dodge City* (US 39); *El Paso* (US 49); *Fort Worth* (US 51); *Guadalajara* (Mex 43); *Havre* (Fr 86); *Honolulu* (US 39); *Houston, Texas* (Fr 81); *Istanbul* (US 57) (Bel 84); *Jakarta* (US 88); *Kalamazoo* (Can 87); *Karachi* (Nor 88); *Khartoum* (GB 66); *Lahore* (Ind 53); *Laramie* (US 49); *Lisbon* (US 56); *London* (GB 26); *Madrid* (Sp 87); *Malacca* (Swe 86); *Malaga* (GB 54); *Manaos* (It/Mex/Sp 80); *Mandalay* (US 34); *Maracaibo* (US 58); *Marbella* (It 86); *Matewan* (US 87); *Miami* (US 24); *Monte Carlo* (US 26) (US 30); *Montevideo* (FRG 52) (FRG 64); *Naples and Sorrento* (It 30); *Nashville* (US 75); *New Orleans* (US 29) (US 47); *New York* (US 16) (US 27); *New York, New York* (US 77); *Palm Beach* (Aus 79); *Palm Springs* (US 36); *Paris* (US 26) (US 29); *Paris, Texas* (FRG 84); *Paris-New York* (Fr 40); *Port Arthur* (Cz 37); *Port Said* (US 48); *Prague* (Cz 85); *Quebec* (US 51); *Reno* (US 23) (US 30) (US 39); *Rimini, Rimini* (It 87); *Rio* (US 39); *Rome* (It 71); *Saigon* (US 48) (US 88); *San Antonio* (US 45); *San Francisco* (US 36) (Bel 83); *Santiago* (US 56); *Santa Fe* (US 51); *Shanghai* (US 35); *Shiraz* (Ger/Ind 28); *Sofia* (US 48); *Soweto* (GB/Nigeria 88); *Suddenly* (US 54); *Talpa* (Mex 57); *Tangier* (US 46); *Teheran* (GB 47); *Tel Aviv-Berlin* (Isr 87); *Texas City* (US 52); *Timbuctoo* (GB 33); *Timbuktu* (US 59); *Tobruk* (US 66); *Tombstone* (US 42); *Tucson* (US 49); *Tulsa* (US 49); *Union City* (US 80); *Valencia* (Ger 27); *Valparaiso, Valparaiso!* (Fr 71); *Vegas* (US 78, TVM); *Vera Cruz* (US 54); *Virginia City* (US 40); *Washington* (Iran 83); *Wetherby* (GB 85); *Wichita* (US 55); *Yuma* (US 71, TVM).

When *Men* (US 86) was playing at the Ritz Five in Philadelphia, it was reported that the usherettes had their work cut out redirecting male patrons from the other four auditoria who had mistaken the meaning of the sign over the entrance.

Date Titles

1514 (Hun 62); *1740* (Can 77); *1776* (US 06); *1776* (US 72); *1778* (Fr 78); *1789* (Fr 73); *1810* (Arg 60); *1812* (Rus 12); *1812* (Ger 23); *1812* (USSR 44); *1812* (GB 65); *1812* (Hun 73); *1814* (Fr 11); *1848* (Rom 80); *1860* (It 32); *1861* (US 11); *1866* (It 33) —English language title; *1880* (Fr 63); *1884* (GB 83); *1900* (US 72); *1900* (It/Fr/FRG 77); *1905* (USSR 52); *1907* (Rom 76); *1913* (Bul 85); *1914* (GB 15); *1914* (Ger 31); *1917* (GB 70); *1918* (Fin 55); *1918* (USSR 58) —English language title; *1918* (US 85); *1919* (Sp 83); *1919* (GB 85); *1922* (Gre 79); *1925* (Bul 76); *1929* (Cz 74) —English language title; *1929* (Fin 79); *1931* (GB 32); *1933* (Can/US 67); *1936* (It 81); *1936* (Jap 87); *1939* (Swe 88); *1941* (US 41); *1941* (US 79); *1945* (Ger 45); *1948* (Fr 48); *1958* (Nor 80); *1967* (US 67); *1968* (US 68); *1969* (US 88); *1970* (US 70); *1971* (Ven 71); *1972* (FRG 73); *1983* (GB 83); *1984* (GB 56); *1984* (GB 84); *1985* (US c. 70); *2010* (US 84); *2084* (Aus 85).

Battle Shock (Isr 87) starring Alon Abouthoul is not to be confused with *Battle Shock* (Isr 87) also starring Alon Abouthoul. Two entirely different movies, one is directed by Yossi Zomer, the other by Yoel Sharon.

Title Changes

☆ *Livingstone* (GB 25), was reissued in America in 1933 as *Stanley*. (Livingstone was British; Stanley an American.) Numerous British films have needed title changes for the USA—*Carleton Browne of the F.O.*/US: *Man in a Cocked Hat* (GB 59) and *Never Take Sweets from a Stranger*/US: *Never Take Candy from a Stranger* (GB 60) are two obvious examples, but there is only one recorded instance of a simultaneous title change *within* Britain. *This England* (GB 41), a wartime flagwaver with Emlyn Williams and Constance Cummings, was retitled *Our Heritage* for release in Scotland.

☆ In China *Great Expectations* (GB 46) was released as *Bleeding Tears of Lonely Star, Nicholas Nickleby* (GB 46) as *Hell on Earth,* and *Oliver Twist* (GB 48) as *Lost Child in Foggy City*. Olivier's *Hamlet* (GB 48) became *The Prince's Revenge.*

☆ *Peyton Place* (US 57) played in Paris as *The Pleasures of Hell*, in Munich as *Glowing Fire Under the Ashes* and in Hong Kong as *The Cold and Warmth in the Human World*. *Guys and Dolls* (US 55) was *Heavy Youths and Light Girls* in Germany, Indonesia changed *I'll Cry Tomorrow* (US 55) to *To Relieve Yourself From the Grief of Your Passions*, while Hong Kong looked for something catchier than *Not as a Stranger* (US 55) and came up with *The Heart of a Lady as Pure as a Full Moon Over the Place of Medical Salvation.*

☆ The Tokyo office of United Artists translated *Dr No* (GB 62) as *We Don't Want a Doctor*. The solecism was noticed just in time to stop the posters being printed. No such last minute rescue prevented *Eine Nacht in London* (Ger/GB 34) from being released in Britain as *One Knight in London.*

☆ *Chicago, Chicago* was not the mid-west release title of *New York, New York*, but the Spanish title of Norman Jewison's *Gaily, Gaily* (US 69).

☆ *Dracula 72* (GB 72) did not reach France until a year after its release in Britain. When it did, the title had become *Dracula 73*. Similarly *Airport '79* (US 78) became *Airport '80* on its late arrival in the UK.

☆ The working title of United Artists' *Foxes* (US 80) was *Twentieth Century Foxes* until another film company intervened.

☆ The Spanish word for *Grease* (US 78) is *grasa*, but this translates literally as 'fat'. In Spain the movie was released as *Brillantina/Brilliantine* and in Venezuela as *Vaselina/Vaseline.*

☆ The first movie version of Barrie's play *The Admirable Crichton* had its title changed to *Male and Female* (US 19) after it was discovered some exhibitors were billing it as *The Admiral Crichton*. *Flaming Love* (US 25) was released under that title in New York, but it was considered a bit strong for the hicks in the sticks; for out-of-town dates it became *Frivolous Sal.*

☆ *The American Success Co* (US 79) started out under that title without much success, so was recut and re-released in 1983 as *American Success*. American it may have been . . . Three years later the distributors tried again with another cut, this time titled simply *Success*. When that did not bring in the crowds either they just had to accept that for them *Success* meant failure.

☆ Among the odder title changes was from the explicit *North Seas Hijack* (GB 80) —which gives a clear idea of what the film is about—to the US release title *ffolkes*, which happens to be the name of the character played by Roger Moore.

☆ *Down and Out in Beverly Hills* (US 85) was released in Italy as *Up and Down Beverly Hills*—sounds similar, is dissimilar.

☆ Paramount considered 250 alternative titles for the American release of Australian smash-hit *Crocodile Dundee* (Aus 86). After rejecting them all, the distributors decided on one small change for US consumption—the first word was put in quotes, as they felt *'Crocodile' Dundee* would help to avoid the misconception that the film was about crocodiles.

Particular key words tend to recur in film titles, according to the spirit of the age. In the last five years the dominant words have been 'hotel' and 'dance' (or 'dancing'). Namely: *Hotel Central* (Bul 83); *Hotel New Hampshire* (US 84); *Hotel on the Island* (USSR 84); *Hotel delle Ombre* (It 85); *Hotel Particulier* (Bel 85); *Hotel New York* (US 85); *The Rosebud Beach Hotel* (US 85); *The TV and the Hotel* (Sp 85); *Hotel de France* (Fr 86); *Hotel Colonial* (US/It 87); *Bates Motel* (US 87, TVM); *Motherland Hotel* (Tur 87); *Starlight Hotel* (NZ 87); *Hotel California* (US 87); *Hotel du Paradis* (Fr/GB 87); *Roach Hotel* (GB 87, TVM); *Hotel London* (US 87); *Hotel St Pauli* (Nor 88); *Hotel Terminus* (Fr 88); *Screwball Hotel* (Can 88); *Heartbreak Hotel* (US 88). *Flashdance* (US 83); *Breakdance 2* (US 84); *Dance with a Stranger* (GB 85); *Dances Sacred and Profane* (GB 85); *Dancing in the Dark* (Can 85); *The Second Dance* (Ice 85); *That's Dancing* (US 85); *Dancing Rink* (USSR 86); *Tough Guys Don't Dance* (US 87); *Dance of the Puppets* (Bra 87); *Slam Dance* (US 87); *Square Dance* (US 87); *Dirty Dancing* (US 87); *Dancers* (US 87); *Anita—Dances of Vice* (FRG 87); *One for the Dancer* (Mex 87); *Dancing Through the Summer* (Swe 88); *Dancing in the Forest* (US 88); *Shadow Dancing* (US 88); *Sweetheart Dance* (US 88); *The Dancer* (FRG/Jap 88).

Star Titles

When a performer's name was billed above the title, that meant real stardom. But an even greater accolade of fame is for a star's name to appear *in* the title—particularly when the star is not in the movie. (Where the title is marked with an asterisk, the star did appear.) Omitted from this list are star biopics and also titles containing the names of performers like Abbott and Costello who always played a fictitious version of themselves. The first title listed, therefore, is on account of Karloff rather than the comedy duo. *Abbott and Costello Meet the Killer, Boris Karloff* (US 48)*; *Adolf and Marlene* (FRG 77)—with Margit Carstensen as Marlene Dietrich; *Bela Lugosi Meets a Brooklyn Gorilla* (US 52)*; *The Black Dragon Revenges the Death of Bruce Lee* (HK 75); *Chaplin! Who Do You Cry* (Jap 32)—porno; *Charlie Chaplin and the Kung Fu Kid in Laughing Times* (HK 81); *Charlie Chaplin Na Vitoscia* (Bul 24); *Come Back to the 5 and Dime, Jimmy Dean, Jimmy Dean* (US 82); *The Curse of Fred Astaire* (US 84); *Dear Brigitte* (US 65)*; *F comme Fairbanks* (Fr 75); *Garbo Talks* (US 86); *Gary Cooper, Who Art in Heaven* (Sp 81); *Ginger and Fred* (It 86); *The Gracie Allen Murder Case* (US 39)*; *Happy Birthday, Marilyn!* (Hun 81)— Yes, it does refer to MM; *In Like Flynn* (US 85); *Ist Eddy Polo Schuldig* (Ger 28)*; *The Kiss of Mary Pickford* (USSR 26)*—shot clandestinely without the star knowing she was in it; *The Little Valentino* (Hun 79); *The Man with Bogart's Face* (US 80); *The Semester We Loved Kim Novak* (Sp 80); *Shirley Temple se enamora* (Mex 38); *Valentino Returns* (US 86); *The Woman Who Married Clark Gable* (Ire 85).

The only film with the main title at the end instead of the beginning was Henry King's *Who Pays?* (US 16). The picture, King's first, was about a girl who has an illegitimate baby and marries another man after the father has been erroneously reported killed. The father eventually reappears. King decided it would be more appropriate to pose the question when the audience knew why it was being asked.

Meaningless or Misleading Titles

☆ *The Bible* (It 13) was not a biblical epic as its title suggested, but a 6-reel melodrama which included a riot in a theatre, a revolver fight on stage, a car chase, a motorcycle blowing up, and people falling out of trains, fighting to the death in rivers, and kidnapping children. Somewhere amongst all this activity a bible was worked into the plot. Warner's *Tracked by the Police* (US 27) was a Rin Tin Tin vehicle whose title was decided before the script was written. The completed film was certainly about tracking, but the tracker was Rin Tin Tin with never a policeman in sight from first reel to last. Edgar Ulmer's *The Black Cat* (US 34) had nothing to do with the Poe story of the same name (despite a credit to Poe) and nothing

to do with a black cat other than the fact that a cat crept in and out of a few scenes, to justify the title.

☆ *The Axe* (US 77) was released in Britain as *California Axe Massacre*, though it was set nowhere near California. *Big Hand for a Little Lady* (US 66) had its title changed in Britain to *Big Deal at Dodge City*. Whoever thought this one up had not seen the picture. It was set in Laredo. *Exiled To Shanghai* (US 37) was not about anyone being exiled and the story did not play in Shanghai, while *Roundup Time in Texas* (US 37) was about roundup time on the South African veldt and *Adventures in Iraq* (US 43) was set in Syria. *The Malibu Bikini Shop* (US 86) is about a boardwalk swimsuit store in Venice, California, not in Malibu.

☆ Dore Schary, head of production at MGM and RKO in the forties and fifties, recalled that in his early days in Hollywood at Columbia, it was customary to assign a writer a title and expect him to develop an appropriate story. His first assignment was to devise a plot for the title *Fury and the Jungle* and this was followed by *Fog, The Most Precious Thing in Life* and *Man of Steel*. The titles were deliberately kept general enough to admit of almost any plot line.

☆ *Never Say Never Again* (GB 83), the film in which Sean Connery made his reluctant comeback as James Bond, was so called because the Scottish star had said 'Never Again' after *Diamonds Are Forever* (GB 71).

☆ Gene Wilder's *Haunted Honeymoon* (US 86) is about an engaged couple staying in a spooky old house. Story ends well before the honeymoon.

☆ Rather confusingly *As You Like It* (Bul 85) is based on *Romeo and Juliet*.

☆ Audiences might be forgiven for not knowing that the difficult-to-pronounce *Rocinante* (GB 87), starring John Hurt and set against a background of the 1984 miners' strike in Britain, was actually the name of Don Quixote's horse. Or if they did know it, for failing to see the connection with a recent industrial dispute.

☆ In the early 1930s, piracy of ideas was rife in the Indian film industry and director Dhiren Ganguly was wont to evade questions about the title of his next film with a courteous 'Excuse me, Sir' before hastily switching to another topic. After a while people began asking him when *Excuse Me, Sir* was due to be released, so he decided to call his current project by that title. *Excuse Me, Sir* (Ind 31), released in Hindi and Bengali versions, was one of the most successful pre-war Indian comedies.

☆ Equally meaningless, and for not dissimilar reasons, was the title of a Warner movie starring Errol Flynn. During the thirties there was a Hollywood convention of using the wholly fictitious title of *Another Dawn* for films purportedly showing at any cinema in a film story. When Warner's ran out of ideas for something catchy to title the somewhat slender story for Flynn's next exhibition of sexual bravado, they tagged it *Another Dawn* (US 38).

> MGM's Louis B. Mayer, like many Hollywood moguls, had a deep distrust of literature. Silent star John Gilbert, an erudite man with a strong story sense, had a pet project for making a film based on John Masefield's poem *The Widow in the Bye Street*. Mayer rejected the proposal with derision. With the connivance of director Monta Bell, Gilbert got his way. Bell changed the title to *Man, Woman and Sin* (US 27) and Mayer enthusiastically endorsed the script without realizing it was the same story.

☆ Universal executives admitted that they had no idea what relevance *You Can't Cheat an Honest Man* (US 39) had on the subject matter, nor what writer-star W. C. Fields meant by this scarcely tenable aphorism.

☆ In *Her Twelve Men* (US 54), Greer Garson played a teacher in charge of a class of 13 boy pupils. The original story by Louise Baker, on which the film was based, was called *Miss Baker's Dozen*, which aptly and accurately tallied the 13 young men.

☆ *The Amorous Prawn* (GB 62) was about a general's wife who opens their official home in the Highlands to American paying guests. In America the title was changed to *The Playgirl and the War Minister*, despite the fact that there was no playgirl and no War Minister in the film—the date explains the choice, since 1962 was the height of the Profumo Affair. Similarly *Marilyn and the Senator* (US 75) had nothing to do with Marilyn Monroe and Senator Kennedy, despite its promotors' obvious intention to mislead, and the girl entangled with a senator is not even called Marilyn.

☆ *The Seagull* (Ban 79) was indeed a film based on a classic work of literature. It was not, however, a movie version of Chekhov's celebrated play but of Jack London's famous novel *The Sea Wolf.*

☆ Many people who saw and enjoyed Hitchcock's fast-moving thriller *North by Northwest* (US 59) left the cinema wondering what the title had to do with the story. Those of a literary bent may have devined that it was a reference to the character played by Cary Grant, who feigns madness. The words in the title are slightly misquoted from *Hamlet*: 'I am but mad north-northwest; when the wind is southerly, I know a hawk from a handsaw.'

☆ *Waterloo* (Aus 81) is not a reconstruction of the battle, but an Australian documentary on urban planning. On the other hand *Ran-xerox* (Fr 84), which might be taken to be an industrial film about photocopying, is in fact an erotic feature based on a lascivious French comic strip.

☆ *South of Rio* (US 49) took place well north of it and *Krakatoa, East of Java* (US 68) wasn't. Krakatoa was 200 miles *west* of Java.

The editor's personal selection of recent titles which have failed to entice him away from his fireside: *Cannibal Hookers* (US 87); *Fat Guy Goes Nutzoid* (US 87); *Girls School Screamers* (US 87); *I Was a Teenage TV Terrorist* (US 87); *Amazon Women on the Moon* (US 87); *Nymphette Goes Hollywood* (US 87); *I Was a Teenage Zombie* (US 88); *Demented Death Farm Massacre* (US 88); *Young Werewolves in Love* (US 88); *Bitchin' Sorority Babes* (US 88); *The Dirty Filthy Slime* (US 88); *Creepzoids* (US 88); *Space Sluts in the Slammer* (US 88); *Slave Girls from Beyond Infinity* (US 88); *I Was a Teenage Sex Mutant* (US 88); *Assault of the Killer Bimbos* (US 88); *Return of the Killer Tomatoes* (US 88); *Sorority Babes in the Slimeball Bowl-O-Rama* (US 88).

INTER-TITLES AND SUBTITLES

The earliest known use of inter-titles was by R. W. Paul in *Our General Servant* (GB 98), at 320 ft the longest story film then produced in Britain. Presented in four scenes, with linking inter-titles, it related how a new maid was compromised by the master of the house. **The earliest known European example** is Georges Méliès' *L'Affair Dreyfus* (Fr 99) and **the earliest American example**, Edwin S. Porter's *Uncle Tom's Cabin* (US 03). **The earliest known use of dialogue in inter-titles** occurs in Edwin S. Porter's *The Ex-Convict* (US 04).

Subtitles superimposed over action—as in foreign language films today—**were first used** in a Lubin serial *Road o' Strife* (US 15) in order to avoid interrupting the fast-paced narrative. The only other silent picture examples known are another serial, *Judex* (Fr 17), the monumental *Ben Hur* (US 25) and *Walking Back* (US 28). The reason it was not done more often appears to be the problem presented with foreign-language versions.

The silent film with the most inter-titles in relation to its length was *Every Woman's Problem* (US

> The Italian religious epic *The Old Testament* (It 22) was released in America in three versions with different inter-titles—one for Protestants, one for Roman Catholics and one for Jews. The titles were approved by the ecclesiastical committees of each denomination to 'accord with their several doctrines'.

25), starring Dorothy Davenport. Nat Levine, then sales manager with a Kansas City film exchange, bought the 2300 ft negative, with no titles, for a bargain basement $10,000. By adding 2600 ft of inter-titles he increased it to acceptable feature length and, by choosing an enticing main title, did well enough at the box office to gross four times his investment. Levine used his profit to go into production on his own account, founding the famous Poverty Row studio of Mascot Pictures. *Every Woman's Problem* was probably the only film in which the titles occupied more time than the action.

Silent films with no inter-titles—Murnau's *The Last Laugh* (Ger 25) has often been described as the first feature-length silent movie to rely solely on the action for the development of the narrative, to the exclusion of explanatory titles. Those that preceded it were: Max Reinhardt's *Eine Venzianische Nacht* (Ger 14); Alexander Tairov's *Le Mort* (Rus 15); *A Page from Life* (It 16); *Remorse* (Den 20); *The Rail* (Ger 21); *The Old Swimming Hole* (US 21); *Warning Shadows* (Ger 22); Karl Grune's *The Street* (Ger 23); Lupu Pick's *Sylvester* (Ger 23); *Lily of the Alley* (GB 23); *The Audacious Mr Squire* (GB 23).

A title at the beginning of *Bill* (Fr 23) warned the audience that the film contained no love interest and no mechanical thrills.

An American Werewolf in London (GB 81) had an end title congratulating HRH Prince Charles and Lady Diana Spencer on their wedding. Release of the film was concurrent with the happy event.

CREDITS

The first screen credits went to André Heuzé for the films he wrote for the French production company Pathé Frères from 1906.

The first person to receive screen credits in the USA was G. M. Anderson, as the leading man of the Broncho Billy westerns in 1908. As producer and author of the films, and part-owner of the Essany studio, Anderson was in a strong position to promote his own name. Generally performers in American films did not receive screen credit until 1911, when the Edison Co. and Vitagraph Co. led the way.

LOCAL GIRL NEARLY MADE GOOD
During the early thirties supporting player Dorothy Jordan was always given the star billing when her films were shown in her home town of Clarksville, Tennessee, however minor the role.

The first British film known to have included screen credits was the Gaumont Co.'s *Lady Letmere's Jewellery* (GB 08), with Maisie Ellis in the title role. The credits were pictorial, each leading character being portrayed next to a card bearing his or her name and role. It is possible that Gaumont had adopted the practice of screen credits earlier the same year when they released a film version of the Lyceum Theatre production of *Romeo and Juliet* (US 08), with Godfrey Tearle and Mary Malone. In this case the cast had been billed in the advertising for the film.

The film-maker with most screen credits was Cedric Gibbons (1893–1960), whose name appeared as art director on over 1500 films between 1917 and 1955. The feat was achieved by Gibbons' insistence on a clause in his 1924 contract with MGM to the effect that every film produced by the studio in the USA would credit him as art director. In practice the art direction for the majority of these films was in the hands of his subordinates.

Demagogic movie mogul Harry Cohn's legendary ruthlessness extended even to the credits on Columbia's releases. Ken Hall's *Smithy* (Aus/US 46), a biopic of the great Australian aviator Sir Charles Kingsford Smith, was made under contract to Columbia by the Australian production company Cinesound with an all-Australian cast and crew. The sole interest of the Hollywood studio was to use up dollar assets frozen in Australia. When Cohn saw the finished product, he ordered fictitious credits substituted for the real ones to disguise its Australian origin. Cohn was nothing if not thorough; even the acknowledgements to the Sydney Symphony Orchestra and the Royal Australian Air Force ended up on the cutting-room floor.

The first pre-credit sequence was in Ben Hecht and Charles MacArthur's *Crime Without Passion* (US 34), which opens with an extreme close-up of the barrel of a gun. The gun fires and blood drips on to the floor. The three Furies of Greek mythology ascend from the puddle of blood in flowing robes and fly over a modern metropolis inciting various crimes of passion. One cf the Furies sweeps her arm over the face of a skyscraper, shattering the window glass, which showers down until it forms the words *Crime Without Passion.*

The longest pre-credit sequence lasts for a full half-hour before the opening title of Dennis Hopper's *The Last Movie* (US 71).

The longest credit sequence lasted for 12 minutes in Sergio Leone's *Once Upon a Time in the West* (It/US 68).

WOMEN ... With One Prayer in Their HEARTS ..."GIMME"
WOMEN ... With One Word on Their LIPS ..."MEOW"
WOMEN ... With One Thought on Their MINDS ..."MEN"

METRO · GOLDWYN · MAYER Presents

Norma SHEARER
Joan CRAWFORD
Rosalind RUSSELL

SHEARER...as
a wife fighting
for her man

CRAWFORD...
as a girl who takes
what she wants

RUSSELL...
as a slandering
society she-cat

"*The* WOMEN"

with
Mary BOLAND · Paulette GODDARD
Phyllis POVAH · Joan FONTAINE
Virginia WEIDLER · Lucile WATSON

GODDARD...
as a woman who
was almost a wife

Screen Play by
Anita Loos and Jane Murfin
From the Play by CLARE BOOTH
By Arrangement with
Max Gordon Plays and Pictures Corp.

BOLAND...as a
Cowboy Romeo's
inamorata

BEAUTY PAGEANT DICTATES FASHIONS
of 1940! Hollywood's most glamorous lovelies in a stunning display
of famous Adrian's style creations for the coming year...
All in TECHNICOLOR!

Directed by George CUKOR · Produced by Hunt Stromberg

THEATRE

There were 126 other women with speaking roles in *The Women* (US 39) (see p. 93) besides the nine who got the billing.

The largest number of names credited was 457 for *Superman the Movie* (GB 78).

Unusual Credits
In *The Terror* (US 28), the novelty of sound inspired Warner's to have the credits spoken by a caped and masked Conrad Nagel. Other films in which the credits have been spoken rather than written include Orson Welles' *The Magnificent Ambersons* (US 42), Truffaut's *Fahrenheit 451* (GB 66), Tony Richardson's *Hamlet* (GB 69) and Robert Altman's *M*A*S*H* (US 70). The last named had a recurring theme of the front line field hospital's nightly film show being announed over the Tannoy. The last film to be so announced is *M*A*S*H* itself, with full credits. A film called *Episode* (Aut 35) was released with conventional credits at home, but with spoken cred-

its in Nazi Germany. In this case the reason was more sinister than a mere desire for novelty. The director of the picture, Walter Reisch, was Jewish. The credits were spoken against a musical background and when Reisch's name was reached, the music swelled to make it inaudible.

One of the only recorded examples of sung credits features in *Por que te engana tu marido/Why Does Your Husband Deceive You* (Sp '69). The vocalists are a priest and his choirboys.

Slim Carter (US 57) had novelty credits whereby the cast signed their own names on the screen.

When Broadway was a Trail (US 14) was an early feature film about star-crossed lovers in Dutch colonial New York, then New Amsterdam. The performers were introduced in period costume on the roof of a skyscraper in modern (1914) Manhattan. The end title showed them in modern dress silhouetted against a background of Broadway at Times Square.

Although performer credits have often been superimposed over the image of each performer named, only once have production credits been treated in this way. In the Douglas Fairbanks movie *When the Clouds Roll By* (US 20), the director's credit pictures him wielding his microphone, the cameraman's credit shows him grinding the camera, the scriptwriter's credit has him hunched over the typewriter and so on.

The credits for *Gettin' Back* (US 74) list five different camermen, one designated simply as 'Paul'. The mystery lenser, per *Variety*, 'split before telling anybody his last name'. *Hell's Angels Forever* (US 83), a documentary ten years in the making, credited the various directors and producers of the film with the dates of their participation.

Probably the only film which managed to spell its star's name wrong in the credits was *The Bit Part* (Aus 87), with topliner Chris Haywood billed as 'Heywood'.

In Mike Snow's curiously titled ↔ (Can 69), the credits appear in the middle of the film.

Notorious credits include two for authors. *The Taming of the Shrew* (US 28) bore the attribution 'by William Shakespeare, with additional dialogue by Sam Taylor'; while *The Black Cat* (US 34) was credited to Edgar *Allen* Poe, a misspelling of his middle name. (The fact that the film had absolutely nothing to do with Poe's story did not seem to trouble anyone.)

Fritz Lang's *Hangmen Also Die* (US 43) is probably the only film with credits distinguishing the scriptwriter who wrote the script that was used (Fritz Lang) from the scriptwriter who wrote the script that was not (Bertold Brecht). Incensed that Lang had departed so far from his intended ideas, Brecht won a court decision that allowed him a credit disassociating his script from the shooting script.

Adrian Lyne's *Fatal Attraction* (US 87) boasts one of the odder script credits with 'screenplay, James Dearden, for the screenplay based on his original screenplay'. This last was the screenplay for a 45-minute film called *Diversion* (US 79), rescripted and reshot as a full-length feature under a new title.

Escapade (US 35) ended with William Powell speaking to camera to tell the American public about his co-star, newcomer Luise Rainer, and MGM's high hopes for her Hollywood career. Miss Rainer herself then appeared and was introduced to the audience by Powell.

The role of Crystal Kingsby in *The Lady in the Lake* (US 46) is given as Ellay Mort. In fact the character never appears, because she is dead. Ellay Mort is 'elle est mort'. Story credit for *Lt Robin Crusoe USN* (US 66) went to the somewhat obscure Retlaw Yensid. Reversed it reveals the rather better known Walt Disney.

Marie-Sophie Pochat is billed as Marie-Sophie L. in Claude Lelouch's *Attention Bandits* (Fr 87). The discreet identification masks the fact that the L stands for Lelouch—the director married her immediately after the completion of the picture.

Hollywood feminism is even taking over the credits. The Best Boy on *Slam Dance* (US 87) is credited as 'Electrical Best Person'.

Diangaka (SA 65) had a credit which read 'Original African music composed by . . .' followed by a number of European names.

The sombre Australian melodrama *In Search of Anna* (Aus 78), featuring a pooch called Billy, had a closing credit which informed audiences that 'Billy eats Loyal Dog Food'. Dusan Makavejev's *The Coca Cola Kid* (Aus 85) contained an unusual testimonial in the credits: 'Catering—Kaos (Highly recommended by the whole cast and crew)'. What appears to be an Australian preoccupation with comestibles stimulated another testimonial at the end of *The Marsupials: The Howling III* (Aus 87), which has a credit to the restaurant director Philippe Mora goes to for his Eggs Benedict.

Making of *The Cotton Club* (US 85) involved so much litigation that the credits even included one for the law firm representing the successful litigants.

Night Patrol (US 84), a knockabout comedy about offbeat Los Angeles cops, had all the credits in French for some inexplicable reason.

Unique credit on a unique version of *Casablanca* (US 43) is 'Copyright Infringements by Joao Luiz Albuquerque'. Brazilian cinéaste Albuquerque recut the classic movie for a private showing at the 1987 Rio Film Festival. In the celebrated airport-scene Ingrid Bergman does not get on to the plane leaving Casablanca and comes back into the arms of Bogey.

'Diversions by Irving Schwartz' among the credits for *The Sand Pebbles* (US 66) was, apparently, in tribute to a mysterious, unknown correspondent whose letters proved a morale booster to cast and crew during trying location work in Hong Kong and Taiwan.

Other unusual credits include one for the 'Roach Wrangler' on George Romero's *Creepshow* (US 59) —the film contains a scene involving thousands of cockroaches; for the 'Technical Consultant on Vampire Bats' on *Chosen Survivors* (US 74); for 'Ant Consultant' in *Empire of the Ants* (US 77); for 'Orgy Sequence Adviser' on *Solomon and Sheba* (US 59); for the perfume worn by the leading players in *Marjorie Morningstar* (US 58); for the shoe polish brightening the cast's shoes in *Scent of Mystery* (US 60); for 'Spiritual Counsel' on *Hallelujah the Hills* (US 63); for the 'Second Second Assistant Director' on *Reform School Girls* (US 86); for the 'Assistant to the Assistant to the Unit Publicist' on *The Greek Tycoon* (US 78); and to Frederico Fellini, who was not on the picture, 'for encouragement at the right time' in *The World's Greatest Lover* (US 77). *The Killing Fields* (GB 84) displayed the enigmatic credit 'Assistant Footsteps Editor', while Gary Graver's low-budget horror pic *Trick or Treats* (US 82) credits Orson Welles as 'Magical Consultant'. 'Fangs by Dr Ludwig von Krankheit' in Polanski's *Dance of the Vampires* (GB 67) should probably be taken with a pinch of garlic salt.

Never credited—if they were it would destroy the illusion—are the actors and actresses who do the voice-overs for other performers with unsuitable voices. Dave Prowse, the giant actor who played the sinister Darth Vader in *Star Wars* (US 77) has a West-Country accent, so he was dubbed by black American actor James Earl Jones. Several of the Bond girls—Ursula Andress, Shirley Eaton, Eunice Gayson and Claudine Auger—had difficulty matching an alluring voice to their undoubted physical attributes. In each case they were dubbed by aspirant actress Nikki van der Zyl, now practising as a barrister. On *Doctor No* (GB 62) she did every female voice except Miss Moneypenny and a Chinese girl, an assignment that earned her a modest £150. Miss van der Zyl also dubbed Raquel Welch's voice in *One Million Years BC* (GB 66). Although only required to grunt in the picture, Miss Welch's middle-western accent sounded insufficiently prehistoric and Miss van der Zyl was called in to grunt the straight Neanderthal way.

ELEVEN

CENSORSHIP

The first film known to have been suppressed was taken by Lumière cameraman Francis Doublier in Moscow in the summer of 1896 and showed Prince Napoléon dancing with the 'lady of his affections', a professional dancer. The film was seized by the Russian police and destroyed.

Later the same year *Delorita's Passion Dance* (US 96) became **the first film to be banned in the USA** when it was prohibited from exhibition in Atlantic City, NJ, by order of the Mayor.

The world's first regulated film censorship was introduced under a Chicago City Council Ordinance of 4 November 1907 'prohibiting the exhibition of obscene and immoral pictures'. Effective 19 November 1907, the Ordinance required that every film be shown to the Chief of Police before it was exhibited publicly and an exhibition permit obtained. Penalty for violation was a fine of $50–100 (£10–20), each day of exhibition without a permit to be regarded as a separate offence. One of the first films to fall foul of the censorship in Chicago was a Vitagraph production of Shakespeare's *Macbeth* (US 08), banned by a zealous police lieutenant on the grounds that 'Shakespeare is art, but it's not adapted altogether for the five cent style of art'. He explained: 'The stabbing scene in the play is not predominant. But in the picture show it is the feature.'

The first country to establish a State Censorship Board was Sweden. The Statens Biografbyrå was founded on 4 September 1911 and all films released in Sweden after 1 December 1911 were required to be certified by the Board.

Censorship USA

The USA is one of four countries where the film industry has a self-regulatory censorship independent of government (the others are Britain, Germany and Japan). The following is a brief chronology of American censorship as regulated by the Motion Picture Producers of America (MPPA).

1922 The Motion Picture Producers and Distributors of America founded March under the presidency of former Postmaster General Will H. Hays in an attempt to regulate the industry from within and combat growing demands for government intervention. At this date there were already eight State Censorship Boards (Maryland, New York, Florida, Ohio, Pennsylvania, Virginia, Kansas, Massachusetts) plus 90 municipal boards of varying degrees of severity.

Roscoe 'Fatty' Arbuckle, the world's highest paid entertainer, became **the first screen star to be banned**. The announcement was made by Will H. Hays of the MPPDA on 18 April, six days after Arbuckle had been acquitted of the manslaughter of 'good time girl' Virginia Rappe. Shortly afterwards Hays drew up a list of 200 people considered morally dangerous whom it was intended to bar from the industry. Heading the list was Wallace Reid, probably the most popular male star in America prior to Fairbanks' ascendancy, whose drug habit was to finish his career before the MPPDA was able to finish it for him.

1924 The 'Hays Formula' introduced—members agreed to submit scripts in advance for comment and guidance. Few did so unless the script was known to be innocuous.

The 'Index' of forbidden books and plays was introduced.

1927 Hays' list of 'Don't's and Be Carefuls' adopted in June. Eleven 'Don'ts' include 'any licentious or suggestive nudity', 'miscegenation', 'ridicule of the clergy', 'any inference of sex perversion' and 'the illegal traffic of drugs'. 'Be Carefuls' included 'brutality and possible gruesomeness' and 'the sale of women, or of a woman selling her virtue'. Largely ineffective.

1930 First Production Code—known as 'The Hays Code'—drawn up by Martin Quigley, publisher of *Motion Picture Herald*, and Fr Daniel A. Lord of St Louis University. Introduced 31 March. No penalties for evasion.

1931 Prior submission of scripts made binding on members.

1934 Production code Administration Office established in June. 'Resolution for Uniform Interpretation' required producers to abide by Code. Penalties for evasion introduced.

First Seal of Approval granted by Hays Office to Fox's *The World Moves On* 11 July.

1943 Howard Hughes caused the first serious breach of the Code when he exhibited *The Outlaw* (US 43) without a Seal of Approval. Billy the Kid, a criminal and moral transgressor, and his girl Rio, a moral transgressor only, were able to ride off into the sunset without reaping any of the just deserts demanded by the Code. (Or by history—in reality Billy the Kid was shot.)

1954 Code seriously breached when Preminger distributed *The Moon is Blue*, a comedy about virginity, without a Seal of Approval.

1955 *The Man with the Golden Arm* awarded Seal despite explicit treatment of drug addiction.

1956 Revised Code introduced. Nudity, profanity and obscenity remained forbidden in all circumstances. Most other former prohibitions modified.

1961 *The Children's Hour* granted Seal despite theme of sexual deviation—in this case lesbianism.

1964 Sidney Lumet's *The Pawnbroker* was passed uncut with a scene showing a woman naked to the waist. This was the first time nudity had been allowed on screen since the setting up of the Production Code Administration Office 30 years earlier.

1966 The 'blue language' barrier finally crashed by *Who's Afraid of Virginia Woolf*, the Production Code Administration agreeing to give it a Seal (with audiences restricted to over 18's) because it reflected 'the tragic realism of life'.

Code revised again, with no positive prohibitions remaining. Approved films were now divided into 'general audience' and 'mature audience'.

1968 Production Code Administration defied when they refused to approve two British films which contained scenes of oral sex: Michael Winner's *I'll Never Forget Whatshisname* (GB 67) and Albert Finney's *Charlie Bubbles* (GB 68). They were released through subsidiary companies of the intending distributors which were not members of the Association. This device enabled any major distributor to circumvent the Administration and hastened its end.

Code replaced by ratings system under the Motion Picture Association of America Ratings Board, effective 1 November. Four classifications: G = General audience; M = Mature audience; R = Restricted (over 18); X = Over 21 only. M was replaced by GP (General patronage) in 1970, as 'mature' was being misinterpreted as 'X+' By 1975 R had changed to allow accompanied children under 17, the X restriction had been lowered to over 17, and GP had become PG (Parental guidance). The X rating can be self applied to obviate any requests for cuts.

1981 The last State Censorship Board—Maryland—dissolved after 65 years of activity. During its last full year of operation, the Maryland Censor Board viewed 559 movies and banned eight.

1984 A new PG-13 rating introduced 27 June to designate films which require 'special guidance' from parents for children under 13.

Censorship GB

The British Board of Film Censors (BBFC) was inaugurated by the Kinematograph Manufacturers' Association in October 1912 with powers effective from 1 January 1913. The moving spirit behind the venture was the film producer Will Barker, who was concerned at the increase in the number of films being produced 'for the smoking room', which he considered would bring the whole industry into disrepute. Together with Col A. C. Bromhead and Cecil Hepworth, two leading pioneer film-makers, he persuaded the Kinematograph Manufacturers' Association that it was up to the trade to put its own house in order, and with the approval of the Home Secretary the Board was established under the Presidency of G. A. Redford, formerly a playreader for the Lord Chamberlain.

The original classification was into 'U' (Universal) and 'A' (Adult). **The first U Certificate** was granted to the Barker production *Mary of Briarwood Dell* (GB 13) and **the first A Certificate** to the Clarendon picture *A Strong Man's Love* (GB 13), both on 1 January 1913. The A Certificate was originally advisory only. It was not until 1923 that the London County Council prohibited unaccompanied children under 16 from attending A films. Most other local authorities in England and Wales followed suit by the end of the decade, though in Scotland the A Certificate always remained advisory only.

The BBFC began its life with only two firm prohibitive rules: no film depicting the living figure of Jesus Christ and no film which contained scenes of nudity would be granted a Certificate. During the first year of operation, the Board examined 7510 films (6861 'U'; 627 'A'), of which only 22 were rejected outright. Reasons included 'indelicate or suggestive sexual situations', 'holding up a Minister of Religion to ridicule', 'excessive drunkenness' and the portrayal of 'native customs in British lands abhorrent to British ideas'. In 1917 the new Chairman, T. P. O'Connor, declared that he would not grant a Certificate to any film in which crime was the dominant feature and warned producers that no criminal was to be portrayed as a victim of social deprivation. By 1925 the following were also among the 'Don'ts': 'Women fighting with knives'; 'Animals gnawing men, women and children'; 'Insistence upon the inferiority of coloured races'; and 'Salacious wit'.

An 'H' Certificate (advisory only) was introduced in 1933 to designate horror films, and 'X' for 'Adult Only' in 1951. A revised rating system took effect in 1970 with the A Certificate reverting to advisory status, a new AA classification signifying a minimum admission age of 14, and a raising of the admission age from 16 to 18 for X films. It was found that few people understood the status of A and AA films and by the end of the seventies Britain was one of the only countries still using X for respectable adult films, often of artistic merit; elsewhere it was being used solely as a label for pornography. The current ratings system, introduced in December 1982, retained the

U for Universal, but replaced A with PG (Parental Guidance) and AA and X with a simple numerical classification of 15 and 18 respectively to denote the minimum age for admission. It also added an 18R category to classify porno and violent films only for showing in specially licensed cinemas.

The Board's function and powers have remained fundamentally unchanged since its inception, despite modification of its criteria for certification in line with changing social and moral standards. An aide-mémoire states: 'The power of censorship is in the hands of Local Authorities. The BBFC exists to act as an intermediary between Local Authorities and the film industry. Its success or failure can be measured simply in terms of the acceptability of its judgements to the majority of Local Authorities in Britain.'

Local Authorities have the power to alter the Certificate issued by the BBFC or to permit the showing of an uncertified film. They also remain the only agency with the power to refuse the right of exhibition.

Censorship was extended to home video movies in Britain in 1985. The renamed British Board of Film Classification's first annual report since the introduction of the new measure revealed that 6.4 per cent of the 652 videocassettes classified had required cuts. Half of the cuts involved scenes of violence and brutality. Others depicted drug use and criminal techniques that might be imitated.

The first cut made by censors in a soundtrack was of offensive words sung by Winnie Lightener in a 1927 Vitaphone short produced by Warner Bros.

The first film to receive an X-rating (adults only) under the British Board of Film Censors system of classification was La Vie commence demain/Life Begins Tomorrow (Fr 50), which opened in London on 9 January 1951. The reason for the X Certificate was a sequence dealing with artificial insemination. Previously the film would have had to have been either banned or cut. By the end of the permissive 1960s the number of X films had surpassed the number of A and U films combined.

The first film to receive an X-rating under the Motion Picture Association of America system of classification was Brian de Palma's anti-establishment Greetings (US 68) with Robert de Niro, which opened in New York on 15 December 1968.

The first film containing a scene of sexual intercourse to be passed fit for juvenile (accompanied) audiences in Britain was Siddhartha (US 72), starring Shashi Kapoor and Simi Garewal and based on the Hermann Hesse bestseller.

The largest number of cuts known to have been ordered by a censor to one film is 103 in respect of Faria de Almeida's Catembe (Por 64), a critical film by a Mozambique director about the then Portuguese Colony. The most cuts to a Hollywood film was 60 in the case of D. W. Griffith's Way Down East (US 20), a heart-rending Victorian melodrama which had been reducing stage audiences to tears for the previous 30 years without apparently undermining their morals. The pivot of the story concerns the waif-like heroine's (Lillian Gish) illegitimate baby and it was this to which the Pennsylvania State Censorship Board took grave exception. Scenes ordered to be cut in their entirety included the mock marriage (the heroine having been deceived), the mock honeymoon, the heroine announcing that she was with child, and all sequences relating to its birth. Indeed the baby made its first, unheralded appearance in the cut version only shortly before it expired, much to the bewilderment of Pennsylvania audiences. (The Board also insisted, for reasons undisclosed, that the title 'I can never be any man's wife' be changed to 'I can never marry any man'.)

The Japanese censor board insisted on more than 450 'blurs' before permitting the release of Bob Guccione's notorious production of Caligula (US 79).

> According to the USA's National Coalition on Television Violence, which in recent years has turned its attention to the large screen, Rambo (US 85) rates '161 brutal violent acts per hour'. The same source reveals that in Cobra (US 86), the character played by Sylvester Stallone 'kills four times as many people as the entire Miami police force in the whole of 1985'.

The most banned film is open to dispute, but a recent contender is Make Them Die Slowly (US 83), billed as 'The Most Violent Ever'. Publicity for the picture proudly proclaimed that it had been banned in 31 countries.

The country to have imposed the most outright bans, apart from Saudi Arabia, which bans all films, is Abu Dhabi with a cumulative total of some 2400. Most of the films affected were declared obscene, anti-Islamic or favourable to Jews.

The first country to abolish censorship of films was Russia under the Kerensky government in March 1917. It was formally reimposed in 1922, though in practice there had been a strong measure of control since the accession of the Bolsheviks to power. In the Stalinist era the Soviet censorship became the most rigorous in the world, to the point of nearly extinguishing the film industry in the 1950s. It probably remains so.

The brief flowering of liberty in the revolutionary Russia of 1917 had resulted in nothing more stimulating than a spate of anti-Tsarist films, most of them centring on the depraved monk Rasputin as the architect of decay. When Germany abolished censorship in December 1918, the worst fears of its upholders were confirmed by the rash of sex films that followed. Their titles in no way belied their content: *Frauen, die der Abgrund verschlingt/ Women Engulfed by the Abyss* (Ger 18), *Verlorene Töchter/Lost Daughters* (Ger 19), *Die Prostitution* (Ger 19), *Hyänen der Lust/Hyenas of Lust* (Ger 19), etc. Homosexuality (q.v.) was also treated on the screen for the first time. It is doubtful whether anything so explicitly sexual was encountered again in films until the 1960s. Censorship was restored by the National Assembly in May 1920.

No other country abolished censorship for adult audiences until 1969, when Denmark took a lead which was to be followed in the 1970s by Austria, Uruguay, Portugal and Upper Volta and in the 1980s by Panama, Argentina and Peru. Belgium is unique in never having exercised any censorship of films for adults.

RIPE FOR CENSORSHIP
The first demand for censorship in Britain came from the cheese industry in 1898, when Charles Urban released one of his scientific films taken through a microscope which revealed the bacterial activity in a piece of Stilton.

The Unkindest Cuts

The vagaries of censorship have taken many forms. Here are some of them.

☆ The State of Illinois demanded excision of the scene in *The Kid* (US 20) in which Jackie Coogan smashes windows. For similar reasons the censorship board of Ohio tried to ban *Treasure Island* (US 20) altogether lest it should encourage children to piracy.

☆ *The Muppet Movie* (US 79) was cut by the New Zealand censor on grounds of gratuitous violence. The offending scene showed Fozzie Bear being menaced by a drunken sailor with a broken bottle. Sweden banned *E.T.* (US 82) for children under 11 because it was claimed the film showed parents being hostile to their offspring.

☆ 20th Century Fox was obliged to cut a shot of a Botticelli nude from its art documentary *Birth of Venus* (US 52) at the insistence of the Hays Office.

☆ The films of Libertad Lamarque, one of Argentina's major stars of the thirties, were banned in Argentina when Perón came to power in 1945. The reason was that Senorita Lamarque had slapped the face of Perón's mistress Eva Duarte—Evita—on the set of *Circus Cavalcade* (Arg 43) because the aspiring actress had sat in the star's personal chair. When Eva Duarte became the nation's First Lady as Eva Perón, Libertad Lamarque had to flee into exile.

☆ *Bloody Cry* (Chn 34) was banned by the Kuomintang censors because the villain bore a certain physical resemblance to Chiang Kai-shek. Things did not improve after the revolution. By order of Mao in 1949, no Chinese government leaders were allowed to be portrayed on screen, however favourably.

☆ *Sea Dogs of Australia* (Aus 14) was a victim of historical circumstance. Premièred a week after war broke out in August 1914, it was promptly banned by order of the Australian defence authorities because scenes shot aboard HMAS *Australia* were thought to be a security risk.

☆ When the script of *Zaza* (US 39) was returned from the Hays Office, a line in which the heroine screams at the villain 'Pig! Pig! Pig! Pig! Pig!' had noted in the margin against it: 'Delete two pigs'. The Hays Office permitted the saloon queen Frenchie (Marlene Dietrich) to push money down her cleavage in *Destry Rides Again* (US 39), but insisted on the deletion of the accompanying line 'There's gold in them thar hills!'

☆ The Syrian Ministry of Information banned *Kadr* (Syr 81) on grounds that 'it is badly directed and filled with vulgar scenes which are neither edifying nor interesting, that it is cheaply sensational and lacks a coherent plot'.

☆ *La Coquille et la Clergyman* (Fr 28), the surrealist fantasy directed by Germaine Dulac, was banned by the British Board of Film Censors with the comment: 'This film is so cryptic as to be almost meaningless. If there is a meaning, it is doubtless objectionable.'

☆ *Limelight* (US 52) was banned in the USA for 20 years after its release because director–star Charles Chaplin was politically *persona non grata*. When it was eventually shown in America in 1972, it won an Oscar for the best original dramatic score—a uniquely belated Academy Award.

☆ Karate films were banned in Iraq in 1979.

☆ In 1964 the Peking Cinema Institute banned, along with *Hamlet* (GB 48), *Othello* (US/Fr 51) and *The Three Musketeers* (US 48), an educational film titled *Elementary Safety in Swimming in Rivers, Lakes and Seas.* The safety element was considered a bourgeois tendency likely to undermine revolutionary daring.

☆ No films depicting two-piece bathing suits were allowed on Malta's screens before 1964; a similar ban on bikinis applied to Malta's beaches. In that year an English tourist was charged with indecent exposure for having revealed her midriff while sunbathing, but was found not guilty. The court ruling had an immediate effect on film censorship. A large number of banned youth movies, including the whole Elvis Presley repertoire, were given the censor's seal of approval.

☆ *The Wicked Lady* (GB 45), in which Margaret Lockwood played a high-born lady highwayman, had

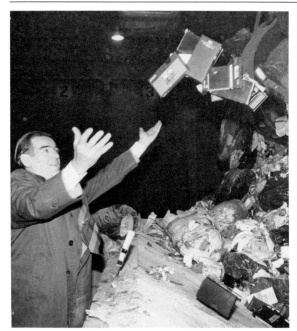

Destroying 'video nasties' in London in 1983. Most people were in favour of this form of censorship. (*Popperfoto*)

to be almost entirely reshot for the USA due to the depth of Miss Lockwood's *décolletage*.

☆ In New Zealand, two of Shakespeare's works were barred from the University of Wellington's Shakespearian Film Festival in 1985—*The Merchant of Venice* for 'anti-semitism' and *The Taming of the Shrew* for 'sexism'. Doubtless the organizers would have approved of the Act of Parliament passed by the Indian government in 1986 which prohibits the denigration of women in films. Penalty for infringement is up to two years in gaol and a fine equivalent to $200.

☆ Mickey Mouse was banned in Romania in 1935 on the grounds he was frightening to children.

☆ Peter Ustinov's *Memed, My Hawk* (GB 82), from the Turkish novel of the same name, was banned in Turkey lest it 'attract the interest of that portion of the population which is illiterate'.

☆ The name 'Pussy Galore', a character played by Honor Blackman in Bond movie *Goldfinger* (GB 64), caused problems with the American censors. United Artists were preparing to change it to 'Kitty Galore' when publicist Tom Carlile stepped in. He arranged for Prince Philip to be photographed with Honor Blackman at the première of *Goldfinger* in London and syndicated the picture worldwide under the caption 'Pussy and the Prince'. Producer Cubby Broccoli took the press clippings to the censors and was able to convince them that what was good enough for HRH was good enough for the great American public.

☆ In 1937 the Nazis succeeded in censoring a Holly-wood film—not just in Germany, but everywhere else too. James Whale, who had directed the classic anti-war drama *All Quiet On the Western Front* (US 30), made another impassioned plea for peace with *The Road Back* (US 37), also based on an Erich Maria Remarque World War I novel. The German consul in Los Angeles wrote to the 20 featured performers in the film, the leading crew members and the head of Universal Studios, warning that all future films of everyone involved would be blacked in Germany if the film went ahead. Shooting continued and Goebbels then gave Universal an ultimatum that all their films, past, present and future, would be banned in Germany unless *The Road Back* was remade in a form acceptable to the Nazis. The studio capitulated and replaced Whale with a new director, cut 21 scenes and reshot others, and released a film which should forever bring shame on those who were prepared to meet the demands of an odious and tyrannical regime.

☆ John Milius's *Red Dawn* (US 84) was passed by the Zimbabwe Board of Film Censors, but banned after the Soviet and Cuban ambassadors, who considered the film 'derogatory and offensive' to Communists, persuaded the Zimbabwe government to 'intervene'.

☆ Frank Capra's *The Miracle Woman* (US 31) was based on the life of flamboyant evangelist Aimee Semple McPhereson, whose weekly take from the faithful was regularly listed in *Variety*'s showbiz columns. In England the film was banned for 'irreverence'.

☆ Joseph Strick's *Ulysses* (GB 67), from the long banned novel by James Joyce, was only passed by the British Board of Film Censors with the deletion of the more outrageously obscene dialogue from the soundtrack. Strick then took the film to the GLC, who as the licensing body for London could ignore the Board's decision. The GLC passed the film without a single cut. It was later revealed that the sound reproduction in the GLC projection room was so faulty that none of the censors had heard a word of the dialogue.

☆ In contrast to the above, Louis Malle's sexually explicit *Les Amants* (Fr 59) passed the British Board of Film Censors only to fall foul of London Transport. The poster, which showed Rodin's beautiful sculpture of a couple in tender embrace, *Le Baisir*, was banned from buses and the Underground.

☆ *The Grapes of Wrath* (US 40) was allowed to be shown in the USSR, because the authorities considered it painted a sufficiently unattractive picture of the life of the American proletariat during the depression. It was later banned when they found that audiences were immensely impressed by the fact that the itinerant family of the story, intended to represent America's dispossessed, owned an automobile.

☆ After 1942 no photos of Gandhi were allowed on

The Soviet authorities allowed *The Grapes of Wrath* (US 40) to be released in Russia because they thought it painted a sufficiently harrowing picture of Depression-hit America. But they banned it when they found that their toiling masses were envious of jobless Americans who owned automobiles like this one.

the screen in Indian films, even as incidental props. Prior to World War II many Indian producers and directors had demonstrated their support of the outlawed Indian National Congress by using the Gandhian symbol—the spinning wheel—as decoration, or by having pictures of Gandhi and Nehru on the walls, or by introducing a few bars of a Congress anthem into the sound-track.

☆ Hatred has been a regrettably potent factor in censorship. All German films were banned in Britain after World War I (a ban imposed by the exhibitors themselves) and until recent years no German film was admitted into Israel. *All Quiet on the Western Front* (US 30), generally acknowledged as one of the greatest pacifist films, was banned in France until 1962 because of its moderate stance towards the Germans. When it was finally released it was booed by Paris audiences. Local censorship boards in the southern states of America between the wars customarily demanded cuts in films that depicted blacks in any role other than a menial one. Even after World

War II the Memphis censor cut Lena Horne sequences from MGM musicals and a scene from *The Sailor Takes a Wife* (US 46) in which a white character tips his hat to a black.

☆ On the outbreak of World War II, the neutral Irish Republic banned war scenes from newsreels.

☆ Films have sometimes been banned by different censors for diametrically opposite reasons. *Die Reiter von Deutsche Ost-Afrika/The Riders of German East Africa* (Ger 34) was banned by the Nazi government in 1939 as pacifist and by the Allied authorities in Germany in 1945 as militarist.

☆ Franklyn Barrett's *The Breaking of the Drought* (Aus 20) was an early Australian film classic, presenting a raw and undiluted view of the hardships as well as the rewards of life in the outback. The drought scenes were considered 'harmful to the Commonwealth' and the film was banned for *overseas* release.

☆ The five-member panel of the Ontario Film Review Board banned *The Toxic Avenger* (US 86) after only 40 minutes of screen time and refused to see the other 45 minutes. The panel gave as its reason the 'graphic and prolonged scenes of gratuitous violence, torture, crime, cruelty, horror, rape, degradation to humans and animals and exploitation of the blind and children, as well as indignities to the human body in an explicit manner'.

Now you see him, now you don't. Soviet censors have 'unpersoned' Stalin from Mikhail Romm's classic *Lenin in October* (USSR 37).

The deletion of 'unpersons' from Soviet encyclopaedias and the retouching of historical photographs to eliminate 'enemies of the state' like Trotsky are familiar practices in the Soviet Union. Evidence has reached the West that a similar revision of history was undertaken with classic films during the Brezhnev era. Writing in *Sight and Sound*, Alexander Sesonske reports how he showed Mikhail Romm's distinguished *Lenin in October* (USSR 37) to a class of film students in 1983. The original film, as Sesonske knew, had attributed to Stalin a leading role in the October Revolution second only to that of Lenin himself; and in nearly every scene depicting Lenin, the tyrant was shown at his right hand, dispensing wise advice and supporting him loyally in committee against Trotsky and other revisionists. The print shown to the students had not a single image of Stalin; he had been eliminated from the film entirely. Some shots had been simply deleted, others cut at the point that Stalin should have appeared. The majority, however, had been skilfully doctored by back projecting the film, then rephotographing the images after placing a large foreground figure, usually a Baltic sailor, to block out Stalin from view. Ironically the revised version of *Lenin in October* is far closer to historical truth than Romm's original.

☆ Not all censorship comes from censorship boards, nor is it always to protect the public interest. Many of the scenes in which leading lady Barbara Bates romanced with Danny Kaye in *The Inspector General* (US 49) ended up on the cutting room floor—at the command of Sylvia Fine, aka Mrs Danny Kaye.

☆ Censors have been known to demand the most alarming distortions of history. The only way Herbert Wilcox could get *Nell Gwynn* (GB 34) released in the US was by shooting a special scene for America only in which Charles II marries the orange girl.

☆ The British are peculiarly sensitive about the treatment of animals in films. Two Australian films fell foul of the British Board of Film Censors the same year. They banned *Orphan of the Wilderness* (Aus 36), a much-loved children's film about a boxing kangaroo, on the grounds that it had involved cruelty to animals. The Board was undeterred by the fact that the Australian RSPCA and the NSW Department of Education had both endorsed the picture. The BBFC was equally adamant about *Thoroughbred* (Aus 36), objecting to a scene of a stable fire. In vain the producers protested that the scene had been shot with rear projection to simulate the flames and that the horses had never been exposed to them. Animal scenes remain contentious not only in Britain but also in former outposts of the Empire. A supernatural thriller called *Calamity of Snakes* (Tai 82), in which the snakes have a bad time, was banned outright in British Columbia.

☆ *The Cow* (Iran 69) was produced under the auspices of the Iranian Ministry of Culture and Arts. On completion it was promptly banned—by the same Ministry of Culture and Arts.

☆ In 1918 the burghers of Villefranche-sur-Rhône banned *Othello* (It 14) from local exhibition because they objected to Desdemona being killed in it.

☆ There was a unique instance in American censorship of a ban on a particular individual being portrayed on the screen. It applied to gangster John Dillinger, whose heroic stature in the mass consciousness had considerably unnerved the American authorities by the time he was gunned down in 1934. For ten years the Hays Office would consider no scripts featuring the gangster, though eight Dillinger movies have been made since 1945.

☆ In 1967 the manager of Center Theater at High Point, NC, USA, was arrested for showing a Julie Andrews picture declared to be obscene. The film,

Hawaii (US 67), contained scenes of chaste but bare-bosomed native girls. Under a local ordnance, in force since the mid-19th century, any depiction of unclad breasts was an indictable offence.

☆ Probably the most liberal censorship of sexual content during the thirties was that of Naxi Germany. It is doubtful whether such erotic comedies as *Der Ammenkönig* (Ger 35) or Carl Froelich's *Wenn wir alle Engel wären/If We were All Angels* (Ger 36) would have passed any foreign censor. This may well have been because of Josef Goebbels' own sexual predelictions and he was the Chief Censor not only in name but in practice. During the twelve years of the Third Reich he personally viewed every one of the 1363 films produced, as well as all newsreels, cartoons, documentaries and other shorts, before they were passed for public showing. There was one exception to the generally permissive tone. Hitler himself had personally ordered that any woman character in a film who broke up a marriage must die before the end.

☆ There is at least one attested case of a film being refused certification unless the title was changed. *Pure Shit* became *Pure S* (Aus 73).

☆ One local police chief in Sweden about the time of World War I censored all films in which china was smashed—presumably to prevent housemaids from getting the idea that the practice had the endorsement of moviemakers.

☆ A sequence in the iconoclastic *Inter Nos* (Ice 82) in which the Icelandic national anthem is presented in a rock version, escaped censorship but resulted in a special Act of Parliament making it illegal to tamper with the tune.

☆ An unusual, though probably very justified, act of censorship was the cutting of a scene in *Love and Bullets* (GB 79) in which Charles Bronson is shown constructing a lethal blowpipe from readily available items in his hotel room. The British Board of Film Censors thought that some spectators might try emulating him, with possibly fatal results.

☆ The Hindi film *Itihas* (Ind 87) only got the green light for exhibition after a scene in which a criminal is referred to by his name, Mohammed, was cut to satisfy the susceptibilities of Muslims.

☆ Thirty-one story treatments of *Shanghai Gesture* (US 41), from John Colton's play, were submitted to the Hays Office before Arnold Pressburger got the 32nd through. The price paid was changing the Shanghai brothel into a gambling hall and the name of its proprietor from Madam Goddam to Mother Gin Sling.

☆ *The Adventures of Barry McKenzie* (Aus 73)—funded by the Australian government—fell foul of the New Zealand censor, who observed that he could only pass it if one cut was made—from 'the beginning to the end'.

☆ *Dynamite* (Swe 47), from a 1938 novel about a dynamite saboteur, was held up for several months by the Swedish censors while a real dynamite saboteur was on the loose.

☆ The Mexican censor lopped more than half an hour from *Silkwood* (US 83), representing all the scenes in which Cher was depicted as a lesbian.

☆ In 1984 Syria banned *Sophie's Choice* (US 82) because it was 'anti-Arab and aroused sympathy with Jews'; *The Birth of the Beatles* (GB 79) because the distributor dealt with Israel; and *Giant* (US 56) because it topSlined Elizabeth Taylor, a supporter of the Israeli cause.

☆ In August 1913 Russia banned films showing strikes, 'the life of indentured peasants' and 'difficult forms of labour'. Mexico banned imported films that depicted Mexicans as villains in 1926. The ban was ignored by Hollywood, but the effect on exports south of the border was sufficiently serious for the Hays Office to order no more Mexican heavies in 1930. As a quid pro quo, the censors let it be tacitly understood that it would be quite acceptable for the stock foreign undesirable to be portrayed as Russian, in retaliation for Soviet restrictions on Hollywood imports. France in the twenties had an instruction written into its code 'No displeasing Mexicans, Chinese or Niggers', while Poland at this time banned 'films tending to provoke emigration agitation'. India, meanwhile, had accumulated a list of 50 prohibited subjects, including 'representation of nude statues', 'references to race suicide', 'unnecessary exhibition of female underclothing', 'bathing scenes passing the limits of propriety', 'indecorous dancing', 'vulgar accessories', 'references to controversial politics', 'unpleasant details of medical operations', and 'scenes . . . bringing into disrepute British prestige in the Empire'. The latter piece of chauvinism was matched by Mussolini in 1928. He banned all foreign war films from Italian screens because they gave insufficient credit to Italy's contribution in World War I.

☆ Indian pictures have been banned in Pakistan for over 20 years. In June 1981 it was reported from New Delhi that Pakistani customs officials had made a bonfire of 1375 Indian films which had been smuggled into the country. They are also banned in Bangladesh, with the result that plagiarists reproduce popular Indian hits shot-by-shot, line-by-line and costume-for-costume with their own casts. Two big-budget films, *Laila Manju* (Ban 79) and *Bashar Ghar* (Ban 79) were banned by the Bangladesh government in 1979 in an attempt to halt the practice.

TWELVE

AUDIENCES AND EXHIBITORS

CINEMAS

The first cinema was the Cinématographe Lumière at the Salon Indien, a former billiard hall in the Grand Café, 14 boulevard des Capucines, Paris, opened under the management of Clément Maurice on 28 December 1895. The proprietors of the show were Auguste and Louis Lumière, the pioneer cinematographers whose films made up the programme. The opening performance included *Le Mur, L'Arrivée d'un train en gare, La sortie des Usines Lumière, Le goûter de Bébé, La pêche des poissons rouges, Soldats au manège, M. Lumière et le jongleur Trewey jouant aux cartes, La rue de la République à Lyon, En mer par gros temps, L'arroseur arrosé* and *La destruction des mauvaises herbes.* Returns from the box office on the day of opening were disappointingly low, as only 35 people had ventured a franc to see the new form of entertainment. This barely covered the rent of 30 francs a day, and the owner of the Grand Café, M. Borgo, doubtless congratulated himself that he had refused Maurice's offer of 20 per cent of the receipts in lieu of rent. Later he was to come to regret his decision, when the Cinématographe Lumière became the sensation of Paris and box office receipts rose to 2500 francs a day. Most historians have assumed that the Cinématographe Lumière at the Grand Café was simply a temporary show and consequently it has usually been claimed as the first presentation of films before a paying audience (which it was not) instead of the first cinema. Although the exact date of its closure is not known, there is contemporary evidence that it was still functioning as late as 1901. The fact that it operated continuously for at least 5 years should be sufficient to justify any claim based on permanence.

The first cinema in the United States was Vitascope Hall, opened at the corner of Canal Street and Exchange Place, New Orleans on 26 June 1896. The proprietor of the 400-seat theatre was William T. Rock and his projectionist was William Reed. Most of the programme was made up of short scenic items, including the first British film to be released in America, Robert Paul's *Waves off Dover* (GB 95), but there was sometimes more compelling fare, such as *The Irish Way of Discussing*

Permanent cinemas were preceded by fairground booths. This glorious wood and canvas castle was photographed at a temporary resting place on the outskirts of Manchester in 1900.

USA and UK cinemas from 1945 (total number of screens)

	USA	UK		USA	UK
1945	20,457	4723	1967	13,000	1736
1946	19,019	—	1968	13,190	1631
1947	18,607	—	1969	13,480	1581
1948	18,395	4706	1970	13,750	1529
1949	18,570	4800	1971	14,070	1482
1950	19,016	4584	1972	14,370	1450
1951	18,980	4581	1973	14,650	1530
1952	18,623	4568	1974	15,384	1535
1953	17,965	4542	1975	15,969	1530
1954	19,101	4509	1976	15,976	1525
1955	19,200	4483	1977	16,554	1547
1956	19,003	4391	1978	16,755	1563
1957	19,003	4194	1979	16,965	1604
1958	16,000	3996	1980	17,372	1590
1959	16,103	3414	1981	18,144	1562
1960	16,999	3034	1982	18,295	1439
1961	—	2711	1983	18,772	1327
1962	—	2421	1984	19,589	1226
1963	12,800	2181	1985	—	1226
1964	13,750	2057	1986	22,384	1237
1965	14,000	1971	1987	22,719	1250
1966	14,350	1847			

Politics (US 96) or *The Lynching Scene* (US 96). A major attraction was the movie *May Irwin Kiss* (US 96), which may be said to have introduced sex to the American screen. Admission to Vitascope Hall was 10¢ and for another 10¢ patrons were allowed to peep through the door of the projection room and see the Edison Vitascope projector. Those possessed of a liberal supply of dimes could also purchase a single frame of discarded film for the same price.

The first cinema in Britain: The earliest attempt at establishing a cinema in Britain was made by Birt Acres, whose Kineopticon opened at 2 Piccadilly Mansions at the junction of Piccadilly Circus and Shaftesbury Avenue on 21 March 1896. The manager was Mr T. C. Hayward. The opening programme (admission 6d) consisted of *Arrest of a Pickpocket*, *A Carpenter's Shop*, *A Visit to the Zoo*, *The Derby*, *Rough Seas at Dover* (original title of *Waves off Dover* mentioned above), *The Boxing Kangaroo* and *The German Emperor Reviewing his Troops*. After only a few weeks operation, Acres' cinema was gutted by fire.

The first cinema in Britain of any permanence was Mohawks' Hall, Upper Street, Islington, opened by the Royal Animated & Singing Picture Co. on 5 August 1901. The manager was Henry N. Phillips. Principal attractions of the inaugural programme were *The Rajah's Dream or The Enchanted Forest* (Fr 00), billed as 'the finest mysterious picture ever placed before the public', and a number of primitive 'talkies' featuring vocalists Lil Hawthorne, Vesta Tilley and Alec Hurley. There were also war films from South Africa and China, scenes of rush hour at the Angel, a 'graphic representation of the sensational sporting spectacle *Tally Ho* taken at the London Hippodrome', a newsreel of King Edward VII presenting medals to the South African war heroes, and scenes of a motor car explosion, Count Zeppelin's airship and 'a visit to a spiritualist'. The show was nightly at 8 p.m., with matinees on Thursdays and Saturdays, and prices of admission were 6d, 1s, 2s and 3s—considerably more than the average of 3d or 6d that most cinemas charged at the time of World War I. The Mohawk, though, was an ambitious enterprise, for while later cinemas were content to offer a piano accompaniment to the films, the Royal Animated & Singing Picture Co. engaged the 16-piece Fonobian Orchestra under the direction of Mr W. Neale. Within a few days of opening, the Mohawk advertised that it was 'besieged at every performance'. Evidently the cinema-going public was fickle, for within a few months the Mohawk had been forced to close its doors. After a period as a music hall, it was reopened as a cinema in 1908 as the Palace, changed hands ten years later to become the Blue Hall Cinema, and finally became a Gaumont before closing in 1962. The building was demolished in 1985 to make way for the Business Design Centre.

First Cinemas Worldwide

The cinemas listed below were the first to be established permanently (or intended to be permanent) in their respective countries.

ARGENTINA (1901) 467 Calle Maipu, Buenos Aires
AUSTRALIA (Dec 1896) Salon Cinématographe, 237 Pitt Street, Sydney
AUSTRIA (1903) Münstedt-Kino, the Prater, Vienna
BELGIUM (1897) Théâtre de Cinématographie, boulevard du Nord, Brussels
BRAZIL (31 Jul 1897) Salão de Novidades, 141 Rua do Ouvidor, Rio de Janeiro
BULGARIA (1908) The Modern Theatre, Sofia
CANADA (Oct 1907) The Electric Theatre, Vancouver
CHINA (1903) estab. Shanghai by Antonio Ramos
CUBA (c. 1904) Florodora, Palationo, Havana
CZECHOSLOVAKIA (1907) Blue Pike, Prague
DENMARK (7 Sept 1904) Kosmorama, Copenhagen
EGYPT (1904) Pathé Cinema, Cairo
FINLAND (1901) Kinematograph International, Helsinki
FRANCE (28 Dec 1895) Cinématographe Lumière, 14 boulevard des Capucines, Paris
GERMANY (Jul 1896) 21 Unter den Linden, Berlin
GREECE (1907) Constitution Square, Athens
HONG KONG (c. 1909) Bi Zhao Cinema
ICELAND (1906) Biógraftheater, Reykjavik
INDIA (1907) Elphinstone Cinema, Calcutta
IRAN (1905) Avenue Cherâq Gaz, Teheran
IRELAND (EIRE) (1909) Volta Cinema, Dublin (manager: James Joyce)
ITALY (c. 1898) Cinema Silenzioso, 21 Corso Vittorio Emanuele, Milan
JAPAN (Oct 1903) Denkikan, Asakusa
LEBANON (1909) Zahret Sourya, Beirut
MAURITIUS (1912) Luna Park, Port Louis
MEXICO (1901) Salon Pathé, 5 Calle de la Profesa, Mexico City
NEW ZEALAND (1910) King's Theatre, Auckland
NORWAY (1 Nov 1904) Kinematograf-Teatret, 12 Storthingsgd, Oslo
PORTUGAL (1904) Salão Ideal, Lisbon

ROMANIA (May 1909) Volta, Bucharest
SOUTH AFRICA (19 Dec 1908) New Apollo Theatre, 39 Pritchard Street, Johannesburg
SPAIN (c. 1897) Salón Maravillas, Glorieta de Bilbaô, Madrid
SWEDEN (27 Jul 1902) Arkaden Kino, Gothenburg
SWITZERLAND (11 May 1906) Grand Cinématographe Suisse, 17 Croix d'Or, Geneva
SYRIA (1916) Janak Kala'a, Damascus
THAILAND (1907) The Bioscope, Bangkok
TUNISIA (16 Oct 1908) Omnia Pathé, Tunis
TURKEY (1908) Pathé, Istanbul

UNITED KINGDOM (5 Aug 1901) Mohawk's Hall, Upper Street, Islington
UNITED STATES (26 Jun 1896) Vitascope Hall, Canal Street, New Orleans
USSR (RUSSIA) (1903) The Electric Theatre, Moscow
YUGOSLAVIA (CROATIA) (1900) Znasstveno Umjetničko Kajilšte, Zagreb

It is apparent from this list that the oft repeated claim that the first cinema in the world was the Nickelodeon opened by Harry Davis in Pittsburgh, Pa. in June 1905 is wholly without foundation.

CINEMAS WORLDWIDE

AFGHANISTAN
1939-1; 1952-9; 1972-20; 1977-45

ALBANIA
1935-10; 1939-18; 1950-14; 1960-176; 1970-189; 1979-450 (includes mobile); 1985-300

ALGERIA
1935-130; 1939-165; 1950-200; 1962-550; 1979-304; 1988-300

ARGENTINA
1923-800; 1930-1608; 1939-1021; 1950-1855; 1960-1739; 1970-1767; 1979-1794; 1988-425

AUSTRALIA
1919-760; 1925-1216; 1930-1250; 1935-1090; 1939-1371; 1945-1600; 1950-1674; 1960-1800; 1970-1349; 1978-900; 1984-813; 1988-687

AUSTRIA
1921-516; 1925-580; 1930-736; 1935-850; 1949-957; 1956-1210; 1964-1248; 1970-820; 1977-533; 1983-536; 1988-455

BANGLADESH
1976-230; 1984-420; 1988-600

BARBADOS
1981-8; 1988-4

BELGIUM
1920-811; 1930-700; 1939-1100; 1950-1550; 1960-1550; 1972-1081; 1979-545; 1983-652; 1987-435

BELIZE
1988-1

BERMUDA
1985-1

BOLIVIA
1925-16; 1935-23; 1947-60; 1954-60; 1976-41; 1984-160

BRAZIL
1930-1431; 1939-1450; 1947-1514; 1958-3113; 1968-3234; 1978-3200; 1988-1200

BULGARIA
1920-93; 1925-48; 1935-128; 1939-111; 1947-240; 1957-1400; 1967-2957; 1979-3529; 1987-3250

BURMA
1939-131; 1950-150; 1960-380; 1985-435

CAMBODIA
1933-4; 1951-15; 1975-50; 1979-0

CAMEROON
1985-70

CANADA
1922-1087; 1937-1121; 1947-1493; 1955-2085; 1960-1756; 1968-1142; 1977-1392; 1984-2004

CHILE
1930-215; 1939-243; 1947-268; 1960-450; 1972-336; 1988-145

CHINA
1925-120; 1930-185; 1935-276; 1939-275; 1949-596; 1953-770; 1958-1386; 1965-2000; 1982-2670; 1988-3100

COLOMBIA
1930-207; 1939-276; 1947-435; 1972-819; 1980-1000; 1984-700; 1988-536

COSTA RICA
1930-21; 1939-40; 1947-52; 1950-77; 1972-136; 1988-68

CUBA
1939-375; 1947-450; 1950-515; 1972-444; 1976-453; 1985-550

CYPRUS
1985-56

CZECHOSLOVAKIA
1919-490; 1925-680; 1930-1200; 1939-1254; 1945-1656; 1951-1928; 1955-2268; 1966-3584; 1972-3469; 1978-3248; 1984-2847; 1987-2801

DENMARK
1930-270; 1935-340; 1939-370; 1947-430; 1955-458; 1960-500; 1970-382; 1978-442; 1984-457; 1987-404; 1988-390

DOMINICAN REP.
1984-150; 1988-80

ECUADOR
1930-25; 1935-29; 1939-37; 1950-75; 1960-260; 1977-330; 1983-500

EGYPT
1908-11; 1925-40; 1930-60; 1935-89; 1939-118; 1946-285; 1950-226; 1960-389; 1972-384; 1979-215; 1986-160

FIRE
1945-212; 1950-345; 1955-327; 1960-290; 1970-300; 1975-230; 1980-131; 1988-153

EL SALVADOR
1988-67

ETHIOPIA
1939-33; 1950-11; 1974-31

FINLAND
1911-80; 1922-120; 1927-245; 1932-195; 1937-274; 1942-421; 1947-460; 1952-523; 1957-613; 1962-581; 1970-330; 1979-314; 1983-368; 1987-344; 1988-238

FRANCE
1920-1525; 1925-2947; 1930-3113; 1935-4000; 1939-4600; 1950-5300; 1955-5732; 1960-5821; 1965-5454; 1970-4381; 1975-4328; 1984-5031; 1988-5063

GERMANY
1912-1500; 1918-2299; 1920-3731; 1925-3878; 1930-5266; 1935-5100; 1940-6900; 1945-11,150. FRG: 1950-5930; 1955-5100; 1960-6950; 1965-5209; 1970-3634; 1975-3094; 1979-3110; 1984-3687; 1987-3242. GDR: 1960-1550; 1968-1300; 1975-880; 1980-839

GHANA
1984-80

GREECE
1915-147; 1925-138; 1930-224; 1935-122; 1939-170; 1947-300; 1955-450; 1960-1000; 1970-1034; 1979-1504; 1983-1200; 1987-508

GUAM
1986-19

GUATEMALA
1930-25; 1939-34; 1950-42; 1975-106

HONDURAS
1925-6; 1930-27; 1950-28; 1972-60; 1984-105; 1988-99

HONG KONG
1920-6; 1950-27; 1954-62; 1972-99; 1978-73; 1981-82; 1987-105

HUNGARY
1907-127; 1912-270; 1921-362; 1930-495; 1939-524; 1945-972; 1951-586; 1960-1200; 1972-981; 1979-1045, 1987-1047. (NB: Figs refer to 35 mm cinemas only.)

ICELAND
1912-2; 1930-3; 1988-31

INDIA
1910-5; 1920-148; 1924-171; 1930-309; 1936-910; 1941-1136; 1946-1700; 1950-1950; 1960-3200; 1970-4500; 1975-5363; 1979-6232; 1984-7248; 1988-8409. (NB: Excluding mobile cinemas.)

INDONESIA
1930-196; 1939-170; 1950-260; 1960-750; 1972-675; 1982-1581; 1987-2215

IRAN
1925-4; 1930-10; 1939-35; 1945-78; 1950-80; 1972-520; 1976-438; 1984-256

IRAQ
1935-7; 1939-20; 1950-71; 1972-137; 1979-87

ISRAEL
1947-216; 1960-226; 1970-257; 1975-227; 1980-230; 1984-156; 1988-160

ITALY
1907-500; 1922-2019; 1930-2405; 1935-3794; 1939-4049; 1955-9543; 1960-10,500; 1970-9680; 1979-7495; 1988-3000

IVORY COAST
1980-60

JAMAICA
1930-19; 1939-17; 1950-28; 1972-54; 1981-28; 1988-31

JAPAN
1920-600; 1925-1050; 1930-1120; 1935-1600; 1939-1749; 1947-1477; 1950-2157; 1955-7400; 1960-8477; 1963-6164; 1966-4119; 1970-3246; 1973-2974; 1975-2443; 1977-2453; 1979-2392; 1983-2239; 1986-2109

JORDAN
1950-17; 1972-34; 1988-15

KENYA
1935-8; 1950-44; 1972-28; 1979-35; 1985-50; 1988-44

KOREA
1935-45; 1939-60; 1950-116. South Korea: 1960-273; 1970-658; 1977-752; 1985-443

KUWAIT
1962-4; 1979-10; 1985-11

LEBANON
1949-48; 1960-82; 1972-170

LIBYA
1951-12; 1962-35; 1972-60; 1977-52

LUXEMBOURG
1933-26; 1939-30; 1950-39; 1955-41; 1972-52; 1975-36; 1979-17; 1988-20

MADAGASCAR
1925-5; 1933-14; 1950-24; 1974-31

MALAYSIA
1925-10; 1935-58; 1939-97; 1950-100; 1960-220; 1972-430; 1977-425; 1984-322; 1988-118

MALTA
1915-30; 1950-26; 1960-49; 1972-39; 1979-35; 1982-34; 1988-9

CINEMAS WORLDWIDE (continued)

MAURITIUS
1988-40
MEXICO
1930-615; 1935-701; 1939-823; 1946-1369;
1950-1726; 1960-2232; 1972-1850; 1981-
3020; 1988-2995
MONACO
1985-3
MOROCCO
1933-51; 1939-62; 1950-90; 1972-155; 1977-
276; 1988-c. 300
NETHERLANDS
1925-264; 1930-236; 1935-308; 1939-333;
1950-461; 1955-573; 1960-565; 1966-490;
1970-435; 1975-387; 1980-507; 1987-436
NEW ZEALAND
1925-350; 1930-443; 1935-366; 1939-576;
1945-568; 1950-570; 1960-581; 1970-260;
1975-228; 1979-200; 1984-154; 1988-117
NICARAGUA
1925-11; 1939-24; 1950-47; 1972-85; 1988-
127
NIGER
1983-10
NIGERIA
1939-11; 1950-25; 1973-112; 1979-131
NORWAY
1925-252; 1930-212; 1935-241; 1939-247;
1947-291; 1951-452; 1955-508; 1960-668;
1971-442; 1975-464; 1979-455; 1984-467;
1988-450
OMAN
1988-20
OUTER MONGOLIA
1952-50; 1977-60; 1982-59
PAKISTAN
1947-250; 1957-360; 1960-419; 1970-527;
1975-623; 1979-725; 1984-750; 1988-800
PANAMA
1988-55
PARAGUAY
1930-9; 1939-15; 1950-40; 1972-30; 1988-100
PERU
1925-60; 1930-70; 1935-110; 1939-205; 1950-
235; 1960-400; 1972-363; 1977-400; 1985-
480; 1988-400
PHILIPPINES
1935-273; 1950-450; 1960-634; 1972-704;
1977-900; 1980-1200; 1984-946; 1988-800

POLAND
1925-383; 1935-728; 1939-769; 1950-574;
1967-3694; 1977-3232; 1984-2112; 1987-
2045. (NB: Figs 1967 onwards include 16 mm
cinemas.)
PORTUGAL
1925-127; 1939-215; 1950-301; 1967-336;
1975-410; 1984-397; 1988-352
PUERTO RICO
1988-115
ROMANIA
1925-304; 1930-357; 1935-380; 1939-372;
1948-383; 1955-350; 1968-573; 1972-462;
1977-578; 1984-635; 1987-630
SAINT HELENA
1985-1
SENEGAL
1975-87; 1979-75
SEYCHELLES
1988-1
SINGAPORE
1985-57
SOUTH AFRICA
1925-380; 1935-350; 1945-465; 1950-470;
1970-521; 1979-700; 1985-507; 1988-432
SPAIN
1914-900; 1921-570; 1925-1500; 1930-2074;
1935-3252; 1939-3500; 1948-3251; 1955-
7325; 1960-6459; 1970-6627; 1974-5178;
1978-4430; 1981-4096; 1984-3663; 1986-
2640; 1988-2234
SRI LANKA
1930-24; 1939-19; 1950-82; 1960-206; 1970-
315; 1975-365; 1984-320; 1987-210
SWAZILAND
1988-5
SWEDEN
1920-600; 1930-1182; 1935-843; 1939-1907;
1947-2493; 1955-2494; 1966-1733; 1975-
1192; 1979-1210; 1984-1220; 1988-660
SWITZERLAND
1920-178; 1930-302; 1941-351; 1950-410;
1960-615; 1972-539; 1977-494; 1985-437;
1988-431
SYRIA
1925-14; 1935-26; 1950-50; 1960-70; 1972-90;
1977-70; 1983-70
TAIWAN
1960-542; 1972-668; 1986-567

TAHITI
1988-9
TANZANIA
1988-35
THAILAND
1915-3; 1925-42; 1935-68; 1939-80; 1950-118;
1960-238; 1970-501; 1977-376; 1986-577
TONGA
1985-10
TRINIDAD
1988-26
TUNISIA
1933-61; 1950-50; 1972-65; 1979-76; 1984-85
TURKEY
1925-40; 1930-104; 1939-120; 1950-275;
1960-700; 1970-790; 1979-3000 (claimed)
UK
1914-3170; 1928-3760; 1934-4305; 1939-
4901. For 1945-1987 see p. 178.
URUGUAY
1925-101; 1930-122; 1935-137; 1945-175;
1950-177; 1972-223; 1979-94; 1984-79; 1988-
85
USA
1910-9480; 1913-15,700; 1923-15,000; 1929-
23,344; 1935-15,273; 1940-19,042. For 1945-
1987 see p. 182.
USSR
1987-5257[1]
YEMEN
1985-20
YUGOSLAVIA
1921-231; 1930-397; 1939-383; 1950-736;
1960-1585; 1967-1765; 1977-1385; 1983-
1278; 1987-1345
VENEZUELA
1930-121; 1939-147; 1950-350; 1954-575;
1964-741; 1975-650; 1984-450; 1988-380
VIETNAM
1912-10; 1925-29; 1930-34; 1939-110; 1950-
80; 1960 (S. Vietnam only) -189; 1970 (S.
Vietnam only) -102; 1977-199
ZAMBIA
1988-8

[1] (NB: At the time of the revolution in 1917 the
number of Russian cinemas was 1045. No
reliable figures are available for the interim years
because the USSR counts projection points, not
cinemas proper.)

The first purpose-built cinema was the Cinéma Omnia Pathé, on the boulevard Montmartre, Paris, which opened with *Le Pendu* (Fr 06) and supporting programme on 1 December 1906. The world's first luxury cinema, and the first with a raked floor so that everyone could see above the heads in front, it was decorated in classical style with columns and Grecian friezes. The screen, measuring 20 ft by 13 ft, was one of the largest ever installed in a cinema at that time. Admission for the two-hour show ranged from 50c to 3fr—prices at other cinemas were generally in the range of 25c to 2fr.

The first purpose-built cinema in Britain was established by Joshua Duckworth of the Premier Picture Co., a former magic-lantern showman and kinetoscope proprietor, whose Central Hall, Colne, Lancs, was erected at a cost of £2000 and opened on 22 February 1907. At first Duckworth presented both films and variety, but abandoned the latter when he found that pictures alone were a sufficient

attraction. In his two-hour programme, he always liked to 'include an educational or travel subject; this I find gives dignity to the show. Good drama and pathetic subjects are always appreciated. The greatest difficulty is experienced in satisfying an audience to which you are playing week after week, with humorous and comic subjects—breaking crockery, tumbling over furniture, or running against the banana cart fails to draw a smile if not positive disapproval.' (*Kinematograph Weekly* 2.7.08). The building continued in operation as a cinema until 1924, then became a spiritualist chapel and later an engineering training workshop. It now houses the Robotics Division of Cleveland-Guest Engineering Ltd, but the exterior remains unchanged from when it was first built.

The large purpose-built cinema followed soon after. First to seat over a thousand people was the 1200 Gem in Great Yarmouth, which opened for business on 4 July 1908 under the management of

Britain's first thousand-seat cinema, the 1908 Gem at Great Yarmouth, illuminated with 1500 light bulbs. Men and women were not allowed to sit together, by council decree.

C. B. Cochran—later to become famous as a West End impresario. The Gem was an impressively ornate building in the Renaissance style with twin cupolas surmounting towers on either side of the entrance. At night it was lit by 1500 powerful electric bulbs—with that engaging disregard for the literal truth which has always characterized cinema publicity, the management dubbed it 'The Palace of 5000 Lights'. One of the odder characteristics of this pioneer venture in bringing mass entertainment to mass audiences was a condition of the licence granted to Cochran by the local authority. Men and women were not allowed to sit together, presumably for fear of what they might get up to in the dark. The Gem had another curious distinction, being one of the very few purpose-built cinemas ever to have been converted into a theatre. It still operates as the Windmill Theatre, mainly for summer shows and amateur productions. There is even the occasional film show, usually cartoons for the younger holidaymakers.

The first British cinema with a sloping floor was the Picture Palace at St Albans, Hertfordshire,

opened by Arthur Melbourne-Cooper of the Alpha Trading Co. in 1908. It was also the first to depart from standard theatre practice by charging more to sit at the back of the stalls than the front. The *Bioscope* reported: 'This arrangement was somewhat resented at first by patrons of the higher-priced seats, but when they found the specially raised floor gave them a better view than could be got from the front, they appreciated the innovation'. The idea was suggested to Melbourne-Cooper by his usherette, whom he later had the good sense to marry.

The first cinema to erect a neon sign was the West End Cinema in Coventry Street, London in 1913. It was also the first building of any kind in Britain to be emblazoned with neon and remained the only one for another ten years.

The first air-conditioned cinema was the Central Park Theater in Chicago, opened in 1917 by former nickelodeon operators Abraham and Barney Balaban and their partner Sam Katz.

The first arts cinema, specializing in minority interest films of artistic merit, was the Studio des Ursulines opened in Paris on 14 January 1926 by Laurence Myrga and Armand Talliser.

The first arts cinema in Britain was established by Elsie Cohen when she took over the Palais de Luxe in London's Great Windmill Street in 1929. The following year it was converted into the Windmill, one of the rare instances of a cinema becoming a theatre.

Social Acceptance of the Cinema

Although the cinema was primarily a proletarian form of entertainment in the USA and UK prior to World War I, elsewhere it achieved social acceptance at an earlier date. The first countries in which this was manifest were Russia and Japan, a phenomenon partly accounted for by high admission charges. In Japan seat prices of the earliest cinemas (c. 1903) were generally in a range equivalent to 6d (12¢)–3s 9d (90¢), well out of the reach of peasants or artisans. The respectability of the cinema in Russia was attested by the fact that the exclusive Hotel Metropole in Moscow saw fit to open its own cinema in 1906. The interest of the Tsar and Tsarina in films—the court photographer was kept constantly employed filming the Royal Family at leisure—did much to make movies fashionable. An American wrote to a US trade publication in 1913 that the audiences he saw in Russia were of a far better class—and the seats more expensive—than elsewhere in Europe. Cinemas were attended, he said, even by 'very high officials in uniform'.

In France the stage-bound but much admired productions of Film d'Art, with casts drawn from the illustrious Comédie-Française, catered from 1908 for the kind of audiences who looked to film as a silent record of great theatre drama. Around 1910, at a time when even minor American players would only deign

USA and UK weekly cinema attendance (millions)

	USA	UK		USA	UK
1922	40	—	1955	46	22.7
1923	43	—	1956	47	21.2
1924	46	—	1957	45	17.6
1925	46	—	1958	40	14.5
1926	50	—	1959	42	11.2
1927	57	—	1960	40	9.6
1928	65	25.2	1961	42	8.6
1929	95	—	1962	43	7.6
1930	90	—	1963	44	6.9
1931	75	—	1964	—	6.6
1932	60	—	1965	44	6.3
1933	60	—	1966	38	5.6
1934	70	18.3	1967	17.8	5.1
1935	75	—	1968	18.8	4.6
1936	88	—	1969	17.5	4.1
1937	85	—	1970	17.7	3.7
1938	85	—	1971	15.8	3.9
1939	85	—	1972	18	3.0
1940	80	—	1973	16.6	2.6
1941	85	25.2	1974	19.4	2.7
1942	85	28.7	1975	19.9	2.2
1943	85	29.6	1976	18.4	2.0
1944	85	30.3	1977	20.2	2.1
1945	90	30.5	1978	21.7	2.4
1946	90	31.4	1979	22.1	2.5
1947	90	28.1	1980	19.8	2.0
1948	90	29.1	1981	20.5	1.6
1949	87.5	27.5	1982	22.4	1.2
1950	60	26.8	1983	23.0	1.3
1951	54	26.2	1984	22.9	1.0
1952	51	25.2	1985	20.3	1.4
1953	46	24.7	1986	21.8	1.4
1954	49	24.5	1987	23.8	1.5

The wrong way to receive patrons being demonstrated at the School for Cinema Managers, Finchley, in 1951. The young man with the slicked-back hair has committed three transgressions: smoking on duty, having his jacket unbuttoned and wearing suede shoes with evening dress. (*Popperfoto*)

to appear in films under the strictest cloak of anonymity, the fact that the leading stars of the Budapest National Theatre were prepared to be seen on screen gave the Hungarian cinema its artistic imprimatur. In Germany *Der Andere* (Ger 12), directed by Max Mack with the distinguished stage actor Albert Basserman in the lead, was the first film to receive serious critical attention in the press and consequent patronage from a new type of cinema audience. The emergence of Denmark's Asta Nielsen as the first star specializing in tragic roles had a profound influence on the cinema in Scandinavia and Central Europe from 1910 onwards, demonstrating the drawing power of original screen drama and 'name' stars to middle-class audiences. As the artistic quality of motion pictures improved, new luxury cinemas opened designed to accommodate the kind of audiences at which these films were aimed. Foremost was the giant Gaumont-Palace in Paris (1911), with a seating capacity of 5000; others included Berlin's

2000-seat Alhambra Platz (1911), the Panellinion in Athens (1911), also with 2000 seats, and Copenhagen's majestic 3000-seat Palads-Teatret (1912).

In America the era of the 'super cinema' began a little later, dating from the opening of the Regent on 116th Street and 7th Avenue in February 1913 and the Vitagraph Theater and the Strand on Broadway in 1914. There has been a tendency to oversimplify American film history by suggesting that the cinema remained a primitive entertainment controlled by unlettered immigrants and largely aimed at immigrant audiences until the advent of D. W. Griffith, whereupon, it is said, the movies became an art form. In fact the influence of Griffith in making the cinema socially acceptable is probably less significant than the emergence of the feature-length film in the United States in 1912–13, a development that took place later than it did in Europe. While the simple one-reeler remained standard, the primitive nickelodeon was an appropriate showplace. The rise of the full-length drama, which was contemporary with the creation of the 'star system', broadened the appeal of the movies and stimulated the erection of theatres adequate to their presentation in an atmosphere of 'comfort and refinement'.

In Britain the feature film was also late in supplant-

THE CINEMA AS AN EDUCATIVE FORCE.

Tommy (a regular attender at cinematograph shows, during the performance of a society drama). "IS THAT THE TRUSTING HUSBAND OR THE AMOROUS LOVER?"

The cartoon weekly *Punch* has always been something of a social barometer. When *Punch* publishes a cartoon about a new trend, it is probably here to stay. Note the middle-class audience in this 1912 drawing.

Between the wars every big cinema had its own restaurant. This one, opened in 1918, was at the Stoll Picture Theatre in Newcastle upon Tyne. During the 1930s, cafés like this served a four-course luncheon with a roll and butter and coffee for as little as 1s 6d (7½d). The last cinema café, at the Odeon in Southampton, closed in May 1982.

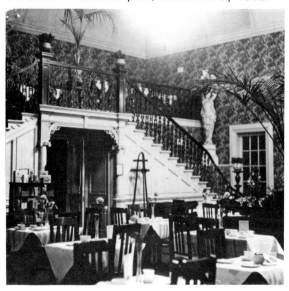

ing the modest one-reel melodramas and comedies of predominantly backstreet picture houses. Significantly the humour weekly *Punch*, generally alert to social trends, did not publish its first cartoon about cinema-going until 1912. By that date artist Charles Pears was able to show what was clearly intended to represent a sophisticated, middle-class audience. Few of the 4000 cinemas estimated to be operating in Britain by 1912, however, would have aspired to such a level of patronage unless they were of the standard of London's first luxury cinema, Cinema House in Oxford street (1910), with its oak-panelled auditorium, adjoining restaurant, and seats upholstered in a 'delicate shade of Rose du Barri velvet'. Generally speaking, middle-class cinema-going in Britain came in with World War I and was due to a combination of circumstances: the relaxation of chaperonage, the provision of better appointed and more luxurious cinemas, the feverish desire for entertainment by officers home on leave, and not least, the vastly improved standard of film-making after 1914.

The largest cinema in the world is the 5041-seat Fox Theater in Detroit. Originally opened in 1928, the Fox is now principally a live entertainment theatre but still shows movies on an occasional basis. After a downward career as the site of Motown revues in the 1960s, a Kung Fu film palace in the 1970s and a rock 'n' roll emporium in the 1980s, the magnificent Fox, its fading Taj Mahal interior still partially intact, was bought by retired

Ford employee Chuck Forbes for $1 million in 1984 and subsequently underwent an $8 million restoration.

The largest cinema ever was the Roxy, built in New York at a cost of $12 million and opened under the management of Samuel Rothapfel (after whom it was named) on 11 March 1927. With an original seating capacity of 6214, the Roxy employed a total of 300 staff, including 16 projectionists and 110 musicians. The Roxy closed on 29 March 1960.

Europe's largest-ever cinema was the Gaumont Palace, opened in Paris with a 6000 seat auditorium in 1931.

The largest cinema in Britain is the Odeon, Leicester Square, with 1983 seats.

The smallest cinema in the world to operate as a regular commercial venture was the Miramar at Colon, Cuba, which was reported in 1926 to have 25 seats.

The smallest cinema in the USA was the Silver Star Theater in Silver Star, Montana, which had a seating capacity of 26 in 1925. Silver Star, population 75, boasted two cinemas, with a total seating capacity (126) exceeding the number of citizens. Only eleven of the 15,000 cinemas operating in the US at that date had under 100 seats, of which five were in the State of Montana.

The smallest licensed cinema in Britain is the 30-seat CBA Cinema Toftwood in Dereham, Norfolk. Owned by the CBA group (ABC backwards), which arguably can claim to be Britain's smallest cinema chain—it runs one other cinema in Dereham—it has a 6 × 10 ft screen, cherry-red drapes on the walls, and a miniature cinema organ which rises from below the floor to serenade arriving patrons. Four flavours of Aldous ice cream, a Norfolk speciality, are available at 25p a cornet.

The smallest auditorium in a multiple cinema is in the six-screen Biohoellin at Reykjavik, Iceland, which seats 17.

The highest cinema attendance in the world is in China, with 21,000 million admissions in 1986 (about 57.5 million daily). Not all these are paid admissions, however, as cinema shows in public parks and in rural areas are often free. China also has the highest number of attendances per capita, with 21 p.a. The highest in the western world is 10 to 11 p.a. in Iceland.

The country with the largest number of cinemas in relation to population is San Marino, with one cinema for every 3190 inhabitants (a total of 7). In comparison the USA has one cinema for every 11,000 inhabitants, the USSR has one cinema for every 53,000 inhabitants and the UK, television dominated, has one cinema for every 45,000 inhabitants.

At the other end of the scale comes Saudi Arabia (pop. 8 million) with no cinemas, the public pres-

The Chinese are the most ardent cinemagoers in the world, averaging 21 visits a year each. Enjoying one of those visits is this crowd of patrons at Kunming, who will see the show for the equivalent of 5p. (See p. 192.)

entation of films being illegal as contrary to strict Islamic belief.

The capital city with the fewest cinemas in relation to its population is Cairo with ten for 12 million inhabitants. (Jedda has none, but movies are illegal.)

The highest number of admissions for a film per capita of population was achieved by the historical epic *Khan Asparoukh* (Bul 82), of which the first of three parts was seen by 6.5 million of Bulgaria's 8.5 million population, equal to 76.5 per cent. Total admissions for the first run of all three parts (shown separately) were 12 million.

Despite the devastation of the blitz, the Luftwaffe proved remarkably unsuccessful at destroying Britain's cinemas during World War II. Out of the 300-strong Odeon chain, the only one to suffer bomb damage too severe for rebuilding was the Canning Town Odeon. Opened in 1939, it survived just two years. Twenty years later TV succeeded where Goering had failed.

Special Amenities for Cinema Patrons

These were offered by some exhibitors from an early date. A correspondent of the *Kinematograph Weekly* reported in 1907 that it was customary for Italian cinemas to be furnished with a reading-room stocked with the current newspapers and illustrated journals for the benefit of patrons waiting for their friends.

Berlin's first super-cinema, the 2000 seat Alhambra Platz of 1911, served beer during the performance. Each seat had a tip-up tray on the back, similar to those on airliner seats, for the person behind to rest his tankard on. The first air-conditioned cinema was opened in America in 1917, but in hot countries efforts had been made to keep the patrons cool before that date. China Theatres Ltd, which operated a chain of cinemas in the Chinese Treaty Ports, provided cold towels for the audience's comfort. *Moving Picture World* recorded: 'The picture is stopped about every reel for an interval to permit him (the Chinaman) to whizz his towel across to the attendant in the aisle, who immediately wets it in icy water and whizzes it back.'

Many American cinemas have provided a crèche where mothers could leave their babies, the earliest recorded being at the Alhambra, Milwaukee in 1913. The Strand, opened in New York in April 1914, would take telephone calls for patrons, who were asked to notify the Captain of Ushers, in advance, where they were sitting. In the thirties, London's Cameo cinema allowed patrons to telephone out for nothing, besides giving them free cups of tea and free pre-stamped postcards.

A New York cinema which opened in 1925, the Knickerbocker, had a separate 'Carriage Entrance' for the kind of wealthy clientele the movies were beginning to attract. A resident chiropodist ministered to patrons of the Capitol, NY in the 1920s. Club-like amenities existed at New York's Little Carnegie Theater, which opened in 1928 with a ping-pong room, a bridge salon and a dance floor. The Fox, San Francisco, contained an art gallery with paintings personally selected in Europe by Mrs Fox.

Nothing could compare with the 6000-seat Roxy in New York, with its permanent choir of 100 voices, 50-strong ballet troupe, lavishly appointed drawing room, its own broadcasting station and a fully-equipped hospital with separate male and female wards. No less than 12,900 cases were treated in the Roxy's first year (1929–30) and it was claimed that eight lives were saved. There was also the Bilmarjac Seat Indicator System, which consisted of aisle boxes with a row of discs corresponding to the seats. When a seat was vacated, the disc lit up.

After the Roxy, anything offered elsewhere seemed tame by comparison. However, a Paramount representative who visited Australia in the 1940s was particularly impressed with the 'Crying Rooms', in which mothers nursing infants could watch the film from behind a soundproof glass screen. In addition, there would often be a similar room with glass screen for the use of private parties, a facility that the Paramount representative thought highly desirable as Australians visiting the cinema in a group were often drunk.

A novel device that failed to catch on elsewhere was the automatic ticket dispenser installed at Loew's 175th Street Theater, New York, about 1960. It would take either coins or notes and give change; if the change was paper money it came in the form of a bill rolled like a cigarette and hygienically wrapped in tissue.

In 1979 the Edmonds Theater, Seattle, made a determined pitch for the teenage market by ripping out 40 seats and installing a dance floor. Live bands played for dancing after each performance, the $3 admission covering both the picture and the rock session.

Open-air cinemas are common in Mediterranean countries, but until recently the Oriente cinema in Barcelona enjoyed the special seasonal amenity of a sliding roof which enabled audiences to sit beneath a star-studded sky in summer—and, less romantically, enabled urchins to lob dead cats over the walls.

The first cinema to present a double bill of feature films was the Glacarium in Melbourne, Australia, on 15 May 1911. The programme for the week was *The Lost Chord* (Aus 11) and *The Fall of Troy* (It 10).

During the 1950s small cinemas in Japanese villages would show up to six features on a single programme. This invariably arose from competition between two rival cinemas, one advertising a triple feature, the other outbidding with a quadruple, and so on.

The longest non-stop show took place at the Variety Arts Center in Hollywood on 29–31 May 1983, when 37 low-budget classics were shown in continuous sequence during a 50-hour 'B Movie Marathon'. Tickets cost $15 for the entire show, patrons bringing their own sleeping bags, food and drink, and what *Variety* described as 'assorted life suppport systems to get them through the gruelling early morning hours'.

The oldest cinema in Britain is the Cannon Royal, Charing Cross Road, which opened as the Cinema de Paris on 12 February 1910. In the interim the cinema became the Cameo (1926), the Cameo Revudenews (1936), the Cameo-Royal (1956), the Classic Royal (1972), the Royal (1977), the Classic Leicester Square (1979) and the Classic Royal again (1983). It acquired its present name in 1985.

The oldest building ever converted to use as a cinema was the Music Hall Cinema, Chester, which was in service as a 'common hall' as early as 1280 and as a place of entertainment by 1616. The building was converted into a legitimate theatre in 1773 and a music hall in 1855. Films were first exhibited there in 1910, but only in 1921 was it reconstructed as a permanent cinema. It closed in 1962 to undergo yet another conversion, this time an ignominious transformation into a supermarket.

The largest cinema chain in the world is the United Artists Theater Circuit of East Meadow, New York, which controls 2048 screens at 485 locations in 34 states, Puerto Rico and Hong Kong (end 1987 figs). Cineplex Odeon of Toronto, however, controls more cinema buildings, with 1644 screens at 492 locations in 20 American states, the District of Columbia and six Canadian provinces. United Artists' holding represents 9 per cent of all cinema screens in the USA. There are 91 cinema chains in America with 12 or more screens.

The oldest cinema chain is the 108-screen Wehrenberg Corp. of St Louis, Mo, which was established in 1906.

The largest cinema chain in Britain is the Cannon Group, which now includes what were formerly ABC and Classic cinemas, with 408 screens at 154 sites. (Feb 1988 figs.) This represents 30 per cent of Britain's screen total.

The largest UK cinema chain of all time was Rank's Odeon circuit, with 596 cinemas in 1950.

The highest box office gross for a cinema in any one week was the $468,173 receipts for *Crossed Swords/UK: The Prince and the Pauper* (US 78) at New York's Radio City Music Hall during the week commencing 2 April 1978.

Not a notable box-office success elsewhere, the film's remarkable drawing power on this occasion may not have been entirely unconnected with the fact that the closure of Radio City Music Hall had been announced for the following week.

> General Cinema Theatres, America's fourth largest cinema chain with 1328 screens, conducts what is literally a straw poll every presidential election. In the months running up to the vote, they issue some two million drinking straws identified with the two major candidates. People buying soft drinks are invited to take the straw of their choice and stock depletion is carefully counted.

The last silent cinema in Britain was the Electra at Royton, Lancs, run by the Progress Film Co. In contrast to their name the proprietors refused to countenance anything so new-fangled as talkies and only closed down in 1935 when the renters were unable to maintain a supply of silent films.

Elsewhere the silent cinema survived longer. According to US statistics, there were 36 silent pic-ture houses remaining in 1937, though it is possible that some of these were buildings still licensed to show films, but which had ceased to operate. Finland is said to have had some silent houses running during World War II and as late as 1952 only 50 out of the 150 cinemas in Burma were wired for sound. Thailand continued to produce silent films until the mid-1960s (see Silent Film, p. 150).

The longest continuous run of any film at one cinema was 10 years 8 months in the case of *Emmanuelle* (Fr 74), which opened at the Paramount City, Paris on 26 June 1974 and closed on 26 February 1985. In this time it was seen by 3,268,874 patrons. The film then moved to the Paramount Montmartre in the ninth *arrondissement*, where it is still running.

The longest continuous run at one cinema in Britain was 4 years 9 months for the double bill *Young Frankenstein* (US 74) and *The Rocky Picture Show* (GB 75) at the Times Centa in Baker Street, London from January 1981 until October 1985. *South Pacific* (US 58) ran at the much larger Dominion, Tottenham Court Road, for 4 years 22 weeks ending on 30 September 1962.

The shortest run of any film with a general release was that of *The Super Fight* (US 70), a feature-length movie of a mock championship fight between the then two undefeated heavyweight champions of history, Rocky Marciano and Muhammad Ali, which was released globally on 20 January 1970. In accordance with conditions laid down by the distributor, bonded guards collected all prints after a single showing and took them to be incinerated.

The longest name ever given to a cinema was conferred on a mobile picture show operated by Spanish showman José Fessi Fernandez in the Bordeaux region of France around 1902. It was called the Lentielectroplastiscromomimocoliserpentographe.

The longest name of a cinema currently in operation is the comparatively terse Cinema-I-Anjuman-I-Khairiya-I-Niswan, a 200-seat picture house in Kabul, Afghanistan. **The longest single word name** is borne by the Kannikaparameswari in Turyvegere, India.

The shortest name ever given to a cinema was borne by the K in Mattoon, Ill. in 1925.

Unusual Cinema Names

These have abounded since the Cabbage opened in Liverpool in 1914 and the Decadence in Harbin, China, the same year. A Bradford clergyman, the Rev. S. Thomas, opened The World's Window about this date and while Brussels offered High Life, Moscow promised Magic Dreams. Brno, Czechoslovakia made an honest declaration with The Illusion, while Estonia's Bi-Ba-Bo may have meant anything at all, even in Estonian. A name which definitely cloaked a secret was the 555 at Brown's Bay, New Zealand, owned by Mrs Olga Brown—it was 'a private family joke, believed to concern cards'. The first cinema in Peking to show talkies was inappropriately called the Peace and Quiet. The Yank Theatre was located far from any indigenous Yanks, in the Grand Duchy of Luxembourg, and it was unnecessary to travel to Milan to attend La Scala when there was one in the Irish village of Letterkenny, Co. Donegal. Greenland Theatre was nowhere near Greenland, but in Pala-code, India. The image of suburban gentility conjured up by Bristol's Kosy Korner Kinema was matched by Mon Repos, only the latter was located in the untamed frontier atmosphere of Russia's Baku oilfield in 1916. In India many cinemas are still called 'Talkies', such as Swastika Talkies in Bihar, Tip Top Talkies at Gopichettipalayam, Jolly Talkies in Muttom and Molly Talkies in Nedunganpara, or Baby Talkies, Thiruvarar. English Talkies in Ahmedabad shows movies in Gujarati, not English. The Roxy, now no more than a fading memory to New Yorkers, lives on in Motihari, Champaran, Bohar, and Bombay. The White Elephant and the Black Cat both belonged to WWI Glasgow, as did a Cinerama long before today's wide-screen spectacle was ever thought of. The Buffalo in Ashington, Northumberland, opened about 1912, was so named because it specialized in westerns.

The oddest names are undoubtedly those found in the United States: Amusu (Lincolntown, Ga.); Hobo (Shawneetown, Ill.); The No Name (Moreauville, La.); Tootles (St Joseph, Mo.); U-No-Us (Rensselaer Falls, NY); Muse-Us (Dayton, Ohio); Tar Heel (Plumtree, NC); Dazzleland (Philadelphia); Glory B (Miami, Okla.); C-It (Ashtabula Harbor, Ohio); The Vamp (Barnwell, SC); Fo To Sho (Ballinger, Texas); Ha Ha (Minneapolis); Hoo Hoo (Doucette, Texas); The Herring (Winton, NC); Cinderella (Detroit); OK (Simpson, Ill.); My (Indianapolis); Your (Detroit); Our (Sparta, Mich.); Why Not (Greenfield, Ind.); It (Huntingdon, W. Va.); Try-It (Buffalo, NY); Hi-Art (Lockport, NY); Good Luck (Seattle, Wash.); Sour Wine (Brazil, Ind.); Oh Gee (Edwardsville, Ill.); Happy Jack (Abilene, Texas); Uses Pictures (Butlerville, Ind.); No Home (Dalton City, Ill.); Pa and Ma's (Cobsden, Ill.); Red Apple (Omak, Wash.); Fattie's (Winchester, Texas); Silent Prayers (Sprigg, W. Va.); Za Za (Plainfield, Ind.); Zim Zim (Cumberland, W. Va.). The Norka in Akron and the Idol in Lodi were simply the town name spelt backwards. In Thibodaux, La., there were two cinemas before the war. The larger was the Grand. Its smaller rival was the Baby Grand.

The largest number of cinemas in one city was 986 in New York in 1913.

The post-war record was held by Tokyo, which had over 600 cinemas in 1958, two and a half times as many as New York.

The largest number of cinemas showing the same film in the same city at the same time was 246 in New York when the sensational sex film *Traffic in Souls* (US 13) was first released.

The first multiple cinema in Britain was the Regal Twins, Manchester, opened in 1930. It is now known as Studios 1 and 2. The present nationwide movement into multiples began with the twinning of the Odeon, Nottingham in July 1965. **The first triple** was the ABC Lothian Road in Edinburgh, opened on 29 November 1969.

A choice of films at the same cinema was not unknown even before the advent of the multiple. In 1926 the Spanish correspondent of the German film journal *Lichtbildbuehne* reported that he had visited a cinema in Cairo with twin screens in one auditorium showing two different films at the same time.

The first multiplex in the USA was the Alhambra Twin at Alhambra, California, which opened in 1923 as a single auditorium cinema and had a second auditorium added in 1939 when proprietors Edwards Theatres bought up and converted an adjacent grocery store. The original buildings were demolished in 1987 and replaced by a new eight auditoria multiplex.

The largest multiplex in the world is the 7000 seat Bruparck in Brussels, Belgium, opened in September 1988 and containing 27 auditoria. Proprietor Albert Bert declared that he could have accommodated 8500 patrons, but preferred to trade extra seating for extra comfort. The distance from the back of one seat to the back of another is four feet, obviating a need to skew the knees sideways to admit the passage of other patrons. The front row in each auditorium is the same distance from the screen as the height of the screen; in the case of the auditorium showing IMAX films on a giant screen this means 60 ft of unoccupied space.

The largest multiplex in Britain is the 11 screen Showcase opened by National Amusements at Nottingham in June 1988. It cost £6 million and seats 2600. Planning permission was granted to the Maybox Group in October 1987 for the conversion of the Apollo Theatre, Glasgow, into a 14-screen multiplex and Cannon have announced plans to erect a 17-screen multiplex off Piccadilly Circus.

The northernmost cinema in the world is the 329-seat North Cape Municipal Kino at Honningsvåg (pop. 5000), Norway, which lies on latitude 71° 1', 300 miles north of the Arctic Circle.

The southernmost cinema in the world is the Cine San Martín in Ushuaia (pop. 2200), Tierra del Fuego, Argentina, just north of latitude 55°.

Unusual Cinemas

Cinemas have been located in odd places ever since someone thought of putting one on top of Mt Portofino, Genoa, in 1907. Motion pictures entered the Arabian harem the same year when one Mehdi Russi Khan persuaded Shah Mohammed Ali to allow him to relieve the boredom of the many royal wives with a 'ladies only' cinema showing Pathé films imported from France. Meanwhile in the less exotic atmosphere of one of London's ancient churches, St Mary Axe, the Rev. Wilson Carlisle was relieving the ennui of his parishioners by introducing elevating and instructive movies into his Sunday services. Some years later, in the early 1920s, the Crawford Memorial Methodist church at 218th Street, New York, began doubling as a cinema. The Rev. Lincoln

> One of the more picturesque pieces of roguery to engage the attention of the American judiciary in recent times was a 1987 case in which the owner of the Bala cinema in Philadelphia was found guilty of conspiring to have malodorous skunk oil spread inside the rival Narberth cinema. The foul deed was never actually consummated, as the man the Bala's owner paid $100 to perpetrate the crime, one Marrandino, turned out to be a government informer.

The outdoor daylight cinema was a French idea of 1922. (*ILN*)

Caswell was worried about dwindling congregations and started up Saturday night cinema performances with full-length features plus a supporting programme of comedies and a newsreel, borrowing the films for nothing from an obliging neighbouring theatre. The following night he would preach on the moral pointed by the 'big picture'. As a further inducement the stars themselves were invited along, one notable patron being Lillian Gish.

There have been occasional misguided attempts to establish open-air cinemas in Britain, among them the Garden Cinema at Hull, which opened for business on a balmy summer's night in July 1912. Patrons sat on deck chairs in an open-sided marquee. Not surprisingly the cinema was forced to close with the onset of winter and never reopened again. Another attempt was made in 1915, when a roof-top cinema seating 150 was established by Pathé Frères on a building in Wardour Street, London. Two years later an open-air cinema was inaugurated in the middle of Trafalgar Square for the benefit of soldiers and sailors on leave.

In 1913 Secretary of State William Jennings Bryan established a cinema inside the State Department, Washington, for the leisure-time entertainment of the staff.

There is no record of cinemas in prisoner of war camps, but Allied civilians interned at Ruhleben Internment Camp during World War I enjoyed the benefit of a well-appointed picture house.

One Nazi concentration camp is known to have had a cinema. In November 1944 a barracks at Dora, a concentration camp adjacent to Buchenwald, was converted into a cinema as a special privilege for the slave labourers engaged on the assembly of Hitler's V1 and V2 rockets.

In England during World War II, Chislehurst Caves were converted into shelters at the height of the blitz, special trains being run nightly from London. Some people even moved in with their own furniture and a cave cinema was operated to keep the temporary refugees amused during the long winter evenings.

A number of cinemas have been devoted to the films of a single star. The Crystal Hall on 14th Street, New York, showed only Chaplin movies for nine years, 1914–23, with the exception of one week when they decided to vary the programme. Business was so bad they reverted to Chaplin. In Moscow in 1925 there was a cinema devoted entirely to old Clara Kimball Young movies, despite the fact that Miss Young's career was already over by this date. (She had refused to diet when the fashion for slim figures overtook America. In Russia the rotund look never went out.) There are two cinemas which show only Bond movies—the Camera cinema in Berlin and the Kolosseum Kino in Vienna. The 007 pictures are shown strictly in rotation, each one for a week three–four times a year. In Madras there is a cinema which shows only Sivaji Ganesan movies.

In May 1931 the Grand Cinema in Auckland, New Zealand, changed its name to the London and initiated a policy of showing only British films 'for the first time in the whole Empire'. It was also the last time. Modern-day Helsinki has a Soviet government-owned cinema, The Cosmos, which shows exclusively Soviet films. It runs at a prodigious loss—total box-office take in 1981 was only $83,000.

Cinemas catering to minorities have included one for lepers opened in Trinidad in 1921 and Britain's first and only cinema for negroes, established in Cardiff in 1935. A cinema for children called Smile is run by the pupils of a boarding school at Almetievsk in the Tatar Republic of the USSR. The Harmonic cinema in Frankfurt has women-only performances once a fortnight—the films shown are either made by women or specifically about women. Another cinema with a female bias is the Kineca Omori in Tokyo, which is run by and located in a supermarket. It specializes in European films and silent classics: the people most attracted by such fare in Japan are female and over 25, so supermarket shoppers are prime target audience.

The first cinema in a train was established on the Trans-Siberian Railway by a French company in 1913. Admission was 50 kopeks (12½¢ or 1s). In Britain cinema coaches on trains were introduced by the LNER on the *Flying Scotsman* between Kings Cross and York in March 1924. The premier presentation was *Ashes of Vengeance* (US 23) with Norma Talmadge. 'Talkie Trains' were inaugurated by the LNER in May 1935 and continued in service till outbreak of war.

A floating cinema was instituted in the USA on the Erie Canal between Troy and Newark, NY in 1907. Called the *Star Floating Palace*, it was a converted canal boat with a 'wainscoted inside' which plied the canal towns giving shows at each. In later years the idea was borrowed by Soviet Russia. When the 'agit-steamboat' *Red Star* was dispatched on a propaganda tour down the Kama and Volga Rivers in 1919, Molotov and Lenin's wife Krupskya, who were in charge, arranged for the construction of a 800-seat cinema on a barge, which was towed behind the *Red Star*.

A cinema called the Fly-In was opened at Asbury Park, NJ, in 1948 with space for 500 cars and 50 aeroplanes.

> The only cinema in the world which has never had a change of programme is Screen 6 of Atlanta's CNN Centre 6, which shows *Gone With the Wind* (US 39) twice a day every day of the year.

Berlin 1931 and the impact of the talkies. Photographs of audience reaction like this are extremely rare. (*Backnumbers*)

There is nothing unusual about watching movies in the air, but cinemas are curiously rare at airports. The only one in Europe is at Prague, where it is greatly appreciated by those subjected to the haphazard scheduling of East European airlines. It shows full-length features, mainly Italian westerns with Czech sub-titles, and admission is free to passengers.

A conventional cinema run in an unconventional way was the Picture House in the little Yorkshire village of Denholme, established as a co-operative venture in 1935 and operated entirely by voluntary labour. A hundred villagers contributed the £200 capital needed and the management of the cinema was in the hands of a committee elected annually. Old Age Pensioners were admitted free, others paid 3d–9d.

A village cinema of the present-day offers the amenity of a pint of ale with the film and supper in the interval. The locale is the Bear Inn, a 16th-century timbered building in the Shropshire village of Hodnet, where a large upstairs room has been converted into a cosy 60-seater cinema with performances on two evenings a week.

The Globe Cinema, a 300-seat picture house in Norwich, was built in 1934 by 14-year-old Alfred Warminger on a £1500 loan from his father. Alfred himself was manager and projectionist, while his two sisters acted as usherettes, with a boy to sell chocolates. There were two shows a night, the cost of admission to the 5 o'clock performance being a penny and to the 7 o'clock performance twopence.

The first children's Saturday matinees were inaugurated by Sidney Bernstein (now Lord Bernstein) of the Bernstein Group of Theatres (later Granada Theatres) with a performance at the Empire, Willesden, on 23 March 1928. Two thousand children paid 3d each to attend a programme which included *Robinson Crusoe* (GB 27), a *Topical Budget* and two shorts.

The first cinema club for children in Britain was the Mickey Mouse Club, the earliest recorded branch being established at the Arcade Cinema, Darlington, in 1933. There were 200 Mickey Mouse Clubs by May 1937. Gaumont–British cinema clubs were in being by 1936 and the Granadiers, organized by the Granada circuit, were founded in 1937.

South Bay Galleria in Redondo Beach, California, boasts a Kidpix cinema where moms can leave their tots for a 95-minute performance while they do their shopping. Each child is numbered on admittance and only handed over at the end of the show to an adult producing the correct ticket stub. Parents are supplied with bleepers free of charge so that they can be summoned in an emergency.

The first gaol to institute film shows for prisoners was Goulburn Gaol, Sydney, New South Wales, commencing on 3 January 1911 with a programme presented by the Methodist chaplain, the Rev. J. H. Lewin. The *Melbourne Argus* reported: 'Some of the long-sentence prisoners had never previously seen moving pictures and they more especially enjoyed the entertainment. The pictures were of course of an elevating character, including *Waterways of Holland, Dogs of Various Countries,* and *The Visit of the American Fleet.*'

In Britain the first regular film shows for gaol inmates were instituted on a weekly basis at Maidstone Prison in November 1937. The inaugural programme was rather dauntingly described as 'three hours of educational and cultural films, specially selected for reformative treatment of prisoners'. The shows were held in the 100-seat prison chapel, admission according to a three-weekly rota (Maidstone held 350 prisoners) being permitted to inmates who had earned a certain number of good conduct marks. The projector was operated by 'lifers'.

The first drive-in cinema was the Camden Automobile Theater, opened by Richard Hollingshead on a 10-acre site off Wilson Boulevard, Camden, NJ, on 6 June 1933 with a presentation of *Wife Beware* (US 33), with Adolphe Menjou. The screen measured 40 ft (12 m) by 30 ft (9 m) and there was accommodation for 400 cars. The sound came from high-volume screen speakers provided by RCA–Victor.

The 'In-Car' speaker was introduced by RCA–Victor in 1941. The screen speakers of the pioneer drive-ins had been replaced in the meantime by multiple-site speakers providing sound for two cars side by side.

The expansion of drive-ins began very slowly; twelve years after the opening of the Camden there were still only 60 in the whole of the United States. The growth years were the same as for television, for no clear reason. In 1949 there were 1000 drive-ins and the peak was reached in 1958 with 4063 against 12,291 hard-tops. There are now (1988) 2,148.

The first news theatre was the Embassy, Broadway and 46th Street, New York, which opened on 2 November 1929. It ceased showing newsreels and sports films in November 1949 owing to the competition from television—probably the first cinema to close for this reason.

Britain's first news theatre was the Pavilion, Shaftesbury Avenue, opened in 1930.

News theatres were seldom devoted exclusively to newsreels. In 1934 *Kinematograph Weekly* reported that on average only a third of the programme would be news, the rest consisting of general interest shorts, one-reel comedies, cartoons and serials. By the outbreak of World War II there were 22 news theatres in Britain, 16 of which were in London, and the only one showing solely newsreels was the GB Movietone in the West End. **The first all-cartoon cinema**, the Cameo-Royal in Charing Cross Road, had been opened in 1937. With the decline of newsreels in the late fifties and early sixties, most of the surviving news theatres evolved into cartoon theatres. **The last surviving cinema devoted to short films** in Britain was the Cartoon Cinema by the side of platform 19 at Victoria Station. Originally a news theatre, it closed down on 27 August 1981 after 47 years in operation. It enjoyed the curious distinction of being the only cinema in Britain without a lavatory. Fidgety patrons had to make a dash for the BR convenience on platform 15.

The first sex cinema in Britain was the 185-seat Compton Cinema Club, London, opened by Tony Tenser in November 1960. The first film shown was

Birth of the in-flight movie—Imperial Airways, April 1926. (*Backnumbers*)

Private Property (US 60). The cinema's club status enabled it to show films which would not have been eligible for a censor's certificate. Membership was 10s a year.

The first in-flight movie was First National's production of Conan Doyle's *The Lost World* (US 25), shown during a scheduled Imperial Airways flight from London to the Continent in April 1925.

America's first in-flight presentation was a more modest affair consisting of a *Universal Newsreel* and a couple of cartoon shorts shown aboard a transcontinental Air Transport Inc. Ford transport aircraft on 8 October 1929.

The first airline to introduce regular in-flight movies was TWA, commencing with the presentation of *By Love Possessed* (US 61), with Lana Turner and Efrem Zimbalist Jnr, in the first-class section during a scheduled New York–Los Angeles flight on 19 July 1961.

The world's airlines are estimated to spend about $45 to $50 million per annum on acquiring rights to films. A major airline like Australia's QANTAS pays in the region of $30,000 per picture, with a minimum of about 350 showings. The average age of the in-flight audience is about 20 years older than theatrical audiences, hence films that do well at the box office do not necessarily meet the same response a mile up in the air. Conversely a film like *Raise the Titanic* (US 80), which bombed at the box office, won plaudits from air passengers.

Cinema Cinema

A prodigious number of movies have been made about the business of movie making, from *Merton of the Movies* to *A Star is Born* and beyond. Not many movies have the showing of films as a central theme. Here are the few which do.

☆ *Paybox Adventure* (GB 36) Enid Stamp Taylor as heiress who works as ticket seller in cinema.

☆ *Contraband* (GB 40) Michael Powell–Emeric Pressburger, spies using cinema as a front.

☆ *The Smallest Show on Earth* (GB 57) Bill Travers and Virginia McKenna as young couple who think they have inherited a luxury picture palace, but find that it is in fact a run-down little flea-pit. Charming story recounts how they make it pay (e.g. turning the heat up during desert movies and then selling iced drinks).

☆ *Targets* (US 68) Peter Bogdanovich's second movie, in which a crazed sniper terrorizes the audience of a drive-in. Notable for Boris Karloff's last major performance.

☆ *The Projectionist* (US 70) A projectionist fantasizes he is Captain Flash under the baleful eye of tyrant cinema manager.

☆ *The Last Picture Show* (US 71) Peter Bogdanovich's evocation of small town life in Texas c. 1950, with the single cinema as the main centre of entertainment and social intercourse.

☆ *The Picture Show Man* (Aus 77) Rivalry between travelling picture shows in 20s backblocks Australia.

☆ *The Enchanted Sail* (It 82) Two brothers take a travelling cinema wagon round rural Italy in 1920s.

☆ *Variety* (US 83) Set in a sex cinema called Variety, in which the box office girl finds herself being drawn to events on screen and becomes entangled with one of the patrons.

☆ *Mr Love* (GB 85) Barry Jackson as cinema projectionist in Southport who plays Bogey live on stage to the usherette's Bergman when the projector breaks down during *Casablanca*.

☆ *American Drive-In* (US 85) Rare example of a film in which the whole of the action takes place in a cinema—in this case a hick town drive-in during the showing of a double bill of *Hard Rock Zombies 1* and 2. Mainly a study of audience types, including a biker gang, a hooker, two little old ladies who turn out to be dope dealers, and an intellectual couple who earnestly analyse the hokum on screen.

☆ *The Purple Rose of Cairo* (US 85) Woody Allen's ultimate movie fantasy, in which the fictional hero of a topper and tails thirties society movie walks out of the screen to romance unhappily married working girl and besotted movie fan Mia Farrow.

☆ *Demons* (It 85) Horror movie set in cinema showing horror movie.

☆ *Dead-End Drive-In* (Aus 86) Relates the story of a group of unemployed in 1990 imprisoned in a sinister drive-in.

☆ *Prunelle Blues* (Fr 86) French Algerian owner of cinema in Barbes quarter of Paris who discovers it is centre of a drugs ring.

☆ *Rhosyn a Rhith/Coming Up Roses* (GB 86) Filmed in Aberdare, charming Welsh language pic (with subtitles) is about a decaying cinema whose projectionist and ice cream lady turn it into a flourishing mushroom farm when it closes down.

☆ *Anguish* (Sp 87) Horror hokum with a homicidal eye doctor, main character in a gore movie being shown in tacky LA flea pit, appearing in the auditorium to dispatch various members of the audience.

*T*ICKETS

The highest seat price (excluding charity performances) was for Kevin Brownlow's reconstruction of Abel Gance's silent classic *Napoleon* (Fr 27) when it was shown in Tokyo in October 1981. Top price was 12,000 yen or $44. Both showings were a sell-out. The same picture carried a price tag of £17 top when it was shown at the Empire Leicester Square the previous March.

The lowest seat price recorded was a farthing by a cinema in London's Whitechapel Road in 1909, though the concessionary admission applied only to four children purchasing tickets together. The regular price for children at the Star Kinema in Newcastle upon Tyne about the time of World War I was ½d, but admission could be obtained by presenting a clean glass jam jar instead. In 1925, during a temporary slump in moviegoing, a desperate cinema manager in Covington, La., admitted patrons in exchange for empty beer bottles. He took $23 and 1812 empties. The cheapest seats noted in the Report of the Indian Cinematograph Committee (1928) were priced at one anna—slightly over one penny. These were 'seats' in a figurative sense, since the lowly price meant only a lowly place on the ground. In the late 1930s some cinemas in Karachi were wont to give free shows, consisting of shorts and long trailers, when their rivals were showing a blockbuster. A cinema opened in Cardiff in 1935 for 'coloured people' only charged a flat rate admission of 1d. Even cheaper was a picture house on Sixth Avenue, New York, which advertised *c*. 1912 a movie of a negro lynching for 1c. On at least one occasion any price for a seat has been accepted. In Victoria, BC, a cinema manager running *The Luck of Ginger Coffey* (Can 64) allowed patrons to pay whatever they thought the film was worth.

Currently the lowest admission charges are in China, where tickets range from the equivalent of 6c to 10c in the cities and are reported to be even cheaper in the country areas. The cheapest tickets in Europe are in Hungary, where the price of seeing a Hungarian-made film is 6 forints or 10p (14c). Foreign films are more expensive—up to 50 forints. In the USSR, the government recently announced the first price hike in 50 years—from 27 kopecs (25p or 42c) to around 40 kopecs.

ECONOMY AT THE CINEMA DE LUXE.

Mrs. Jones (completing her fourth hour). "I USED TO STAY ONLY TWO HOURS; BUT ONE 'AS TO MAKE THREEPENCE GO FURTHER THESE DAYS."

In 1916, when this cartoon appeared in *Punch*, cinema was already a mass entertainment. Two hours of relaxation for 3d was within reach of almost all.

Probably the cheapest cinema in the USA is Akron's Civic Theatre, whose weekend seat prices are 50c for main floor and back balcony seats and 65c for *loge* seats—exactly the same admission as when it first opened in 1929.

The highest tax on cinema admission prices is levied by the state government of the Punjab in Pakistan, where it was raised to 150 per cent on 1 July 1978.

> Robert Jacobsen will never buy a cinema ticket again. The internationally renowned sculptor designed the Danish Film Academy's Oscar, called the Alta, which was first presented in 1984. Instead of a fee, he opted for a free pass for life to every cinema in Denmark.

*A*UDIENCES

The largest audience ever to view a film simultaneously in the same locale was 110,000 on the occasion of the screening of D. W. Griffith's *Boots* (US 19) at the Methodist Centenary celebration held at the Oval Amphitheater, Columbus, Ohio, on 4 July 1919. Fifty thousand of the audience were accommodated in the stands, the remainder in the arena. The film was projected on a giant screen, with a picture size of 100×75 ft.

The highest number of times a patron has seen the same film is 940 by Mrs Myra Franklin of Cardiff, Wales, whose favourite picture can only be *The Sound of Music* (US 65).

The film seen by the most cinemagoers. There are no reliable figures to authenticate the most popular film of all time in terms of the highest number of paying patrons. However, *Mother India* (Ind 57), which has been on almost continuous release in various parts of India since 1957, is claimed by some authorities on Indian cinema to have been seen by more cinemagoers than *Gone With the Wind* (US 39).

The film seen by the least cinemagoers. Of films which have actually secured a release, the lowest reported audience was achieved by Luis Vera's *Accomplished Facts* (Chile 86) with 1880 spectators.

Fan Mail

Mail began to be sent to the uncredited performers of the early silents even before the advent of named stars. Mary Pickford recalled an occasion at the Biograph Studios in about 1912 when she enquired about a letter she was expecting, and was told that it had probably been thrown away together with the hundreds of other letters addressed simply to 'the Girl with the Curls' or 'the Biograph Girl'. She was amazed to learn that people she had never met should feel impelled to write to someone who had no more substance for them than a mute shadow on a silver screen. Biograph's high-handed method of disposing of unsolicited correspondence did not long survive the onslaught of the fan magazines, which soon took to publishing the stars' studio addresses in response to eager enquiries from the fans. Producers came to realize that a mail count was one method of assessing a rising star's popularity and consequently his or her box office potential, while the stars themselves knew that it was in their own interest to maintain a devoted fan following, even at the cost of the $250 a week it was estimated in the twenties that a major star would need to spend on photographs and postage.

The largest fan mail of the immediate post World War I period was received by 'America's Sweetheart' Mary Pickford, with an average of 18,000 letters a month. It was maintained that Miss Pickford employed a fleet of 18 secretaries to answer them.

Mary Pickford's popularity began to decline in the 'flapper era' and in 1927 it was reported that Colleen Moore was leading the fan mail league table with 15,000 letters a month. Miss Moore was obliged to dispatch an average of 12,000 photographs of herself monthly at a cost of 12c each, including postage. A year later she had been overtaken by Clara Bow, whose count for the month of April 1928 was no less than 33,727 items of mail. The cost of replying was $2550 including $450 for three full-time secretaries.

> Donald O'Connor made six films with Francis the Talking Mule but surrendered his leading role to Mickey Rooney when he discovered the mule was getting more fan mail than he was.

The most popular male star at that time was, somewhat surprisingly, Charles 'Buddy' Rogers, with 19,618 letters. Douglas Fairbanks, generally thought of as the most consistently popular male star of the twenties, rated only 8000 letters, which gave him equal place in the league table with a dog, Rin Tin Tin. Chaplin, who had once created a fan mail record with 73,000 letters in the first three days of his return home to London in 1921, could muster no more than 5000.

The coming of sound virtually ended the screen careers of Colleen Moore and Clara Bow, but ushered in a host of new stars, one of whom was to create a fan mail record which has never been broken. Mickey Mouse, reported Walt Disney at the end of 1933, had received 800,000 letters that year, an average of 66,000 a month. He stressed that all these communications had been addressed to Mickey personally, and not to his creator.

In that heady period of Hollywood history known as 'the era of the Great Stars', neither Gable nor Garbo could compete with a mouse, a child and a singing cowboy. By 1936 seven-year-old Shirley Temple was receiving just over 60,000 letters a month, an all-time record for a mere human being. As age crept up on the golden-curled moppet, the fickleness of film fans once again asserted itself. By the time she had reached the mature age of ten, Miss Temple was no longer at the top. Her place had been taken by the guitar-strumming cowboy Gene Autry, though it may have been some consolation that his peak of 40,000 letters a month came nowhere near her best.

World War II brought a new element into star appeal with the advent of the pin-up picture, and it is probable that a high proportion of the dogfaces who wrote from far-away places to the new record holder, the fighting forces' own Betty Grable, had never seen any of her films. The attraction of her million dollar legs, however, was attested by the average of 30,000 letters a month they inspired.

A number of factors contributed to the decline of fan mail after World War II, chief amongst them the parallel decline in the star system, the rise of other cult heroes such as pop singers and sportsmen, and dwindling audiences in the wake of television. Even in recent years, however, it has been possible for stars held high in public esteem to inspire prodigious quantities of mail at times when they are the focus of news attention, as evidenced by the 150,000 letters received by John Wayne from loyal fans during the two months following his heart operation in June 1978.

Intimate Snapshots of Film Favorites

No. 1

Clara Bow spends a quiet evening amidst her fan mail

Left: This 1928 cartoon was not too much of an exaggeration. Clara Bow really did have three full-time secretaries answering 30,000 fan letters a month.

The nature of the fan letter writer has seldom been examined, but in April 1927 *Variety* published the results of a survey in which they reported that 10 per cent of all fan mail sent from within the USA came from Poles (or people with Polish names), while up to 8 per cent of the 32,250,000 letters received annually from fans worldwide by Hollywood studios originated from South American countries. The greater proportion of requests for photographs, said *Variety*, came from people who never went to the movies—'they are of the poor kind who cannot afford it and simply pick up coupons or read names on billboards of the various stars ...'. An analysis made the following year at Paramount, the studio which received the most fan mail, revealed that 75 per cent of the correspondents were women, despite the fact that female stars received more letters than men.

Fan mail being traditionally associated with film stars, it is worthy of note that no actor or actress has received in the course of a career the number of letters delivered to Charles Lindbergh following his transatlantic flight—a total of 3,500,000.

Space precludes more than the briefest selection of the last 60 years of fan mail:

☆ To Kathlyn Williams 1916: 'Dear Miss Williams, You are my favourite moving picture actress. I would appreciate it so much if you would give me one of your old automobiles, any one, I wouldn't care how small.'

☆ To Enid Bennett 1920: 'I am making a collection of pictures of the most notorious actresses. Please send me yours.'

☆ To Emil Jannings (whose looks were certainly subordinate to his artistry) 1928: 'Dear Miss Jannings, You are my favourite actress. I go to see all your pictures because I like the way you wear your clothes. To me you are the best-dressed actress on the screen, as well as the most beautiful. I try to imitate your clothes and your stylish way of wearing your hair.'

☆ To Una Merkel (following a request for a signed photo) 1933: 'Do not send picture. Am moving and decided I don't want it.' Miss Merkel to fan: 'Picture is sent. You'll take it and like it.'

☆ To Glenn Ford 1946: 'I am 22, pretty, but I never saved my money. You did. That is the real reason I would like to marry you. Please let me know soon, as I have also written to Dick Powell and Larry Parks.'

☆ To Virginia Mayo from Arab Sheik 1948: 'You are the surest proof to me of the existence of God.'

☆ To Frank Sinatra, from girl fan proposing marriage 1956: 'We've never met, but I'm a singer and I feel I can do so much for your career.'

Film Fans, Famous and Infamous

Royalty have been among the most fervent supporters of the cinema since its earliest days. At a time when 'animated pictures' had scarcely moved out of the fairground, Queen Victoria was enjoying frequent film shows at Windsor Castle. An ardent film fan, the Queen had a special predilection for movies about children and her favourite was said to be a Riley Bros production called *The Pillow Fight* (GB 98), in which four mischievous schoolgirls bombarded each other with pillows in their bedroom.

The first royalty with private cinema theatres in their palaces were the Crown Prince of Siam and Tsar Nicolas II, both in about 1913. When war broke out and the Tsar took command of his forces in the field, he missed his cinema at the Tsarkoye Selo palace so much that he had another one installed at the Stavka, headquarters of the Russian Army. The Tsar's favourite film was *The Exploits of Elaine* (US 14), a cliff-hanger type serial which he watched weekly at Stavka throughout the second half of 1916. The deposed Emperor of China, Henry P'u Yi, had a cinema built at the Palace of Established Happiness about 1920, where a steady flow of Charlie Chaplin and Fatty Arbuckle films were maintained, until the emergence of Harold Lloyd, who displaced them as Imperial Favourite. The Emperor's owlish horn-rimmed glasses were said to have been acquired in tribute to the American comedian.

Queen Alexandra's favourite film was *True Heart Susie* (US 19), in which Lillian Gish played the kind of simple, joyful country girl the Queen sometimes wished she could have been. A private print of the film was kept at Buckingham Palace. Queen Mary's taste, on the other hand, ran to rather more robust fare, her favourite star being the romantic and extremely athletic hero of Hollywood adventure movies Eddie Polo. (Reputedly Queen Mary was the only member of the Royal Family who was not a Charlie Chaplin fan—the reason, according to one fan magazine writer, being the fact that she was not endowed with a very developed sense of humour.) The Queen was said to be the Royal Family's most enthusiastic filmgoer and during World War II, when living at Badminton, she gave a weekly film show for servicemen. However, her youngest son, the Duke of Kent, seems to have rivalled her in his passion for the pictures. When he married Princess Marina in 1934,

---

Under a local decree of 1984 in the Maharashtra town of Nandurbar, Muslim women are forbidden to visit the cinema. The penalty for violation is the equivalent of $10. Any man reporting a woman in the audience receives a reward of $5.

the Earl of Dudley had a squash court converted into a cinema at his seat, Himley Hall, where the Royal Couple were to spend their honeymoon. During the twelve days of their stay, the Duke and Duchess watched 18 feature films, nine comedies, an unspecified number of documentaries, five newsreels and a specially made life-story of His Royal Highness. Every night of the honeymoon was spent at the movies reported an ecstatic Gaumont–British, who had supplied the 202 reels of film shown.

Both the Duke's brothers shared his delight in the cinema. The Duke of York, later King George VI, was reported in America to have a particular weakness for the films of Nancy Carroll. A greater sensation, though, was the revelation in *Photoplay* in 1931 that the Prince of Wales (later Edward VIII) was in the habit of making incognito visits to one of London's less exclusive suburban cinemas, the Grand in Edgware Road, at least once or twice a week. The Prince always attended with the same girl, it was alleged, she taking her seat at 8.45 p.m. and he slipping into his at precisely 9 p.m., after the house lights had gone down.

No recent information is available about H.M. The Queen's taste in films, the Palace being prepared to say only that 'she most often asks to see those of which she has read favourable reviews'. According to a newspaper report of the late 1950s, however, her favourite stars were then Gary Cooper, Laurence Olivier and Dirk Bogarde. Curiously Her Majesty

> Few fans attain the degree of devotion that black superstar Michael Jackson accords to Elizabeth Taylor. One of the rooms in his 50-room Malibu mansion is a shrine to the much-married star, decorated throughout in her favourite violet. Videos of her films play 24 hours a day with or without an audience.

does not have a private cinema. At Sandringham the shows are held in the Ballroom, at Balmoral in the Large Drawing Room and at Windsor Castle in the Waterloo Room. Films are not shown at Buckingham Palace. Royal film shows are the responsibility of the Equerry in Waiting, who selects the films unless the Queen has made a particular request.

World leaders have also been in the forefront of the world's film fans. Both Stalin and Churchill named *Lady Hamilton* (GB 42) as their favourite film, the British Prime Minister seeing it four times. Churchill's passion for films was not shared by all his wartime colleagues, a number of whom have testified to their displeasure at the PM's habit of breaking off the evening's work to watch the ritual movie and then expecting them to match his alertness and vigour as top-level discussions continued until three in the morning. At Kremlin film shows, according to

Khruschev, Stalin 'used to select the movies himself. The films were usually what you might call captured trophies: we got them from the West. Many of them were American pictures. He liked cowboy movies especially. He used to curse them and give them their proper ideological evaluation but then immediately order new ones.'

Hitler's favourite movie at the time he became Chancellor of Germany was *The Blue Angel* (Ger 30), of which he had a private print. Trenker's *The Rebel* (US 33), was said to be his favourite American film. *The Blue Angel* was later displaced in his affections by Willi Forst's *Mazurka* (Ger 35), which he watched as often as two or three times a week in the small hours of the morning when he was suffering from insomnia. Such was the Führer's devotion to the film, a rumour spread that its star, the bewitching Pola Negri, was under his special protection. In fact Miss Negri had never met Hitler, but found that whenever she went to Nazi Germany she was treated with the kind of privileged deference accorded only to intimates of the Reichs Chancellor. (She later won a libel action against the French cinema magazine *Pour Vous*, which alleged she was Hitler's mistress.)

The Führer is said to have indulged in film shows of a less conventional kind. Pauline Kohler, who served on the staff at Berchtesgaden, claimed that Hitler had a special film made of a prominent German star stripping and exhibiting 'various exercises' which 'threw a terrible light on the perversity of Hitler's sexual desires'. This was shown in the Führer's private cinema at Berchtesgaden, where a selected group of staff were invited to view it on Christmas Day 1937.

Arturo Alessandri, President of Chile in the 1930s, was besotted with the infant Shirley Temple. He had each of her films shown at his official residence in Santiago as soon as it was released and prevailed upon the Chilean Navy to adopt her as their official mascot.

President Anwar Sadat of Egypt watched a movie every day. President Tito of Yugoslavia saw an average of 200 a year—one virtually every night he was in Belgrade. His favourite was the Humphrey Bogart–Bette Davis movie *The Petrified Forest* (US 36), about a group of travellers at a way-station in Arizona who are held up by gangsters.

With the passing of Presidents Sadat and Tito, the most devoted film fan among current heads of state is President Bongo of Gabon. He is reported to watch 'several films every night' at the Presidential Palace, mainly karate movies from Hong Kong and Hindu melodramas. He has personally financed the making of three feature films, two of them scripted by his wife Joséphine and the third, *Demain un jour nouveau* (Gab 78), based on his own autobiography.

American Presidents have been enjoying films at the White House since June 1914, when Giovanni

Pastrone's epic *Cabiria* (It 14) was screened before President Wilson and his Cabinet. The President's favourite star was the statuesque Katharine Mac-Donald, known as 'The American Beauty'. If FDR had any preferences when it came to the ladies, he was not letting on to his wife. Eleanor Roosevelt confided that 'the President never has an evening of his own planning without at least one Mickey Mouse film'. It is not recorded whether President Truman was obliged to sit through *The Scarlet Pimpernel* (GB 34) the 16 times his daughter Margaret—a devotee of Leslie Howard—had it screened at the White House. Eisenhower's favourite films while President were *Angels in the Outfield* (US 52) —described by Leslie Halliwell as 'unamusing, saccharine whimsy' —*Springfield Rifle* (US 52), *To Catch a Thief* (US 55), and *Rear Window* (US 54). The latter two starred his favourite actress, Grace Kelly. President Kennedy left the selection of films to aide Arthur Schlesinger, who arranged a show every Sunday evening at the White House. *Patton* (US 69) was President Nixon's favourite, while President Carter though unwilling to name a favourite film, was enrolled as an honorary member of Britain's Errol Flynn Fan Club. It behoves the present incumbent of the White House to be discreet about his preferences. The President and Mrs Reagan see films at weekends at Camp David and the White House, making their choices, per the White House Director of Media Relations, 'from movies recommended by friends and staff members, and they enjoy watching some of the old classics . . .'. In answer to the obvious question, the Director of Media Relations reveals that the President 'has viewed one of his own films at the request of his staff'.

> Some 80 per cent of Japanese cinemagoers are women, a phenomenon accounted for by the fact that men work long hours and are expected to fraternize with co-workers in bars until late in the evening. In the UK the split between male and female cinemagoers is exactly 50/50.

PREMIERES

The largest audience to attend a world première were the 23,930 persons who paid $2.50 to $50 each to see Robert Altman's *Brewster McCloud* (US 70), starring Bud Cort and Sally Kellerman, at the Houston Astrodome on 5 December 1970. A special 70 mm print was made exclusively for the première at a cost of $12,000, since a standard gauge film would have given insufficient definition on the 156×60 ft 'astroscreen'. The *Houston Chronicle* reported in inimitable Texan style: 'The reaction was what you might call mixed. The audience was mostly your younger hip crowd, but the low intelligibility and the film's wierdness in general caused things to be a bit subdued. Miss Kellerman runs around nekkid a lot and there are what you might call bad words . . .'.

The largest number of simultaneous openings was for Paramount's *Crocodile Dundee II* (US/Aus 88), starring Paul Hogan, which opened at 2837 North American sites on 25 May 1988.

The first performer to achieve simultaneous premières on stage and screen was Marie Dressler, who opened in *A Mix Up* at the 39th Street Theater on the same night, Monday 30 December 1914, that her feature length comedy *Tillie's Punctured Romance*, in which she starred together with Charlie Chaplin and Mabel Normand, had its world première at the New York Theatre.

Unusual Premières

Not all premières take place in glittering and star-studded surroundings. *Oliver Twist* (US 22) had its British Première at London's historic Foundling Hospital, presumably in tribute to the protagonist's orphan origins; while the world première of MGM's Agatha Christie whodunnit *Murder at the Gallop* (GB 63) took place in a tent at a church garden party in rural Cheshire. The Barbara Stanwyck starrer *My Reputation* (US 46) was premièred in a Nissen hut on an airfield 'somewhere in England'. After this somewhat downbeat launch, it went on to become a major box office success in America.

There was only one place to hold the world première of *Dodge City* (US 40). The last of the real razzmatazz preems before the austerities of war, the celebration began with a special train bringing 150 Warner Bros executives and stars, including the movie's topliners Errol Flynn and Olivia de Havilland, which was escorted into Dodge City by an aerial fleet of 50 private aircraft. Overnight the little Kansan town underwent a temporary population explosion from 10,000 to 150,000.

There was no problem in accommodating everyone who wanted to come to the world première of *King of the Coral Sea* (Aus 54), an adventure story about pearlers in the South Seas. It took place on the tiny Pacific atoll of Thursday Island. With a population of less than a thousand, everyone was invited.

The première of *The Incredible Mr Limpet* (US 64) was held underwater. The oddball story of a man who turned into a fish, the picture was preemed by Warner Bros on the ocean floor with a submerged screen at Weeki Wachi, Fla. The invited audience of 250 sat in a glass tank 20 ft below the surface.

The only world première held in the air was organized by master showman Joseph E. Levine, who held the first showing of Lewis Gilbert's *The Adventurers*

(US 70), glitzy filmization of the Harold Robbins novel, in a jet airliner crossing the USA.

Far-flung simultaneous opening are not so rare, but when Stanley Kramer decided to hold the world première of *On the Beach* (US 59) on both sides of the Iron Curtain at the same time there was certainly no precedent. Based on Nevil Shute's novel about the doomed survivors of a nuclear holocaust, the film opened in 17 cities on 17 December 1959, including New York, Moscow and the city in which the story was set, Melbourne.

If Kramer's intent was to stimulate unity against war among nations, very different sentiments must have actuated the Nazis' decision to première Veit Harlan's epic *Kolberg* (Ger 45) in the besieged fortress of La Rochelle. *Kolberg* was about the fortitude of the inhabitants of the Baltic town of that name during the Napoleonic Wars; the staging of its première in such unpropitious circumstances a symbolic act. Since the print could not be brought through the lines of the besieging army, it was dropped into the town by parachute.

The most belated première of a feature film took place at the Cinémathèque Française in Paris in April 1984, when the completed version of André Antoine's 64-year-old *L'Hirondelle et la Mésange* (Bel 20) was presented for the first time. Six hours of unedited rushes had been discovered in the State Film Archive and edited by Henri Colpi as he perceived Antoine had intended. The reason the unedited film had been shelved in 1920 was that distributor Charles Pathé was so disconcerted by the rushes, which revealed a story of canal life shot in cinéma verité style, that he refused to release it. The audience at the première, by contrast, were captivated by the film's lyrical beauty as well as its understated realism.

*R*OYALTY

The first occasion on which a ruling monarch attended a public film performance was on 11 June 1896, when King Christian IX of Denmark (reigned 1863–1906) visited Vilhelm Pacht's exhibition of Lumière films at his Kinoptikon in Copenhagen's Raadhuspladsen.

The first member of the British Royal Family to visit a public cinema was Queen Alexandra (1844–1925), daughter of King Christian IX of Denmark (see above), who attended a performance at the Kinomatograph Theatre, Christiania (Oslo), in September 1907 accompanied by the Dowager Empress of Russia.

The first British monarch to attend a public cinema performance was King George V (reigned 1910–36) who, accompanied by Queen Mary, saw a matinee showing of *Quo Vadis?* (It 13) at the Albert Hall on 5 May 1913. The visit was described

as 'strictly private', meaning it was not a Command Performance.

The first Royal Command Film Performance was held at Marlborough House on 21 July 1896 before 40 royal guests who had assembled for the marriage of Princess Maud the following day. The show was occasioned by a request from pioneer cinematographer Birt Acres of New Barnet, Herts, to be allowed to exhibit publicly a film he had taken the previous month of the Prince and Princess of Wales attending the Cardiff Exhibition (see News Film, p. 220). Before giving his permission, the Prince of Wales commanded Acres to bring the film to Marlborough House for inspection. It was screened in a specially erected marquee together with 20 other short films, including Tom Merry the Lightning Artist drawing Mr Gladstone and Lord Salisbury, the Derby races of 1895 and 1896, Henley Regatta, and scenes showing a boxing kangaroo, a Great Northern Railway express train, and the pursuit of a pickpocket. The royal film was shown twice by popular demand.

The first Royal Command Performance before the Sovereign was held in the Red Drawing Room at Windsor Castle on 23 November 1896, when HM Queen Victoria (reigned 1837–1901) saw a film of the Royal Family taken by W. Downey at Balmoral the previous month (see News Film: Monarch to be Filmed, p. 220). The Queen brought her opera glasses to ensure that she missed none of the action. This was the first of many such performances before the aged Queen, who became something of a cinema addict in the closing years of her life.

The first feature film presented by Royal Command was Cecil Hepworth's production of *Comin' Through the Rye* (GB 16), starring Alma Taylor, which was shown before Queen Alexandra (1844–1925) in the State Dining Room of Marlborough House on 4 August 1916. Hepworth was no stranger to Command Performances, having been present at the very first one when he had acted as assistant to Birt Acres.

The first feature film to be presented by Command of the Sovereign was *Tom Brown's Schooldays* (GB 17), which Lew Warren exhibited before King George V (reigned 1910–36) and Queen Mary at Buckingham Palace on 25 February 1917.

The first Royal Command Performance at a public cinema and the first of the present series of annual Command Performances took place at the Empire, Leicester Square, on 1 November 1946, when King George VI (reigned 1936–52) and Queen Elizabeth, accompanied by Princess Elizabeth and Princess Margaret, saw David Niven and Marius Goring in *A Matter of Life and Death* (GB 46). The novelty of seeing the King 'going to the pictures' caused crowds to gather ten hours before his arrival.

ROYAL COMMAND PERFORMANCE FILMS

1946 *A Matter of Life and Death* (GB)
1947 *The Bishop's Wife* (US)
1948 *Scott of the Antarctic* (GB)
1949 *The Forsyte Saga* (US)
1950 *The Mudlark* (GB)
1951 *Where No Vultures Fly* (GB)
1952 *Because You're Mine* (US)
1953 *Rob Roy the Highland Rogue* (GB)
1954 *Beau Brummel* (GB)
1955 *To Catch a Thief* (US)
1956 *The Battle of the River Plate* (GB)
1957 *Les Girls* (US)
1958 No Performance
1959 *The Horse's Mouth* (GB)
1960 *The Last Angry Man* (US)
1961 *The Facts of Life* (US)
1962 *West Side Story* (US)
1963 *Sammy Going South* (GB)
1964 *Move Over Darling* (US)
1965 *Lord Jim* (GB)
1966 *Born Free* (GB)

1967 *The Taming of the Shrew* (It/US)
1968 *Romeo and Juliet* (GB)
1969 *The Prime of Miss Jean Brodie* (GB) —first X film
1970 *Anne of the Thousand Days* (GB)
1971 *Love Story* (US)
1972 *Mary Queen of Scots* (GB)
1973 *Lost Horizon* (US)
1974 *The Three Musketeers* (Panama)
1975 *Funny Lady* (US)
1976 *The Slipper and the Rose* (GB)
1977 *Silver Streak* (US)
1978 *Close Encounters of the Third Kind* (US)
1979 *California Suite* (US)
1980 *Kramer vs Kramer* (US)
1981 *Chariots of Fire* (GB)
1982 *Evil Under the Sun* (GB)
1983 *Table for Five* (US)
1984 *The Dresser* (GB)
1985 *A Passage to India* (GB)
1986 *White Nights* (US)
1987 *84 Charing Cross Road* (US)
1988 *Empire of the Sun* (US)

HM Queen Elizabeth was not amused by the portrayal of her ancestor George IV in *Beau Brummel* (GB 54). For a while it looked like the end of the Royal Film Performance, as recently declassified Cabinet papers reveal. *(SI)*

Recently declassified Cabinet Papers dating from 1955 reveal that the Queen was so dissatisfied with the standard of films shown at the Royal Film Performance that she threatened to stop attending. The particular film which so aroused her ire that she complained to Prime Minister Winston Churchill about it was *Beau Brummel* (GB 54), in which Stewart Granger played the title role and Peter Ustinov his 'fat friend' the Prince Regent. Churchill told Sir Frank Lee, President of the Board of Trade, to carpet the hapless Alfred Bromhead, chairman of the selection committee, who admitted that a 'grievous mistake' had been made in choosing the film. As the controversy raged within the inner councils of government, the Queen let it be known that an invitation to the 1955 Royal Film Performance would be regarded as 'by no means appropriate'. The matter was resolved by appointing Lord Radcliffe as 'neutral' chairman of the selection committee with absolute powers of veto—the unfortunate Alfred Bromhead had been outvoted when he sought to dissuade his colleagues from the choice of *Beau Brummel.* In February 1955 the PM was advised: 'The film industry can be regarded as having done its best to ensure that the fiascos of recent years are not repeated. In the circumstances, Her Majesty will be advised to attend a Performance this year.' She did and to everyone's huge relief, Hitchcock's *To Catch a Thief* (US 55) with Cary Grant and soon-to-be-royal Grace Kelly was reported to have found favour with Her Majesty.

PROJECTORS

The first projector manufactured for sale was the Lumière Cinématographe, produced under licence by Jules Carpentier of Paris, early in 1896.

The first British projector manufactured for sale was the Theatrograph, produced by R. W. Paul at his Saffron Hill factory, of which the first model to be sold was purchased by conjurer David Devant for £100 and installed at the Egyptian Hall, Piccadilly, on 19 March 1896. It was at just about this time that Paul Cingqueralli arrived in London to offer the Edison Vitascope, which had yet to make its American debut, to prospective purchasers at $25,000 each. Not surprisingly the margin between £100 ($500) and $25,000 effectively dissuaded anyone from purchasing what was later said to be an inferior projector.

The first motorized projector was the Kinematograph designed and manufactured by J. H. Rigg of Skinner Lane, Leeds, and demonstrated publicly at the Royal Aquarium, London, on 6 April 1896. Powered by a four-volt electric motor, it was available for sale by the end of the year through the Anglo-Continental Phonograph Co. of London and Rigg's American agent in Philadelphia.

The most powerful projector ever built was the Canadian developed IMAX, made by the Multiscreen Corporation for use at Japan's *Expo '70*, where the Fuji Group used it to show the specially produced multi-image film *Tiger Child* (Can/Jap 70). The projector's ten-element Canon 150 mm F/20 high-precision lens and 25,000 watt Xenon short arc lamp were capable of reproducing a high-fidelity image nine storeys tall. The illumination was four times as great as the most powerful lamp hitherto available. Although the size of the Fuji Co.'s pavilion at *Expo '70* limited the screen size to 60 × 40 ft, the projector was theoretically capable of rendering a sharp image on a screen measuring 126 × 88 ft.

FILM REEL

The largest film reel holds 20,200 ft of film, against the 1000 ft capacity of a standard 35 mm reel. Produced by the Imax Systems Corporation of Toronto, Canada, for use with Imax projectors, the reel is 4 ft in diameter.

SCREEN

The largest screen ever used for projecting a motion picture was the 115 × 85 ft installation at the Tsukuba Expo '85 in Japan, on which a 20 minute $2 million production *Skywards* (Can 85) was presented by the Canadian Imax system. The largest ever video screen, the 131 × 82 ft Sony Jumbotron, featured at the same exhibition.

It had taken 'state of the art' technology 87 years to catch up with and surpass the previous record for the largest screen image, set by Louis Lumière in 1898 at the Galérie des Machines on the site of the forthcoming Paris Exposition with a picture measuring 99 ft × 79 ft 2 in. The distance from the projector was 650 ft and the screen was kept wet to increase its reflection of light, a task undertaken by the Paris Fire Brigade, who trained their hoses on the mammoth sheet before the show began.

The largest screen in the world today belongs to the Imax Theatre at the Taman Mini Park in Jakarta, Indonesia and measures 96 ft × 70 ft 6 in.

The largest screens in the USA are two identical 70 ft 6 in × 96 ft screens at Marriott's Great America Parks at Santa Clara, California and Gurnee, Illinois. They were manufactured by Harkness Screens of Boreham Wood, Herts, England, and are used in conjunction with Canadian Imax projection systems.

The largest screen in Britain measures 62 × 45 ft and is used with the Imax projection system at the National Museum of Photography, Film and Television at Bradford. The screen is the height of a five-storey building.

The widest screen ever used for projecting motion pictures was erected at the Palais d'Electricité et de la Lumière at the Paris Exposition of 1937 for showing Henri Chrétien's *hypergonar* films, the precursor of Cinerama. The concave screen had a breadth of 195 ft and was 32 ft 6 in high. By comparison the Cinerama screen size was 90 × 26 ft.

> Hamburg's annual 'Low-Budget Film Festival' boasts something unique in film presentation—a floating screen. It is moored on the Alster and anyone who cares to can simply sit on the bank and enjoy the midnight shows for free.

The widest screen in use today was installed at the Mercury Cinema, Paris, in 1981 and measures 133 ft in breadth.

360° screens, with the audience wholly surrounded by the projected image, exist at the China Pavilion of Walt Disney's EPCOT Center in Florida, where the system is called 'Circle Vision'; and at the L'Espace Gaité cinema in Paris, which presents the 'Panrama' system on a 350 square metre screen.

The giant screen used by the Lumière brothers,
Paris, 1898.

THIRTEEN

PRESS AND PRINT

The first book on cinematography was *The History of the Kinetograph, Kinetoscope and Kineto-Phonograph*, by W. K. L. and Antonia Dickson, New York, 1895. Dickson was Thomas Edison's assistant and the inventor of the Kinetoscope 'peep show' motion picture apparatus and Kinetograph camera patented in his employer's name. The book was published in Britain in October of the same year by the Continental Commerce Co. of New York as a give-away to publicize their Oxford Street Kinetoscope parlour.

The first British work on the subject of cinematography was *Animated Photography, or the ABC of the Cinematograph* by Cecil Hepworth, published by Hazell, Watson & Viney Ltd of London in 1897.

The first poem to mention the cinema was in the British journal *Truth* on 30 July 1896. Titled 'The St Stephens Music Hall', it was about the various attractions to be found at this mythical establishment, including the new-fangled films:

Then, of course, of 'Living Pictures' there are some at which to laugh,
And repeated presentations of 'The Animatographe'.

The first work on the aesthetics of the cinema was an essay entitled *The Cinematograph* by a certain O. Winter in *The New Review* of May 1896. Written, astonishingly, only two months after the first-ever public film show in Britain, Winter's essay is scornful of the adulation the early films were receiving. He believed that their apparent realism was a delusion because they reproduced nature without selection and for this reason films would have no artistic future.

The first book on the aesthetics of cinema was Vachel Lindsay's *The Art of the Moving Picture*, published in the USA in 1915.

The first short story about the cinema was 'Our Detective Story' from the *Referee*, a London newspaper, of 24 January 1897. Written by G. R. Sims under the pseudonym 'Dagonet', it centres around a husband whose suspicions are aroused when his wife temporarily disappears in Spain. He has almost forgotten the incident when, some time later, he and she are watching a series of actuality films of Spain at a music hall. Suddenly a lady and gentleman appear on screen arm in arm. It is the wife with the husband's partner: 'The woman was looking up into the man's face . . . His arm stole round her waist—she put up her face—he stooped and kissed her. The audience yelled with laughter.' The husband is outraged and a divorce follows, the films being produced as evidence in court.

Researching the early fiction of the cinema, film historian Stephen Bottomore has identified some 15 short stories published before 1912 which deal with films. Of these, strangely enough, all but two or three deal with a similar theme to 'Dagonet's', i.e. the revelation of some hitherto hidden facts through the showing of a film. The facts in question are usually to do with marital infidelity, but sometimes reveal the perpetrator of a more serious crime.

This constant theme in the fiction of early cinema may have had some basis in reality. As early as January 1897 the well-known British detective Henry Slater was advertising that he would employ the 'Animatographe' for surveillance 'in all cases and . . . produce the pictures in Court in evidence. Consultations free.' In subsequent years there were persistent reports of husbands or wives seeing their spouses two-timing them in newsreel pictures.

The first play to mention the cinema was *Hans Huckebein* by Oskar Blumethal and Gustav Kadelburg, premièred at the Lessing Theatre, Berlin on 16 October 1897. It is a farce about a man, Martin, married to the suspicious Hildegard. She goes to a filmshow and sees a scene shot on a beach, with Martin about to kiss a girl. Hildegard is angry with Martin and things look bleak for him until the end of the play when the girl turns up and reveals that she was hired by the film producer to kiss men on the beach to spice up the films. The piece was successful enough to be staged in London and New York before the end of the year.

The earliest allusion to the cinema in a novel appears in Frank Norris's *McTeague*, published in February 1899. The plot has McTeague taking his girlfriend Trina and her family to see the Kinetoscope. They are all very impressed except Trina's mother who announces 'I'm too old to be fooled . . . dot's nothun but a drick'. The novel was later made into a famous film directed by Erich von Stroheim, called *Greed* (US 23).

Britain's first allusion to cinema in a novel is in E. F. Benson's *Mammon and Co* (London 1899). An elderly lady called Mrs Murchison, much given to malapropisms, visits the Palace Theatre to 'see the Biography'. She reports that 'Most interesting it was, and the one from the front of the train made me feel quite sick and giddy—most pleasant.'

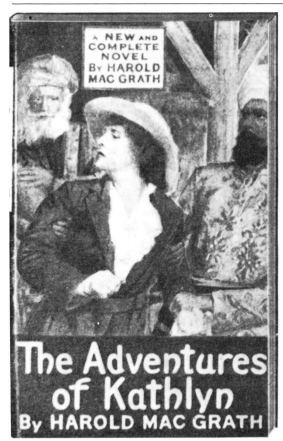

The first novelization of a movie. Harold MacGrath had written the scenario of the successful 1913 Selig serial on which the novel was based. Published in 1914, it was illustrated with stills.

The first book-of-the-film was a special illustrated 'photoplay edition' of Ralph Ince's Vitagraph three-reeler *The Mills of the Gods* (US 12), published by Grosset and Dunlap of New York at 50c.

The first original work of literature based on a film was Stuart Edward White's *Oil on Troubled Waters*, published in the *Saturday Evening Post* in 1913. Director Allan Dwan had written the film scenario and approached White, a distinguished novelist, with the idea of paying him simply for the use of his name as the supposed author. White was so impressed with the plot, however, that he decided to turn it into a genuine short story for publication. One of the most notable examples of literature derived from a motion picture is Budd Schulberg's novel *On the Waterfront*, adapted from the screenplay of his 1954 film. Novels had been written from screenplays before, but as with cheap paperback adaptations today this was simply a means of publicizing a film at the same time as producing a book with high readership potential. Schulberg's 'book-of-the-film' was probably the first to be conceived as a serious work of literature exploring themes beyond the capacity of the movie camera.

Economically, the book-of-the-film is seldom more than a subsidiary merchandizing operation. In what is believed to be a unique case, however, respecting the Faye Dunaway starrer *The Eyes of Laura Mars* (US 78), the highly-successful paperback is reputed to have made a larger profit than the lacklustre movie.

Another book born of a film was *The Jazz Singer*. In this case a newspaper serial was adapted from the novel (by Arline De Haas), which was based on the film script (by Alfred A. Cohn) of the 1927 talkie, which in turn was a rendering of the Broadway show (by Samson Raphaelson), which had been dramatized from a short story called *The Day of Atonement* (also by Samson Raphaelson).

Similarly, the 1972 TV series *Anna and the King* was a spin-off of the film musical *The King and I* (US 56), an adaptation of the stage musical of the same name, derived from the straight movie version of the story, *Anna and the King of Siam* (US 46), taken from Margaret Landon's fictionalized biography which was based on the autobiography of Anna Leonowens.

Not even Shakespeare is immune. Huddersfield Theatre Royal advertised *Hamlet* in April 1952 as 'The Play of the Famous Film'.

The first university thesis written on the subject of the cinema was sociology major Ray LeRoy Short's *A Social Study of the Motion Picture*, which earned its author an MA degree from the University of Iowa in 1916.

The first film script to be published in book form was by Carl Mayer for Lupu Pick's *Sylvester* (Ger 23), about a grocer (Eugen Knopfer) who is unable to resolve the jealousy between his wife and his mistress and hangs himself, which was published in Berlin in 1924.

The first dialogue film script to be published in book form was Henri Ette's *The North Pole*, described as 'A 100% Tone and Speaking Picture with Songs, Choruses and Dances', issued by Ette Publications, Faroe Isles, 1931.

The first script of an American movie issued in book form was *The Mighty Barnum* by Gene Fowler and Bess Meredith, published by Covici-Friede, New York, 1934.

The first script of a British movie issued in book form was *The Private Life of Henry VIII*, story and dialogue by Lajos Biro, edited by Ernest Betts, and published by Methuen at 3s 6d in 1934.

Only one script has ever been published by a studio: *In Old Chicago*, by Lamar Trotti and Sonya Levien, Twentieth Century Fox Film Corp., Beverly Hills, 1937.

The first autobiography of a star was Pearl White's *Just Me*, published by Doran of New York in 1916. It is a lively and wholly unreliable account of her rise as the Queen of the Silent Serials.

The star with the largest number of biographies is Charles Spencer Chaplin (1889–1977), whose life and art have been expounded in 289 book-length works. (A full bibliography by Swedish scholar Lennart Eriksson is due for the Chaplin centenary.)

The most biographied female star is Marilyn Monroe (1926–62), with 56 life stories, followed by Greta Garbo (1905–) with 26.

The highest advance for a star's autobiography was the $1 million paid by New York publisher Dick Snyder to Greta Garbo in 1977. Under the terms of the contract her life story, told by Miss Garbo to Antony Gronowitz over a period of five years, will not be published until after her death.

The first film journal was *Le Bulletin Phonographique et Cinématographique*, established in Paris as a fortnightly during the summer of 1899.

The first film journal in Britain was *The Optical Lantern and Cinematograph Journal*, monthly, price 3d, which commenced publication in November 1904. The opening number included an interview with pioneer producer Charles Urban, in which he deplored films 'depicting crime, immorality, foolhardiness, drunkenness and other vices': reviews of *Lady Plumpton's Motor* (GB 04), *The Jonah Man*

(GB 04) and a rather daring Gaumont offering (of which Mr Urban was doubtless disapproving) called *Mixed Bathing* (GB 04); and such items of trade intelligence as 'The National Sunday League have introduced animated pictures into their Sunday programmes' and 'Look out for a new style of home cinematograph projector, at two guineas'.

The first American film journal was *Views and Film Index* in 1906.

The first fan magazines were Italy's *Il Cinematagrafo* and Spain's *El Cinematagrafo*, both established in 1907.

America's first fan magazine was *Motion Picture Story Magazine*, founded by J. Stuart Blackton of Vitagraph as a monthly in February 1911.

The first fan magazine in Britain was *Pictures*, weekly 1d, founded on 21 October 1911. It consisted mainly of fiction based on film scenarios, illustrated with stills from the films summarized, but a regular feature called 'Picture Notes from All Parts' retailed such interesting snippets of information as the fact that four million people went to the pictures daily (1911), that Florence Lawrence was making 300 films a year and was America's highest paid star at £50 a week, that newsreel producers had paid £200 for special positions on the Coronation route, and that Leyton Public Library was blaming local cinemas for a decline in the number of books issued.

In 1931 *Film Favourite* offered the factory girls of depression-hit Britain the dream of becoming a star . . . while *Movie Fan* preferred a role model for 6d.

The most extensive cinema press in the world belongs to India, which had 630 film magazines of all kinds at the latest count. During the silent period, Japan had the most prolific film press, with 104 fan magazines existing in 1926, including one of the only journals ever devoted solely to a single star—*Kurishima Notebook*, for fans of the Japanese 'Queen of the Silents' Sumiko Kurishima.

The august and sober *Financial Times*, headlining its story of the 1987 takeover of America's showbiz bible *Variety* by British conglomerate Reed International: '*Variety* in splice of life: Tinseltown Telegraph Finds Reed All About It.'

The first cartoon about the cinema was published in France in the satirical newspaper *Le Charivari* on 19 April 1896. It shows a man giving a cinematograph camera to a couple of newlyweds and advising them cynically: 'In 45 years time you'll be able to see again the only agreeable moment of your marriage.' No less than three other cartoons about the cinema followed in *Le Charivari* in May and several others over the next year, some of which used the movies as a vehicle for political satire.

The first-ever cartoon about the cinema—in this case home movies. *Le Charivari*, 19 April 1896. (Stephen Bottomore)

Britain's first cartoon about the cinema. *Scraps*, 16 January 1897. (Stephen Bottomore)

Farmer, Ruggles (at the Eldorado Palace): "Here, I want to see this Annie Mattygraph. What time does she come on?"

The first cartoon concerning films to be published in a newspaper was also a vehicle for political satire. This was in the *Cape Register* (South Africa) of 19 September 1896 and showed the Edison Vitascope in a political lampoon about excessive customs charges.

Britain's first cartoon about the cinema was in the comic paper *Scraps* for 16 January 1897. It was a simple joke with a country bumpkin, Farmer Ruggles, seeing a poster for the Animatograph and thinking that it was a performer, 'Annie Mattygraph'.

America published its first cartoon on cinema in the comic journal *Judge* on 20 February 1897. It shows Cyrus Jayson walking home along the railway track, somewhat the worse for drink. A train approaches but he thinks it's just a film because he's 'seen them kinettyscope pictures before'.

The first painting on a cinematic theme is an oil of 1907 by American artist John Sloan (1871–1951) titled *Movies, five cents*. It shows a nickelodeon audience watching a film of a couple kissing and is in a private collection in New York.

The first British work of art about the cinema is Malcolm Drummond's *In the Cinema* of 1912–13.

The first regular film column in a newspaper began appearing in the *New York Morning Journal* in 1909.

The first regular film column in a newspaper in Britain was a weekly feature titled 'Around the Cinema Palaces' written by W. G. Faulkner for the *Evening News*, commencing 17 January 1912. It was to be many years, though, before editors were to regard screen journalism as having any connection with the arts. In 1921 the editor of a leading London newspaper remarked that their film page was intended solely for East End readers, the only film news worthy of attention outside slumdom being the activities of Mary Pickford or Charlie Chaplin.

Film Criticism

This was born with a brief review of *May Irwin Kiss* (US 96) in the *Chap Book* for 15 June 1896: '. . . absolutely disgusting'.

In the early days of screen journalism the trade journals used to carry plot outlines, but there was little attempt to assess the merits of the new films.

The first regular film critic was Frank Woods, who began reviewing for the *New York Dramatic Mirror* with the issue of 1 May 1909. Woods used

---

A review of *Luffar-Petter/Peter the Tramp* (Swe 22) in the Swedish magazine *Swing* commented of one of the supporting players: 'Since Miss Gustafsson has so far had only the dubious pleasure of having to play a "bathing beauty" for Mr Erik Perschler in his fire department film, we have received no impression whatever of her capacity. It pleases us, though, to have the opportunity of noting a new name in Swedish films, and we hope we have a chance to mention it again.'

It was mentioned again, but by then the name had changed to Garbo.

---

the pen-name 'Spectator'. His salary was $20 a week.

None of the performers were identified in early reviews. *Variety* seems to have been the first to discard this anonymity, the issue for 21 January 1911 referring to Mary Pickford's 'cute ways and girlish manner' in *The Italian Barber* (US 11).

The first newspaper to carry film reviews was *Vilag* (*World*), a Budapest daily, which engaged Sándor Kellner as its critic in August 1912. Kellner's sojourn with the paper was brief, since he was determined to get into the production side of the movie business, which he did with spectacular success as (Sir) Alexander Korda.

The first American newspaper to employ a regular film critic was the *Chicago Tribune* with the appointment of John Lawson in 1914. Lawson was killed in an accident soon after and his place was taken by Miss Audrie Alspaugh, who wrote under the by-line 'Kitty Kelly'. Movie historian Terry Ramsaye recalled: 'Kitty Kelly could make or break a picture in the Middle West . . . Her column was a large success, and she became the best disliked name in the world of the film studios'.

Chicago to New York might seem a long way to go for the sake of just ten seconds of screen time, but it was not too far for the Windy City's ace critics Siskel and Ebert. The film they flew to see was the X-rated version of Alan Parker's *Angel Heart* (US 87), which is just 10 seconds longer than the R-rated version for general release. Less mobile critics outside New York had to be content with reviewing the cut version and exercising their own imaginations about what had so exercised the censor's imagination. For the curious, the scene that was scissored depicted Mickey Rourke making love to a 17-year-old black girl, played by Lisa Bonet, while blood gushed down on to them from the ceiling.

Stay Away Crits

Verbal annihilation has been the stock in trade of the film critic ever since the very first review. Here are a few intimations that the critic did not think the picture deserved his unqualified approval.

☆ Anthony Slide on Marguerite Duras's *India Song* (Fr 75) 'Without question the most boring, pretentious feature ever foisted on the general public'.

☆ Alan Brien of the *Sunday Times* on Irwin Allen's *The Swarm* (US 78) 'Simply the worst film ever made'.

☆ *Variety* on *The Gong Show Movie* (US 80) 'Bong-g-g-g-g'.

☆ Vincent Canby on the $48 million *Inchon* (US/Kor 82) 'The most expensive B-movie ever made'.

☆ *Variety*: 'Lonesome Cowboy is Andy Warhol's best movie to date, which is like saying a three-year-old has graduated from smearing faeces on the wall to the occasional use of finger paints'.

☆ Anonymous critic on *Cleopatra* (US 63) 'Elizabeth Taylor is the first Cleopatra to sail down the Nile to Las Vegas'.

☆ *New York Daily News* on *Hawk of Powder River* (US 48) 'Eddie Dean's latest is in black and white rather than color but the improvement is hardly noticeable; you can still see him'.

☆ Judith Crist on *The Agony and the Ecstasy* (US 65) 'All agony, no ecstasy'.

☆ *Variety* on *Way Back Home* (Bel 81) 'So poor that it gives amateurism a bad name'.

☆ Gary Arnold of the *Washington Post* on Ken Russell's biopic of Tchaikovsky *The Music Lovers* (GB 71) 'Awful . . . the worst experience I ever had in a cinema'.

☆ *Variety* on *Les Enfants du Paradis* (Fr 44) —which is probably the most universally admired foreign language film of all time 'Downright dull'.

☆ Colin Bennett of the *Melbourne Age* on Australia's first sexploitation movie *The Set* (Aus 70) 'At last my 18-year search for the worst film ever made has ended'.

☆ Alan Parker on *The Draughtsman's Contract* (GB 83) 'A load of posturing poo poo'.

☆ John Simon on *Camelot* (US 67) 'This film is the Platonic idea of boredom, roughly comparable to reading a three-volume novel in a language of which one knows only the alphabet'.

☆ James Agee on *You Were Meant For Me* (US 48) 'That's what you think'.

☆ *Variety* on *Movie Movie* (US 78) 'Awful Awful'.

☆ David Aasen of *Newsweek* on *A Dream of Passion* (US 78) 'As one endures the spectacle of Mercouri bearing her soul . . . it seems one has wandered into the home movies of a demented culture maven'.

☆ C. A. Lejeune on *No Leave No Love* (US 46) 'No Comment'. (This was the complete review.)

☆ *Variety* on *The American Prisoner* (GB 29) 'Save for direction, story, dialog, acting and being a period picture, this is a good one'.

☆ The *Reporter* magazine on *Guess Who's Coming to Dinner* (US 67) 'Abie's Irish Rose in Blackface'.

☆ 'Cart' of *Variety* on *The Lion with the White Mane* (Cz 87) 'All concerned should run and hide . . .'.

☆ Pauline Kael on *Blue Collar* (US 78) 'Jukebox Marxism'.

☆ *Variety* on Vadim's *And God Created Woman* (Fr 57), which became the most successful foreign film ever released in America, 'Just average for any US possibilities . . . questionable attributes of the new star here, Miss Bardot'.

☆ David Denby of *New York* magazine on Sylvester Stalione's *Cobra* (US 86) 'Senselessly crude, laughably unbelievable . . . unimaginably degraded'.

Variety gave the thumbs down to Vadim's sensationally successful *And God Created Woman* (Fr 57) due to 'the questionable attributes of the new star here, Miss Bardot'. Well, it was the Doris Day era . . . (*Kobal*)

FOURTEEN

AWARDS AND FESTIVALS

The first film awards were made in respect of a festival which opened in Monte Carlo on New Year's Day 1898. The competition was open to professionals and amateurs alike but subjects had to be taken in Monaco. The first prize was worth £80, and there were two others worth £40 and £20. The following year the competition was expanded. Prize money was increased to a total of £1200 (30,000 francs) plus a number of honourable mentions and this time it was purely for amateurs. It was organized by the Societé des Bains de Mer who stipulated that each competitor must send in three films of any place or subject which should never previously have been exhibited. The jury was to be composed of 'artists and amateurs' and films were judged on 'originality, artistic merit and photographic quality', according to the *British Journal of Photography*. The prizes were awarded in February 1900 by the Prince of Monaco and the winning entries were shown at the Palais des Beaux Arts. The titles of the winning films are not recorded.

Among the more recondite awards made at film festivals is the one presented at Varna International Film Festival in Bulgaria for 'artistic impact and subtlety in treating maternity as a basic human value'.

The first award winning film known by name was Giovanni Vitrotti's *Il Cane riconescente* (It 07), an Ambrosio production which won a gold plaque awarded by the Lumière brothers at an international contest held in Italy in 1907.

The first award made to a feature film was also won by Ambrosio. The Grand Prix of 25,000 francs at the International Exhibition at Turin in 1912 went to *After Fifty Years* (It 12), an historical drama set in the Austro–Italian War of 1859.

The first annual awards and the oldest extant were instituted in 1917 by America's National Board of Review of Motion Pictures.

Britain's first film festival was the International Festival of Women's Films, held in London in 1928. The first prize went to Dorothy Arzner's *Fashions For Women* (US 27). The only other pre-war festival on record was a non-competitive event held at Malvern in 1931, notable chiefly for the pre-release presentation of the first Bernard Shaw talkie, *How He Lied to Her Husband* (GB 31) with Edmund Gwenn.

The first regular film festival was held as part of the Venice Biennale and took place at the Hotel Excelsior from 6 to 21 August 1932, the purpose behind it being an attempt to revive the depression-hit tourist trade. A total of 18 pictures were entered by Germany, the USA, France, Italy and the UK, three of them directed by women. No awards were made.

The only floating film festival was CineKid '87, which was held aboard a boat which journeyed down the Rhine from Switzerland to Amsterdam (where the Festival took to dry land for a week) during the summer of 1987. The vessel contained two cinemas and wherever she berthed along the way, local children were invited aboard to see the festival selections for free.

A Selection of Specialist Festivals

Red Cross and health films: Varna
Mystery films: 'Mystfest', Cattolica, Italy
Ecological: 'Nature, Man and His Environment'— held each year in different Italian city
Trailers: Promo Film Festival, Maddona di Campiglio, Italy
Black films: Berlin Festival of Black Cinema
American Indian films: San Francisco
Art films: Montreal
Agrarian films: Zaragoza, Spain
Celtic films: Inverness, Scotland
Sci-fi films: 'Imagfic', Madrid
Children's films: Bhopal, India
Youth films: Laon, France
Erotic films: Madrid
Low-budget films: Hamburg
Student-made films: Tours, France

Generally reckoned the most originally-themed festival of 1987 was 'The Seven Deadly Sins Festival' held in New York. The sins were represented by the following pictures: Greed— Erich von Stroheim's *Greed* (US 24); Lust— F. W. Murnau's *Sunrise* (US 27); Envy—Joseph L. Mankiewicz's *All About Eve* (US 50); Gluttony—Percy Adlon's *Sugarbaby* (FRG 85); Sloth—Nikita Mikhalkov's *Oblomov* (USSR 79); Pride—Orson Welles's *The Magnificent Ambersons* (US 42); Anger—Fritz Lang's *Fury* (US 36).

Banned films: San Francisco
Silent films: Pordenone, Italy
Aboriginal films: Pincher Creek, Alberta
Women's films: 'Silence, Elles tournent!', Montreal

A CADEMY AWARDS

These were instituted by the Academy of Motion Picture Arts and Sciences and first presented on 16 May 1929. The awards that year were to dignify the efforts of film-makers during the 12 months August 1927 to July 1928—and at the same time to dignify, the Academy hoped, the somewhat tarnished reputation the film industry had earned itself in the 'roaring twenties'.

Oscar, the Academy Award trophy, is the figure of a man with a crusader's sword standing on a reel of film. Until 1931 it was known simply as 'The Statuette', but in that year Academy librarian Margaret Herrick chanced to remark 'He looks like my Uncle Oscar' and the name stuck. Plated in 10 carat gold, Oscar has always stood 13½ inches tall, except in war time when the trophy consisted of a gold-plated plaster plaque with the Oscar figure in relief. The value of an Oscar is about $150. Recipients pledge never to sell their statuette except back to the Academy, who will pay $10 for it. Between 1936 and 1939 the members of the Board of the Academy had to pay for the Oscar statuettes out of their own pockets as the Academy was so short of funds. Double Oscar winning scriptwriter Frances Marion says that she sees the statuette as 'a perfect symbol of the picture business: a powerful athletic body clutching a gleaming sword, with half of his head, that part which held his brains, completely sliced off'.

The most awards in any category have been won by Walt Disney (1901–66), who was honoured with 26 regular and six special trophies.

The most awards for individual creative achievement are the eleven won by Cedric Gibbon (1893–1960) of MGM for art direction; the most won by a woman are the eight by costume designer Edith Head (1907–81).

The largest number of films qualifying for consideration for an Academy Award was 264 for the 47th Awards in 1974. During the 1980s the figure has fluctuated around the 250 mark, representing a little less than half the films released annually in the USA. To qualify a film has to have played publicly in Los Angeles for at least a week within specified dates.

The most awards won by any one film went to *Ben Hur* (US 59) and numbered eleven: Best Picture; Best Director; Best Actor; Best Supporting Actor; Cinematography; Art Direction; Sound; Music Score; Film Editing; Special Effects; Costume.

The most awards won by a British film went to *Gandhi* (GB 83) and numbered eight: Best Picture; Best Actor; Best Director; Best Original Screenplay; Cinematography; Film Editing; Art Direction; Costume Design.

The most nominations for awards were made in respect of *All About Eve* (US 50) with 14. It won six.

The most nominated films to receive no awards were *The Turning Point* (US 77) and *The Color Purple* (US 86), each with 11 nominations.

Only two films have won 'The Big Five' major awards—Best Picture; Best Director; Best Actor; Best Actress; Best Screenplay. They are: *It Happened One Night* (US 34)—Frank Capra; Clark Gable; Claudette Colbert; Robert Riskin; and *One Flew Over the Cuckoo's Nest* (US 75)—Milos Forman; Jack Nicholson; Louise Fletcher; Lawrence Hauben and Bo Goldman.

The most Best Director awards have been made to John Ford, who won four times: *The Informer* (US 35); *The Grapes of Wrath* (US 40); *How Green was my Valley* (US 41); *The Quiet Man* (US 52).

The only time that all five Best Director nominations went to non-American directors was

Casting the Oscars at the Southern California Trophy Company in 1949. The 'high hats' were knocked off before the figures were dipped in a bath of liquid gold. (*Popperfoto*)

in 1988: Bernardo Bertolucci (It) for *The Last Emperor*; John Boorman (GB) for *Hope and Glory*; Adrian Lyne (GB) for *Fatal Attraction*; Lasse Hallström (Swe) for *My Life As a Dog*; and Norman Jewison (Can) for *Moonstruck*. The winner was Bernardo Bertolucci.

The most Best Actor awards have been won by four actors, each with two Oscars: Spencer Tracy for *Captains Courageous* (US 37) and *Boys Town* (US 38); Fredric March for *Dr Jekyll and Mr Hyde* (US 32) and *The Best Years of our Lives* (US 46); Gary Cooper for *Sergeant York* (US 41) and *High Noon* (US 52); and Marlon Brando for *On the Waterfront* (US 54) and *The Godfather* (US 72). Tracy, though, received nine nominations during his career, against seven for Brando and five each for March and Cooper. Sir Laurence Olivier has equalled Tracy's nominations, but won only a single Best Actor award for *Hamlet* (GB 48). Perhaps Tracy should also take first place by virtue of the fact that Katharine Hepburn is on record as saying that one of her Academy Awards was doubtless intended for both of them.

The most Best Actress awards have been won by Katharine Hepburn, whose four Oscars were awarded for *Morning Glory* (US 33), *Guess Who's Coming to dinner* (US 67), *The Lion in Winter* (GB 68) and *On Golden Pond* (US 81). Miss Hepburn also enjoys the distinction of having received the most nominations of any performer (13), and of having the longest award-winning career, spanning 48 years.

The first co-stars to win Best Actor and Best Actress award in the same year were Clark Gable and Claudette Colbert, for *It Happened One Night* (US 34). Miss Colbert was so sceptical of her chances of winning the Oscar that she decided not to postpone a trip to New York on a train scheduled to leave on the evening of the ceremony. She was just stepping into the carriage when officials of the Academy arrived to tell her she had won. A motorcycle escort rushed her to the Biltmore Bowl to receive the award, still dressed in her travelling clothes.

Other co-stars who won in the same year have been: Jack Nicholson and Louise Fletcher: *One Flew Over the Cuckoo's Nest* (US 75); Peter Finch and Faye Dunaway: *Network* (US 76); Jon Voight and Jane Fonda: *Coming Home* (US 78); Henry Fonda and Katharine Hepburn: *On Golden Pond* (US 81).

The only tie for Best Actor was between Wallace Beery in *The Champ* (US 31) and Fredric March in *Dr Jekyll and Mr Hyde* (US 31).

The only tie for Best Actress was between Barbra Streisand in *Funny Girl* (US 68) and Katharine Hepburn in *The Lion in Winter* (GB 68).

The following members of the same family have won Oscars in the same year: brother and sister Douglas and Norma Shearer, he for Sound Recording on *The Big House* (US 30), she as Best Actress in *The Divorcee* (US 30); father and son Walter and John Huston, both for *The Treasure of the Sierra Madre* (US 47), as Best Supporting Actor and Best Director, respectively; brothers Richard M. and Robert B. Sherman for Best Song, 'Chim-Chim Cher-ee' in *Mary Poppins* (US 63); and father and son Carmine and Francis Coppola, both for *The Godfather Part II* (US 74), as composer of Best Original Dramatic Score and Best Director respectively.

The shortest performance to win an Oscar was Anthony Quinn's eight-minute *tour de force* as Gauguin in *Lust for Life* (US 56), which won him the 1956 Best Supporting Actor award.

The first Oscar winning debut performance was by Gale Sondegaard in *Anthony Adverse* (US 36), for which she won the Best Supporting Actress Award.

The first performer to win an award for a foreign language film was Sophia Loren, whose role in *Two Women* (It 61) secured her the Oscar for Best Actress.

Only two non-professionals have won acting Oscars: Canadian war veteran Harold Russell for his role as the handless ex-soldier (Russell himself had had his hands blown off) in *The Best Years of Our Lives* (US 46); and Cambodian refugee Dr Haing S. Ngor for his moving performance as a victim of Cambodia's Pol Pot regime in *The Killing Fields* (GB 84).

The youngest Oscar winner was Shirley Temple, who won a Special Award at the age of six for 'her outstanding contribution to screen entertainment during the year 1934'.

The youngest person to receive a regular Academy Award was 9-year-old Tatum O'Neal, who won the Oscar for Best Supporting Actress for her role in *Paper Moon* (US 73).

The oldest Oscar winner was George Burns, who was 80 when he collected his Best Supporting Actor award for *The Sunshine Boys* (US 75).

The first black Oscar winner was Hattie McDaniel, who was awarded Best Supporting Actress for her role as Mammy in *Gone with the Wind* (US 39). Twenty-four years elapsed before another black performer won a regular Oscar: Sidney Poitier was awarded Best Actor for *Lilies of the Field* (US 63).

The only western to win Best Film was *Cimarron* (US 31).

The only sequel to win Best Film was *The Godfather Part II* (US 74). *The Godfather* (US 72) also won.

The first Award winner to refuse an Oscar was Dudley Nichols, voted Best Writer (Screenplay) for *The Informer* (US 35). Nichols gave as his reason loyalty to the Writers Guild, which together with other unions was trying to force a boycott of the Academy Awards in their fight for recognition by the studios.

The first performer to refuse an Oscar was George C. Scott, winner of Best Actor for *Patton* (US 70).

The longest acceptance speech was made by Greer Garson on receiving the Best Actress award for *Mrs Miniver* (US 42) —it lasted over an hour.

The first person to know the identity of the Oscar winners is the anonymous auditor at accountancy firm Price Waterhouse & Co. whose job it is to count the votes from the 4200 voting members of the Academy of Motion Picture Arts and Sciences.

THE ACADEMY AWARD FOR THE BEST FILM

Dates given are year award was made
1929 *Wings* (US)
1930 *Broadway Melody* (US)
1931 *All Quiet on the Western Front* (US)
1932 *Cimarron* (US)
1933 *Grand Hotel* (US)
1934 *Cavalcade* (US)
1935 *It Happened One Night* (US)
1936 *Mutiny on the Bounty* (US)
1937 *The Great Ziegfeld* (US)
1938 *The Life of Emile Zola* (US)
1939 *You Can't Take It With You* (US)
1940 *Gone with the Wind* (US)
1941 *Rebecca* (US)
1942 *How Green was my Valley* (US)
1943 *Mrs Miniver* (US)
1944 *Casablanca* (US)
1945 *Going my Way* (US)
1946 *The Lost Weekend* (US)
1947 *The Best Years of Our Lives* (US)
1948 *Gentlemen's Agreement* (US)

1949 *Hamlet* (GB)
1950 *All the King's Men* (US)
1951 *All About Eve* (US)
1952 *An American in Paris* (US)
1953 *The Greatest Show on Earth* (US)
1954 *From Here to Eternity* (US)
1955 *On the Waterfront* (US)
1956 *Marty* (US)
1957 *Around the World in 80 Days* (US)
1958 *The Bridge on the River Kwai* (GB)
1959 *Gigi* (US)
1960 *Ben Hur* (US)
1961 *The Apartment* (US)
1962 *West Side Story* (US)
1963 *Lawrence of Arabia* (GB)
1964 *Tom Jones* (GB)
1965 *My Fair Lady* (US)
1966 *The Sound of Music* (US)
1967 *A Man for All Seasons* (GB)
1968 *In the Heat of the Night* (US)
1969 *Oliver!* (GB)

1970 *Midnight Cowboy* (US)
1971 *Patton* (US)
1972 *The French Connection* (US)
1973 *The Godfather* (US)
1974 *The Sting* (US)
1975 *The Godfather, Part Two* (US)
1976 *One Flew Over the Cuckoo's Nest* (US)
1977 *Rocky* (US)
1978 *Annie Hall* (US)
1979 *The Deer Hunter* (US)
1980 *Kramer vs Kramer* (US)
1981 *Ordinary People* (US)
1982 *Chariots of Fire* (GB)
1983 *Gandhi* (GB)
1984 *Terms of Endearment* (US)
1985 *Amadeus* (US)
1986 *Out of Africa* (US)
1987 *Platoon* (US)
1988 *The Last Emperor* (It/GB/Chn)

THE BERLIN FILM FESTIVAL AWARD FOR BEST FILM

The Berlin Film Festival was established in 1951. There was no overall Best Film award in the first year and from 1952–55 the films were voted for by the audience. The Golden Bear award for Best Picture was inaugurated 1956.
1952 *She Danced for the Summer* (Swe)
1953 *The Wages of Fear* (Fr)
1954 *Hobson's Choice* (GB)
1955 *The Rats* (FRG)
1956 *Invitation to the Dance* (GB)
1957 *Twelve Angry Men* (US)
1958 *The End of the Day* (Swe)
1959 *The Cousins* (Fr)
1960 *Lazarillo de Tormes* (Sp)
1961 *La Notte* (It)
1962 *A Kind of Loving* (GB)

1963 *Oath of Obedience* (FRG); *The Devil* (It)
1964 *Dry Summer* (Tur)
1965 *Alphaville* (Fr)
1966 *Cul de Sac* (GB)
1967 *Le Depart* (Bel)
1968 *Ole Dole Doff* (Swe)
1969 *Early Years* (Yug)
1970 No award
1971 *The Garden of the Finzi-Continis* (It)
1972 *The Canterbury Tales* (It)
1973 *Distant Thunder* (Ind)
1974 *The Apprenticeship of Duddy Kravitz* (Can)
1975 *Orkobefogadas* (Hun)
1976 *Buffalo Bill and the Indians* (US) —award declined

1977 *The Ascent* (USSR)
1978 *The Trouts* (Sp); *The Words of Max* (Sp)
1979 *David* (FRG)
1980 *Heartland* (US); *Palermo Oder Wolfsburg* (FRG)
1981 *Di Presa Di Presa* (Sp)
1982 *Die Sehnsucht der Veronica Voss* (FRG)
1983 *Ascendancy* (GB); *The Beehive* (Sp)
1984 *Love Streams* (US 84)
1985 *Wetherby* (GB); *Die Frau und der Fremde* (FRG)
1986 *Stammheim* (FRG)
1987 *The Theme* (USSR)
1988 *Red Shorghum* (Chn)

BRITISH FILM ACADEMY

Best British Film Award (1948–68)
Best Film Award (1969–)
1948 *Odd Man Out*
1949 *The Fallen Idol*
1950 *The Third Man*
1951 *The Blue Lamp*
1952 *The Lavender Hill Mob*
1953 *The Sound Barrier*
1954 *Genevieve*
1955 *Hobson's Choice*
1956 *Richard III*
1957 *Reach for the Sky*
1958 *The Bridge on the River Kwai*
1959 *Room at the Top*
1960 *Sapphire*

1961 *Saturday Night and Sunday Morning*
1962 *A Taste of Honey*
1963 *Lawrence of Arabia*
1964 *Tom Jones*
1965 *Dr Strangelove*
1966 *The Ipcress File*
1967 *The Spy who Came in from the Cold*
1968 *A Man for All Seasons*
1969 *The Graduate* (US)
1970 *Midnight Cowboy* (US)
1971 *Butch Cassidy and the Sundance Kid* (US)
1972 *Sunday Bloody Sunday* (GB)
1973 *Cabaret* (US)

1974 *La Nuite Americaine/Day for Night* (Fr)
1975 *Lacombe, Lucien* (Fr)
1976 *Alice Doesn't Live Here Anymore* (US)
1977 *One Flew Over the Cuckoo's Nest* (US)
1978 *Annie Hall* (US)
1979 *Julia* (US)
1980 *Manhattan* (US)
1981 *The Elephant Man* (GB)
1982 *Chariots of Fire* (GB)
1983 *Gandhi* (GB)
1984 *Educating Rita* (GB)
1985 *The Killing Fields* (GB)
1986 *The Purple Rose of Cairo* (US)
1987 *A Room with a View* (GB)
1988 *Jean de Florette* (Fr)

CANNES FILM FESTIVAL

Palme d'Or for Best Film
1946 *La Bataille du Rail* (Fr)
1946 *Antoine et Antoinette* (Fr)
1948 No festival
1949 *The Third Man* (GB)
1950 No festival
1951 *Miracle in Milan* (It); *Miss Julie* (Swe)
1952 *Othello* (Mor); *Two Cents Worth of Hope* (It)
1953 *Wages of Fear* (Fr)
1954 *Gate of Hell* (Jap)
1955 *Marty* (US)
1956 *World of Silence* (Fr)
1957 *Friendly Persuasion* (US)
1958 *The Cranes are Flying* (USSR)
1959 *Black Orpheus* (Fr)
1960 *La Dolce Vita* (It)

1961 *Viridiana* (Sp); *Une aussi longue absence* (Fr)
1962 *The Given Word* (Bra)
1963 *The Leopard* (It)
1964 *The Umbrellas of Cherbourg* (Fr)
1965 *The Knack* (GB)
1966 *A Man and a Woman* (Fr); *Signore e Signori* (It)
1967 *Blow-Up* (GB)
1968 Festival disrupted; no awards
1969 *If* (GB)
1970 *M*A*S*H* (US)
1971 *The Go-Between* (GB)
1972 *The Working Class Goes to Paradise* (It); *The Mattei Affair* (It)
1973 *Scarecrow* (US); *The Hireling* (GB)
1974 *The Conversation* (US)

1975 *Chronicle of the Burning Years* (Alg)
1976 *Taxi Driver* (US)
1977 *Padre Padrone* (It)
1978 *L'Albero Degli Zoccoli* (It)
1979 *The Tin Drum* (FRG); *Apocalypse Now* (US)
1980 *All That Jazz* (US); *Kagemusha* (Jap)
1981 *Man of Iron* (Pol)
1982 *Missing* (US); *Yol* (Tur)
1983 *The Ballad of Narayama* (Jap)
1984 *Paris, Texas* (FRG)
1985 *When Father Was Away On Business* (Yug)
1986 *The Mission* (GB)
1987 *Under the Sun of Satan* (Fr)
1988 *Pelle the Conqueror* (Den)

VENICE FILM FESTIVAL

Best Foreign Film Award (1934–42)
Best Film Award (1946–68)
Golden Lion for Best Film (1980–)
1932 No official award
1933 No festival
1934 *Man of Aran* (GB)
1935 *Anna Karenina* (US)
1936 *Der Kaiser von Kalifornien* (Ger)
1937 *Un Carnet de Bal* (Fr)
1938 *Olympia* (Ger)
1939 No award
1940 *Der Postmeister* (Ger)
1941 *Ohm Kruger* (Ger)
1942 *Der grosse König* (Ger)
1943–45 No festival
1946 *The Southerner* (US)

1947 *Sirena* (Cz)
1948 *Hamlet* (GB)
1949 *Manon* (Fr)
1950 *Justice is Done* (Fr)
1951 *Rashomon* (Jap)
1952 *Forbidden Games* (Fr)
1953 No award
1954 *Romeo and Juliet* (It/GB)
1955 *Ordet* (Den)
1956 No award
1957 *Aparajito* (Ind)
1958 *Muhomatsu no Issho* (Jap)
1959 *Il Generale della Rovere* (It)
1960 *Le Passage du Rhine* (Fr)
1961 *Last Year at Marienbad* (Fr)
1962 *Childhood of Ivan* (USSR)

1963 *Le Mani sulla citta* (It)
1964 *Red Desert* (It)
1965 *Of a Thousand Delights* (It)
1966 *Battle of Algiers* (It)
1967 *Belle de Jour* (Fr)
1968 *Die Aristen in der Zirkuskuppel* (FRG)
Jury and award system discontinued 1969–80.
1980 *Gloria* (US); *Atlantic City* (Fr/Can)
1981 *Die Bleierne Zeit* (FRG)
1982 *The State of Things* (FRG)
1983 *Prenom Carmen* (Fr/Swz)
1984 *Year of the Quiet Sun* (Pol)
1985 *Sans toit ni loi aka Vagabonde* (Fr)
1986 *Le Rayon Vert* (Fr)
1987 *Au Revoir les Enfants* (Fr)

THE GREATEST AMERICAN FILMS OF ALL TIME (1977)

These were selected in 1977 by means of a ballot of the 35,000 members of the American Film Institute, each of whom was asked to name his or her Top Five. A total of 1100 films were nominated, from which the AFI compiled a list of 50 which had received the most 'votes'. A second ballot was then held, the members being asked to select their Top Five from the list of 50. Considering the effort put into this survey, it is less than reassuring to find that four British productions were included amongst the 50 'Greatest American Films' and that two of these (*2001: A Space Odyssey* and *The African Queen*) emerged in the final Top Ten listing, a permutation based on the results of the second ballot. The titles of the AFI's Top Ten Greatest American Films of All Time are, in order of greatness:

1 *Gone with the Wind* (1939)
2 *Citizen Kane* (1941)
3 *Casablanca* (1942)
4 *The African Queen* (1952)
5 *The Grapes of Wrath* (1940)
6 *One Flew Over the Cuckoo's Nest* (1975)
7 *Singin' in the Rain* (1952)
8 *Star Wars* (1977)
9 *2001: A Space Odyssey* (1968)
10 *The Wizard of Oz* (1939)

BFI MEMBERS' TOP 30 FILMS

On the occasion of its 50th anniversary, the British Film Institute polled 1200 members on their best 30 films of all time. Over 2000 films were nominated and the top 30 were presented at the National Film Theatre in September 1983. Programme director Ken Wlaschin wrote: 'Analysing the results, the top 30 films range in date from 1935 to 1979 but include no silent pictures (Keaton's *The General* came in at number 31). America won 16 positions, Britain four, France seven and Japan, Italy and Germany each one. Three directors had two films selected: Billy Wilder, Jean Renoir and John Ford. Most genres were represented, with a preference for comedies and musicals and only one Western and one SF film.' The results:

1 *Casablanca* (US 42)
2 *Les Enfants du Paradis* (Fr 43–5)
3 *Citizen Kane* (US 41)
4 *Singin' in the Rain* (US 52)
5 *2001: A Space Odyssey* (GB 68)
6 *Some Like It Hot* (US 59)
7 *Seven Samurai* (Jap 54)
8 *Gone with the Wind* (US 39)
9 *The Third Man* (GB 49)
10 *One Flew Over the Cuckoo's Nest* (US 75)
11 *Céline and Julie Go Boating* (Fr 74)
12 *The Graduate* (US 67)
13 *Death in Venice* (It 71)
14 *La Grande Illusion* (Fr 37)
15 *Brief Encounter* (GB 45)
16 *Manhattan* (US 79)

17 *Top Hat* (US 35)
18 *Kind Hearts and Coronets* (GB 49)
19 *Apocalypse Now* (US 79)
20 *The Searchers* (US 56)
21 *Orphée* (Fr 50)
22 *Cabaret* (US 72)
23 *Psycho* (US 60)
24 *Henry V* (GB 44)
25 *Jules et Jim* (Fr 61)
26 *La Règle du Jeu* (Fr 39)
27 *Aguirre, Wrath of the Gods* (FRG 72)
28 *Monsieur Hulot's Holiday* (Fr 53)
29 *The Grapes of Wrath* (US 40)
30 *Double Indemnity* (US 44)

FIFTEEN

ANIMATION

The first animated film using the stop-motion technique to give the illusion of movement to inanimate objects was Vitagraph's *The Humpty Dumpty Circus* (US 98?). Albert E. Smith, who conceived the idea, borrowed his small daughter's toy circus and succeeded in animating the acrobats and animals by shooting them in barely changed positions one frame at a time—the same principle as that used for animated cartoons.

The earliest known British example of animation is an untitled advertising film made by Arthur Melbourne Cooper of St Albans, Herts, for Messrs Bryant & May. Dating from 1899, it consists of an appeal for funds to supply the troops in South Africa with matches, as it seems this was something the Army authorities had overlooked. The animated 'performers' are match-stick men who climb up a wall and form themselves into the legend: 'Send £1 and enough matches will be sent to supply a regiment of our fighting soldiers'.

Some years later, Melbourne Cooper made two charming films featuring animated toys, *Noah's Ark* (GB 08) and *Dreams of Toyland* (GB 08). Strutting teddy bears were featured in the latter with particularly engaging effect.

Meanwhile, in the United States, J. Stuart Blackton, Albert E. Smith's co-partner at Vita-

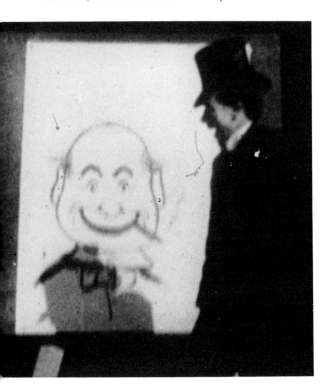

graph, had produced an unusual novelty with *The Haunted Hotel* (US 07), in which furniture moved about seemingly by its own agency.

The following year Pathé pioneered the animation of paper cut-outs in *Paper Cock-a-Doodle* (Fr 08) —the cut-outs being in the shape of exquisitely wrought birds. The pioneer of animation in Russia was Ladislas Starevitch, who applied the stop-motion technique to bring dead insects 'alive' in *The Grasshopper and the Ant* (Rus 11) and *The Stag Beetles* (Rus 11).

The first cartoon film was J. Stuart Blackton's *Humorous Phases of Funny Faces* (US 06), produced for the Vitagraph Co. of New York. Like nearly all early American film cartoonists, Blackton used the technique of showing an artist drawing a still picture which then magically came alive and moved. Most of the illusions were created by means of cardboard cut-outs, but a few genuinely animated drawings featured at the beginning of the film, showing a man and a woman rolling their eyes and the outline of a gentleman with bowler and umbrella apparently drawing himself.

The first British cartoon film was the Charles Urban production *The Clown and His Donkey* (GB 10), drawn by Charles Armstrong.

The first cartoon film to tell a story was Emile Cohl's *Fantasmagorie* (Fr 08), which was premièred at the Théâtre du Gymnase in Paris on 17 August 1908. Cohl made the film for Léon Gaumont, by whom he was employed as a scenarist. Prior to this, nearly all cartoon films were of the artist-drawing-a-living-picture genre. Robert Desnos has described Cohl as the first to 'cut the umbilical cord which still linked the life of the characters on the screen with the secretions of the fountain pen'. He made about 100 cartoons between 1908 and 1918 and can thus be regarded as **the first professional screen animator.**

The first use of matte photography to combine live action and animation together was by Emil Cohl in *Clair de Lune espagnol/Man in the Moon* (Fr 09). The film shows how Pedro the Matador,

The first step towards cartoon animation. In this Edison film of November 1900, *The Enchanted Drawing* (US 00), J. Stuart Blackton drew a humorous face which changed its expression while the artist stood aside. This was done by jump cutting and there was no illusion of movement. It was another six years before Blackton pioneered true animation in *Humorous Phases of Funny Faces* (US 06). (*Library of Congress*) having been captured by aliens from outer space, discharges various missiles at the Man in the Moon. Pedro is played by an actor, while the Moon's changing facial expressions are worked by animation. The most impressive illusion occurs when Pedro hurls a hatchet at the Moon. It starts as a real hatchet, but in mid-flight turns into a drawing of a hatchet, continuing on its way to land on the Moon's nose.

The first cartoon series was inaugurated by Emile Cohl with the debut of his character Fantôche, a kind of match-stick man combatting the cruel world, in *Le Cauchemar du Fantôche* (Fr 09). **The first cartoon series in America**, also inaugurated by Cohl, was Eclair's *The Newlyweds*, starting with *When He Wants a Dog, He Wants a Dog* (US 13). Based on George McManus's popular cartoon characters in the *New York World*, this was also **the first cartoon series adapted from a comic strip**. In addition to these innovations, the series also gave a new descriptive term to the vocabulary of film-making. It was an advertisement for *The Newlyweds*, appearing in *Moving Picture World* for 15 February 1913, that contained **the first use of the term 'animated cartoon'**.

The first British cartoon series was *Adventures of Slim and Pim* (GB 18), drawn by Leslie Dawson for Charles Urban's Kineto Co. Slim and Pim were two characters prone to Laurel and Hardy-type misadventures. First to feature animal characters was *The Wonderful Adventures of Pip, Squeek and Wilfred* (GB 21), 26 one-reel episodes based on the popular children's strip in the *Daily Mirror* by A. B. Payne and B. J. Lamb. The series was drawn by Lancelot Speed for Astra Films.

The first animal cartoon character was Old Doc Yak, a tail-coated billy-goat in striped pants, who was brought to the screen by *Chicago Tribune* cartoonist Sidney Smith in a Selig Polyscope series started in July 1913. It was the much-loved animal cartoon characters who eventually gave animated films a distinct appeal of their own as suitable entertainment for children. This development can best be dated from the advent of Pat Sullivan's Felix the Cat in 1919, an animal who 'kept on walking', and who was the first cartoon character to attain the celebrity of a human star. Felix was also **the first animated cartoon character to be merchandised**, both as an image on packaging and, in 1926, as a phenomenally successful cuddly toy.

The first cartoon talkie was *The Audion* (US 22), an animated physics film on the working of the three-element vacuum tube. Made by E. B. Craft of Western Electric, it was premièred at Woolsey Hall, Yale University, on 27 October 1922. The synchronized disc sound system used later developed into Vitaphone.

The first cartoon talkie for theatrical release was Max Fleischer's Koko Song Kar-Tune *My Old Kentucky Home* (US 26), in which Bimbo the dog plays a trombone and speaks the words: 'Now let's all follow the bouncing ball and sing along'. It was produced by Inkwell Studio Productions with sound-on-film accompaniment by DeForest Phonofilm.

The first all-talking cartoon was Paul Terry's 'Aesop's Film Fable' *Dinner Time* (US 28), produced by Van Beuren Enterprises in the RCA Photophone sound system and premièred at the Mark Strand Theater in New York on 1 September 1928. Walt Disney dismissed it as 'a lot of racket and nothing else'. His own initial venture in talkies, *Steamboat Willie* (US 28), presented at New York's Colony Theater on 18 November 1928, was more auspicious; it marked the debut of the most successful cartoon character of all time, Mickey Mouse.

The first British cartoon talkie was *The Jazz Stringer* (GB 28), with 'Orace the 'Armonious 'Ound, made at Wembley Studios by Joe Noble and his brother George ('Orace's voice) for British Sound Productions and premièred at the Tivoli Cinema in the Strand on 15 December 1928. It was claimed as 'the first lip synchronized cartoon in the world'.

Louis B. Mayer, notwithstanding the advice of MGM studio executives, refused to put aspiring cartoon-maker Walt Disney under contract in 1928 after seeing a preview of the first Mickey Mouse movie because he thought that pregnant women would be frightened of a 10-ft high rodent on the screen.

The first colour cartoon was *The Debut of Thomas Kat* (US 20), a Paramount release produced by the Bray Pictures Corporation of New York in the Brewster natural-colour process. The drawings were made on transparent celluloid and painted on the reverse, then filmed with a two-colour camera. An unfortunate kitten, Thomas Kat, had been taught by his mother to catch mice, but inadvertently mistook a rat for the smaller breed of rodent. There was no follow-up to this remarkable pioneering endeavour until 1925, when *The Flying Elephant* (US 25) was made in the Natural Color Kelly Process.

The first colour cartoon talkie was Ted Esbaugh's *Goofy Goat* (US 31), made in two-colour Multicolor and previewed at Warner's Alhambra Theater, Los Angeles, on 6 July 1931.

The first Disney colour cartoon (often erroneously claimed as 'the world's first colour cartoon'), and the first cartoon made in a three-colour process, was the Silly Symphony *Flowers and Trees*

(US 32), made in Technicolor and premièred at Grauman's Chinese Theater on 15 July 1932.

Britain's first cartoon talkie in colour was *On the Farm* (GB 33), produced in Raycol Colour and animated by Brian White, Sid Griffiths and Joe Noble from designs by *Punch* cartoonist H. M. Bateman.

The first feature-length cartoon film was Don Frederico Valle's 60-min *El Apostol* (Arg 17). Based on the book by Alfredo de Lafarrere, the film was a political satire on Argentina's President Irigoyen. The team of five animators was headed by Diogones Tabora, a well-known caricaturist, and between them they produced 50,000 drawings for the completed film.

The first full-length cartoon talkie was also surprisingly produced in Argentina. Made by Quirino Cristiani in 1931, *Peludopolis* was another satire on President Irogoyen and used the Vitaphone sound-on-disc system of synchronized sound. Running time was one hour. These two Argentinian cartoon features, and an Italian production *The Adventures of Pinocchio* (It 36), preceded the film which has generally been hailed as the world's first full-length cartoon feature. In fact Walt Disney's *Snow White and the Seven Dwarfs* (US 37) was only the first

George Orwell's *Animal Farm* was the subject of Halas and Batchelor's 1954 film, Britain's first full-length cartoon for theatrical release. The book has just been published in the USSR for the first time. Could the film follow? (*SI*)

Clarence Nash (1904–85), the immortal voice of Donald Duck, may have been incomprehensible quacking in his native American, but he could be equally hard on the ear in French, Spanish, Portuguese, Japanese, German and Chinese. None of these languages could he understand—Nash had the words written out phonetically and gabbled them in Duckspeak for the delight of audiences from Paris to Peking.

American cartoon feature, though the world's first to be made in both sound and colour. (A curiosity with the uninviting title of *Einstein's Theory of Relativity* (US 23), produced by Premier Productions in 7 reels, has sometimes been claimed as America's first cartoon feature. According to recent research by Denis Gifford, it would appear that this lost film was mainly live action, with some animated sequences by Max Fleischer.)

Britain's first feature-length cartoon was *Handling Ships* (GB 46), an instructional film made for the Admiralty by Halas and Batchelor. The first made for commercial release was Halas and Batchelor's *Animal Farm* (GB 54), from George Orwell's savage satire on Soviet repression.

The first 3-D cartoon was Norman McLaren's abstract subject *Around is Around* (Can 51).

The first full-length animated feature in 3-D was the Australian science-fantasy rock musical *Abracadrabra* (Aus 82), directed by Alexander Stitt.

In 1939 work began on what would have been Britain's first full-length cartoon feature film had World War II not intervened. Produced by Alexander Korda, *Around the World in Eighty Days* had the voice of Donald Pleasance as Phileas Fogg. Completed sequences include the beginning of the adventure, with Fogg making the celebrated wager in his London club, and his travels through India with the faithful Passe-Partout. These were assembled by the British Film Institute in 1955 and presented under the title of *Indian Fantasy*.

The first cartoon to be X-rated in Britain was UPA's *The Tell-Tale Heart* (US 53).

The first cinemascope cartoon was Walt Disney's *Toot, Whistle, Plonk and Boom* (US 55); the first feature Disney's *Lady and the Tramp* (US 56).

The most expensive cartoon ever made was Walt Disney's *The Black Cauldron* (US 85), which cost $25 million. One of the least successful of the Disney cartoon features, it returned less than $10 million in North American rentals.

The highest grossing cartoon film of all time is Walt Disney's *Snow White and the Seven Dwarfs* (US 37), with worldwide rentals of $380 million to the end of 1987.

The longest cartoon ever made was Osamu Tezuka's erotic feature *A Thousand and One Nights* (Jap 69), which had a running time of 2 hr 30 min in the original Japanese version.

Feature Cartoon Output

Up to the end of 1987, a total of 436 all-cartoon feature films (excluding compilations) had been produced by 31 countries. The most prolific country was Japan, with 137 full-length cartoon features, followed by the USA (80), France (30), Hungary (22), Australia (16), Italy (16), USSR (15), Belgium (13), Spain (11), West Germany (10), UK (10), Czechoslovakia (10), Denmark (9), China (8), Canada (6), S. Korea (6), Sweden (6), Bulgaria (3), Cuba (3), Poland (3), Netherlands (2), Iraq (2), Hong Kong (2), Finland (2), Colombia (2), Mexico (2), Brazil (2), Israel (1), Thailand (1), Romania (1), New Zealand (1), Yugoslavia (1), Taiwan (1) and the United Nations (1).

*C*ARTOON DEBUTS

BETTY BOOP
Max Fleischer's boop-boop-a-doop flapper of the thirties debuted in *Dizzy Dishes* (US 30). Betty started life as a small dog with long ears and only became a human girl in 1932. Her baby-talk voice was done by five different actresses, of whom Little Ann Little (who spoke in boop-boop-a-doop language in real life) and Mae Questel were the best known.

BUGS BUNNY
Started as a hare rather than a 'wabbit' in Ben Hardway and Cal Dalton's Looney Tune *Porky's Hare Hunt* (US 38). The character only began to assume his real Brooklyn bunny persona in Tex Avery's *Wild Hare* (US 40).

DAFFY DUCK
Tex Avery's Looney Tune *Porky's Duck Hunt* (US 37). After disappearing from cinema screens with his 126th movie in 1964, Daffy made his comeback 33 years later in WB's *The Duxorcist* (US 87).

DONALD DUCK
Walt Disney's *The Wise Little Hen* (US 34). His opening (and only) words were: 'Who—me? Oh no! I got a bellyache!' Clarence Nash, always Donald's voice, recalled: 'I had an ambition to be a doctor and somehow or other I became the biggest quack in the country.' He was still quacking 49 years later in *Mickey's Christmas Carol* (US 83).

DROOPY DOG
Created by Tex Avery in MGM's *Dumb-Hounded* (US 43).

FELIX THE CAT
Inspired by Kipling's *The Cat that Walked by Himself* in the *Just So Stories* (1902); created for Pat Sullivan by animator Otto Messmer. Prototype Felix, as yet unnamed, debuted in Paramount's *Feline Follies* (US 19). First of the anthropomorphic animal characters to attain the kind of celebrity accorded to human stars; also first to be merchandised. Television debut WXB2S New York 1930.

GOOFY
Walt Disney's *Mickey's Revue* (US 32).

MICKEY MOUSE
Born 18 November 1928 with première of *Steamboat Willie*. The artist for the MM cartoons was not Disney but UB Iwerks, though Walt himself did Mickey's voice. By 1934 the Mouse was receiving more fan mail than any other Hollywood star. There were a total of 119 MM cartoons, of which the majority—87—were made in the thirties. There was a 30-year interval between *The Simple Things* (US 53) and the mouse's triumphant return in *Mickey's Christmas Carol* (US 83). Mickey was voiced in his Dickensian role by Wayne Allwine, who was born the year of the previous Mickey Mouse film.

MR MAGOO
UPA's *Ragtime Bear* (US 49).

PLUTO
Walt Disney's *The Chain Gang* (US 30).

POPEYE
Debuted in Max Fleischer's *Popeye the Sailor* (US 33); head animator Seymour Kneitel. The voice was that of William Costello, better known as Red Pepper Sam, whose experience as a talking gorilla on a radio show was thought to qualify him for the role. Success went to his head and he was fired as too temperamental, so Jack Mercer, an artist at the Fleischer Studio with a bent for imitations, took over. Popeye's friend Wimpy gave his name to a disagreeable type of British hamburger.

PORKY PIG
Warner Looney Tune *Haven't Got a Hat* (US 35).

ROAD RUNNER
Together with the Coyote, created by Chuck Jones and Michael Maltese in *Fast and Furry-ous* (US 48).

SPEEDY GONZALES
The Fastest Mouse in all Mexico debuted in Warner Bros' *Speedy Gonzales* (US 55).

SYLVESTER
Kitty Kornered (US 45). His constant prey Tweety Pie had preceded him on screen (see below).

TOM AND JERRY
Hanna-Barbera's *Puss Gets the Boot* (US 39). The love-hate relationship of the amiable adversaries was condemned in the '70s for its 'mindless violence'.

TWEETY PIE
Birdie and the Beast (US 44). American essayist S. J. Perelman held Tweety Pie personally responsible for what he regarded as a reprehensible British habit of referring to all felines as 'puddy tats'.

WOODY WOODPECKER
Knock Knock (US 40). The distinctive woodpecker voice was that of Grace Stafford, wife of Woody's creator Walter Lanz. It was Grace who had suggested to her husband that he originate the cartoon character to let off steam after a noisy woodpecker had kept annoying them while on honeymoon at Sherwood Lake, California.

SIXTEEN

SHORTS AND DOCUMENTARIES

Two frame enlargements from the earliest surviving advertising film in the world, which dates from 1897. (*Library of Congress*)

ADVERTISING FILMS

The first advertising films were made in France, Britain, and the USA, in 1897. The single surviving American example of that year was copyrighted by the Edison Co. of West Orange, NJ, on 5 August 1897. The Library of Congress Catalogue records: 'The film shows a large, poster-type backdrop with the words "Admiral Cigarettes". Sitting in front of the backdrop are four people in costume: Uncle Sam, a clergyman, an Indian, and a businessman. To the left of the screen is an ash-can size box that breaks apart and a girl, attired in a striking costume, goes across the stage towards the seated men and hands them cigarettes. Then she unfolds a banner that reads, "We all Smoke".'

Advertising films were also made that year by the International Film Co. of New York, who were the first company to specialize in such productions. Their clients included Haig Whisky, Maillard's Chocolate and Pabst's Milwaukee Beer, and the films advertising these products were interspersed with entertainment films, in the manner of modern TV commercials, in a grand open-air free movie show in the centre of New York. The giant screen was set on top of the Pepper Building at 34th Street and Broadway and the films rear projected with a powerful Kuhn & Webster 'Projectorscope'. The projectionist was Edwin S. Porter, later to achieve fame as director of *The Great Train Robbery* (US 03). On this occasion, however, the only fame he achieved was in the police court, where he was charged with being a public nuisance and causing an obstruction by encouraging people to block the sidewalk.

Three different advertising films are known to date from 1897 in Britain. Walter D. Welford made a film called *The Writing on the Wall* for John Samuel Smith and Co. of Borough High Street, Southwark, manufacturers of bicycle tyres. This was shot in Tottenham and showed a man painting the words 'Ride Smith Tyres' on a brick wall. Rather more ambitious was a production by Arthur Melbourne Cooper of St Albans, which brought to light a contemporary poster for Bird's Custard. An old man is seen walking down stairs bearing a large tray of eggs. He misses his footing, trips, and the eggs cascade on to the floor.

> The world's only archive devoted exclusively to advertising films was established in 1982 at the Poster Museum in the rue de Paradis, Paris. It contains some 25,000 publicity films and TV commercials dating back to the turn of the century.

Cook has no need to worry, though, because she has a liberal supply of Bird's Custard Powder. The company made an agreement with Melbourne Cooper that he should be paid £1 for every copy of the film distributed. The third example comes from Nestlé and Lever Bros, who joined forces in 1897 to purchase 12 Lumière Cinématographes for a combined promotional exercise. Their initial effort was called *The Sunlight Soap Washing Competition* and was available free to showmen. Besides producing their own advertising films, Lever Bros and Nestlé's also sponsored films with no advertising content. On 7 February 1898 they premièred a film of the recent

Test Match in Australia at the Alhambra, Leicester Square. This was so successful that it was followed in March by films of the Cambridge crew in training for the Boat Race and later by the Boat Race itself. Mellin's Baby Food also began giving 'advertising entertainments' with the cinematograph the same year.

The most sophisticated of the pioneer advertising films were made by the great French innovator Georges Méliès, who also made the earliest trick films and the earliest 'blue movies'. Méliès' first advertising film, made at his studio at Montreuil-sous-Bois, was for Bornibus mustard. The scene was a restaurant. Two diners get into an argument which grows so heated that they begin to pelt each other with mustard. The camera then cuts to a black table top on which a jumble of white letters are scattered at random. The letters are seen to form themselves into the slogan *Bornibus, sa moutarde et ses cornichons à la façon de la mère Marianne*—all except the 's' of 'Bornibus', which is unable to find its correct place and keeps bumping into the other letters. Méliès recalled that the erratic 's' was always greeted with gales of laughter.

Subsequent Méliès productions advertised shoe polish, flour, Chocolat Ménier, tortoiseshell combs, Moritz Beer, Mystère corsets, Xour Lotion (hair restorer), Delion hats and Dewar's Whisky. In the last named, ancestors step down from family portraits to sample the product. The Delion commercial showed live rabbits being pushed into one end of a Heath Robinson-type machine and emerging as fur hats at the other. An attempt was made to placate the animal lovers in the audience by then reversing the film to show the hats entering the machine and becoming live rabbits again. These films were projected on an open-air screen in the Boulevard des Italiens in Paris by Méliès' young daughter Georgette.

The earliest known advertising film in colour was *Das Wunder/The Wonder* (Ger 25), an animated cartoon coloured directly on to the prints by means of a stencilling process. Directed by Julius Pinschewer, the two-minute film advertised 'World-renowned Kantorwicz Liqueur' and was notable not only for its colour but also its use of expressionism in the animated designs, some of them wholly abstract, of animator Walter Ruttmann.

The first British all-colour advertising film was *It's An Ill Wind* (GB 29), made for Tintex Dyes of London. The film related the drama of an office boy emptying a bottle of ink over the typist heroine's jumper. However, with the aid of Tintex Colour Remover and Tintex Dye, the jumper is made like new in the latest fashionable colour.

The first talkie advertising film was *Die Chinesische Nachtigall/The Chinese Nightingale*

While cinema advertising films have lost much of their appeal to advertisers against the lure of television, a new technique for plugging products from the silver screen has been developed in recent years. New York based Associated Film Productions represents some 70 companies who are willing to pay considerable sums to have their products featured as props in a feature movie. Hence the choice of Cheerios, Budweiser and Quaker State Motor Oil as goods consumed in *Honky Tonk Freeway* (US 81) was by no means fortuitous, any more than the Hormel Chili eaten by Robert Redford in *The Electric Horseman* (US 79)—a story, incidentally, about one man's rejection of commercial sponsorship—or the Anhauser Busch beer commercials watched by Peter Sellers in *Being There* (US 79). Associated plugs 200 different brands and guarantees 'positive visibility' in five films a year for a fee in the region of $100,000—strictly small change compared to the cost of a TV commercial. The rewards can be considerable. Sales of Reese's Pieces, a type of peanut-butter candy, spiralled by 85 per cent after a plug in *E.T. The Extra-Terrestrial* (US 82) that not only got noticed on screen but mentioned in many of the reviews as well.

(Ger 28), an animated silhouette version of the Hans Andersen fairy tale made by the Tri-Ergon Co. of Berlin to advertise a new process they had developed for disc recording. Although the use of synchronized discs was common to many early sound film systems, the process Tri-Ergon were promoting had no apparent connection with film-making, their advertising talkie being made by the sound-on-film process they had pioneered six years earlier.

Britain's first advertising talkie was *Meet Mr York* (GB 29), a cartoon with animation by John Noble which was directed by Bertram Phillips of British Publicity Talking Pictures for Rowntree & Co. of York.

Between 1914 and 1942 the standard length for advertising films in Britain was five minutes. Generally they contained some element of narrative and often featured famous stars, such as Jack Hulbert and Cicely Courtneidge in a 1926 comedy made for Rufflette Curtain Tape. Shortage of film stock brought the 'story' advertising film to an end in World War II. In the USA, the use of major stars was rarer, partly due to the contract system but also because most advertising films were made in New York. One notable example, however, was a General Electric advertising film of 1933 which had Dick

The world's most beautiful woman? Nobody would have said so when this 16-year-old appeared in an advertising short called *How Not to Wear Clothes* (Swe 21), but they did when she conquered Hollywood as Greta Garbo.

Powell and Bette Davis cast as a suburban couple extolling the virtues of dishwashers and garden floodlighting. Advertising films could also be an entrée for those who had yet to receive the summons to Hollywood. When the Bergström Department Store of Stockholm allowed a 16-year-old salesgirl to play a small role in *How Not to Wear Clothes* (Swe 21) they were unwittingly launching the screen career of Greta Garbo.

The first X-rated advertising film was made by Ray Selfe of Norwood Entertainments Ltd in 1974 to promote the movie magazine *Cinema X*. It showed a nude girl rising and walking away from the tracking camera, intercut with shots of picture spreads from the magazine. At the climax she turned and the title *Cinema X* was animated across those parts of her body which, had they been revealed, would have denied the film any certificate at all. According to the director, the film had to be submitted to the British Board of Film Censors several times because 'the lady examiner couldn't understand that the optical work which would obscure the pubic region couldn't be carried out until they had agreed to awarding the film a certificate'.

AERIAL FILM

The first film shot from an aeroplane was taken by L. P. Bonvillain, a Pathé cinematographer, piloted by Wilbur Wright at Camp s'Auvours, France, in September 1908. This was over a year before the first still photograph from an aeroplane was taken at Rheims.

The first aerial film of a topical event (non-aeronautic) was made by the Warwick Trading Co. for its *Bioscope Chronicle* newsreel on 21 April 1913. The film showed the Royal Yacht *Victoria and Albert* bearing King George V across the Channel on a visit to Paris, and the arrival at Calais. The pilot, B. C. Hucks, flew the cameraman straight back to Hendon, where a representative of the film company was waiting to rush the canister back to the laboratories. The complete film of the King's journey from London to Paris, including the aerial sequences, was shown during the matinée performance at the Coliseum at 5.20 p.m. the same day.

DOCUMENTARY

The term 'documentary' was first used by L. d'Herbeumont in the January 1924 issue of *Cinéopse* (Paris), referring to sponsored and industrial films. Its earliest use in English was by John Grierson in February 1926 in his review of Robert Flaherty's *Moana* (US 26) for the *New York Sun*. Flaherty is generally acknowledged as the first to have brought form and structure to documentary films, commencing with his study of Eskimo life. *Nanook of the North* (US 22); while Grierson himself is regarded as the father of Britain's between the wars 'documentary movement'.

The first documentary film: The majority of pre-1900 films were actualities, but the first of sufficient length to be considered a legitimate documentary record of its subject was *The Cavalry School at Saumur* (Fr 97), which ran for 1330 ft, about 20 min. At around the same time Joseph Perry of the Salvation Army's Limelight Division at Melbourne, Vic., Australia, began shooting some 2000 ft of film illustrating the social work of the Salvation Army. Melbourne had been the first place in the world where the Salvation Army embarked on an organized programme of social work in addition to its traditional evangelism.

The first British documentary was Robert Paul's one-reel production *Army Life, or How Soldiers are Made* (GB 00), premièred at the Alhambra in London on 18 September 1900.

The first feature-length documentaries were Paul Rainey's eight-reel *African Hunt* (US 12); a dramatized production in five reels called *One Hundred Years of Mormonism* (US 12); and Akaky Tsereteli's *Journey Along the Racha and Lechkhuma*

(Rus 12) by the Georgian director Vasily Ama-shukeli.

The first sound documentary for theatrical release was Tri-Ergon's *Life in a Village* (Ger 23), premièred at the Alhambra Theatre, Berlin in September 1923.

NEWS FILMS

The first news film (other than sporting events, q.v.) was made by photographer Birt Acres of High Barnet, Herts, on the occasion of the opening of the Kiel Canal by Kaiser Wilhelm II (1859–1941) on 20 June 1895. Besides the arrival of the Kaiser at Holtenau aboard his yacht *Hohenzollern*, Acres took films of the laying of a memorial stone, and of a number of other events held as part of the celebrations, including scenes of the Kaiser reviewing his troops at Hamburg and leading a procession through the streets of Berlin. He also filmed a charge of Uhlan Lancers at the Tempelhof Feld in Berlin, starting a news cameraman's tradition of taking risks in the cause of film reportage by arranging with their commander that the horsemen should charge direct at the camera. Seized with the desire to run for his life as the troop thundered towards him with drawn lances, he nevertheless continued to grind the handle of his camera and was afterwards congratulated by the CO as 'the pluckiest fellow he had ever met'. The first screening took place before the Royal Photographic Society on 14 January 1896.

The first news film shot in Britain was taken by Birt Acres on 27 June 1896 and showed the arrival of the Prince and Princess of Wales at the Cardiff Exhibition. Acres secured special permission to film the Royal party, on the proviso that he himself was not seen. Accordingly, a small aperture was cut in a canvas screen forming one side of a private walkway along which the Prince and Princess would approach the exhibition entrance. Since there was no corresponding hole for the viewfinder, Acres had to begin shooting on receipt of a signal from an official. He filmed the whole scene without being able to see anything of his subject. The film was premièred at a Command Performance at Marlborough House on 21 July 1896.

The first British monarch to be filmed was Queen Victoria (1819–1901) during her autumn holiday at Balmoral in 1896. She recorded the event in her diary for 3 October: 'At twelve went down to below the terrace, near the ballroom, and we were all photographed by Downey by the new cinematograph process—which makes moving pictures by winding off a reel of film. We were walking up and down, and the children jumping about. Then took a turn in the pony chair, and not far from the garden cottage Nicky and Alicky planted a tree.'

Downey was the Royal Photographer. The children who jumped about included the late Duke of Windsor, who must consequently have had one of the longest records of film appearances (including three acting roles) when he died in 1972. 'Nicky and Alicky' were the Emperor Nicholas II (1868–1918) and the Empress Alexandra Feodorovna (1872–1918) of Russia, who had arrived at Balmoral for an informal visit ten days earlier. The film was 'premièred' in the Red Drawing Room at Windsor Castle on 23 November 1896.

The first American President to be filmed was Grover Cleveland (1837–1908), outgoing President on the occasion of President-designate William McKinley's inauguration at Washington DC on 4 March 1897. The inaugural parade, covered by Edison, Biograph and Lumière cameramen, and by one E. H. Amet, included shots of Cleveland, then in the last hour of his Presidency. McKinley had been filmed by Biograph cameraman Billy Bitzer on 18 September 1896, shortly before the Presidential election.

The first Pope to be filmed was Pope Leo XIII (reigned 1878–1903) by Biograph cameraman W. K. L. Dickson in 1898. The film, which showed the Pope in his carriage, riding in his sedan chair, walking, seated on his favourite bench in the Vatican gardens, and bestowing the Papal blessing on an audience, was premièred at Carnegie Hall in New York on 14 December 1898 in the presence of Archbishop Corrigan.

NEWSREELS

The first newsreel was *Day by Day*, produced by Will G. Barker and presented at the Empire Theatre, Leicester Square, in 1906. It was issued daily except when fog prevented filming.

The first newsreel produced for general distribution was *Pathé-Faits Divers*, founded in Paris early in 1908 under the direction of Albert Gaveau. The name was soon changed to *Pathé-Journal*. Japan's *Daimai News* is variously claimed to have been founded in 1908 and 1909. This was literally intended as a moving-picture newspaper, having been established by the influential daily *Osaka Mainichi*, *Pathé-Journal* did a reverse operation, founding a weekly illustrated newspaper of the same name in November 1912. The photographic news reportage consisted of stills from the newsreel.

The first general newsreel in Britain was *Pathé's Animated Gazette*, founded in 1910, which survived, as *Pathé News*, until February 1969.

The first newsreel in the United States was *Pathé's Weekly*, of which the first issue came out on 8 August 1911, just ten days before its rival *The Vitagraph Monthly of Current Events*. In 1914 it was replaced by *Pathé Daily News*, but in 1917 it was no longer possible to obtain the safety film stock from France which gave Pathé the advantage over its rivals of being able to distribute daily by mail, and the newsreel reverted to weekly issue as *Pathé News* until its closure in 1956.

Local Newsreels

This phenomenon seems to have begun with *Paterson's Pictorial Review*, inaugurated by an enterprising cinema owner in Aberdeen in 1907. Generally they emanated from the larger centres of population, such as Marcus Loew's *New York Weekly* (1914) and the San Francisco newsreel *Golden Gate Weekly* (1914), or they could be statewide, such as *Iowa News Flashes* (c. 1935), or regional, like Britain's *Northern Topical News Gazette* (1915) and the *Scottish Moving Picture News* (1917). A rare example of a local sound newsreel was *The Tatler News Reel*, serving the Merseyside area, which was instituted by Capital & Provincial News Theatres Ltd in October 1936. Smaller centres were also represented: Bradford Playhouse started showing 9.5 mm and 16 mm newsreels made by local amateurs in 1938 and the same year The Rex at Brighton introduced a local newsreel produced by the manager, Mr J. C. Howe. Probably the smallest town in Britain to support a regular locally produced newsreel was Beverley, Yorks, where the manager of the Picture Playhouse, Mr Ernest Symmons, brought the events of the 10,000 strong community to the screen of his own cinema. America could boast a local newsreel serving an even smaller population. Skilled amateur cinematographer W. H. Miller, proprietor of the two cinemas in Cloquet, Minnesota, captured the doings of his 6000 fellow citizens in *The Cloquet Newsreel* which he founded in 1927.

The first regular sound newsreel was *Movietone News*, presented at the Roxy Theater, New York, on 28 October 1928. The subjects covered included Niagara Falls, the Army-Yale football game, 'Romance of the Iron Horse', and Rodeo in New York. Regular weekly issue of *Movietone News* to cinemas throughout the USA commenced 3 December 1928.

The first British sound newsreel was *British Movietone*, commencing with an issue showing the Derby and the Trooping of the Colour which was released on 9 June 1929. It survived as the last remaining newsreel produced in Britain.

The first unscheduled event to be captured by the sound newsreel camera was the assassination attempt on Prince Humbert of Italy on 24 October 1929. Cameraman Jack Connolly of *Movietone* had hidden himself behind the Tomb of the Unknown Warrior in Rome in order to secure forbidden pictures of the Prince and Princess pay-

FAMOUS OUTLAWS
CLYDE BARROW
Terror of the Southwest and his Gun Moll
"BONNIE" PARKER
Modern tigress, fast shooting, cigar smoking, blond Jezebel MEET DEATH AT GIBSLAND, LA.

ACTUAL AUTHENTIC PICTURES
Taken immediately after the death of these murderous lovers at the hands of the law.

See the Texas Cop Killers - Slayers of 10 men - Extra Feature -
'BEYOND THE RIO GRANDE'
WITH 5 FAMOUS WESTERN STARS--- Featuring Jack Perrin, Buffalo Bill Jr., Pete Morrison, Franklin Farnum, Edmund Cobb and Starlight the Wonder Horse.
An All-Talking Western for the Whole Family to See and Hear!

It was not often that the newsreel was billed above the feature. In this case though the slaying of Bonnie and Clyde took precedence over any horse opera.

ing tribute to the Italian war dead. He had just been discovered by the police when a shot was fired at the Prince, but fortunately the camera was still running and the sound equipment operating.

The first newsreel footage of an execution was taken by Universal Newsreel's Cuban cameraman Abelardo Domingo, who happened to walk into a prison yard with his camera one day in 1935 just as bandit Jose Costiello y Puentas was about to face the firing squad. Domingo shot the grisly scene unobserved and shipped the film over to New York for inclusion in the newsreel. As soon as it was released in Cuba, Domingo was arrested and condemned to death—also by firing squad. He was released only after Universal's manager in Cuba had paid the appropriate financial sum.

The last newsreel in the United States was *Universal Newsreel*, founded as *Universal Animated*

Weekly in 1913, of which the final issue was released on 22 December 1967. At its peak it was showing in 3300 cinema theatres, but with the competition of television declined to a circulation of 1100.

The last newsreel in Britain was *Movietone News*, founded as *British Movietone* in 1929 (see above), which suffered a decline from its circulation of over 2000 a week at the peak in World War II to only 200 a week when the final issue was released on 27 May 1979. The sign-off items were the Chelsea Flower Show, 'Our Capital City' (London from the air) and 'Highlights of 50 Years'.

Early sound newsreels were often shot silent and sound effects added afterwards. According to *Picturegoer* (30 April 1932), 'one firm who owned a specially good crowd track put it on every crowd scene they issued. It was easily recognizable to anyone in the trade because at a certain point a dog barked.'

The major remaining producer of newsreels is China, with over 20 studios devoted to their production.

The most costly newsreel ever made was the *Gaumont British* edition of 24 October 1934, which included scenes of the Centenary Air Race shot at Melbourne, Victoria. The Australian footage was transmitted to Britain frame by frame by beam wireless for 68 hours at a cost of some $4000 a foot or $30,264 for the brief sequence of 160 frames. It was shown in 1500 cinemas within 48 hours of transmission.

The only woman news cameraman was Dorothy Dunn, a member of the *Universal Animated Weekly* crew in America during World War I.

Kinematograph Weekly on newsreels, 25 October 1934: 'Television, of course, will not supplant the celluloid reel for many obvious reasons'. Evidently the reasons were too obvious to be worth stating.

Specialized Newsreels

These have catered to various minorities and sectional interests since the early twenties. The first all-black newsreel was produced by the Renaissance Co. of New York in 1922 and a sound newsreel for blacks called *All-American News* was established in 1942. The last newsreel to be established anywhere in the western world, Heyns Films' *Topical News*, was founded as recently as 1975 to cater to the black population of South Africa. A number of newsreels for women were produced in America, including *Eve's Film Pictorial* in the early 1920s, the world's first colour newsreel, *McCall Fashion News* (1925), and

Fox's *Fashion Forecast*, which ran from 1938 to 1940.

Children were catered to in America by *The Junior Newsreel* (1934). Other newsreels were made by young people themselves. In England the boys of Mill Hill public school started the *Mill Hill School Animated News* in 1920. On the other side of the Atlantic *Dartmouth College News* (1928) was a regular 16mm newsreel made by the college film club for circulation to alumni, and Culver Military Academy was producing a weekly newsreel in 1929.

A sponsored newsreel, the *Ford Animated Weekly*, was produced by the Ford Motor Co. between 1914 and 1921, succeeded by the *Ford News*, which was for circulation to Detroit theaters only, in 1934. A different type of sponsored newsreel, *Kinograms*, which had commercials interspersing the news items, was introduced on 28 August 1931. The sound was recorded on disc—the only sound newsreel ever to use the synchronized disc system.

Newsreels in Britain were never subject to censorship, except the self-imposed censorship exercised by the newsreel producers. Their timidity, avoiding any controversial issues, was notorious during the 1930s. *World Film News* (July 1937), commenting on the newsreels' non-coverage of labour disturbances and the abdication, said that world events of the past year had conspired to show them up 'at their most cowardly and incompetent'. The report continued: 'On May 25th, four men walked into the shining new offices of British Movietone News in London's Soho Square. They were R. S. Howard, Editor of Gaumont-British News; Cecil Snape of Universal; Louis Behr, of Pathé; and G. T. Cummins of Paramount. Inside they were met by Gerald Sanger, Movietone's Production Chief, for a hush-hush heart-to-heart. Within a few minutes they had reached complete agreement. The Wedding of the Duke of Windsor was BARRED from every screen in Britain . . . The newsreels' official statement that they were "respecting the Duke of Windsor's desire for privacy" was plainly ridiculous, when every newspaper was screaming headlines round the world . . .'.

Naked capitalism was matched by a socialist newsreel called *The Workers' Newsreel*, of which 16 issues were produced in the USA (1931–32) by the Film & Photo League, an offshoot of the militant Workers' International Relief.

The William J. Ganz Co. of New York began issuing a monthly *Highlights of the News* for home-movie buffs in 1927. A similar enterprise in Britain was Fox Photos' *Film-at-Home News*, inaugurated in September 1933 at an annual subscription of £25 for a 200 ft reel monthly.

Israel produced a *Monthly Newsreel for Immigrants* between 1966 and 1968.

The only all-cartoon newsreel was *Topical Sketch*, founded in Britain in July 1915. Wallace Carlson's *Canimated Nooz Pictorial*, released weekly by Essany from May 1916 to mid-1917, had photographic heads on pen-and-ink bodies. A regular comedy newsreel, titled *Crazy Newsreel*, was issued by 'Gaumont-Skittish News'—otherwise Gaumont-British—from 1937 to 1939.

Soviet Russia has a satirical newsreel called *Fitil/ The Fuse*, which deals chiefly with the shortcomings of the bureaucracy. Established in the days of Khruschev's 'thaw', and allowed to survive as a safety valve against discontent, each ten-minute monthly issue comprises a playlet, a documentary report and a cartoon. The documentary sequence of a recent *Fitil* showed children walking to school in the rain, despite regulations enjoining local authorities to supply transport. When the bureaucracy replied that the situation had now been rectified, another issue of *Fitil* showed the same schoolchildren still walking to school, this time in a snowstorm.

SERIALS

The first serial was the 12-episode Edison production *What Happened to Mary* (US 12), starring Mary Fuller as a foundling seeking her lost inheritance, of which the first episode was released on 26 July 1912. It has been claimed that the film was not a true serial, but a *series* of episodes each complete in itself. Although it is true that the cliffhanger element, an essential element of later serials, was missing from *What Happened to Mary*, in fact the denouement was not revealed until the final episode, and the various adventures were all part of a continuing storyline. *The Adventures of Kathlyn* (US 13) added the missing ingredient, leaving audiences in an agony of suspense at the end of each episode until the final triumph of the heroine.

The first talkie serial was Mascot Pictures' 10-episode jungle yarn *King of the Kongo* (US 29), starring Jacqueline Logan, Walter Miller and Boris Karloff.

The longest serial was *The Hazards of Helen*, directed in 119 one-reel episodes by J. P. McGowan and James Davis for Kalem, and starring Helen Holmes (episodes 1–26), Elsie McLeod (episodes 27–49) and Helen Gibson (episodes 50–119). The first episode was released on 7 November 1914; the last on 24 February 1917. The complete picture had a running time of over 31 hours.

The last Hollywood serial was Columbia Pictures' unremarkable *Blazing the Overland Trail* (US 56), directed by Spencer Bennet.

During the 44-year life of the episode film, American studios put out an estimated 350 silent serials and 231 talkies.

SPORTS FILMS

The first film of a sporting event was taken at the Edison Laboratories, West Orange, NJ, and depicted a six-round boxing match fought between Mike Leonard and Jack Cushing on 14 June 1894. Leonard, the better known fighter, was paid $150 for his services and his opponent $50. The ring was only 12 ft square, in order that all the action might be followed by the immobile camera. Having knocked Cushing out in the last round, Leonard summed up after the fight: 'I hit him when I liked and where I liked. I'd hit him oftener, only Mr Edison treated me right and I didn't want to be too quick for his machine. I generally hit 'im in the face, because I felt sorry for his family and thought I would select the only place that couldn't be disfigured.' The film was premièred at a Kinetoscope parlour at 83 Nassau Street, New York, probably at the beginning of August 1894. From a commercial point of view it was not a complete success, as each round was shown in a different Kinetoscope peep-show machine for which a separate charge was made. At 10c a round, it cost 60c to see the whole fight, so most patrons opted to pay a single dime to witness the knock-out round only.

The first British sports film and the first anywhere in the world of a regularly scheduled sporting contest was made by Birt Acres of the Oxford and Cambridge Boat Race on 30 March 1895.

The first motion picture of a horse race was also taken by Acres, of the Epsom Derby on 29 May 1895.

The earliest known film of a football match was made by R. W. Paul at Newcastle upon Tyne, England, in November 1896.

Baseball was the subject of a dramatic movie, Edison's *Casey at the Bat* (US 99), just before the turn of the century.

The earliest known record of a basketball game was filmed by American Mutoscope & Biograph at Missouri Valley College (a girls' school) in 1904.

When heavyweight contenders James J. Jeffries and Tom Sharkey battled 25 rounds together on a sweltering night at Coney Island on 3 November 1899, the fight was filmed by the light of a battery of arc lamps suspended just over their heads. By the end of the fight the exhausted men, barely able to stand, were both bald. Their hair had literally been grilled to a frazzle.

TRAVELOGUE

The first travelogue of sufficient length and variety to warrant the term was R. W. Paul's *Tour in Spain and Portugal* (GB 96), a 600-ft film made by cameraman Henry Short during a five-week tour of the two countries in September 1896. It comprised 14 scenes of Lisbon, Madrid and Seville, including a bullfight, and was premièred at the Alhambra Theatre in London on 22 October 1896. At the end of October, Paul issued a booklet publicizing the film, a forerunner of the exhibitors' campaign book.

The term 'travelogue' was coined by Burton Holmes, who presented his first such movie, a 50 ft view of St Peter's, Rome, at Oak Park Presbyterian Church, Chicago, in 1897.

WAR FILM

The first war to be filmed was the Graeco-Turkish War of 1897. Sole cameraman in the field was British war correspondent and pioneer cinematographer Frederick Villiers (1852–1922), who filmed the Battle of Volo in Thessaly, Greece, in April. He wrote in his memoirs: 'Luckily I was well housed during the fighting in front of Volo, for the British consul insisted on my residing at the consulate. To me it was campaigning in luxury. From the balcony of the residence I could always see of a morning when the Turks opened fire up on Valestino Plateau; then I would drive with my camera outfit to the battlefield, taking my bicycle with me in the carriage. After I had secured a few reels of movies, if the Turks pressed too hard on our lines I would throw my camera into the vehicle and send it out of action, and at nightfall, after the fight, I would trundle back down the hill to dinner.' These first historic war films were destined never to be seen by the public. When he finally arrived back in London, Villiers found to his consternation that Star Films of Paris had already flooded the market with dramatized reconstructions of the campaign and there was no demand for the genuine article. He was equally unlucky the following year when he filmed the Battle of Omdurman from a gunboat on the Nile. As the gunboat's battery opened up, the camera tripod collapsed and Villiers' camera hit the deck, the magazine fell out and the film was exposed to the light.

The earliest surviving news film taken during a military campaign consists of scenes of the 5th Northumberland Fusiliers at Orange River, South Africa, during the Boer War of 1899–1902. Made by John Bennett Stanford on 12 November 1899, it is preserved in the National Film Archive.

In the days when newsreel reportage was as important a means of communication as television news today, it was not unknown for battles to be delayed pending the arrival of the cameramen. On 3 January 1914 the Mexican bandit General Pancho Villa signed a contract with the Mutual Film Corporation assigning them the rights to all battle coverage and undertaking that, whenever possible, battles would be fought in daylight hours and at such times as were convenient to the Mutual cameramen. Villa was as good as his word. He postponed his attack on the city of Ojinaga until the camera operator, engaged elsewhere, arrived to record the victory. In a more savage theatre of war, the Nazi destruction of Gdynia in Poland in 1939 was delayed to allow time for cameramen to move forward and film the German forces from in front as they attacked.

John Grierson, pioneer of the documentary film movement, succeeded in making a film specifically designed for Hitler to see. After the Dieppe raid in 1942, the Führer had the captured Canadian prisoners put in chains. As head of the Canadian National Film Board, Grierson produced a film showing the humane treatment of German POWs in Canada and arranged for a copy—indeed the only copy—to fall into Nazi hands. It was duly viewed by Hitler, as intended, and the Führer was sufficiently impressed by the film to order the Canadian prisoners to be released from their chains.

SEVENTEEN

TELEVISION AND THE MOVIES

'Television will be the world's greatest box-office and turnstile killer'—*World Film News* April 1937.

The first film shown on television was British Sound Film Productions' *The Bride* (GB 29), featuring George Robey, which was transmitted experimentally from the Baird Television Studios in Long Acre, London, on 19 August 1929.

The first television station to show films as part of their regular programme service was the De Forest Radio Corporation's W2XCD Passaic, NJ, commencing 1 March 1931. These were mainly documentary and travel shorts, two of the earliest to be aired being *People Who Live in the Desert* (US 30) and *Lumbering in British Columbia* (Can 30). Five days later the Baird Co. followed suit in Britain, starting with a boxing short and airing a Chaplin comedy with the Keystone Cops on 9 March.

The first full-length feature film shown on television was *Police Patrol* (US 25), transmitted in six daily episodes by W2XCD Passaic, NJ, 6–11 April 1931. Directed by Burton King for Gotham Productions, it related the story of a New York policeman (James Kirkwood) who arrests a girl thief (Edna Murphy) the exact double of his sweetheart (also Edna Murphy).

The first feature films shown on television uninterrupted were Cecil B. DeMille's *This Day and Age* (US 33), with Richard Cromwell, and John Cromwell's *The Texan* (US 30), with Gary Cooper, which were both aired by Don Lee Television of Los Angeles on stations W6XS and W6XAO during September 1933. The TV image had 80-line definition.

The first feature film shown in scheduled service in Britain was *The Student of Prague* (Ger 35), starring Anton Walbrook and Dorothea Wieck, transmitted by the BBC on 14 August 1938.

The first film made for television was a short silent comedy titled *Morgenstude hat Gold im Munde/The Early Bird Catches the Worm* (Ger 30), produced by F. Banneitz of Commerz-Film AG, Berlin, on behalf of the German Reichs-Rundfunkgesellschaft. Intended specially for transmission by low-definition television, the actors' movements were exaggerated for visual emphasis and the costumes were designed for greater tonal contrast than in a normal cinema film.

The first film drama made for high definition television was *Wer fuhr IIA 2992?/Who was Driving Car Number IIA 2992?* (Ger 39), a thriller scripted by Gerhart W. Göbel of the Reichspost and produced by UFA in Berlin. Göbel devised the plot after seeing a police announcement on television appealing for help in a murder case. The scenario centred round a hit-and-run driver, since the Nazi Propaganda Ministry would not allow murder as a theme for films to be shown abroad. The film was first shown during television demonstrations in Bucharest and Sofia in 1940 and was also used after the war when the German Post Office resumed experimental transmissions in 1950.

The first British television film drama and **the first TV film aired in scheduled service** was *A Dinner Date with Death* (GB 50), a pilot for a TV series titled *The Man who Walks by Night*, shot at Marylebone Studios by Vizio Films Ltd, 11–14 July 1949, and transmitted by BBC Television on 28 September 1950. Produced by Roy Plomley of *Desert Island Discs* fame, the film was directed by Eric Fawcett, scripted by Duncan Ross, and starred Patricia Jessel and James Cairncross. Designed for a half-hour programme with a break for commercials, it was also **the first British television drama to be televised on network TV in America.**

The first of the major Hollywood studios to enter television production was Columbia, when Ralph Cohn, nephew of production chief Harry Cohn, asked for $50,000 to start a subsidiary

Television attracted the attention of the movies in its infancy. A newsreel called the *Empire News Bulletin* secured exclusive rights to illustrating the Baird television system and the first issue of the *Bulletin*, released on 3 May 1926, featured John Logie Baird and his original TV apparatus. A few years later, in 1932, *Gaumont Graphic* devoted a whole issue to showing the low-definition programme service run from the BBC television studio in the basement of Broadcasting House. A copy of this newsreel survives in the Visnews Film Library and represents the earliest film record of the public broadcasting of television as an entertainment medium.

for filming TV product. Cohn Snr complied on condition that the $50,000 should be the first and last demand. It was. On 12 June 1952 Columbia Screen Gems, as the subsidiary was named, announced a contract to produce 39 *Ford Theater* programmes for the Ford Motor Co., who would pay 75 per cent of the cost of the first-run rights. The decision of the majors to join television rather than to fight it was a wise one; ultimately it was to mean the survival of Hollywood.

The first feature-length television film or TVM was *High Tor* (US 56), a whimsical ghost story starring Bing Crosby as an idealist who refuses to sell High Tor, a peak of the Palisades on the Hudson River, to property speculators. The film, networked coast-to-coast on 10 March 1956, was shot in twelve days at a cost of $350,000 and is chiefly notable for the fact that it featured Julie Andrews in her American TV debut. *Films in Review*'s critic commented: 'The commercials were a welcome relief'.

The first TVM shot on tape was Metromedia's *Sandcastles* (US 72), starring Bonnie Badelia as a lonely young girl who has a ghostly romance with a young man killed in a car accident. The cameraman was Alan Stensvold.

The first of the major Hollywood studios to sell televison rights to its films was RKO in December 1955. The studio's entire pre-1949 film library of 740 features was purchased from Howard Hughes by Thomas F. O'Neil of General Teleradio Inc. for a package deal price variously reported as $15 million and $25 million. First of the RKO package to reach the small screen was *King Kong* (US 33) early in 1956. New York's WOR-TV was so overwhelmed at its good fortune in having a genuine Hollywood release to play—formerly only foreign product had been aired—that they transmitted it twice every day for a week. Once RKO had breached the big studios' agreement to have no truck with the tube, the others followed suit, Warner Bros selling off their pre-1949 library to Associated Artists Productions for $21 million in February 1956.

The first motion picture based on a television play was a Merton Park 'B' picture directed by Michael McCarthy titled *Assassin for Hire* (GB 51), scripted by Rex Rienits from his own 1950 TV production.

The first American film from a TV play was Delbert Mann's *Marty* (US 55), with Ernest Borgnine, from writer Paddy Chayevsky's acclaimed TV production about a shy New York butcher courting an equally shy schoolteacher. The motion picture version, which won Academy Awards for Best Picture, Best Director, Best Actor and Best Screenplay, was very much in the TV genre of simple narratives about simple people in a familiar setting, and at variance with Hollywood's fantasy world of the rich and successful living in a world of opulent but emotionally wrought make-believe.

The first television series based on a film was the BBC's 20-year long marathon *Dixon of Dock Green*

The first major screen actor to establish a reputation on television before entering films—nowadays the classic route to Hollywood—was Charlton Heston. During the late 1940s he played Antony in *Julius Caesar* and Heathcliff in *Wuthering Heights*, among other significant roles in TV plays, and these performances attracted the attention of Paramount, leading to his large screen debut in *Dark City* (US 50) when he was 27.

(1955-76), starring Jack Warner in the role of Dixon, who had actually been killed off in *The Blue Lamp* (GB 49). In the USA *Peyton Place* (US 57) gave rise to the 1964-69 TV series of the same name.

The first motion picture based on a television series was *Dragnet* (US 54) with Jack Webb, who also starred in the radio and TV versions. The first British example was *It's a Great Day* (GB 56), with the original cast of Roland and Michael Pertwee's television series *The Groves*.

The country with the highest number of televised films is Italy, where over 500 stations transmit more than 2500 films a week. The total of approximately 130,000 movies annually (many of course duplicated) equals the entire world output of feature films for the last 30 years.

Family Business (US 82) was a rare example of a documentary film developed into a television comedy series. A *cinéma-vérité* study of a family-run pizza business in smalltown Middle America, the film resulted in the pizza parlour's proprietor, ex-Marine Colonel Howard Snider, signing a contract with Henry 'the Fonz' Winkler in April 1982 for this story of everyday pizza folk to be adapted for television.

TV Versions of Theatrical Motion Pictures

Films shown on television are generally cut to fit the available programme time, but occasionally the reverse takes place. The TV versions of *Requiem for a Heavyweight* (US 62), *Earthquake* (US 74), and *Airport 77* (US 77) were all expanded by the inclusion of footage edited out of the theatrical version. The two *Godfather* movies (US 71 and US 74) were combined in 1978 to make one marathon TVM lasting 7½ hours. Titled *Mario Puzo's The Godfather. The Complete Novel for Television*, the new version was not only resequenced, so that the saga was related chronologically, but also set a record for expansion—some 75 minutes of out-takes, equivalent to a short feature by itself, was added to the film. The material added to *Earthquake* actually introduced a new character (played by Debralie Scott) and in the case of

Joseph Losey's *Secret Ceremony* (GB 68), the producers shot additional scenes three years later to enable the film to fit a two-hour slot on American television. The additions, according to Losey, 'exactly reversed the meaning and intention of my film'.

Why does exactly the same version of *The Sound of Music* (US 65) run nearly seven minutes longer on US TV than on British TV? In fact all standard versions of films are shorter when they are shown on television in Britain. The Americans run films on television at 24 frames per second, the same as in cinemas; the British television stations run films at 25 f.p.s.

The most popular film ever shown on US television was *Gone with the Wind* (US 39), which scored a Nielsen rating of 47.6 (ie 47.6 per cent of all sets monitored were showing the film) and a 65 share (65 per cent of all sets turned on in monitored homes were tuned to the film) when the first part was aired on 7 November 1976. The second part was transmitted the following day, scoring a Nielsen rating of 47.4 and a 64 share.

The highest rating for a TVM (television movie) on US television was 46.0 and a 62 point share for *The Day After* (US 83), a nuclear holocaust drama shown on the ABC network on 20 November 1983.

The movie most often repeated on US television, according to a survey conducted by *TV Guide*, is *Casablanca* (US 42), with *King Kong* (US 33) second. The most repeats on US network television is 16 for *The Wizard of Oz* (US 39) since its original transmission by CBS on 3 November 1956.

The most prolific producer of feature films in Britain today is Channel 4, which has financed or co-financed over 140 feature-length movies since 1982. Many go into theatrical release before being aired on television and the web has been credited with 'changing the face of British cinema'.

The longest film shown on television in a single day was the 8 hr 27 min epic *War and Peace* (USSR 67), transmitted by Mexico's Channel II on 28 February 1981. **The longest on British television** was Tony Palmer's *Wagner* (GB 83), with Richard Burton, which ran for 5 hr 15 min (including commercial breaks) on Channel 4 on 6 January 1985.

The first 3-D film shown on television was *Miss Sadie Thompson* (US 53), transmitted by SelecTV on its pay-TV systems in Los Angeles and Milwaukee in December 1980. First to be shown via the airwaves was *Revenge of the Creature* (US 55) by WGNO-TV New Orleans on 9 February 1982. Some 400,000 pairs of 3-D spectacles were sold through a local convenience store at 50¢ a pair.

The highest fee paid for television rights to a movie was $35 million by CBS to MGM in April 1978 to televise *Gone with the Wind* (US 39) 20 times over the following 20 years. The value of the TV rights represented about 6½ times the production cost of the film.

The highest fee paid for television rights to a British movie is an unconfirmed $20 million to Goldcrest Films by Embassy Communications for US-Canada TV and cable airing of *Gandhi* (GB/Ind 83).

The highest price paid for British TV rights to a movie was an unconfirmed £2,250,000 by the BBC for *The Sound of Music* (US 65) in 1978.

The lowest fees paid for film rights by any national TV network are by Bermuda, where US product may earn as little as $90. Zambia pays in the region of $100 and Haiti from $100 to $200. The most profitable market outside the US is Great Britain, where the two networks pay within the $60,000–250,000 price range for quality product and more for blockbusters.

In the US home market, new films with star names but only modest box-office potential sell to the networks for figures in the $4–6 million region.

*V*IDEO FILMS

The first video films were offered for hire by Sears, Roebuck in the USA at $3–6 each in the spring of 1972. Titles included *Stagecoach* (US 39), *Hamlet* (GB 48), *High Noon* (US 52), *The Bridge on the River Kwai* (GB 57), *Cactus Flower* (US 69) and *The Anderson Tapes* (US 71). They were for showing on the Avco Cartavision video player, which retailed at $1600. The first video films for sale were put on the market by Andre Blay of the small Michigan-based company Magnetic Video, who acquired the rights to 50 Fox productions in 1977. The initial titles, which included *M*A*S*H*, *Hello Dolly* and *Patton*, sold for $50 per cassette.

The first film produced expressly for the video market (excluding pornography) was *Tangier* (GB 82), starring Billie Whitelaw.

The first 3-D feature film to be released on videocassette was the martial arts picture *Dynasty* (Tai 77) by America's OVC Corporation in October 1987. Cassettes were packaged with the special spectacles needed for viewing in 3-D.

The highest sales of a video film were achieved by Walt Disney Home Video's *Lady and the Tramp* (US 55), released for Christmas 1987. Within weeks it had overtaken the previous record of 2,900,000 units achieved by Paramount's *Top Gun*

(US 86) and by February 1988 had become the first video film with sales in excess of three million.

The highest sales of a video film in Britain were achieved by Paul McCartney's *Rupert Bear and the Frog Chorus* (GB 84), originally released theatrically with *Give My Regards to Broad Street* (GB 84). Virgin Video sold 150,000 units during the 12 months following the video release in December 1985. Top-selling feature film in Britain is CBS/Fox Video's *Crocodile Dundee* (Aus 86), which had outsold US and world record holder *Top Gun* (US 86) by 65,000 units to 48,000 at end 1987.

The only major film to have earned more on video than in theatrical release is Disney's *Sleeping Beauty* (US 59). The first million video sales earned Disney $19.5 million, against $15.8 million in North American film rentals.

The highest fee paid for video rights was $60 million by Warner Bros for the foreign rights to the entire United Artists catalogue in 1983. The US rights were bought by Magnetic Video for $44 million—the second highest fee. World rights for individual Hollywood films range between $50,000 and $1 million.

The highest fee paid for video rights to an individual movie was an estimated $15 million by CBS/Fox Video in 1984 for the George Lucas production *The Empire Strikes Back* (US 80).

> Homevideo has already overtaken cinema in the US in terms of revenue. While cinemas garnered $4.25 billion at the box office in 1987, sales and rentals of videocassettes amounted to $7.46 billion.

The country with the largest number of video-cassette recorders is the USA, with an estimated 42 million units at end 1987. Japan is only marginally behind with 39 million VCRs, way ahead of the two European leaders, Britain with 11 million sets and West Germany with 10.4 million. France has nearly 5 million, Spain 2.6 million and Italy and the Netherlands 2 million. The USSR, with only 500,000 VCRs, has fewer than its small neighbour Finland (550,000).

The highest penetration of VCRs is in Kuwait, where 92 per cent of homes have sets. Among major countries, Australia has the highest penetration with an estimated 63 per cent at end 1987, followed by Britain and Japan at 55 per cent (some estimates for Japan are higher). It is now more common for British households to have a VCR than to take a holiday abroad or own a freezer. US penetration is 52 per cent (January 1988), while the American city with the highest penetration is Fairbanks, Alaska, where 75.6 per cent of homes had a VCR in 1987.

Video Vistas

☆ Probably the most insatiable homevideo viewers in the world are the citizens of war-torn Beirut, from whence come reports of video-library customers renting as many as 900 films a year.

☆ Some 800,000 homes in Spain, over half of them in Andalucia, are wired for what is known as 'community video'. Tenants in blocks of flats share the cost of wiring, then appoint someone—often the doorman—to rent video films and transmit them from one central point to any of the subscribers wanting to tune in. Some apartments have a choice of as many as five or six films a day. Distributors and video rental outlets are strongly opposed to the practice, claiming it has had a disastrous effect on the homevideo market, but their attempts to have it outlawed failed with a ruling by Spain's Supreme Court in January 1987 that community video was both legal and constitutional.

☆ The double-bill programme may not be common in many cinemas any more, but for the Czechs at least it is standard for home viewing. All videocassettes contain three hours of programming, most of them two full-length features.

☆ The price of the standard VCR on sale in the USSR, the Elektronika VM 12, is 1200 rubles ($1800). The average worker's annual income is 2250 rubles ($3375). There is a 10-month waiting list even at this price. New foreign films cost $15 a night to hire.

☆ Unemployed teenagers in the UK watch an average of four videocassettes a week each.

☆ The country with the most stringent homevideo censorship law is Finland, where no film banned for under 18-year-olds at cinemas may be rented as a videocassette by anyone of *any* age. Films like *The Godfather* (US 71) can be shown on television but not on video.

☆ For $19.95 American homevideo viewers can have *Dinner with a Naked Lady* (US 87). The half-hour videocassette allows every solitary male to indulge his fantasy of dining a beautiful girl tête-à-tête and persuading her to remove her clothes during the course of the meal. The part of the naked lady is played by Vanessa Giorgio as the 'quintessential airhead', per producer Terri Mandell. By way of contrast, *Goldfish* (GB 86) is just that—a 30-minute videofilm of six goldfish swimming round a tank, consisting of one shot taken with a static camera. Producer/director Adrian Munsey calls it an 'ambient audiovisual entertainment relaxant' and certainly tired British businessmen may find it more restful than Ms Mandell's offering for their American counterparts.

☆ The most video swamped city in the world is undoubtedly Bombay, with 15,000 video libraries—over three times the UK total of 4500. At the other end of the scale is Moscow, with a total of two.

*I*NDEX